S0-BSX-094

PUBLIC ADMINISTRATION
An Action Orientation

Third Edition

PUBLIC ADMINISTRATION
An Action Orientation

Third Edition

ROBERT B. DENHARDT
University of Delaware

with

JOSEPH W. GRUBBS
University of Delaware

Harcourt Brace College Publishers
Fort Worth   Philadelphia   San Diego   New York   Orlando   Austin   San Antonio
Toronto   Montreal   London   Sydney   Tokyo

Publisher	Earl McPeek
Acquisitions Editor	David Tatom
Developmental Editor	Steven Stembridge
Project Editor	Michael E. Norris
Art Director	Vicki Whistler
Production Manager	Serena Barnett

ISBN: 0-15-505524-0

Library of Congress Catalog Card Number: 98-71721

Copyright © 1999 by Harcourt Brace & Company

Cover illustration by Kevin Tolman

Several parts of this book were adapted from previously published works. The material on strategic planning in Chapter 7 was revised from "Strategic Planning in State and Local Government," *State and Local Government Review* 17 (Winter 1985): 174–179, by permission of the Carl Vinson Institute of Government, University of Georgia. A part of Chapter 8 originally appeared as "Implementing Quality Circles in State Government," *Public Administration Review* 47 (July/August 1987): 304–309 (with James Pyle and Allen Bluedorn), copyright © 1987 by the American Society for Public Administration. All rights reserved. Chapter 12 draws on material from "Image and Integrity in the Public Service," *Public Administration Review* 49 (January/February 1989): 74–77 (with Edward T. Jennings, Jr.); and "Frontiers of Public Service," *American Review of Public Administration* 16 (March 1988): 1–7.

All rights reserved. No part of this publication may be reproduced or transmitted in any form or by any means, electronic or mechanical, including photocopy, recording, or any information storage and retrieval system, without permission in writing from the publisher.

Requests for permission to make copies of any part of the work should be mailed to: Permissions Department, Harcourt Brace & Company, 6277 Sea Harbor Drive, Orlando, FL 32887-6777.

Portions of this work were published in previous editions.

Address for Orders
Harcourt Brace College Publishers, 6277 Sea Harbor Drive, Orlando, FL 32887-6777
1-800-782-4479

Address for Editorial Correspondence
Harcourt Brace College Publishers, 301 Commerce Street, Suite 3700, Fort Worth, TX 76102

Web site address
http://www.hbcollege.com

Printed in the United States of America

9 0 1 2 3 4 5 6 7   039   9 8 7 6 5 4 3 2

For Michael and Cari

ABOUT THE AUTHORS

Robert B. Denhardt is Charles P. Messick Professor of Public Administration in the School of Urban Affairs and Public Policy at the University of Delaware. A fellow of the National Academy of Public Administration, Dr. Denhardt is a past president of the American Society for Public Administration, the leading national association promoting excellence in public service.

Dr. Denhardt is the author of several books, including *The Pursuit of Significance, In the Shadow of Organization,* and *Theories of Public Organization,* and the editor of several others, including *Executive Leadership in the Public Service, The Revitalization of the Public Service, Public Administration in Action,* and *Pollution and Public Policy.* He has published more than fifty articles in professional journals, primarily in the areas of public sector management, strategic planning and public productivity, and organization behavior.

Prior to joining the faculty at the University of Delaware, Dr. Denhardt taught at the universities of Colorado, Missouri, Kansas, New Orleans, and Central Florida. He has held several major administrative positions in these universities, serving as vice provost at the University of Missouri–Columbia. He served as chair of the Governor's Advisory Council on Quality Productivity for the state of Missouri and was a Fulbright scholar in Australia in 1990.

Joseph W. Grubbs received his doctorate from the University of Delaware's School of Urban Affairs and Public Policy. His research focuses on organizational change, organizational culture, interagency collaboration, and citizen participation in governance. He also specializes in program evaluation and performance measurement at the state and local levels. In addition to numerous conference presentations, his work has appeared in the *American Review of Public Administration, International Journal of Public Administration,* and *Journal of Policy Analysis and Management.* He holds a bachelor's in history from the University of North Florida and a master's in public administration from the University of Central Florida.

PREFACE

The third edition of *Public Administration: An Action Orientation* updates the text, taking it into the late 1990s and the second Clinton administration. But it also adds new material of importance to those becoming acquainted with the field of public service. We have especially made efforts to incorporate current information with respect to intergovernmental relations, administrative law, budgeting and financial management, and human resources management, including quite prominently the "new public management" and the National Performance Review. In addition, we have included important new material dealing with the global dimensions of public policy and administration today and the increasingly important connection between public administration and civic action or citizenship. This book also provides the latest approaches to management in the public sector and continues to pay special attention to the skills needed for administrators at all levels of government and in nonprofit organizations.

Like previous editions, the third edition contains subtle but telling differences from other books in the field. We assume that students in an introductory course in public administration don't want to learn about the profession only in the abstract, but are interested in influencing the operations of public agencies, as managers from the inside or as citizens from the outside. They want to acquire the skills necessary for changing things for the better.

For this reason, it is important that the text not only introduce students to the scholarly literature of public administration, but also help them develop the insights and abilities that will make them more effective and responsible actors. This book contains a good deal of material that is basic to working in or with public organizations; at the same time, the discussion attends to the complex and often confounding values that distinguish work in the public sector. Most significant, however, is the focus on the technical expertise and interpersonal skills that are crucial to effecting change in public organizations.

Another feature of the book is its balanced attention to the work of managers at all levels of government and in nonprofit organizations. Although the federal government is a powerful model for the study of public administration, managers of state and local agencies are important actors in the governmental process, and their work is acknowledged and examined as well. Similarly, we show how managers of associations, nonprofit and "third sector" organizations, and even traditionally private organizations are now confronting the same issues faced by administrators in the public sector. In fact, we use the term *public organizations* to describe all such groups involved in the management of public programs.

We also have sought to give proper attention to the global dimensions of public administration today. No longer are administrators confined in their work to their own organizations or even their own jurisdictions. The complexity of modern life means, among other things, that administrators must be attentive to developments around the world as well as those at home. Decisions made in a foreign capital may affect the work of a public administrator even more significantly than those made only miles away. Today, knowledge of international affairs and comparative issues is important not only to those who work in other countries but to all who work in public administration.

Public Administration: An Action Orientation is perhaps most distinctive in its treatment of the ethics of public service. Not only is the topic of ethics thoroughly covered in a separate chapter, references to ethical concerns appear throughout the text. Ethical issues cannot be separated from action; indeed, every act of every public servant, at whatever level of government or in any related organization, has an important ethical dimension. For this reason, we have made a strong effort to be attentive to the ethical considerations that are a part of all administrative activities.

Finally, this edition of *Public Administration: An Action Orientation* is the first such text to be fully integrated with the Internet resources that are available to assist public administrators and those studying public administration. In each chapter, we have highlighted "networking" resources available to students, including Web sites that contain material that supplements the text, provides examples and case studies, and links the student to other materials available online.

In this text we talk about action, but we also invite students to act. At the end of each chapter are self-diagnostic materials and exercises (cases, simulations, discussion points, and so on) designed to supplement students' cognitive learning with behavioral practice. These activities impart a sense not only of what public administration looks like to the impartial observer, but also what it feels like to the manager or private individual engaged in public action. Students have opportunities to test, practice, and improve their skills. Each chapter also contains a list of key terms and definitions (which reappear in the glossary) and recommendations for further reading.

There are very exciting possibilities in public administration today. Working to solve important public problems, sensing the human drama involved in such work, and gaining the satisfaction of doing something really worthwhile make being involved in public organizations quite fascinating. The perspective adopted here, focusing on the experiences of people acting in the real world of public organizations and on the skills needed for managerial success, permits a lively and interesting presentation of the field. We particularly hope to convey, in a personal and direct manner, the challenges and rewards of public service.

ACKNOWLEDGMENTS

Many people contributed to this book. From our work with members of the American Society for Public Administration, we have gained special appreciation of the complexity of public management and of the dedication and hard work required for public service. We hope we have conveyed the commitment and concern that guide the work of the best public managers; they deserve great credit and respect.

In the first edition of the text, Bob's colleagues in the Department of Public Administration at the University of Missouri–Columbia were a great source of help and support. More recently, both Bob and Joe Grubbs have called upon good colleagues and friends at the University of Colorado, the University of Central Florida, the University of Delaware, and Wichita State University, who have contributed substantially to the second and third editions. We especially want to acknowledge the help and support of Maria Aristigueta, Bill Boyer, Linda Chapin, Peter and Linda deLeon, Mark Glaser, Jay

Hakes, Ed Jennings, Arno Loessner, John Nalbandian, Jan Perkins, Jeff Raffel, Dan Rich, and John Thomas.

While we have been going forward with this work, others have provided balance in our lives, and their help in maintaining our sanity should be acknowledged. Bob is especially appreciative of the warmth and support of the poets and pickers of the Tyree Basement String Band; for the support, help, and generosity of friends and colleagues from Missouri to Colorado to Florida to Delaware, especially Mark, John, Jan, Ann, and Steve; and for the incredible support, tolerance, and patience of a hapless group of very forgiving golfers.

Joe would like to give special thanks to his wife, Heidi, for defining what love and strength can be and laboring with him through every challenge; to his mother, Dorothy, and members of his family, Charles, Lucy, Barbara, Jessica, Maggie, and Seamus, for their undying support and spiritual guidance; and to his first academic mentor at the University of North Florida, David Courtwright, for instilling a sense of responsibility.

Finally, this book is dedicated to Bob's children, Michael and Cari, who have been a constant source of joy, confusion, and wonderment, and to the memory of Joe's father, Robert I. Grubbs, Jr., a man who devoted his life to his faith, to his family, and to public service. Thanks to all.

Robert B. Denhardt
with Joseph W. Grubbs

CONTENTS

Chapter 1

PERSONAL ACTION
IN PUBLIC ORGANIZATIONS

Public administration is concerned with the management of public programs. Public administrators work at all levels of government, both at home and abroad, and they manage not-for-profit organizations, associations, and interest groups of all kinds. The substantive fields within which public managers work range across the varied interests of government and public affairs, from defense and national security to social welfare and environmental quality, from the design and construction of roads and bridges to the exploration of space, and from taxation and financial administration to personnel and human resources management. Though public administration varies tremendously in its scope and substance, those who work in public organizations share certain commitments. Among these, none is more important than a commitment to *public service*.

In this book, we will examine the work of public administrators in many different kinds of organizations. We will seek a clear understanding of the political and historical context within which public organizations operate; we will examine the commitments that underlie the notion of public service and the opportunities and constraints they place on public action; we will examine the many technical fields, such as planning, budgeting, personnel, and evaluation, with which public administrators must be familiar; and we will consider the personal and interpersonal talents needed by successful public managers. Most importantly, we will emphasize the knowledge, skills, and values that *you* will need to be both effective and responsible as you act in the public interest.

Although we will introduce you to many different areas of public administration, we will do so from a particular point of view that will provide a unifying theme in our examination of administrative work in public organizations. Briefly stated, that point of view is that there is something very special about public administration: your work in public organizations is distinguished by its pursuit of democratic values, and this concern affects nearly everything you do as a public manager. As a public administrator, you are obligated not only to achieve efficiency and effectiveness, but to be responsive to the many bodies that help define the public interest—elected officials, members of the legislature, client or constituent groups, and citizens generally. This special obligation requires that you be ever mindful of managerial concerns, political concerns, and ethical concerns, and that you develop structures and processes that take into account all three. The result is a particularly complicated approach to getting things done, but one that has special rewards. From service to the public, you may gain a very special sense of accomplishment and personal satisfaction, one that comes from helping others and from pursuing the public interest.

WHAT IS PUBLIC ADMINISTRATION?

We have already described public administration as the management of public programs. But to elaborate on this definition, it helps to know a little history. Happily, there is only a little history to learn because public administration at least in this country is a relatively young field of study. Of course, people have been engaged in the management of public programs for thousands of years. (For example, imagine the administrative headaches involved in building the Egyptian pyramids!) However, the self-conscious study of public administration is a fairly recent development, often dated to the work of French and German scholars in the late nineteenth century. Public administration as we know it today in the United States began as the study of government administration, and that study began as part of late nineteenth-century efforts to reform governmental operations. Most scholars and practitioners date the beginnings of the self-conscious study of public administration in this country to an 1887 essay written by Woodrow Wilson (then scholar, later president). While some have recently questioned the influence Wilson had on the field, there is no question his essay marks the symbolic beginning of American public administration.

Wilson's essay was basically reformist in nature, and highly practical. It was designed to address the inefficiency and open corruption that had become a part of government during the late 1880s, and to suggest certain remedies within the administration of government. Wilson argued that while scholars and practitioners had focused on political institutions (such as Congress or the presidency), too little attention had been paid to administrative questions—the questions of how the government actually operates. The result, according to Wilson, was that it was becoming "harder to run a constitution than to frame one" (Wilson, 1887, p. 200). Wilson first wanted the work of government agencies to be accomplished more effectively. He felt that such organizations would operate best if they pursued the private sector's commitment to efficient or "businesslike" operations. Wilson, of course, wrote in a period during which business, industry, and technology were developing in rapid and surprising new ways. Like others, he admired the managerial philosophies that business seemed to be developing. Among these notions, Wilson particularly favored the idea of concentrating power in a single authority atop a highly integrated and centralized administrative structure. His recommendation of a strong chief executive has been echoed by writers (and chief executives!) even to the present.

The men and women who followed Wilson in discussions of what came to be called public administration were very practical people, concerned with reforming governmental structures and making them more efficient. But they were also quite careful to place these concerns within the context of democratic government. How might the principles of democracy, including such lofty ideals as liberty and justice, be extended throughout government and throughout society? Indeed, Leonard D. White, one of the most thoughtful of the early writers, commented that "the study of public administration . . . needs to be related to the broad generalizations of political theory concerned with such matters as justice, liberty, obedience, and the role of the state in human affairs" (White, 1948, p. 10). As we will see, a continued concern for operating efficiently while at the same time operating in a way consistent with democratic values marks the field of public administration even today.

VALUES OF DEMOCRACY

Since their commitment to democratic values so clearly affects the work of those in public organizations in this country, it may be helpful to briefly review some of the key commitments we associate with democratic governance. The term **democracy** well reflects its roots—the Greek words *demos,* meaning "people," and *kratis,* meaning "authority. Generally speaking, democracy refers to a political system in which the interests of the people at large prevail. However, it is clear that within these broad parameters there are many different conceptions of democracy. As one illustration, at the end of World War II, representatives of the United States, Great Britain, France, and Russia met to consider the "democratization" of Germany. Yet, it soon became apparent that the Russian idea of democracy was quite different from the Western view. While Westerners associated democracy with such ideas as free elections, freedom of the press, freedom of movement, and the freedom to criticize the government, the Russians had quite a different conception. For them, democracy did not necessarily mean government by or of the people but rather, whether government policy is carried out *in the interest* of the people.

Even today the term *democratic* is used in many different ways by many different people. Yet, in the American experience, there is general agreement that democracy refers to a political system—a way of ordering power and authority in which decision-making power is widely shared among members of the society. Or, to put it in terms of control, democracy is a system in which many ordinary citizens exercise a high degree of control over their leaders. (In either case, the opposite would be an **oligarchy,** government by the few, or an **autocracy,** government by one.)

But democracy is defined not only in terms of processes or procedures (for example, rule by many, etc.), but also by several important cultural values that are typically pursued in a democratic society. Among these, three—**individualism,** equality, and liberty—have been of special importance to those who have helped shape the American idea of democracy. The first is individualism, the idea that the dignity and integrity of the individual is of supreme importance. Individualism suggests that achieving the fullest potential of each individual is the best measure of the success of our political system. It is the idea of individualism that is reflected in the familiar phrasing of the Declaration of Independence—that all persons are endowed by their Creator with certain inalienable rights and that it is the purpose of government to secure those rights.

Second is the idea of **equality,** not the idea that all persons are equal in their talents or possessions, but that each individual has an equal claim to life, liberty, and the pursuit of happiness. In this view, each person should be seen as an end, not a means; no one should be a mere tool of another. Moreover, equality in the field of government would suggest that differences in wealth or position are not sufficient reasons for giving one group preference over another. In a democracy, each one has an equal claim to the attention of the system and should be able to expect just outcomes.

A third central value of a democratic society is **liberty** or *freedom.* This idea suggests that the individual citizen of a democracy should have a high degree of self-determination. You should have the maximum opportunity to select your own purposes in life and to choose the means to accomplish these. Liberty is more than just the absence of constraints; it suggests the freedom to act positively in pursuit of one's own ends. Only by allowing individuals the freedom to choose, it is argued, will social progress occur.

That these themes have influenced the development of public administration is undeniable. Though, as we will see, people differ over the degree to which they influence the day-to-day operations of public agencies. Similarly, the way in which democracy has been operationalized in the American political tradition has had important influences on the operation of public organizations. For example, take the traditional separation of legislative, executive, and judicial functions. While the primary task of the legislative branch is to make policy through the enactment of legislation, the primary task of the executive branch is the faithful execution or implementation of policy, and the primary task of the judicial branch is the interpretation of the law, especially as it relates to constitutional guarantees.

David Rosenbloom of American University has argued that these three functions of government are related to three views of the role of public administrators in American society (Rosenbloom, 1993, p. 15).

1. The *managerial approach* to public administration, which Rosenbloom connects to the executive function, emphasizes the management and organization of public organizations. As with Wilson, this view sometimes suggests that management in the public sector is very much like that in the private sector, in that it is primarily concerned with efficiency.
2. The *political approach* to public administration, related to the legislative function in government, is more concerned about assuring constitutional safeguards, such as those already mentioned. Efficiency becomes less a concern than effectiveness or responsiveness.
3. Finally, the *legal approach* to public administration, related to the judicial function, emphasizes the administrator's role in applying and enforcing the law in specific situations. It is also concerned with the adjudicatory role of public organizations.

While we will examine these various approaches in more detail as we move through the book, it is important to understand at the outset that all the actions of public administrators take place within an important political context: a commitment to democratic ideals and practices. Yet today that ideal is somewhat tarnished. Americans' trust in government has been steadily declining over the last several decades. Questions are being raised not only about the quality and productivity of government, but about the responsiveness of government to the people (see Box 1.1). This tension will be a persistent theme as we examine contemporary approaches to the study and practice of public administration. Borrowing a phrase from earlier times, the task of public administrators still today is to "make democracy suitable for modern conditions." Doing so in a time of confusion and mistrust will be a special challenge to those in public administration as we move into the twenty-first century. Keep this issue in mind as we examine the various approaches and techniques that are appropriate to public administration today.

BOX 1.1

The Democratic Dream

The predominant American political belief—attained, pretended, or otherwise—from before the establishment of the Republic and throughout the nation's history has been the democratic dream, nominally based on some version of popular representation and governance. Virtually every political structure and reform . . . have been predicated on some mode of the democratic, egalitarian ethos, even as they oscillated back and forth between its Jeffersonian and Hamiltonian poles.

Indeed, to imagine a widespread domestic political movement (and probably foreign policy initiative) that does not in some very visible manner drape itself in the sacred vestment of democracy is inconceivable.

It is this ambience that American political philosophies, politics themselves, and even certain professions (e.g., public administration) were created and nurtured.

Not surprisingly, public service and public administration in the United States have shared a similar democratic coloration. From the early days of the professional public administrator—when Woodrow Wilson temporarily partitioned "politics" and "administration" into separate entities—we find a solid stream of democratic theory underpinning and underlining contemporary public administration.

But the Constitution cannot serve as a singular political poultice for whatever ails the body politic. Within the country at large, there is a tangible sense that as often appeals are made to the nation's democratic benchmarks, these are more calls to a fading faith than references to reality. Americans are apparently disenchanted with their politics, both in terms of substance and process. ". . . Our public life is rife with discontent. Americans do not believe they have much to say about how they are governed and do not trust government to do the right thing."

Source: Peter deLeon, *Democracy and the Policy Sciences* (Albany: State University of New York Press, 1997).

CONTRASTING BUSINESS AND PUBLIC ADMINISTRATION

One issue, however, deserves further comment up front. As we have just seen, even though work in public organizations is guided by commitments to democratic ideals, it is also involved with management, and, for that reason, public administration is often confused with business management. Indeed, such confusion has occasionally been quite prominent in the field of public administration. (As we have already seen, early writers in the field often suggested that government should become more like business, a phrase heard even today.) Certainly, there are some similarities between business and public administration. Managers in both sectors are involved in questions of organizational design, the allocation of scarce resources, and the management of people. But most observers would agree that the primary distinction between business and government is that business is primarily concerned with making a profit, while government is concerned with delivering services or regulating individual or group behavior in the public interest. All would agree that the context of public management significantly alters the work itself. Three differences are most apparent.

Ambiguity

A first difference between government and business lies in the purposes to be served. In most businesses, even those with service objectives, the bottom-line profit is the basic measure of evaluating how good a job the organization is doing. In turn, the performance of individual managers can, in many cases, be directly measured in terms of their unit's contribution to the overall profit of the company. The same is not true in public agencies, where the objectives of the organization in which one works may be much more ambiguous and where making or losing money is not the main criterion for success or failure.

Often the objectives of public organizations are stated in terms of service; for example, an agency's mission may be to protect the quality of the environment or to provide an adequate level of rehabilitative services to the disabled. Yet such service objectives are much harder to specify and to measure. What does "quality" mean with respect to the environment? What level of service to the disabled is "adequate"? The difficulty of specifying objectives such as these makes it harder to assess the performance of government agencies and in turn their managers. Moreover, most businesses wouldn't tolerate a money-losing operation in a depressed area, but a public organization, though equally attentive to the money being spent, might well consider meeting human needs more important than the financial "bottom line."

Pluralistic Decision Making

A second difference between work in government and in business is the fact that government—at least in a democratic society—requires that many groups and individuals have access to the decision process. As a result, decisions that might be made rapidly by one individual or a small group in a business might, in a public organization, require input from many diverse groups and organizations. Consequently, it is difficult to speak of specific decision centers in government. W. Michael Blumenthal, a business executive who became secretary of the treasury in the Carter administration, described the situation in this way:

> If the President said to me, you develop [an economic policy toward Japan], Mike, the moment that becomes known there are innumerable interest groups that begin to play a role. The House Ways and Means Committee, the Senate Finance Committee, and every member on them and every staff member has an opinion and seeks to exert influence. Also the Foreign Relations Committee, the oversight committees, and then the interest groups, business, the unions, the State Department, the Commerce Department, OMB, Council of Economic Advisers, and not only the top people, but all their staff people, not to speak of the President's staff and the entire press. (Blumenthal, 1983, p. 30)

The pluralistic nature of governmental decision making has led many business executives who have worked in government to comment that this feature of public service makes government management much more difficult than management in the private sector. But, as Blumenthal points out, "the diversity of interests seeking to affect policy is the nature and essence of democratic government" (Blumenthal, 1983, pp. 30–31). Many have also found that this aspect of government service is particularly challenging and rewarding.

Visibility

Finally, managers in government seem to operate with much greater visibility than their counterparts in industry. The work of government in a democratic society is subject to constant scrutiny by the press and by the public. Donald Rumsfeld, another who has worked in both government and business, once commented that "in government, you are operating in a goldfish bowl. You change your mind or make a blunder, as human beings do, and it's on the front page of every newspaper" (Rumsfeld, 1983, p. 36). The media seems to cover everything you do, and this may be a mixed blessing. On the one hand, media coverage enables the leaders of the organization to communicate rapidly both to external and internal audiences. On the other hand, the media's constant scrutiny of policy positions and their labeling inconsistencies as weaknesses can be somewhat limiting to free discussion of issues in their formulation stage. And, of course, the occasional intrusions of the press into even the most mundane personal matters can be excessive; one local newspaper even reported a problem a new city manager moving to the community was having with his refrigerator! Yet, executives in government realize that it is essential to a democratic society that their work be visible to the public and subject to the interest and control of the citizenry.

THINKING ABOUT PUBLIC ADMINISTRATION TODAY

With this background, we can now think more carefully about how the field of public administration has traditionally been described and how we might develop an action orientation toward the study of public administration. In terms of definition, many early writers spoke of administration as a function of government, something that occurred in many shapes and forms throughout government. There were obviously administrative activities performed in the executive branch, but there were also administrative functions performed in the legislative and judicial branches. Some even noted that from time to time any single official might engage in both legislative or administrative functions.

Somewhat later, public administration came to be viewed as merely concerned with the activities of the executive agencies of government. In the words of an early text, public administration is concerned with the "operations of the administrative branch only" (Willoughby, 1927, p. 1). By the fifties, such a perspective was so firmly entrenched that the leading text of that period stated, "By public administration is meant, in common usage, the activities of the executive branches of national, state, and local governments; independent boards and commissions set up by Congress and state legislatures; government corporations; and certain other agencies of a specialized character" (Simon et al., 1950, p. 7). More modern definitions of public administration have tended to return to the traditional view, including attention to administrative officials in all branches of government and even focusing on those in nonprofit organizations.

For our purposes, a formal definition of the field may be less important than trying to discover how public administration is experienced by those in the "real world." Our commitment to an action orientation suggests that we try to determine the kinds of activities engaged in by public administrators and the environmental factors that help to shape their work. We have already seen how the ambiguity of service objectives, the pluralistic nature of governmental decision making, and the visibility of management in the public sector create a context in which managerial work is significantly different from that in other settings. From the standpoint of the real-world administrator, the things that really make the difference in the way you operate are not whether you are employed by a government agency but rather whether you work under circumstances that feature an ambiguity of objectives, a multiplicity of decision centers, and high public visibility.

NETWORKING

The leading national organization for those in the field of public administration is the American Society for Public Administration. See http://www.aspanet.org/. Other related organizations with helpful Web sites include the National Academy of Public Administration at http://www.napawash.org; the Alliance for Redesigning Government, http://www.clearlake.ibm.com/Alliance; Association for Public Policy Analysis and Management at http://qsilver.queensu.ca/~appamwww/; Council for Excellence in Government at http://www.excelgov.org/; the American Political Science Association, http://www.apsanet.org/; and the Academy of Management, Public and Not for Profit Sector Division, http://www.fsu.edu/~spap/orgs/aom/aom.html.

Publicness

These features in turn all derive from the simple fact that the public manager is pursuing public purposes. In terms of the actions and experiences of the public administrator, therefore, we may say that it is the "publicness" of the work of the public manager that distinguishes public management from other similar activities. This view of the administrator's role suggests that, as a public manager, you must operate with one eye toward managerial effectiveness and the other toward the desires and demands of the public. It recognizes that you are likely to experience an inevitable tension between efficiency and responsiveness as you work in public organizations, a tension that will be absolutely central to your work.

Let us point out some of the implications of this orientation. Many commentators point out that the distinction between public and private management is no longer simply a distinction between business and government, or between profit and service. In fact, more and more frequently, we encounter situations in which traditionally public organizations are pursuing enhanced revenues (profits?) and traditionally private organizations are concerned with the provision of services. What is important is not merely what is being sought, but rather whose interest is being served. On this basis, a private enterprise would be one in which private interests privately arrived at are paramount; a public organization, on the other hand, would be one in which public interests publicly arrived at are paramount.

There is a trend in our society for greater openness and responsiveness on the part of many organizations. Most associations and nonprofit organizations would fit this mold, and managers in those organizations must certainly be attentive to both efficiency and responsiveness. But many corporations as well are now finding it important to open their decision-making processes to public scrutiny and involvement. The range of public organizations (and the applicability of public management) seems ever-increasing.

On the other hand, our understanding of the public manager's role would suggest that there could be managers in government agencies who would be pursuing interests other than those of the public. Certainly, those operating agencies in totalitarian countries could hardly be considered to be pursuing publicly defined values. They would more likely be pursuing the privately defined interests of a political elite. Similarly, we might question from time to time whether all managers in our democratic society have a proper concern for the public interest. Certainly, in cases where managers pursue their own personal agendas, as in cases of empire-building, we would question the "publicness" of their actions.

We now have a notion of the complexity of work in the public sector—the complexity inherent in the technical work of public agencies, but, even more important, the complexity of the political and ethical context in which public managers operate. Indeed, as noted before, this complexity will provide a theme that ties together many aspects of your work as a public manager. The way you set objectives, the way you develop budgets and hire personnel, the way you interact with other organizations and with your own clientele, the way you evaluate the success or failure of your programs—all of these aspects of your work as a public manager, and many more, are directly affected by the fact that you will be managing in the public interest.

WHY STUDY PUBLIC ADMINISTRATION?

Students come to introductory courses in public administration for many different reasons. Many students recognize the vast array of positions in government (and elsewhere) that require training in public administration and hope that the course will provide some of the basic information and skills that will move them toward careers as public managers. These students seek to understand the field of public administration, but also to sharpen their own skills as potential administrators.

Other students, whose interests lie in technical fields as wide-ranging as engineering, teaching, natural resources, social work, and the fine arts, recognize that at some point in their careers their jobs may involve management in the public sector. The engineer may become director of a public works department; the teacher may become school principal; the natural resources expert may be asked to run an environmental quality program; the social worker may administer a welfare program; the fine arts major may direct a publicly supported gallery or museum. In these cases and others like them, the individual's technical expertise may need to be complemented by managerial training.

NETWORKING

The National Association of Schools of Public Affairs and Administration is the accrediting body for programs in public administration and pursues other educational matters. See its home page at http://www.unomaha.edu/~wwwpa/nashome.html; NASPAA and its list of accredited MPA programs at http://www.unomaha.edu/~wwwpa/ nasrost.html.

Other students may have no expectation whatever of working in a public agency, but recognize that as corporate executives, as businesspeople, or merely as citizens, they are likely to be called upon to interact with those in public organizations. Someone who owns a small business might wish to sell products or services to a city, a county, or some other governmental body; partners in an accounting firm might seek auditing contracts with a local or state government; a construction firm might bid on the design and construction of a new public building. In each case, knowledge of the operations of public agencies would not only be helpful, it would be essential.

A final group of students, a group overlapping with any of the previous three, might simply recognize the importance of public agencies in the governmental process and the impact of public organizations on their daily lives. They might wish to acquire the knowledge and skills that would enable them to more effectively analyze and influence public policy. Some will find the world of public administration a fascinating field of study in its own right and pursue academic careers in public affairs. Because understanding the motives for studying public administration will also give us a more complete view of the variety and the importance of managerial work in the public sector, we will examine each in greater detail.

PREPARING FOR ADMINISTRATIVE POSITIONS

You may be among those who wish to use the introductory public administration course as a stepping-stone to a career in the public service. If so, you will find that these careers take many forms. We sometimes make distinctions among program managers, staff managers, and policy analysts. **Program managers** range from the executive level to the supervisory level and are in charge of particular governmental programs, such as those in environmental quality or transportation safety. Their job is to allocate and monitor human, material, and financial resources to meet the service objectives of their agency. **Staff managers,** on the other hand, support the work of program managers through budgeting and financial management, personnel and labor relations, and purchasing and procurement. Meanwhile, **policy analysts** provide important information about existing programs through their research into the operations and impacts of the programs; moreover, analysts help bring together information about new programs, assess the possible effects of different courses of action, and suggest new directions for public policy. Managers and analysts may work with the chief executive, with the legislature, with officials at other levels of government, and with the public in framing and reframing public programs.

As we will see, the work of public organizations also encompasses a wide variety of substantive areas. Think for a moment of the range of activities the federal government engages in. The federal government touches upon nearly every aspect of American life, from aeronautics, air transportation, and atmospheric sciences; to helping the homeless, juvenile delinquents, and migrant workers; to working with waste management, wages standards, and water quality. In each area, skilled managers are called upon to develop, to implement, and to evaluate government programs. But the work of managers at the federal level represents only a part of the work of those trained in public administration.

At the state and local levels, even more opportunities exist. As we will see in Chapter 2, whereas there is only one federal government in this country, there are over eighty thousand state and local governments! (These include cities, counties, and special districts.) Consequently, state and local government employment in this country amounts to over 13 million persons (compared to just under three million civilians employed at the federal level).

Obviously, the work of government at the state and local levels is different from that at the federal level. State and local governments, for example, do not directly provide for the national defense; however, most have police forces, which the federal government does not. There are also other positions at the state and local levels that do not have exact counterparts at the federal level. For example, consider the president or chancellor of your state university a public administrator with significant and unusual responsibilities, or consider the city manager in a local community a professional administrator appointed by a city council to manage the various functions of local government.

Work in public organizations, however, is not limited to work in government. Beyond working in federal, state, or local government, those trained in public administration will find many other opportunities. Directors of nonprofit organizations at the state and local levels, as well as those in similar associations at the national level, often find that the skills required for their jobs—skills that combine managerial training with an understanding of the political system—are the skills developed in public administration courses. Again, to demonstrate the breadth of these activities, we might note that there are large numbers of nonprofit associations at the national level alone, ranging from well-known groups like the American Medical Association or the American Bar Association, to trade groups such as the American Frozen Food Institute and the National Association of Bedding Manufacturers, to professional associations such as the American Society for Public Administration and those representing a particular field of interest, such as the Metropolitan Opera Guild. There is even an association of association executives—the American Society of Association Executives. Beyond these groups at the national level, there are numerous nonprofit groups operating at state and local levels; examples include the local United Way organization, a local food bank, an art league, or a historic preservation group.

Finally, those with training in public administration may work in a private corporation's public affairs division. Because of the increasing interaction between business and government, corporations often need special assistance in tracking legislation, developing and monitoring government contracts, and influencing the legislative or regulatory process. Thus, the combination of managerial and political skills possessed by someone with training in public administration can be highly valuable. The career possibilities in the field of public administration are seemingly endless.

COMBINING TECHNICAL AND MANAGERIAL TRAINING

Many students seek positions in the public service as a primary career objective, while many others see the possibility of work in public administration as secondary, but nonetheless important, to their main field of interest. As noted, the work of government spans many areas; consequently, the people who work for government (one out of every six people in this country) come from a wide variety of professional backgrounds. There are engineers who work in the Defense Department and for NASA at the federal level, in state highway departments, and in local public works departments. Persons interested in natural resources may work for the U.S. Forest Service and the Environmental Protection Agency, in state conservation departments, and local parks departments. Medical personnel work for the Veterans Administration or the National Institute for Mental Health, for state health departments, and for local hospitals and health offices.

Governments at all levels hire social workers, planners, personnel specialists, accountants, lawyers, biologists, law enforcement officers, educators, researchers, recreation specialists, and agricultural specialists, just to mention a few. To illustrate the magnitude of government employment of technical specialists, some 154,000 engineers and architects, 134,000 medical personnel, and 123,000 accountants and budget specialists work for the federal government alone.

People who have worked for some time within a technical field in a public organization are often promoted to managerial positions. A surgeon may become chief of surgery, a water pollution specialist may be asked to direct a pollution control project, or a teacher may become a school principal. Despite having started out in a technical field, these individuals find themselves in a managerial position; they are public administrators. Some people may desire promotion to a managerial position; others may not. (There are some jurisdictions in which continued advancement practically requires moving into an administrative position.) But whatever one's motivation, the new administrator soon discovers a completely new world of work. Now the most pressing questions are not the technical ones, but rather those having to do with management, with program planning and design, with supervision and motivation, and with balancing scarce resources. Often the situation is quite bewildering; it's almost as if one has been asked to change professions in midcareer from technical expert to public manager.

The fact that so many people from technical fields eventually find themselves in managerial positions in the public sector has led many of them to seek training in public administration. For this reason, it is no longer unusual for students majoring in technical fields to take courses in public administration or for students to combine undergraduate training in a technical field with graduate training in public administration (even at midcareer). This, then, is a second reason for studying public administration—to prepare for the eventuality that work in a technical field of interest might lead you to a managerial position in the public sector.

INTERACTION OF BUSINESS AND GOVERNMENT

Even for students who never work for a public agency of any type, understanding the processes of policy formulation and implementation can be enormously helpful. One of the most important trends in American society is the increasing interaction of business and government. Clearly, the decisions of government affect the environment within which business operates, but government also specifically regulates many businesses, and, of course, serves as the biggest single customer of business.

Those in business recognize that governmental decisions affect the economic climate. Most obvious are the effects of governmental decisions at the federal level; note, for example, the impact of government economic pronouncements on the stock market. But state and local governments also affect the business climate. The governors of many states have begun major campaigns to attract industry to their states, providing not only information and advice, but specific incentives for plants and industries that might relocate. Similar activities are being undertaken in more and more local communities, as cities recognize that they are in competition for economic development. At a minimum, business recognizes that the political climate of any locality directly affects the area's economic climate.

But the influence of government on business is more specific. At the federal level, major regulatory agencies, such as the Federal Communications Commission and the Federal Trade Commission, provide specific guidelines within which certain businesses must operate. Moreover, requirements of agencies such as the Environmental Protection Agency and the Occupational Safety and Health Administration restrict the operations of business so as to ensure the quality of air and water and the safety of working conditions. Similarly, at the state level, some agencies directly regulate specific businesses, while others act more generally to prevent unfair or unsafe practices. Even at the local level, through licensing and zoning practices, public organizations directly regulate business practice.

Government is also important as a consumer of business products and services. At the federal level, over $116 billion is spent each year on goods and services; in the Defense Department alone, the figure is over $85 billion per year. Similarly, at the state and local levels, expenditures for products and services amount to $176 billion. Business is attentive to its customers, so it is not surprising that business is attentive to government!

For all these reasons, people in business are becoming increasingly aware of the need to understand in detail the work of government—how policies are made, how they are implemented, and how they may be influenced. Not only are more and more businesses developing public affairs offices to specialize in governmental operations, to track policy developments, and to try to influence policy, but they are placing a greater premium upon having executives at all levels who understand how government agencies operate. Even if you plan a career in business, understanding the work of public organizations is an essential part of your training.

INFLUENCING PUBLIC ORGANIZATIONS

Any of the motives for studying public administration we have discussed so far may bring you to an introductory course; however, there is another more general reason you may wish to study public administration—to understand one important aspect of the governmental process so as to be able to deal effectively with public issues that directly affect your life. We are all affected by the work of government, so it is helpful, and sometimes even essential, to understand the operations of public organizations.

We have become so accustomed to the pervasiveness of government and the range of its influence that we sometimes forget just how often our lives are touched by government. Imagine a typical day: we awake in the morning to the sounds of a commercially regulated radio station or National Public Radio coming over a patented and FCC-registered clock radio operating on power supplied either by a government-regulated power company or by a public utility. We brush our teeth with toothpaste produced under a government patent and trust that it has been judged safe (if not effective) by a federal agency. We use municipally operated water and sewer systems without thinking of the complexity of their operation. We dress in clothes produced under governmental restrictions and eat food prepared in accord with government regulations and inspected by the government. We drive on a public highway, following government-enforced traffic laws, to a university substantially funded by federal, state, and sometimes local dollars to study from books copyrighted and catalogued by the Library of Congress. Though the day has hardly started, our lives have been already touched by government in many, many ways.

The importance of government and public administration in daily life is tremendous; consequently, the decisions made by governmental officials (and not just elected officials) can affect us quite directly. Imagine, for example, that one day you discover that the loan program that is helping to finance your college education is being reviewed and will likely be revised in such a way that you will no longer be eligible for funding. In such a case, you might well want to take some action to try to maintain your eligibility. Obviously, knowing something about the operations of government agencies, especially some of the ways administrative decisions can be influenced, would be of great help.

As citizens affected by government, understanding the operations of public organizations is helpful; it is even more important if one becomes personally involved in some aspect of the governmental process. For those reading this book, such involvement is actually rather likely. Indeed, if you are a college graduate, regardless of your major or field of interest, chances are quite good that at some point in your life you will engage in some kind of formal governmental activity. You may be elected to local, state, or national office; you may be asked to serve on a board or commission; or your advice concerning government operations in your area may be sought in other ways. You may also become involved in the work of nonprofit organizations or charities in your local community. In any of these cases, a thorough knowledge of the structure and processes of public organizations, both government and nonprofit organizations, will be of great importance.

Finally, those who are interested in understanding the work of public organizations may indeed find the field of public administration interesting from a more academic standpoint: studying and commenting upon the operations of government and nonprofit organizations contribute to our understanding of the process of policy development and support the work of those in public organizations. The opportunities for academic careers in public administration positions involving teaching and research are many, and you may find yourself drawn to those opportunities. Even here, however, one begins with a concern for action.

MAKING THINGS HAPPEN

Of the many reasons to learn about public organizations, one theme seems to tie together the various interests—an interest in making things happen. Whether you are preparing for a career in the public sector, covering the possibility that you might someday manage a public agency, or simply preparing to affect the course of public policy and its implementation as it directly affects you or your business, your interest is in taking action, in influencing what goes on in public organizations. It's one thing to gain knowledge of the field in the abstract, but most students want to learn those things that will make them more effective *actors* in the governmental process. Some of the more promiment actors are discussed in Box 1.2.

BOX 1.2

Public Service: A Distinguished Profession

For my part, when I think of government service, in uniform and out, I think of individual men and women of genuine distinction who have served this country over the years and also of the amazing diversity of a service that can range from defending our borders to delivering our mail, curing disease to exploring outer space. I was looking at a civil service publication the other day containing an alphabetical list of well-known employees through the years . . . and found it began with a career civil servant named Neil Armstrong who went on TDY (temporary duty) to the moon . . . and concluded several pages later with Walt Whitman, the poet, who worked in the Department of the Interior and the U.S. Attorney [General's office]. How's that for diversity? Incidentally, the group also included four Nobel Prize winners and several important inventors, including Alexander Graham Bell, who among his other associations worked for the Census Bureau. There also were some other familiar names of people who shared your proud profession: Clara Barton, Washington Irving, Abraham Lincoln, Charles Lindbergh, Knute Rockne, Harry Truman, and James Whistler, to name but a few.

In my own experience, as one who served the federal government for some years, I look back on those periods as among the most exciting, challenging, and thoroughly demanding in life. I have often said, and still say, that I never worked harder than I did in my years as a public servant. I worked alongside some of the finest, most competent, thoroughly committed people I have ever known. I realize this does not comport with everything that you read in the papers or see on television but I never miss a chance to point it out.

My own experience in government left me with an abiding respect for the men and women who serve this nation as public employees."

SOURCE: Norman R. Augustine, Chairman and Chief Executive Officer of Martin Marietta Corporation, Address to the Federal Executive Board, Denver, Colorado, April 26, 1989. Text provided by The Council for Excellence in Government, Washington, D.C.

This book is oriented toward action, toward how to make things happen in public organizations. Our perspective will be that of the actor not the scholar, although an understanding of the world of administrative action is the basis for good scholarship as well. Action first requires a base of knowledge; there are certain things that you simply need to know about government and the administrative process to be effective. There are also value questions that must be settled in the course of making and carrying out public decisions. And, finally, there are both technical and interpersonal skills you must acquire to be effective in working with others in your chosen field. Selecting an action orientation, therefore, commits you to emphasizing all three areas—the knowledge, values, and skills that will help you to become more effective and responsible in your work in and with "real life" public organizations.

ISSUES IN PUBLIC ADMINISTRATION THEORY AND PRACTICE

Throughout the chapters to come, our primary emphasis will be on action—those things that real-world actors do in order to be successful in public organizations. But action never stands alone. Without some degree of reflection, action is sterile and unguided. For this reason, we will outline here two themes that have traditionally characterized work in public organizations and that continue to be of great importance today. As such, these themes—politics and administration, and bureaucracy and democracy—provide a part of the intellectual and practical context of public administration. While our purpose here will be simply to introduce these two themes, we will suggest that they are most often manifest in contemporary public administration in a tension between efficiency and responsiveness. This tension is one that is absolutely central to the work of public administrators today and one to which we will return frequently within the context of specific discussions of administrative action.

POLITICS AND ADMINISTRATION

Even though the supposed dichotomy between politics and administration is one of the oldest issues in public administration, it continues to hold great relevance for administrators today. You will recall that an early essay by Woodrow Wilson framed the initial study of public administration in this country. In addition to his emphasis on businesslike practices, Wilson was concerned as well with isolating the processes of administration from the potentially corrupting influences of politics. With respect to this issue, Wilson wrote, "Administration lies outside the proper sphere of politics. Administrative questions are not political questions. Although politics sets the tasks for administration, it should not be suffered to manipulate its offices" (Wilson, 1887, p. 210). In other words, while policies were to be debated and decided by politicians, they were to be carried out by a politically neutral, professional bureaucracy. In this way, the everyday conduct of government would be isolated from the potentially corrupting influence of politics.

Other early writers joined Wilson in talking, at least analytically, about the distinction between politics (or policy) and administration. More practical reformers went further, creating governmental forms, such as the council-manager plan for local government, that were based on a separation of policy and administration. As we will see later in this form of government, the council presumably makes the policy and the city manager carries it out. The council is engaged in politics (or policy) and the manager in administration.

Over the first few decades of this century, however, the distinction between policy and administration was increasingly broken down, even in council-manager governments. Managers found that they had expertise that was needed by policy makers and began to be drawn into the policy process. By about the middle of the century, Paul Appleby of Syracuse University would write simply, "Public administration is policy-making" (Appleby, 1949, p. 170).

The increasing involvement of administrators in the policy process was in part attributable to the fact that the operations of government were becoming more complex and the technical and professional skills needed to operate public agencies were dramatically increasing. As people with such skills and expertise became a part of public organizations, they were inevitably called upon to present their views. At the same time, the legislative branches of government (at all levels) found it difficult to be knowledgeable about every detail of government and, consequently, were forced to rely more and more on the expertise of those in public agencies. Additionally, the complexity of government meant that legislative bodies often found it necessary to state laws in general terms, leaving those within the agencies of government considerable discretion to interpret those laws as they saw fit, and, therefore, make policy daily.

Ensuring Accountability

The contemporary acknowledgment of the interaction of politics and administration does not make the question of their relationship any easier. If public administrators make policy, how can we be sure that the policies they make are responsible to the people (as we would expect in a democratic society)? Presumably legislators must be at least somewhat responsive or, come the next election, they will no longer be legislators. But what of administrators? Traditionally, the answer was that the administrators were accountable to the legislators who, in turn, were accountable to the people. But even that argument is somewhat tricky today. Those in public agencies do indeed both work with and report to legislatures, but they also shape public opinion through the information they provide. They mobilize for support within the government and outside, and they bargain with a variety of public and private groups. To a certain extent, they act as independent agents.

For this reason, more contemporary discussions of the issue of accountability (which we will elaborate on in Chapter 4) place an emphasis on measures that would supplement accountability to the legislature by either seeking a strong subjective sense of responsibility on the part of administrators or by providing structural controls to ensure responsibility. As we will see, some people have tried to assert professional standards in public organizations, while others have developed codes of ethics and standards of professional practice. Others have sought greater legislative involvement in the administrative process or more substantial legislative review. Still others have described mechanisms such as public participation in the administrative process or surveys of public opinion that would bring the administrator in closer alignment with the sentiments of the citizenry.

The relationship between politics (or policy) and administration will be a theme that recurs throughout the remainder of this book. While the classic dichotomy between politics and administration has fallen, as the role of public administrators in the policy process has become more apparent, the question of the relationship between politics and administration remains central, simply because it goes to the heart of what public administration is all about. If public organizations differ from others in our society, that difference must surely rest in the way in which public organizations participate in and respond to the public interest. But that question merely leads us to another—the relationship between bureaucracy and democracy.

BUREAUCRACY AND DEMOCRACY

A second theme that grew from the earliest discussions of public administration in this country had to do with the potential for conflict between democracy and bureaucracy. Let's start once again with democracy. One writer has defined the moral commitments of a democracy in terms of three standards. First, democratic principles assume that the individual is the primary measure of human value, and that the development of the individual is the primary goal of a democratic political system. Second, democratic morality suggests that all persons are created equal—that differences in wealth, status, or position should not give one person or group an advantage over another. Third, democratic morality emphasizes widespread participation among the citizens in the making of major decisions (Redford, 1969, p. 8).

Set against these tenets of democracy are the ideals of bureaucratic management. The early scholars and practitioners in public administration were, of course, writing at a time when businesses were growing rapidly and beginning to use both new and more complicated technologies and new ways of organizing appropriate to those technologies. To some extent the public sector looked to the field of business for models of organization. They found that the growth of large-scale business had led to the development of large and complex bureaucratic organizations, organizations that were built around values quite different from those of democracy. (While the term *bureaucracy* is often used in a pejorative sense, as in "bureaucratic red tape," we will use it here in its more neutral and scientific sense, as one of the many ways of organizing work.) Consequently, the bureaucratic model of organizing was brought into the public sector.

The values of bureaucracy included first the need to bring together the work of many individuals in order to achieve purposes far beyond the capabilities of any single individual. Second, bureaucratic systems were to be structured hierarchically, with those at the top having far greater power and discretion than those at the bottom. Third, bureaucratic organization generally assumes that power and authority flow from the top of the organization to the bottom rather than the other way around. (We will examine the concept of bureaucracy in greater detail in Chapter 7.)

In contrast to the democratic value of individuality, there stood the bureaucratic value of the group or organization; in contrast to the democratic values of equality, there stood the bureaucratic hierarchy; and in contrast to the democratic values of participation and involvement, there stood the bureaucratic value of top-down decision making and authority.

How these values were to be reconciled became a difficult issue for early scholars and practitioners in the field of public administration, as it continues to be today. A variety of questions are raised. For example, is it proper for a democratic government to carry out its work through basically authoritarian organizations? But the key issue turns out to be an emphasis on efficiency as the sole measure of agency success.

EFFICIENCY VERSUS RESPONSIVENESS

As those in public administration have wrestled with the issues of polities and administration and democracy and bureaucracy, public managers have begun to experience more frequently the problems they face from day to day in terms of efficiency versus responsiveness. Indeed, in a sense, the two earlier issues seem to have dissolved into the single issue of efficiency versus responsiveness. On the one hand, there is the hope that public organizations will operate in the most efficient way possible, getting things done quickly and with the least cost to taxpayers. On the other hand, public managers must be constantly attentive to the demands of the citizenry, whether those demands are expressed through the chief executive, through the legislature, or directly.

A practical and contemporary expression of this difficulty is presented in case study number 5 at the end of the chapter. (You might want to read that case study at this point; see No. 5 under "Cases and Exercises" at the end of this chapter.) The case relates a dispute that arose in the course of developing a new housing loan program. While the case presents several different issues, most students reviewing the case focus their attention on the different interpretations that John and Carol have of their work. At first glance, John appears to be solely interested in doing things efficiently, while Carol appears to be much more concerned with responding to the needs of the client group. The case appears to be a classic illustration of the tension between efficiency and responsiveness, and indeed it is. But, at a deeper level, the case also illustrates how complex the issues really are. You might say, for example, that John was trying to be efficient in response to the demands of those clients who had been waiting for their loans to be processed. You might also say that Carol, through her educational efforts, was helping to ensure a more efficient, long-term operation.

The main point, of course, is that, in public organizations, you may quite frequently encounter difficulties in reconciling efficiency and responsiveness. A key to resolving the ethical questions raised in situations such as that faced by John and Carol is first understanding the various moral values represented on each side of the equation, and second engaging in ethical deliberation (and perhaps dialogue) in order to arrive at a proper approach to the problem. Interestingly enough, in this particular case, the real-life characters represented by John and Carol got together and talked through the differences in their respective approaches. The result was a course of action they both agreed upon, one they felt met both their obligations to be efficient and to be responsive. In the real world, dialogue sometimes works!

To summarize this point, the themes of politics and administration and bureaucracy and democracy have marked much of the history of the field of public administration. Today those themes seem often manifest in the tension between efficiency and responsiveness. Are public agencies to attend only to creating the desired outcomes in the most efficient manner possible? Or are such agencies to be responsive to the public interest and the public will, even though the public interest and public will may not have been explicitly articulated by elected officials, especially those in the legislature? Time after time, you'll find evidence of this tension in discussions on public policy, human resources management, budgeting and financial management, and so on. The tension between efficiency and responsiveness remains an "unsolved mystery" of public administration. But, perhaps for that reason, it is a tension that helps make public administration such a fascinating and dynamic field.

WHAT DO PUBLIC ADMINISTRATORS DO?

An action orientation to public administration requires that we focus on what public managers actually do—how they act in real-world situations. How do they spend their time? What skills do they require to do their work well? What are the rewards and frustrations of public service? From the perspective of the administrator, we can ask: What characterizes the most effective and responsible public management? What are the demands on administrators? What are the satisfactions that public managers draw from their work?

We will approach these issues by concentrating on the skills managers need to accomplish their work. In a classic article in the Harvard Business Review, Robert Katz provided the first major description of the general types of skills all managers need: conceptual, technical, and human (Katz, 1974).

1. Conceptual skills include the ability to think abstractly, especially in regard to the manager's concept of the organization. This category also involves the ability to see the organization as a whole, how all the parts or functions work and fit together, and how making a change in one part will affect other parts. Conceptual skills also include the ability to see how the organization, or parts of it, relate to the organization's environment.
2. Technical skills refer to an understanding of and proficiency in the methods, processes, and techniques for accomplishing tasks. These are, for example, the skills of an accountant who can conduct an audit or develop an income statement or the skills of a mechanic who can repair an engine.
3. Human skills involve the capacity to work effectively as a member of a group, or the ability to get others to work together effectively. ("Others" may include subordinates, superiors, managers at the same level, or virtually anyone with whom one might work on a given project or assignment.)

All these skills are important to managers, but not equally important to all managers. Katz makes a strong argument that technical skills are most important to managers at the supervisory level who manage day-to-day operations but become less and less important as the level of management increases. On the other hand, conceptual skills are most important to top-level managers who must deal with the organization as a whole rather than with just one or a few parts of it. Conceptual skills are less important at the middle-management level and least important at the supervisory level.

Human skills, however, maintain a constant, high level of importance; they are critical regardless of one's level. How managers' human skills are employed may vary from level to level (e.g., top managers lead more meetings than supervisory managers), but as a category, human skills remain the one constant for managerial success. In this book, we will consider the knowledge and values associated with public management (conceptual skills), the techniques public managers require in such areas as budgeting and personnel (technical skills), and the personal and interpersonal qualities that help managers work effectively with others (human skills).

AN INVENTORY OF PUBLIC MANAGEMENT SKILLS

One way to elaborate on an action approach is to create an inventory of the skills and competencies required for successful public management. There are many ways such an inventory can be constructed; one of the best ways is to talk with public managers about their work, as we suggest in exercise one at the end of the chapter. Several research studies have sought to answer this question by identifying the skills that are critical to managerial success. Of these studies, research by the federal government's Office of Personnel Management (OPM) is particularly helpful (Flanders & Utterback, 1985). The OPM study was based on information gathered from a large number of highly effective federal managers and produced a description of the broad elements of managerial performance at all levels supervisory, managerial, and executive. These sets of competencies were divided into two subcategories: (1) management functions (the "what" of management, its content responsibilities) and (2) effectiveness characteristics (the "how" of management, the style found most effective). (See Appendix A at the end of this chapter.)

NETWORKING

Major federal organizations dealing with management issues include the Office of Personnel management http://www.opm.gov/, and the National Performance Review, http://www.npr.gov/. In addition to the journals listed in the back of the book, you might be interested in the Web sites of the following: Governing *magazine, http://www. governing.com/;* Government Executive *magazine, http://www.govexec.com/, the* Government Technology *magazine, http://www.govtech.net/, and* Public Manager, *http://www.feiaa.org/Public%20Manager.htm.*

According to the OPM study, the competencies of public managers include such things as being sensitive to agency policies and national concerns; representing the organization and acting as a liaison to those outside the organization; establishing organizational goals and the processes to carry them out; obtaining and allocating necessary resources to achieve the agency's purposes; effectively utilizing human resources; and monitoring, evaluating, and redirecting the work of the organization. But the OPM researchers recognized that managerial excellence requires not merely doing the job, but doing it well. For this reason, they developed a set of skills, attitudes, and perspectives that seemed to distinguish the work of highly successful managers.

Displaying these characteristics in terms of several concentric circles (see Box 1.3) makes a point about their importance at different organizational levels—that as managers move up the organizational ladder, they must accumulate increasingly broader sets of skills. The researchers suggest, for example, that first-line supervisors must apply communication skills, interpersonal sensitivity, and technical competence to ensure effective performance on their own part and within the work unit. In addition, their actions must begin to reflect those characteristics in the next ring: leadership, flexibility, an action orientation, and a focus on results.

Middle managers, on the other hand, must demonstrate all these characteristics of effectiveness and begin to acquire the skills listed in the outer ring: a broad perspective, a strategic view, and environmental sensitivity. Executives at the highest levels of government who are responsible for the accomplishment of broad agency objectives must

BOX 1.3

Management Excellence Framework

SOURCE: U.S. Office of Personnel Management, *The Management Excellence Framework* (Washington, DC: Office of Personnel Management, 1985).

demonstrate the full complement of effectiveness characteristics to be most successful. Some of these characteristics are shown in Box 1.3. Clearly, a wide diversity of skills, regardless of how the job is constructed or of the style with which it is executed, will be essential to your success as a public manager.

VOICES OF PUBLIC ADMINISTRATORS

Studies such as that of the OPM are helpful in understanding what you need to know and what you must be able to do to be successful in public management. But how does it actually "feel" to work in a public organization? The best way to answer this question is to let some public administrators speak for themselves. Recently, we spoke to three outstanding professionals in the field of public administration about their views of the field and their feelings about their work. The following accounts are based on those interviews. Jan C. Perkins is city manager of Fremont, California. When asked about her motivations for entering the field of public administration, she replied:

> I was interested in improving the quality of life for all people and increasing the access of women and minorities. I believed that I could have the most impact by being involved in local government at a management level.
>
> The most rewarding aspects of my work have been being able to articulate the mission of the city and focus my resources and efforts in effectively meeting that mission, solving the problems of residents, and seeing employees grow and develop.
>
> Those considering public service careers should understand that managing in the public arena is different from that in a private corporation. It requires a commitment to values—of providing quality services for all and dealing with all people on an equal level. It is very important that people who enter the public service do so with a high standard of ethical behavior and an ability to deal honestly and directly with all people!

Michael Stahl works for the federal government in the Environmental Protection Agency:

> I entered public service because I viewed (and still do) government as an instrument to solve social problems. Democratic government can be a tremendous positive force in society, and in spite of recent political rhetoric and prevailing political ideology, I am convinced that the institutions and programs of government are of vital importance to the nation and that public service is a noble calling.
>
> There is great satisfaction in knowing that your work has made an impact on persons who could only have been helped through the intervention of the government. In my own experience, for example, schoolchildren across the country have been helped by elimination of exposure to asbestos in their schools that were unable to remove asbestos materials without federal financial assistance from a program I helped implement. Government service provides opportunities to help people through means that are beyond the capabilities of the private sector.

If you are considering a career in the public service, take the time to reflect on your motivation for entering the public service, because there are "right" reasons and "wrong" reasons. You are entering for the right reasons if you want to make a contribution to the solution of social problems, promote democratic values and ethical standards on using the powers of government, and if the concept of serving the public good is a passion. You are entering for the wrong reasons if you are looking for public adulation and recognition for your accomplishments, seeking material or financial rewards as compensation for your hard work, or expecting to acquire levels of power and change the world according to your own plan. Those entering for the wrong reasons will be bitterly disappointed. . . . Yet, for those whose passion is to contribute to the public good, government service can represent the single most satisfying way of translating your passion into ideas and events for improving the quality of life for scores of people. Very few professions offer this kind of opportunity and that is why public service will always be an exciting, challenging, and satisfying endeavor.

Cheryle A. Broom is legislative auditor for the state of Washington. She describes her reasons for entering the public service:

I was working in business and felt the need to make a change to a career where my efforts might make more of a difference in terms of addressing public needs. While I had a somewhat idealistic goal to serve the public, I recognized my orientation was not toward professions such as social work or K-12 teaching.

Problem solving and proposing solutions to significant public issues have been the emphasis of my work. It is particularly rewarding when these efforts influence policy and administrative changes that, hopefully, improve service delivery and cost effectiveness of public programs.

Individuals with an interest should be encouraged to explore careers in the public service and to develop the skills necessary to be successful in their chosen field. I think it is also important to keep a perspective, ie., it won't be easy nor will you do it single-handedly, but you can make a difference.

Obviously, these three professionals, as well as Tom Downs, the "public service junkie" (see Box 1.4), take very seriously their commitment to serving others. In making such a commitment, these administrators participate in a long and proud tradition. Indeed, the public service has historically been considered one of the highest callings in our society and has been even more highly regarded in other countries, such as France and Japan.

Without question, the public service in the United States, especially at the federal level, has come under considerable attack in the past several decades. Both political leaders and ordinary citizens have sought to blame the bureaucracy for many of the problems our society faces. Consequently, many today question the efficacy of the public service and wonder about the opportunity it presents. However, other groups, such as the American Society for Public Administration's National Campaign for Public Service and the National Commission on the Public Service (the Volcker Commission), have sought to restore a greater sense of dignity and worth to the idea of public service. We will

BOX 1.4

Reflections of a Public Service Junkie

In reviewing my own motivations for staying in public service, I found several, rather than one single answer.

First, there is a joy in the use of skills learned through a long apprenticeship. After twenty years in public service, I realize my skills and abilities were not easily or painlessly acquired. My education in public service has been costly, and I feel an obligation to repay the resources, energy, and interest others have invested in teaching me.

A second factor is the conviction that the work is important. There is an underlying assumption in public service that we are all part of an effort that leads to a better life for individuals in our society. Public service is ultimately based on the view that the human condition can be improved, an optimism which perhaps forms the core of the motivation for staying in public service. In order to remain in government, you have to believe that your actions can have some small impact on the public good.

Only in public service can you find the sense of completion that comes from working on a successful program to reduce infant mortality, for example, and then realizing that thirty-five more children are alive this year as a result of that effort. Only in public service can you participate in a process that helps move individuals from mental hospitals back into the community. The opportunity to help solve a community problem and then to witness the changes that occur is the cement that binds us to public service.

A final motivation for public service is the importance of constantly reaffirming the legitimacy and credibility of government services in the public's mind. One vital way to reaffirm our ability to govern ourselves, to control our own fate, is to have government, at all levels, that delivers the services expected of it. This presupposes a cadre of individuals who can understand and manage public institutions. If there is no response when the public demands action, then it confirms our sense of alienation and powerlessness, and we lose our ability to cooperate. If, as public servants, we are rusty, rundown, obsolete tools of government, then there will only be further reaction against the institution of government. The challenge is to be there whether or not we are wanted, to be committed to the public's business whether or not we are noticed, to carry the public trust whether or not we are asked, and to pick up the garbage.

In the end, regardless of the personal reasons to stay in public service, the process of government demands dedicated professionals to make it work. The ability to continue day-to-day government operations in the face of all difficulties is what public service is about. That ability is what creates a legitimate government, what creates the public trust. If that is too abstract, then let us say that public service is about babies living, fires being extinguished, garbage collected, crimes solved, people moved. That is all there is, ever.

SOURCE: Thomas Downs, "Reflections of a Public Service Junkie," *Public Management* 70, (March 1988): 7–8; International City Management Association, Washington, D.C. (Tom Downs, a former city manager, is currently president of AMTRAK.)

examine these debates in more detail later. For the time being, we should simply note that the idea of serving others has great appeal, in part because of the great joy and satisfaction it brings. Those working in public organizations experience almost daily the rewards of public service.

SUMMARY AND ACTION IMPLICATIONS

As noted, our focus in this book will be on the individual administrator or the individual citizen seeking to influence public policy through the agencies of government or through other public organizations. We will consider in some detail the institutions, processes, and techniques required for work in the public sector. But, most importantly, we will examine the "real world" of public administration, the world as it is experienced by the administrator.

That world, as we have seen, is one for which you will need to develop certain capabilities to operate effectively and responsibly. Among these we include an understanding of the institutions and processes of government; an appreciation of the values underlying public service; technical skills in such areas as program design, budgeting, and personnel; interpersonal skills in communications, leadership, and decision making; and a capacity to "put it all together" to integrate knowledge, skills, and values appropriately.

Ideally, in studying the issues discussed in this book, you will develop a good sense of the political context of public administration; a sound understanding of your role in both policy development and policy implementation; a sensitivity to the moral and ethical questions inherent in the notion of public service; technical competence in such areas as planning and program development, budgeting, personnel, and productivity; facility with interpersonal relationships (including leadership, decision making, and communications), and the self-confidence and self-awareness to act effectively and responsibly in real-life situations. Though public administration in the abstract sometimes appears lifeless and remote, the real world of the practicing public administrator is a quite lively and interesting place, filled with challenging problems and unique opportunities.

Terms and Definitions

Autocracy: Government by one.

Democracy: A political system in which decision-making power is widely shared among members of the society.

Equality: The idea that all persons have an equal claim to life, liberty, and the pursuit of happiness.

Individualism: The idea that the dignity and integrity of the individual is of supreme importance.

Liberty: The idea that individual citizens of a democracy should have a high degree of self-determination.

Oligarchy: Government by the few.

Policy analysts: Persons who provide important information about public programs through research into the operations and impacts of the programs.

Program managers: Persons ranging from the executive level to the supervisory level who are in charge of particular governmental programs.

Public administration: The management of public programs.

Staff managers: Persons who support the work of program managers through budgeting and financial management, personnel and labor relations, and purchasing and procurement.

Study Questions

1. Discuss some of the career opportunities available to those trained in public administration.
2. "One of the most important trends in American society is the increasing interaction of business and government." This quotation signals the need for better recognition and understanding of the interactions between business and government. Discuss the importance of this interaction and why a clear understanding of the relationship between the public and private sector is necessary.
3. The differences between public administration and business management are profound. Explain how the two fields differ and why the two terms are not interchangeable.
4. How did early scholars, such as Woodrow Wilson, view the role of public administration in a democracy?
5. The term democracy can be interpreted in a variety of ways. What significant concepts helped form the democratic society within which American government operates?
6. What is the role of "publicness" in defining the work of public managers?

Cases and Exercises

1. Interview a public administrator. Locate one or more people who work as a manager or analyst in a public organization and interview them. The interviewees might work in a public university, a local government, a state or federal agency, or a nonprofit organization. They might be a university, a city manager or department director (public works, parks and recreation, etc.), a county official (such as a county clerk), a manager in state government (perhaps someone in a welfare office or the highway department), a federal government manager (in a local office of a department such as Social Security, Agriculture, or the FAA), or someone such as an association executive. They might be a program manager, a staff manager, or a policy analyst.

Ask the people you interview to describe their jobs, including the range of responsibilities they have and the knowledge, values, and skills that are important to them in their work. The following are some examples of questions you might want to ask:

- Describe the work you do and how you came to this position. What is your educational and work background?
- What impact does the work you do have on the community/state/nation/etc.?
- What do you find different or unusual about working in a public organization? How do you think your job compares to work at a comparable level in business or industry?
- What knowledge, values, and skills are important to your work? For instance, if you were hiring someone to take your place, what would you look for?

2. Consider the following case. As an administrative assistant in the Department of Finance of a midsize suburban community, you are asked by the director to contract with an accounting firm to audit the books of the ten major city departments. You develop a request for bids, advertise in the local newspaper, and send written notices to all the local accounting firms. In response, you receive five proposals, four from local firms and one from a Big Eight accounting firm based in a nearby city. The proposals are essentially the same with respect to cost and expected quality of work; however, one firm, Jones and Denham, appears to have considerably more experience, having done similar audits locally in the past. Having gathered all the information you feel you need to make a decision, you make an appointment to report to the director early Tuesday morning. At lunch Monday, however, a friend who knows you are working on the auditing contract casually mentions that a certain Mr. Howard, of the Firm T. P. Howard and Co., is the brother-in-law of the mayor. T. P. Howard and Co. is one of the five firms that has submitted bids for the auditing contract. Later that afternoon, you receive a call from the mayor, asking for a report on the auditing contract. What do you say to the mayor? What do you recommend be done about the contract? What does this case say about the relationship between business and government?

3. Consider the following case. There wasn't much that David Wood couldn't do. He was an excellent teacher, a dedicated scholar, and a good department chair. He had been called to the chancellor's office to comment on a new curriculum proposal, one his faculty and he had discussed and one they firmly opposed. The chancellor began the meeting by commenting on the excellent administrative work that David had been doing and on the possibility that he might be considered for a deanship that was coming open soon. David had always wanted to be a dean. He voiced very mild objection to the curriculum proposal, then promised to try to convince his faculty to support it.

Moving from an academic position into an administrative position or from any technical position into an administrative position puts you in a different world, one with greater complexity and different pressures. What are some of the factors that affect those holding managerial jobs as opposed to technical jobs?

4. Recently fraternities and sororities at a major midwestern university were informed that the property tax classification for their houses was being changed from "residential" to "commercial," a change that would increase the assessed values of the

properties from 19 percent to 32 percent and would cost the Greek houses thousands of dollars in new taxes. The Greeks felt the change was inappropriate because, as one member stated, "There's not a fraternity or sorority on campus that makes a profit." On the other hand, a county official pointed out that the houses contain more than "four dwelling units," as the law describes it. Moreover, fraternities and sororities are probably not residential enterprises and are definitely not agricultural ones (as specified in the law), so they are relegated to the third "catch-all" category, "commercial and all others."

If you were advising the Greek organization as to how they might seek relief, what would you recommend? What kind of action should they take? Where should an appeal originate? How might it proceed?

5. Consider the following real-life case study (see the discussion under "Efficiency versus Responsiveness" earlier in this chapter):

John Taylor and Carol Langley worked for a local community development agency. Following a rather massive reorganization of the agency in which a number of new programs were taken on, John was asked to supervise a new housing loan program, and Carol was asked to assist him. The program was designed to provide low-interest loans to assist persons in rehabilitating housing in certain parts of the city. Although John and Carol had experience in related areas, neither was familiar with this particular program. To make matters worse, seminars to provide help in establishing such programs had been held some months earlier. John and Carol were simply given a manual and told to begin.

The program involved a number of new activities and took considerable time to set up. For example, it was necessary to train new housing inspectors to coordinate their inspection activities with those provided by the city, and relationships had to be established with the many agencies that would provide information about the applicants being processed.

John soon began receiving considerble pressure to complete the processing of the first group of applications within a brief period of time. For one thing, the first group of applicants consisted of some forty persons who had originally applied for other programs but had been turned down. Since their applications had been on file in the agency for as long as a year, they were quite anxious to have their applications processed quickly. Initial visits and phone calls from several of the applicants made John quite aware of their feelings. In addition, however, John was aware that this particular loan program would have a significant impact on the community and that, consequently, his doing an efficient job under these difficult circumstances would be important to the agency and in turn important to his own future in government service.

Carol recognized the necessity to do the work as quickly as possible, but she also felt a special obligation to the applicants themselves. She took seriously the agency director's comment that the agency could use this opportunity to help "educate" the applicants about the procedures involved in such projects. She felt it was very important to check periodically on the inspections, cost estimates, loan amounts, financial information, and terms and conditions of the loans. Unlike John, who spent most of his time in the office, she talked frequently with the applicants, many of whom she knew personally from her previous position in the agency.

For each applicant, John and Carol were to accumulate a complete file of information about financial status and about the rehabilitation project the applicant had in mind. This file was to be received and signed by the applicant, then forwarded to the federal regional office of HUD for its action on the loan.

John felt the process could be completed more quickly if Carol would simply get the applicants to sign a blank set of forms that could be kept at the office. When information was received regarding a loan, the appropriate items could be entered on the signed forms, bypassing the time involved reviewing each form with the applicant. Also, this procedure would eliminate the often lengthy process of coordinating several office visits to discuss the material.

When John asked Carol to obtain the signed forms, she refused. Not only was she concerned that the applicants see and understand the materials before signing, she was afraid that getting people to sign blank forms might be illegal. When she talked with John's supervisor about the request, she was told that the procedure was not illegal and had been used before by persons in the regional office.

For Additional Reading

Ban, Carolyn. *How Do Public Managers Manage?* San Francisco: Jossey-Bass, 1995.

Cohen, Steven, and William Eimicke. *The New Effective Public Manager.* San Francisco: Jossey-Bass, 1995.

Doig, Jameson W., and Erwin C. Hargrove. *Leadership and Innovation.* Baltimore, MD: Johns Hopkins University Press, 1987.

Frederickson, H. George. *The Spirit of Public Administration.* San Francisco: Jossey-Bass, 1997

Ingraham, Patricia, and Donald F. Kettl, eds. *Agenda for Excellence.* Chatham, NJ: Chatham House, 1992.

Kettl, Donald F., and Brinton Milward, eds. *The State of Public Management.* Baltimore, MD: The Johns Hopkins University Press, 1996.

Lane, Frederick S., ed. *Current Issues in Public Administration.* 5th ed. New York: St. Martin's Press, 1994.

Lynn, Naomi B., and Aaron Wildavsky, eds. *Public Administration: The State of the Discipline.* Chatham, NJ: Chatham House, 1990.

Naschold, Frieder. *New Frontiers in Public Sector Management.* Berlin: Walter de Gruyter, 1996.

Perry, James. *Handbook of Public Administration.* 2d ed. San Francisco: Jossey-Bass, 1996.

Rohr, John A. *The President and Public Administration.* Washington, DC: American Historical Association, 1989.

Waldo, Dwight. *The Enterprise of Public Administration.* Novato, CA: Chandler and Sharp, 1980.

Wilson, James Q. *Bureaucracy: What Government Agencies Do and Why They Do It.* New York: Basic Books, 1989.

APPENDIX A

OPM Inventory of Management Skills

The "What" of Management: Functions

1. External awareness: Identifying and keeping up-to-date with key agency policies and priorities and/or external issues and trends (e.g., economic, political, social, technological) likely to affect the work unit.
2. Interpretation: Keeping subordinates informed about key agency and work unit policies, priorities, issues, and trends and how these are to be incorporated into work unit activities and products.
3. Representation: Presenting, explaining, selling, and defending the work unit's activities to the supervisor in the agency, and/or persons and groups outside the agency.
4. Coordination: Performing liaison functions and integrating work unit activities with the activities of other organizations.
5. Work unit planning: Developing and deciding upon longer-term goals, objectives, and priorities; and developing and deciding among alternative courses of action.
6. Work unit guidance: Converting plans to actions by setting short-term objectives and priorities; scheduling/sequencing activities; and establishing effectiveness and efficiency standards/guidelines.
7. Budgeting: Preparing, justifying, and/or administering the work unit's budget.
8. Material resources administration: Assuring the availability of adequate supplies, equipment, facilities; overseeing procurement/contracting activities; and/or overseeing logistical operations.
9. Personnel management: Projecting the number and types of staff needed by the work unit, and using various personnel management system components (e.g., recruitment, selection, promotion, performance appraisal) in managing the work unit.
10. Supervision: Providing day-by-day guidance and oversight of subordinates (e.g., work assignments, consultation, etc.); and actively working to promote and recognize performance.
11. Work unit monitoring: Keeping up-to-date on the overall status of activities in the work unit, identifying problem areas, and taking corrective actions (e.g., rescheduling, reallocating resources, etc.).
12. Program evaluation: Critically assessing the degree to which program/project goals are achieved and the overall effectiveness/efficiency of work unit operations, to identify means for improving work unit performance.

The "How" of Management: Effectiveness Characteristics

1. Broad perspective: Broad, long-term view; balancing short- and long-term considerations
2. Strategic view: Collecting/assessing/analyzing information; diagnosis; anticipation; judgment
3. Environmental sensitivity: "Tuned into" agency and its environment; awareness of importance of nontechnical factors

4. Leadership: Individual; group; willingness to lead, manage, and accept responsibility
5. Flexibility: Openness to new information; behavioral flexibility; tolerance for stress/ambiguity/change; innovativeness
6. Action orientation: Independence, proactivity; calculated risk taking; problem solving; decisiveness
7. Results focus: Concern with goal achievement; follow-through, tenacity
8. Communication: Speaking; writing; listening
9. Interpersonal sensitivity: Self-knowledge and awareness of impact on others; sensitivity to needs/strengths/weaknesses of others; negotiation; conflict resolution; persuasion
10. Technical competence: Specialized expertise (e.g., engineering, physical science, law, accounting, social science)

SOURCE: Loretta R. Flanders and Dennis Utterback, "The Management Excellence Inventory," *Public Administration Review* 45 (May/June, 1985): 403–410. Reprinted with permission from Public Administration Review; © 1985 by the American Society for Public Administration (ASPA), 1120 G Street NW, Suite 500, Washington, D.C. 20005. All rights reserved.

Chapter 2

THE POLITICAL CONTEXT
OF PUBLIC ADMINISTRATION

Your involvement in public organizations, whether in your career or as a private citizen, will inevitably center on the development and implementation of public policies. You may work for an agency charged with devising new approaches to familiar problems, you may want to see that a particular policy or proposal is framed in a way that is consistent with your beliefs, or you may simply want to better understand the implications of a particular direction in national policy. In any case, it will be helpful for you to know how public policies are developed and implemented.

Talk of public policy is, of course, quite familiar. From one day to another, we hear criticisms of the U.S. policy in the Middle East, calls for a more effective drug enforcement policy, challenges to a school district's approach to violence in the schools, ideas for changing a city's policy toward the homeless, or proposals for altering an organization's hiring practices. Our uses of the term *policy* are many and varied, and the process by which policies are developed is even more complex.

We may think of a **policy** as a statement of goals and intentions with respect to a particular problem or set of problems, a statement often accompanied by a more detailed set of plans, programs, or instructions for pursuing those goals. **Public policies** are authoritative statements made by legitimate governmental actors (the chief executive, the legislature, public agencies, etc.) about important, and sometimes not so important, public problems. We expect public officials at all levels to spend considerable time and energy dealing with such topics as foreign affairs, health, education, employment, the economy, civil rights, the environment, energy, transportation, housing, agriculture, law enforcement, and myriad other issues. But in each of these areas, public policy is simply what an agency or the entire government decides to do or not do.

Public organizations are deeply involved in carrying out public policy—executing or "implementing." But public organizations are also involved in developing policy. The agencies of government are key actors in shaping public policy. Proposals are written and submitted by agency personnel; testimony and other expert advice are presented; and representatives of various agencies, especially political appointees who head agencies, often seek to build public support for particular ideas. Those in governmental agencies are often asked to elaborate on or clarify legislative intentions, and, in doing so, they continue the process of policy development.

Moreover, other public organizations, such as nonprofit organizations and associations, not only develop policies that guide their own activities, but also seek to influence the course of public policy in behalf of their members or other constituencies. Many such groups limit their activities to providing public information and seeking to affect indirectly the formation of policies in their area of interest. But others are far more direct, employing lobbyists and others whose specific job is to influence the policy process.

To understand the conduct of public organizations in the policy process, you must have some understanding of the context in which public organizations operate. That context is not merely physical; it includes the beliefs and values that shape our expectations of public organizations as well as the structures we have developed to try to maintain those values. In large part, the complexity of the policy process in this country is the result of the Founding Fathers' fear of concentrated power, a fear they sought to allay by organizing the federal government into three branches—executive, legislative, and judicial—so that no one branch could exert itself above the others. As we will see, our political system has evolved in such a way that the relations between and among the various branches remain a central issue in conducting public programs. This chapter focuses on the process of public policy and especially the relations between public administrators and the executive, the legislature, and the judiciary as they work together to seek important policy goals.

ADMINISTRATIVE ORGANIZATIONS AND EXECUTIVE LEADERSHIP

As we saw in Chapter 1, public administrators work in the federal, state, and local governments and in nonprofit organizations and associations. But, understandably, the federal government, simply by virtue of its size and the range of its activities, has become the model against which others are often judged. For that reason, we will begin our discussion of the structure of American public administration by examining the development of the national administrative system and the role of the chief executive in that system.

Again it is helpful to begin with a brief historical review, primarily because some of the arguments that characterized discussions of administration in the early days of our nation are quite similar to those that continue to confront us. Take, for example, the difference between the Federalist view, expressed most forcefully by Alexander Hamilton, and that of the Jeffersonians, led by (you guessed it!) Thomas Jefferson. Hamilton and his Federalist colleagues argued for a strong centralized government, staffed and managed by men of wealth, class, and education. "The Federalist preference for the executive branch was a faithful reflection of their distrust of the people. An intelligent perception of sound public policy, in their view, could come only from well-educated men of affairs, men with trained minds and broad experience—in short from the upper classes" (White, 1948, p. 410).

The Jeffersonians, on the other hand, saw the administration of government as intimately connected to the problem of extending democracy throughout the nation. They thus preferred a more decentralized approach to the executive function and sought formal legal controls on the executive so that executive power would not be abused (Caldwell, 1994). These democratic views reached their pinnacle in the administration of

Andrew Jackson, known for its openness to the "common man." But the Jacksonian era was also notable for extension and formalization of the administrative apparatus of government; the administration of government began to form "a link between the nation's political authorities and its citizens" (Crenson, 1975, p. 10; see also Nelson, 1982).

Despite these developments, the president's role as chief executive officer, the head of the federal bureaucracy, was not clearly established until well into the twentieth century, when Franklin Roosevelt was able to assert his administrative management of the executive branch and to set a model for all the presidents who have followed him. Some changes were inevitable: the growing size and scope of governmental activity simply required greater attention to management and organization. Others were more reflective of a greater understanding of the administrative process, how the work of government might be accomplished more effectively.

In 1936, President Roosevelt appointed a committee on administrative management, chaired by Louis Brownlow, that included a number of respected scholars and practitioners in the emerging field of public administration. The Brownlow committee concluded that "the president needs help" and recommended a series of possible steps to improve the president's management of the executive branch (Karl, 1963). Though initially sidetracked in the wake of the president's attempt to "pack" the Supreme Court, the major recommendations of the Brownlow committee were finally approved in the Reorganization Act of 1939. This act authorized the president to take the initiative in reshaping and reorganizing the executive branch, subject only to congressional veto. The Reorganization Act also allowed President Roosevelt to create the Executive Office of the President, composed of six assistants, to give the president the help he needed. (The Executive Office of the President continues today, though now it employs nearly 2,000 people.)

All presidents since Roosevelt have continued to assert their executive power in various ways. President Nixon, for example, sought to further centralize managerial power in the White House; President Carter sought greater managerial responsiveness through the Civil Service Reform Act. Presidents Reagan and Bush pursued the same ends, by extending political control further into the bureaucracy while also developing programs to reduce costs and increase productivity. President Clinton has pledged to streamline government and improved quality and productivity through implementing the National Performance Review.

The President's National Performance Review, and the larger "Reinventing Government" movement of which it is a part will be examine in much greater detail in later chapters. However, it is important that you understand generally what that effort is and why it was undertaken. Basically, the NPR was a Clinton administration initiative headed by Vice President Gore and aimed at increasing the trust of the American people in their government through a broad range of improvements in the quality and productivity of government (as well as through reductions in the size of government). The National Performance Review, first presented to President Clinton in September 1993 and implemented over the next several years made hundreds of recommendations aimed at cutting unnecessary red tape and burdensome regulations, empowering federal employees to make decisions while holding them accountable for the results, and emphasizing service to "customers." The general orientation of the NPR is outlined in Box 2.1

BOX 2.1

Reinventing Government

President Bill Clinton, March 27, 1995, White House Press Release

In Washington, we're engaged today in a great debate over what the role of the government here ought to be. Just about everybody has rejected the past view that there is a big one-size-fits-all government that can solve all the big problems of America. Now the rage in Washington is to argue that the government is the source of all of our problems and if just there simply weren't one, we'd have no problems. Sooner or later, the American people will come to agree—and I think they are quickly coming to agree—that the old one-size-fits-all view was wrong, but the new rage of no government is wrong as well; that we need a government that can be a partner to our people, to help them to compete and prosper in a global economy which is changing very rapidly and which presents great opportunity, but also real challenges as well. It's basically an old-fashioned social compact about citizenship—citizenship for the twenty-first century—that requires us to get rid of yesterday's government and replace it with a new government.

Vice President Al Gore, December 5, 1994, White House Press Release

It is time to get rid of the old way of managing the federal government where control is centralized and direction comes only from the highest levels. While that system was effective in the early 1900s, it no longer meets the needs of government's customers, the American people. What's needed instead is an entirely new model of leadership based on clear sets of principles, flexibility, innovation, accountability, and customer service.

Federal executives are where this revolution starts or stops. In each of their departments and agencies, they must be responsible for leading the change from the old way of doing the government's business to a more efficient, effective system where employees are empowered to provide the American people with the best service possible.

The information age has made possible "flatter" organizations, wider spans of control, and quicker information sharing. It is now possible for a president—whether of a company or a country—to decentralize, yet keep field operations accountable. It means empowering employees to do their jobs, yet holding them accountable for the results.

Specifically, federal executives should:

- Encourage innovation and culture change: managers should help paint a clear vision and specify a mission for workers.
- Implement the laws of the United States: the expectations of the president should be shared with every employee.
- Be accountable to the public: use surveys and goal-setting measures to provide better customer service and empower front-line workers.
- Manage and empower other government employees: give employees freedom to accomplish goals within broad guidelines.

Experience has shown that painting a vision of what needs to be done and allowing those closest to the processes to find the best way of doing it is a powerful tool to increase productivity and efficiency.

One important tool that presidents have employed is the **executive order,** a presidential mandate directed to and governing, with the effect of law, the actions of government officials and government agencies. Over time, the executive order has become a chief instrument of presidential power. President Clinton, for example, used his first executive order (no. 12834, January 20, 1993) to detail ethics commitments required of every single executive appointee in his administration (see Chapter 4). In this case and many others like it, the president is essentially making law by decree, occasionally in direct opposition to the wishes of Congress (Cooper, 1986).

The president, as the chief executive officer of the federal government, exercises power over an enormous and wide-ranging set of public organizations. There are some 2.9 million civilians employed by the federal government and another 1.5 million uniformed military personnel. In addition, the federal government supports and pays for the work of a wide variety of activities in which the actual work is performed by someone other than a federal civil servant. The Defense Department, for example, supervises almost two million persons in private industry involved, directly or indirectly, in defense-related work. While the size of government actually grew some 8 percent during the 1980s, it has decreased nearly 7 percent in the 1990s under President Clinton.

ADMINISTRATIVE ORGANIZATIONS

You are probably already familiar with many of the agencies of government at the federal level; however, several types are particularly important: (1) the Executive Office of the President; (2) the cabinet-level executive departments; (3) a variety of independent agencies, regulatory commissions, and public corporations; and (4) administrative agencies that support the work of the legislature and the judiciary.

The Executive Office of the President

The various administrative bodies located in the Executive Office of the President both advise the president and assist in formulating and implementing national policy. Several offices have come to play especially important policy roles; the *Office of Management and Budget,* for example, assists the president in preparing the budget, submitting it to Congress, and administering it. OMB is also involved in reviewing the management of various agencies, suggesting changes in structures and procedures, and searching out capable executives for service in government. *The National Security Council* is charged with integrating domestic, military, and foreign policy; it is made up of the president, vice president, and secretaries of state and defense and is directed by the national security adviser. (Recall that in late 1986, charges that John Poindexter and Oliver North, among others on the NSC staff, were exceeding their statutory authority and engaging in covert military operations led to the Iran-Contra affair, and, among other things, a reorganization of the NSC.) Finally, the *Council of Economic Advisers* consists of three economists who develop proposals to "maintain employment, production, and purchasing power." The council also develops a variety of economic reports.

Obviously, each of these groups, and others in the Executive Office of the President, are used in different ways by different presidents, according to the personality of the president and the particular issues that are most pressing at that time. Some presidents, such as

Eisenhower and Reagan, have relied very heavily on their staffs, while others, such as Carter, have been much more personally involved in management and policy development.

NETWORKING

To locate information about the executive branch of the federal government, check out the following sites: http://www.Whitehouse.gov/; http://www.Thomas.gov/; http://www.fedworld.gov/; and http://www.rams-fie.com/.

Cabinet-Level Executive Departments

These agencies are among the most visible, if not always the largest, of the federal executive agencies. There are currently thirteen cabinet-level departments. In decreasing order of size, they are the Departments of Defense, Health and Human Services, Treasury, Agriculture, Interior, Transportation, Justice, Commerce, State, Labor, Energy, Housing and Urban Development, and Education. Several departments, such as Treasury and State, date back to the nation's founding; others have been created by Congress as needed.

Each cabinet-level department is headed by a secretary, who, along with a group of top-level staff people, is appointed by the president with the approval of the Senate. Each cabinet-level department is organized into smaller units, such as offices, services, administrations, branches, and sections. The Department of Health and Human Services, for example, includes the Public Health Service, which in turn includes the Food and Drug Administration, the National Institutes of Health, and the Center for Disease Control and Prevention. Though each department is headquartered in Washington, D.C., their offices are, of course, spread across the country. Indeed, just over 10 percent of the federal workforce lives in or around the District of Columbia.

The cabinet-level secretaries, along with a few others, such as the director of the Office of Management and Budget and the ambassador to the United Nations, constitute the president's cabinet, a group that some presidents have used sparingly and primarily for formal matters and others have employed extensively for help and advice. Inevitably, a president will come to rely informally on certain advisors, cabinet members, or others outside the formal inner circle for advice and consultation. Historically, for example, President Kennedy relied heavily on the advice of his brother, Robert, during the Cuban Missile Crisis, even though as attorney general his brother held no formal position that would involve him in foreign affairs.

Independent Agencies, Regulatory Commissions, and Public Corporations

A variety of **independent agencies** have been created intentionally outside the normal cabinet organization. Some are engaged in staff functions in support of other agencies. The Office of Personnel Management, for example, oversees the federal personnel function, and the General Services Administration oversees the government's property. Other agencies have simply not been viewed as appropriate to include in cabinet-level departments; among these are the Environmental Protection Agency, the Small Business Administration, and the Veterans Administration. With rare exceptions, these independent agencies are directed by persons appointed by the president with the confirmation of the Senate.

Regulatory commissions, which are formed to regulate a particular area of the economy, are structured quite differently. Typically, they are headed by a group of individuals (variously called directors, commissioners, or governors) appointed by the president and confirmed by the Senate. These persons are protected in various ways from removal by the president; in some cases, their terms of appointment overlap presidential terms. Presumably, the regulatory commissions are to perform their tasks independently and objectively, free from undue influence either by the political incumbent or by the affected clientele. As we will see later, however, the nature of regulatory work makes this task exceedingly difficult. (Note that not all regulatory bodies are located outside the cabinet departments; for instance, the Food and Drug Administration is part of the Department of Health and Human Services.)

Public corporations are employed where the objective of the agency is essentially commercial, where the work of the agency requires greater latitude than would be typical, and where the agency will acquire at least a portion of its funding in the marketplace (Walsh, 1978). The Tennessee Valley Authority, which has provided power in the Tennessee Valley for over fifty years, is a classic example of a public corporation. Somewhat more recent additions to the growing list of government corporations include the U.S. Postal Service and the National Rail Passenger Corporation (AMTRAK), both established in 1970. (Periodically, there are questions raised about the status of these two operations, indicating that the structure of public organizations is constantly subject to question.)

Agencies Supporting the Legislature and the Judiciary

Whereas both the legislative and judicial branches require considerable direct administrative support for their members (legislative staff, committee staff, court administrators), there are also several specific agencies attached to the legislative branch that are of special significance. Among these, you are probably familiar with the Government Printing Office and the Library of Congress. But, although less is known about the General Accounting Office (GAO), its duties have become increasingly important. Established in 1921, the GAO is responsible for auditing funds to see that they are properly spent. In recent years, however, the agency's mission has broadened to include formal program evaluations within various agencies (Rourke, 1978). Finally, Congress is supported by the Office of Technology Assessment and the Congressional Budget Office, whose operations we will examine more carefully in Chapter 5.

THE STATE LEVEL

The organization of state governments varies considerably, according to each state's policy interests and political development; however, there is little question that state government in this country is "big business." One recent study compared the financial activity of state governments with *Fortune* magazine's ranking of the 500 largest industrial firms. On this basis, California would rank fourth between Wal-Mart and Exxon, while New York would be sixth, just above the General Electric Corporation. Even Delaware, a small state, would rank in the top 500 near such corporate well-knowns as OfficeMax and Estee Lauder.

Recent efforts to decrease federal involvement in domestic policy have combined with a general growth in the range of activities undertaken at the state level to support a vast increase in state activity. Between 1980 and 1995, state government employment rose from 3.7 million to 4.7 million, with an even more dramatic rise in state expenditures. Though spurring economic development is a major focus in this growth of activities, their primary areas of emphasis and expenditure continue to be education, social services, and highways.

The organization and structure of state government in many ways mirrors that of the national government, but there are some distinctive features. You should note, for example, the large number of elected administrative officials in most state governments. In most states, the people elect not only the governor and lieutenant governor, but also the attorney general, the secretary of state, and the state treasurer. Many states still elect the head of the Department of Agriculture by popular vote, and it is not uncommon to have members of various boards and commissions (e.g., the Public Service Commission) elected by the public. Obviously, these latter offices are filled at the federal level by presidential appointment. (The large number of elected officers at the state and local level is a carryover from a period in which democratic tendencies in this country were especially strong and it was felt that nearly all major officials of government should be elected directly by the people.)

In addition, many state departments do not report directly to the governor, but rather to boards or commissions isolated from executive control in the same way as regulatory commissions at the federal level. For example, a Department of Conservation may report to a commission appointed by the governor for periods exceeding those of the governor and, indeed, may have dedicated sources of revenue essentially outside the governor's budgetary control. Obviously, under such circumstances, the governor's power as chief executive is severely limited.

Despite structural limitations on gubernatorial powers, contemporary governors exercise a broad range of political and executive powers that enable them to play a major, even central role in the operations of state government. Most important, governors play a major symbolic role, helping to set the political agenda and to focus the attention of other political and administrative actors on a limited number of special topics. In addition, most governors have accumulated special powers with respect to the budget process through which they are able to dramatically affect the allocation of state resources and to mediate policy disputes among executive agencies (Bowman & Kearney, 1986, p. 54).

Beyond these somewhat informal powers, the strength of the governor's formal executive powers is often gauged by three measures: the presence or absence of the item veto, the ability of the governor to reorganize state agencies, and the number of other elected officials. In all states but North Carolina, the governor (like the president) has the power to veto legislation. Most states also give the governor the power of an item veto (also called "line-item veto"), the capacity to veto specific items within an appropriations bill (as opposed to accepting all or nothing), which is a helpful tool in shaping legislation according to the governor's preferences. (President Clinton, himself a former governor, supported passage of the line-item veto at the federal level and used it frequently in his second term, despite the fact that the veto was being challenged in court.) The gubernatorial power to reorganize is more limited. Roughly half the states require either statutory or even constitutional action to reorganize. Finally, as we have seen, nearly all states have a variety of statewide elected officials in addition to the governor and lieutenant governor. Indeed, most states have between four and eight agencies that are controlled by individuals elected statewide rather than appointed.

NETWORKING

For information about state governments, start with the Council of State governments: http://www.csg.org/. Then see the state and local gateway at http://www.statelocal.gov/; the National Council of State Legislatures, http://www.ncsl.org/; and these two library-based sites: http://www.loc.gov/global/state/stategov.html; and http://www.law.indiana.edu/law/v-lib/states.html.

The growing importance of state government suggests that governors will likely continue to assert their executive leadership role and will seek greater control by reorganizing the executive branch. So far, however, relatively few structural moves have been made. However, some procedural changes have occurred; for example, many states have moved in the direction of more clearly establishing the governor's leading role in the budgetary process and establishing centralized management improvement programs.

Although the organization of government varies considerably from state to state, most states have a variety of substantive agencies concerned with state and local needs (Natural Resources, Highways and Transportation, etc.), as well as several agencies, such as the Department of Social Services, that largely administer programs funded by the federal government. These agencies are likely to be assisted by a central management support unit, called an Office of Administration or some similar title, that provides budget, personnel, and other general services. As mentioned, if there is one trend in the reorganization of state agencies, that trend would seem to be creation of a greater number of state departments devoted to economic development. In some cases, these departments seek to coordinate many economic development activities; in others, there is a more specific focus on small business or on providing incentives for industrial location or relocation.

THE LOCAL LEVEL

According to the most recent data available, there are over eighty-five thousand local governments (see Table 2.1). Many of these are municipalities, cities, and towns of varying sizes offering a full range of services; others are counties, typically more limited in their role but still embracing a variety of governmental functions. But most are special districts, created to serve one particular function, such as education, fire protection, or parks and recreation. (Only special districts have substantially increased in numbers over the past several years.)

TABLE 2.1

Number of Governmental Units, by Type of Government

Type of government	1,992
Federal	1
State	50
Local	84,955
County	3,043
Municipal	19,279
Township and town	16,656
School district	14,422
Special district	31,555
Total	85,006

SOURCE: U.S. Bureau of the Census, *Statistical Abstract of the United States* (Washington, D.C.: U.S. Government Printing Office, 1995).

Cities

American cities are organized in three ways. The *mayor-council* form is used by about 49 percent of all municipalities, about 56 percent of those having a population over 250,000, and three-fourths of those with a population over one million. In all cases, both the council and the mayor are elected, the latter either by direct popular vote or a council election. One variation of the mayor council form features a *strong mayor*, with almost total administrative authority, including preparation and administration of the budget. Policy making in this form is a joint endeavor of the mayor and the council. The *weak mayor* type places primary administrative control, including most appointments and development of the budget, in the hands of the council.

The power of the mayor as chief executive is obviously greater in the strong mayor system and, consequently, that system is used in most large, industrial cities. At least in a formal sense, however, several large cities, including Chicago, still maintain a weak mayor system, although even under such circumstances, a particular mayor may assert considerable strength. The legendary Mayor Richard Daley of Chicago, for example, was able to utilize a well-oiled political machine to assert substantial administrative power. Though he operated in a weak-mayor system, Daley was unquestionably a strong mayor.

One interesting recent variation on the mayor-council form is the use of a professionally trained chief administrative officer (sometimes called a "deputy mayor") to oversee the administrative operations of city government (e.g., Los Angeles, New Orleans, Washington, D.C.). We find this administrative arrangement in many big cities, where mayors are often more interested in campaigning and in working with external constituencies and like to have someone else oversee the internal management of the city. But city administrators are also being hired in an increasing number of smaller mayor council communities as well, mostly in an effort to bring professional expertise to local government.

The *council-manager* form of local government is of special interest in that it represents a structural effort to solve the classic question of the relationship between politics (or policy) and administration. In this form, the city council, usually five to seven people, has responsibility for making policy, including passing appropriations and supervising in a general way the administration of city government. The primary executive responsibility, however, lies with a full-time professionally trained city manager; the mayor has no involvement in the administration of the city and performs primarily ceremonial duties and legislation. In its classic formulation, therefore, the council-manager form is designed so that the council makes policy and the city manager carries it out.

The council-manager plan was first tried in Staunton, Virginia, in 1908, and a few years later was adopted in Dayton, Ohio, with great success. Several reform organizations, such as the National Municipal League, felt the council-manager plan would be a good way to insulate the management of city government from the vagaries of local politics and consequently added their endorsement.

NETWORKING

For information about local government, see the local government home page and the various organizations linked to that site: http://localgov.org/. And don't miss the National Civic League at http://www.cais.com/nlc and the National League of Cities at http://www.nlc.org/. See also the Local Government Institute, http://www.lgi.org/, the Local Government Network http://www.civic.net/lgnet and the U.S. Conference of Mayors home page at http://www.usmayors.org/uscm/home.html.

The number of council-manager governments has grown steadily throughout this century and continues to increase. Today, some 42 percent of American communities employ the plan. Where the mayor-council system is associated with larger, industrialized, and heterogeneous cities, the council-manager plan is most frequently found in medium-sized cities. Over 60 percent of American cities with populations between 25,000 and 250,000 operate with the plan, and 32 percent of the cities with a population below 5,000 have adopted it. Although a number of large cities, such as Dallas, Kansas City, Phoenix, San Antonio, and San Diego, use the plan, it is rare among cities over one million in population. The council-manager form continues to grow, however, with the number of council-manager adoptions outrunning those of the mayor-council form by three to one over the past twenty years. Those favoring the council-manager plan usually argue that it emphasizes professional expertise and administrative accountability; those favoring the mayor-council plan emphasize its adaptability and its responsiveness to community needs.

A small number of American cities use the commission form of government. Under this form, the people elect a set of commissioners. Each acts as a council member, but also as director of a particular city department; for example, one commissioner might head the Parks Department and another the Public Works Department. The commission form is fading; we find it today primarily in smaller rural communities, though it is still found in such cities as Portland, Oregon, and Tulsa, Oklahoma. These larger cities usually hire a chief administrative officer to provide the necessary coordination of city government.

Counties

Counties (or variations, such as *parishes* in Louisiana) are found in nearly every state and range in population from very small to huge. Once considered the "dark continent" of local government, counties are emerging as important actors in the modern governmental system. Counties have traditionally provided a range of services in behalf of state government, a role that has expanded considerably in the past few years. In addition, counties have recently assumed a wide range of new services (such as mass transit, mental health, waste disposal, and police services) that, for one reason or another, cannot be offered by individual municipalities (Dodge, 1988, pp. 2–3).

The traditional form of county government has been a combination of a county commission and a series of elected administrative officials, such as sheriff, auditor, treasurer, and so on. An emerging trend in county government, however, is the use of appointed county administrators, similar in many ways to the city manager at the municipal level. Still another type of county government, also increasing in use, involves the combination of a city council and an elected executive. In this system, a chief executive is elected by the people and holds powers similar to that of a governor in a state system. For example, the elected executive often has veto power over council actions (Henry, 1980, pp. 158–164). Trends toward a greater range of activities, especially in the social services, combined with the increasing professionalism of county government, make this often overlooked area one of the most interesting arenas for public service today.

Native American Tribes

Native American tribes have had a special relationship with the United States government. This relationship was first articulated by Supreme Court Justice Marshall in three decision between 1827 and 1832 known as the Marshall Trilogy. In these decisions Marshall acknowledged that Indians had inherent rights to possess and use their land, and that they had sovereignty to run their own affairs. But even though they were seen as nations, the tribes were not foreign nations. They could not sell their land without the consent of the federal government. And the federal government had responsibilities to protect Indian land from incursions from the states and others. Marshall described this relationship as similar to guardianship.

In the last 150 years this relationship has evolved. Influenced greatly by European settlers' desire to move westward, Congress made treaties, fought wars, and otherwise moved Indians out of the way of the western expansion. Despite these efforts to assimilate Indians into the dominant culture, many Indians have clung to their heritage and maintained their tribal governance systems. Today, the Department of the Interior recognizes more than four hundred tribes who have sovereignty over their internal affairs. Non-Indian public administrators who work near or with tribes need to be aware of the legal history that has led to Indian rights that are unique in America.

Special Districts

Finally, we should note again the large number of special districts that exist at the local level. These limited-purpose districts, which may operate in the areas of natural resources, fire protection, libraries, schools, housing and community development, and so forth, are typically governed by an appointed part-time governing board and a full-time general manager or executive director, who plays the most significant role in the operation of the district. Critics claim the proliferation of special districts causes fragmentation and lack of coordination, but others argue that such districts remain important because they are "close to the people."

Nonprofit Organizations and Associations

A multitude of public organizations fall somewhere between what we think of as the "public sector" and the "private sector." These may be described as belonging to an independent or third sector of our economy. For the most part, third-sector organizations do not have producing a profit as one of their major objectives; they exist instead to meet the needs of the public at large, a particular portion of the public, or the needs and interests of their own members (McLaughlin, 1986). Technically, **nonprofit organizations** are defined as those prohibited by law from distributing surplus revenues (profits) to individuals (typically, members). Such organizations may in fact make a profit; however, the profit must be used for the purposes of the organization.

Nonprofit organizations may include churches, civic organizations, schools and colleges, charitable organizations, social and recreational groups, health service organizations, membership organizations (including labor unions and fraternal organizations), conservation and environmental groups, mutual organizations (including farmers' cooperatives), trade associations, community chests, youth activities (such as Boy Scouts), community betterment organizations, advocacy groups of all kinds, and many others. Their numbers range into the millions, depending on how they are counted, and, as noted earlier, include some 23,000 national nonprofits (see Table 2.2).

NETWORKING

For information of nonprofit organizations, see the Support Center for Nonprofit Management at http://www.supportcenter.org/sf/. See also several sites listing foundations and other nonprofits at http://www.law.indiana.edu/law/v-lib/orgs.html; http://www.cof.org/; and http://www.foundations.org/.

While private nonprofit organizations account for between 6 percent and 10 percent of employment in the United States (depending again on how you count), the voluntary effort that is expended in support of these groups makes their impact far greater. Nearly 100 million American adults devote volunteer time to such organizations, an investment of time that has been estimated as the equivalent of over $200 billion a year. Over the last twenty years, the third sector has been the fastest-growing segment of our economy.

The importance of volunteering was highlighted in President Clinton's Summit for America's Future, led by Colin Powell and held in Philadelphia in 1997. The Summit called on all Americans to give of their time to serve others, but was especially oriented toward involving young people in public service activities. Various youth service organizations have pledged to involve more youth in service projects, perhaps doubling the number involved in service projects by the turn of the century.

TABLE 2.2

National Nonprofit Organizations by Specialty, 1993

Category	Number
Trade, business, and commercial organizations	3,755
Environmental and agricultural organizations	1,124
Legal governmental, public administration, and military organizations	780
Engineering, technology, and sciences	1,381
Educational organizations	1,310
Cultural organizations	1,918
Social welfare organizations	1,934
Health and medical organizations	2,453
Public affairs organizations	2,113
Fraternal, nationality, and ethnic organizations	541
Religious organizations	1,230
Veteran, heredity, and patriotic organizations	745
Hobby and vocational organizations	1,548
Athletic and sports organizations	836
Labor unions, associations, and federations	245
Chambers of commerce and trade and tourism	160
Greek and non-Greek letter societies, associations, and federations	337
Fan clubs	491
Total	22,901

SOURCE: Encyclopedia of Associations, 29th ed., vol. 1 (Detroit, MI: Gale Research Company, 1996).

Many of these organizations are concentrated in the human services, especially in such important areas as health, education, and welfare. As efforts have been made to "privatize" certain traditionally public functions (a trend we will explore later), nonprofit organizations have come to carry an increasing share of the delivery of major services. Nonprofit organizations are involved in such key service areas as hospitals, museums, colleges and universities, the performing arts, religion, advocacy, and research (Young, 1983, p. 9). It has been estimated that over 50 percent of the human services delivered in major urban areas are delivered not by government but by other groups, mostly nonprofit organizations.

Nonprofits can be categorized in many ways, but perhaps most easily according to their purposes and source of financial support. Some nonprofits are *charitable* or *public benefit organizations,* which provide services to the public at large or to some segment of the public. These organizations, such as social service organizations or art museums, may receive some funding from government and some from private contribution; they are generally tax-exempt under federal statutes. Other nonprofits are *advocacy organizations,* groups that espouse a particular cause and seek to lobby for that cause, or *mutual benefit organizations,* which produce benefits primarily for their members. The former would include groups like Common Cause and the Sierra Club; the latter would include trade associations, professional organizations, labor unions, and others that directly promote the interests of their own members. Obviously, however, from these examples, the line between the two is not completely clear. Finally, *churches* are obviously charitable organizations, but are difficult to classify in the categories mentioned.

Indeed, the entire "third sector" is sometimes confusing to categorize. For one thing, the distinctions among the three sectors are not clear, even to the point that a particular individual might find the same service provided by one or more sectors. For example, you can play golf at a municipal course (public sector), a private driving range (private sector), or a country club (third sector). Moreover, the sources of funding are often intermixed. For example, both governments (public sector) and private corporations (private sector) often contribute financial support to local chambers of commerce.

The fact that nonprofit organizations are required to pursue a public interest is reflected in their legal structure (and tax-exempt status). Typically, so that the government can feel that a public purpose is being carried out, there are requirements that the organization be governed by a board of trustees (or directors or commissioners), the purpose of which, at least in legal terms, is to promote and to protect the public interest that is involved (Wolf, 1984, p. 21). Such persons will also likely establish the mission and operating policies, hire an executive director, and generally oversee fiscal and programmatic operations. The executive director is responsible for day-to-day operations and often becomes the organization's chief spokesperson. Most nonprofit associations are highly dependent on their executive director's leadership. More and more, such persons (and other major staff persons in nonprofit organizations) are coming from a background in public administration.

RELATIONSHIPS WITH THE LEGISLATIVE BODY

In examining the political context of public organizations, we have thus far emphasized the importance of executive leadership. For example, we noted the emergence of the president as the chief executive officer of our national government and the pivotal role of the chief executive in state and local governments and in nonprofit organizations and associations. But though we tend to associate public agencies with the executive branch of government, there are numerous administrative bodies associated with the legislative and judicial branches. More importantly, wherever agencies are located, their role in the policy process will be especially clear in their relationship with the legislature. In discussing the relationship between public agencies and legislative bodies, we will focus much more directly on the policy process.

THE POLICY PROCESS

Before we examine the role of public organizations in developing public policy, we should review the process by which public policies are developed. We may think of the policy process as involving three stages: agenda setting, policy formulation, and policy implementation (see Box 2.2). Whereas public organizations are the primary actors in

BOX 2.2

Stages in the Policy Process

- Agenda setting
- Policy recognition
- Policy generation
- Political action
- Policy formulation
- Policy implementation

Adapted from John W. Kingdon, *Agendas, Alternatives, and Public Policies* (Boston: Little, Brown, 1984).

implementing public policy (indeed, most of this book focuses on ways to effectively carry out public policy), they are also significant players in the first two phases.

Agenda Setting

Obviously, before policies are acted upon, they must get the attention of major decision makers. From among all the many and competing claims on their time and interests, decision makers must select issues that will be given priority and those that will be filtered out. Through the **agenda-setting** phase, certain problems come to be viewed as needing action, while others are postponed. Naturally, there is a great deal of ebb and flow in what is considered most important. In the 1970s and 1980s, U.S. foreign policy was dominated by concerns for Soviet movement into such areas as the Middle East; in the 1990s attention shifted to a variety of "flash points" such as Somalia and Bosnia. Similarly, any particular issue area can gain or decline in prominence over time, as has the attention to energy policy over the past fifteen years.

Many people contribute to setting the public policy agenda. The president, for example, has a special claim on the attention of the American people and their elected representatives; a presidential speech or press conference can significantly affect what decision makers see as important. But there are many others whose actions can give certain topics greater or less visibility. Members of Congress, executive branch officials, political parties, interest groups, the media, and the general public can all significantly shape the question of what will be considered important. Think, for example, how concern for teen pregnancy has been recently brought to public awareness. Who have been the leaders in shaping public opinion on this issue?

The agenda-setting process may be viewed as the confluence of three streams of events: policy recognition, policy generation, and political action (Kingdon, 1984). The first, *policy recognition,* has to do with the way certain topics emerge as significant issues that demand action. As you can well imagine, decision makers are subject to many influences in choosing what items are significant. They may respond to particular indicators that come to public view, such as an increase in air traffic problems or a rise in unemployment. Or they may get feedback on current programs that indicates some need to reassess the status of a particular issue. Finally, some items are brought to the policy agenda by events that simply demand attention, such as starvation in Africa or the damage brought about by hurricanes or other natural disasters.

There are many ways people try to affect the degree of attention given to particular items. Sometimes called **policy entrepreneurs,** those who are willing to invest personal time, energy, and often money in pursuit of particular policy changes can use a variety of personal tactics, such as publicity campaigns, direct contacts with decision makers (letters, phone calls), petition drives, and many others. Or they can involve themselves in major institutions, such as the media, political parties, or interest groups, that provide access to decision makers. Election campaigns, for example, often help clarify or focus the policy agenda.

A second phase of the agenda-setting process may occur almost simultaneously. At the same time that attention is focusing on a particular issue, it is likely that many will be involved in trying to *generate solutions* to the problem. Ideas may come from decision makers themselves, members of their staffs, experts in the bureaucracy, members of the scientific community, policy think tanks (such as the Brookings Institution or the American Enterprise Association), or from the public generally. Typically, proposed solutions swirl around through speeches and articles, papers, and conversations until a few ideas begin to gain special currency. Most often these will be the ideas that not only seem to correctly address the problem, but seem also to be politically acceptable.

NETWORKING

For material on specific policy areas see policy.com at http://www.policy.com/news/index.html. See also the home pages of various "think tanks" such as the Brookings Institution http://www.brook.edu/ and the American Enterprise Institute at http://www.aei.org/. Especially interesting is the site for the Urban Institute: http://www.urban.org/.

A third stream of events affecting the policy agenda is concerned with *political action.* For a proposal to reach the top of the policy agenda, it must be consistent with emerging political realities. Items that are consistent with the prevailing political climate, those that are favored by the incumbent administration and legislative majority, and those that have interest group support (or at least lack organized opposition) are more likely to reach the top of the agenda. These political realities, the proposed ideas or solutions, and the recognition of particular topics represent streams that must come together at just the right moment for action to occur. The windows of opportunity for policy action are narrow, and it takes great skill in managing the various streams so that one's interests are best served.

Policy Formulation

Formulation of public policy involves development of formal policy statements (legislation, executive orders, administrative rules, etc.) that are viewed as legitimate. Again, we will focus here on policy making by the legislature and on the role of public administrators in the legislative process. The basics of how a bill becomes law are well known. At the federal level and in most state governments, a bill is introduced and referred to a committee (and perhaps a subcommittee), hearings are held, the committee reports to the larger body, a vote is taken in both houses, a conference committee works out any differences in the two versions, and the bill is sent to the chief executive for signature. In most other jurisdictions, a similar, though often simplified, approach is used. In any case, the complexity of the legislative process, and the fact that many different decision points must be passed before anything is final, means there are many occasions when those seeking to shape legislative outcomes can seek to exert their influence.

The president, of course, has both formal and informal means of influencing legislation, most notably through program initiatives and budget proposals. Others in the government, including many agency personnel, interact with Congress on a regular basis and may also affect policy outcomes. At the same time, those outside the government—from individual citizens to well-organized interest groups—also seek access and influence. Agency personnel become involved in the legislative process in several ways. In many cases, agencies actually send program proposals to the legislature for its consideration. Such proposals are usually submitted to the legislative leadership, then passed on in turn to the appropriate committee chairs. Though a member of Congress will actually be the one to introduce the proposed legislation, that person may depend on those in the agency for background information and other support. Whether or not legislation has been submitted by an agency, agency personnel will often be called upon to provide testimony regarding particular proposals. As you might imagine, those who staff major public agencies constitute an important source of expertise concerning public issues. For example, it's hard to imagine a group of people better able to understand the tax laws of a particular state than those who work in the state revenue department.

Over time, the relationship between agency personnel and representatives of Congress (either members or staff) can become quite strong. After all, the two groups share common interests and concerns, along with representatives of certain interest groups. A subcommittee on aging, a senior citizen's lobbying organization, and the Social Security Administration, for example, are likely to agree on the need for more Social Security benefits. When the relationship among such interest groups, agency personnel, and members of Congress becomes especially frequent and intense, the resulting alliances are sometimes called *subgovernments* or **iron triangles.** These coalitions can often exert great, possibly even unwarranted, influence.

You should be aware of some of the special considerations facing public administrators at the local level and in nonprofit organizations as they are called upon for advice and help during the process of policy development. As noted, the council-manager form of government was actually founded on a separation of policy and administration—the council made policy and the city manager carried it out. Over time, however, many city managers have become valued by their councils for their expertise in local government and frequently find themselves commenting on or even proposing particular policies. While this situation is quite at odds with the theory underlying council-manager government, it is the reality in most council-manager cities. The same is true of executives in nonprofit organizations and associations. Such situations are not without risk, however, for a delicate balance must be maintained between the executive and legislative functions. Council or board members who feel that their policy-making territory has been intruded upon may exercise another of their council prerogatives—firing the manager or executive!

POLICY IMPLEMENTATION

Members of public organizations play important roles in building the policy agenda and shaping legislative policy, but they are also involved in policy making as part of the implementation process. By its very nature, legislation is general and lacking in detail. Legislators cannot foresee all the individual questions that might come up in implementing a program. Moreover, legislators don't want to tie the hands of program managers by being too restrictive. Consequently, legislation typically leaves a great deal of discretion to public managers in working out the details of a particular program. The Federal Trade Commission, for example, is instructed to prevent deceptive advertising, but has to decide what is deceptive; the Occupational Safety and Health Administration is asked to define and set safety standards for the workplace, but must define more clearly what that means (Meier, 1987, p. 52). In these and many other cases, managers develop administrative rules or policies to give detail to the legislation or to fill in the gaps and, in effect, they make policy.

An early case involving the Environmental Protection Agency illustrates the latitude administrators are often given by Congress (and other legislative bodies) and the difficulties they can cause (Reich, 1985). The EPA is required by law to develop national standards limiting the emission of hazardous air pollutants so as to provide an "ample margin of safety" to protect the public health. But there is no definition in the legislation of ample. This question was especially problematic in the case of a copper smelter in Tacoma, Washington. The EPA determined that, in the absence of any controls on emissions of arsenic from the plant, four new cases of cancer each year could be expected. Even with the very best control equipment, there would still be one new case each year. On the other hand, requiring actions to eliminate the threat would cost the company so much money that it could not afford to continue operations, and its annual $23-million payroll would be lost to the Tacoma community. Obviously, EPA administrator William Ruckelshaus faced a difficult exercise of discretion. (We'll see in Chapter 4 what he did.)

There have been several recent debates concerning the amount of discretion given to administrative agencies. Some analysts argue that broad grants of discretion amount to an abdication of legislative power; others point to the advantages of expertise and flexibility residing in the agencies or with the executive. Currently, the trend appears to be in the direction of greater detail in federal legislation, though occasionally less so at other levels. In any case, there inevitably remain many opportunities for the exercise of administrative discretion.

TYPES OF POLICY

The government develops and carries out several different types of policies, and the involvement of public organizations in the policy process varies somewhat according to type. We will examine four types: regulatory, distributive, redistributive, and constituent policy (Meier, 1987). These classifications are not precise, however, and indeed, many agencies work in several different areas at the same time.

Regulatory policy is designed to limit the actions of persons or groups so as to protect the general public or a substantial portion of the public. For example, people are prohibited from selling certain drugs, polluting the air and water, and engaging in monopolistic business practices. One form of regulation simply focuses on illegal criminal activity; it is a crime to do certain things. State and local governments have special responsibilities in this area, and certain federal agencies, such as the Drug Enforcement Administration, are active here as well. Another form of regulation focuses on American business and seeks to assure fair and competitive practices. Indeed, the first major regulatory effort in this country came in 1887, when the federal government created the Interstate Commerce Commission to regulate the railroads. Similar regulatory agencies today monitor securities (Securities and Exchange Commission), commodity exchanges (Commodity Futures Trading Association), and labor relations (National Labor Relations Board), among others.

A more modern regulatory area is concerned with limiting access to certain goods available to the public generally, such as the airwaves (regulated by the Federal Communications Commission) or clean air and water (regulated by the Environmental Protection Agency). Other regulatory bodies focus on protecting health and safety, in such areas as consumer protection (Consumer Product Safety Commission), air travel (Federal Aviation Administration), food (Food and Drug Administration), and workplace safety (the Occupational Safety and Health Administration).

While federal regulation of economic activities has seen several waves of growth through the past century (Ripley & Franklin, 1987), the last two decades have seen somewhat of a movement in the opposite direction. Late in the Carter administration and extending through the Reagan administration, there were several efforts to deregulate certain industries. The Civil Aviation Board was disbanded in 1984, and significant areas of transportation, telecommunications, and banking were deregulated. Moreover, regulations were eliminated or enforcement slowed down in areas such as the workplace, auto, and consumer products safety.

Distributive policy, perhaps the most common form of government policy, uses general tax revenues to provide benefits to individuals or groups, often by means of grants or subsidies. If the country faces a large agricultural surplus, for example, the federal government may provide incentive payments to farmers not to produce crops that would add to the surplus. Similarly, the federal government provides direct grants to state and local governments for a variety of purposes. Finally, governments often create "public goods" that all citizens can enjoy. In some cases, such as national defense, the good is provided for all; in others, such as city, state, or national parks, it is anticipated that some citizens will use the benefit and others will not. (In Chapter 3, we will examine the growing trend toward employing user fees for certain of these traditionally public goods.)

Unlike regulatory agencies that are often at odds with a clientele group they are seeking to regulate, agencies that carry out distributive policies often develop close relationships with their constituencies and, in turn, with interested members of Congress. The growth of veterans' benefits over the past several decades is an almost classic example of the operation of such a subgovernment. The Veterans Administration is now one of the largest federal agencies and provides a broad range of health benefits, educational assistance, pensions, and insurance for veterans. Such a development would not have been possible without the VA's close relationship with veterans' groups (such as the American

Legion and the Veterans of Foreign Wars) and with the veterans' committees in Congress.

Redistributive policies take taxes from certain groups and give them to another group. On rare occasions, redistribution is from the less well off to the better off; many charge that capital gains proposals are of this type. Redistribution is, however, generally thought of as benefiting less advantaged groups at the perceived expense of the advantaged. Among major redistributive policies are those that deal with (1) income stabilization, helping to support those who are unemployed or retired; (2) social welfare, providing either direct payments to individuals or supporting state and local efforts for the indigent; and (3) health care programs, such as Medicaid and Medicare. Most federal agencies active in the redistributive area, such as the Social Security Administration or the office of Human Development, are located in the Department of Health and Human Services.

Since redistributive policies are often (though sometimes incorrectly) viewed in win-lose terms—that is, if one group benefits, another will surely lose—they generate perhaps more intense discussion than any other area of public policy. Despite this controversy, every American president since Roosevelt and prior to Reagan has supported some major redistributive efforts. Presidents Reagan and Bush, however, took the opposite position, seeking to limit and even reduce redistributive programs. Although support for such programs in the Congress remained substantial, and few programmatic changes came about through legislation, budget reductions and administrative actions substantially diminished social programs. While President Clinton's administration is more favorably inclined toward such programs, its efforts to stimulate growth and reduce the federal budget have limited what is possible in this area.

Constituent policies (Lowi, 1972, p. 300) are intended to benefit the public generally or to serve the government. Foreign and defense policies are good examples of the first set of constituent policies, as well as good examples of the operations of a significant subgovernment. The Air Force had lobbied since the 1960s to build the B-1 bomber as a mainstay of our air defense. In 1978, President Carter was able to "kill" the B-1; however, only three years later, a combination of Defense Department officials, representatives from the defense industry (especially contractors), and congressional supporters of increased military capabilities helped President Reagan resurrect the B-1. (Incidentally, even though today more than a hundred B-1 bombers have been built and are in service, the B-1 remains controversial.)

The other set of constituent policies are those directed toward the agencies of government itself. Legislation affecting the structure and function of government agencies, as well as policies governing their operations, falls in this area. President Carter was especially interested in this area and was instrumental in such changes as a reorganization of the federal personnel system and a reemphasis on affirmative action in hiring practices. Presidents Reagan and Bush were more interested in matters of technical efficiency in government and problems of waste in government. President Clinton, early in his term, expressed an interest in managerial issues, pledging to implement some version of Total Quality Management in the federal government, as he had done in Arkansas. And, of course, later President Clinton, assisted in significant measure by Vice President Gore, developed the National Performance Review, an effort to make government work better and cost less (and a topic we will examine in detail later).

SOURCES OF BUREAUCRATIC POWER

There are several reasons governmental agencies have become so influential in the policy process. First, those who staff the agencies constitute an enormous source of expertise with respect to their areas of interest. No president, governor, mayor, or legislator could ever be expected to gain comparable expertise in all areas. Consequently, to make informed decisions, elected officials must often rely on those in the various agencies. It is often said that information is power; the information that is stored in government agencies is a distinct source of power.

Second, as noted earlier, legislation is often both inevitably and intentionally vague, leaving considerable discretion to the administrator. In some cases, legislators simply wish to defer to the expertise of those in the agencies to provide detailed rules and interpretations. In others, they are recognizing the necessity of some flexibility in administering public programs. In still others, they are responding to the pressures of the legislative process itself, where specificity leads to disputes, and vagueness can often promote agreement.

Administrative discretion is also necessary because changing conditions necessitate changing policies, and it is not always possible to wait for new laws to be passed. In the 1960s, for example, the Department of Agriculture sought to maintain farm income by lowering the supply of agricultural products. Following shortages in the 1970s, the department sought increased production (Anderson, Brady, & Bullock, 1984). In the 1980s, the policy once again became one of limiting production. Flexibility is also needed as new information is discovered; for example, a few years ago, the surgeon general sent a brochure to all households in the country outlining the latest information about AIDS, an action not mandated by Congress but, in the judgment of the surgeon general, required by emerging events.

Through their expertise and discretionary power, those in public agencies help shape public policy. But there are more active and more political ways in which certain agencies become involved in the policy process. Whereas all agencies participate in making policy at some level, some agencies clearly are more politically adept than others. The Defense Department and the Veterans Administration, for example, both wield considerable power, whereas the Government Printing Office has little.

The power, influence, and, in turn, the resources an agency is able to generate depend on several factors, some external to the agency, some internal (Meier, 1987, pp. 54–72). Obviously, shifts in public opinion concerning the agency's task are likely to affect the support the agency receives. The National Aeronautics and Space Administration has experienced wide variations in public support over the years, riding a crest of popularity with the first lunar landing, but later coming under special scrutiny in the wake of the *Challenger* disaster. More recently, the agency has been fighting desperately to maintain projects such as the space station in the light of proposed budget cuts. Not surprisingly, there seems to be a close correlation between favorable public opinion concerning an agency's area of interest and the support it receives from Congress.

More specific support comes from clientele groups, members of the legislature, and others in the executive branch. We have already noted the support certain agencies receive from clientele groups who benefit from the agencies' actions. Obviously, the larger and more powerful the supporters of the agency, the more powerful the agency is likely to be. But agencies also develop opposition, which can be damaging to the agencies' programs. The Environmental Protection Agency, for example, interacts with many different groups, including businesses, state environmental agencies, members of the scientific community, and groups like the Sierra Club or the National Wildlife Federation; the EPA is likely to receive support from some groups and opposition from others.

Special support can also come from individual members of the legislature who decide, for whatever reason, to champion an agency's cause. Rep. Claude Pepper of Florida, for instance, became associated with improved benefits for older Americans and, in that role, worked closely with the Social Security Administration and related social welfare agencies. As we have seen, the combination of congressional and clientele support can lead to the development of "subgovernments" within particular policy areas. These subgovernments come about, in part, because each group has something to give and something to gain from the relationship. The agency can provide quick and favorable responses to congressional requests for help as well as rulings favorable to clientele groups. In return, the agency might receive support for expansion of its budget and programs.

Support may also come from other members of the executive branch. Presidential support is obviously important, whether it is diffuse support of the general area of an agency's work or specific, as in a president's support for AIDS research, increased drug enforcement, or a particular new weapons system. But agencies are also attentive to their relationships with other agencies. The development of a new state park may raise environmental issues, economic development issues, and health issues. The Parks Department will clearly fare better if all the relevant groups and agencies are "on board."

In addition to the external sources of bureaucratic power, there are several internal sources of power (Meier, 1987, pp. 66–72). We have already noted the importance of the *information* and expertise of agency personnel. Especially in highly technical areas, such as medicine or agricultural economics, those in the agencies are likely to be far more knowledgeable than many others involved in setting policies and priorities. If they can employ their expertise credibly, demonstrating effective performance over time, the agency will surely benefit.

Agencies are also likely to benefit by their **cohesion,** the degree to which members are uniformly committed to the organization and its goals. An agency that is seen as divided over major issues will suffer a loss of credibility. Conversely, a sense of unity within an agency is likely to make the agency more effective, both internally and externally.

Finally, agencies benefit from strong and effective *leadership.* For example, James Baker became known as a highly effective leader (as well as an effective politician) in his several roles during the Bush administration. As Secretary of State, Baker played a strong leadership role in U.S. policy in the Middle East and elsewhere. Similarly, in the Clinton administration, Madeline Albright quickly emerged as a strong Secretary of State and enjoyed a good relationship with Congress, especially in her early days in office. On the other hand, the impact of effective versus ineffective leadership is illustrated by the change in the EPA under the highly effective William Ruckelshaus and the ineffective Anne Burford.

The power of particular agencies, therefore, is the result of interaction between the agency and its environment, a process to which the agency brings certain strengths, but must also exercise considerable skill to reach its goals. The external support an agency can generate and the internal combination of its knowledge, cohesion, and leadership affect the amount of power and influence it can command. Whatever an agency's degree of power and influence, however, that power and influence must be exercised judiciously. The agency is a creation of the legislature, and its programs are always subject to the legislature's review, alteration, and even termination.

LEGISLATIVE SUPERVISION: STRUCTURAL CONTROLS

Obviously, most governmental programs (and the agencies that administer them) first take shape in the legislative process. In response to public demands and perhaps also executive leadership, the Congress or a state legislature or a city council or a board of directors passes legislation or policies to correct a particular problem. The problems vary widely, from federal environmental policy to state education requirements to local trash collection practices to the establishment of local health centers, but in most cases legislation authorizes the program. Typically, especially in larger jurisdictions, money to operate the program is separately authorized through an appropriations process. With a program authorized and money appropriated, the building (or expansion) of a public organization can commence.

NETWORKING

For information on Congress, see the following: http://www.loc.gov/ for the Library of Congress; http://www.thomas.loc.gov/ for Congress; http://www.house.gov/ for the House; and U.S. http://www.senate.gov/ for the Senate.

Legislation is, however, somewhat limited as a device for controlling the day-to-day activities of public organizations, especially at the federal and state levels. (Remember that legislation is usually intentionally vague at some points.) But legislation can be used as a control device. After a program is under way, legislation may be passed to prevent members of the executive branch from taking certain actions (Meier, 1987, pp. 140–141). For example, the Boland Amendment sought to prevent covert action in support of the Contras in Nicaragua in the mid-1980s. Whereas legislation authorizing programs must inevitably be somewhat general, legislative prohibitions on administrative actions can be quite specific. However, as in the Iran-Contra scandal, members of an administration may go to great lengths to reinterpret legislation to avoid even those specific prohibitions.

Legislative Veto

One specific device legislatures employ to control public agencies is the **legislative veto,** a statutory provision that essentially says that any action proposed by the executive (or administrative agency) under provisions of a particular piece of legislation is subject to the approval or disapproval of Congress (or some portion of Congress), usually within thirty to ninety days. For example, legislation might authorize a new highway program, but require legislative consent to undertake specific projects. The legislative veto was first used in the 1930s to permit the president to reorganize, subject to review by Congress. In the 1970s and early 1980s, however, the legislative veto began to be used in many other areas, most notably in the War Powers Resolution of 1973, which required the president to notify Congress of military action and to cease such action within sixty days unless Congress acts to continue it.

The effect of a legislative veto provision on a public agency is illustrated in the experience of the Federal Trade Commission in the late 1970s and early 1980s. An aggressive consumer protection effort by the FTC in the late 1970s was countered by business groups in Congress, which successfully passed legislation to the effect that Congress could disapprove any FTC rules it didn't like. Congress used that provision in 1982 to disapprove an FTC rule, which had been developed over a ten-year period, requiring used-car dealers to disclose defects in cars they sold (Ripley & Franklin, 1987, pp. 141–142). In a similar case that found its way to the Supreme Court as *Immigration and Naturalization Services v. Chadha* (1983), the Court ruled the legislative veto unconstitutional. The Court's argument was that the constitutional process for passing legislation requires the involvement of the president, and actions under a legislative veto provision fail to involve the executive.

Despite the unconstitutionality of the legislative veto, the interest of Congress in controlling the work of administrative agencies has not diminished. Indeed, Congress has found a variety of ways to get around the *Chadha* ruling, either informally, or by adding detailed rules to legislative authorizations, or by simply continuing to include veto provisions in legislation despite the court's ruling. From the day that the *Chadha* decision was rendered to the end of 1990, approximately two hundred new legislative vetoes were enacted into law (Fisher, 1991). Other vetoes have been created by informal agreements, such as an agreement made during the Bush administration by Secretary of State James Baker regarding release of funds for the Contras in Nicaragua. Some have even charged that congressional involvement in the details of administration (sometimes called *micromanagement*) has increased as a result of the *Chadha* ruling (*PA Times,* 29 April 1988, p. 1). According to this argument, Congress, lacking the legislative veto, has sought to exert its influence through increasingly detailed legislation, which may unduly limit administrative flexibility. (The *Chadha* ruling in a federal case does not itself limit the use of the legislative veto at the state level, where use of the veto has been rapidly growing. Those few cases that have been decided in state courts, however, have followed the *Chadha* lead in ruling the legislative veto unconstitutional [Johnson, 1983]. At the same time, state legislatures have also continued vetolike actions.)

Sunset Laws

Another control device that legislatures employ, to assess the performance of agencies and to eliminate those that are not successful, is the **sunset law.** Sunset laws are based on the assumption that certain governmental programs should periodically terminate, to continue only after an evaluation of the program's effectiveness and a specific vote by the legislature. A classic case on the problem of program continuation is the military commissary system, which was created to provide foodstuffs to the cavalry on the western plains in the 1800s. The program continues today, although nearly all military commissaries are within ten miles of two or more supermarkets!

Sunset laws became popular in the late 1970s and early 1980s, after the state of Colorado, at the urging of Common Cause, passed a set of laws requiring that certain regulatory agencies be terminated at a given point unless given new life by the legislature. Soon dozens of other states and many municipalities passed general sunset laws, applying termination dates to a set of programs, or included sunset provisions in legislation creating new programs. Proposals containing sunset provisions were also presented at the federal level.

The purpose of specifying a particular life span for a program is to force careful evaluation of the program at some future point. Critics of automatic terminations point out several problems, not the least of which is the cost of evaluations and the burden to the legislature and legislative staff if all programs were periodically evaluated in great detail. Questions also arise about whether sunset legislation actually changes our assumptions about continuing most programs; for example, no one would seriously anticipate that a police or fire department would be eliminated. Finally, critics point out that most programs are reviewed periodically anyway and that highly ineffective programs are often eliminated even without "sunset" provisions.

A final mechanism through which legislative bodies formally exert control over administrative agencies is passage of broad legislation to govern agency conduct. Such legislation, applicable to all agencies, might affect administrative procedures, contracting or purchasing arrangements, human resources management, or other areas. A good example is the continuing congressional interest in access to governmental information. Following World War II, governmental agencies, probably in keeping with the military mentality of the war years, could legally classify as "confidential" all records for which there was "good cause" to hold secret. As you can imagine, it was not difficult to come up with all kinds of "good causes" or reasons to withhold records. The practice of keeping secrets became so widespread that one congressional investigating group found that the Pentagon had classified as secret the construction of the bow and arrow and the fact that water runs downhill! Similarly, the General Services Administration had decided photographs could not be taken in federal buildings without permission of the janitor (Archibald, 1979, p. 314).

As a result of findings such as these, and in the belief that the public has the right to information gathered by the government, Congress passed the Freedom of Information Act in 1966. The law was based on the assumption that the public has the right to know, except in clearly defined and exceptional cases; in other words, it limited those in the executive branch from classifying documents for ill-defined purposes. Implementation of the new law was hindered by confusion about certain of its parts and by some agency officials who still tried to maintain as much secrecy as possible. These problems were addressed in a series of amendments passed over the veto of President Ford in 1974. The amendments required agencies to respond to inquiries quickly and even sought to penalize government officials who hid government records from the public. Although problems with the act have persisted, nearly all federal agencies have now implemented the Freedom of Information provisions.

Sunshine Laws

These examples of constraints on the operation of government agencies are closely related to **sunshine laws** that require various agencies, especially regulatory agencies, to conduct business in public view (except under specific conditions). For example, early in 1993, based on a Freedom of Information request from a New York artist, NASA released forty-five photographs of wreckage of the space shuttle *Challenger*, which had exploded some seven years earlier.

Florida's Government-in-the-Sunshine Law provides the public a right of access to governmental proceedings at the state, county, and municipal levels, as well as other political subdivisions such as authorities and special districts. This law requires that any gathering of two or more members of any board or commission be subject to the requirements of the Sunshine Law if they discuss any matter that will foreseeably come before that board for action. The three basic requirements of the law are: (1) meetings must be open to the public, (2) reasonable notice of such meetings must be given, and (3) minutes of the meetings must be taken. In effect, the law prohibits members of any board or commission from having informal or casual discussions of board business outside an open public meeting for which reasonable notice was given.

All fifty states now have "sunshine" provisions for their own legislative bodies, for administrative agencies, and for local governments. In all these cases, the legislative body, in expressing its concern for the public's right to be informed about the public's business, has exercised control over a broad range of administrative agencies.

LEGISLATIVE SUPERVISION: OVERSIGHT

In addition to the "structural" mechanisms for legislative control, the legislature also exercises continuing supervision of administrative agencies through what is called the oversight function. Each house of Congress has a government operations committee charged with overseeing the activities of all government agencies, including their relationships with other levels of government. In addition, each of the other congressional committees exercises oversight responsibility with respect to its particular area of interest and expertise (e.g., defense, welfare, the post office). Oversight is especially connected to the legislative and appropriations processes (see Box 2.3), but may occur at any time. For this reason, it is not unusual to see a cabinet secretary, complete with charts and documents, testifying before a congressional committee that is interested in his or her programs.

Holding hearings is probably the most visible oversight activity of Congress, at times assuming a circuslike atmosphere. The Iran-Contra hearings, for example, were essentially an investigation of the activities of the National Security Council, an executive agency, but they became the arena for considerable political in-fighting concerning the Reagan administration's conduct of foreign policy. (They were also noteworthy for their revelations of intentional efforts by Lt. Colonel Oliver North and Undersecretary of State Elliot Abrams to deceive Congress in the course of normal oversight activities.)

The exposure that hearings provide members of Congress is obvious. Politicians from Harry Truman to Sam Ervin to Daniel Inouye to Fred Thompson have built national reputations through their involvement in congressional hearings. But hearings can also provide excellent opportunities for administrative officials at the federal, state, and

BOX 2.3

Testifying before the Appropriations Committee

The most important thing in a committee hearing is creating an atmosphere of confidence—so that you have confidence in the committee and they have confidence in you. I tell my people to be perfectly honest and to have a full, free, and frank discussion with the committee, even if it hurts you a little bit. That will mean more than anything else in getting your money. Nobody likes to admit things and cast reflections on his own shop, but don't try to fool the congressmen. You can't. They have a sixth sense when someone is not talking freely and frankly. If you have a perfectly open discussion, they'll have more confidence in you, and your appropriations troubles will be minimized.

SOURCE: An agency budget officer quoted in Richard F. Fenno, Jr., *The Power of the Purse* (Boston: Little, Brown, 1966), 298.

local levels, and in nonprofit organizations, to tell their side of the story, to help educate members of the legislature and the public generally, and to build support for their programs. Consequently, most agencies devote considerable time and attention to legislative relations, often, at the federal level, working through a legislative liaison office, or, at the state and local levels, on a more individual basis.

Nationally, Congress can also exercise oversight through its staff agencies, most of which were significantly enhanced by legislation in the early 1970s that created the Congressional Budget Office and charged it with furnishing certain program information to Congress, and also shifted the focus of the General Accounting Office from its traditional financial auditing to program evaluations. Now, in addition to holding hearings, Congress can exercise oversight responsibility through staff evaluations of agency operations by requesting information from the Congressional Budget Office or by initiating audits or program evaluations by the General Accounting Office. Although legislative staff capabilities at the state and local levels are considerably less, and often more focused on policy development than oversight, all levels of government have witnessed a general increase in legislative staff over the past twenty years.

Finally, there are myriad informal relationships between legislators and those in executive agencies. In fact, such nonstatutory controls may be the most common form of congressional oversight (Davidson & Oleszek, 1990).

Despite the array of oversight activities available to members of Congress and despite devoting increased staff resources to oversight, questions remain concerning the effectiveness of legislative oversight of executive branch operations. Part of the problem is simply that many legislators have relatively little interest in oversight activities. Instead, they tend to focus on policy issues, recognizing that they are much more likely to build their reputations in the policy arena than in oversight. Moreover, interest in oversight activities is likely to vary from time to time, increasing in times of crisis or public outcry, when new and different program requests are forthcoming from an agency, or when a member feels a particular agency has not been responsive to constituent groups. Generally, when a member has high confidence in a set of leaders and tends to agree with policies, the motivation for oversight decreases; conversely, when trust is low or when the member's favored programs are being ignored, the incentive for oversight is greater.

LEGISLATIVE SUPERVISION: CASEWORK

Legislators also interact with those in public agencies on an individual basis, usually in behalf of their constituents. Obviously, legislators who wish to be reelected must be attentive to requests for information or influence from those in their districts. And, on the other side of the coin, individual citizens have come to expect that they can and should receive help from their senator or representative in dealings with government. Thus, members of the legislature receive a multitude of requests for assistance, from someone who needs help to collect Social Security benefits to someone who hopes to influence the award of a particular governmental contract. Intervention in behalf of individuals or groups that need assistance with or access to government agencies is called legislative casework.

At the federal level, providing services for constituents has become one of the most time-consuming and important activities for Congress members. Requests for assistance are typically handled by congressional staff members who specialize in casework. If the request requires an inquiry into an agency activity, the staffer will likely approach the agency's congressional liaison office or perhaps go directly to the agency head or a regional office. In most instances, inquiries are responded to promptly, and information about the case and any necessary explanations of the agency's action are returned quickly to the member of Congress.

Federal officials, in both the legislature and the agencies, feel the process is useful not only in providing a mechanism for review, but in clarifying agency policies and procedures and assessing agency performance (Johannes, 1984). Occasionally, however, pressure to "bend the rules" or to play political favoritism occurs. Several years ago, for example, Congressman Daniel Flood of Pennsylvania was charged with conspiracy, bribery, and perjury in connection with his efforts to obtain certain federal grants and loans for a hospital in his district.

Casework activities seem less routine and institutionalized at the state and local levels. Here there appear to be both benefits and costs (Elling, 1980). On the one hand, casework activities serve to "humanize" the bureaucracy; on the other, there are disadvantages in the disruption of administrative processes and in the possibility of political influence. Certainly in the more highly professionalized governmental agencies, agency heads view legislators' involvement positively (Abney & Lauth, 1982).

In many European countries, and in some American states and localities, the legislature's casework function has been paralleled or even turned over to the office of the **ombudsman,** a permanent office that receives complaints and acts on behalf of citizens in securing information, requesting services, or pursuing grievances. Many other jurisdictions have created similar, though less formal, structures, such as public advocates, citizens' assistance offices, and so on (Hill, 1982).

RELATIONSHIPS WITH THE JUDICIARY

The relationship between administrative agencies and the judiciary derives, as you might expect, from the legal foundations of administrative actions, some of which are quasi-legislative and others of which are quasi-judicial. Those that are *quasi-legislative* elaborate the details of legislation. As we have noted, most legislation is necessarily and intentionally general, leaving considerable room for interpretation or discretion on the part of the administrator. For example, an agency might be required by law to set safety standards for nuclear-powered electric utilities but receive little guidance about which specific standards should be employed. The agency would seek to determine appropriate standards, then develop rules to govern implementation of the legislation. **Rule making** is concerned with establishing general guidelines that would apply to a class of people or a class of actions in the future.

 NETWORKING

Basic issues in administrative law are listed in the Administrative Law index at http://www.law.indiana.edu/law/v-lib/admin.html.

At the federal level, rule making by administrative agencies, as well as many other aspects of administrative law, is governed by the Administrative Procedures Act. (Similar statutes exist in each state to provide the legal framework for administrative actions.) The act seeks to assure that rules are based on proper legal authority, that there are both adequate notice of the rule making and an opportunity for citizens to be heard, that the rule is clear and unambiguous, and that people are given sufficient advance warning that the new rule will take effect (*Federal Administrative Procedures Source Book,* 1992, p. 416).

In 1996, the APA celebrated its fiftieth anniversary, an anniversary that had some questioning whether the act still provided an adequate framework to resolve the increasingly complex legal questions in contemporary society. Recent challenges to the APA have centered on issues of regulatory reform, including efforts by the Republican-controlled Congress to curb powers of administrative agencies. The discourse on Capitol Hill, however, has tended to be divided along partisan lines, with only a trace of common ground to advance the reform agenda, and, in fact, most of the recent criticism from Congress had little to do with "poor administrative practices." The courts, on the other hand, remain favorable to the APA and during the past three years have sustained the act's administrative framework. So while the legislative debate goes on, the APA continues to be the primary guide for the practice of administration.

In most cases, rule making is fairly straightforward, involving notice, comment, and steps to assure an adequate record; in others, legislation requires greater detail and great formality in the rule-making process. Food and Drug regulations and others that involve high risks require a formal rule-making process. Formal rule-making procedures require that the agency issue its rule only after trial-type hearing procedures are completed.

The Negotiated Rule Making Act of 1990 continued a trend toward the use of alternative means of dispute resolution—that is, mechanisms for resolving disputes that would not require formal legal processes. As with other alternative means of dispute resolutions, "negotiated rule making provides a means of using consensual techniques to produce better, more acceptable results, reducing the likelihood of protracted legislation." Essentially, negotiated rule making brings together various parties involved in a particular issue to discuss potential rules and to try to arrive at consensus in advance of the structure and content of those rules.

Like other forms of dispute resolution, such as mediation or arbitration, no agency is forced to use these techniques; however, many public agencies are finding it very helpful to do so (*Federal Alternative Procedures Source Book,* 1992).

Other administrative actions are quasi-judicial in that they produce orders relating to individual cases. For example, following the issuance of safety standards for nuclear power plants, an administrator might have to decide if a particular plant has met those standards. Similarly, an administrator might have to decide if a specific individual is eligible for workers' compensation. In such cases, the administrator is making decisions that determine one's status under the law. The substantive decisions are obviously important, but so are the procedures under which they are resolved. For example, a woman denied welfare support might request a hearing to argue her case before a final decision is made. The administrator's decision to grant or refuse the hearing represents another kind of quasi-judicial administrative action.

In quasi-judicial administrative actions, often called *adjudication,* procedural issues such as those just mentioned are of special importance. There is a desire that citizens be treated fairly and not subjected to arbitrary decisions. Consequently, where standards of due process are applied, notice of the proposed action must be given, there must be a chance for the affected party to respond, and there must be an independent decision maker and an opportunity for appeal.

The courts may review administrative actions (in rule making, adjudication, or other areas) through *judicial review.* Such review typically occurs when a party "suffering legal wrong because of agency action, or adversely affected or aggrieved by agency action" seeks judicial remedy (5 U.S.C., Section 702). The court reviews the case in light of constitutional, statutory, and executive provisions and determines the appropriateness of the administrative action. Generally speaking, courts may find unlawful and set aside agency actions that are unconstitutional, that extend beyond the limits of statutory authority, that are "arbitrary, capricious, or an abuse of discretion," that are procedurally unfair or without substantive justification (5 U.S.C., Section 706). However, following the Supreme Court's finding in *Chevron* v. *National Resources Defense Council* (1984), if a statute is silent or ambiguous with respect to the issue at hand, the agency's interpretation of the statute must be upheld if its interpretation is a reasonable one.

The deference to administrators underlying *Chevron,* a position referred to as contemporaneous administrative construction, stems from the court's belief that an administrative agency responsible for implementing a piece of legislation has the most knowledge of the policy and of existing legislation concerning the issue. The courts may ultimately disagree with the agency interpretation, but they start with a heavy presumption that the agency was correct. While some suggest that *Chevron* is being called into question, recent Supreme Court decisions have reinforced the doctrine of judicial deference to administrative agencies. In four recent cases, rulings made by the high court during the "post-*Chevron*" era relating to the U.S. Treasury Department and the federal tax code, the Supreme Court relied on *Chevron* in supporting the validity of the department's regulation. Such consistency, when considered with lower court decisions during the same period, suggests that the judiciary will continue to maintain the capacity and scope of administrative agencies.

That is not to say that the court always rules in favor of the administrative agency. Of particular interest are those cases in which the court determines that the agency has misinterpreted (or gone beyond) the intent of the legislation. As an example, the statute creating the Occupational Safety and Health Administration (OSHA) in the Department of Labor charged the agency with developing a standard for toxic substances in the workplace "which assures, to the extent feasible . . . that no employee will suffer material impairment . . . even if such employee has regular exposure to the hazard . . . for the period of his working life" (Cooper, 1983, p. 192). After extensive studies, OSHA determined that exposure to the toxic substance benzine created a risk of cancer and other health hazards and set a standard accordingly.

The American Petroleum Institute sought judicial review that led the courts to a discussion of two rather interesting issues. One aspect of the case had to do with legislative intent. The Fifth Circuit Court focused on this issue, finding that the phrase "to the extent feasible" in the legislation meant that a standard had to be both technologically and economically feasible. For this reason, the court set aside the OSHA standard. The Supreme Court concentrated more on the health aspects of the case, with the majority concluding that existing standards were not dangerous and the new standard was not necessary. The justices who dissented argued that the Court should not substitute its own judgment on the technical merits of the case for that of experts within the agency. The case illustrates several of the most important difficulties that face the courts in reviewing administrative actions.

The courts lately have more frequently acted not only to review agency actions, but to compel agency action "unlawfully withheld or unreasonably delayed" (5 U.S.C., Section 706). A few years ago, the Food and Drug Administration received a petition from a group of death row inmates to determine whether the materials used for lethal injections were safe and painless or whether they might leave the prisoner conscious but paralyzed, a witness to his or her own slow death. The FDA responded that it did not have jurisdiction to review the practices of state corrections systems in cases such as this; however, on review, the circuit court concluded that the FDA did indeed have jurisdiction. The court wrote, "In this case FDA is clearly refusing to exercise enforcement discretion because it does not wish to become embroiled in an issue so morally and emotionally troubling as the death penalty. As a result of the FDA's inaction, appellants face the risk of cruel execution" (Cooper, 1985, p. 649).

Closely related to the FDA's failure to undertake an investigation are cases in which the agency refuses to make rules or delays the issuance of rules required by statute. But there have also been several recent cases in which agencies have been found to have exceeded their authority in rescinding previously established rules.

CONCERNS FOR DUE PROCESS

At the heart of our system of jurisprudence is the assurance that people will be treated fairly, that they have a right to present arguments and evidence in their own behalf, and that those who make the decisions will be unbiased and impartial. As with issues of due process in administrative adjudication—whether a hearing is required, at what point, and the format of the hearing—some patterns have emerged in the Supreme Court's evaluation of administrative matters. During the 1950s, 1960s, and early 1970s, the Court sought to protect the rights of citizens from arbitrary action on the part of administrative agencies by requiring that a person be allowed an opportunity to challenge a proposed action before being made to suffer serious harm. The Court would not allow cost or inconvenience to the agency as an excuse for causing harm to an individual.

Through the 1970s and 1980s however, the Supreme Court, under the leadership of Chief Justice Warren Burger, began to alter its approach to administrative due process, treating administrative hearings not as a means of protection but as devices for fact-finding. Most frequently, the Court has employed a "balancing test," weighing the interests of the individual (rather narrowly defined), the value of additional safeguards, and the government's interest (including the fiscal and administrative burdens that additional procedural safeguards might impose). The material is Box 2.4 illustrates the application of this balancing test. As a result, it has become much more difficult for someone who feels that adequate protections have not been provided to prevail in the courts (Cooper, 1982).

The flexibility in administrative law for due process has contributed to a variety of alternative dispute resolution (ADR) strategies, namely mediation and arbitration. In fact, the adoption of the Alternative Dispute Resolution Act of 1990 helped remove many of the barriers administrators face to such alternative approaches. For the most part, ADR strategies are easier to employ in less complex cases. Yet ADR should not be used to obtain settlements that fail to protect the public interest. The spirit and letter of the agreement must be clear or else face considerable challenge, and potential failure, during the implementation stage.

THE COURTS AND AGENCY ADMINISTRATION

Over the past twenty years, one of the most dramatic developments in the relationship between administrative agencies and the judiciary is the direct involvement of federal district courts (and some state courts) in agency administration, including decisions on spending, personnel, organization, and management. This involvement has come about through court rulings in *administrative equity* cases, wherein individual rights, such as the prohibition against cruel and unusual punishment, have been violated by state and local administrative organizations.

Two landmark cases in the early 1970s set precedents for such rulings. In the first, prisoners in the Arkansas penitentiary system alleged a large number of abuses, including dangerous and unhealthy conditions in the prisons. The court ruled that confinement in the Arkansas system amounted to cruel and unusual punishment and ordered corrections officials to devise a plan to remedy the problems. Similarly, in Alabama a federal district court judge found "intolerable and deplorable" conditions in that state's largest

BOX 2.4

The Spotted Owl and Agency Interpretation of the Law

When a court reviews an agency's construction of the statute it administers, it is confronted with two questions. First, always, is the question of whether Congress has directly spoken to the precise question at issue. If the intent of Congress is clear, that is the end of the matter; for the court, as well as the agency, must give effect to the unambiguously expressed intent of Congress.

If, however, the court determines Congress has not directly addressed the precise question at issue, the court does not simply impose its own construction of the statute, as would be necessary in the absence of an administrative interpretation.

Rather, if the statute is silent or ambiguous with respect to the specific issue, the question for the court is whether the agency's answer is based on a permissible construction of the statute.

Given the ubiquity of ambiguity in regulatory statutes, *Chevron* looked like a recipe for judicial acquiescence to agency interpretations. It hasn't worked out that way. Sometimes, to be sure, the Court gives full scope to the doctrine announced in *Chevron*. Other times, however, the Court virtually ignores the *Chevron* test. Most importantly, only three years after *Chevron,* the Court recognized a major escape hatch from the doctrine of deference to agency interpretation.

Babbitt v. *Sweet Home Chapter of Communities for a Great Oregon*—the celebrated Spotted Owl case—illustrates the indeterminacy of the *Chevron* doctrine. At issue was the meaning of the term *harm* in the Endangered Species Act. The act prohibits the "taking" of endangered animals and defines "take" to mean "to harass, harm, pursue, hunt, shoot, wound, kill, trap, capture, or collect[.]" According to Secretary of the Interior Bruce Babbitt, "harm" includes destruction of habitat that has the effect—although not the purpose—of harming endangered wildlife. Oregon business interests challenged this interpretation as contrary to the statute.

The fundamental problem in administrative law is that a congressional majority typically favors some federal response to a problem, but no congressional majority favors any particular response. Rather than do nothing, Congress adopts general language and leaves it to the agencies—and the courts—to make the controversial choices. The Endangered Species Act is a good illustration of this. Congress knew quite well that habitat destruction poses the biggest threat to endangered species. Congress also knew, however, that regulating habitat destruction would conflict with economic development. So Congress waffled.

The only clear intention Congress had regarding habitat destruction is a clear intention to have no clear intention. The problem calls less for lawyerly interpretations of authoritative language than for a policy decision made by an institution that is familiar with the problem and is held politically accountable. The agency has the advantage (over) the courts on both counts.

SOURCE: Donald A. Dripps, *Trial* 32, no. 2 (February 1996): 70–71.

mental health facility and ordered corrective actions. The court also established a constitutional right to treatment, detailing actions required to meet that constitutional standard (Gilmour, 1982, pp. 26–29).

The involvement of courts in the management of public agencies is especially well illustrated in a federal judge's order demanding reform of the New Orleans Parish Prison. In addition to ordering adequate medical services, improved security, and development of recreational facilities, the judge directed that "the management and operation of the prison be improved immediately," that a professional penologist be hired to manage the prison, and that personnel practices (filling vacancies, raising wages, etc.) be improved in specific ways. Although court actions such as this have obviously corrected constitutional inequities, there are questions as to whether the courts are well suited for involvement in the details of administration. Moreover, many states and localities argue that court-ordered expenditures of funds on projects such as desegregation or prison reform take money away from other needed services, such as education, social welfare, or mental health. Indeed, for these various reasons, the Supreme Court has recently taken steps to limit the involvement of courts in the work of administrative agencies, requiring carefully tailored plans of limited duration based on specific constitutional violations.

SUMMARY AND ACTION IMPLICATIONS

This chapter has explored the political context of public administration, including things you will simply need to know to operate effectively in or with public organizations. The material in this chapter (and in Chapter 3) constitutes a knowledge base on which to build your action skills. Understanding the political context of work in the public sector will enhance the effectiveness of your actions.

Public managers work in many different institutional settings, but those institutions all reflect important political values that lie at the heart of a democratic system. Whether at the federal, state, or local level, in government or in the nonprofit sector, a democracy's values, especially a concern for operating in the public interest, affect the structure of public organizations. For example, the division of powers at the federal level expresses a fear of concentrated power; similarly, the council-manager plan expresses one way to view the relationship between politics and administration. Finally, the structure of nonprofit organizations reflects their operation in the public interest. Knowing something about how democratic values are reflected in the structure of public organizations and knowing something about the role of executive leadership in administrative organizations will enable you to act with greater confidence and authority.

As a public manager, you may have important interactions with a legislative body, either the national Congress, a state legislature, a local city council, or a nonprofit organization's board of directors. Those in public organizations participate in one way or another in nearly all policy areas—a situation that our political system encourages. The distinction Woodrow Wilson suggested between politics (or policy) and administration no longer accurately describes the relationship between the legislative and the executive branch. Today, the legislature and the various agencies of government share in the policy process, either working together in developing policy or making separate decisions in different realms.

As a public manager, you will also deal with the legislature in many other ways. Most importantly, the legislature will establish the tasks your agency or association will undertake and provide human and financial resources to carry them out. Moreover, the legislative body will exercise continuing, though sometimes intermittent, supervision over your work. Thus, you may spend a great deal of time developing effective working relationships with those in the legislature.

The involvement of the courts in the work of administration is both intense and inevitable. For this reason, your understanding of the legal system and your ability to interact with legal and judicial officers will improve your effectiveness as a public manager. Whether you are dealing with the legislative body or the courts, your relationship with either need not be adversarial. Indeed, in many cases, the legislature and the courts can help to substantially improve administrative practices.

By now you should be coming to realize that your behavior as a public manager is bounded by a vast and complicated network of relationships in which you are but one of many players. Within this network, you must be attentive to questions of executive leadership, legislative intent and oversight, and judicial interpretation. The world of the public administrator is indeed complex!

Terms and Definitions

Agenda setting: Phase in public policy process when certain problems come to be viewed as needing attention.

Cohesion: Degree to which members of a group are uniformly committed to the group and its goals.

Constituent policy: Policy designed to benefit the public generally or to serve the government.

Distributive policy: Policy involving use of general tax funds to provide assistance and benefits to individuals or groups.

Executive order: A presidential mandate directed to and governing, with the effect of law, the actions of government officials and agencies.

Independent agencies: Agencies intentionally created outside the normal cabinet organization.

Iron triangle: Term given to a coalition of interest groups, agency personnel, and members of Congress created to exert influence on a particular policy issue.

Legislative veto: Statutory provision that gives Congress the authority to approve or disapprove certain executive actions.

Nonprofit organizations: Organizations prohibited by law from distributing surplus revenues to individuals.

Ombudsman: Permanent office that receives complaints and acts on behalf of citizens to secure information, request services, or pursue grievances.

Policy: Statement of goals and intentions with respect to a particular problem or set of problems.

Policy entrepreneur: A person willing to invest personal time, energy, and money in pursuit of particular policy changes.

Public corporation: An essentially commercial agency where work requires greater latitude and acquires at least a portion of its funding in the marketplace (e.g., Tennessee Valley Authority).

Public policy: Authoritative statements made by legitimate governmental actors about public problems.

Redistributive policy: Policy designed to take taxes from certain groups and give them to another group.

Regulatory commission: Group formed to regulate a particular area of the economy; usually headed by a group of individuals appointed by the president and confirmed by the Senate.

Regulatory policy: Policy designed to limit actions of persons or groups to protect all or parts of the general public.

Rule making: Administrative establishment of general guidelines for application to a class of people or a class of actions at some future time.

Sunset law: Provision that sets a specific termination date for a program.

Sunshine law: Provision that requires agencies to conduct business in public view.

Study Questions

1. What do we mean by the term *public policies?*
2. Describe how the president's role in the administration of government has changed since the framing of the Constitution.
3. Describe the administrative system at the federal level.
4. State and local governments have been designed to operate similarly to the national level; however, both have distinct structures for administering government initiatives. Explain each level's structure and the different approaches to operating the government bureaucracy.
5. Describe the policy process and actors who play significant roles in shaping administrative issues.
6. What are the four types of policy? Define and give examples.
7. How do agencies maintain a power base within the government?
8. Describe some of the structural controls on bureaucratic power and how government, as a whole, benefits from these controls.
9. Discuss several ways the legislative and judicial branches interact with the bureaucracy. Explain why these interventions are necessary and useful.

Cases and Exercises

1. We have discussed the various powers, both formal and informal, that affect the governor's ability to exercise executive power in the administration of state government. Among the informal powers that governors exercise are political powers (including agenda setting), budgetary powers, and executive leadership.

   Among the formal powers are the presence or absence of an item veto and the ability of the governor to reorganize state agencies. Another indicator of gubernatorial power is the number of other elected statewide officials. Analyze the power of the governor in your state, giving special attention to the governor's power to exercise executive leadership over the agencies of state government. How do your governor's executive powers compare to those of the president of the United States? How do they compare to those of your local mayor?

2. The *United States Government Manual* is the handbook or encyclopedia of federal government programs and activities. It contains descriptions of the many programs the federal government operates, as well as information about how the government is organized to conduct those programs. Obtain a copy of the *Manual* and analyze the organization and structure of one cabinet-level department, such as Transportation or Health and Human Services. Then, using local sources, try to develop similar information about how your state and your local government are organized to deal with the same subject matter. What are the similarities and what are the differences? How do you explain them?

3. Attend a meeting of a congressional or state legislative committee, of your local city council, or of the board of directors of a local nonprofit organization. Watch the pattern of interaction between elected members of the legislative body and full-time administrators. (The latter may be agency staff called to testify, legislative support staff, a city manager or executive director, or many others.) What strengths does each side bring to the exchange? What is the level of cooperation or competition? If possible, try to follow up with the administrator to see how he or she felt about the interchange. To what extent did the legislative body set a clear direction for the administrator's ensuing actions? What discretion did the administrator have (or claim to have) following the meeting?

4. Consider the following case: Billie Jackson was city manager of a small community in Colorado. For six years, Billie had been trying to interest members of her city council in purchasing an abandoned downtown hotel for conversion to a city-owned long-term care facility. Billie felt strongly that the community needed such a facility and that the city had a golden opportunity to meet that need through purchase of the hotel. The problem was that several extremely conservative members of the council felt differently. In their view, the city shouldn't get into providing social services, especially where the need might be met by a private firm at some point in the future. Moreover, they felt the cost of the purchase and renovations would be more than the community could bear.

   The hotel issue was once again on the council agenda, and Billie was determined to make the strongest appeal possible. With the help of a nearby university, she had prepared a lengthy report documenting the need for the facility and the desirability of purchasing the hotel. Just as she was beginning her presentation, one of the conservative council members said, "Mrs. Jackson, we have heard more on this topic than we care to. I just don't want to go through all this again. I move to table the issue indefinitely." The motion to table carried by a quick and somewhat confused voice vote.

Assume the role of Billie Jackson. What is your immediate response? What would you do in the days and weeks that followed? Would you consider resignation? Why or why not?

5. Read the following case: The U.S. Supreme Court has let stand a ruling requiring Alaska to collect rent or royalties from miners of gold, silver, and other hard rock, despite the fact that collections will be so low that the money won't even cover state paperwork costs.

Under the Alaska Statehood Act, the state received more than 100 million acres of land and was directed to devise a system to protect its mineral rights. The legislature decided to collect royalties from companies involved in the lucrative search for oil, gas, and coal, but waived the requirement for the mining of gold, silver, and other hard rock because it did not generate much money.

Alaska received more than $1 billion a year in royalties from companies that mine for oil and gas, the state's major resources. The state has argued that royalties for hard rock mining would amount to only $100,000 a year, not enough to make the paper work worthwhile.

A coalition of environmental, fishing and native Alaskan groups had originally filed suit to force the state to collect fees for the mining for hard rock, accusing Alaska of violating the Alaska Statehood Act.

SOURCE: *City and State* 4 (June 6, 1988). Reprinted by permission.

Discuss your response to this case. Under what circumstances, if any, do you think it is appropriate for a federal court to order a state or locality to undertake an action it has chosen not to take and that will cost the state or locality to administer?

For Additional Reading

Aaron, Henry, Thomas Mann, and Timothy Taylor, eds. *Values and Public Policy.* Washington: Brookings Institution, 1994.

Ammons, David N., and Charldean Newell. *City Executives: Leadership Roles, Work Characteristics and Time Management.* Albany, NY: State University of New York Press, 1989.

Anderson, James E. *Public Policymaking: An Introduction.* 2d ed. Boston, MA: Houghton Mifflin Co., 1994.

Bailey, Mary Timney, and Richard T. Mayer, eds. *Public Management in an Interconnected World: Essays in the Minnowbrook Tradition.* New York: Greenwood Press, 1992.

Baker, Randall. *Comparative Public Management.* Westport, CT: Praeger Publishers, 1994.

Bingham, Richard D., et al. *Managing Local Government.* Thousand Oaks, CA: Sage Publications, 1991.

Cochran, Clarke E., et al. *American Public Policy: An Introduction*. 4th ed. New York: St. Martin's Press, 1993.

deLeon, Peter. *Democracy and the Policy Sciences*. Albany: State University of New York Press, 1997.

Ehrenhalt, Alan. *The United States of Ambition: Politicians, Power and the Pursuit of Office*. New York: Times Books, 1991.

Fiorina, Morris. *Divided Government*. New York: Macmillan, 1992.

Gies, David L., J. Steven Ott, and Jay Shafritz, eds. *The Nonprofit Organization*. Pacific Grove, CA: Brooks/Cole, 1990.

Goodsell, Charles T. *The Case for Bureaucracy*. 3d ed. Chatham, NJ: Chatham House, 1994

Holden, Matthew. *Continuity and Disruption*. Pittsburgh: University of Pittsburgh Press, 1996.

Johnson, David B. Public Choice: *An Introduction to the New Political Economy*. Mountain View, CA: Mayfield, 1991.

Meier, Kenneth J. *Politics and the Bureaucracy*. 2d ed. Pacific Grove, CA: Brooks/Cole, 1987.

Mier, Robert. *Social Justice and Local Development Policy*. Newbury Park, CA: Sage Publishers, 1993.

Nalbandian, John. *Professionalism in Local Government: Transformation in Roles, Responsibilities and Values of City Managers*. San Francisco, CA: Jossey-Bass, 1991.

National Academy of Public Administration. *Beyond Distrust: Building Bridges between Congress and the Executive*. Washington, D.C.: National Academy, 1992.

Palumbo, Dennis J. *Public Policy in America*. Englewood Cliffs, NJ: Prentice Hall, 1988.

Peters, B. Guy. *American Public Policy: Promise and Performance*. 3d ed. Chatham, NJ: Chatham Books, 1993.

Pfiffner, James P., ed. *The Managerial Presidency*. Pacific Grove, CA: Brooks/Cole, 1991.

Pops, Gerald M., and Thomas J. Pavlak. *The Case for Justice: Strengthening Decision Making and Policy in Public Administration*. San Francisco: Jossey-Bass, 1991.

Reich, Robert. *Trapped in the Cabinet*. New York: Alfred A. Knopf, 1997.

Ripley, Randall B., and Grace A. Franklin. *Congress, the Bureaucracy, and Public Policy*. 4th ed. Pacific Grove, CA: Brooks/Cole, 1987.

Roberts, Nancy C., and Paula J. King. *Transforming Public Policy*. San Francisco: Jossey, 1996.

Seidmen, Harold, and Robert Gilmour. *Politics, Position, and Power*. 4th ed. New York: Oxford University Press, 1986.

Svara, James H. *Official Leadership in the City: Patterns of Conflict and Cooperation*. New York: Oxford University Press, 1990.

Chapter 3

THE INTERORGANIZATIONAL CONTEXT OF PUBLIC ADMINISTRATION

As a public manager, you will interact not only with many others at your level of government or nonprofit management, but also with those throughout government, to say nothing of those in client groups, businesses, interest groups, and associations of all types. More and more, public administrators recognize that managing an agency requires paying attention to what happens in other organizations and that relations with those outside the agency are just as important as relations with those inside. This chapter will examine the interorganizational context in which public administrators operate.

The traditional focus in public administration has been the agency, and that is the focus we have largely taken so far. In many cases, however, especially those involving various levels of government, those involving both the public and private sector, and those that bring together many different organizations in the delivery of human services, it may be more helpful to focus not on the individual agency but on the *relationships* among many different groups. Today, the effectiveness of public programs depends on the ability of various agencies to cooperate in delivering services.

Federal grant money, whether in housing, social services, transportation, or other areas, goes to states and localities to fund particular programs. This finding is typically accompanied by specific guidelines and reporting requirements to assure that the money is properly spent. In turn, the states and localities may either develop their own capabilities to run the programs or they may rely on other groups, including nonprofit organizations or even private businesses.

The Job Training Partnership Act, for example, designed to help the unemployed prepare for the world of work, provides for grants to the states to conduct job-related training and development. The states, in turn, are required to create Private Industry Councils composed of public- and private-sector representatives at the local level to serve as a board of directors for encouraging, developing, and providing at least partial funding training programs. The councils then rely on a variety of other groups to actually run the programs—city or county governments, community action programs, councils of government, private nonprofit organizations, and even chambers of commerce. These administrative bodies deliver some services themselves, but also contract with other organizations, such as public school systems, private vocational schools, or private businesses to operate specific programs. The job training a particular individual receives may well be the product of work at all levels of government and perhaps the public, private, and nonprofit sectors.

This example illustrates the complexity of the interactions triggered by federal policies. But equally complex relationships can grow from the bottom up as well. A local community that wants to attract new industry might develop a coalition of government, business, labor, and education groups to promote the city's image and to work with groups at other levels of government. These groups might include a state Department of Economic Development to help contact prospective employers wishing to relocate. Or the city might request that the state or federal government designate a particular area in the city as an *enterprise zone,* thus permitting special tax incentives and other benefits for businesses willing to locate there. Again, a variety of government and nongovernment entities are involved in the task of economic development.

One can easily understand why the effectiveness of many public programs depends on the quality of the relationships among various organizations. For this reason, some analysts emphasize the importance of the **interorganizational networks** that develop in various policy areas. Obviously, the various groups and organizations involved in any policy arena do not report to a single director, nor are they structured in a typically hierarchical fashion. Rather, they are loosely joined systems that often have overlapping areas of interest, duplication of effort, and lack of coordination. Hult and Walcott write, "Governance networks link structures both within and across organizational boundaries. Like governance structures, networks may be permanent or temporary, formal or informal. They may be consciously designed, emerge unplanned from the decisions of several actors, or simply evolve. A given governance structure may be part of one or several networks" (Hult, 1990, p. 97).

Whether the growing dependence on such systems is a helpful development is a matter of some debate. Many experts have suggested that the use of intermediaries in the delivery of services is a major reason for the difficulties many programs encounter. On the other hand, many such networks have proven enormously stable over time, while others have capitalized on the inherent flexibility and adaptability of such systems. In any case, because interorganizational networks are such an important part of the management of public programs, they deserve our attention.

THE DEVELOPMENT OF INTERGOVERNMENTAL RELATIONS

In terms of your ability to operate public programs effectively and responsibly, you must understand the relationships among levels of government. There are various ways to describe the relationship between a larger comprehensive unit of government and its constituent parts. A *confederation,* for example, is a system in which the constituent units grant powers to the central government, but do not allow it to act independently. A unitary system is one in which all powers reside with the central government, and various units derive their powers from that unit. France and Sweden, for instance, are characterized by unitary systems, as is the relationship between states and localities in the United States; localities hold only those powers specified or permitted by the state.

The relationship between our national government and the states, however, is *federal* in that it involves a division of powers between the two levels of government—federal and state/local. As you know, some powers are granted specifically to the central government (to conduct foreign relations, to regulate interstate commerce, and so on); some are reserved by the states (to conduct elections, to establish local governments, etc.), and some are held by both levels (to tax, to borrow money, to make laws, and so on). (This system of governance is also referred to as "federalism.") A federal structure has many advantages in that it allows for diversity and experimentation, but it has also led to the development of a highly complex intergovernmental system, a fact of life with important implications for the management of public programs.

The term **intergovernmental relations** is often used to encompass all the complex and interdependent relationships among those at various levels of government as they seek to develop and implement public programs. The importance of intergovernmental relations has been recognized in several structural developments. At the federal level, a permanent Advisory Commission of Intergovernmental Relations was established in 1959 and continued to operate until the mid-1990s. All states and nearly all major cities have a coordinator for intergovernmental relations (though the specific titles vary). Finally, many scholars and practitioners have begun to emphasize the managerial processes involved in intergovernmental relations by employing the term *intergovernmental management*.

A key to understanding intergovernmental relations in this country is understanding the changing patterns used to fund public programs. Although intergovernmental relations involve much more than money, financial questions are inevitably at the core of the process, so definitions of various types of **grants,** transfers of money (and property) from one government to another, are a helpful starting place.

NETWORKING

Some basic information on federal-state-local interactions can be found at the Federal Information Exchange at http://web.fie.com/ and the State and Local Gateway at http://www.statelocal.gov/.

Some grants give more discretion to the recipient than do others. **Categorical grants** or **project grants** may be spent for only a limited purpose, such as building a new sewage treatment plant. Categorical grants have historically been the predominant form of grants in this country; however, in recent years, many categorical grants have been consolidated into **block grants,** which may be used for nearly any purpose within a specific functional field, such as housing, community development, education, or law enforcement. The recipient government might spend a law enforcement grant on police training, new equipment, or crime prevention programs. Finally, **revenue sharing,** when it has been used, has made funds available for use by the recipient government in any way its leaders choose (within the law).

Grants may also be classified in terms of how they are made available. A **formula grant** employs a specific decision rule indicating how much money any given jurisdiction will receive. Typically, the decision rule is related to the purpose of the grant (for example, money for housing might be distributed to qualified governments based on the age and density of residential housing). A project grant, on the other hand, makes funds available on a competitive basis. Those seeking aid must submit an application for assistance for review and approval by the granting agency.

Grants may also be categorized as to the purposes they serve. **Entitlement grants** provide assistance to persons meeting certain criteria, such as age or income; for example, Aid to Families with Dependent Children or Medicaid. **Operating grants** are for use in the development and operation of specific programs, such as those in education or employment and job training. **Capital grants** are for use in construction or renovation, as in the development of the interstate highway system.

Finally, grants may vary according to whether they require matching funds from the recipient agency. Some federal grants require the state or locality to put up a certain percentage of the money for the project; in the case of the interstate highway system, states contribute $1 for every $9 of federal money. Other grants require different matching amounts, and some will require no matching at all. Note that the different types may be combined in different ways to create quite a variety of grant possibilities. A specific grant might be made available on a competitive basis strictly for use in programs for job training and may require local matching funds.

DUAL FEDERALISM

Historically, the various grant types have been employed in different ways and in different times. The earliest period in our country's intergovernmental history, a period that lasted well into this century, was characterized by what has been called **dual federalism**, a pattern in which the federal and state governments both sought to carve out their own spheres of power and influence and during which there was relatively little intergovernmental cooperation—indeed, there was substantial conflict.

However, some programs cut across the strict divisions of federal, state, and local responsibility associated with dual federalism. A notable example is the Morrill Act of 1862, which granted land to universities to establish agricultural programs and was the basis for the eventual development of "land-grant" colleges. It was important in the development of higher education, but it was also precedent-setting in terms of the structure of its grants (Nathan et al., 1987). No longer were grants made in a fairly open-ended fashion; specific instructions were attached, requiring that they be used for "agriculture and the mechanical arts." In addition, new reporting and accounting requirements were added as a condition of receiving the grants.

The adoption of grant programs such as the Morrill Act was accompanied by considerable anguish, because some saw such programs as a drastic departure from the dual federalism they preferred. The Morrill Act itself, signed by President Lincoln, had previously been vetoed by President Buchanan, who commented: "Should the time arrive when the State governments shall look to the Federal Treasury for the means of supporting themselves and maintaining their systems of education and internal policy, the character of both Governments will be greatly deteriorated" (Nathan et al., 1987, p. 25).

In any case, the period of dual federalism was marked by considerable conflict among the various levels of government. The federal government sought to deal effectively with the increasingly broad issues being raised in a more complex, urbanized society by developing new grant programs in such areas as highway construction and vocational

BOX 3.1

Images of American Federalism

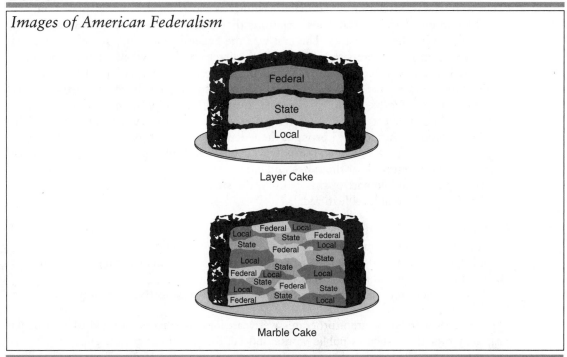

education. The states, though they appreciated federal money, were cautious of federal interference in their spheres of responsibility. The localities, though creatures of the state and dependent on state grants of authority or money, sought to build their own political bases. The resulting pattern of federalism resembled a layer cake, with three levels of government working parallel to one another but rarely together (see Box 3.1).

COOPERATIVE FEDERALISM

If the layer cake was the prevailing image associated with dual federalism, the marble cake was the image for the period that followed, notable for its increasing complexity and interdependence. As opposed to the conflict and division of the earlier period, the emerging era of **cooperative federalism** was characterized by greater sharing of responsibilities. The marble cake image implied a system in which roles and responsibilities were intermixed in a variety of patterns vertical, horizontal, and even diagonal (see Box 3.1).

The great impetus for the development of cooperative federalism was the Roosevelt program for economic recovery following the Great Depression. Although the majority of President Roosevelt's programs were national in scope and could have been national in execution, a political choice was made to operate many of the programs through the states and their localities. The pattern of intergovernmental relations that emerged revealed a dramatically increased federal role, accompanied almost paradoxically by greater federal/state/local sharing of responsibilities. In addition, there was greater attention to vertical relationships within functional areas such as social welfare or transportation.

The pattern of federal/state/local relations that emerged from the New Deal is illustrated by several key programs. The first was the Federal Emergency Relief Administration, which provided grants to states for both direct relief and work relief and was able to revitalize many rather weak state relief agencies. A variety of public works and employment security programs were also attempted to supplement relief efforts; the best known was the Works Progress Administration (WPA), a program that used federal money to hire state-certified workers for locally initiated construction projects. Finally, the Social Security Act of 1935 brought the federal government to an even greater degree into the area of direct relief for the poor, disabled, and unemployed, an area that had previously been reserved for the states and cities.

Through the middle part of this century, the structure of the various grant programs initiated at the federal level featured:

1. Federal definition of the problem
2. Transfer of funds primarily to the states (rather than localities)
3. A requirement that plans for use of funds be submitted to the federal government
4. A requirement for state matching funds
5. A requirement for federal review and audit of the programs (Nathan et al., 1987)

For the most part, these grant programs were categorical—that is, directed to a particular category of activity, such as public works. Indeed, the use of categorical grants as the primary mechanisms for federal/state transfers continued until the 1970s. Throughout this period, various groups appointed to review the state of intergovernmental relations returned the same verdict: the federal government and the states should begin "cooperating with or complementing each other in meeting the growing demands on both" (quoted in Nathan et al., 1987, p. 33). Today, the principle of cooperative federalism is well established.

PICKET-FENCE FEDERALISM

Through the 1960s, 1970s, and 1980s, there were dramatic shifts in the pattern of intergovernmental relations. Nowhere were these shifts more striking than in the contrast between the activism of the Kennedy and Johnson years and the cutbacks of the Reagan and Bush years. President Johnson used the phrase **creative federalism** to describe his approach to intergovernmental relations, which included a huge increase in the number and amounts of federal grants available to states, localities, and other groups. Over three years, the number of available grants from the federal government grew from about fifty to nearly four hundred. Federal aid to states and localities rose from $7 billion in 1960 to $24 billion in 1970 (Wright, 1987, p. 236). Interestingly, state aid to local governments also nearly tripled during this period.

The new federal programs focused mainly on urban problems and problems of the disadvantaged. Medicaid, for example, the largest of the new grant programs, provided funds to states to assist in medical care for low-income people. (Medicaid is largely administered by the states [eligibility requirements vary from state to state], but it also requires state matching funds, which became a fiscal problem for many states.) But there were also new programs in education aimed directly at school districts, new programs in employment and training run by cities and other independent providers, and new programs in housing and urban development in major metropolitan areas.

Probably the most publicized domestic program of the Johnson years was the "War on Poverty," launched with the passage of the Economic Opportunity Act of 1964. The War on Poverty and other Johnson programs were significant for both their size and shape. Substantially more aid was aimed directly at local governments, school districts, and various nonprofit groups, as opposed to the previous pattern of aid primarily to states. Second, there were requirements for detailed planning and for streamlined budgeting systems, as well as demands for public participation in management of the programs. Third, and most important, the majority of the new programs involved project grants, requiring grant applications for specific purposes. States and localities began to spend enormous amounts of time playing the federal grant game trying to obtain grants, searching for matching funds, and trying to meet planning and reporting requirements. As a result, intergovernmental relations took on an increasingly competitive tone (Wright, 1988, pp. 81–90).

Through this period, the intergovernmental system was becoming increasingly dominated by the relationships among professionals within various substantive areas at various levels of government. In a particular program area, the relationship among mayor, governor, and president might be less important than that involving a local health department official, someone from a state department of health, and the manager of a federal program in health care. A new image emerged, replacing the "cakes" of earlier periods—that of **picket-fence federalism.** The horizontal bars of the fence represented the levels of government, and the vertical slats represented various substantive fields, such as health, welfare, education, employment, and training (see Box 3.2).

President Nixon's administration brought about a reaction against many of the developments we have just described. Claiming that the programs of the Great Society were simply too detailed in their requirements to administer effectively at the local level and that subgovernments within particular substantive areas were coming to dominate the intergovernmental system, Nixon proposed what he termed a *New Federalism* that would reestablish greater local autonomy in the use of federal funds. Although a part of his program involved administrative changes, lessening certain requirements, the most notable changes President Nixon proposed involved changes in the structure of grant programs.

One way to return power to state and local leaders, especially elected leaders as opposed to program professionals, was through general revenue sharing. The Nixon plan for general revenue sharing involved transfers of money from the federal government to states and localities to use for any purpose they wished. The funds were distributed based on a complex formula, but once in the hands of the state or local political leadership, they could be used for tax reduction, transportation, community development, law enforcement, or any other area. First passed in 1972, the Nixon revenue-sharing program provided approximately $6 billion a year for five years and was continued through the Nixon, Ford, Carter, and early Reagan years before being eliminated in 1986.

The Nixon administration also sought to consolidate large numbers of categorical grants into block grants, two of which were passed. The Comprehensive Employment and Training Act (CETA) provided funds to local "prime sponsors," usually a local government or group of governments, for manpower training. Which specific programs would be developed was up to the prime sponsor at the local level. Similarly, two weeks after President Nixon resigned, President Ford signed the Community Development

BOX 3.2

Picket-Fence Federalism

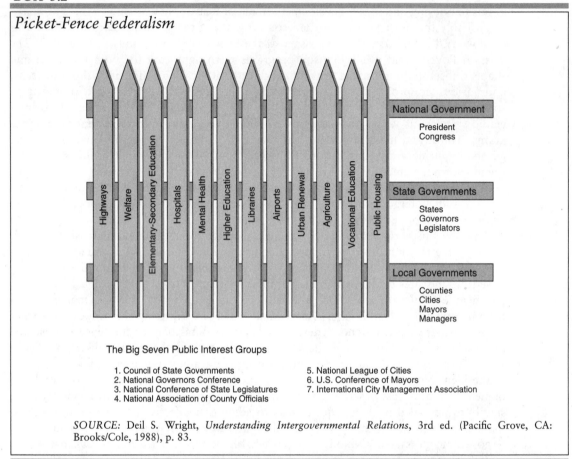

The Big Seven Public Interest Groups

1. Council of State Governments
2. National Governors Conference
3. National Conference of State Legislatures
4. National Association of County Officials
5. National League of Cities
6. U.S. Conference of Mayors
7. International City Management Association

SOURCE: Deil S. Wright, *Understanding Intergovernmental Relations*, 3rd ed. (Pacific Grove, CA: Brooks/Cole, 1988), p. 83.

Block Grant program (CDBG) consolidating several categorical grant programs, including **urban renewal** and the model cities program. Despite these successes in altering the pattern of federal grants, the Nixon and Ford years actually increased the total amount of aid available to states and localities.

The dependency of state and especially local governments on federal aid became more apparent during the administration of President Carter. The Carter years saw few dramatic departures in intergovernmental relations, continuing the general revenue sharing and block grants of the Nixon administration, though there was a greater tendency to target funds through categorical grants. Among the more important initiatives were expansion of public service employment under CETA, so that local government jobs would be filled by the unemployed, and passage of the Urban Development Action Grant program to stimulate economic development in especially distressed cities.

As a former governor, President Carter was attentive to the needs of state and local governments to more effectively operate intergovernmental programs, so he proposed a

BOX 3.3

Forget Washington: Social Issues Shift to the States

Republican and Democratic candidates alike declared, "Power to the People!" in the 1996 campaign. They were not invoking 1960s radicalism but expressing their enthusiasm for returning power from Washington to state and local governments.

Republicans have long championed shrinking big government. Since the Reagan administration and, more recently, since taking control of Congress in 1995, they have sought credit for shifting decision making closer to the people for whom decisions are made. Democrats are also echoing the theme. Last year's national party platform blared, "For years, Republicans talked about shifting power back to states and communities—Democrats are doing it." New Devolution States' Rights as a slogan was once associated with more conservative causes, like resistance to federal court decrees guaranteeing civil rights legislation and to legalization of abortion. Now Democrats and Republicans, liberals and conservatives, are circumnavigating Washington to choose sides on gun control, immigration, campaign finance, education reform, assisted suicide, and privatization.

Yet the cause of what is now popularly called devolution is far more complicated than partisan sloganeering might suggest.

Rather than federal lawmakers voluntarily ceding authority to the states, frustrated local governments have seized many issues that for years languished at the federal level. In perhaps the most obvious example, welfare reform, many governors argued that the Washington turnabout involving block grants was motivated not out of a desire to give states more influence but to shed a difficult and costly problem.

Some local officials complain that while congressional Republicans are eager to leave social matters to the states, they are no less meddlesome than their Democratic predecessors in grabbing big issues like telecommunications and securities regulation and attempts to nationalize product liability laws.

There is no shortage of state governments daring to take on issues that failed in Washington. The struggle over gun control, for example, has moved to Washington, Massachusetts, and other states, where proponents of tougher regulations say they feel less pressure from the gun lobby. The shift also has been spurred by the Supreme Court, which has been a vigorous ally of states and earlier this year struck down a federal provision requiring local authorities to do background checks on firearms buyers.

Georgia and North Carolina have enacted several education reforms like heavy investment in Head Start and tax credits for higher education that Democrats are considering on a national level. And on the Republican side, while Congress is stymied, California has adopted measures restricting affirmative action and benefits to immigrants.

"I bet that half the states have done things on the conservative or liberal side of the ledger that are essentially filling a vacuum left by inaction at the federal level," said Vermont Governor Howard Dean, a Democrat who has been more successful than President Clinton in expanding health insurance coverage.

continued

continued from previous page

States have long been seen as more innovative than the federal government, and that has been especially true as Washington suffers from partisan gridlock. State governments are often not as partisan, and have begun to record budget surpluses that give them more freedom to innovate. And many governors with presidential ambitions (mostly Republican) are eager to claim credit for flashy initiatives with national ramifications.

Delaware Governor Thomas Carper, a Democrat who served a decade in Congress before he was elected governor in 1992, said he has had far more success achieving welfare reform in his state.

"Delaware's a tiny little state with less than a million people," he said, "and Democrats work with Republicans here. Governors tend to be consensus builders and pragmatic problem solvers. In Washington, the politics and the inertia of the place can be paralyzing."

But many Washington politicians are not ready to concede that the government is a dinosaur.

"One of the reasons people like deciding questions nationally is that you do it one time and you do it as a nation," said Senator Bob Graham, D-Fla., who also served as governor.

But Thad L. Beyle, a political science professor at the University of North Carolina at Chapel Hill, warns that the shift is real. "The states are getting to be where a lot of the action is," he said. "And it will continue that way until we have a major depression or other catastrophe."

SOURCE: Richard L. Berke, *New York Times*, October 19, 1997.

series of administrative steps for improving intergovernmental management. In this effort, he worked closely with a group of seven major public interest groups, known as the PIGS, that had come to be increasingly active in the intergovernmental system. These included such groups as the Council of State Governments, the National League of Cities, the National Governor's Association, and others (see Box 3.3). Later in the Carter years, however, a new mood of fiscal restraint combined with Carter's own fiscal conservatism to limit the amount of money available, something states and localities found difficult to handle. But, from the standpoint of state and local governments, the reductions of the late Carter years were just the beginning.

THE REAGAN AND BUSH YEARS

The Reagan and Bush administrations brought major structural changes in the pattern of fiscal federalism, including elimination of general revenue sharing and a reworking of the block grant system. However, these years were more significant (in intergovernmental terms) for the administration's efforts to reduce the size of the federal government through a variety of tax and spending cuts and to return responsibility for major areas, especially social welfare, to the states.

A strong ideological commitment undergirded President Reagan's efforts to eliminate federal funding and federal regulation of state and local activity wherever possible. In his inaugural speech, the president stated, "It is my intention to curb the size and influence of the federal establishment and to demand recognition of the distinction between the powers granted the federal government, those reserved to the states or to the people" (Reagan, 1981). One way he proposed to do so was by turning back responsibility for a variety of federal programs, and the resources to pay for them, to the states. (President Bush employed the same ideology, emphasizing the term *turnovers* rather than *turnbacks,* in promoting his programs.)

Proposals along these lines, however, quickly became intertwined with the president's 1981 efforts to reduce taxes and spending under the banner of **supply-side economics,** an approach that holds that decreased taxes and spending will stimulate capital investment and in turn economic growth (Stone & Sawhill, 1984). The defense budget was protected by the Reagan administration, so the majority of cuts were sought in federal grant programs and general government operations. Indeed, during 1981, the Reagan administration achieved the first absolute decline in federal expenditures in decades. As part of these reductions, federal grants were lowered from about $95 billion in fiscal year 1981 to about $88 billion in fiscal year 1982, with a major portion of the cuts coming in employment and training programs (Beam, 1984, p. 420).

Meanwhile, state and local officials decried the depth of the cuts and the administration's failure to make available any revenue sources to pick up the slack, especially as the tax cuts failed to produce the expected economic growth. Moreover, concerns were increasingly voiced that efforts to balance the budget had been especially damaging to the poor, for example, by reducing eligibility for Aid to Families with Dependent Children (AFDC) payments (Nathan et al. 1987, pp. 52–57). Whereas the public was apparently concerned about excessive spending, it became clear that neither the Congress nor the public always considered spending for social welfare, environmental protection, and infrastructure maintenance excessive.

Thus, by the middle of the second Reagan term, eligibility requirements in AFDC were restored; the environmental Superfund, designed to clean up toxic wastes and repair leaking underground tanks, was funded by Congress at a significantly higher level than the president requested; and use of the Highway Trust Fund for improved highways, including urban mass transit, was passed over Reagan's veto.

On the other hand, reductions continued in specific areas, most notably in general revenue sharing. Recall that the Nixon general revenue-sharing program had been continued through the Carter administration; however, early in the Reagan years, revenue sharing for states was eliminated. Finally, in 1986, revenue sharing for local governments was also ended. Many saw general revenue sharing as a way to equalize the disparity between rich and poor communities and allow greater flexibility at the local level; others saw revenue sharing as providing too much money and too much discretion, especially to wealthy communities.

President Bush continued the Reagan approach to federalism, making important, but largely stylistic gestures to the states and localities. In part, he could do little else. The budget deficit continued unabated and led to the Budget Enforcement Act of

1990. Under the new law, as we will see later, any legislation that exceeds the budget ceiling in its category will trigger an across-the-board cut in that category. In this way, the BEA effectively pits each domestic program against all others. When this legislation was combined with the savings and loan bailout, there was little enthusiasm left for expanding domestic spending, including state and local aid.

As mentioned earlier, President Bush continued the Reagan strategy of turning back or turning over various programs to the states, but just as in Reagan's case, there was great skepticism about whether the proposed turnovers were based on a commitment to states' rights and responsibilities or whether they were just a strategy for placing more of the burden for funding various programs in the hands of the states. For example, the administration's highway plan proposed to turn over four-fifths of the federal highway system to the states with funding to be on a 60-40 basis, federal to state. According to Transportation Secretary Skinner, the proposal was designed not only to permit greater local flexibility, but also very clearly to turn over more financial responsibility to the states, shifting the burden to the states.

THE CLINTON PRESIDENCY

During the Clinton presidency, the philosophical foundation of New Federalism has remained mostly in place. The primary themes continue to be regulatory reform and shifting decision-making authority to state and local governments. However, the character and scope of this devolution of power have been interpreted in vastly different ways by the president, the Republican House, and the more moderate leadership in the Senate. In the past few years state and local governments, too, have offered their own ideas on federalism and the overall system of intergovernmental relations. Such diversity of viewpoints has generated a number of questions concerning not only the state of federalism but also the implications for government practice.

Early on, President Clinton left little doubt as to his administration's position on intergovernmental relations, a position characterized by a sensitivity to state and local governments. The president quickly showed his gubernatorial roots, for example, by choosing four of his cabinet members from the subnational level. And, within months of taking office, the administration identified the removal of burdensome federal regulations as a primary objective. President Clinton in September 1993 issued Executive Order 12866, which along with a subsequent order prevented federal agencies from imposing mandates without financial support. Although administrative agencies would gain regulatory powers under the order, central review was to be continued to ensure that new regulations conformed with the president's priorities. The president reinforced his stance a month later by issuing Executive Order 12875, establishing a system of state and local review of intergovernmental regulations.

The Clinton administration's New Federalist philosophy also carried over into programmatic areas. In supporting new approaches to health care, the administration issued an unprecedented number of Medicaid waivers, enabling subnational governments to shape reforms to meet their particular needs. Moreover, in the president's primary community and economic development initiative, the Empowerment Zone/Enterprise Community Program, as well as its key education initiative, Goals 2000: Educate America Act, "the administration persuaded Congress to expand state and/or local discretion" (Walker, 1996, p. 274).

Underlying this approach was the belief that by reducing federal regulations and handing decision-making power to the state and local level, those closest to the issue would be in a better position to effect innovation and change in the given policy area.

Vice President Al Gore further advanced the administration's position on intergovernmental relations. In his National Performance Review (NPR) and related efforts, the vice president highlighted a variety of alternative strategies for managing public programs. These strategies, which echoed Osborne and Gaebler's *Reinventing Government,* injected a new spirit of entrepreneurialism into the federal government. Gore's NPR called for "a new customer service contract with the American people, a new guarantee of effective, efficient, and responsive government." Although the vice president focused mainly on the national level, the philosophy driving his reinvention agenda fostered a greater appreciation for innovation by local and state administrators. NPR also featured several practical measures that affected intergovernmental relations, such as collapsing categorical grants into more flexible funding streams and removing unfunded federal mandates.

On this latter issue, the adoption of New Federalist ideals extended beyond the Clinton administration. Regulatory reform and the removal of unfunded mandates became key issues for the 104th Congress. As cited in the Republican Contract with America, conservatives argued that federal agencies placed too great of a burden on state and local administrations by imposing regulations without adequate financial resources for their implementation. Republican lawmakers thus returned to two measures from the preceding Congress (H.R. 4771 and S. 993) and, with assistance from the Clinton administration, revised the bills into the Unfunded Mandates Act (1995). Under the resulting act, the cost of any future mandate would need to be spelled out by the Congressional Budget Office. The act also raised the President's Executive Orders cited above to a statutory level, binding agencies by law to find less expensive, more flexible ways of instituting regulations.

During President Clinton's second term, however, ties with the Republican Congress have degenerated into political gridlock. Though the two camps have come together on measures to eliminate the federal deficit and reform the nation's welfare system, the prevailing story from Washington in the past few years has been one of partisan extremism. And, even the hallmarks of the period have faced a troubled reception among state and local governments. Many governors and mayors, while recognizing the need for fiscal constraint and welfare reform, are concerned that the cost of the measures will fall primarily on the subnational administrations. How this will play out over the next few years, and into the next presidential administration, remains to be seen. What is certain is that changes in federal spending and public assistance will redefine the nation's system of intergovernmental relations. Whether the Clinton administration can or will change the face of American federalism, of course, remains to be seen. However, some of the political ingredients for such a change seem present.

Recent work in Grand Rapids, Michigan, reveals the local response to changes in intergovernmental relations during the Clinton presidency. About twenty-four local governments operate in the Grand Rapids metropolitan area, which contains more than a half-million residents. From 1991 to 1995, these administrations faced increased demands, brought on by cuts in federal spending and shifts in decision-making capacity to the local level. They answered by building more cooperative relationships among themselves and with citizens.

The first step toward this new cooperation involved a public "visioning" process, in which citizens and community organizations worked with public officials to map out a governance structure for the future. This visioning produced a development plan to help participating local governments ensure that land use and service delivery matched with citizen-driven needs. While adhering to the plan remains discretionary, most of the local governments have signed on to the agreement. Transportation and utility plans also have been developed. Yet, due to the stringent nature of federal and state requirements for transportation spending, the transportation plan is more binding on the local governments.

To date, much of the cooperation between local governments has been in the area of water and sewer services. About 53 of the 151 agreements in Grand Rapids have involved these service areas. The remainder has targeted fire services and commitments for mutual aid. Despite this record, though, intergovernmental ties have not been made in many of the potential service areas, such as public safety, parks and recreation, public works, and planning and development.

In fact, officials suggest that the metropolitan administrations have moved only about halfway to where they need to be with regard to interlocal cooperation. While the Grand Rapids story is still unfolding, many believe that such engagement between local governments will become the norm in the post-Clinton era. However, implicit in this shift to the local is a unique opportunity for the public to be restored to the center of public decision making. As the Grand Rapids case revealed, citizens and civic organizations have become increasingly involved in the governance process. And, consequently, the relationship between citizens and the institutions of governance can be expected to have a dramatic effect on our emerging system of intergovernmental relations.

Not only have changes in the system of intergovernmental relations during the Clinton presidency been characterized by a shift in power down to the local level, as revealed by recent deliberations over the Intermodal Surface Transportation Efficiency Act (ISTEA), such a transformation in the balance of power also has triggered increased tension between the federal, state, and local layers.

In 1991, Congress passed ISTEA as a way to revamp the nation's deteriorating transportation system, based on locally driven priorities. The six-year, $151 billion act handed local governments a level of decision-making previously unseen. Under its provisions, local officials—not the federal government—would determine how to spend revenues generated by a 14-cent-per-gallon gas tax. And, targets for the $26 billion a year in spending have ranged from highways to local roads, from mass transit to alternative systems such as bikeways.

However, ISTEA was slated to expire in September 1997, and some critics of the legislation suggested using the reauthorization process to remove, or at least reduce, the local influence. State officials, in particular, say that the current legislation forces state governments to work with too many smaller jurisdictions, which often are represented by municipal planning organizations (MPOs). ISTEA requires that jurisdictions with populations of 200,000 or more be allowed to determine how the resources will be used. Some have launched a campaign to have that threshold lifted to cities and counties of more than 1 million.

Local officials, on the other hand, argue that the influence of the smaller communities must remain, that thanks to the MPOs those with significant transportation-related needs have been allowed at the table. Led by the National Association of Counties and the National League of Cities, these critics challenge the notion of raising ISTEA's 200,000-population threshold. In fact, they suggest lowering the cutoff to incorporate the interests of smaller jurisdictions (see discussion in Barlas, 1997).

How this dispute will be resolved remains to be seen. Some have suggested splitting gas tax revenues into two separate funds, one for state and another for local initiatives. Others believe that the federal tax should be lowered, with states instituting their own gas tax to fund necessary improvements. Yet underlying these deliberations lie important questions concerning the relationship between federal, state, and local governments. Indeed, the fate of ISTEA may reveal important insights into the future of intergovernmental relations in the post-Clinton era.

JUDICIAL INFLUENCE

One final point relates to the role of the judiciary in shaping intergovernmental relations. Through the 1980s and early 1990s, students of federalism became increasingly aware of the role of the judiciary, especially the Supreme Court, in defining the relationship between the federal government and states and localities. The results were mixed. In some cases, the Court seemed to hold for the states, but in others an increasing federal role was supported. Three Missouri cases indicate the complexity of federalism in the 1990s. In *Webster* v. *Reproductive Health Services* (109 S.Ct. 3040, 1989) the Court sent the explosive abortion issue back to the states, giving the states greater leeway in abortion legislation. On the other hand, in *Missouri* v. *Jenkins* (109 S.Ct. 1150, 1990) the Court held unanimously that a federal district court judge could not "levy a tax" to pay for his or her court order, in this case, a school desegregation plan. The Court did rule, however, that the judge could order a local government—in this case, the school district—to levy an increase. For some the distinction was too subtle. In still another Missouri case, *Gregory* v. *Ashcroft* (33 IJSLW 4714, 1991), the states fared better. Here the Court ruled that the Missouri constitution's rule that state judges retire at age seventy does not violate the federal Age Discrimination Act, as the Equal Employment Opportunity Commission had ruled. Justice O'Connor's opinion emphasized the notion of dual sovereignty and the importance of states determining the qualifications of their officials.

THE STATE AND LOCAL PERSPECTIVE

We have described the system of intergovernmental relations primarily from the federal perspective, but states and localities are also major actors in the intergovernmental system, both as they participate in federal programs and as they interact with one another state to state, state to locality, and locality to locality. Here also intergovernmental relations have been changing. While budgetary shifts have created serious problems for state and local governments, state and local governments have proven remarkably well equipped to deal with these problems, both financially and administratively.

FUNDING PATTERNS

As we have seen, while federal grant dollars declined in the early 1980s, this trend was soon reversed somewhat, with aid growing from $88 billion in 1982 to $182 billion in 1992. Similarly, federal grants for state and local governments declined from 539 in 1981 to 404 in 1984, but increased again to 557 by 1991 (Kincaid, 1993, p. 1). This roller-coaster ride created severe problems for state and local governments and still has not returned aid to its earlier point in terms of its importance to those governments. In 1980, grants-in-aid amounted to 15.5 percent of the federal budget; by 1991, aid to states and localities was still under 12 percent.

Throughout the 1980s, the impact on state and local governments, as well as other service delivery organizations, was severe. As we see in Table 3.1, in 1980 the federal government provided over 25 percent of the money spent by state and local governments. That percentage dropped during the late 1980s to about 17 percent and has risen only to 20.5 percent. All of these changes occurred at a time in which state governments were experiencing significant fiscal stress related to other factors such as the recession, inelastic tax systems, growing expenditures in health, poverty, and immigration, and so on. As an example, twenty years ago, the states spent approximately $2.7 billion on Medicaid, about 4 percent of their budgets. These costs rose to $31 billion (13 percent) in 1990 and have continued to rise steadily. The levels of fiscal stress experienced by the states were especially difficult in 1991, a year in which twenty-nine states cut back expenses below the levels appropriated and thirty-four states raised taxes (Gold, 1992, p. 35). Consequently, state and localities found it necessary to curtail or even terminate many programs, while at the same time trying to develop new sources of revenue.

TABLE 3.1

Federal Grants-in-Aid, 1980–1991 (in billions of current dollars)

Federal Grants-in-Aid as a Percentage of Total Outlays

Fiscal Year	Total State/Local Outlays	Total Federal Outlays
1980	26.3	15.5
1985	21.3	11.2
1988	18.6	10.8
1989	18.6	10.7
1990	18.7	10.8
1991	19.5	11.7
1992	20.8	12.9
1993	21.2	13.7
1994	21.8	14.4
1995	22.2	14.8

SOURCE: ACIR, *Significant Features of Fiscal Federalism*, vol. II (Washington, D.C.: Advisory Commission on Intergovernmental Relations, 1996), 60.

Without question, the last several decades have presented a variety of fiscal challenges to state and local governments. One surprising development, however, is that the states have proven able to manage their new responsibilities far better than many predicted. Indeed, while the federal government has a huge deficit, the states continue to operate balanced budgets, albeit often with great difficulty.

Once considered a weak link in the federal system, the states have been able, over the past twenty-five years, to dramatically increase their capacities. Although there are still considerable variations in the capacities of the states, most have undertaken important institutional reforms (such as developing legislative audits), expanded the scope and professionalism of their operations (to include new services in areas such as energy planning and conservation or new programs in areas such as productivity improvement), and demonstrated remarkable fiscal restraint. Indeed, the states are operating balanced budgets, and some are even making investments for the future (Beckman, 1988, p. 438).

The states also are moving into areas of responsibility once thought to rest at the federal level. The field of international trade is one area where some shifting in roles already seems to be taking place. Whereas the federal government has traditionally played the leading (if not the exclusive) role in foreign affairs, economic forces are precipitating much greater state and local activity in the international arena. For example, all states have offices of economic development involved in some way with international economic development. Through such units, the states provide local businesses with seminars and conferences on how to market themselves overseas. Over forty states also maintain permanent offices overseas, with some of the larger states having offices in several countries.

PREEMPTIONS AND MANDATES

Preemptions

Although our federal system of government establishes certain federal powers, reserves certain powers to the states, and permits certain actions at both levels, there has long been controversy about the exact definition of these categories. This controversy has been especially intense where the question concerns the power of the federal government to preempt the traditional powers of the states and localities or where the federal government coerces states and localities into doing (or not doing) certain things.

As a case in point, the Fair Labor Standards Act of 1938 set the minimum wages and maximum hours that could be worked before overtime pay was required. Whereas the act originally applied only to the private sector, 1974 amendments applied its provisions to all state and local governments. Many state and local officials argued against the amendments, citing the difficulties in applying the standards to government; for example, how do you measure the hours a firefighter works in off-and-on shifts of several days' duration? Soon the amendments were challenged in court and, in the case of *National League of Cities* v. *Usery* (1976), the Supreme Court decided that the functions of "general government" were part of the powers "reserved" to the states by the Tenth Amendment and therefore could not be regulated by the federal government. Consequently, the FLSA did not apply.

Confusion remained, however, about which areas were included in the phrase "general government." The confusion persisted until, nearly ten years later, the Court reviewed a case that sought to determine whether the San Antonio transit authority was performing "general government" functions and was therefore exempt from the Fair Labor Standards Act. In *Garcia* v. *San Antonio Metropolitan Transit Authority* (1985), however, the Court went beyond the narrow question of whether transit is a general government function and decided that Congress did in fact have the power, under its responsibilities to regulate commerce, to intervene in the affairs of state and local governments.

The effect of *Garcia*, a direct reversal of the Court's earlier position in the *Usery* case, was to remove questions about the scope of the federal government's powers from the realm of judicial inquiry. The Court essentially held that the states have sufficient input into the national legislative process, through the election of members of Congress and the influence of their governors and mayors, to be able to protect themselves politically from burdensome legislation. That being the case, the question of whether the federal government could act in areas previously believed reserved to the states should be decided through legislation rather than judicial action. The rights of the states were, therefore, viewed as raising political rather than judicial questions (Howard, 1985).

A similar argument was developed by the Court in *South Carolina* v. *Baker* (108 S.Ct. 1355, 1988), a case viewed by many as putting a nail in the coffin of the Tenth Amendment rights of the states. *South Carolina* asked whether the federal government had the right to dictate the form of bonds issued by the states. The Court not only answered "yes," but also indicated that the federal government had the right to tax income earned on tax-exempt bonds. Obviously, if the federal government had this right, then the states would have to compete directly with private firms issuing bonds. While political leaders tried to assure the bond market that the federal government would not try to balance its budget by intruding on the states' abilities to issue tax-exempt bonds, several such proposals were in fact introduced in Congress. As you can imagine, states and localities were incensed at this intrusion into a critical area of state financing, but again the states were precluded from a judicial remedy and asked to rely on their political power to see that Congress did not act to tax state and local bonds.

The *Garcia* and especially *South Carolina* cases potentially open the door for the federal government to move into more areas once thought to be the province of state and local governments. Certainly state and local officials, who have seen the federal government act in areas from rat control to minimum drinking ages, have been skeptical of the self-restraint of Congress. At a minimum, *Garcia* and *South Carolina* set a precedent for expanded federal action directed at state and local governments.

Whereas these cases deal with the powers of the federal government over states and localities, similar but somewhat less complex issues have been raised with respect to the powers of the states over local governments. As noted, our intergovernmental system does not allocate separate spheres of power to state and local governments, but rather treats local governments merely as "creatures of the state," having only those powers granted by the state. In what has come to be known as **Dillon's Rule**, Judge John Dillon declared in 1911 that municipalities had only those powers granted in their charters, those fairly implied by the expressed powers, and those essential to the purposes of their being granted a charter. In other words, Dillon's Rule allowed for state control over all but a narrow range of local activities. Dillon's Rule has been somewhat relaxed, especially in states that permit cities greater autonomy through *home-rule* provisions, but the powers of local government continue to derive directly from the actions of the state.

There are various mechanisms involved in the relationship between the federal government and the states and between the states and localities. **Preemptions** involve the federal government preempting state action traditionally associated with the lower level of government. For example, the federal Nutrition Labeling and Education Act of 1990 preempted many state and local laws regarding food labeling. Such assumptions of power have been particularly significant in the last few years. For example, federal preemptions of state and local authority more than doubled after 1970. More than 50 percent of the preemption statutes enacted in the entire history of our country were enacted in the last twenty years. Not even Ronald Reagan, despite his rhetoric promising a return of more power to the states, was exempt from this trend, endorsing federal limits on the regulation of business, as well as restraints in health and the environment (Kincaid, 1990, p. 149).

Mandates

The *Garcia* case deals with what are called **direct orders**, requirements or restrictions enforced by one government upon another (the federal government on states and localities, the states on the cities). Direct orders might include a federal requirement that cities meet certain clean water standards or a state requirement that a city pay part of the costs of certain welfare programs. Another way control may be exercised over another government is through *conditions* tied to grants-in-aid. These conditions are typically of the type parents use with children: "You can go outside to play, if you first clean up your room." Conditions of aid might require land-use planning or an assurance of making facilities accessible to the handicapped prior to a capital construction project.

Because cities derive their powers from the states, most state requirements are in the form of direct orders. But most federal requirements are conditions-of-aid tied to a particular grant program. "Conditions-of-aid" are of two varieties. **Cross-cutting requirements** are rules that apply to most, if not all, grant programs; for instance, the federal government requires environmental impact statements before undertaking capital projects, certain personnel provisions in agencies receiving grant funds, and compliance with civil rights legislation. Other conditions-of-aid are program specific, applicable only to the particular program. They may include rules about program planning, implementation, and evaluation; for example, a particular program might prescribe certain maximum salaries for individuals employed under the grant or some form of citizen participation in program design (most federal programs have this latter requirement) (Kettl, 1983).

The term **mandate** has been used to embrace both "conditions-of-aid" and "direct orders," in either case an order requiring a government to do something it might not otherwise do. Mandates often require states or localities to spend money they would not otherwise spend. Today it is estimated that federal mandates cost state and local governments an estimated $100 billion a year. State spending mandated by the recent immigration bills alone is estimated to be over $1 billion. Moreover, states and cities claim that mandates unduly impinge upon the autonomy of their level of government. Consequently, mandates have become a source of considerable frustration for those on the receiving end. It's no wonder that former Mayor Edward Koch described the "mandate millstone" around the necks of state and local officials as "a maze of complex statutory and administrative directives [threatening] both the initiative and the financial health of local governments throughout the country" (Koch, 1980, p. 42) Koch was joined then and now in his argument by mayors and governors across the country—the mayors concerned with both federal and state mandates, the governors concerned primarily with federal mandates.

At the federal level, every president since Nixon has pledged to reduce the burden of mandates on states and local governments. In his 1992 State of the Union address, President Bush said, "We must put an end to unfinanced Federal Government mandates. . . . If Congress passes a mandate, it should be forced to pay for it and to balance the cost with savings elsewhere. After all, a mandate just increases someone else's burden, and that means higher taxes at the state and local level" (Bowman & Pagano, 1992, p. 4). However, shortly after the president made his remarks, he signed a budget agreement that contained twenty new mandates expected to cost state and local governments about $17 billion over the next five years.

An important step forward was taken in March of 1995, when President Clinton signed the Unfunded Mandates Reform Action of 1995, presumably an effort to limit the effects of federally imposed mandates. While this bill does not provide federal funding for all mandated activities, it does require that Congress recognize the implications of mandates for state and local activities and, in some cases, authorize funding for such mandates. However, there seem to be a variety of "loopholes" through which Congress might avoid funding. While most state and local government associations (such as the Big Seven Public Interest Groups) actively supported the act, most also now realize that it provides limited relief from federally imposed mandates. And, we should note that the act does nothing about mandates imposed on local governments by state governments.

SUBNATIONAL RELATIONSHIPS

Even focusing on state and local activities, we find the federal government involved in some way—at a minimum, in providing funds for states and localities. But important intergovernmental activity also occurs at the subnational level: state to state, state to local, and local to local.

State to State

Relationships between and among states are mentioned several times in the U.S. Constitution, most notably in the requirement that states recognize the rights and privileges of citizens of other states and give "full faith and credit" to the public acts and legal proceedings of other states. Some of the most important intergovernmental relationships involving various state governments are not based in constitutional doctrine, however, but are rather the result of political practices over the years.

Relationships among states are not without conflict. States may differ over census counts (important in determining the number of representatives in Congress), may dispute shifting state boundaries (as when a river changes course), and may debate a variety of substantive policy issues (such as the rights to underground water or the degree to which dumping pollutants into a river affects water quality in states downstream). In addition, states must increasingly compete with one another for economic development; for example, when General Motors announced its plans to build a major new plant to produce the Saturn, many states entered an intense bidding war, each hoping GM would locate the plant within its boundaries.

States also cooperate. There are many opportunities for officials in one state to seek the advice of those in other states with respect to policy alternatives or new administrative arrangements. Many organizations, including the Council of State Governments, the National Governor's Association, the National Council of State Legislators, and groups that bring together state officials in personnel, budgeting, purchasing, social welfare, health, and so forth, have been created to help officials share information and expertise. These groups, along with the Washington offices of various states, constitute an important lobbying group in Washington.

One way the states come together to resolve potential disputes or work together on common problems is through *interstate compacts*. These agreements have historically been bilateral, involving only two states; however, increasingly, compacts are being developed to involve a number of states within a region or even all fifty states. Originally used to resolve boundary disputes, interstate compacts today cover a wide variety of topics, most arising from the fact that today's policy problems do not confine themselves neatly to the borders of one state. Imagine, for example, the common interests of people in several states sharing the same underground water supply. Think also of the problems that are of interest to all who live in metropolitan areas, such as Cincinnati or Kansas City, that cross the boundaries of two or even more states. It is not uncommon in such areas to find interstate compacts covering air and water pollution, transportation, law enforcement, and so on.

States may also use interstate compacts to symbolize their agreement to cooperate in especially important policy areas. For example, Congressional legislation mandates that states assume responsibility for the disposal of low-level radioactive wastes and encourages such efforts to be undertaken through interstate compacts. In 1992, forty-two states had formed nine compacts to deal with this problem. In all cases, an interstate compact provides a way to formalize resolution of a dispute or to arrange to work together without involving the federal government.

State to Local

We have seen that the relationship between states and localities is unitary—that is, local governments have only those powers granted by the state. However, the nature of the powers may vary considerably. Most cities operate under some form of **charter,** the local government equivalent of a constitution. But a state may grant charters in several ways. Some states develop *special charters* for each individual local government; others take exactly the opposite approach and grant a *general charter* for all local governments. The *classified charter* approach seeks to avoid the restrictive nature of the special charter and the rigidity of the general charter by granting charters to various classes of cities. For example, all cities over 1 million in population might be designated Class A and have one set of charter provisions, while cities from 250,000 to 1 million might be in Class B and have a different set of provisions. A final means of chartering cities, called **home rule,** permits cities to write their own charters, within very broad state guidelines and generally subject to voter approval.

Home rule obviously provides the greatest flexibility for local governments in terms of basic structure; however, even under home rule, there is substantial state involvement in local government affairs. For one thing, the states are an important source of funding for local activities. Indeed, at a time when federal aid has leveled somewhat, state aid to local governments has increased dramatically. Between 1980 and 1995, for example, state aid to local governments increased from about $83 billion to well over $200 billion, with most of that targeted for education and lesser amounts for welfare, highways, and other purposes.

But states not only provide money; they also regulate local government activities. State governments tell local governments what taxes they can levy, what services they can provide, and what types of management systems they must employ. In doing so, states provide needed uniformity, as in the case of highway signs, as well as ensure minimum standards of performance, as in education or welfare programs. Since states have virtually unlimited power over local governments, there is an obvious temptation to compel local governments to assume new responsibilities. In most states, there are twenty to thirty statutes that impose substantial financial burdens on local governments. The total number of mandates or regulations may number in the thousands (Berman, 1992, p. 53).

Just as states complain about federal mandates, many local officials view state mandates as unnecessary intrusions on local prerogatives that may require local expenditures that might not otherwise be made. Recently, localities have complained especially about *sneaky mandates,* actions that are required of local governments by the inaction of state governments. For example, Georgia failed to pick up prisoners housed "temporarily" in county jails, resulting in overcrowding in the prison system, to say nothing of the additional financial burden on the counties. There is, however, new sympathy for localities in terms of mandates and about one-third of the states now have requirements for at least partial reimbursements of expenses created by mandates (MacManus, 1992).

Localities are not powerless in their relationship with the states, especially as they are an important base of political support for those in the legislatures. Local representatives and senators can and often do voice the local message loudly and clearly in the state legislature. Moreover, various patterns of state/local cooperation have emerged in the past several years. Many states, for example, have developed state-level equivalents of the federal Advisory Commission on Intergovernmental Relations. These state commissions bring together state and local officials to discuss problems in the intergovernmental system and devise ways to work together more effectively. Among the recommendations that have emerged are suggestions for greater local discretionary authority and for reductions in the number of state mandates. Despite these recommendations, the states still maintain a dominant position in their relationships with cities.

Local to Local

In discussions of intergovernmental relations, there is an understandable tendency to focus on national patterns, but for those who work at the local level, relationships with other local governments are extremely important. One reason is that many citizens live in one jurisdiction, work in another, shop in another, and pay taxes to several. They naturally expect services, such as the quality of the streets or law enforcement, to remain fairly constant as they move from one place to another.

From a political standpoint, the fragmentation of government, especially in urban areas, often means that problems are separated from the resources that might be employed to solve them. Wealthier cities have the money; poorer cities have the problems. But even where resources are fairly evenly distributed, it is difficult to get several local governments together to resolve common problems. Where this is the case, citizens often turn to higher-level governments for help, thus taking the problem (and its solution) out of the hands of local authorities (Nice, 1987, p. 191).

But many interlocal problems are resolved at the local level. Natural, though informal, patterns of cooperation develop, especially in the relationships among local professionals. The police chief in one community talks with other police chiefs, the health officer talks with other health officers, and so on. More formally, one government may actually purchase services from another, contracting for police or fire protection, wastewater treatment, or trash collection. Los Angeles County, for example, provides a variety of services to local governments through contract arrangements. Additionally, **councils of government** (COGs), oversight bodies representing various localities, may be created to help coordinate local affairs.

Finally, special districts may be created to solve problems that cross governmental boundaries. As mentioned, **special districts** are local governments created for a specific purpose within a specific area (not necessarily coinciding with the boundaries of a city or county). Although special districts may promote coordination of health, education, or other services, they also add to the number of governments within a particular area. Thus, one city block may be governed by the city, a county, and several special districts; a resident may have difficulty figuring out which government can help with a particular problem. The difficulties in coordinating efforts are substantial, as are the problems of holding the various governments accountable.

WORKING WITH NONGOVERNMENTAL ORGANIZATIONS

It is not unusual for one level of government to make use of another in carrying out its policies. The federal government uses the states to carry out programs in transportation, criminal justice, and health and human services; the states use local governments to carry out policies in education and human services. But governments at all levels may also utilize private and nonprofit organizations to help carry out their policies. The National Aeronautics and Space Administration, for example, contracts with private companies to build space shuttles; state governments use both private and nonprofit organizations to conduct job training and provide employment services; local governments often contract with private firms for trash collection or towing services.

Many governments have entered into private partnerships to conserve revenues, to reduce crime in blighted areas, and to promote economic growth. The city of Daytona Beach, for example, entered into a public/private partnership with a developer to renovate a dilapidated boardwalk area and build a beachfront hotel. In each case, the interorganizational relationships that arise are important to the success or failure of public programs. For this reason, many argue that looking solely at intergovernmental relations is insufficient; it is better to use the more inclusive term *interorganizational relations*.

The use of private and nonprofit organizations in the delivery of public services has grown markedly in the last several years. Figure 3.1 compares, at the federal level, civilian employment and overall governmental expenditures. Between 1950 and 1990, government spending increased by over 400 percent, even holding inflation constant, but government employment grew only about 25 percent, with practically no significant growth in the last

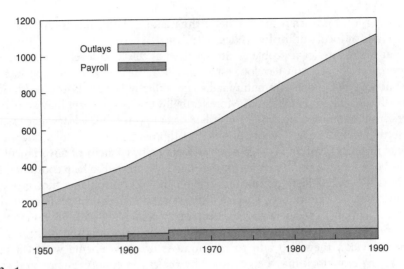

FIGURE 3.1

Federal Payroll and Government Spending, 1950–1990 (in millions of constant 1987 dollars)

twenty-five years. This substantial growth in federal programs, occurring without comparable growth in federal employment, is explained by the fact that parties other than the federal government are actually conducting the programs and delivering the services. Federal money, for example, goes to private firms, such as defense contractors or banks that administer school loan programs, and to nonprofit organizations, especially those that provide human services such as care for the homeless or disabled.

PRIVATIZATION

The movement toward greater involvement of private and nonprofit organizations in the delivery of public services is partly ideological. Some people simply feel that services should be provided by those outside government wherever possible. But the movement has also been stimulated by recent restrictions on government spending and a resulting effort to find more efficient ways to conduct the public's business. Both motives have been discussed under the heading **privatization,** the use of nongovernmental agencies to provide goods or services previously provided by government, but since the term is used several different ways, it is important to be clear about its various meanings (Kolderie, 1986).

In its broader sense, privatization refers to efforts to remove government from any involvement in either the design or conduct of a particular service. In Great Britain, for example, major industries such as steel or coal, once nationalized, are returning to private control, typically through direct sales to individuals, firms, or other groups. In the United States, most such major industries, including most utilities, are already in private hands, so there are relatively few examples of such magnitude (the sale of Conrail and certain petroleum reserves are exceptions). There are many more limited examples of privatization, however; a city might, for example, sell a golf course to a country club development, thus ending the government's involvement in golf. Box 3.4 describes another example of privatization.

BOX 3.4

Building Partnerships for Successful Job Training—Project QUEST

A manufacturing plant on the south side of San Antonio closed about five years ago, laying off more than one thousand workers. Most were low-income Hispanic women. Following the shutdown, community-based organizations helped locate new jobs for the former employees. Finding local job-training programs grossly inadequate, the groups decided to take matters into their own hands. They initiated research, started grass-roots organizing in churches and homes, and built alliances with business and government. Out of these efforts, Project QUEST was born.

Project QUEST differs from many job-training programs in its focus on preparing people for highly skilled positions, not entry-level jobs. The training is rigorous, typically taking eighteen to twenty-four months. The goal is to help workers qualify for long-term jobs that pay at least $7.50 per hour—sufficient to break out of poverty. Project QUEST is especially important in San Antonio, which has an unusually large minimum-wage workforce. Although the city's jobless rate is a relatively modest 4.5 percent, personal income is nearly 20 percent below the national average.

Project QUEST is unusual not only because of its long-range focus, but also because of its continuing link to the community-based organizations that pioneered the program and its close association with employers. The QUEST network also includes sixty community, corporate, and educational organizations, including the local community college system.

Project QUEST grew out of the efforts of two community-based organizations in San Antonio—Communities Organized for Public Service (COPS) and Metro Alliance. Today, COPS and Metro Alliance provide the community outreach necessary for recruiting and supporting QUEST trainees. The groups provide mentors to the trainees and provide links with the local government, business community, and educational institutions. Child-care subsidies, transportation, and referrals to health and other support services are available to trainees, as needed, under agreements with area agencies.

By the end of 1995, 825 enrollees had begun Project QUEST training and more than 300 have been placed in jobs, at an average wage of more than $7.80 per hour. Funding for the program, about $2.7 million per year, comes from a variety of sources, including federal and state governments and the city. Participating employers now number more than sixty, up from twelve in 1992. Other key program supporters include the Alamo Community College District (ACCD) and the San Antonio Chamber of Commerce. ACCD staff help ensure that training responds to employers' needs in target occupations. The Chamber of Commerce has helped coalesce business support. Business leaders, especially from banking and health, have taken an active role in the program.

NETWORKING

To trace some innovative practices in government, check out the Ford Foundation Innovations Awards program at http://ksgwww.harvard.edu/~innovat. Also see the National Center for Public Productivity at http://andromeda.rutgers.edu/~ncpp/.

The rationale for removing government from a particular area varies. In some cases, people may feel that clients will receive more personal attention from a nongovernmental or private group, such as one that operates a drug abuse program or a day-care center. Others suggest that privatization enhances competition among service providers, thus ensuring that the new means of delivering services will provide higher quality at a lower cost to the client. Programs also can be turned over to the private sector because the programs seem inappropriate to government or because the private firm can operate more efficiently.

Privatization is used in a more narrow sense (and more frequently) to refer to various devices through which a government retains a policy role regarding a particular service but engages someone else to actually deliver the service. A federal agency might decide to contract with a private firm rather than handle all its computer programming itself; a state might contract with a nonprofit organization to deliver services to welfare recipients; or a local government might lease a public hospital to a private firm. In each case, the services would be spelled out in detail by the government and some, if not all, funding might be provided, but day-to-day operation of the program would be the responsibility of the private or nonprofit agency.

A recent survey of privatization activities in state government reveals that during the past decade more and more jurisdictions have turned public services over to private and nongovernmental firms. The Council of State Governments reported that over half of the respondents said their state had expanded the number of privatization initiatives during the study period, with another one-third indicating they had maintained the current level. Furthermore, nearly all of the respondents said that, with increasing legislative support, privatization would only increase during the next five years. Most identified benefits such as cost control, government efficiency, and enhanced productivity as the primary reasons for the move. The survey report also stated that while monitoring of the privatization activities had been, at best, episodic, many of the respondents said the initiatives had generated significant cost savings.

CONTRACTING

There are various mechanisms through which relationships are established among government agencies and private and nonprofit organizations. By far the most common way to involve nongovernmental bodies in the conduct of public business is by *contracting* for goods or services. A decision to contract for goods or services may arise for several reasons. The government agency may not have (or wish to develop) the capacity to produce certain items; it may be easier to purchase a hammer, automobile, or tank from a private firm than to build one. Or those in the agency may feel that a private firm would be able to produce a good or deliver a service more efficiently, given their greater flexibility, different labor costs, or economies of scale.

On the other hand, private firms may become more concerned with profit than with the quality of service and, similarly, may neglect values such as equity in their pursuit of efficiency. Moreover, it is not always certain that the private firm will operate more efficiently. Mayor George Lattimer of St. Paul has commented:

> The private sector also has its problems in delivering expensive and desirable products: the private sector has had a decline in productivity, slackening investment in research and development, an unwillingness to consider external effects of private actions, a lack of capital investment, a trend to see short-term benefits, resistance to experiment with creative management, a loss of competitive strength . . . , and problems with the public sector contracting out enormous sums of dollars to private businesses where we have seen delays, cost overruns, and sometimes frauds. (Hatry, 1983, pp. 8–9)

Interestingly, after allowing public and private groups to bid on service contracts, jurisdictions have found that sometimes the private group wins and sometimes the public group wins!

DEFENSE CONTRACTING

One of the most publicized examples of government contracting in recent years has been the Defense Department's procurement of new weapons systems. The Pentagon oversees contracts totaling more than $150 billion a year and, perhaps not surprisingly, has had its share of problems with these contracts. Several aspects of the procurement process have proven especially troublesome. First, there may be difficulties in identifying just what the government wants. Detailed specifications may be required even for simple items. For example, at one point, the contract specifications for fruitcakes that are fed to military personnel are eighteen pages long and describe such things as the size of the nuts and the types of raisins that are allowed (Kettl, 1988, p. 35)! But as the requested items become more complex, the process of writing specifications also becomes more difficult. The Pentagon has its own experts who are responsible for writing specifications; however, since the size of Pentagon procurement offices was reduced during the 1980s, outside help has become necessary. The drafting of specifications is increasingly done by technical consultants hired by the government for their expertise in weapons technology. This arrangement has led to difficulties when consultants "rigged" specifications in favor of particular contractors or wrote specifications for the government, then helped contractors respond to the specifications.

Second, there is the question of government oversight of the contractor's performance. Recent investigations reveal a variety of abuses by contractors, including the widely ublicized $700 pliers and $600 toilet seats. Oversight has also revealed other questionable items charged to the government, such as country club dues, corporate parties, and even boarding an executive's dog (Carrington & Pound, 1988, p. 4). Although these investigations have demonstrated abuse of the system, contractors often complain that government oversight has become too detailed and hinders the contractor in getting the job done. Sanford McDonnell, head of McDonnell-Douglas, cited thousands of visits by government auditors and accused the federal government of "overmanaging, overspecifying, and overscrutinizing" defense contractors (Kettl, 1988, p. 40).

Third, recent policies that sought to create more competition for defense contracts have run into unexpected difficulties. In the past, the Pentagon worked closely with single contractors on a *sole-source* basis to develop new systems, but now competitions are held to determine who will receive a contract. Whereas competition has generated some savings on major items such as attack submarines and fighter plane engines, it has also created a new market for "inside" information that would give companies an edge in the competition. "Operation III Wind," a 1988 investigation into defense procurement practices, revealed that a combination of consultants, government officials, and contractors apparently conspired to exchange information that would give certain companies an advantage in the bidding process. Following these revelations, a major reform of the defense contracting process was undertaken.

HUMAN SERVICES

A quite different set of issues has emerged as states and localities have contracted for human services. One motive for contracting out is to obtain reductions in cost; however, in the social services, other motives also enter in. Most state social service agencies use federal Title XX funds to contract with private and nonprofit organizations for services, but competition for the funds is rare, because the number of agencies that operate in any one field—say, geriatric day care—is small. Moreover, groups that provide social services have not traditionally considered themselves subject to the same pressures for profit making as others, such as trash collection services. Quite appropriately, they have been more concerned with changing the lives of their clients than meeting some "bottom-line" financial figure. The determining factor in a contract for human services is likely to be the capacity of the organization to effectively deliver high-quality services.

Even the operation of correctional facilities has been contracted to private and nonprofit organizations. Prison services, such as medical care or drug treatment programs, have been contracted for many years. More recently, however, as incarceration rates have soared and the cost of operating prisons has risen, entire prisons have been contracted to outside organizations. Many states have passed legislation permitting privately run jails and prisons, but the moral and philosophical questions raised by such efforts are both obvious and complex. For example, how can a jurisdiction be sure that the rights of prisoners will not be violated by private entrepreneurs seeking higher profits?

Equity in delivery of services is important in the human service areas. Sylvester Murray, former city manager of Cincinnati, described contracting for garbage collection: one particular area of the city, "Over the Rhine," according to Murray, deserved garbage collection two or three times a week rather than once a week. As he put it, poor people accumulate more trash because they don't have garbage disposals and don't buy packaged goods as often. "The richer person will buy one giant-sized box of Tide and use that for three weeks. In the lower-income area, a person buys a small box every week . . . " (Murray, 1985, p. 4). An equitable solution would be to collect garbage more often from poorer neighborhoods than from richer neighborhoods. According to Murray, "What frightens us . . . about contracting out [for trash collection] is that the independent entrepreneur may not even think about [the equity issue]. He may not even consider it something that we ought to be concerned about, because he is so particularly interested in just the input and the output" (Murray, 1985, p. 4). Throughout the last twenty years, of course, one problem facing governments and their contractors was how to effectively and equitably cut back on existing services.

In the late 1980s, for example, Connecticut faced nearly a one-third reduction in funds for social services, with the decision about what to eliminate left to the state (Kettl, 1988, pp. 66–68). In making its decisions, the state followed a recommendation of the Kettering Foundation and used what is called a negotiated investment strategy, bringing together representatives of all the affected groups to set priorities for funding under the remaining block grant. Representatives of the fourteen state agencies involved, of nearly one thousand nonprofit groups involved in grant activity, and of the local governments affected by the grants met with skilled mediators to try to reach an agreement that all could sign. The questions were obviously difficult: Is child care more important than family planning? Is emergency shelter more important than recreation? (In both of these areas, the group answered "yes.") After an extended period of bargaining and negotiation, an agreement was reached that participants felt represented a fair and equitable solution to the state's dilemma.

STATE AND LOCAL GOVERNMENT CONTRACTING

Several initiatives at the state and local level have captured national attention as being best practices for privatization. In Massachusetts, for example, the state Highway Department sold off a variety of its maintenance operations to a private firm in order to increase quality of service and rein in expenditures. The decision came when state officials realized that more than two-thirds of the department's vehicles were beyond average life expectancy and that outlays for staff overtime had grown to excessive levels. Quality also had become a problem, particularly in that grass along roadways was cut only once a year and that, even then, the department had to use borrowed equipment. In the first-year privatization trial period, Massachusetts saved approximately $4.4 million, with an estimate $3 million to $7 million in savings to follow in subsequent years.

The state of Kansas also became a model for privatization by handing off its child-care services to nonprofit providers. State Department of Social and Rehabilitative Services officials said that the previous arrangement of state services simply had broken down. Agencies involved in adoption services had failed to place even half of their young clients into families; and, in foster care, some children were being shuffled through as many as eight different homes. The system had reached a crisis when, in 1990, the ACLU filed suit against the department on behalf of children. Recognizing that piecemeal attempts at change would not be good enough, the state opened its child-care system to a network of private providers. Proponents say that the result has been not only cost savings for the state, but that children in Kansas are getting the attention and assistance they need.

The experience of the state of Massachusetts illustrates some of the forces driving privatization efforts across the country. A few years ago, the Massachusetts Highway Department found itself on the edge of disaster. Most of the bridges in the state had not been washed in several years. Grassy areas lining the state roadways were cut only once a year, and then with borrowed equipment. About two-thirds of the department's vehicles already had exceeded average life expectancy.

Despite this poor service quality, the department was experiencing cost overruns. Personnel estimates suggest that for every two employees the agency had one foreman and that many of these foremen were earning more than $40,000 in overtime alone. Contracting out for highway services had served only to magnify the problem, as the department was paying more on contracts than other states but still had more workers on the payroll.

Under the direction and, to some degree, prodding of Governor William Weld, the department in 1992 handed over highway maintenance and drawbridge operations in Essex County to a private firm, Middlesex Corp. of Chelmsford, Massachusetts. The deal featured a $3.7 million, quantity-based contract for a one-year trial period. The contract required that Middlesex Corp. provide one hundred hours for washing bridges, cut the grass along the highways five times per year, patch roadways, and repair bridges.

The state of Massachusetts reported that in the first year, the agreement had saved the state approximately $4.5 million, including $2 million in operations, $1.5 million in reallocated personnel, and $1 million in reallocated equipment. And, the state said it would save between $3 million and $7 million if the privatization activity is continued. A separate study released by Harvard University's John F. Kennedy School of Government said the privatization initiative had enhanced service quality and that operations performed by Middlesex Corp. had been significantly more cost effective than the state's had been.

Some local governments, too, are turning to privatization for many of their service delivery areas. A recent study of four major city administrations revealed that service quality and cost efficiency were the driving factors. In New York, the administration of Mayor Rudolph Giuliani enhanced the city's financial condition by selling off many of its services, particularly in the areas of refuse and facilities maintenance. Mayor Ed Rendell's administration in Philadelphia reaped similar gains by privatizing park maintenance and the operation of parking garages. And Indianapolis, under Mayor Stephen Goldsmith, opened up most of its services to private bid prior to 1994. However, according to the study, the leader at the local level remains the city of Phoenix, where privatization became the norm more than a decade ago.

While cases such as this lay out the gains possible through privatization, each example comes with an equally strong argument for keeping public services under the purview of government. The most immediate source of conflict for any privatization initiative generally will be from organized labor. Union officials and some government workers see selling off service delivery as a way for administrations to avoid having to pay union wages. Private firms may hire nonunion personnel, or even temporary workers, who can be paid less and do not demand costly benefit packages. Others suggest that by handing off the delivery of public services to private firms, government is simply removing its responsibility to protect the public interest. By concentrating simply on efficiency, critics contend, government has become less responsive to the needs of citizens.

Arguments against privatization may not be with the practice itself but rather with the system in which it is carried out. For example, a recent survey of privatization activities by state government found that only about one-fourth of the respondents "use a formal decision-making process for privatization process [and that] overall they initiate privatization projects without standard decision-making, monitoring, or evaluation processes." While state and agency administrators admitted that a clear set of policy guidelines should precede any attempt at privatization, in most cases the process remains arbitrary and at the discretion of the project administrator. Indeed, critics contend that too often privatization serves more as a system of political reward than a cost-conscious strategy for providing public services.

OTHER MECHANISMS FOR PRIVATIZATION

Contracting is the most common technique for privatizing public services, but a variety of other mechanisms are used as well (see Box 3.5). A **franchise** can be awarded to a private firm to perform a certain service within a state or locality. The firm charges citizens directly for the services it provides. Typically, rates and performance standards are established by the government, and there is often some continuing regulation of the firm. Examples include electric power, taxi services, cable television, and emergency ambulance services. Similarly, governments may provide *grants* or *subsidies* to private or nonprofit organizations that are performing needed public services. The government provides full or partial support for activities that will benefit the community but which the local government, for financial or other reasons, does not wish to operate on its own. Examples include local government support for the arts, child care, or shelter for the homeless.

All levels of government have experimented with the use of *vouchers*. In a voucher system, citizens receive vouchers or coupons to redeem for goods or services from a variety of suppliers. The federal food stamp program, for example, provides recipients with coupons with which to purchase food, but permits the individual to choose both the supplier and the items to be purchased (within stated limits). At the local level, several cities have experimented with voucher systems for taxis to provide transportation to elderly citizens. This kind of system is considered more cost effective than providing more extensive mass transit.

Another means of privatizing public services is through the involvement of citizens in activities that were previously the work of government. **Coproduction,** as this technique is known, involves supplementing or perhaps supplanting the work of government officials with local residents' volunteer activity. Private citizens and government workers share in providing a particular service. Many cities, for example, have called on volunteers to assist in police, fire, parks and recreation, and education. Others have asked citizens to "adopt a park" or "adopt a highway" and to share in its maintenance.

What is important in all of these efforts to privatize public services is that they bring government officials into new relationships with nongovernment agents, whether contractors, service providers, or volunteers. Thus, it is no longer sufficient to

BOX 3.5

Privatization Gains in American Cities

Since the mid-1980s local governments have been working to provide better services in often faltering economies. But opposition to raising taxes to pay for local services, coupled with eroding tax bases, has made that difficult.

In answer, a number of local governments have embraced the notion of privatizing, mainly in the form of contracting out or introducing competition and the profit motive in order to contain and even lower the burdens of taxation.

Privatization in the 1990s has involved contracting out of government services and the sale or divestment of government assets. Hiring a firm to manage the billing for a government water utility or contracting with a company for trash removal services are examples. The government usually allows the firm to choose how it will satisfy the contract.

For example, a contract may specify trash removal services for the area residents a certain number of times per week. The firm is normally allowed to choose the methods it will use to perform the requirements of the contract, the trash trucks used, and the number of workers on each trash truck. The profit motive will encourage the firm to produce the services efficiently at the least cost, a motive absent in government provision of services.

Alternatively, a government may grant a franchise to a firm to remove trash in a certain area and allow that firm to charge residents governmentally determined prices for the service.

But this form of privatization is much less common than simple contracting out.

The question, then, is: What are the characteristics of the service that allow for it to be contracted out? In short, the work and the targeted population can be specified precisely, and the resulting performance can be monitored and measured.

The trend has been to rely increasingly upon privatization to introduce efficiency into government goods and services. In its "Tenth Annual Report on Privatization," the Reason Foundation noted that between 1987 and 1995, the percentage of local governments contracting out certain services grew substantially. In 1987, slightly more than 50 percent of the 120 local governments in thirty-four states surveyed by the Mercer Group contracted out their janitorial services. In 1995, that percentage had increased to 70.

The privatization trend is also apparent from the highly publicized efforts of cities like Indianapolis, Phoenix, Philadelphia, and New York. Indianapolis, under Mayor Stephen Goldsmith, privatized most of its services between 1991 and 1994.

In 1994 alone, Philadelphia, under Mayor Ed Rendell, opened up eleven services to competition, including park maintenance and the operation of parking garages. In 1995, New York City, under Mayor Rudolph Giuliani, subjected forty municipal services to competition.

Their results have provided a boost to the privatization movement. Giuliani, for instance, has predicted that competition created by privatization will lower costs and provide better services for New Yorkers.

Rendell noted, "Ironically, privatization is the most effective way we know to re-store productivity and the taxpayers' faith in government."

And Goldsmith stated that ". . . the moral of the story is that competition can cre-ate quality and better government, and even the residual government institutions are better off after competition."

SOURCE: Edwin Blackstone and Simon Hakim, "Private Ayes: A Tale of Four Cities," *American City and Count* 111, no. 2 (February 1997).

focus on intergovernmental relations alone; we must now speak of the importance of interorganizational relations. Moreover, these new circumstances raise important value questions. Where government programs are run directly by government, respon-sibility for their success lies squarely with the government agency. But where such programs are actually delivered by those in the private or nonprofit sector, traditional mechanisms for control and accountability may not work. Maintaining a proper con-cern for democratic values such as equity and responsiveness may, in the long run, prove more difficult than the managerial challenges of creating appropriate interorga-nizational policy networks.

THE GLOBAL DIMENSIONS OF PUBLIC ADMINISTRATION

As we view public administration in an interorganizational context, we also must extend our vision beyond national borders, for during the past generation the processes of gov-ernance have become increasingly international. Administrators in today's society not only must understand the challenges confronting their counterparts around the world, but also recognize that global issues affect us all. We cannot, for example, simply pass off environmental problems as localized phenomena, or believe that structural factors in the economy remain limited to a particular region. Their impacts go well beyond the lo-cality, the state or region, or even the nation-state. Responding to such issues will require new ways of thinking about public administration.

Over the years, studies comparing public administration in various countries have helped administrators gain a greater appreciation of the field's global dimensions. Comparative studies point out the common challenges we as public administrators face, while taking account of the diversity within our respective regions. They also help identify major trends being confronted by the international community. Most re-cently, four primary trends have emerged that characterize the international concerns in public administration: globalization, decentralization, civil society, and profession-alism. Each of these introduces a unique set of demands for public administrators; together they reinforce the idea that public administration truly has become a global endeavor.

GLOBALIZATION

The first trend has to do with the globalization of our social, economic, and political lives. Advancements in information and other forms of technology have removed past barriers posed by geography and distance. Our society has become what some call a "global village," in which we share based more on our common interests than on some sense of duty to an artificial geographic boundary. Such a shift has been influenced by economic forces. No longer do we think of ourselves as existing within isolated markets. The primary economic issues of today no longer have to do merely with national viability, but include the impact of multilateral foreign investment, international trade, the protection of intellectual property, and other global concerns. Consequently, our systems of governance have been forced to ensure both the public interest domestically and the sustainability of the jurisdiction within the international community.

Responses to globalization have been mixed. On one hand, some fear that by concentrating on international issues we may lose sight of those at home who remain in need. Challenges to recent trade deals, such as the North American Free Trade Agreement (NAFTA) and the General Agreement on Tariffs and Trade (GATT), exemplify this concern. Critics state that by removing measures that protect the environment and each nation's workers, such agreements will generate negative consequences far exceeding the gains from free trade. However, proponents counter that the emerging global marketplace will offer greater opportunities for employment and wealth creation, that in the long term the global village as a whole will benefit. They argue that protectionist ideals are a thing of the past and that remaining barriers should be removed in order to enhance the globalization trend.

While these positions reflect extreme views on internationalism, they share a common trait with regard to the practical implications of globalization—that is, a growing sense of interdependence among nations. Regardless of one's philosophical position, the truth in today's world is that social arrangements, economic markets, and government processes overlap with those in other countries. In turn, government institutions at the national, regional and local levels have begun to form transnational relationships to help manage the complexity. Formation of the European Union (EU) and the Asian-Pacific Economic Cooperation alliance (APEC), for instance, are indicative of such ties among nation-states. Likewise, states and localities, through formal partnerships like the Sister City program, have established working relationships with their counterparts worldwide.

DECENTRALIZATION

The global dimensions of public administration, however, do not end with changes in international relationships. During the past decade the balance of power also has shifted within national boundaries. We have noted the trend toward decentralization in the U.S. system of federalism—a devolution of authority from the national government down to the state and local level. Yet this trend in intergovernmental relations has also been playing out, in varying degrees, in democratic nations around the world. Structural forces at the supranational and the subnational levels have contributed to this trend. Specifically, the nation-state has been caught between the rise of the global on one hand, and the gaining influence of regional and local powers on the other.

In the past decade, national governments have taken on more of a figurative role within the social, economic, and political environment. Decisions of importance generally have been made through multilateral arrangements, or by ties between regional or local authorities. Indeed, in many areas the principal economic engines and the primary institutions of government have been at the provincial or municipal level. The nation-state, therefore, has found it necessary to hand over authority to subnational powers. Systems of governance, once characterized by highly centralized, bureaucratic organizational structures, have become decentralized, more flexible, and based on power-sharing networks among participating groups. Local administrations in particular have gained a greater capacity for policy decision making.

Despite the opportunity provided through such decentralization, such as the chance to shift power to a level that promotes engagement by citizens and communities, many local governments lack the framework and governance processes necessary for self-rule. A primary challenge confronting public administrators, then, involves the development of more effective systems of governance at the subnational level. In this regard, a distinction should be made between political decentralization and administrative decentralization. While much of the discussion has centered on political decentralization, or the shifting of formal authority from the national to the subnational level, not enough attention has been paid to administrative decentralization, the more practical aspects of handing over administrative functions to regional and local governments. Over the next generation, this latter area will become even more salient for students and practitioners of public administration.

CIVIL SOCIETY

An important concept underlying administrative decentralization involves the participation of citizens in the governance process, which many have called the development of a "civil society." In the past, government decisions were made by the central government and then handed down to local administrative arms for implementation. Citizens had little reason to engage subnational institutions, whose primary role was to carry out orders. The decentralization trend has turned this system on its head. Local governments exercise unprecedented power to initiate policies and programs. They can target governance strategies to meet the specific needs of their constituent population. Thus, citizens play an important role not only as recipients of government services but also as coproducers of the policies that affect their lives.

Of course, citizen participation is not a new concept in existing theories of democracy. At the very heart of our governmental system lies the principle of interaction between institutions and the public, either directly or by representation. Though over the past few centuries we have tended toward the representative form, the notion of civil society implies a return to more direct means of democratic engagement. Citizens are being challenged to go beyond merely casting a vote on election day, to think in terms broader than their self-interest and for the good of their community. Through civic organizations and nongovernmental groups, the public is being called upon to help shape a system of self-governance that, to paraphrase a popular saying, "thinks globally but acts locally."

The building of such a civil society carries important implications, not to mention significant challenges, for public administrators. Perhaps the most apparent of the challenges, though, is the requirement that citizen participation becomes a meaningful part of the governance process. Too often, civic engagement is reduced to simply being a source of legitimation for public decisions; citizen input is solicited for decisions already made within the elite power structure. Processes of this nature result not only in policies that are detached from the actual needs of affected populations, but over time create barriers between the local institutions and citizens. Thus, the forms of engagement must remain meaningful, with citizens playing a central role in the design, implementation, and evaluation of public policy.

PROFESSIONALISM

In order to achieve this vision, administrators around the world are seeking ways of enhancing professionalism and ethics in the public service. Primary goals include the creation of more responsive and accountable processes of government, more horizontal distributions of power, and transparent organizational structures that facilitate substantive engagement with citizens. Where in the past institutions of government were based on an internal orientation, with the primary objective being the enhancement of bureaucratic efficiency, the emerging system of administration features an external orientation, one that takes account of citizen priorities and remains open to public scrutiny. As a consequence, the underlying notion of public management has been transformed from one situated on established, rational administrative mechanisms, to an interactive, dynamic process occurring within the civil society.

Though this changing environment has ushered in unprecedented demands on government, particularly at the local level, public administrators continue to face declining resources. Cutbacks in spending allocations and personnel have left many leaders struggling to achieve significant outcomes. However, the environment also has triggered a change in the way we define leadership. Around the world, traditional systems of authority have been replaced with more lateral forms of leadership and decision making. Members throughout governmental organizations have been encouraged to take the initiative for innovating better, more cost-effective ways of meeting public demands. The result has been the development of more responsive and efficient means of delivering public services.

But professionals have also been concerned about ethics. As we will see in Chapter 4, a major concern during the past few years has been toward instituting more ethical processes of administration and management. For example, public administration research in the last decade has included a substantial increase in the number of scholarly publications relating to ethics; entire journals have been developed dedicated to the subject. Practitioners have begun exchanging views on ethical decision making with their counterparts worldwide, and professional associations, such as the American Society for

Public Administration, have created codes of ethics to help guide the education and practice in the field.

In all these ways, public administration has begun to be thought of in much more broad-ranging terms than before. All of the concerns just examined affect administrators not only in this country but around the world. Whether you plan to work in other countries or to spend you entire career in this country, you will need to understand trends that reach far beyond your local, state, or national boundaries. A city manager in Missouri once commented that he needed to know as much about economic decisions in Tokyo as those in the state capital. Administrators of all types will find that their knowledge of global developments will be essential to their work, wherever they live.

SUMMARY AND ACTION IMPLICATIONS

Given the complexity of modern society, your work as a public administrator will likely involve a complex set of relationships with all kinds of external groups. Many of these groups will be agencies at other levels of government. Our federal system has evolved from a pattern in which the various levels of government were relatively distinct to a pattern in which funding and programmatic relationships are extremely intense.

The fact that public programs today operate through vast and complex networks of people and organizations—public, private, and nonprofit—means that new skills are required of the public manager. Any particular program may involve various levels of government, organizations from all sectors of society, and clients or citizens with many different interests and concerns. As a public manager, you must be able to identify the network that is or should be involved in a particular situation and assess the effectiveness of that network.

To make that judgment, you will need to consider several factors. The first is *communications,* the type of information that goes from one organization to another and how it is transmitted. Second, you might focus on *exchanges* of goods and services, money, and personnel among the organizations involved. Third, you might examine the normative aspect of the relationship—that is, what each organization expects of the other and what each is willing to contribute to the relationship. Examining these same categories may also suggest ways to improve the effectiveness of interorganizational networks.

The interorganizational nature of modern public administration also has interesting implications for the interpersonal skills you must bring to the job. Increasingly, the government official responsible for a given program must be skilled in negotiating relationships with those outside the agency to ensure that the program proceeds effectively and responsibly. More and more, the public administrator works in a world in which older images of organizational hierarchy and control are quickly giving way to newer images of "managing in ambiguity" and "negotiating organizational boundaries." The interorganizational nature of public administration today has a direct effect on what skills managers need.

Terms and Definitions

Block grants: Grants in which the money can be used for nearly any purpose within a specific functional field.

Capital grants: Grants for use in construction or renovation.

Categorical or project grants: Grants requiring that the money may be spent for only a limited purpose; typically available on a competitive basis.

Charter: Local government's equivalent of a constitution.

Cooperative federalism: Greater sharing of responsibilities between federal and state governments.

Coproduction: Using volunteer activity to supplement or supplant the work of government officials.

Councils of government: Oversight bodies representing various localities to help coordinate local affairs.

Cross-cutting requirements: Rules that apply to most grant programs.

Dillon's Rule: Municipalities have only those powers granted in their charters; cities are creatures of the state.

Direct orders: Requirements or restrictions that are enforced by one government over another.

Dual federalism: Pattern in which federal and state governments are struggling for power and influence with little intergovernmental cooperation.

Entitlement grants: Grants that provide assistance to persons who meet certain criteria.

Formula grants: Grants that employ a specific division rule to indicate how much money any given jurisdiction will receive.

Grants: Transfers of money (and/or property) from one government to another.

Home rule: Provision allowing cities greater autonomy over local activities.

Intergovernmental relations: A term encompassing all the complex and interdependent relations among those at various levels of government.

Interorganizational networks: Pattern of relationships within and among various groups and organizations working in a single policy area.

Mandate: Order requiring a government to do something.

Negotiated investment strategy: Bringing together representatives of all affected groups to set priorities for funding.

Operating grants: Grants for use in development and operation of specific programs.

Picket-fence federalism: Pattern of intergovernmental relations in which the horizontal bars represent levels of government and the vertical slats represent various substantive fields.

Preemption: Federal government efforts to preempt an area traditionally associated with state government.

Privatization: Use of nongovernmental agencies to provide goods and services previously provided by government.

Revenue sharing: Grant pattern in which the money can be used any way the recipient government chooses.

Special districts: Local governments created for a specific purpose within a specific area.

Supply-side economics: Argument that decreased taxes and spending will stimulate capital investment and economic growth.

Study Questions

1. Although intergovernmental relations involve more than financial matters, funding programs have a significant role in the process. Define and give examples of the various kinds of grants and funding programs.
2. Compare and contrast "dual federalism," "cooperative federalism," and "coercive federalism." Describe the approach to federalism used during the Clinton presidency.
3. In the last decade, states and localities have faced significant changes in funding from the federal government. Discuss the reasons for the changes and how they affect relations among the various levels.
4. How do governmental mandates and regulations affect operations at the state and local levels?
5. Government has been moving to "privatization" of some goods and services. How will this trend affect intergovernmental relations?
6. Explain the importance and use of contracting for services and goods.

Cases and Exercises

1. Analyze the relationship between state and local governments in your state. What legal requirements govern state/local relationships? What, if any, bodies exist to help in intergovernmental cooperation? What kinds of mandates has the state imposed on local governments? What has been the reaction to these? How do you think state/local relations could be improved?

2. Assume the role of a member of a task force that has been asked to consider ways your local parks and recreation services could be delivered at less cost to the city government. (You may be able to obtain a budget, a list of services, and existing fees from the Parks and Recreation Department.) Consider alternatives such as special charges, citizen involvement in service delivery, and limitations on services. At the same time, consider what minimal level of parks and recreational services the city should provide as part of its general operations.

3. John Kincaid, a prominent student of intergovernmental relations, offers a list of trends emerging during the 1990s that characterize what he calls America's system of coercive federalism. Discuss each trend and predict its impact on the future of intergovernmental relations.

- Aid reduction: A decline in federal aid to state and local governments.
- Aid reduction to persons: A cutback in federal assistance programs, such as Medicaid and Aid to Families with Dependent Children.
- Aid conditions: An increase in federal mandates attached to aid programs to state and local governments.
- Mandates: A rise in federal mandates, despite recent initiatives by President Clinton and Congress to curb such measures.
- Preemption: A displacement of state and local government power by executive, legislative, and judicial actions at the federal level.
- Intergovernmental tax immunities: An intrusion on the part of the federal governments on the tax base of state and local governments.
- Uncooperative programming: A deterioration in the level of cooperation toward intergovernmental programs.
- Judicial indifference: A lack of concern on the part of the courts toward state and local government interests.

4. Divide the class into several groups of six to eight students each. Have one group assume the role of a granting agency charged, by legislation, with providing funds to local communities to help in projects that "improve the economic potential of the community and assist low-income and disadvantaged groups in the community." Assume that the agency has $50 million to distribute, but that the legislation has given the granting agency the authority to determine all other details of the grant program.

The agency group must first define as clearly as possible the intent of the legislation, then prepare guidelines outlining the types of projects that will be funded under the program. A written Request for Proposals (RFP) should then be prepared and distributed to a set of potential applicant communities, each represented by one of the other groups in the class. The RFP should contain, at a minimum, a description of the program, criteria by which proposals will be evaluated, examples of projects that might be funded, and instructions for submitting proposals for funding (including a deadline for applications).

Each community group will then prepare a grant application to support a project or projects it wants for its community. Members of each community group may communicate with one representative of the agency designated as liaison to that community, but should not talk with other agency members. Community groups can communicate with one another if they wish. By the deadline contained in the RFP, all proposals should be submitted to the agency. The agency will then determine which, if any, projects will be funded and at what levels. The results should be communicated to all the communities.

Following the exercise, the class as a whole should discuss the entire process. You might want to focus on issues such as these:

- What is the role of the agency in defining the kinds of projects that will be funded?
- What types of instructions are necessary to enable communities to compete fairly and effectively?
- What was most attractive about the proposals that were funded?
- For what reasons were other proposals not funded?
- What effect on the final decisions did communications between the community and the liaison from the agency have?
- Did "politics" play any role?

For Additional Reading

Bernstein, Susan R. *Managing Contracted Services in the Nonprofit Economy*. Philadelphia: Temple University Press, 1991.

Bowman, Ann O., and Richard C. Kearney. *The Resurgence of the States*. Englewood Cliffs, NJ: Prentice Hall, 1986.

Cook, Brian J. *Bureaucracy and Self-Government*. Baltimore: Johns Hopkins University Press, 1996.

Cooper, Phillip J., and Chester A. Newland. *Handbook of Public Law and Administration*. San Francisco: Jossey-Bass, 1997.

Cooper, Phillip J., et al. *Public Administration for the Twenty-First Century*. Fort Worth: Harcourt Brace College Publishers, 1997.

Gage, Robert W., and Myrna P., Mandell, eds. *Strategies for Managing Intergovernmental Policies and Networks*. Westport, CT: Greenwood Press, 1990.

Hill, Kim Quaile, and Kenneth R. Mladenka. *Democratic Governance in American States and Cities*. Pacific Grove, CA: Brooks/Cole, 1992.

Hill, Larry B., ed. *The State of Public Bureaucracy*. Armonk, NY: M. E. Sharpe, Inc., 1992.

Jennings, Edward T., Jr., Dale Krane, Alex N. Pattakos, and B. J. Reed, eds. *From Nation to States*. Albany: State University of New York Press, 1986.

Judd, Dennis R., and Todd Swanstrom. *City Politics. Private Power and Public Policy*. New York: HarperCollins College Publishers, 1994.

Jun, Jong S., and Deil S. Wright, eds. *Globalization and Decentralization: Institutional Contexts, Policy Issues, and Intergovernmental Relations in Japan and the United States*. Washington, DC: Georgetown University, 1996.

Kemp, Roger L., ed. *Privatization. The Provision of Public Services by the Private Sector.* Jefferson, NC: McFarland & Company, 1991.

Kettl, Donald F. *Government by Proxy.* Washington, D.C.: Congressional Quarterly Press, 1988.

Kettl, Donald F. *Sharing Power: Public Governance and Private Markets.* Washington D.C.: The Brookings Institution, 1993.

Levin, Martin, and Mary Sanger. *Making Government Work.* San Francisco: Jossey-Bass, 1994.

McLaughlin, Curtis. *The Management of Nonprofit Organizations.* New York: Wiley 1986.

Nathan, Richard P., Fred C. Doolittle, et al. *Reagan and the States.* Princeton, NJ: Princeton University Press, 1987.

National Academy of Public Administration. *Privatization: The Challenge to Public Management.* Washington, DC: National Academy, 1989.

Nice, David C. *Federalism: The Politics of Intergovernmental Relations.* New York: St. Martin's Press, 1987.

Peirce, Neal R., Curtis Johnson, and John Stuart Hall. *Citistates: How Urban America Can Prosper in a Competitive World.* Washington, DC: Seven Locks Press, 1993.

Peterson, Paul. *The Price of Federalism.* Washington, DC: Brookings Institution, 1995.

Rivlin, Alice M. *Reviving the American Dream: The Economy, the States, and the Federal Government.* Washington, DC: The Brookings Institution, 1992.

Rusk, David. *Cities without Suburbs.* Baltimore: Johns Hopkins University Press, 1993.

Salamon, Lester, ed. *Beyond Privatization.* Washington, DC: Urban Institute Press, 1989.

Smith, Steven Ragbeth, and Michael Lipsky. *Nonprofits for Hire: The Welfare State in the Age of Contracting.* Cambridge: Harvard University Press, 1993.

Waters, Malcolm. *Globalization.* London: Routledge, 1995.

Wright, Deil S. *Understanding Intergovernmental Relations.* 3d ed. Pacific Grove, CA: Brooks/Cole, 1988.

Chapter 4

THE ETHICS OF PUBLIC SERVICE

So far we have focused on the context of public administration—the values, structures, and relationships you need to understand to act effectively and responsibly in public organizations. Now we begin a transition to more skill-based issues by exploring the ethical issues raised in public service. An ethical posture toward work in public organizations requires not only knowing the right answers, but being willing and able to do what is right. You must be prepared to act.

Over the last several years, there has been a surge of interest in ethical issues in public organizations. A recent set of *Time* cover stories asked the question, "What Ever Happened to Ethics?" The articles commented on ethical dilemmas in business, education, and even religion, but gave special attention to the ethics of those in government. In one article, Sissela Bok, a philosophy professor at Brandeis University, stressed that moral leadership must come first from those in public office. "Aristotle said that people in government exercise a teaching function. Among other things, we see what they do and think that is how we should act. Unfortunately, when they do things that are underhanded or dishonest, that teaches too" (*Time,* May 25, 1987).

Certainly the concerns Bok and others expressed about the ethical behavior of public officials have been triggered by such dramatic public events as Watergate and the Iran-Contra scandal. But in fact, ethical issues permeate public organizations as they do all organizations. Every action of every public official—whether in the formulation or implementation of public policy—carries value implications. Given this situation, it is not surprising that both President Bush and President Clinton used their first executive orders to deal with ethical issues and that states and localities across the country have struggled mightily with ethical concerns.

As a public manager, you will often face difficult ethical choices. These choices may present themselves in several ways. "Dilemmas arise for decision makers when responsibilities conflict, when the obligations they undertake or the rules to which they are subject are unclear, or when they are unsure how to weigh their responsibilities against personal needs or desires" (Fleishman & Payne, 1980, p. 17). Understanding the moral implications of your actions and resolving the dilemmas they pose is one of the most difficult problems you will face working in the public sector. Consequently, your ability to understand the context in which public problems arise and to work them out in a careful, reasoned, and ethical fashion will be essential to your success (and your own sense of personal well-being).

In this chapter we examine a variety of ethical issues faced by public managers. Some involve concerns that might arise in any organization—cases of lying, cheating, or stealing, or questions about what to do when you feel compelled to refuse an order from your boss. Others are more directly connected to the special values that underlie public service, involving the relationship between political leaders and career civil servants or between competing demands for efficiency and responsiveness.

APPROACHES TO ETHICAL DELIBERATION

Ethics is, of course, a branch of philosophy and is concerned with the study of moral principles and moral action. To properly define *ethics,* therefore, we must first understand the meaning of morality. **Morality** is concerned with those practices and activities that are considered right or wrong; it is also concerned with the values those practices reflect and the rules through which they are carried out within a given setting (DeGeorge, 1982, p. 12). The morality of a society, a political system, or a public organization concerns what is considered to be right or wrong within that group. Morality expresses certain values that members of the group hold to be important and is reflected in laws, rules, and regulations, or in policies and procedures. Moral action, in turn, is action that is consistent with the group's morality—that which expresses the group's most basic commitments about what is right and what is wrong.

Ethics, on the other hand, can be defined as "a systematic attempt through the use of reason to make sense of our individual and social moral experience in such a way as to determine the rules which ought to govern human conduct. . . ." (DeGeorge, 1982, p. 12). Ethics is concerned with the process by which we clarify what is right and wrong and by which we act on what we take to be right; ethics involves the use of reason in determining a proper course of action. Ethics is the search for moral standards.

Though we have defined ethics as the study of morality, the two terms are often used almost interchangeably. For example, we often call an action that is morally correct an ethical action. Similarly, we speak of codes of moral conduct as codes of ethics. Despite the overlapping uses of the terms, the distinction between morality and ethics is important not only for philosophical reasons, but because focusing on ethics emphasizes the individual's active involvement in searching out morally correct positions. Ethics calls us into action; it requires us to reason, to analyze, and to seek guidance as to the proper course of action.

This deliberative aspect of ethics is important because the issues you will face in public organizations are rarely black or white. Should you lie to a legislator so as to carry out a policy you think is correct? Should you bend the rules to benefit a client in need? Should you follow orders from an organizational superior even if you know you are being asked to do something wrong? These questions and the thousands of others you may encounter in public organizations don't have easy answers. To act properly, you must be able to sort through the many and often competing values that underlie your work, and you must be able to come to a reasoned conclusion that will form the basis for action.

It's not enough to simply say, "It depends," and go about your business, though such a position has gained widespread currency in our society. **Ethical (or moral) relativism** is the belief that actions that are immoral in some places or circumstances are moral in others and that one can make moral judgments only by taking into account the context in which an action occurs. According to this view, there are no universal rules of conduct that apply in all situations. A defense of the relativist position is that different cultures have different rules of conduct. One culture may consider it proper to leave old people to die alone, while another may give the elderly considerable care and attention.

Such arguments, however, often fail to take into account larger and more unifying moral principles, such as respect for the elderly. Furthermore, the relativist position seems at odds with our moral experience. When we make the judgment that murder is immoral, we don't mean that it is immoral for some individuals and not others. We don't even mean that murder is immoral in some countries and not in others. We claim that murder is immoral for all people at all times—and we can defend our statement on both rational and emotional grounds. This position suggests that there is really only one right answer to moral questions (even though that answer may be hard to find!). Nevertheless, by understanding the context in which an action occurs, working through the various arguments in behalf of one position or another, and arriving at a set of guidelines for action, one can at least act with greater clarity and confidence.

What are the steps in ethical deliberation? First, you should attempt to *clarify the facts*. Although most ethical issues involve both facts and values and the facts alone are not likely to resolve the issue, it is important to establish the facts as clearly as possible. A pollution control policy may require precise measurements of pollutants released into the air; knowing the exact measurements, rather than speculating about them, may resolve the issue. In other cases, merely becoming clearer about the facts will help resolve certain ethical problems.

Second, it is easier to resolve ethical issues if those involved come to some agreement about *basic principles*. These may be broad moral standards (such as freedom or justice); they may be laws or other rules accepted by the society; or they may be standards of behavior appropriate to a particular group or organization. These ideas are, of course, deeply held by members of any society or organization, so disagreements may be marked. For example, two detectives may have dramatically different views about how to treat criminals, but if they clarify their agreement on the basic goal of fighting crime, they may be able to reconcile their differences. Generally speaking, any progress you can make in establishing a common ground or in bringing about agreement on basic principles will help resolve the issue.

Third, one of the central aspects of ethical deliberation is the *analysis of arguments* presented in behalf of various viewpoints. The arguments may be articulated by different individuals or different groups, or they may simply be arguments and counterarguments you think through yourself. In either case, you will need to consider the evidence presented, the justifications for various viewpoints, and possible fallacies of the justifications. Throughout the process of argumentation, dialogue is extremely helpful in clarifying one's position. (If the problem is one you are considering alone, finding someone to talk through the issues with you is a good idea.) Ultimately, however, you will need to make a decision and act on it. Ethical deliberation will lead you to a decision, but acting in a way that is consistent with that decision is also important, though often difficult.

REASONING, DEVELOPMENT, AND ACTION

You will be better prepared to deliberate if you become familiar with some basic approaches to ethical reasoning: moral philosophy, moral psychology, and moral action. In each case, we will present only a brief overview. You should be aware that there are many varying and sometimes conflicting interpretations of these issues, and you may find others (perhaps including your teacher) who disagree with the formulation presented here. Consider this material merely an invitation for further learning!

Moral Philosophy

Regarding *moral philosophy*, we can ask: given a particular set of circumstances, how do we determine what is right and what is wrong? In other words, how do we go about figuring out the proper course of action? One approach is to consider who will benefit and who will suffer from each of various alternative actions, then ask which course of action provides the greatest benefit at the least cost. Another approach is to search for a moral principle or rule against which to measure aspects of the particular case. In the first approach, one focuses on the consequences of the action; in the second, one looks for universal rules of conduct.

One of the most common forms of ethical deliberation, which focuses on the consequences of actions, is utilitarianism. **Utilitarianism** holds that an action is right, compared to other courses of action, if it results in the greatest good for the greatest number of people (or at least the minimum harm). Proponents of this view contend that there are no universal principles that can guide action, but rather that the likely benefits and costs associated with any action must be calculated to judge that practice either moral or immoral.

Obviously, this view leans toward relativism; according to a utilitarian, telling the truth cannot be judged a priori either right or wrong—rather, the rightness or wrongness of telling the truth depends on a calculation of who is helped and who is harmed by the act. Only then can a moral judgment be rendered. In the utilitarian view, "Actions themselves have no intrinsic values. They are simply means to attain things which do have value" (DeGeorge, 1982, p. 40).

An administrator employing a utilitarian approach to moral reasoning in a specific situation would ask what the likely outcomes of one course of action or another might be. If building a new highway through a particular neighborhood would inconvenience a few people but benefit many others, then building that highway in that location would be considered a proper course of action. The administrator would not follow any predetermined moral principle, such as that citizens should not be arbitrarily displaced, but would calculate costs and benefits relative to the specific case. Moreover, the administrator would not generalize beyond the specific case; each act would be judged on its own merits.

A contrasting approach to moral reasoning based on the search for general rules or principles of conduct is often called deontological. **Deontology** holds that broad principles of rightness and wrongness can be established and that these principles are not dependent on the consequences of a particular action. Those who hold this view tend to focus on duties or responsibilities (*deontology* derives from the Greek word for "duty"). Quite simply, one's duty is to do what is morally correct and to avoid doing that which is morally wrong, regardless of the consequences of one's actions (DeGeorge, 1982, p. 55). Deontologists thus tend to focus on broad principles of right and wrong, such as those embodied in concepts like "rights" or "justice."

Using the deontological approach, an administrator would seek to act in accord with generally accepted moral precepts, such as honesty or benevolence. Administrators are expected, for example, to tell the truth, keep their promises, and respect the dignity of the individual. Their doing so does not derive from laws or codes of ethics but from generally accepted moral principles. In particular situations, these actions might even be harmful to the overall interests of the organization or the society, but, because the actions could be justified as consistent with a shared sense of moral order, the administrator should feel strongly compelled to act in that way (Denhardt, 1988, p. 46).

One contemporary deontological theory that has received considerable attention is that of philosopher John Rawls. His approach emphasizes fairness or equity in policy decisions (Rawls, 1971). An interesting argument that Rawls develops to explain his theory suggests that if decisions were made under conditions in which the decision makers had no knowledge of whether they would personally accrue harm or benefit by choosing one way or another, then fairness would likely prevail. Imagine a city council committee deciding where to spend $1 million on street improvements. If all members of the committee acted in their own interest, they might spend the money in their own neighborhoods (and those would likely be the more affluent neighborhoods). On the other hand, if all members of the committee acted under a "veil of ignorance," not knowing where they lived or whether or not they were affluent, they would most likely spend the money so as to bring the poorer streets up to some standard level (and in doing so, they would likely spend more in less affluent neighborhoods). If all public decisions were rendered by acting out of concern for fairness rather than self-interest, Rawls argues, a far different moral order would prevail—one that was much more consistent with the basic principles of liberty and justice.

Moral Psychology

Psychologist Lawrence Kohlberg devised a scheme outlining three levels of moral development through which people pass: the preconventional, conventional, and postconventional stages (Kohlberg, 1971). According to Kohlberg, most people operate on one of the first two levels of moral development, and no one operates exclusively on the third level.

At the *preconventional level,* children begin to develop certain ideas about right and wrong. They interpret these ideas in terms of the consequences of their actions or the physical power of those around them. At an early stage, the ideas are associated with punishments; for example, if the child writes on the wall with a crayon, the child will be scolded. To avoid the negative consequences associated with writing on the wall, the child avoids that behavior. Later on, the child begins to behave in certain ways to receive rewards, such as parental praise. Whether to avoid negative consequences or to receive praise, the child begins to behave in ways that we characterize as right rather than wrong. Of course, from the child's point of view, there is no moral code; the child is merely doing things to avoid punishments or to seek rewards. At this level of moral development, therefore, the consequences of our actions—the rewards or punishments we receive—determine whether we consider our actions right or wrong. The preconventional orientation is, of course, one that we all carry into adulthood.

At the *conventional level* of moral development, people behave morally in terms of conformity to various standards or conventions of the family, group, or nation. The individual seeks to conform to given moral standards and, indeed, to actively support and maintain those standards. This level involves two stages. Kohlberg calls the first the

"Good Boy/Nice Girl" stage, at which we conform to expectations of parents or teachers or peers and to the norms we learn at home, in church, or at school. We come to develop moral rules or codes, standards of right and wrong, though what we think of as good behavior is really just that which meets the expectations of others.

A second stage in the conventional level of moral development is the "Law and Order" orientation. At this stage, we develop an orientation toward authority and the social order; we learn what it means to be a "good citizen"; and we come to accept the importance of living by the conventional rules of the society. Notions of duty and honor tend to dominate one's moral perspective at this level. We recognize that certain behaviors are wrong—lying, cheating, stealing—but if asked why, we can only answer, "Because everyone knows they are wrong" (DeGeorge, 1982, p. 25). Most adults continue to operate, at least in part, at this level of moral development.

Few adults reach the final level, the *postconventional,* but some do. At this level, people accept moral principles and behave according to those principles, not merely because someone says they should, but because they know themselves what makes these principles right. The individual seeks to define moral principles for himself or herself and to understand how those values operate independently of any group or society. A first postconventional stage is called the "social-contract" or "legalistic" stage, which has a strong utilitarian bias. The individual recognizes the rights of other individuals, including the right to one's own beliefs and values, and how societies are constituted to support those rights. The result is a legalistic viewpoint, though it recognizes the possibility of changing the legal order (rather than freezing it, as in the previous level). Changes of this sort are often supported based on the greatest good for the greatest number.

The second stage of the postconventional level represents the highest stage of moral development. At this stage, the individual freely chooses to live by a particular set of abstract moral principles, such as justice, equality, and respect for individual dignity. One chooses to follow these precepts not for rewards or punishments and not to meet others' expectations, but because one understands why the principle should be supported and freely chooses to live by that standard. The actual standards one follows may be the same in both level two and level three, but there is an important difference in the *reason* one holds an action to be right or wrong.

Although we have focused on Kohlberg's work here, we should point out that there are several alternatives to his interpretation that have been voiced recently. One important alternative, for example, is that suggested by Carol Gilligan. Gilligan argues that, in contrast to the rational and impartial perspective of Rawls and Kohlberg, one may interpret moral theory in terms of care and relationships. According to Gilligan, a final and mature morality involves an interaction between the concerns of impartiality and those of personal relationship and care (Blum, 1988, pp. 472–491).

As you work in and with public organizations, you will come to recognize that many of the ethical decisions you make are based in one or another level of moral development. We do certain things because they will lead to rewards or punishments and we do other things because we must adhere to laws or organizational standards of conduct. For example, you may obey an order from a superior so that you won't be fired, or you may purchase a new piece of equipment through a bidding process rather than from a friend because that's the law. But you will also encounter cases that will require you to think much more carefully and much more personally about the standards you are willing to live by. For example, purchasing a piece of equipment might be complicated by the fact that your supervisor *ordered* you to purchase the equipment from a friend without other bids. In cases such as these, postconventional or "principled" reasoning may be essential. Certainly if you recognize that not all the answers can come from the power or expectations of others and that careful deliberation concerning moral principles is often quite appropriate, you will be better positioned to make the correct ethical decisions, time after time.

Moral Action

Knowing the proper and correct course of action is not enough. You must indeed act in a way that is consistent with what you consider to be right. (After all, we describe people as having "integrity" not merely on the basis of what they believe, but on the basis of how they act.) This concern is especially significant for a public manager (or, for that matter, any other professional) who wishes to act ethically. Questions of ethics in the public service are not abstract; they are real. And they have immediate and sometimes serious human consequences. It is thus important to consider how we can ensure moral actions in public organizations.

A long philosophical tradition holds that putting principles (whether utilitarian, deontological, or otherwise) into action requires the development of "character" on the part of the individual. In other words, it is necessary to apply a complex set of general principles to specific cases—something that requires more than abstract knowledge. Aristotle spoke of the importance of gaining "practical wisdom" so as to make morally correct judgments in specific situations. This practical wisdom or "virtue" requires that the individual not simply know how to apply given principles, but rather why to do so. That is, to bring moral knowledge to bear in the "real world," the individual needs a strong sense of what is ideal in human conduct. Terry Cooper, for example, argues that virtues are traits of character that are acquired through reflection and conduct. They involve an integration of both thought and feeling where potentially conflicting tendencies are brought under control (Cooper & Wright, 1992, p. 6).

This "ethics of virtue," then, is not merely another philosophical approach but a way of developing the skills one brings to the problem of ethical decision making. Aristotle speaks of developing the skills of virtue in the same way we develop other skills, that is, by practice: "The virtues we get first by exercising them. . . . For the things we have to learn before we can do them, we learn by doing them. . . . We become just by doing just acts, temperate by doing temperate acts, brave by doing brave acts" (McKeon, 1941, p. 952).

But what are the virtues that we must practice? Obviously, this question has challenged philosophers over the centuries. Answers range from honesty, courage, and trustworthiness to kindness, fairness, and dependability, but most seem to center around concerns for *benevolence* and *justice*. If this is the case, then all persons should practice these virtues, while members of specific professions (such as public administrators) should practice applications of these virtues in their specific situations (Tong, 1986, pp. 91–92).

How, then, does one sort out the various philosophical and psychological approaches one might employ to make ethical choices in the "real world"? First, if you set about solving difficult moral problems through the application of broad moral principles in specific situations, you need to understand the principles and moral reasoning that underlie them. Second, you must engage in careful and consistent ethical deliberation, through self-reflection and dialogue with others. Third, you must understand how virtues such as benevolence or justice are played out in public organizations; that is, you must recognize the political and ethical context that conditions the moral priorities of the public service (Bailey, 1965, p. 285).

As you approach particular questions, it may be helpful to consider first the utilitarian position—what are the costs and benefits, and which alternative will bring the greatest benefits? Next, you might ask whether the alternative you chose will infringe upon the rights of others and, if so, whether there are overwhelming factors that justify such an outcome. You might next ask whether the chosen alternative violates principles of equity and fairness and, if so, whether again there are overwhelming factors that would justify the outcome. Finally, you might ask whether the alternative is consistent with your ideals with respect to human conduct (especially the conduct of public affairs) and whether by choosing this alternative you will be acting in a way you consider to be virtuous. At any point, you may find that the alternative comes up short, and you must search for another. Remember that your ultimate goal is the development of virtue and the application of sound ethical reasoning to public problems.

ISSUES OF ADMINISTRATIVE RESPONSIBILITY

People who work in or with public organizations face literally dozens of ethical dilemmas. Some—like lying, cheating, or stealing—are the same problems that many others face. But some, like the public manager's commitment to democratic standards or feelings about the political involvement of public employees, are peculiar to public organizations.

One of the most troublesome "broad-range" issues in the field of public administration is that of administrative responsibility. (In the section that follows, we focus much more specifically on issues where personal values, such as honesty, equity, and justice, become deeply intermingled with the broader values of public service.) As a public manager, you may often confront the potentially conflicting demands of operating as efficiently as possible while, at the same time, being fully responsive to administrative superiors, to the legislature, to the citizenry, and to the principles of democratic governance generally. This tension between *efficiency* and *responsiveness* characterizes many of the problems public managers face.

As we have seen, the tension between efficiency and responsiveness grows from two other issues that are deeply rooted in the history of public administration—the issue of politics and administration and the issue of bureaucracy versus democracy. Early writers in the field sought a clear distinction between *politics* and *administration,* arguing that, wherever possible, administrative activities should be insulated from the potentially corrupting influence of politics. Obviously, this idea was based on the assumption that policy making could be distinguished from policy implementing. Making such an assumption allows easy resolution of questions of democratic responsibility—the legislature, charged with making policy, should be responsive to the people; the administrative agencies, charged with implementing policy, should be responsive to the legislature. The requirements of democracy will be met by a neutral and competent public bureaucracy that follows the mandates of the legislative body; this is called the doctrine of **neutral competence.** Most writers and practitioners clearly preferred this somewhat narrow view of administrative responsibility. Indeed, the doctrine of neutral competence, and the politics-administration dichotomy on which it is based, continues to influence the field. But there were and are many who recognize the difficulty of maintaining a neutral public bureaucracy. Some even argue that the role administrative agencies play in the policy process is not only inevitable, but proper.

NETWORKING

For general discussions of ethics in government, see the following: Center for Public Integrity, http://www.publicintegrity.org/; Institute for Philosophy and Public Policy, http://www.puaf.umd.edu/IPPP/; Center for the Study of Values in Public Life, http:// divweb.harvard.edu/csvpl/; and Josephson Institute at http://www.josephsoninstitute. org/. Organizations that seek to promote citizen action include the Center for Civic Networking at http://civic.net/ccn.html and the Center for Democracy and technology at http://www.cdt.org/.

THE LIMITS OF ADMINISTRATIVE DISCRETION

We have noted that administrators take their primary cues from the actions of legislatures that initiate programs and from executives who are charged with carrying out the programs. If you are hired to manage a new agency, one of your first priorities will be to familiarize yourself with the legislation that created the agency and with any executive orders or other directives outlining the agency's responsibilities. But if your situation is typical, you will find that neither the legislation nor the directions you receive from the executive are sufficiently detailed to answer all the questions your work raises. There will be a need to develop policies regarding these issues; policies that are, in effect, merely more detailed pieces of "legislation." In addition, as you get into the work, you may find it necessary to ask the legislature or the chief executive to make certain changes in the rules and regulations under which you operate.

The problem, of course, is to make sure that your policies or recommendations for change are consistent with the wishes of the citizenry (see Box 4.1). In most jurisdictions, of course, the legislature and the chief executive are popularly elected, and their reelection depends on their response to the public's perceived needs and interests. For them, the electoral process assures responsiveness, at least in theory. As long as you are acting in a way that is clearly consistent with legislative intent, you are likely to be considered appropriately responsive. But because most situations aren't that clear, the question becomes, "How can we assure that the administrator is exercising discretion in a way consistent with the will of the people, whether expressed in the Constitution, the laws of the land, or the preferences of citizens?"

Historically, two answers have been posed to this question. In an important debate in the pages of the *Public Administration Review* and other journals some forty years ago, Herman Finer argued that, to maintain responsiveness to the public, managers in public

BOX 4.1

Putting Citizens First

Over the past thirty to forty years, the public's trust in government has declined dramatically. Where only a few decades ago three out of four people said that they "trusted the government in Washington to do what is right" most or all of the time, today that percentage is less than one out of four. People see their elected officials, especially those at the federal level, as being dishonest, callous, and unwilling to listen. They see the government as "out of control."

At the same time, the level of citizen interest and involvement in public affairs is being questioned. In a historic context, citizenship meant working for the common good. Yet too often today we hear people respond to public issues by saying "What's in it for me" or "Not in my backyard." Citizens are not well-educated with respect to the operations of government, nor are they well tuned in to public affairs.

An interesting and important effort to address these basic concerns has been occurring over the past year and a half in Florida. On April 4, 1995, Linda W. Chapin, the first elected county chairman of Orange County, Florida (the county surrounding Orlando), addressed a large gathering of community leaders and volunteers. In her remarks, Chapin pointed out that success in any policy area—whether the environment, transportation, criminal justice, or schools—ultimately depends on the pride and commitment of citizens. Arguing that a rekindling of the idea of civic engagement lies at the base of all efforts to improve community life, Chapin called for a program to put "Citizens First!"

The idea of "Citizens First!" starts with the proposition that people acting as citizens must demonstrate their concern for the larger community, their commitment to matters that go beyond short-term interests, and their willingness to assume personal responsibility for what happens in their neighborhoods and the community. After all, these are among the defining elements of effective and responsible citizenship.

But the "Citizens First!" theme cuts in another way. Chapin remarked, "To the extent that people are willing to assume (the role of citizens), those . . . in government must be willing to listen—and to put the needs and values of citizens first in our decisions and our actions. We must reach out in new and innovative ways to understand what our citizens are concerned about. And we must respond to the needs that they believe will help make a better life for themselves and their children. In other words, those of us in government must put citizens first."

SOURCE: Robert B. Denhardt, "Local Governments Learn to Put 'Citizens First,'" *PA Times*, v. 20, no. 1 (February 1997): 1.

organizations should be subjected to strict and rigid controls by the legislature. His question was straightforward (though perhaps overdrawn): "Are the servants of the public to decide their own course, or is their course of action to be decided by a body outside themselves?" (Finer, 1972, p. 8). His answer was equally direct: Only through specific and detailed legislation carefully limiting the work of public managers could responsiveness to the legislature be maintained. This interpretation of how to assure responsiveness is often called **objective responsibility,** depending as it does on objective external controls.

Carl Friedrich, on the other hand, argued that the increasing complexity of modern society made such detailed legislation difficult, if not impossible; consequently, Friedrich felt that the administrator's own concern for the public interest was often the only real assurance that his or her actions would be responsive to the electorate. Fortunately, wrote Friedrich, the growing number of professionals in government increases the likelihood that a sense of democratic responsibility will be a part of the administrator's makeup (Friedrich, 1972).

Others, following Friedrich's lead, noted the growing number of governmental officials receiving training in schools of public affairs and public administration. These schools take quite seriously the need to expose students to the ethical issues they may encounter in public organizations and to ways these issues might be resolved. This way of assuring responsiveness is often called **subjective responsibility,** depending as it does on the subjective nature of the individual.

Recently, Terry Cooper has argued that the notion of citizenship involves both rights and responsibilities and that the citizen must assume a positive role in the betterment of society as a whole. In doing so, he or she acts in pursuit of the common good and in accord with values such as political participation, political equality, and justice. When a citizen becomes a public administrator, he or she assumes the role of "citizen-administrator, both a citizen and someone working for the citizenry." In this case, the administrator's ultimate obligation is to deliver public goods and services "in ways that enhance the common good of community life through which character and civic virtue are formed" (Cooper, p. 161).

One approach to assuring responsiveness that cuts across the objective/subjective distinction is *representative bureaucracy*—the idea that public agencies whose employees reflect certain demographic characteristics of the population as a whole are likely to operate more in line with the policy preferences of the general citizenry. According to this view, an agency with a substantial number of women or minority employees is more likely to take into account the views of women and minorities in the population than would an agency of white males. Experience with representative bureaucracy has produced mixed results. Whereas we might indeed expect greater responsiveness with respect to race and gender in the example, there is no reason to think that such an agency would be more or less representative on other types of issues. Moreover, there is no real assurance that a person from one particular group would necessarily or always reflect that group's policy preferences. Those preferences might well be displaced by the professional or bureaucratic norms that person adopts.

AVENUES FOR PUBLIC PARTICIPATION

Another way to assure that public managers and employees act in a way consistent with the desires of the public is to involve citizens directly in the decision-making process through membership on advisory boards, open hearings, or direct polling. Such techniques, which have now become widespread, took their initial impetus from passage of the Economic Opportunity Act of 1964, legislation that required the "maximum feasible participation" of the poor in the design and conduct of antipoverty programs. In this case, the question of involvement itself became quite an issue, especially as the representatives of the poor came into direct confrontation with those holding established positions of power in local communities. The movement toward widespread citizen participation was soon well established, however, and spread quickly to local school boards, universities, and a variety of other government agencies. Today, for example, the practice of holding hearings prior to administrative decisions is commonplace at all levels of government.

There are questions, of course, as to whether real power is transferred to the citizens or whether citizen involvement is merely a device for defusing protests. Some use the term **co-optation** to describe situations in which citizens are given the feeling of involvement but little real power. On balance, it is probably accurate to say that there are some cases in which citizens have been co-opted through involvement in advisory boards or even public hearings, but in most cases, administrators are truly interested in receiving input from the public that will help them make difficult decisions.

The complexities of public involvement in administrative decision making are illustrated in the following "classic" case, actually a continuation of one we encountered in Chapter 2. As we learned, the Clean Air Act required the EPA to set national emissions standards for hazardous air pollutants to protect the public health. But no definition was given as to what would be considered "an ample margin of safety."

The issue received national attention in 1983 when EPA was trying to decide what, if anything, should be done about inorganic arsenic, a cancer-causing pollutant produced when arsenic-content ore is smelted into copper. The problem was particularly serious in the area around Tacoma, Washington, where the American Smelting and Refining Company (ASARCO) operated a copper smelter. The EPA had concluded that, in the absence of any controls on ASARCO's arsenic emissions, approximately four new cases of lung cancer would be contracted each year in the Tacoma area. Even after installation of the "best available" pollution-control equipment, there would still be one new case of cancer per year. But there was an important consideration on the other side of the issue as well. If the EPA were to impose any more onerous conditions on ASARCO—requiring, for example, that it use ore containing less arsenic or install a new and far more expensive electric smelter—the company could not afford to continue to operate the plant. ASARCO employed 570 workers, with an annual payroll of approximately $23 million; the company bought an additional $12 million worth of goods from local suppliers. Closing the plant therefore would pose serious economic problems for the local economy.

William Ruckelshaus, then administrator of the EPA, decided that the citizens of the Tacoma area ought to wrest with the problem. Accordingly, Ruckelshaus flew to Tacoma to announce a series of three public workshops to be held during the summer of 1983. The purpose was to acquaint residents with the details of the pollution problem, help them prepare for subsequent formal hearings, and enable them to deliberate about what should be done.

Some questions concerned technical matters, like the reliability of the proposed control equipment and the risk figures and epidemiological studies on which the EPA had based its estimates. Other questions revealed the inadequacy of the EPA's explanation of the relative health risk posed by the smelter: One resident asked whether that risk was greater than the risk posed by auto emissions.

Residents were not solely concerned, however, with the factual basis for the agency's claims. Several residents wanted to discuss the effects of the arsenic emissions on their gardens, their animals, and on the overall quality of life. Several residents expressed hostility toward the EPA for involving them in this difficult decision making in the first place. These issues are very complex, and the public is not sophisticated enough to make these decisions. This is not to say that EPA doesn't have an obligation to inform the public, but information is one thing—defaulting its legal mandate is another.

These numerous workshops, together with the national attention that Ruckelshaus had deliberately drawn to them by traveling to Tacoma to announce them, created considerable and often unfavorable press coverage. In an editorial on July 16, 1983, entitled "Mr. Ruckelshaus a Caesar," the *New York Times* argued that "Mr. Ruckelshaus has it all upside down. . . . What is inexcusable is for him to impose such an impossible choice on Tacomans:" An article in the *Los Angeles Times* pointed out the difficulties "in taking a community's pulse. . . . [Should one] poll the community . . . [or] count the pros and cons at the massive hearing?" Ruckelshaus was not surprised by the controversy. He said, "Listen, I know people don't like these kinds of decisions. . . . [W]elcome to the world of regulation. People have demanded to be involved and now I have involved them, and they say, 'Don't ask that question.' What's the alternative? Don't involve them? Then you are accused of doing something nefarious." (Reich, 1985.)

SOURCE: Reprinted by permission of the Yale Law Journal Company and Fred B. Rothman & Company. From *The Yale Law Journal,* Vol. 94, pp. 1617–1641.

The outcome of the case is anticlimactic: Before the EPA promulgated its regulations, declining copper prices led to the closing of the ASARCO smelter anyway. The case does, however, point out some of the difficulties in designing adequate programs for public participation. Certainly there is every reason to think that Ruckelshaus really wanted to test the pulse of the citizens before making regulations. But his attempt was met not only with ambivalence, as is often the case, but with outright hostility. Moreover, despite his efforts, there were few clear signals to the agency with respect to what to do. The ethical issues posed by the requirements of administrative responsibility are indeed complex.

THE ETHICS OF PRIVATIZATION

We noted in Chapter 3 the increasing involvement of private and nonprofit organizations in the delivery of public programs. Especially as governments have contracted for or otherwise sought to "privatize" services, private and nonprofit organizations have become major providers of public services. But, as we also saw, transfer of responsibility may raise significant ethical questions regarding equity and accountability. The government might find it necessary or expedient to contract out for garbage collection, for example, but neither necessity nor cost savings would justify allowing contractors to engage in discrimination or other unethical practices.

The issue is particularly critical for private-sector providers, who could have a tendency to maximize profits even at the sacrifice of some other public value. A private organization might be tempted to provide either more services than necessary for clients (to increase payments and therefore revenues) or less services than necessary (to cut costs). Actions such as these, clearly motivated by concern for profit, are less likely to occur in service delivery by nonprofit organizations, simply by virtue of their service "ethos," but even they require mechanisms to assure equity and accountability (Rubin, 1990).

In any privatization arrangement, the government's responsibility is not only to assure quality and cost consistent with stewardship of public resources, but also to promote democratic ideals and assure constitutional protections. There are at least two different types of delegation to consider: those that involve no transfer of discretionary authority and those that do. Obviously, many contracts involve no transfer of authority; public works contracts, for example, can usually be standardized and highly specified so as to grant virtually no discretionary public authority to contractors (though even here there are exceptions, as we saw with Rochester). The government retains responsibility for exercising public authority (e.g., determining eligibility for and frequency of garbage collection or street repair) and for holding contractors accountable for quality, quantity, and cost of work.

Other arrangements may involve transfer of discretionary authority; for example, the authority to determine details of eligibility requirements for student loans or the authority to decide what services to provide to inmates of a privately operated prison. In situations such as these, appropriate accountability structures must be in place to assure responsiveness to the government agency that administers the contract as well as to the public generally. Developing contractual arrangements that fully incorporate appropriate concerns for the public interest presents one of the most significant challenges of efforts to privatize public services.

ETHICAL PROBLEMS FOR THE INDIVIDUAL

Even the most straightforward ethical problems may be problematic, especially in the context of work in public organizations. Think for a moment about telling the truth. At first glance, nothing could seem more obvious than to tell "the truth, the whole truth, and nothing but the truth." But is that really the proper ethical position (outside a courtroom)? Should you be prepared to lie to protect matters vital to the national defense? Should you tell the whole truth in response to questions from the press about confidential matters affecting your clients? Is it proper to "stretch" research findings so they better support a policy position you feel is in the public interest? These are just a few of the most pressing and difficult questions you may face that will test not only your principles but also your willingness to act in accord with those principles.

INTERACTING WITH ELECTED OFFICIALS

The relationship between public managers and elected officials, either chief executives (such as mayors or governors) or members of a legislative body, presents a unique but nearly pervasive set of issues for the public manager. Whether as a department head working with a legislative committee, a city manager working with a city council, or an executive director working with the board of a nonprofit organization, the relationship between manager and the legislative body presents special problems.

We have examined some of the implications of this relationship for the development of public policy; but we should also be aware of possible ethical implications.

On the one hand, an administrator should be accountable to the legislative body; on the other hand, responding blindly to legislative decree may not always be in the public interest.

The latter situation might arise in several ways. Certainly, differing strongly with members of the legislature on policy questions presents great difficulties. As an administrator, to what extent should you seek to persuade the legislature to your position? Is it proper for a manager to try to build a power base in the legislature to enable special consideration of legislation favorable to the agency? If the legislature acts contrary to your strong beliefs, should you continue in your position or should you resign? If you continue, is it proper to try later to shape implementation of the legislation to fall more closely in line with your beliefs?

Similarly difficult questions might arise if the manager is asked to do something improper. For instance, what would you do if a legislator asked you to do something illegal, such as permitting health care payments to an ineligible client? How would your decision change if the legislator only asked you to "bend the rules" a little bit? How would your decision change if the legislator chaired the committee that passed on your agency's appropriation?

These issues may arise in any public organization; however, they are especially well illustrated at the local level with the council-manager form of government, which is built around the distinction between policy and administration. Theoretically, the council is responsible for determining policy and the manager is responsible for carrying it out. In practice, however, the line between policy and administration is never so clear; inevitably, the manager becomes involved in policy matters and the council in administrative matters.

Because of this overlap, the Code of Ethics of the International City Management Association contains several statements that bear on the council-manager relationship. The code's first item emphasizes the manager's dedication to "effective and democratic local government by *responsible elected officials*" and recognizes the contribution professional management can make in this regard. More specifically, on the manager's policy role, the code suggests that the manager "submit policy proposals to elected officials; provide them with facts and advice on matters of policy as a basis for making decisions and setting community goals, and uphold and implement municipal policies adopted by elected officials." Similarly, the manager is advised to "recognize that elected representatives of the people are entitled to the credit for the establishment of municipal policies; (while) responsibility for public execution rests with the members."

Despite these helpful guidelines, city managers often face difficulties in relationships with city councils. One city manager disagreed strongly with a council move to limit widening a particular city street, an improvement the manager felt was essential to local economic development; another city manager felt that a council member was acting irresponsibly in proposing legislation that would help his contracting business; still another city manager was asked to process travel vouchers that included payment for personal vacation expenses. Simply figuring out how to respond effectively to these situations is hard enough, but the problem is even greater when you remember that the city manager who forces an issue of policy or ethics may be seen as "attacking" his or her bosses— and may, at any time, be summarily fired. It's no wonder that the average tenure of city managers in this country is only between four and five years!

FOLLOWING ORDERS

Another problem has to do with limits to organizational authority. What would you do if your boss asked you to do something you felt was morally wrong? Suppose you are asked to "bury" a report on toxic wastes you consider potentially dangerous to the public, or that, under pressures of time, you are asked to give quick approval to a piece of equipment that might be unsafe. Or imagine that you are asked to approve an expense reimbursement for your boss, when you know the amount has been "padded."

In cases such as these, you face difficult choices—choices made even more difficult by the very logic that causes us to employ bureaucratic means of organizing. Bureaucratic organizations are attractive because they enable people to accomplish large-scale tasks they would not otherwise be able to undertake, but bureaucracy as a social form also demands a certain amount of obedience to authority. Presumably, if orders are not obeyed, the whole system falls apart—so there are strong pressures for individuals to follow orders rather than their consciences.

The most dramatic historical example of the problem of unquestioning obedience to authority comes from Hitler's attempt to exterminate the European Jews during World War II. Although the killings were ordered by political leaders, they were carried out through the German bureaucracy. The problem faced not only those at the top of the organization but those throughout. Raul Hilberg, author of a classic study of the Holocaust, writes:

> Most bureaucrats composed memoranda, drew up blueprints, signed correspondence, talked on the telephone, and participated in conferences. . . . However, these men were not stupid; they realized the connection between their paperwork and the heaps of corpses in the East. And they realized, also, the shortcomings of those rationalizations which placed all evil on the Jew and all good on the German. That was why they were compelled to justify their individual activities. The first rationalization was the oldest, the simplest, and therefore the most effective: the doctrine of superior orders. First and foremost there was duty. No matter what objections there might be, orders were given to be obeyed. A clear order was like an absolution; armed with such an order, a perpetrator felt that he could pass his responsibility and his conscience upward. (Hilberg, 1961, p. 649)

This manner of justifying one's actions became central to the defense of those accused at the Nuremberg trials. Many defendants argued, as did General Alfred Jodl, that it is "not the task of a soldier to act as a judge over his superior commander" (Arendt, 1963, p. 133). But despite the rationale of "superior orders," for the German bureaucrats and for their more contemporary counterparts, the moral dilemma posed by such orders remains.

One might argue, of course, that the German example is overdrawn—that such a thing could never happen in a democratic society such as ours. But perhaps it could. Indeed, a remarkable series of studies conducted by Yale psychologist Stanley Milgram many years ago suggests that Americans are often quite willing to obey, even where doing so causes them extreme moral discomfort. In an elaborate series of experiments, Milgram asked subjects to administer shocks to a person supposedly involved in a memory experiment. Even though the person receiving the shocks writhed in pain (he was actually an actor and an accomplice), the subjects continued to follow Milgram's orders to administer the painful shocks—simply because they were told to do so! Milgram concluded that "a substantial proportion of people do what they are told, irrespective of the content of the act and without limitations of conscience, so long as they perceive that the command comes from a legitimate authority" (Milgram, 1974, p. 189).

Contemporary examples of problems with orders from above are perhaps less dramatic than the German illustration, but they present equally difficult choices for the individual. You may, of course, protest the action, either directly to your superiors or more indirectly, though in doing so, you may place yourself in jeopardy. Or you may leave the organization, resigning in protest, even though the available alternatives—such as unemployment—may not be attractive. Or you may simply keep quiet and do what you are told. The latter alternative is certainly the easiest in most cases—by obeying orders, you feel you have someone else (your superior) to blame if something goes wrong—and, in any case, there is a strong feeling that if people in large organizations fail to follow orders, things won't get done. Unfortunately, rationalizations such as these don't allow you to escape the moral consequences of your actions.

CONFLICTS OF INTEREST

Another area of potential ethical difficulties for public officials involves conflicts of interest. Finding ways to avoid conflicts of interest, especially financial, has been central to federal, state, and local ethics legislation for the past twenty-five to thirty years. At the federal level, legislation proscribing the ethical behavior of public officials has deep historical roots; however, the tone of modern ethics legislation was set by Executive Order 11222 issued by President Johnson in 1965. In part, the policy reads as follows:

> Where government is based on the consent of the governed, every citizen is entitled to have complete confidence in the integrity of his government. Each individual officer, employee, advisor of government must help to earn and must honor that trust by his own integrity and conduct in all official actions.

The executive order then provides a set of "standards of conduct" that covers such topics as accepting gifts, financial conflicts of interest, misuse of federal property, and limitations on outside employment. The policy also bars use of public office for personal gain or for the gain of those with whom the individual has family, business, or financial ties.

The Johnson policy also initiated public disclosure of financial statements, something that was given greater prominence in the Ethics and Government Act of 1978. This act codified many of the previously established standards and created the Office of Government Ethics to establish more detailed regulations to monitor the behavior of public servants and provide ethics training for managers and other officials.

President Bush, in keeping with his desire to set a high moral tone for his administration, used his first executive order to establish a Commission on Federal Ethics Law Reform. In establishing the commission, the president sought four key principles: "(1) ethical standards for public servants must be exacting enough to ensure that the officials act with the utmost integrity and live up to the public's confidence in them; (2) standards must be fair, they must be objective and consistent with common sense; (3) the standards must be equitable across all three branches of the federal government; finally we cannot afford to have unreasonably restrictive requirements that discourage citizens who are able from entering public service" (President's Commission, 1989, p. 2). Central to the Bush recommendations were provisions dealing with conflicts of interest.

Under existing legislation, officers of the executive branch of the federal government are required to refrain from participating "personally and financially" in deciding, approving, recommending, or advising with respect to matters in which they or family members or close associates have a financial interest. An official facing a possible conflict of interest has a number of avenues available. First, the official can simply withdraw from participating in the particular case. Second, the official may seek a waiver, especially when his or her interest is not considered substantial or the relationship is too remote to affect the integrity of the action. Third, the employee may choose to place his or her assets in a "blind trust." Or fourth, the official can sell, give away, or otherwise divest himself or herself of the financial interest in question.

Other parts of the federal ethics legislation restrict outside income and the acceptance of gifts or favors. For example, as a federal employee, you are prohibited from accepting any salary or contribution from any source other than the federal government. The law also limits the acceptance of meals, entertainment, and gifts; for example, meals can usually be accepted if offered during the course of a working meeting, but there are prohibitions on "one-on-one" meals in which you are being treated.

There are also prohibitions on what a federal employee can do after leaving government. Sections of the Ethics and Government Act prohibit former officials from representing outside parties before the federal government with respect to matters in which they had some personal involvement or official responsibility for a period of two years. There is also a one-year "cooling-off period," during which you cannot represent parties before your agency even on matters that were not your responsibility while working for the government. The Bush commission recommended strengthening provisions dealing with activities of former federal officials by requiring a prohibition not only against personally representing outside interests before government agencies but also "aiding or advising any other person." The proposal would eliminate not only direct representation, but "behind the scenes" advice and counsel as well.

Legislation such as this is obviously intended to prevent "influence peddling" by those who have recently left government and to limit the "revolving door" phenomenon, wherein persons move in and out of government to acquire knowledge and information valuable to external groups. This issue became particularly prominent during the Reagan administration, when several officials, including Michael Deaver and Lynn Nofziger, were accused of using their previous contacts to unduly influence the governmental decision process. Moreover, the defense procurement scandals of the Reagan years underlined the need for stricter controls on information exchange that could influence purchase of defense materials or contracts.

Finally, the potential for conflicts of interest is decreased by requirements for financial disclosure on the part of executive officials. The Bush commission, for example, wrote "financial disclosure has been variously described as the linchpin of the ethical enforcement system, as the disinfectant sunlight which makes possible the cleaning up of abusive practices" (President's Commission, 1989, p. 5). Though financial reporting requirements have sometimes been criticized as excessively detailed and intrusive, they have been, in the view of most ethics experts, highly valuable in maintaining public confidence in the integrity of government. If nothing else, the reports have meant that individuals are forced to carefully review potential conflicts of interests that they may bring with them to government, and thus be more aware of those interests should conflicts arise.

The recommendations of the Bush commission led in February 1993 to new standards creating greater uniformity across all agencies of the federal government. The rules cover seven areas: (1) gifts from outside sources, (2) gifts between federal employees, (3) conflicting financial interests, (4) impartiality in performing official duties, (5) seeking other employment, (6) misuse of position, and (7) outside activities. In many respects, these standards reflected the new president's pledge for a return to values-based leadership. As a candidate, President Clinton had voiced sharp criticism against the ethical shortcomings of preceding administrations. Then, on Inauguration Day, the president had used his first executive order to require new ethics commitments of executive branch appointees, requirements restricting an appointee's lobbying or otherwise trying to influence an agency where he or she worked.

NETWORKING

The primary federal agency dealing with ethics issues is the Office of Government Ethics at http://www.usoge.gov/.

However, despite the efforts of the Clinton administration to set a high moral tone, it is unlikely that the Clinton presidency will be remembered for its stance on ethics. The removal of several staff members in the White House travel office, and their replacement with individuals more favorable to the new administration caused many to question whether President Clinton intended to live up to his promise on ethics. Furthermore, more recent concerns stemming from the first family's private financial dealings and the Clinton administration's campaign fund raising have cast a shadow on the president's early pledge. Though the legal and practical outcomes of these concerns remain to be seen, it can be said that the cause of ethics in public service has not been well advanced during the mid to late 1990s.

Many of the same provisions for preventing conflict of interest in federal ethics legislation have been paralleled at the state level. Many states have passed detailed ethics legislation, often using financial disclosure as a chief mechanism for preventing abuse. Indeed, almost all states have some form of financial disclosure provision for some state employees. In addition, more states have adopted ethics codes and ethics commissions. For example, in 1991, the state of Texas established an ethics commission to review the conduct of lobbyists, candidates, and elected officials. Similarly, given the influence of money in politics, other states have sought to establish controls on political money. Florida, for example, reduced the limits on campaign contributions and has created a fully funded public campaign finance system. Many states have adopted similar versions of the federal conflict of interest legislation passed during the Bush administration. Across the country, many states have passed detailed ethics legislation, often using financial disclosure as a chief mechanism for preventing abuse.

WHISTLE BLOWING

There has been a marked increase over the last twenty years in employee disclosure of problems in public organizations. Public employees have exposed defense contract overruns; spoken out against corruption in local police departments; and revealed abuses of the merit system, improper enforcement of toxic waste legislation, and other matters.

Alan Campbell, director of the Office of Personnel Management during the Carter administration, described these public disclosures, or "whistle blowing," in this way: "Quite simply, I view whistle blowing as a popular short-hand label for any disclosure of a legal violation, mismanagement, a gross waste of funds, an abuse of authority, or a danger to public health or safety, whether the disclosure is made within or outside the chain of command" (Bowman, 1983, p. 91). In other words, the *whistle blower* reveals information about fraud, waste, or abuse in government, including actions that might endanger the safety or liberty of other government employees or citizens at large.

Generally, employees who decide to blow the whistle move through several stages. First, the employees become aware of an organizational practice that is unethical or dangerous; second, they express concern to their immediate supervisor or those further up in the hierarchy; and, third, unsatisfied that anyone in the organization will take appropriate action, they take the issue outside, either through "leaks" to the press or to external public interest groups. (The press, of course, may independently play an important role in revealing instances of wrongdoing.)

Unfortunately, whistle blowers in both government and in industry have often been subjected to abuse and retaliation by superiors. One study of whistle blowers shows a large number who were fired or forced to resign or retire, as well as others who were refused promotions or given less desirable work assignments. Others felt excluded from communication within the organization and were avoided by both supervisors and coworkers (Truelson, 1986, p. 9). Studies show that, as a result, many public employees who have knowledge of corruption don't bother to report it, and many who do report abuses suffer reprisals (Bowman, 1983, p. 91).

Obviously if you discover improper actions on the part of persons in your organization, you have a strong obligation to report those actions; however, you should be careful that your allegations are based on fact and are properly reported. Norman Bowie suggests that an act of whistle blowing can be justified if the following conditions are met:

1. If it is done with an appropriate moral motive
2. If all internal channels of dissent have been exhausted
3. If it is based on evidence that would persuade a reasonable person
4. If analysis has been made of the seriousness, immediacy, and specificity of the problem
5. If it is commensurate with one's responsibility
6. If it has some chance of success (Bowman, 1983, p. 91)

At the federal level, codes of conduct have encouraged public servants to expose corruption wherever it is discovered, and protection for whistle blowers has been provided through the Civil Service Reform Act. Moreover, some agencies have established formal *dissent channels,* confidential patterns of communications outside the normal chain of command, that allow a potential whistle blower or someone who merely disagrees with a proposed policy to express a dissenting opinion without fear of reprisal. Consequently, whistle blowing has become somewhat more common at the federal level. But wherever you work, if you decide to blow the whistle, you should be fully aware not only of potential dangers, but also of the protection available to you based on rights of free speech and of prohibitions against discriminatory actions. Encouraging greater communication by providing freer and more open channels of dissent is one way to ensure more ethical behavior in public organizations (see Box 4.2).

BOX 4.2

Whistle Blowing

The following is a resolution passed by the American Society for Public Administration:

> The American Society for Public Administration endorses the growing public demand for improved accountability of government employees in order to achieve more efficient, effective, and ethical enforcement of the laws, and more competent conduct of the public business, recognizing that most whistle blowing results from different perceptions of accountability.

Therefore, in order to improve accountability at all levels of government, ASPA recommends that federal, state and local governments take the following actions:

1. *Establish and enforce policies and procedures that clearly describe the ethical bases for public employment and the penalties for violating them.*

   Adherence to such codes would result in improved accountability by public employees, especially managers, for their decisions and actions. This should result in a concomitant decrease in the need for whistle blowing aimed at exposing criminal activity, abuse of process, waste, withholding or distortion of information, and other unethical or illegal behavior.

2. *Establish and enforce policies and procedures for more adequately communicating to each public employee the expectations of the governmental employer with respect to job performance, ethics, accountability, rewards, penalties, and regulations.*

   Since well-informed and well-supervised employees reflect good management practices, individual employees who know what is expected of them may be more likely to meet accountability standards and less likely to refuse responsibility for their performance or to choose nonlegitimate whistle blowing as a vehicle for communicating. Workshops and other forms of training programs are useful in helping managers and their employees cope with dissent and change.

3. *Establish and enforce policies and procedures for internally reporting, investigating, assessing, and acting on allegations of illegality, mismanagement, waste, or unethical behavior.*

   Complaint-handling offices such as inspectors general and other appropriate mechanisms should be created and adequately supported to receive, and promptly and objectively investigate internal allegations of wrongdoing in order to diminish the need for the public gesture of whistle blowing. To be effective as well as efficient, such offices must inspire the trust and confidence of both managers and employees to avoid the aura of police-state intimidation. They must not tend first to accuse or impugn the motives of the person making the allegation.

continued

continued from previous page

4. *Establish and enforce policies and procedures that permit and encourage legitimate dissent and constructive criticism and protect dissenters from retaliation.*

   Many public employees take an oath of office to uphold, obey, and enforce the law in accordance with their sworn responsibilities. Therefore, perceived violations of that oath which result in differences of opinion about wrongdoing should be viewed as manifestations of accountability, rather than as rejections of supervisory authority, unless proven otherwise.

5. *Create and support dissent channels to permit contrary or alternative views on policy issues to be reviewed at a higher level.*

   Where disaffection grows not from allegations of wrongdoing but from honest professional disagreement over policy decisions, what converts the grieved dissenter into an angry whistle blower is often the lack of any channel for additional senior review of the policy dispute. Good public administration in any institution includes provision for such open review at higher levels. Equating productive dissent or constructive criticism with disloyalty violates democratic principles of free speech and tends to discourage accountability, creativity, and standards of excellence.

6. *Establish and enforce policies and procedures that require management to focus on the message rather than the messenger when an employee expresses either substantive dissent as a professional difference of opinion or makes an allegation of wrongdoing.*

   In most instances, whistle blowing may be averted by giving serious consideration to the merits of the message and by taking appropriate and timely action. By focusing only on the assumed motivations of dissenters or whistle blowers, attention is diverted from the substance of their dissent or the merits of their allegations, to the detriment of the organization, its mission, and the general public.

7. *Create and use program evaluation, monitoring, and other oversight methods to increase and improve the availability of reliable information for decision making.*

   Top management needs accurate and timely information produced by competent staff who are encouraged to make recommendations and to energetically advocate them without fear of reprisal. Since an organizational pattern of absent, distorted, or unnecessarily suppressed information tends to produce demands for such information on the grounds of accountability, the systematic collection, analysis, dissemination, and use of verified facts should help to diminish or eliminate the motivation to blow the whistle.

SOURCE: Copyright © by the American Society for Public Administration (ASPA), 1120 G Street NW, Suite 500, Washington, D.C. 20005. Reprinted with permission. All rights reserved.

PROHIBITIONS ON POLITICAL ACTIVITIES

Political neutrality has traditionally been considered important to effective democratic governance. President Jefferson, for example, issued an early order against federal government employee partisanship, an order whose essence was repeated by Presidents Grant and Hayes. Legislative action occurred with the adoption of the Pendleton Act in 1883, which "prohibited political assessment, solicitations, subscriptions or contributions from or by any employee of the United States." The most sweeping ban on political activity, however, occurred during Theodore Roosevelt's administration. He declared that classified civil service employees "shall take no active part in political management or in political campaigns" (Masters & Bierman, 1985, p. 519). Later, Congress passed the Hatch Political Activities Act in 1939, stating that "no officer or employee of the executive branch of the federal government, or any agency or department thereof, shall take any active part in political management or in political campaigns." (A set of amendments passed in 1940 extended the ban on political management and campaigning to state and local employees whose programs were financed fully or in part by federal funds.)

Under the Hatch Act, public employees can register to vote, contribute money to campaigns, assist in voter registration drives, and express opinions about candidates and issues; however, certain other activities are prohibited:

1. endorsing partisan candidates
2. listing or raising money for political action committees
3. participating in partisan voter registration and get-out-the-vote drives
4. distributing campaign material on behalf of candidates
5. serving as a delegate to a political convention
6. making campaign speeches
7. seeking public office in partisan elections (Masters & Bierman, 1985, pp. 519–520)

Although the Hatch Act seeks both to protect public employees from political harassment and the political process from special influence, it has been subject to various interpretations and has proven confusing in its application. Moreover, many have claimed that it unduly restricts public employees' political freedoms by essentially disenfranchising them from important political activities during the time they hold government employment. Others have pointed out that the Hatch Act places more stringent restrictions on United States government employees than on those of Great Britain, Canada, and Australia. For this reason, there have been recent efforts in Congress to change the Hatch Act, to permit a greater range of political activities by those in government. Many support the proposed legislation, especially those in public employee unions, who feel that public employees should be able to run for office and solicit campaign funds on their own time. Others, however, have argued that the Hatch Act is still necessary to prevent coercion of political officials. Reform of the Hatch Act has been considered for a number of years, with Congress passing major reform legislation in 1991 (though it was vetoed by President Bush). In 1993, Congress changed the Hatch Act, generally strengthening those sections dealing with activities while on-duty and expanding the off-duty activities of federal employees. Basically, with the exception of running for office, which is still prohibited, the new act permits federal workers to participate in a full range of political activities on their own time, though not to do so on the job (*Congressional Quarterly Weekly*, 1993, p. 511).

MANAGING ETHICS

How does a manager promote more ethical practices in an organization? First, of course, there are a variety of formal controls, including legal, on the behavior of those in public organizations—the courts may direct public officials to undertake specific actions or to "cease and desist" from certain courses of action. They may also be required, on behalf of their agencies, to provide individuals with damages or other compensation. And, of course, any public employee may be prosecuted for breaking the law. But what if you are sued as an individual for actions you have undertaken in the course of your official duties?

Actually, this question has been the subject of considerable legal debate throughout our country's history. Whereas early interpretations of the law generally protected public officials against suits, claiming they violated an individual's rights in the course of one's duties, more recent interpretations have severely limited the immunity granted to public officials. Speaking broadly, there are two types of immunity: absolute immunity and qualified (or "good faith") immunity. Absolute immunity, which means that an official is not liable for damages under any circumstances, has been granted to certain legislative and judicial officers and, in limited cases, to members of the executive branch while performing their official duties. (The president has been granted absolute immunity but state governors have not.)

Most other officials have only qualified immunity—they may be sued, but can defend themselves by showing they were acting in good faith to carry out their duties. That is, they must show that they were unaware of the impropriety of an act at the time they were carrying it out and that any reasonable person might have acted similarly. Although the current legal position allows most officials to be sued, relatively few suits have been successful; most public managers have been found to have acted in good faith. In any case, knowing something about public officials' liability for their actions will better enable you and those in your organization to avoid problems in the first place, or to respond to them when they arise.

Besides legal proceedings, other formal devices protect against waste or fraud on the part of public officials or the private individuals or groups with which they interact. For example, most major federal agencies have an Office of the Inspector General to investigate possible cases of fraud, waste, and abuse in government. The inspectors general are charged with looking into situations in which federal employees or funds are being used improperly. Targets of investigations may be either public employees or private individuals, such as contractors, who might attempt to defraud the government.

Through their internal investigations of federal agencies, the inspectors general have occasionally revealed major problems. For example, the Office of the Inspector General of the Department of Health and Human Services recently initiated several studies related to excessive billings for Medicaid payments. Selling samples, billing Medicaid at higher prices than charged the general public, and billing for brand drugs while dispensing generic drugs are among the expected abuses. Similarly, the inspector general's office in the Defense Department announced plans recently to probe the military fastener industry—makers of bolts, screws, and other hardware—to see if substandard parts contributed to military accidents. In a related case, two Maryland defense contractors pleaded guilty to a decade-long scheme to sell cheap, low-grade fasteners for military equipment. The contractors admitted to substituting commercial-grade bolts, screws, and other fasteners for more expensive military-grade hardware ordered by defense contractors for radar and sonar systems, satellites, Trident submarines, and armored earthmovers like those used in the Persian Gulf War (*Washington Post,* 1992).

ESTABLISHING AN ETHICAL CLIMATE

In addition to formal controls, you can help promote ethical behavior by providing strong ethical leadership, creating a climate in which ethical behavior is valued, and encouraging free and open communications throughout the organization. "Managing ethics involves more than making public statements espousing a particular set of values and more than selecting employees with good moral character. Managing ethics also involves careful analysis of the organizational culture, working to develop a cultural environment that places high value on ethical integrity and developing policies and procedures and systems that enable organization members to act with ethical integrity" (Denhardt, 1989, p. 1). Unfortunately, most organizations, including most public organizations, have not undertaken active programs to promote ethics (see Box 4.3).

Many organizational members feel that, in the absence of an ethics program, the requirements of large bureaucracies tend to promote unethical, dishonest, and inhumane behavior. "Managers perceive that the bureaucratic environment is less ethical than their

---

BOX 4.3

Intervention Techniques for Integrating Ethics into Agency Operations

- Do both compliance and integrity training and counseling.
- Give briefings on common ethical problems on the job for new hires.
- Give termination briefings on potential postemployment problems.
- Designate senior manager(s) for integrity issues, separate from compliance/investigative unit.
- Require annual sign-off on prospective commitment and compliance.
- Attend to ethical values and character in recruitment.
- Integrate ethical performance into promotional exams and annual reviews; link ethical behavior to incentives.
- Publicize positive, noteworthy role models.
- Raise ethical concerns at meetings and through regular communication channels.
- Train middle managers to recognize and commend subordinates' statements about ethical concerns.
- Review management practices and administrative routines at every level and in every type of unit in the organization.
- Get the whole team—all employees, all levels, all units to participate; ethics is not a spectator sport.
- Give earnest attention to ethical treatment of subordinates, clients, and others.

SOURCE: Carol W. Lewis, *The Ethics Challenge in Public Service* (San Francisco: Jossey-Bass, 1991), 181.

own values and beliefs, that they are under pressure to compromise personal standards to achieve organizational goals, and that their supervisors are interested only in results not how they were obtained" (Bowman, 1983, p. 74).

A first step in promoting more ethical practices in your organization is to analyze the basic ideas, beliefs, and attitudes that guide the behavior of the organization's members.

One device for assessing the prevailing beliefs of your organization is an **ethics audit,** an assessment of the value premises that guide action in the organization. The audit provides a methodical review of the organization's activities and the implicit values that underlie the activities. Importantly, these values may not turn out to be those contained in public pronouncements. One student of organizational behavior concluded that "the key to learning the ethics of individuals or organizations is simple: *do not listen to what they say about ethics, observe what they do*" (Pastin, 1988, p. 92). By clearly establishing the values that guide behavior in the organization, you and other members can more consciously and clearly begin to alter those that seem inappropriate.

As an example, after numerous incidents of defense contract violations, the General Dynamics Corporation brought in an outside consultant to help establish an ethics program. The consultant conducted an ethics audit, which helped members of the organization recognize that they shared a basic, though unstated, assumption that the government was their adversary and that taking advantage of an adversary was quite acceptable. Once this assumption was understood, it could be addressed openly and replaced with more appropriate assumptions about the relationships between government and its contractors. An example of an ethics audit conducted by a public agency is contained in Carol Lewis's book, *The Ethics Challenge in Public Service* (1991, pp. 199–202).

Following an ethics audit, your organization may wish to develop a clearer statement of values to guide individual behavior. That statement should include general moral guidelines, but it should also articulate a vision of the organization's mission—what it stands for, what it seeks to achieve, and how it plans to go about its business. Developing such a statement should involve many members of the organization and have the full support of the top management team. (We will examine statements of values in more detail later.)

Besides developing a statement of management philosophy for your organization alone, you may also wish to employ more general codes of ethics developed by other organizations. The federal government, for example, has promulgated a Code of Ethics for Federal Service, and many state and local government organizations have developed similar codes. Professional organizations such as the International City Management Association also have codes of ethics related to members of their profession. Perhaps the most comprehensive code of ethics for public-sector managers is that of the American Society for Public Administration. The ASPA Code of Ethics and accompanying guidelines illustrate the variety of ethical concerns public managers face and provide guidance for resolving ethical issues (see Appendix A later in this chapter).

After assessing values and adopting statements to express the desired values, you might wish to develop training programs or other devices for communicating these ideals within the organization. The Office of Government Ethics, for example, conducts frequent seminars for federal managers on ethics in the public service. Similarly, organizations such as ASPA and ICMA have developed training programs that are available nationally or can be adapted to local circumstances. Training programs are also available for executives in nonprofit organizations.

As a manager, however, you should not neglect the fact that your own actions will be taken as a "model" of appropriate behavior. The example you set will be one of the most important "training" devices to members of your organization. If you wish them to take the moral "high road," you must demonstrate by example that ethics is a substantial concern and that unethical conduct will not be tolerated.

SUMMARY AND ACTION IMPLICATIONS

As we move from the context of public administration to the ethics of public service, we also move from areas where abstract knowledge is helpful to areas where the ability to act is important. In dealing with the many ethical dilemmas that confront public officials, you must know not only what the correct action is, but be able to act in a way consistent with that judgment. Understanding something about how ethical choices are made is helpful, as is recognizing the importance of deliberation in making ethical decisions. But what will ultimately make the difference will be your willingness to act on the basis of moral principles.

The particular ethical issues you may face range from matters of individual integrity to those that derive from the special value commitments associated with working in the public interest. Most of the latter are associated in some way with the tension between efficiency and responsiveness that seems to pervade public organizations. That tension, as well as issues of accountability and responsiveness to public demands, are especially intense in the relationship between administrators and the legislative branch.

Many of the concerns you may encounter as a public manager are similar to those other managers face, but some are especially conditioned by the fact that you are operating "in the public interest." In either case, you must exhibit the virtues of benevolence and justice (including honesty, trustworthiness, and fairness) in your behavior. In any case, as you face some of the difficulties that arise, careful self-reflection and dialogue with others about ethical concerns will be especially helpful.

It is within your power as an administrator to undertake programs to encourage and facilitate a more ethical climate within your organization. Conducting an ethics audit, developing a statement of organizational philosophy or a code of ethics, and establishing training programs to deal with ethical issues will help improve your organization's ethics. As a manager, however, perhaps the most important message you can send is that communicated by your own actions. If you seem to attach great importance to ethical concerns, others in the organization will attach similar importance. The model you provide can make an important difference in the ethics of your organization.

Terms and Definitions

Co-optation: Situations in which citizens are given the feeling of involvement while exercising little real power.

Deontology: Belief that broad principles of rightness and wrongness can be established and are not dependent on particular circumstances.

Ethical (or moral) relativism: Belief that moral judgment can be made only by taking into account the context in which action occurs.

Ethics: Process by which we clarify right and wrong and act on what we take to be right.

Ethics audit: Evaluation of the value premises that guide action within an organization.

Morality: Practices and activities considered right or wrong and the value those practices reflect.

Neutral competence: The belief that a neutral public bureaucracy following the mandates of a legislative body will meet the requirements of democracy.

Objective responsibility: Assurance of responsiveness through external controls.

Subjective responsibility: Assurance of responsiveness based on an individual's character.

Utilitarianism: Philosophy of the greatest good for the greatest number of people.

Study Questions

1. Although ethics and morality are similar, what is the distinction between the terms?
2. Discuss the steps in ethical deliberation.
3. Compare the two approaches commonly used in moral philosophy.
4. Discuss the three levels of moral development devised by psychologist Lawrence Kohlberg.
5. What is meant by an "ethics of virtue"?
6. Discuss the conflict between efficiency and responsiveness.
7. Explain the limitations on administrators' discretion with regard to responsiveness and efficiency.
8. Discuss some of the ethical problems individuals who work in public organizations encounter and how they can deal with them properly.
9. The Hatch Act defines prohibited activities of public employees. Explain the significance of these prohibitions with regard to an individual's political actions.
10. Explain ways to improve the ethical behavior of those in a public organization and provide examples of managing ethics.

Cases and Exercises

1. To illustrate various aspects of ethical deliberation, read and discuss the following case:

   There is a raging river which can be crossed only by means of a boat. The only boat is owned and operated by a person we shall call A (in order to protect the innocent as well as the guilty). On the tame side of the river, X is deeply and sincerely in love with a person C on the other side of the river. X goes to A asking to be taken across the river, offering to pay whatever the charge for the service. A declines any money, but agrees to take X across the river if X will sleep with A. Person X refuses, of course (!), but argues and then pleads with A to name some other price. A, however, remains firm.

   Person X leaves, but returns a second day to seek a way across the river. A remains as adamant as before. In frustration, X seeks out a third person, B, who hears the situation sympathetically, agreeing that A is certainly a rogue. But B says, "I have other matters concerning me just now and am not able to help you."

   In desperation, X goes to A a third time, only to be met with the same offer for the trip across the river. X finally agrees to the price and sleeps with A, who then delivers X across the river as promised.

   X and C are joyously reunited, until C asks how X got across the river. X truthfully replies, "I had to sleep with A to earn the trip across the river." C replies indignantly, "Out of my life! I will have nothing to do with one who holds honor and principle so lightly!"

   X, of course, is frustrated and desperate again, and appeals to Person D, who replies, "I understand and am deeply sympathetic. I'd do anything I can to help you." (The curtain falls.) (ASPA, n.d.)

   Following your discussion of the case itself, consider to what extent the discussion reflected moral relativism, utilitarianism, or deontology. Then, reconsider the case, following the steps of ethical deliberation presented in this chapter: clarify the facts, find basic principles, and analyze the arguments. How could you establish a moral action?

2. A random check of long distance telephone calls at the Department of Housing and Urban Development, a study conducted by the agency's inspector general, indicated that some 30 percent were personal calls (though charged to the government). The cost of the calls was estimated at $73,000 for the sample and, by extrapolation, $290,000 for the agency as a whole. Many calls were placed to the homes of employees or their relatives, while others were calls to prerecorded messages, such as time and temperature, horoscopes, and financial information. Penalties for unauthorized use of federal telephone lines include fines, suspension, and dismissal.

   Why do you think employees at HUD, and presumably elsewhere, misuse official telephone lines? What, if anything, should be done to limit such excesses? How do you respond to employees who argue that using agency telephone lines for personal business is necessary from time to time? What about those who argue that telephone use is an essential benefit the organization should provide? If you crack down on unauthorized calls, what will happen to morale in the agency?

To put the case in a more intense, real-world setting, imagine that you are secretary of Housing and Urban Development. You have just finished testifying at a congressional hearing. On your way out the door, a senator corners you and waves a copy of the inspector general's report in your face saying, "This is an outrage! These people are stealing from the public and you've been letting it happen! I want some action on this right away!" Next, a reporter, who has seen the report and heard the exchange with the senator, points a microphone toward your mouth and asks, "Well, what are you going to do?" What is your response, both immediately and over the next several days?

3. Consider the following cases:

Sidney Franklin knew that one of his most valued employees, Anderson Hayes, was stealing from the organization—not much, and in a way that no one but Sidney would ever know—but he was stealing. Sidney also knew that without Anderson, his unit could never complete a newly assigned task on time. He decided to do nothing about the stealing incident and secretly hoped that success in the new assignment would bring about a long-desired promotion and get him out of this awkward situation.

George Cave was a former CIA station chief in Teheran. When he heard that the Reagan administration was working with Manucher Ghorbanifar on an "arms for hostages" deal, he was horrified. "But what could he do? The project had the backing of CIA director William J. Casey and the White House. Cave bit the bullet and traveled to Iran in May 1986 as the translator for former national security adviser Robert C. McFarlane" (Ignatius, 1987, p. 15).

Shirley House, a recently appointed city manager in a small community in Tennessee, arrived at work one morning to find an envelope from the mayor filled with receipts from a recent trip he took to an economic development conference. Included were receipts from a four-day vacation the mayor and his wife took at a resort near the conference city. It was clear that the mayor wanted the city to reimburse him for everything included in the envelope.

Analyze and discuss each of these three cases in terms of the moral position that the individual involved should have taken. Then consider the nature of your own ethical reasoning. What types of moral philosophy, moral psychology, or moral action have you been using?

4. Read the following case. Ask who in the class thinks the administrator, Gordon Chase, overstepped the limits of administrative discretion and who thinks he acted properly. Debate the issue, paying particular attention to the ethical justification for each position. What is the basis on which you build your argument? What assumptions are you making?

The Methadone Maintenance Program was developed by Gordon Chase, health services administrator under Mayor John Lindsay. When Chase was appointed to this position in 1969 he had no direct responsibility for programs to combat heroin use. The unit then responsible for addicts was the Addiction Services Agency (ASA). Its approach was to encourage abstinence from heroin through supervised voluntary therapeutic communities operating under strict discipline. Another agency, the State Narcotics Addiction Control Commission, forcibly confined addicts in expensive treatment centers. There were also two private programs that tried to shift the addict's craving from heroin to an inexpensive synthetic drug called methadone. One was located at the Beth Israel Hospital, the other at the Addiction Research and Treatment Corporation (ARTC).

Shortly after taking office Gordon Chase decided that not enough was being done to treat the 100,000 or more heroin addicts on the streets of New York. Lacking formal authority to undertake new programs but believing that he personally should take action to fill the treatment gap, Chase resolved to establish a methadone maintenance treatment program. His first move was to send the mayor's Narcotics Control Council a proposal to treat 15,600 addicts in less than a year. This number was inflated, but Chase thought that his memorandum would help to get key officials to think in terms of large programs and would create momentum. Then even before the mayor authorized him to do so and before funds were available, he began to recruit a dynamic and capable staff. The head of the new Bureau of Methadone Maintenance was Dr. Robert Newman, who was handpicked by Chase. Newman kept up the momentum by opening clinics in existing institutions, maintaining control and accountability through a tight monitoring and reporting system, pressing to meet deadlines, and working to overcome community opposition to clinics for "junkies." By June 1971, the city's methadone programs had treated 6,000 addicts, and by January of 1974 the figure had risen to over 20,000. Moreover, the apparent success of this effort had stimulated the Beth Israel Hospital to expand its intake of patients.

SOURCE: Excerpted from Donald P. Warwick, "The Ethics of Administrative Discretion," in Joel Fleishman, Lance Liebman, and Mark Moore, eds., *Public Duties: The Moral Obligations of Government Officials* (Cambridge, MA: Harvard University Press, 1981), 94–95.

5. As a class, conduct an ethics audit (or survey) of your college or university and recommend ways the institution might begin to develop higher standards of ethical conduct.

   Begin by considering in detail what might be expected from such an audit (or survey) in any organization and what is practical and ethical to expect from such a project conducted by students within the institution. Recognize your available resources, but also the limitations on your work. (You might even want to discuss your project with several university officers before going too far.)

   As a practical matter, consider basing your work primarily on interviews with important decision makers throughout the institution, including administrators, deans and department chairs, members of the faculty (especially members of the faculty council or faculty senate), representatives of the school's athletic programs, and staff support in areas such as budget and accounting and personnel or human resources. Also consider interviews with members of the school's governing board. You might also want to collect material based on public record—newspaper reports, magazine articles, editorials, and so forth. The Chronicle of Higher Education and other materials dealing with higher education show what kinds of efforts other schools have undertaken.

   Throughout your interviews and other research, you should first seek to determine the major ethical concerns facing institutions of higher education. Topics you will likely encounter are plagiarism and other forms of academic dishonesty (on the part of both faculty and students), the integrity of the research process, matters of institutional governance, questions of equal opportunity and affirmative action, institutional policies toward drugs and alcohol, the school's position on certain political issues, and athletic recruiting policies—just to name a few. In going through these matters, you may find that your institution has taken strong moral positions in some areas (perhaps many); you may even find parts of the institution that have undertaken serious and detailed appraisals of their ethical positions—but you may also find that many of these issues simply haven't been considered, at least in terms of ethical implications.

If you can simply develop an inventory of ethical issues that should receive greater attention from members of the institution, you will have done a great service. But you may also identify cases where actual behavior seems to imply an ethical position different from the position espoused by those with whom you talk. If you do discover such cases, be prepared not only to document your findings, but also to present your report in such a way that will be helpful and constructive. Remember that you are seeking to provide a service to the institution, not an exposé.

Based on your research and analysis, prepare a written report for the school's president or chancellor and offer to have a delegation meet with him or her (or a representative) to discuss your findings. Again, your approach should be to provide preliminary findings that will be helpful in terms of institutional ethics. It may be helpful to think of yourselves as members of the president's or chancellor's staff, developing a report upon which constructive action can be taken. As in any such situation, you should be prepared to suggest specific action steps that will enable the school to give serious and sustained attention to its ethical posture.

After you finish your work, spend some time considering as a class what you have learned from this exercise: what you have learned about institutional ethics and the administrative process, and what will make you a more effective and responsible administrator in the future. Try to develop specific action-oriented statements to guide your actions in the future. Finally, consider whether there were any ethical questions you faced in the course of this project. How did you resolve them? Or did you?

For Additional Reading

Bowman, James S., ed. *Ethical Frontiers in Public Management: Seeking New Strategies for Resolving Ethical Dilemmas.* San Francisco: Jossey-Bass, 1991.

Bowman, James, ed. *Public Integrity Annual.* Lexington, KY: Council of State Governments, 1997.

Burke, John P. *Bureaucratic Responsibility.* Baltimore, MD: Johns Hopkins University Press, 1986.

Cooper, Terry L. *The Responsible Administrator: An Approach to Ethics for the Administrative Role.* 3d ed. San Francisco: Jossey-Bass, 1990.

Cooper, Terry L. *An Ethic of Citizenship for Public Administration.* Englewood Cliffs, NJ: Prentice-Hall, 1991.

Cooper, Terry L. *Exemplary Public Administrators: Character and Leadership in Government.* San Francisco: Jossey-Bass, 1992.

Cooper, Terry, ed. *Handbook of Administrative Ethics*. New York: Marcel Dekker, 1994.

Denhardt, Kathryn G. *The Ethics of Public Service*. New York: Greenwood Press, 1988.

Harmon, Michael. *Responsibility as Paradox*. Thousand Oaks, CA: Sage Publications, 1995.

Hodgkinson, Christopher. *Administrative Philosophy*. Pergamon Press, 1996.

Kellar, Elizabeth, ed. *Ethical Insight/Ethical Action*. Washington, DC: ICMA, 1988.

Pasquerella, Lynn, Alfred G. Killilea, and Michael Vocino. *Ethical Dilemmas in Public Administration*. Westport, CT: Praeger, 1996.

Rohr, John. *Ethics for Bureaucrats*. New York: Marcel Dekker, 1978.

Rohr, John. *To Run a Constitution*. Lawrence: University Press of Kansas, 1986.

Rohr, John. *Ethics and Public Administration*. Armonk, NY: M.E. Sharpe, 1993.

Tong, Rosemarie. *Ethics in Policy Analysis*. Englewood Cliffs, NJ: Prentice-Hall, 1986.

Washington, Sally. *Ethics in the Public Service*. Paris: OECD, 1996.

APPENDIX A

Code of Ethics of the American Society for Public Administration

The American Society for Public Administration affirms its responsibility to develop the spirit of professionalism within its membership, and to increase public awareness of ethical principles in public service by its example. To this end, we, the members of the Society, commit ourselves to the following principles:

I. Serve the public interest

Serve the public, beyond serving oneself. ASPA members are committed to:

1. Exercise discretionary authority to promote the public interest.
2. Oppose all forms of discrimination and harassment, and promote affirmative action.
3. Recognize and support the public's right to know the public's business.
4. Involve citizens in policy decision-making.
5. Exercise compassion, benevolence, fairness, and optimism.
6. Respond to the public in ways that are complete, clear, and easy to understand.
7. Assist citizens in their dealings with government.
8. Be prepared to make decisions that may not be popular.

II. Respect the Constitution and the Law

Respect, support and study government constitutions and laws that define responsibilities of public agencies, employees, and all citizens. ASPA members are committed to:

1. Understand and apply legislation and regulations relevant to their professional role.
2. Work to improve and change laws and policies that are counter-productive or obsolete.
3. Eliminate unlawful discrimination.

4. Prevent all forms of mismanagement of public funds by establishing and maintaining strong fiscal and management controls, and by supporting audits and investigative activities.

5. Respect and protect privileged information.

6. Encourage and facilitate legitimate dissent activities in government and protect the whistle-blowing rights of public employees.

7. Promote constitutional principles of equality, fairness, representativeness, responsiveness and due process in protecting citizens' rights.

III. Demonstrate Personal Integrity

Demonstrates the highest standards in all activities to inspire public confidence and trust in public service. ASPA members are committed to:

1. Maintain truthfulness and honesty and to not compromise them for advancement, honor, or personal gain.

2. Ensure that others received credit for their work and contributions.

3. Zealously guard against conflict of interest or its appearance.

4. Respect superiors, subordinates, colleagues, and the public.

5. Take responsibility for their own errors.

6. Conduct official acts without partisanship.

IV. Promote ethical organizations

Strengthen organizational capabilities to apply ethics, efficiency, and effectiveness in serving the public. ASPA members are committed to:

1. Enhance organizational capacity for open communication, creativity, and dedication.

2. Subordinate institutional loyalties to the public good.

3. Establish procedures that promote ethical behavior and hold individuals and organizations accountable for their conduct.

4. Provide organization members with an administrative means for dissent, assurance of due process and safeguards against reprisal.

5. Promote merit principles that protect against arbitrary and capricious actions.

6. Promote organizational accountability through appropriate controls and procedures.

7. Encourage organizations to adopt, distribute, and periodically review a code of ethics as a living document.

V. Strive for Professional Excellence

Strengthen individual capabilities and encourage the professional development of others. ASPA members are committed to:

1. Provide support and encouragement to upgrade competence.

2. Accept as a personal duty the responsibility to keep up to date on emerging issues and potential problems.

3. Encourage others, throughout their careers, to participate in professional activities and associations.

4. Allocate time to meet with students and provide a bridge between classroom studies and the realities of public service.

SOURCE: Copyright © 1994 by the American Society for Public Administration (ASPA), 1120 C Street NW, Suite 500, Washington, D.C. 20005. Reprinted with permission. All rights reserved.

Chapter 5

BUDGETING AND
FINANCIAL MANAGEMENT

Public budgeting and financial management are concerned with the allocation of limited resources to the problems governments and other public organizations face. Just as you may establish a personal budget to track your income and expenses and just as businesses create budgets to aid in decisions affecting profits and losses, so do public organizations of all types employ budgets to help in planning and management. Beyond the budget process, however, public organizations must carefully and responsibly manage large amounts of money and other resources—taking in taxes and other revenues, purchasing innumerable goods and services, and investing surplus funds or managing debt wisely.

From the point of view of the manager or the citizen trying to influence public policy, the budget is an extremely important tool for planning and control. To manage public programs effectively, you must be able to manage resources, both practically and politically. In this chapter we focus on the budget process from the standpoint of the individual public manager, examining how budget decisions are made and how you can influence budgetary outcomes. Although much of the budget process is highly charged politically, specific technical knowledge about budgeting systems will give you a distinct advantage.

The elaborate systems that public organizations have developed to manage their fiscal affairs are relatively recent. Prior to the turn of the century, revenues were easily sufficient to cover the expenses of government, and financial management was merely record keeping. But as the scope of government grew and new demands were placed on its resources, the need for more sophisticated systems of decision making became apparent. Moreover, repeated instances of corruption and waste made more effective control over the public's resources necessary.

In establishing its executive budget process through the Budgeting and Accounting Act of 1921, the federal government was actually following the lead of several local and state governments that had already taken similar actions. The municipal reform movement emphasized the budget process as a means of bringing order to public spending; consequently, by the 1920s, most big cities had established a formal budget process. Similar developments were also occurring at the state level. In 1910, Ohio became the first state to require an executive budget; within the next decade, similar actions took place in most other states. At the federal level, a special Commission on Economy and Efficiency, known as the Taft Commission, recommended establishing an executive budget in 1912; the recommendation was implemented nearly a decade later.

NETWORKING

General information on budgeting organizations can be found at http://www.pubadm.
fsu.edu/abfm/index.html and at http://www.nasbo.org/.

Since the 1920s, the federal budget has grown in both size and complexity, as have
budgets at the state and local levels. This growth means that budgeting and financial
management have come to involve far more than keeping a record of income and expenses. Today, how government spends its money affects many other areas of the economy; consequently, the budget is an instrument of fiscal policy. Moreover, the budget is a
primary expression of government priorities; it constitutes a record of the decisions that
are made concerning various public policies.

THE BUDGET AS AN INSTRUMENT OF FISCAL POLICY

Budgets express the public policy choices of governments and others. Among these are
choices with respect to the impact of the public sector on the economy. **Fiscal policy** is
concerned with the impact of government taxation and spending on the economy generally. Before the Great Depression, little attention was paid to how the federal budget affected the economy; the economy was presumably regulated by what is called the **business cycle.** Periods of economic growth, featuring inflation and high employment, were
followed by periods of recession or depression, featuring deflation and unemployment,
and so on. Meanwhile, the federal government sought to balance its budget each year—
that is, to make revenues and expenditures approximately equal.

Economists soon began to realize, however, that this pattern of government spending
was in fact influencing the economy in a negative way. In periods of economic growth,
government revenues naturally increased, so that, in an effort to balance the budget,
taxes could be lowered to the level of expenditures; in periods of economic decline, the
budget was balanced by lowering spending to meet the lower revenues. The unanticipated result of these actions was to increase citizens' income during good times and decrease their income in bad times—just the opposite of what would be desirable.
Government taxation and spending had the effect of accentuating economic instability
(Pechman, 1983, p. 8).

Economists such as the British scholar John Maynard Keynes argued, in contrast, that
all else being equal, positive government action could lead to greater economic stability.
A key to Keynes's analysis was the relationship between inflation and unemployment.
Keynes noted that periods of rapid economic growth are typically accompanied by high
inflation, which is harmful to individuals because it lowers their purchasing power, especially if they are on fixed incomes. On the other hand, periods of economic decline are

typically accompanied by high unemployment, which not only hurts individuals, but also lowers revenues for government. In either case, government action aimed at achieving greater stability might be both possible and desirable.

There are many ways the federal government can influence the economy, but one important way is simply by varying its own spending or, somewhat more indirectly, by raising or lowering taxes. The capacity of government spending patterns to influence the economy so dramatically is not hard to understand if you recognize the enormous role of government in the economy. The Gross National Product (GNP), the rate of inflation, and the rate of unemployment are the key indicators of economic health. **The Gross National Product,** a measure of total spending in the economy, comprises personal consumption, private investment, and government purchases. Almost two-thirds of our current GNP is private in nature, but over one-third is based on government spending. Based on revenues, the U.S. federal government is the single largest organization in the world, almost ten times the size of General Motors or Exxon. Obviously, decisions at the federal level play an important role in the health and stability of the economy generally.

The key relationships are these. If the economy is experiencing rapid growth—with high inflation and low unemployment—then the government might seek to "cool off" the economy by taking money out of the economy through lowering spending, raising taxes, or both. These actions have the effect of limiting private demand and slowing economic growth. On the other hand, if the economy is experiencing recession or depression—with falling prices and high unemployment—then the government might want to stimulate the economy by putting more money into circulation, through increasing spending, lowering taxes, or both. These actions have the effect of stimulating private demand and increasing economic growth. Creating a surplus, as might occur in the first case, would help restrain private spending during prosperity; creating a deficit, as in the second case, might stimulate spending during a recession.

Cumulative state and local spending also affects the economy. State and local government expenditures constitute close to 15 percent of the GNP and must be taken into account in discussions of fiscal policy. If the federal government seeks to cut taxes, but also cuts aid to states and localities, those governments may find it necessary to raise taxes themselves, thus offsetting any economic gains caused by lower taxes at the federal level (Bahl, 1984, pp. 17–30).

Patterns of spending in many states and in major cities do have some effect on the local economy and, consequently, state and local officials are becoming more cognizant of their role in fiscal policy and especially economic development. These governments, however, often don't have the tools or authority to make certain kinds of decisions. For example, nearly all the states have either constitutional or statutory provisions requiring a balanced budget. (Various political leaders have called for a balanced budget amendment at the federal level as a way to eliminate deficit spending, though if balanced budgets are achieved in other ways, calls for an amendment will be undercut. In any case, such a proposal, though attractive in a symbolic sense, would obviously limit the flexibility of the federal government in seeking to influence the economy.) In any case, it is clear that the budget process has important effects on the economy that must be anticipated in structuring overall patterns of public spending.

Where the Money Comes From

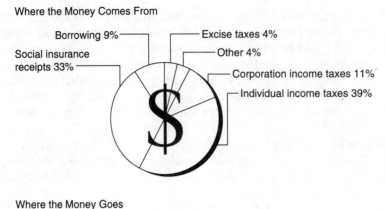

Where the Money Goes

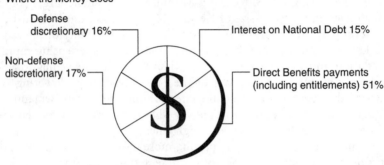

FIGURE 5.1

The Federal Government Dollar: Fiscal Year 1998 Estimate

SOURCE: A Citizen's Guide to the Federal Budget (Washington: Government Printing Office, 1997). Due to rounding, total is not 100 percent in the lower pie chart.

THE BUDGET AS AN INSTRUMENT OF PUBLIC POLICY

Although the overall pattern of spending represented in a government budget has an important effect on the economy, the many individual entries in the budget represent important choices with respect to public policies of all types. The budget is, essentially, a measure of support (or lack of support) for specific programs. Those in favor are funded; those that are out of favor are not. For this reason, discussions of budgetary priorities are of special importance to political leaders, to government officials at all levels, and to representatives of various interests in society. As a manager, you will need to understand both where the money comes from and where the money goes (see Figure 5.1).

WHERE THE MONEY COMES FROM

Governments obtain the funds they need to operate the programs deemed important either from their own sources or through transfers from other governments. There are a variety of ways governments can raise their own revenues, including levying taxes and charging individuals or groups for specific services. Because all public programs are affected by the way governments raise revenues, and because revenue administration is itself an important part of public administration, you will find it helpful to understand the way taxes are structured.

Obviously, developing tax policies requires attention not only to the level of taxes being taken from individuals or groups, but also to the fairness, efficiency, and simplicity of the tax system. Everyone agrees that the tax system should be fair and that everyone should pay his or her "fair share." But what exactly does that mean? Some argue that each should pay according to the benefits they receive; others argue that those who have a greater ability to pay should in fact pay more.

One way to approach the issue is to think in terms of the relationship between one's tax rate and one's income. A tax is said to be **proportional** if it taxes everyone at the same rate. If a tax rate of 10 percent is applied to a $20,000 income (yielding $2,000) and the same rate is applied to a $200,000 income (yielding $20,000), even though the amounts differ, the tax is proportional. A tax is said to be **progressive** if it taxes those with higher incomes at a higher rate. A progressive tax might apply a 10 percent rate to a $20,000 income (yielding $2,000) and a 50 percent rate to a $200,000 income (yielding $100,000). Finally, a tax is said to be **regressive** if it taxes those with lower incomes at a proportionally higher rate than those with higher incomes. If an individual with a $20,000 income and one with a $200,000 income both pay a $400 tax on the same new car, the tax is regressive, taking 2 percent of the first individual's income but a much smaller proportion of the second individual's income (LeLoup, 1977, pp. 193–194).

Individual Income Tax

All methods of taxation involve application of a *tax rate* to a particular *tax base;* the product of the two yields *tax revenue.* The individual income tax, the single most important tax in our country, calls for the individual to add up all income from taxable sources, reduce that amount by certain deductions or exemptions, then apply a tax rate to that base to arrive at the individual's income tax. The current federal income tax, for example, applies rates between 15 percent and 39.6 percent to five income brackets.

All advanced industrial nations use some form of income tax. In the United States, the income tax is the primary source of revenue for the federal government and is used to a lesser extent in many states and some cities. In most cases, a higher rate is applied to higher incomes, making the income tax a progressive tax. For nearly thirty years after its passage in 1913, the federal income tax applied only to a fairly small number of high-income people; however, with the advent of World War II, deductions were reduced significantly and higher rates applied.

Managing the task of collecting an income tax from everyone in the country is obviously difficult. Yet, the Internal Revenue Service (IRS) has developed a relatively efficient mechanism for collection and does so at a cost of less than one-half of 1 percent of the revenues produced. One key to the existing system is the requirement that each individual calculate his or her own tax liability. IRS auditors then select a few returns for closer inspection, concentrating on those with unusual features. The extent of compliance with tax regulations in this country, though far from complete, is considered comparatively high.

However, throughout 1997, testimonies before the National Commission on Restructuring the IRS revealed serious concerns relating to the service's internal and external operations. Witnesses indicated that some IRS officials collected tax information for their personal benefit, that unjustifiable audits were ordered against citizens, and that the organization had inappropriately acquired billions of dollars from taxpayers. Commissioners concluded that the IRS needed a major reorganization, and by year's end a bipartisan effort had been launched in Congress to carry out the commission's recommendations.

Corporation Income Tax

The corporation income tax actually predates the individual income tax by several years and, for most of this century, was a key source of federal revenue. Also a progressive tax, the corporation income tax is justified by its proponents as a way of taxing capital accumulation that is not specifically distributed to individuals. Moreover, the corporation income tax is needed to support the individual income tax; without it, individuals could simply keep their income in corporations and avoid paying income taxes. Though most states have corporation income taxes, the tax is far more substantial at the federal level. Yet even here, the corporation income tax is declining in contrast to other sources of revenue. Where it once yielded more revenue than the individual income tax, the corporation income tax has declined to only about one-tenth of federal revenues.

Payroll Taxes

Taxes on payrolls support a variety of social security and other social insurance programs, such as unemployment compensation and medical care for the aged. (These specific taxes should not be confused with the general income taxes that may be deducted from a payroll check.) These programs are primarily financed by taxes paid either by the employer or by the employer and employee in equal amounts. Because there is a flat rate, with no deductions or exemptions, and maximum amounts above which taxes are not required, payroll taxes overall are regressive. Payroll taxes at the federal level now constitute the second largest source of federal revenue.

Sales and Excise Taxes

Both sales and excise taxes are applied to goods and services. *Sales taxes* are applied to a broad range of goods and services at either retail or wholesale levels and are a popular source of income at state and local levels. There are, however, significant variations in both sales tax rates and items covered by sales taxes; for example, some jurisdictions exempt food, clothing, and medicine from sales tax. **Excise taxes,** on the other hand, are applied to the sale of specific commodities such as gasoline, tobacco, or alcohol, and are the primary form of consumption tax at the federal level. Typically, excise taxes are applied at specific rates (e.g., 2 cents per gallon), but may also be applied to the total sales price. Some excise taxes are, in effect, user charges that help support particular activities. Gasoline taxes, for instance, are typically used to support highway construction and maintenance.

A major issue concerning sales and excise taxes is that of equity. Since the poor consume a greater portion of their income than the rich, the burden of consumption taxes tends to fall more heavily on the poor; that is, the taxes are regressive. These taxes also tend to penalize certain groups, such as those with large families or those just starting a household. On the other hand, these taxes tend to provide more stable revenues, something that is especially important at state and local levels.

Property Taxes

Taxes on personal property are widely used at the local level and provide about half of local government revenues. Administration of a property tax involves assessment of an individual's property, most often land and buildings, then the application of a tax rate. About half the revenue generated by the property tax derives from residential property and half from businesses. Although the property tax is progressive in its effect (those who spend more on housing pay more), administration is difficult and has often not been highly professional. Moreover, recent tax limitations have severely restricted the capacity of local governments to raise additional revenue through the property tax.

Other Revenue Sources

There are, of course, a variety of other sources of government revenues. Whereas public organizations have often charged fees for the use of specific government services, recent limitations on other tax revenues have made such charges increasingly attractive, especially at the local level. For example, fees for the use of parks and recreational facilities are becoming increasingly important. Another recent development in terms of revenues at the state level is the use of lotteries. Nearly half the states and several local governments now conduct lotteries, which provide a highly visible, but relatively small and unstable, source of funds. Lotteries are also highly regressive in their effect (since poorer citizens tend to play the lotteries more); indeed, they are more regressive than even the sales tax (Mikesell & Zorn, 1986, pp. 318–319).

Nonprofit organizations, which lack the power to tax, derive revenues from quite different sources and, indeed, engage in a wide variety of efforts to support their programs. Obviously, membership organizations depend in large measure on member dues for revenue, but such organizations, along with many others, have recently sought to diversify revenues. While grant funding remains an important source of revenue for many nonprofit organizations, recent reductions in federal social service programs have seriously limited grant opportunities for many nonprofits. Additional sources of funds include donations (from individuals, corporations, and foundations), sales of goods and services (from books to coffee cups), and joint enterprises involving commercial firms (such as insurance plans or "affinity" credit cards).

Patterns of Government Revenues

As we have seen, different levels of government vary in their dependence on specific revenue sources. Figure 5.1 shows the distribution of receipts at the federal level. The president's budget for 1997 estimated total revenues of $1.5 trillion, including the following major categories:

Individual income taxes: $645 billion

Payroll taxes: $536 billion

Corporation income taxes: $185 billion

Excise taxes: $60 billion

Although the federal government relies heavily on the income tax, state governments are much more dependent on sales taxes, and local governments are primarily dependent on property tax as a revenue source. All state and local governments combined generated $1,331 billion in revenues in 1993–1994, with $223 billion coming from sales taxes of one kind or another and only $156 billion coming from various income taxes. In addition to tax receipts, the combined governments counted as revenues $215 billion in intergovernmental (primarily federal) transfers. At the local level, the property tax accounts for some $188 billion in revenues.

NETWORKING

For the budget of the United States and how to get to the budgets of other governments, see the Department of the Treasury at http://www.ustreas.gov/. More specifically, see http://www.access.gpo.gov/su_docs/budget/index.html for FY 1998, http://www.access. gpo.gov/omb/omb002.html for FY 1997, and http://www.access.gpo.gov/omb/omb001. html for FY 1996.

WHERE THE MONEY GOES

These revenue figures are staggering, but they hardly match up to the demands on governments at all levels. There simply isn't enough money to meet every need or cure every problem, even if money alone were the solution. Instead, difficult choices must be made each year about which programs will be funded and at what levels. The choices made through the public policy process are reflected in the government's budget. The budget, therefore, stands as a record of the government's priorities.

But government priorities are always shifting. As new conditions arise, new programs are proposed and old programs are expanded or contracted. The emphasis the federal government gives to various areas, as one example, has reflected the condition of the country and the world at various times, as in the large percentage of national resources devoted to national defense during periods of international conflict.

We can also trace budgetary changes over shorter time spans, thus indicating the policy priorities of various presidents, governors, mayors, or other public officials. Certain restrictions, however, have been built into the federal budget over the years that somewhat limit the choices any president or Congress can make. Over the past twenty years, for example, Congress has passed a variety of **entitlement programs** that provide specified benefits to those who meet certain eligibility requirements. For example, legislation might provide benefits to all persons above a certain age or all persons below a certain income level. The implication, supported by several judicial rulings, is that individuals are entitled to or have a right to certain benefits (primarily social welfare benefits).

For these programs, Congress essentially agrees to provide whatever money is necessary from year to year to assure a certain level of benefits to all eligible people. Legislation is typically written so that new action is not required each year to keep the program going. Only a projection of likely beneficiaries is needed to determine the level of expenditures for a given year. Unless Congress takes specific steps to limit benefits or eligibility—something that legislators are reluctant to do—funding of these programs is practically automatic.

But these programs obviously vary in size over time. In a recession, for example, unemployment would be high, and spending for unemployment compensation would rise. Similarly, the changing character of the population—for example, a larger number of older Americans—would also change the amount of money required to provide benefits to that group. Moreover, most entitlement programs have now been *indexed* to the cost of living (or related measures), so that benefit levels automatically rise with inflation. (Indeed, over the past decade, Congress has passed major expansions of indexing in Social Security and Medicare.) Expenditures for entitlement programs thus increase almost every year.

Such programs constituted just over 50 percent of the 1997 federal budget. When they are combined with farm price supports (also indexed), with interest on the national debt (which must be paid), and with expenditures based on previous commitments, these so-called *uncontrollable expenditures* constitute almost two-thirds of the federal budget.

The remainder of the federal budget might be termed **discretionary spending,** meaning the president and the Congress are open to make changes in this relatively small portion of the budget. This includes defense spending (about 16 percent) and domestic discretionary spending (only about 17 percent). These are the areas that generate the most difficult policy choices.

DEFICITS AND DEFICIT REDUCTION

A great deal of political debate in the 1980s and early 1990s has centered on attempts to control the federal deficit. As noted, traditional economic theory does not necessarily disapprove of public borrowing; indeed, there may be benefits to deficit spending in particular years. But at some point, a growing deficit becomes unmanageable, especially as interest payments become such a substantial part of government spending. Large deficits are generally thought to limit both short-term and long-term economic recovery, especially because they limit private investment. Moreover, large deficits contribute to an understandable lack of public confidence concerning their political leaders' ability to deal effectively with the budget.

The budget deficits of the Reagan years were substantial (see Table 5.1). Indeed, the administration's accumulated debt exceeded that of all previous administrations

TABLE 5.1

Deficit by Fiscal Year in Billions of Dollars

Year	Deficit
1980	73.8
1985	212.3
1990	221.4
1991	269.2
1992	290.4
1993	255.1
1994	203.2
1995	163.9
1996	107.3

SOURCE: *Historical Tables, Budget of the United States FY 1998*

The projected deficit assumes that laws are not changed and that discretionary spending keeps up with inflation once the BEA's caps expire.

combined. By 1984 it became clear that if no further actions were taken to reduce the deficit, by the end of the Reagan years, the deficit would total over $2.6 trillion and interest payments alone would require one out of every six federal dollars (Palmer & Sawhill, 1984, p. 9). Facing this prospect, Congress passed the Gramm-Rudman-Hollings Act of 1985. Under this legislation, deficit targets were set for each of the next five budget years and aimed at reducing the deficit to zero in 1990 (though a later amendment pushed the target to 1992). Unfortunately, the president and the Congress were overly optimistic in their economic projections and also employed several questionable budget techniques to evade the restraints set by Gramm-Rudman-Hollings.

With the deficit still out of control in 1990, the president and the Congress faced very difficult budget deliberations. For the 1990 budget, the Gramm-Rudman-Hollings law had targeted a deficit of no more than $110 billion. By October, when the fiscal year began, there was still no agreement on the budget. (As we will see, it is not unusual for a federal fiscal year to begin before the year's budget is approved.) Consequently, automatic, across-the-board spending cuts were applied to all federal agencies.

Finally, in late November, a deficit-reduction plan was approved that would bring the projected deficit below the Gramm-Rudman-Hollings target. The plan that was agreed to, however, contained a number of provisions that appeared to be budgetary "smoke and mirrors." For example, part of the plan would save money by having the government lease rather than buy buildings, something that would obviously save up-front costs within 1990, but would likely increase costs in the long run. Similarly, certain payments to doctors under Medicaid were shifted to the following fiscal year. The biggest reduction item, however, was to simply maintain for another 130 days the across-the-board cuts that had been imposed in October, something that many observers read as a failure of the administration and the Congress to come to grips with the hard choices that deficit reduction requires.

As part of the budget agreement, the Budget Enforcement Act (BEA) was passed to police the deficit even further. The BEA set annual ceilings on several categories of discretionary spending, with violation of the caps requiring across-the-board cuts. BEA also required that legislative actions affecting mandatory spending not increase the deficit in any year. (This is known as the "pay as you go" provision.) Though these provisions seem to have had the desired effect on the budget process, the deficit continued to grow, driven in part by incorrect economic assumptions and in part by increased spending for health care programs and the savings and loan bailout.

In 1997, the Clinton administration led a bipartisan effort in Congress to pass yet another landmark piece of legislation aimed at balancing the federal budget. The budget agreement would eliminate the deficit by 2002, phasing in $121 billion in spending cuts over a five-year period. Much of the savings would come from reductions in Medicare payments to health providers and hospitals. An additional $55 billion would be saved each year through mandates imposed on future spending bills. The budget agreement also featured $95 billion in tax cuts over the five years, including credits for higher education, relief for families with children, and reductions in capital gains. How the legislation will fare with regard to balancing the federal budget remains to be seen. And, many have begun to question if the new spending provisions will remain in place as Congress turns to more pressing concerns, such as fiscal reform of Medicare and Social Security.

NETWORKING

Check out the National Debt Clock at http://www.brillig.com/debt_clock/ and the Treasury Department's FAQs about the budget and national debt at http://www.ustreas. gov/opc/opc0037.html. Also see the simulations that follow: http://www.thirdmil.org/ debt/debt.cgi and http:/uts.cc.utexas.edu/~wphwebpb/tbs.html.

THE CLINTON BUDGET EXPERIENCE

The use of the budget as an instrument of policy change has been well illustrated during the Clinton presidency. Clinton came into office on a platform of so-called New Democratic objectives, a balance between idealistic social activism and pragmatic fiscal conservatism. On one hand, the administration had a clear agenda for community and economic development, for creating economic and employment opportunity, and for enhancing the nation's education and health care systems. On the other hand, the president recognized that such ambitious goals would never be possible under the burden of a $4 trillion national debt. Federal spending would have to be contained and the national budget balanced in order to enhance the country's economic viability.

If the administration's vision seemed challenging at the beginning, the level of difficulty only increased following the 1994 midterm elections, when Republicans gained control of Congress. Conservative lawmakers took the election outcomes as a mandate to relaunch the Reagan administration's assault on "big government." House Republicans, in particular, rallied around the goals of reining in federal spending and cutting the national debt. In fact, fiscal measures such as balancing the budget, giving the president line-item veto authority, and others became key themes in the House Republicans' Contract with America. While both camps agreed in principle to reductions in spending and a balanced budget, the discourse over specific provisions quickly deteriorated into some of the most extreme partisanship Washington had seen in over a generation.

In 1995, budget deliberations stalled when Congress and the president failed to reach a compromise over the four appropriations bills that fund the primary federal agencies, such as the Departments of Labor, Health and Human Services, Housing and Urban Development, Commerce, State, Defense and others. Congress refused to give on its demand for reductions in spending for research, foreign aid, and education. The Clinton administration responded with equal determination, holding to its demand for continued support in these areas. Congress moved ahead with a series of continuing resolutions, short-term authorizations for limited spending that are provided in absence of a formal appropriations agreement. However, as the session continued, both sides warned of the "train wreck" that the federal government would face when these interim measures expired.

And wreck it did, twice. Just before the holiday break the temporary spending provisions ran out and Washington simply shut down. First, in November the federal government closed its doors for four days. Agencies brought in only "essential" personnel, leaving other employees at home and without paychecks. Congress responded by advancing a temporary spending measure, but the provision was short-lived and just weeks later, in December, the government shut down again. This time, the shutdown lasted into January and left an estimated 760,000 employees out of work.

The effects of both shutdowns were unprecedented, as the American public experienced what life would be like without the federal government. Work sites went uninspected, environmental cleanup of hazardous sites was postponed, the investment markets virtually shut down over the lack of key economic and labor reports, and the season's flu epidemic went untracked and unhindered as vaccinations could not be provided by health officials. Estimates indicate that the shutdowns cost American taxpayers about $1.7 billion; however, many say that the cost went far greater than mere dollar amounts.

Before the stalemate ended both Congress and the president had dealt a sharp blow to public trust. Many saw the shutdown as another example of partisan gridlock, a common trait of Washington politics. However, others viewed the crisis as indicative of deeper concerns underlying the nation's system of federalism. Political theorist Sheldon Wolin wrote, "The shutdown was . . . a direct challenge to the principle that in a democracy the government belongs to the people. . . . For the President or Congress to undertake to stop or reconstitute government in order to extract sweeping policy concessions amounts to an attempted coup d'etat by what *The Federalist* . . . would have condemned as a 'temporary majority.'" The government had acted not according to the public will but rather on its own accord to achieve limited outcomes.

As a result of the budget crisis, and the marked decline in public trust that resulted, both sides toned down their partisan rhetoric as they entered 1996 budget deliberations.

Yet the budget process once again became a forum for both sides to advance their policy aims. A bipartisan alliance succeeded in granting the president line-item veto authority, and Congress and the administration reached a landmark deal on reforming the nation's welfare system. The stage seemed well set for a balanced budget agreement. Hoping to have the measure as a plank in his presidential campaign platform, Senate Majority Leader Bob Dole brought the bill to the Senate floor in the spring of 1996. Despite hours of deliberation and compromise, though, the measure failed in the Senate by a single vote.

The spirit of compromise that characterized budget negotiations in 1996 played well with the American public, which in the fall elections returned the Democratic president to a second term and handed the GOP a continued hold over Congress. Lawmakers and administration officials responded by setting an ambitious agenda for the 1997 budget process. Unlike previous years, however, the 1997 spending measures offered provisions that satisfied both sides' policy objectives. Conservatives focused on the cuts in federal spending and reductions in capital gains tax; liberal lawmakers focused on the tax credits for higher education and new spending to provide health care for children. And, by the end of the summer, Congress and the president had accomplished what previously had been impossible—enactment of a balanced budget agreement.

The 1997 measure promised to eliminate the federal deficit by phasing in $121 billion in spending cuts over a five-year period. Reductions in Medicare payments to doctors and hospitals would make up most of the savings, with $55 billion coming from mandates on future appropriations bills. To ensure buy-in from lawmakers, the agreement featured tax credits for families, cuts in capital gains and estate taxes, and incentives for higher education. The legislation also offered $24 billion to cover the cost of health care for uninsured children. Both the Clinton administration and Congress hailed the agreement as a success, with Republicans pointing to aspects that reduced the size of the federal government, and Democrats citing the education and health care provisions.

The long negotiations and the give-and-take required for this bipartisan victory well illustrate the complexity and difficulty of implementing public policies through the budget process. A wide variety of actors influenced the budgetary outcomes, and many different and competing views had to be taken into account. In the end, the resulting agreement reinforced the spirit of compromise between the White House and Congress. Many suggested that only through such bipartisanship could the president and lawmakers succeed in their more pressing concerns, like reforming Medicare and Social Security.

The debate over deficit reduction and indeed the country's near-preoccupation with the deficit issue shifted early in 1998, as President Clinton released his proposed budget for FY 1999, a plan that presented a balanced budget and ended nearly thirty years of deficit spending by the federal government. Lawmakers were soon talking not only about how successfully they had balanced the budget, but also about how to spend the $9.5 billion surplus offered by the president's plan, as well as ways to invest the $1 trillion in surpluses the plan promised over the next ten years—through new programs, debt reduction, and tax relief. Clearly the FY 1999 budget proposal marked an important turning point in the dialogue over the federal deficit.

STATE AND LOCAL EXPENDITURES

Expenditure comparisons at the state and local levels are complicated by our system of intergovernmental transfers. In education, for example, the federal government provides some money directly to individuals (e.g., student grants and loans), but it also transfers large sums to state and local governments. States spend some money directly (e.g., colleges and universities), but they also transfer some money received from the federal government and some raised at the state level to local governments, primarily to support education. Consequently, while local governments provide only less than 30 percent of the money spent on education in this country, they actually are involved in spending 70 percent of that money. If we include intergovernmental transfers spent at the state and local levels in our calculations of state and local spending, the following patterns emerge: states spend the greatest portion of their funds on education, with public welfare next, and highways, health, and natural resources somewhat less. At the local level, the largest amount again is spent on education, with health, public works, and social welfare next (see Figure 5.2).

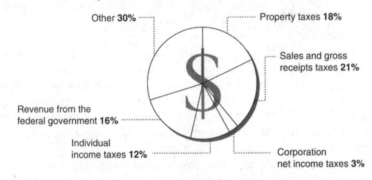

Where the Money Comes From

Other **30%**

Property taxes **18%**

Sales and gross receipts taxes **21%**

Revenue from the federal government **16%**

Individual income taxes **12%**

Corporation net income taxes **3%**

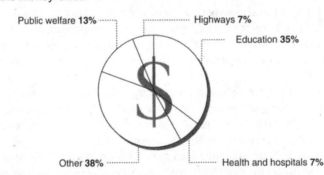

Where the Money Goes

Public welfare **13%**

Highways **7%**

Education **35%**

Other **38%**

Health and hospitals **7%**

FIGURE 5.2

The State and Local Dollar

SOURCE: *The United States Budget in Brief, Fiscal Year 1990* (Washington, DC: U.S. Government Printing Office, 1990), p. 96.

THE BUDGET AS A MANAGERIAL TOOL

As a public manager, you will find that the budget process is critical to your success and that of your agency, quite simply because the budget process establishes the level of funding for your programs and those of others. A variety of steps are required to enable a particular agency to spend money. Legislation must first be passed and signed by the chief executive to authorize the program. This **authorizing legislation** permits the establishment or continuation of a particular program or agency. (Authorizing legislation usually covers multiple years or is even open-ended, though some programs, such as the space program, require new authorization each year.) Next come **appropriations,** whereby the legislature sets aside funds and creates budget authority for their expenditure. Only after both steps have been taken can an agency spend money in pursuit of its stated objectives.

In most cases, governments use a **fiscal year** as their basic accounting period. The federal fiscal year begins on October 1 and runs through September 30 of the following year. The fiscal year carries the name of the year in which it ends; thus, fiscal year 1999, or FY 99, begins October 1, 1998, and ends September 30, 1999. States and localities differ widely in terms of fiscal years; some follow the federal pattern and run from October through September, others start July 1 (as did the federal government until 1976), and others match the fiscal year to the calendar year. Kentucky and a few other states actually have a two-year-long fiscal year because their legislatures meet and pass a budget only every other year.

The fiscal year is the key period in which money is spent, but a variety of steps must be taken both before and after the fiscal year that can affect an agency's expenditures. The budget must be developed, typically by the chief executive (president, governor, mayor), and transmitted to the legislature; it must be approved by the legislature prior to the beginning of the fiscal year; it must be executed during the fiscal year; and it must be reviewed and audited following the fiscal year. At any given point in the *budget cycle,* there are actually several budgets being worked upon. While one budget is being executed (say, FY 98), formulation and approval of another (FY 99) is taking place, as are audits of the previous budget (FY 97).

BUDGET FORMULATION

In the federal government and in many state and local jurisdictions, the chief executive has primary responsibility for preparation of the budget. The budget cycle (see Figure 5.3) typically begins with a letter from a central budget office to the various agencies outlining the timetable for preparation of the budget, transmitting forms for use in the process, and indicating any policy concerns of special priority for the fiscal year. The agencies then prepare their own budget requests and forward them to the central budget office for review (see Box 5.1). Often a series of meetings (or sometimes hearings) are held to negotiate differences in the views of the central budget office (reflecting the priorities of the chief executive) and the agencies. Finally, the budget document is prepared by the central budget office and transmitted by the chief executive to the legislature for approval.

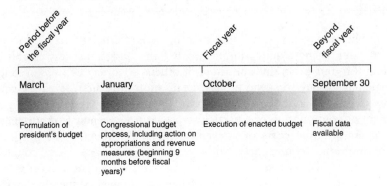

Major Steps in the Budget Process

FIGURE 5.3

The Budget Cycle at the Federal Level

SOURCE: *The United States Budget in Brief, Fiscal Year 1990* (Washington, DC: U.S. Government Printing Office, 1990), p. 96.

BOX 5.1

Financial Management: The Program Manager's Role

Many in government think financial management is the responsibility of financial offices, accountants, and the like. Most program managers, in particular, feel they do not have to be concerned with financial management.

WRONG. Nothing could be further from the truth. Successful program managers appreciate that, in government, they have the responsibility for financial management. They understand what this entails, and thus have a far better chance of successfully delivering their programs despite reduced budgets.

What is financial management? It is nothing more than obtaining and effectively using funds and other resources to accomplish the goals and objectives of the organization. It typically entails:

- Defining people, materials, and services for achieving a program's goals and objectives.
- Defining the sources of resources that can be used to fund the program's costs
- Obtaining the resources
- Managing and minimizing the costs
- Obtaining results from the expenditure of the resources
- Preventing waste in the expenditure of the resources
- Reporting accountability for both the use of resources and delivery of the results.

SOURCE: Harold I. Steinberg, "Improving Financial Management: The Program Manager's Role," *PA Times*, v. 20, n. 11 (November 1997): 1.

In some jurisdictions, responsibility for preparing the budget may not lie completely with the chief executive, and the budget cycle may vary accordingly. In many states, for example, responsibility for budget formulation may be shared among the governor, other elected officials, and members of the legislature. Cities with a strong mayor form usually give responsibility to the chief executive, whereas cities that operate under other forms tend to disperse budget authority. The city manager usually prepares the budget in council-manager cities, though typically with substantial input from the mayor and other council members.

The Office of Management and Budget is the central budget office at the federal level, and has evolved from an office established in 1921. Originally called the Bureau of the Budget, President Nixon renamed the Office of Management and Budget in 1970 to reflect an emphasis on management concerns in addition to budgetary responsibilities. At the outset of the budget process, OMB collects information on projected revenues for the coming fiscal year, as well as information on the outlook for the economy. In addition, OMB develops information on the progress of the current year's budget, as well as the budget being considered by Congress. After a beginning consultation with the agencies to assess their program priorities, OMB works with the president to establish basic policy guidelines for developing the budget.

NETWORKING

Federal organizations involved in budgeting and financial management include the Office of Management and Budget at http://www.whitehouse.gov/WH/EOP/omb, the Congressional Budget Office at http://www.cbo.gov/, and the General Accounting Office at http://www.gao.gov/.

These guidelines are communicated to the agencies, along with detailed forms for budget requests. In turn, managers in the various agencies assess their program priorities and decide the necessary level of funding for accomplishing objectives in the next fiscal year. Starting about September, a period of negotiation occurs with OMB. The central budget office represents the president's policy concerns and usually takes a generalist perspective, in contrast to the more narrow, specialized interests of the agency representatives. About November or December, the president becomes more actively involved in the budget process and makes final decisions with respect to both revenue and fiscal considerations and individual program needs.

The final budget document, which is submitted to Congress early in the new year, represents the culmination of a long process of analysis and interaction among a wide variety of groups.

Obviously, given the magnitude and complexity of the federal government, the process of budget formulation at that level is the most complex in this country. But the difficulties of reconciling different and competing interests in the budget process are significant at all levels of government. In addition, chief executives at the state and local levels face constraints not found at the federal level. For example, most governors are required by constitution or statute to submit a balanced budget to the legislature, making it essential that they project anticipated revenues as closely as possible.

BUDGET APPROVAL

The budget approval phase begins with submission of the budget to the legislature and ends with approval of the budget. The legislature, in most cases, can approve, disapprove, or modify the chief executive's budget proposal; it can add programs or eliminate programs; and it can alter methods of raising revenues. Remember that programs must first be authorized, then money appropriated for their implementation. In some cases, appropriations are contained in one bill that is debated, amended, and passed by the legislative body. In other cases, appropriations may be divided among several different appropriations bills.

In any case, the budget submitted to the legislative body is first sent to the committee or committees responsible for appropriations. These committees review the submitted document and hold hearings involving agency personnel, representatives of interest groups, other legislators, and private citizens. After consideration by the full legislative body, the bill as amended is passed and sent to the chief executive for signature (where approval is required), or, in the case of bicameral legislatures, sent to the other legislative body for similar consideration. If there are differences in the bills produced by the two houses of the legislature, the differences are worked out in a conference committee, and the bill is passed again by the two houses and sent to the chief executive.

Again, there are wide variations in the approval process from jurisdiction to jurisdiction. At the federal level, granting budget authority—the authority to obligate funds for immediate or future *outlays* (government spending)—can come about in several ways. Budget authority for most programs must be granted annually through passage of an appropriations bill. Congress has voted permanent budget authority for some programs, however, so that funds become available each year without further congressional action. In addition, within any given fiscal year, some outlays will be based on obligations made in previous years. Thus, total budget outlays for any fiscal year include the total of previously granted budget authority, authority granted through appropriations for the current year, and money obligated in previous years for spending in the upcoming fiscal year, minus outlays deferred to later years.

Under procedures established by the Congressional Budget Act of 1974, Congress considers budget totals before considering individual appropriations measures. Based on work by the Budget Committees of both houses, a first *concurrent resolution* (a resolution of both houses not requiring the president's signature) is passed by May 15, establishing targets for total revenues and total spending authority within various functional areas for the upcoming fiscal year. Although the president is not formally involved in this part of the budget process, consultation frequently occurs so that all parties will be informed of developments in the approval process. In some cases, the various parties even agree on a set of budget totals to be honored by both the president in his budget submission and the Congress in its approval process.

Congressional review of appropriations requests begins in the House of Representatives, where the Ways and Means Committee considers revenue estimates and the Appropriations Committee (through various subcommittees) reviews spending recommendations. Appropriations are considered within thirteen different appropriations bills covering groups of departments and agencies within related functional areas. After initial passage by the House, all tax bills and the thirteen appropriations bills are forwarded to the Senate for consideration. Differences in the appropriations measures coming from the two houses are worked out in conference committee and, following approval by both houses, are forwarded to the president for signature. The two Budget Committees are charged with drawing up a second concurrent resolution, this one binding in nature, setting limits on total spending. Finally, a separate **reconciliation bill** attempts to reconcile individual actions in taxes, authorizations, or appropriations with the totals.

If action on appropriations for the fiscal year is not completed by the beginning of the fiscal year (October 1), the Congress enacts a **continuing resolution,** which permits the government to keep operating until an appropriations measure is passed. (As we have seen, the term *continuing resolution* became a household phrase during the budget turmoil of 1995–1996. The Clinton administration and Congress both refused to compromise on key provisions of the "big four" appropriations bills, which fund the main federal agencies. A series of continuing resolutions was used to keep government offices open until an agreement could be reached, all to no avail. On two separate occasions, first in November and then in December, the government was forced to shut down as the temporary spending measures ran out and budget deliberations stalled in partisan gridlock. By the end of the crisis, a dozen continuing resolutions were signed to keep the federal government operational.)

Throughout its consideration of the budget, the Congress is aided by the work of Budget Committee staff members (whose numbers have grown substantially in recent years) and by the Congressional Budget Office. This agency provides basic budget information and its own economic forecasts and indicates to Congress how its conclusions differ from those of the executive branch. Such differences have, in several years, led the Congressional Budget Office to predict a more substantial budget deficit than that anticipated by the administration.

An increase in staff capabilities has been among the most important developments in the legislative approval process in most states and in some larger cities. Legislative budget staffs vary in structure and composition; that is, partisan or nonpartisan, centralized or decentralized, joint (both houses) or single house, etc. However, their responsibilities usually include analyzing the governor's budget, forecasting revenues and expenditures, and developing alternatives to the executive budget. In all cases, greater staff capabilities have considerably aided the resurgence of state legislative involvement in the budget process.

One important feature of the approval process at the state level is the existence of the item veto in most states. (The item veto allows the executive to veto specific items in an appropriations bill rather than decide between "all or nothing.") Such authority has been sought at the federal level by recent presidents, but President Clinton became the first chief executive granted such capacity when the federal Line Item Veto Act (P.L. 104-130) took effect in January 1997. The act, though stopping short of extending full constitutional line-item veto power, gives the president authority to strike items from a federal appropriations bill without having to veto the entire piece of legislation. The Clinton administration, like its Republican predecessors, argue that the powers granted under the act, which remains in effect until 2005, will enable the president to make significant cuts in federal spending. Proponents argue that a great deal of time and energy will be saved since the executive and legislative branches will not have to renegotiate an entire budget when only specific items are at issue.

However, critics question whether the act will achieve such meaningful results. They contend that Congress, unlike state legislatures, often appropriates larger lump sums (rather than specific items) in order to give the administrators flexibility. In doing so, Congress can protect its own interests, because these sums would be far more difficult to veto. Moreover, as we have seen, the large percentage of uncontrollable expenditures in the federal budget would limit veto power to a narrow range of programs. Perhaps the most significant argument, though, suggests that by granting the president item veto authority lawmakers have upset the delicate balance between the executive and legislative branches. Many are concerned that the president will enjoy an excessive amount of authority in an area traditionally reserved for Congress. Yet in practical terms it is unlikely that the impact of the Line Item Veto Act will be felt toward any of these extremes. Congress more than likely will find ways of wording legislation and framing line items that limit the presidential powers, and the president, over time, may come to rely on more established means of dealing with lawmakers, perhaps even old-fashioned concepts like negotiation and compromise.

BUDGET EXECUTION

The budget execution stage, generally coinciding with the fiscal year, is that part of the budget cycle in which the agencies of government carry out agreed-upon programs and policies. Obviously, the execution stage involves public administrators in all aspects of the management process—planning, analysis, personnel management, communication, and other interpersonal skills.

Basic financial controls are exercised during the budget execution phase through the mechanism of **apportionment,** a process by which funds are allocated to agencies for specific portions of the year. Typically, the central budget office asks for submission of spending plans indicating what money the agencies anticipate spending in each quarter of the year. Because the agencies may not have received all they wanted in the appropriations process, the apportionment mechanism also acts as the basis for required changes in programs and policies. As soon as there is agreement between the central budget office (acting on behalf of the chief executive) and the agencies on the changes embodied in the apportionment plan, agencies begin receiving **allotments** to spend within a given period.

To assure that funds are in fact expended for the purposes for which they were intended and that there is indeed enough money budgeted to cover a proposed expenditure, some sort of **preaudit** (a review in advance of an actual expenditure) is usually required. Depending on the jurisdiction, the preaudit may be conducted by an agency's own budget office, by an independent agency, or even by an elected state official. Once approval has been given, however, the treasurer will "write a check" for the expenditure.

Even though budgets are not passed until just before (or even well into) the fiscal year, important changes may occur during the year that require changes in an agency's budgeted expenditures. Some changes may require greater funding: for example, when an unexpected natural disaster, such as a drought, places special burdens on farmers. If it is felt that the need must be met prior to the next budget cycle, the president and Congress can work together to provide a **supplemental appropriation,** a bill passed during the fiscal year to add new money to an agency's budget for that fiscal year. Such a bill may simply provide more money for existing programs or money for a newly authorized program.

There are also devices, used primarily by chief executives as a matter of administrative discretion, to restrict agencies' spending below budgeted amounts. Presidents throughout the nation's history have sought to limit agency spending by **impoundment**—withholding—funds authorized and appropriated by law, typically in the case of emergencies or where the purpose of the money had been achieved and budgeted funds still remained. Similarly, at the state level, governors regularly withhold agency funds when revenue projections fall below levels upon which the budget was based.

At the federal level, the impoundment issue became especially intense in the early 1970s, when President Nixon asserted his right to impound funds wherever he felt appropriate to achieve his fiscal goals. Especially annoying to Congress was his refusal to spend money for water pollution control; the money had been passed by Congress over a presidential veto (Pfiffner, 1979, p. 4). Many felt that Nixon's use of impoundment amounted to an unconstitutional item veto.

Consequently, the 1974 Budget Act sought to clarify matters by defining two types of legal impoundments. The first, a **deferral,** is a decision by the president to withhold funds for a brief period. In such circumstances, the president must inform the Congress, and either house of Congress may veto the action. The second, a **rescission,** is a presidential decision to withhold funds permanently; a rescission must receive the positive approval of both houses of Congress. Through these devices, Congress has sought to maintain its involvement in budget execution while at the same time allowing some administrative discretion to the president. (Not surprisingly, recent presidents, including President Clinton, have argued for expanded rescission authority.)

Because situations change, public managers are often accorded some flexibility in the use of allocated funds. Money originally allocated for salaries and wages, for example, might be shifted (with appropriate approvals) to an equipment and expense category. On a broader scale, some agencies engage in *reprogramming*—that is, taking money appropriated for one program and diverting it to another that emerges as a higher priority. This strategy must be undertaken with great care, however, not only because of legal and ethical implications, but because efforts to subvert the legislature's intention arc likely to incur retribution in the next year's budget process.

AUDIT PHASE

The final phase of the budget process is the postexecution or audit phase. *Postaudits* take place following the end of the fiscal year and are concerned with verifying the correctness and propriety of agency operations. These audits were originally designed to assure financial control; as such, they focused on accuracy of record keeping, on compliance with statutes, and on uncovering fraud, waste, and mismanagement. More recently, the concept of auditing has been broadened to include **performance auditing**—analyzing and evaluating the effective performance of agencies in carrying out their objectives.

Three purposes are served by postaudits: (1) financial viability, as indicated by efficient use of resources; (2) compliance with statutes and other limitations; and (3) program performance, including the results of program operations.

Agencies themselves can carry out audits; indeed, we have already seen how the auditing work of inspectors general has revealed waste and fraud in some agencies. There is a clear trend, however, toward broader use of independent agencies. Moreover, to maintain detachment in their review of executive agencies, the postaudit function is increasingly being attached to the legislative rather than the executive branch. In 1921, for example, the federal government created the General Accounting Office as a support agency of the Congress, although President Wilson had previously vetoed such legislation on the grounds that the officers of such an agency should be answerable to the executive rather than the legislature. As we saw, the GAO was originally concerned primarily with the financial auditing of selected federal agencies; however, more recently, it has extended its activities to include program evaluations as well.

At the state level, organizational arrangements vary; however, the trend toward having postaudit agencies attached to the legislature is clear. In 1938, there were five states in which the audit function was part of the legislative branch; in 1960, there were fifteen; today, there are more than forty (CSG, 1993). A large number of states retain an elected state auditor, however, whose office often goes beyond detached analysis and becomes embroiled in political controversy. Finally, a number of large cities, including Dallas and Seattle, have developed legislative postaudit functions.

APPROACHES TO PUBLIC BUDGETING

To be an effective tool in management and decision making, the budget must present information about the purposes of the proposed activity and the resources to be expended. There are a variety of different ways to present such information. Some approaches to budgeting, for example, are based on the assumption that budget decisions are (and should be) largely *incremental*—policy makers start with the given situation (last year's budget) as a base and make only marginal adjustments to that base. Following this approach, managers build budgets by asking for limited increases in spending rather than focusing on major programmatic concerns. Similarly, the legislature focuses on individual expenditures rather than the "big picture." According to proponents of incrementalism, this approach is not only an accurate representation of the actual behavior of decision makers, it is an appropriate way to maintain balance among the many different interests represented in the budget. In contrast, other budget theorists argue for a more rational, comprehensive, and programmatic approach.

Budgets can be categorized according to the purposes they serve. Allen Schick, a leading scholar in the field of budgeting, has suggested that budgets can have at least three different purposes, all of which are reflected in any approach to budgeting. These purposes are planning, management, and control. *Planning* involves the determination of organizational objectives and the development of strategies to meet those objectives; *management* involves the design of organizational means by which approved goals can be translated into action, as well as developing the staffing and resources necessary for execution; *control* refers to "the process of binding operating officials to the policies and plans set by their superiors." According to Schick, each attempt at budget reform changes the balance among the three purposes—sometimes inadvertently, sometimes deliberately. Understanding how budgets are put together will help you present an effective case for program changes.

THE LINE-ITEM BUDGET

Those who established the first systematic governmental budgeting schemes were concerned primarily with assuring the public that expenditures were properly made and accounted for. Consequently, the systems they designed emphasized the control function. Because all agencies purchase essentially the same kinds of goods and services, it was argued, account classifications could be designed that would be broadly applicable to various agencies or departments. It would then be possible for auditors to apply uniform criteria to evaluate the expenditures of all (Lyden & Lindenberg, 1983, p. 67).

Accordingly, in what is called a **line-item** or *objects of expenditure* **budget,** categories of expenditures are listed along with amounts allocated to each. Typically, line-item budgets are organized by departments, so that the budget for one agency might look something like this:

	1998	1999
Salaries and wages	$75,300	$94,400
Utilities	12,320	13,750
Supplies and materials	13,500	13,950
Travel	950	750
Printing	1,200	1,350
Telephone	1,550	1,900

The cost of each object of expenditure is generally based on the agency's past experience and analysis of expected changes during the budget year. Since personnel costs (salaries, wages, and other personal services) typically constitute over half the budget, special attention is given to projected staffing changes, and such changes are often appended to the budget. (Our example projects, among other things, the addition of one clerical person during the upcoming year.)

The line-item budget continues to be widely used, partly because it is easy to understand and partly because it offers political leaders the more palatable option of reducing items (such as travel) rather than eliminating "programs." Moreover, it is well suited to incremental decisions, which make only minor modifications in the previous budget. However, because in the line-item budget the focus is on expenditures, not on their results, it is of little benefit to planning or management. Consequently, budget reformers have sought to balance the line-item budget's advantage of effective control with attention to other purposes as well.

THE PERFORMANCE BUDGET

The 1930s proved a turning point with respect to public budgeting. The federal budget grew tremendously, the Bureau of the Budget became attached to the White House, and, in general, greater attention was paid to the executive management of government agencies. This interest in management was paralleled at the state and local levels, where efforts to relate budget presentations to programmatic activities had been under way for some time. The result was a new approach to budgeting, the performance budget.

The **performance budget** is organized around programs or activities rather than departments and includes various performance measurements to indicate the relationship between the work actually done and its cost. As the Hoover Commission described it, a performance budget "would analyze the work of government departments and agencies according to their functions, activities, or projects. It would concentrate attention on the work to be done or the service to be rendered, rather than the things to be acquired." By focusing on the relationship between available resources and the work to be done, performance budgeting is well suited to the purposes of management.

To construct a performance budget, the manager must first determine appropriate program categories, such as highway safety, then break that program down into appropriate subprograms, such as school visitations or advertising programs. It is then necessary to establish detailed work measures for each activity; for example, a highway safety program might anticipate twenty-seven school visitations during the course of the year. These data would then be related to the cost of making such visits. In its most detailed presentation, a performance budget requires identifying the work activity, establishing an output unit, calculating the cost of each unit, and projecting the units required and the associated costs for the coming year.

Although performance measures are obviously helpful in making budgetary decisions, not all organizations can easily develop such information. A license bureau can report the number of licenses issued and fairly easily calculate the cost per license issued, but a research unit or a group promoting civil rights would find its work much more difficult to measure. Performance budgeting also tends to concentrate on quantity of work rather than quality.

Finally, performance budgeting somewhat diffuses organizational responsibility, because one program or function may be located in several different units. "Public information," for example, may involve work in the mayor's office, police department, fire department, and elsewhere. To sort out costs by department, one would need to construct a crosswalk or matrix of expenditures. A matrix might place various activities on one dimension and departments on another:

| | Activities | | | |
	1	*2*	*3*	*Totals*
Division A	$10,000	$20,000	$15,000	$45,000
Division B	12,000	16,000	10,000	38,000
Division C	5,000	12,000	13,000	30,000
Totals	27,000	48,000	38,000	

A matrix could also be constructed relating activities to traditional objects of expenditure; such calculations are typical in performance budgets.

PROGRAM BUDGETING

Another approach to budgeting had its origins in the Department of Defense in the early 1960s. Soon after taking office as Secretary of Defense, Robert McNamara discovered that his ability to manage the department was severely restricted by the lack of coordination between planning and budgeting. Each service (army, navy, air force) prepared its own annual budget, reflecting its own priorities, then submitted the documents to the secretary. Obviously, this plan failed to give proper attention to systemwide issues. But, equally important, because the budgeting system was based on a one-year time frame, it bore little, if any, relation to the multiyear projections of the department's planning and analysis staff. The development of major weapons systems, for example, involves research and development, assembly, and operations over many years, yet this fact was not clearly reflected in the annual budget submissions.

Consequently, McNamara instituted a new approach, which came to be known as the **planning-programming-budgeting system (PPBS)**, an effort to connect planning, systems analysis, and budgeting in a single exercise. In the Defense Department, PPBS began with the identification of nearly one thousand program elements, each grouped under one of nine major programs or missions—that is, strategic retaliatory forces, continental air and missile defense forces, civil defense, and so on. Not only was extensive study required to identify the right combination of program elements to support each mission, but, once having established the combinations, units in the department were required to submit detailed analyses of proposed program changes. In addition, the new budget system was designed to cover a nine-year period and to show detailed projections for the first six years. President Johnson was so impressed with the operation of PPBS in the Defense Department that he ordered the new system extended to all federal agencies. Each cabinet-level department was asked to identify a limited number of purposes to be served by the agency, then to organize budget requests around those themes. The Department of Health, Education, and Welfare, for example, chose topics such as "social and rehabilitation services" that cut across several agencies within HEW. Costs for each program element were projected five years into the future, and extensive documentation justifying each element was required, especially in areas undergoing significant changes. Most agencies were able to develop their budgets using the new approach, but there was considerable confusion in the implementation of PPBS. As a result of this confusion and for a variety of other political reasons, PPBS was formally terminated by President Nixon in 1971.

During its relatively short tenure, PPBS attracted great attention, with many cities, states, and other countries embracing the new technique. PPBS not only emphasized the planning aspect of budgeting, but it appeared to bring greater rationality and comprehensiveness to the budget process. These goals, however, were accomplished at great cost. Substantial numbers of new staff members were needed, both in the central budget office and in the various agencies to provide the kind of analysis PPBS required. All in all, the process proved extraordinarily time-consuming. Consequently, very few full-blown PPBS systems remain, although many of the principles of PPBS have been incorporated into other approaches, often under the more general label *program budgeting*.

There are important differences between performance budgeting and program budgeting. "As a general rule, performance budgeting is concerned with the *process of work* (what methods should be used) while program budgeting is concerned with the *purpose of work* (what activities should be authorized)" (Schick, 1987, p. 53). Where a performance budget might define the operations of a city garbage department in terms of collecting and disposing of garbage, a program budget might focus instead on the purpose served by collecting the garbage—to prevent infectious disease or to protect property values (Lyden & Lindenberg, 1983, pp. 92–93).

Moreover, although both systems urge measurement of work being done, performance budgeting is more likely to employ measures related to the work (for example, the number of tons of garbage collected) and a program budget might concentrate instead on measures related to the purpose of the work (for example, the rate of infectious disease in the community). Performance data are of great interest to individual managers who seek to improve productivity, but legislators and other policy makers are more likely to be interested in the purposes of various activities.

ZERO-BASE BUDGETING

One of the most recent budget reform efforts is **zero-base budgeting (ZBB)**, a technique developed by Texas Instruments and first applied in government by Jimmy Carter while he was governor of Georgia. As president, Carter mandated the use of ZBB in all federal agencies. ZBB does not mean that agencies must simply start over with each budget cycle, building and rebuilding justifications for all their programs; rather, ZBB seeks to structure the budget so as to present information about the efficiency and effectiveness of existing programs and also highlight possibilities for eliminating or reducing programs (Pyhrr, 1977, p. 1). In contrast to the program development emphasis in program budgeting, the emphasis in ZBB is on cutting back.

The ZBB process begins with identifying a *decision unit*, the lowest organizational unit at which significant program decisions are made. The manager of the decision unit is asked to prepare one or more *decision packages*, which explain each proposed program and contain the purpose, a description of the action to be undertaken, costs and benefits, and workload and performance measures. Top management and the legislature use the decision packages to compare various programs and rank the highest priorities.

As part of developing the decision packages, managers must provide two other types of information. First, they must identify alternative measures for accomplishing the work and indicate why these alternatives were not chosen. For example, an air quality laboratory might recommend using a centralized laboratory to conduct tests rather than conducting tests at regional locations or contracting with a local university (Pyhrr, 1977, p. 4). Second, managers must identify various funding levels: (1) a minimum level, (2) the level necessary to continue current operations, and (3) an improvement level. In each case, the manager must indicate the effects of the funding level on program performance.

For example, a minimum level of $140,000 might permit testing 37,000 air samples, meeting the minimum requirements of those who use the tests, and covering 70 percent of the state's population. An improvement level might require $246,000, but add additional urban areas and cover 90 percent of the population (Pyhrr, 1977, p. 4).

ZBB has been criticized for generating too much paperwork and for failing to provide effective criteria for ranking decision packages. In addition, the minimum funding level requirement has proven difficult to establish; many jurisdictions equate minimum funding with a certain percentage of the current level (e.g., 75 percent). For these and other reasons, ZBB was discontinued by President Reagan, though many agencies still employ some of its elements in their budget process.

OUTCOME-BASED BUDGETING

A recent trend in government budgeting involves increasing the level of accountability for public resources. Citizens, elected officials, and administrators want to be able to determine how much is being spent on each program or agency and the return on the public's investment—that is, the substantive impact of each policy. In practical terms, this requires linking budget information with some type of a performance measurement system. The resulting budget enables administrators to track levels of expenditures and report on the outcomes being achieved.

Unlike performance budgeting mentioned previously, outcome budgeting goes beyond looking at mere issues of productivity and unit cost. It assesses the long-term impact of each policy, program, or agency within its targeted area. Though based on quantitative measures, outcome-based budgeting determines the qualitative results of government initiatives. Many government agencies have incorporated outcome-based budgeting within their strategic planning processes, making it possible to observe the level of resources needed to reach goals and objectives and then use that information for budget decision making.

In Catawba County, North Carolina, local officials used outcome-based budgeting to enhance their government's system of service delivery. The county in the past few years had experienced limited growth in revenues; yet during this time the call for human services continued to rise. County leadership responded by handing decision-making authority to agency administrators, challenging them to reduce costs while more effectively meeting citizen demands. Those who achieved 90 percent of their goals would be able to apply their savings to unrestricted needs. Catawba County administrators embarked on a citizen-driven, outcome-based system of budgeting to ensure that resources were targeted to meet specific community goals. Over time, they not only saved money but also enhanced government responsiveness.

We will see later the way in which performance or outcome measurement has affected the conduct of the public's business at all levels of government. For now, we should simply note that the current federal budgeting system, like most at the state and local levels, is a combination of elements from several of the approaches we have discussed. What is most important is not whether one particular system or another is being used but rather what political and administrative choices underlie the selection of a particular budget approach. That is, what are decision makers trying to emphasize by using the type of budget they select?

BUDGETARY STRATEGIES AND POLITICAL GAMES

Despite all attempts to rationalize the budget process, public budgeting is an inherently political activity. The changing demands on government and its programs, the shifting interests that are brought to bear in policy decisions, and the many different actors (and personalities) that are part of the budget process mean that budget decisions will always occur in a highly charged political environment. As one student of the budget process described the situation, "Budgeting in this environment is a matter of negotiation, persuasion, bargaining, bluff and counter-bluff" (Caiden, 1985, p. 498). Because agency managers typically (and properly) believe in the programs they operate and would like to see the programs be of even greater benefit to the public, they tend to become advocates of an agency position, often seeking to expand the size and scope of the agency's work.

If you can deal effectively with the political environment in which budgeting occurs, you will likely be more successful in expanding, or at least maintaining, your agency's programs. (There are, of course, many cases in which you will be judged on your capacity to hold the line on expenditures or to manage program reductions.) Whatever your intent, understanding the politics of the budgetary process will be helpful.

In discussions of budgetary strategies, two basic concepts will help orient your thinking. The first is the notion of program base. The *base* refers to those elements of an agency's program that everyone expects will be continued from year to year. Under normal circumstances, the program's base is assumed to remain pretty much the same from one year to the next and is not subject to special scrutiny. Having an activity approved for one year is one thing; having that activity considered a part of your agency's base budget is far more important. A second and related concept is that of receiving a *fair share* of the overall budget. Managers often measure success in terms of whether their program receives a proportionate amount of any increases or decreases that the government generally supports. Agency personnel often work for years to build a base that they consider a fair share of the overall budget (Wildavsky, 1988, p. 83).

As we saw earlier, budget requests typically originate with the agencies. They are then reviewed and often changed by a central budget office (acting in behalf of the chief executive) and submitted to the legislature for approval. In constructing a budget request, you need to take into account several different types of expenditures. Many departments at the federal level have a large budget component that is essentially *uncontrollable*. The Department of Health and Human Services, for example, which administers many entitlement programs, has a large percentage of its budget that is essentially fixed. A second part of an agency's budget is likely to be devoted to *adjustments for inflation*. The rising cost of utilities, telephones, postage, and other essential services must be taken into account, either absorbed in the base or covered by increased expenditures. Finally, some part of the agency's budget is *discretionary*, subject to increase or decrease according to the agency's priorities. The discretionary portion of the budget allows you to decide both which new programs to propose and which existing activities to recommend for more (or less) funding. Understanding these categories will help you argue for changes in a particular budget.

STRATEGIES FOR PROGRAM DEVELOPMENT

These choices lead to strategic questions you must answer in building a budget—including the important question of what total amount to request. Although an overall budget is likely to differ only incrementally from that of the previous year, some agencies are clearly more assertive in their requests than others. That is, they are more willing to request large increases rather than small ones. But how assertive to be is conditioned by several factors.

Obviously, support from the chief executive (the president, governor, mayor, and so on) is highly important, whether the support is specific in terms of advocacy for a particular program or more generally an expression of interest in a particular field, such as law enforcement. Similarly, legislative support is also highly important. Agency personnel, in fact, work hard throughout the year to maintain contact with key legislative leaders and to build the kinds of alliances that will be helpful in supporting programs of mutual interest. Finally, your personality—especially your willingness to take risks and defend risky choices—will play a strong role in deciding how much to request.

Aaron Wildavsky, who wrote a landmark study of the politics of the budgetary process, suggested three other strategic elements that not only affect the nature of the request, but also help build political support for it. The first of these is *clientele support*. Obviously, the support of client groups and other associations interested in the agency's work will be helpful in developing testimony and lobbying in behalf of programs. An agency that is confident of the testimony of "satisfied customers" or able to show support for proposed changes will likely fare much better than others. Obviously, the most effective way to build support is to serve a client group well, but agencies may also try to stimulate supportive clientele to communicate with legislators about the agency's good work.

A second element of political support is the *confidence* of higher executives and legislative officials in your character and ability. The magnitude of government budgets is so great that higher officials or legislators simply cannot know all the details necessary for making a purely rational analysis. At some point, they must simply trust the manager. Managers who enjoy a good reputation are typically more successful, especially in dealings with the legislature (see Box 5.2). One administrator commented, "If you have the confidence of your [appropriations] subcommittee your life is much easier and you can do your department some good; if you don't have confidence you can't accomplish much and you are always in trouble" (Wildavsky, 1988, p. 105). There are many ways to build confidence, but highly successful managers seem to agree that a reputation for integrity (telling the whole truth) and responsiveness (keeping in touch and responding completely to inquiries) are particularly important.

Third, agency officials can take certain tactical positions to attempt to develop or protect their favorite programs. One approach, verging on the unethical but nonetheless common, is **budget padding**—that is, proposing a higher budget than is actually needed, on the assumption that after the central budget office and legislature cut it, you will have what you wanted in the first place. (One city manager described including "radio" items in his budget—a radio item was one that "makes a lot of noise but can be unplugged easily." The radio item would attract controversy and deflect attention from other items that were actually more important to the manager.) Another strategy is one Wildavsky

BOX 5.2

Play It Straight

Everyone agrees that the most important requirement for confidence, at least in a negative sense, is to be aboveboard. . . . A lie, an attempt to blatantly cover up some misdeed, a tricky move of any kind, can lead to an irreparable loss of confidence. A typical comment by an administrator states, "It doesn't pay to try to put something over on them [committee members] because if you get caught, you might as well pack your bags and leave Washington." And the chances of getting caught are considerable because interested committeemen and their staffs have much experience and many sources of information.

Administrators believe that punishments for failure to establish confidence are greater than the rewards for achieving it. But at times they do slip up, and then the roof falls in. When Congress limited the amount of funds that could be spent on personnel, a bureau apparently evaded this limitation in 1952 by subcontracting out a plan to private investors. The House Subcommittee was furious:

> *Representative Jensen:* It certainly is going to take a house-cleaning . . . of . . . all people who are responsible for this kind of business.
> *Official:* We are going to do it, Mr. Chairman.
> *Representative Jensen:* I do not mean "maybe." That is the most disgraceful showing that I have seen of any department.
> *Official:* I am awfully sorry.

SOURCE: Excerpted from Aaron Wildavsky and Naomi Caiden, *The New Politics of the Budgetary Process,* 3d ed. (New York: Longman).

---

terms the *camel's nose.* The manager asks for a small amount to begin a program, then later treats this program as part of the base and argues that it would be unfortunate to lose the money already invested by not finishing the job (Wildavsky, 1988, p. 115).

As we have seen, over the past couple of decades, many programs at all levels of government have experienced lower revenues and more limited funding. In some cases, such as in the social services, programs have been reduced or eliminated; in other cases, changes such as the termination of revenue sharing at one level of government have resulted in lower revenues at another; in still other cases, popular efforts to limit either revenues or expenditures, such as Proposition 13 in California, have limited government funds. In any case, many public managers have had to turn their attention from developing new programs to maintaining or even reducing existing ones. This effort has been variously referred to as *managing fiscal stress* or, where serious reductions have occurred, *cutback management.*

As you would expect under retrenchment conditions, many managers have used budgetary tactics of the sort outlined by Wildavsky to lessen the impact of fiscal stress on their agencies (Wildavsky, 1988, p. 113). Any attempt to resist cuts is risky, however, in part because it can quickly undermine the manager's credibility. Moreover, under conditions of long-term fiscal limitations, resistance to cuts is simply not a realistic option for many managers (Levine, 1980, p. 20). Several other ways of dealing with fiscal stress have been tried with some success:

- Following a *multiyear plan* so as to preserve the administrative capacity and the capital investment of the jurisdictions
- *Targeting* cuts in specific programs rather than cutting across the board (all programs cut at the same percentage)
- *Smoothing out* the impact of the cuts (lessening their immediate effect) (Levine, Rubin, & Wolohojian, 1981, p. 210). Smoothing out may occur either through improvements in productivity, so the organization can accomplish more with less, or by generating new revenues, through such moves as imposing new user charges for services.

ASPECTS OF FINANCIAL MANAGEMENT

Although those in public organizations need to budget their resources, they must also attend to other aspects of managing the public's money. They must be concerned with the long-term financing of buildings, roads and highways, and equipment; they must carefully plan and manage borrowing; they must ensure against future losses; and, in all cases, they must try to get the most for the money they spend. (See Chapter 8.)

NETWORKING

For more information on financial management see http://www.financenet.gov/.

CAPITAL BUDGETING

In addition to budgeting annual expenditures, public policy makers and managers need to invest in facilities and equipment that will be used over a period of time. For example, government is primarily responsible for developing and maintaining the country's public works *infrastructure*—streets and highways, tunnels and bridges, sewers and water treatment facilities, and so on. In addition, governments invest in a variety of other major facilities, including schools and universities, hospitals and mental health centers, public housing, and correctional institutions. Finally, innumerable equipment purchases (especially military equipment at the federal level) are intended for long-term use. Expenditures on items that will be used over a period of several years are called **capital expenditures.**

Budgeting for capital expenditures is similar to the process of budgeting for annual expenditures, but it also differs in some ways. In most jurisdictions, with the federal government as the most notable exception, capital expenditures are treated in a separate budget called a *capital budget.* Most states have a separate capital budget, and nearly all give special treatment to capital expenditures in budget presentation; nearly all major cities and most other local governments use a capital budget. For many years, the federal government treated capital spending merely as part of the regular budget; only recently has it begun to provide a special analysis of capital spending. There is still not a separate capital budget at the federal level.

The primary argument in favor of separate consideration of capital items is that the benefits of these items are spread over future generations, and it is therefore not unreasonable to share the burden of repaying the money borrowed. A separate capital budget may also encourage more long-term thinking—the lack of which is often decried in the annual budget process. On the other hand, the capital budget can become a political "pork barrel," in which each legislator seeks to gain his or her share of projects (and their funding). Moreover, a capital budget can become a device for avoiding fiscal responsibility, by pushing expenditures that should be faced immediately into an indefinite future. In any case, whether a separate budget is developed or not, one should keep in mind the relationship between capital and operating expenditures. Building a new swimming pool, for example, implies that annual expenditures will be forthcoming in future years to keep it operating.

Ideally, a capital budget develops in the context of a fairly comprehensive planning process, undertaken either for the government as a whole or by the various agencies within their functional areas (such as health or criminal justice). Whether or not a planning process is in operation, an important intermediate step (and one followed by nearly all governments considering capital projects) is development of a *capital investment program*—a timetable indicating various projects to be undertaken, schedules for their completion, and methods of financing. A capital investment plan is usually written to cover a three-to-five year period and is moved forward each year. The state of Georgia, for example, has a capital budget that is mainly a gathering of capital outlays by agency and project category as these have been requested by the various agencies in their submissions to the budget office. For each category, the financing source is identified (Thomassen, 1990, p. 73).

To undertake such a plan, government decision makers often solicit proposals from the various agencies and then try to bring order to the resulting submissions. Among the criteria decision makers might use would be the essentiality of the project, especially for health and safety; whether the project fills a gap in existing services; whether it builds effectively on existing services; and whether it meets an unforeseen emergency need (Lyden & Lindenberg, 1983, p. 185). Because financing for capital projects is usually spread over many years, as are the benefits, complete analysis of each project is likely to involve detailed consideration of both costs and benefits over time.

DEBT MANAGEMENT

One part of the capital budgeting process is careful consideration of the source of funding. Some jurisdictions try to operate on a "pay-as-you-go" basis, paying in full for all projects during the fiscal year in which they are authorized. (One variation of this idea is the accumulation of money in a *sinking fund,* something like a Christmas Club account, which is then used to pay for the needed improvement.) Other jurisdictions may be willing to borrow money for a project, either because waiting to accumulate funds would simply take too long or because, philosophically, it is felt that the costs as well as the benefits of the project should be spread over a period of years—a "pay-as-you-use" approach.

Borrowing is often used to finance capital improvement projects; but borrowing may be employed to meet a variety of other needs as well. In some cases, anticipated revenues will simply not be available at the time spending is necessary. To solve the resulting "cash-flow" problem, governments undertake short-term borrowing. (In more questionable cases, money is borrowed from future years' revenues to pay operating expenses within the current year. Such a practice was partly responsible for the financial crisis in New York City in the mid-1970s.) Borrowing is also used for emergency needs; for example, a natural disaster, such as fire or flood, might require funds far beyond the capacity of the annual budget. Especially when such spending will be used to reconstruct facilities that will have long-term benefits, borrowing may well be justified. Finally, at least at the federal level, borrowing is sometimes justified as a way of stimulating the economy.

Governments may undertake various types of borrowing; however, the primary mechanism for financing government debt is the issuance of a **bond**—that is, a promise to repay a certain amount *(principal)* at a certain time *(maturity date)* at a particular *rate of interest.* One of the most common bonds is the *general obligation bond,* which pledges the "full faith and credit" of the jurisdiction—in other words, the government provides as security all its revenues and resources. In contrast, *revenue bonds* promise as security the anticipated revenues that a capital project will produce. Revenue bonds might be issued based on the future toll receipts of a new highway or on the gross receipts of a new municipal sports complex.

Both from the standpoint of a jurisdiction, and from the standpoint of potential investors who might purchase the bonds, it is helpful to know something about the jurisdiction's **debt capacity**—if a city, the value of the city's resources combined with the ability of the city government to draw on the city's resources to provide payment. As a service to investors, several firms provide bond ratings for cities and other jurisdictions. The ratings are also important to the jurisdiction, because a lower rating means higher costs of borrowing for the government. Standard and Poor's reference guides rate bonds in descending quality from "AAA" to "AA" to "A" to "BBB" to "BB," and so on. Cities or other government units that carry high ratings will be more successful than others in selling their bonds.

Obviously, the capacity of a government to manage successfully its various financial obligations is of great importance. For example, the Clinton administration proposed altering the mix of securities used to finance the national debt, in order to take advantage of the spread between long-term and short-term debt. Without going into the details of the plan, some experts claimed the idea could save the government more than $16 billion over the next five years (*Congressional Quarterly Weekly,* 20 March 1993, p. 657). (For another example of the complexity of such issues, see Box 5.3.)

RISK MANAGEMENT

Public organizations are subject to a variety of risks that can prove extremely costly. A few years ago, for example, an individual who was driving through a particular city lost control of his car, which bounced off a guardrail into a ditch. The driver suffered serious injuries, then sued the city for several million dollars, arguing that the guardrail had been improperly placed. Similarly, a city employee, with no previous health problems,

BOX 5.3

How to Limit Losses Due to Accidents or Injuries

In the local government workplace every accident, claim or incident may involve uninsured or underinsured losses and/or deductibles that can become costly for municipalities. Although such situations may be virtually unavoidable in the long run, loss control planning can limit their negative consequences.

The costs of accidents can be viewed as the various disruptions of the normal work procedures that occur when the accidents take place. City or county property may be damaged and contractors may need to be hired—not a welcome expense in times of tight municipal budgets. Accidents can result in downtime, extra administrative time, retraining of existing workers and training of replacement workers. Downtime can mean delayed completion of work.

These are just a few of the costs that are absorbed by local governments; in some cases, the costs can exceed the amounts covered by insurance. Effective loss control can help to reduce these costs. A qualified loss control professional can provide safety surveys of local government facilities. He or she can help implement a methodical approach to self inspection, training, and loss prevention.

Developing a safety plan is perhaps the most important component of a methodical approach to loss control. For the plan to be effective, top officials must be committed to it, and someone must be given the responsibility, authority, and budget for seeing the plan through. Carrying out an accident analysis is the first step in developing a successful safety plan. Staff members in charge of the analysis should review and categorize the local government's past accident cases and identify the causes of each case, as well as the patterns and related factors among the different cases.

The next step, communication and training, involves sharing the information compiled through the accident analysis with those who might be affected by similar accidents in the future. The training element of this step can take the form of five- or ten-minute safety talks or more formal training. Department leaders can also supplement the safety training of their employees with informational posters, printed bulletins, paycheck stuffers or novelty gifts as reminders of safety precautions. They can motivate employees to heed these precautions through formal directives and work rules, as well as through contests and incentives.

Supervisors play a critical role in successful safety programs. Thus, training for supervisors is an excellent idea, since they need to understand the goals of management concerning safety, buy into those goals, and be equipped to work with their employees toward the objectives. Supervisors are responsible for field implementation of the safety plan and directives. Supervisors should thus be held accountable for the safety performance of their departments or agencies, just as they are held accountable for their department's general performance.

The next step, inspection, is necessary to ensure compliance with injury control measures, as well as to follow up on the findings of the accident analysis. In areas where physical conditions can be altered to prevent reoccurrence of historical problems, the city or county should issue work orders to solve the problems. If a machine contributed to a past accident, all similar machines should be inspected and altered accordingly.

Insurance costs and uninsured costs are too high for local governments to ignore. Controlling these costs means looking methodically at past problems and striving to make sure they do not reappear.

SOURCE: Salzman, Scott. "Cutting Your Losses in the Workplace." *American City & County* 112, (June 1997): 6.

began to suffer back pains on the job. After several operations, high medical bills, and physical therapy, he was given disability retirement at age twenty-six (Lynch, 1985, p. 316). Another city was sued by residents who lived near the municipal airport, because the noise of aircraft landing and taking off supposedly lessened the value of their property. Over the years, cases such as these involving civil damages, breach of contract, workers' compensation, and related legal problems have cost cities, states, and other jurisdictions millions of dollars.

Risk management concerns how public organizations anticipate and cope with these risks. Obviously, a first step in risk management is to identify potential areas of loss and then to attempt to reduce the probability of losses occurring. Risk reduction programs might include improved work safety, periodic inspections of physical property owned by the city, and employee health programs. But whatever the success of risk reduction efforts, losses do occur. The government has a variety of options for meeting losses, including payment from operating funds or financial reserves, levying special taxes to cover the loss, or even floating bonds.

In anticipation of losses, however, many public organizations purchase insurance often from private firms. In recent years, this option has become more difficult, as insurance rates for governments and other public organizations have risen dramatically and put many traditional forms of insurance beyond reach. (The difficulty of purchasing insurance has also led some jurisdictions to eliminate uninsured services such as some recreation programs.) Another possibility, however, is *self-insurance*, the development of an insurance pool by the jurisdiction itself. After all, many governments are larger than insurance companies, so such an undertaking is not only financially feasible, but provides some administrative control and flexibility that is not present when private firms are used. An increasingly popular means of self-insurance involves pooling risks in a shared program operated by several municipalities.

PURCHASING

A final aspect of financial management in public organizations is the purchase of goods and services. Because public organizations are typically not equipped to produce all the goods and services they require (and in most cases would not find it financially feasible to do so anyway), they must acquire some goods and services from the private sector. Like individuals and businesses, public organizations want to get the most for their money. But at the same time, because government purchasing involves such substantial sums of money and is capable of influencing the structure of the market generally, public purchasing must also take into account social and political goals.

Governments have often found that centralizing purchasing in one agency, rather than having each agency buy what it needs, results in considerable savings. For one thing, a central purchasing unit can buy in sufficient volume to get better prices; for another, those in the purchasing unit can develop expertise with respect to pricing, business conditions, and market practices. Finally, experts in purchasing are likely to be more successful in the negotiating process. Although individual agencies occasionally complain that their specific needs are not met by the purchasing unit, most state and local jurisdictions use centralized purchasing operations.

In most cases, a purchasing unit circulates and advertises the government's needs and solicits bids for the required goods and services. The resulting bids are evaluated in terms of cost, and the lowest bid is usually, though not automatically, chosen. Consideration is also given to the quality of the product and to the ability of the firm to actually deliver the goods or services in a timely fashion. In addition, purchasers are often required to give special preference to certain groups, such as minority-owned firms or in-state companies. Several jurisdictions often join together to cooperate in purchasing activities. In some instances, several local governments may form a common purchasing unit; in other cases, prices negotiated by the state purchasing office are available to local governments as well.

ACCOUNTING AND COMPUTER-BASED
INFORMATION SYSTEMS

Keeping track of the revenues and expenditures of government and other public organizations is an enormously complex task. Not only are there billions of dollars to record and report, but the presentation of financial information must serve several purposes at once. Certainly financial data should be developed and reported in such a way that public officials can be held accountable for the use of public funds, but at the same time, the accounting and reporting system should provide managers with information they can use to operate their organizations more efficiently and effectively. This dual requirement means that financial information should correlate closely with other managerially relevant material, such as personnel data or productivity measures.

GOVERNMENT ACCOUNTING

Accounting, whether in the public or private sector, is simply "the process of identifying, measuring, and communicating economic information to permit informed judgment and decision making by users of the information" (Berne & Schramm, 1986, p. 12). But because the purposes of public organizations differ from those of private organizations, accounting practices also differ. Those in public organizations, for example, are generally not concerned with making a profit; rather, they tend to focus on achieving a balance between revenues and expenditures—what comes in and what goes out. There are some exceptions, such as public corporations, hospitals, and water companies, which are somewhat more like profit-seeking groups; however, in nearly all public organizations, accountability is more important than profit maximization.

Governmental accounting systems reflect these different purposes. The cornerstone of accounting in the public sector is the allocation of resources to various funds, each of which is designed to record transactions within a particular functional area and assure that funds are used in accord with the purposes sought. (Use of such funds is uncommon in the private sector.) The various funds typically reflect policy makers' intent in authorizing certain activities and appropriating funds for them. The legislature may decide, for example, that certain gasoline taxes should be used exclusively for highway maintenance, in which case a separate fund might be created to keep track of money produced by the tax and spent for highways. In all cases, a primary concern is that the accounting system show whether the organization's activities have been consistent with the purposes for which it was created. There are several broad types of funds that are used in public organizations.

1. *General government funds* are used to account for most of the ordinary or routine functions of government. Most important among the general government funds is what is called the **general fund,** which handles the "unrestricted" funds of government, those not restricted to specific purposes (and typically allocated to other funds). The general fund is the dominant fund in most jurisdictions, and handles most of the government's operational activities. Related general government funds might include those that account for special revenues, like a dedicated gasoline tax, or those that monitor expenditures for capital projects.

2. **Proprietary funds** are used to account for government activities or enterprises that more closely resemble private business in their orientation toward profit. This does not mean that all agencies employing funds are required to make a profit; indeed, they may break even or perhaps require a subsidy. What is implied is that a measure of profit is possible and usually desirable in such operations; examples include a local transit system or a state printing operation.

3. Finally, **fiduciary funds** are used when the government must hold assets for individuals (e.g., those in a pension fund) or when the government holds resources to be transmitted to another organization (e.g., property taxes that a county collects for a city) (Berne & Schramm, 1986, pp. 14–15).

Within each fund there is an accounting of the resources available and the flow of funds in and out of the account. On the one hand, there are *assets*—what the government owns; on the other hand, there are *liabilities*—what the government *owes*. Assets include items such as cash, capital facilities, equipment, and money owed to the government; liabilities include items such as bills that the government has yet to pay. When the organization's liabilities are subtracted from its assets, the remainder is called a *fund balance* (and may be expressed either in positive or negative terms). An organization with $2,525,000 in assets and $2,300,000 in liabilities has a fund balance of $225,000. Note that a fund balance does not mean the amount of "cash on hand," but rather signifies a relationship between all assets (including cash) and all liabilities. Broadly, the fund balance is the key measure of the viability of the operation monitored by the fund and is one of many items contained in financial reports issued by governments and other public organizations.

Both accounting practices and financial reporting are guided by standards referred to as "generally accepted accounting practices." The Governmental Accounting Standards Board was established in 1984 to develop standards for accounting and financial reporting at the state and local levels. In its work, the GASB has been especially attentive to multiple users of public financial information, including citizens, taxpayers, legislative bodies, upper-level executives, labor and employee groups, interest groups, contractors, and the press. Again, an important characteristic of governmental accounting is that it must serve multiple purposes, including accountability within a democratic system.

COMPUTER-BASED INFORMATION SYSTEMS

The emergence and widespread use of computers in tracking financial data as well as other program-relevant information has led to what one writer has called a "quiet revolution" in the analysis and use of information in public organizations (Botner, 1983). Not only do computers make easier the accumulation and manipulation of vast amounts of data, they also greatly facilitate analysis of that data in terms that are meaningful to decision makers at all levels. Computers have also increased the probability that information can be provided when it is needed, not weeks later. Consequently, a great deal of attention is being given to design and implementation of computer-based information systems in the public sector and to the political and organizational implications of such changes. Applications in the area of financial management have often led the way in these efforts.

A distinction is often made between management information systems and decision support systems. *Management information systems* collect and summarize routine information as a basis for structuring decision making. Relevant data bases might include budgetary information, expenditures for salaries and wages, and personnel data. The system might be asked, for example, to produce a list of employees eligible for salary increases based on length of service in the agency (McGowan & Lombardo, 1986, p. 581).

Decision support systems, on the other hand, are interactive systems that can assist in the solution of unstructured or nonroutine problems. These systems can range in capabilities from one that allows the manager to manipulate data within the system to produce a specific analysis for a particular decision to one that provides optimization models to use in analyzing a particular policy recommendation. Although most public organizations are developing management information systems of various sorts, the development of decision support systems remains somewhat behind, though we can expect increasing attention to this area in the future.

Applications of computer-based information systems are as wide-ranging as the work of public organizations; however, most organizations are quickly becoming familiar with the use of spreadsheets and statistical packages for budget analysis, financial management packages for revenue and expenditure forecasting, and accounting packages for fund accounting and analysis. But far more extensive applications of information technology have been developed in government agencies. A recent survey indicates that federal agencies vary considerably in use of computer-based information systems, but in the area of financial management, some agencies have developed quite sophisticated systems. The Department of State, for example, has developed and implemented a comprehensive system designed to operate in the department's financial management centers around the world. Other federal agencies have yet to develop agencywide financial management information systems, though all seem to be moving in that direction. In the meantime, all agencies report extensive and varied applications of information technology throughout their organizations.

At the state and local levels, one of the most interesting developments in information technology has been the design and implementation of information systems integrating budgeting, personnel, performance reporting, and auditing. Several states have begun this process of integration, including Michigan, Oregon, Texas, Wyoming, and Washington. Yet efforts of this nature reflect an overall shift on the part of states toward more sophisticated systems of accounting. State governments over the past decade have used information technology to enhance their capacity to generate more detailed financial data, thus allowing for extensive analyses at a variety of organizational and programmatic levels. Over the coming few years, some expect this trend to continue and include forms of cost accounting, which links expenditures with the actual performance or tasks completed.

To the extent that budgetary and performance data are made available to the chief executive and other top managers on a timely basis, more effective management decisions will be possible. In addition, freeing budget analysts from the more mundane aspects of budgetary procedures should allow more attention to planning and analysis. Whether more effective planning results from the increased use of information technology remains to be seen. Some argue that such changes in organizational culture and practice require far more than increased capacity to handle information.

Similar developments have occurred at the local level, especially as the cost and availability of computer technology has made the adoption of information systems possible even in the smallest communities. For example, some local governments have started using microcomputers and the latest spreadsheet applications to simplify complex financial presentations. San Francisco's Public Utilities Commission (PUC) recently employed a new spreadsheet package to condense its 500-page, $400 million budget document into a single page. Commissioners in the past had to sort through a six-inch high stack of data from each of PUC's four divisions, making budget review and financial analysis an exhaustive, time-consuming process. With the new system, however, commissioners can get a quick glance at the cost for each of its diverse operations. In what used to take hours, PUC can in just minutes gain a clear understanding of the revenues and expenditures for the coming fiscal year.

SUMMARY AND ACTION IMPLICATIONS

Budgeting and financial management in public organizations share much in common with those activities elsewhere. But there are also important differences, most of which flow from the necessity for public organizations to be accountable to elected officials and, ultimately, to the people.

The centrality of the budget to any organization can hardly be underestimated; if you want to know what's going on in an organization, look at where the money is going. Establishing budget processes that reflect the organization's priorities, while securing appropriate levels of involvement from all those who will want to affect the budget, is thus extremely important. Finding ways to present budgetary information clearly and comprehensibly is a great aid to decision makers and to the public. Finally, developing mechanisms to assure that the public's money is being spent both efficiently and responsibly is essential. You will find that knowing the technical side of the budget process—being able to follow the budget process and clearly understanding preparation, administration, and review—will be extremely helpful as you try to influence the operations of your organization.

If you work in a central budget office, you will find that the period during which the budget is formulated is intense, and your technical expertise will be put to the test. But you will also recognize that you are playing an important role in shaping public policies. Similarly, if you are managing an agency, you will place your imprint on the policies and directions of your organization through the budget process. Your skill in presenting and supporting requests for programs may determine whether or not they are undertaken.

The budget process at the federal level, and in some state and local jurisdictions, is integrated with a process for long-range planning. Federal agencies are asked to provide certain projections for the two-year period following the year for which the budget is being prepared, thus adding an element of long-range planning to the process.

Budgets and financial management systems are important tools for planning, prioritizing, and operating public programs, as well as important mechanisms for accountability and control. Public access to budgets and financial statements allows citizens to see how their interests are reflected in the actual conduct of government. Budgets and other financial documents that clearly show what is happening in an agency are a necessary part of operating in the public interest.

Terms and Definitions

Accounting: The process of identifying, measuring, and communicating economic information to permit informed judgment and decision making.

Allotments: Amounts that agencies are authorized to spend within a given period.

Apportionment: The process by which funds are allocated to agencies for specific portions of the year.

Appropriation: Legislative action to set aside funds and create budget authority for their expenditures.

Authorizing legislation: Legislative action that permits establishment or continuation of a particular program or agency.

Bond: Promise to repay a certain amount (principal) at a certain time (maturity date) at a particular rate of interest.

Budget padding: Proposing a higher budget than is actually needed.

Business cycle: Periods of economic growth featuring inflation and high employment followed by periods of recession or depression and unemployment.

Capital expenditures: Spending for items that will be used over a period of several years.

Continuing resolution: Resolution permitting the government to continue operating until an appropriations measure is passed.

Debt capacity: Value of a city's resources combined with the ability of the government to draw on them to provide payment.

Deferral: Decision by the president to withhold expenditure of funds for a brief period.

Discretionary spending: That portion of the budget still open to changes by the president and Congress.

Entitlement programs: Programs that provide a specified set of benefits to those who meet certain eligibility requirements.

Excise tax: Tax applied to the sale of specific commodities.

Fiduciary funds: Funds used when government must hold assets for individuals or when government holds resources to be transmitted to another organization.

Fiscal policy: Public policy concerned with the impact of government taxation and spending on the economy.

Fiscal year (FY): Government's basic accounting period.

General fund: Fund that handles the "unrestricted" funds of government.

Gross National Product (GNP): Measure of total spending in the economy; includes total personal consumption, private investment, and government purchases.

Impoundment: Withholding of funds authorized and appropriated by law.

Item veto: Allows the executive to veto specific items in an appropriations bill.

Line-item budget: Budget format for listing categories of expenditures along with amounts allocated to each.

Outcome-based budgeting: Budgeting system that takes into account long-term effects or outcomes.

Performance auditing: Analysis and evaluation of the effective performance of agencies in carrying out their objectives.

Performance budget: Budget format organized around programs or activities, including various performance measurements that indicate the relationship between work actually done and its cost.

Planning-programming-budgeting system (PPBS): Effort to connect planning, systems analysis, and budgeting in a single exercise.

Preaudit: Review in advance of an actual expenditure.

Progressive tax: One that taxes those with higher incomes at a higher rate.

Proportional tax: One that taxes everyone at the same rate.

Proprietary funds: Used to account for government activities that more closely resemble private business.

Reconciliation bill: Legislative action that attempts to reconcile individual actions in taxes, authorizations, or appropriations with the totals.

Regressive tax: One that taxes those with lower incomes at a proportionally higher rate than those with higher incomes.

Rescission: Presidential decision to permanently withhold funds.

Risk management: Ways that public organizations anticipate and cope with risks.

Supplemental appropriation: Bill passed during the fiscal year adding new money to an agency's budget for the same fiscal year.

Zero-base budgeting: Budget format that presents information about the efficiency and effectiveness of existing programs and highlights possibilities for eliminating or reducing programs.

Study Questions

1. Discuss how government uses the budget to affect fiscal policy.
2. Describe some of the ways government obtains funds for operation. Identify the various types of taxes that governments use.
3. How does the government spend the money it collects?
4. The budget cycle consists of four major phases. Discuss government's role in the budget cycle and the components of each phase.
5. Allen Schick suggests three different purposes of the budget. Identify and define these purposes.

6. Compare and contrast the different types of budgeting processes.
7. Explain the two basic concepts of budgetary strategies.
8. Political influence has a major impact on the budgetary process. What are some of the strategies managers use to influence the budget process?
9. Financial management is also an important part of fiscal activities. Discuss some of the concerns fiscal managers deal with, including capital budgeting, debt management, risk management, and purchasing.
10. Discuss the broad types of funds that public organizations use.

Cases and Exercises

1. Revenues, especially at the state and local levels, can vary dramatically from year to year or even month to month, depending on both public actions and economic fluctuations.

   Assume that you are director of Motor Vehicle Registration for your state. Your agency, with offices scattered all across the state, is responsible for registration and licensing of cars, trucks, and other vehicles. About six months into the fiscal year, the governor announces that all state agencies will have to finish the fiscal year with expenditures 5 percent less than originally budgeted. You have already spent half your yearly allocation, so the reduction means you actually have to cut spending by 10 percent over the next six months. How would you go about complying with the governor's order?

2. On December 1, 1988, Larry Rice, the City Manager of Lakewood, Colorado, submitted the 1989 budget to the mayor and city council of Lakewood. Part of that budget dealing with activities in the public works area is shown in Figure 5.4. A public works summary page shows the 1987 actual, 1988 budgeted and estimated, and 1989 proposed expenditures, first by program, then by category of expenditure, then by source of funds.

   Following the summary page, there are two pages detailing public works activities in the area of snow and ice removal (line 9 of the summary page). Information is provided about performance standards, current services, and program objectives. Although the 1989 budget assumes a relatively flat revenue projection, several new budget initiatives are included, one of which is removal of snow from all residential streets when snow depth reaches six inches. (Note the increase in start-up and annual costs this item involves.)

   Analyze these budget pages from the perspective of (1) a city council member who will have to make decisions about which city services to fund; (2) the public works department director who wants to improve services to the community; and (3) an average citizen interested in seeing whether the city's tax dollars are being put to good use. For the purposes of each viewpoint, how complete and clear is the information? Does the budget tell you what you want to know in order to act? Does it present a convincing case for the initiative it contains? How might the budget presentation be improved?

PROGRAM	1987 ACTUAL	1988 BUDGET	1988 ESTIMATED	1989 BUDGET
Public Works Administration	$ 251,388	$ 212,983	$ 199,369	$ 196,298
Traffic Signals	788,913	957,404	1,182,739	934,777
Traffic Control	592,166	648,585	594,926	661,744
Street Lighting	808,501	945,752	901,500	920,652
Design Inspections and Survey	813,850	929,998	816,879	838,401
Development Review	342,080	366,324	354,618	368,022
Street Maintenance	1,604,400	1,561,003	1,607,462	1,592,208
Street Cleaning	423,154	484,322	483,094	497,097
Snow and Ice Removal	417,428	285,397	283,322	409,817
Street Resurfacing/Concrete Rehab.	2,611,102	2,000,342	2,720,000	2,003,384
Drainage Maintenance	379,232	351,007	315,382	304,545
Drainage Improvements	621,173	1,317,500	252,500	600,000
Capital Improvements:				
Street Construction	3,085,010	4,580,205	2,898,500	505,000
Fleet Management	(1,093,554)	(1,169,483)	(1,140,596)	(1,149,398)
Water Utility	400,086	—	558,154	500,333
Sewer Utility	1,385,950	2,852,892	2,165,168	2,731,163
TOTAL	$ 14,524,433	$ 17,493,714	$ 15,333,613	$ 13,063,441

CATEGORY	1987 ACTUAL	1988 BUDGET	1988 ESTIMATED	1989 BUDGET
Personal Services	$ 3,503,068	$ 3,552,303	$ 3,435,311	$ 3,512,808
Operating and Maintenance Supplies	665,666	644,114	655,276	656,050
Charges and Services	3,802,154	4,136,768	4,397,995	5,051,861
Capital Outlay	6,553,545	9,160,529	6,845,031	3,842,722
TOTAL	$ 14,524,433	$ 17,493,714	$ 15,333,613	$ 13,063,441

FUNDS	1987 ACTUAL	1988 BUDGET	1988 ESTIMATED	1989 BUDGET
General	$ 6,141,818	$ 6,325,775	$ 6,160,866	$ 6,323,561
Capital Improvement Fund	4,173,076	4,654,592	4,743,738	3,508,384
Grant Capital Fund	845,269	—	390,000	—
Central Garage Revolving	(1,093,554)	(1,169,483)	(1,140,596)	(1,149,398)
Street Bond	1,578,234	—	1,315,687	—
Nonrevenue Intergovernmental Resource	—	3,660,455	—	—
Water and Sewer Funds	1,786,036	2,852,892	2,723,322	3,231,496
TOTAL	$ 14,524,433	$ 17,493,714	$ 15,333,613	$ 13,063,441

FIGURE 5.4

City of Lakewood: Department of Public Works Budget Summary

3. Consider the following case:

You are Mike Smith, chief procurement officer for a major university. Work generated by your staff of twenty procurement specialists includes writing proposals to vendors and evaluating the vendors' bids. To write those bids, the procurement specialist works with someone from the university agency who is knowledgeable about the project. Tom Drake, a procurement specialist, is currently working with Kathy Kline of the

<u>DEPARTMENT</u>: Public Works   <u>PROGRAM</u>: SNOW AND ICE REMOVAL

<u>FUNCTIONAL DESCRIPTION:</u>

This program provides for the removal of snow and ice from the City street system (not including State Highways) and selected bikeways and sidewalks by plowing and sanding.

<u>SERVICE STANDARDS:</u> Services are standard when:

1.   All plows and sanders are hooked up within 90 minutes after notification of a coming storm and before every weekend and holiday through winter for faster deployment.

2.   75% of crews are on their routes within 1-1/2 hours of being called.

3.   Flowing begins on priority #1 and #2 streets when snow depth reaches 2". Plowing/sanding continues until all priority streets are cleared within 48 hours after the end of the storm.

4.   All residential streets (not priority 1 or 2) are plowed when snow depths reach 6". Plowing is completed within 48 hours after the end of the storm.

5.   Plowing or sanding requests received from citizens are written up for completion by snow removal crews and completed within 72 hours after the end of the storm, except during extremely heavy snowfalls and when this time is increased.

<u>CURRENT SERVICE EVALUATION:</u>

1.   Met.

2.   Met and exceeded.

3.   Met. Plowing starts at 2". Priority 1 and 2 streets are cleared within 48 hours after the end of a storm.

4.   Not met. Non-priority residential streets are currently not plowed except in storms of over 18"–24".

5.   Met.

<u>PROGRAM OBJECTIVES FOR THE COMING YEAR:</u>

1.   Meet service standard #4 to plow all residential streets when snow depth reaches 6 inches, at an annual cost of about $38,000 and $28,000 in initial start up costs.

2.   Computerize record keeping.

3.   Replace worn out sanders and plows in kind.

<u>STATISTICS</u>	<u>1983</u>	<u>1984</u>	<u>1985</u>	<u>1986</u>	<u>1987</u>	1988 Estimated	1989 Estimated
Number of deployments	24	19	21	17	19	15	15
Tons of sand/salt used	7905	3816	8493	4186	11,542	5,000	5,000
Inches of snow	151	118	76	78	107	75	75
Number of complaints	2385	249	528	583	1,648	500	500
Man hours	13,836	7178	10,363	7053	13,900	8,000	8,000

FIGURE 5.4 *continued*

Communications Department to develop a bid proposal to purchase a new campuswide telephone system that includes a quick-dial feature. The university's current telephone system was installed fifteen years ago by Regional Telephone, and over the last few years Regional and one other vendor have sold add-on equipment to five of the university's fifteen departments. This add-on equipment is expensive and represents a major investment to the five departments, one of which is the Communications Department. Departments that have the quick-dial equipment are pleased with the results; departments that do not have quick-dial cannot afford it and are unhappy with Regional.

DEPARTMENT: Public Works   **PROGRAM:** SNOW AND ICE REMOVAL

PROGRAM EXPENDITURE SUMMARY:

	1987 ACTUAL	1988 ESTIMATED	1989 BUDGET
PERSONNEL	$ 133,491	$ 119,727	$ 136,709
SUPPLIES	103,970	50,298	52,298
SERVICES	153,904	113,297	167,310
CAPITAL OUTLAY	26,063	—	53,500
TOTAL	$ 417,428	$ 283,322	$ 409,817

PROGRAM FUND SOURCES:

GENERAL FUND	$ 417,428	$ 283,322	$ 409,817

PERSONNEL ASSIGNED:

	1987 ACTUAL	1988 ESTIMATED	1989 BUDGET
Maintenance Operations Manager	.10	—	.10
Maintenance Supervisor	.40	.30	.30
Maintenance Crew Leader	.40	.40	.40
Clerk III	.25	.25	.25
Maintenance Specialist III	.50	.50	.50
Maintenance Specialist II	1.00	1.00	1.00
Maintenance Specialist I	.70	.60	.60
Maintenance Worker II	.80	.70	.70
TOTAL	4.15	3.75	3.85
Part Time	—	—	3,652 hr.

GENERAL COMMENTS:

The Snow and Ice Control Program has two shifts that are on rotation for 12 hours. There are ten priority #1 routes consisting of 247 lane miles and 6 zones of priority #2 routes with 265 lane miles.

In 1989 smaller units throughout various City Departments will be equipped with plows and used to clear residential streets when snow depth reaches 6 inches. Existing City employees will be utilitzed to operate the plow units.

FIGURE 5.4 *continued*

Tom has updated you on the status of the proposal. The Communications office has insisted throughout the proposal process that the new phone system must be capable of using the existing quick-dial equipment. Tom tells you that if that is the case, only Regional and two or three other vendors would be able to bid on the system. Six other vendors with their own quick-dial equipment would not be able to respond to the bid. Tom explains that in some cases, a whole new system was less expensive than hooking up one of Regional's systems to existing quick-dial equipment. Tom also tells you he has heard that several staff members from the Communications Department have threatened to quit if the bid goes to a company other than Regional. After fifteen years, they feel Regional is the best and only qualified vendor. Tom wants to know how he should proceed to satisfy both the university's needs and the vendors' rights to a fair bidding process.

SOURCE: The preceding case was provided by Bill Carney.

1. How should Tom proceed to ensure that all bidders have an equal chance to participate in the bid process?
2. How can the procurement office avoid the practice of vendors helping buyers to write
   a bid proposal?
3. What about Tom's responsibility to taxpayers? (Several thousands of dollars would be
   wasted if the quick-dial equipment already purchased was scrapped.)
4. The following is an exercise in zero-base budgeting:

   As superintendent of the Highway Patrol, you have been advised by your department head that only $13,950,000 will be available the next fiscal year for expenditure
by the Highway Patrol. You have four decision units that could each achieve several
performance levels with different funding levels. Rank your decision packages in order of decreasing benefit.

Function: Enforcement Activities, Highway Patrol

Decision Units

A. Traffic patrol
B. Criminal investigations
C. Checking of trucks
D. Citizen education

Decision Packages	Increments	Cost per Increment
A-1	1,000,000 miles	$8,000,000
A-2	500,000 miles	4,000,000
A-3	500,000 miles	4,000,000
B-1	3,000 investigations	600,000
B-2	1,000 investigations	200,000
B-3	1,000 investigations	200,000
C-1	10,000 truck checks	500,000
C-2	5,000 truck checks	250,000
C-3	5,000 truck checks	250,000
D-1	500 seminars	100,000
D-2	250 seminars	50,000
D-3	250 seminars	50,000

SOURCE: The preceding case was provided by Stanley Botner of the University of Missouri at Columbia.

5. The following simulation reenacts a series of budget discussions held at the University of Southern Anonymous (USA) during a time of significant budget reductions. To conduct the simulation, divide the class into five groups, each of which will represent one character in the simulation. All students in the class should read the following general description of the situation facing USA. Then members of each group should read only the character description assigned to their group. (It is important that you read only the description assigned to you.) The role descriptions of the following characters can be found after the general description of the situation in the following pages.

Vice President Cooper

Dean Berryderry, College of Liberal Arts

Dean Stevens, Dean of Science

Dean Dudley, Dean of Education

Dean Dollar, Dean of Business

After everyone has had a chance to read the general description of the situation and the specific information pertaining to their character, each character group should meet separately for fifteen to twenty minutes. During this period, the group should (1) select a representative to play the character at a meeting to be held in Vice President Cooper's office, and (2) develop detailed strategies and information for that person to use in representing your group's interests in the meeting.

Following the individual group meetings, the five individuals selected to play the five characters should meet around a table near the middle of the room. Vice President Cooper will call the meeting to order, present any opening remarks he or she wishes to make, then preside over the remainder of the discussion. All other students should remain quiet during this part of the simulation. During the course of the meeting, any member may request a recess to consult with his or her group (for no longer than five minutes). When the meeting in Vice President Cooper's office reconvenes, the person who called the recess will have the floor. The meeting should continue until a consensus is reached concerning the reductions or until Vice President Cooper feels the meeting is stalled and he or she will have to make a decision independently. Enjoy the discussion!

General Description of the Situation

The University of Southern Anonymous (USA) has been informed by the state administration that its budget for the current year will be reduced by several million dollars. The president of the University, I. M. Fearless, has informed Vice President for Academic Affairs Cooper that the various colleges in the university will be required to reduce their budgets by an average of 8 percent. In turn, Vice President Cooper has chosen not to implement across-the-board cuts of 8 percent for all colleges, but has discussed different target percentage reductions with each of the deans of the four colleges—Liberal Arts,

Science, Education, and Business. In response to a request from several of the deans, Vice President Cooper has called a meeting of the four deans to get their reactions to his targeted amounts for each college and to find out how each college plans to implement the required reduction.

By way of background, USA is a medium-sized Midwestern university with the mission of providing students with a broad-based liberal arts education as well as limited graduate programs, primarily in business and education. The school serves a regional constituency in the southern part of the state, though it draws students from around the country, many of whom first heard of USA because of its reputation as a leader in intercollegiate billiards. (In fact, some cynics refer to USA as "Cue U.")

Though the university has traditionally enjoyed a good relationship with the governor and members of the legislature, President Fearless has antagonized many in the state capital with his rough and abrasive manner. Similarly, many on campus see the president as bringing the university the same administrative style he employed as a colonel in the Marine Corps. Despite these difficulties, most academic programs at the university are considered sound, with some exceptions. Similarly, many feel some programs are not suited to the mission of a regional Midwestern university, notably the school's long-standing program in oceanography, which some feel is out of place because the university is seven hundred miles from the nearest ocean.

Character Descriptions

Vice President Cooper

In your five years as vice president at USA, you have never faced such a difficult situation. You recognize that the university's president is in some political trouble and may be asked to resign soon. As a ploy to reduce the heat on his office, he has passed on the largest part of the budgetary reductions to you. If you can come through this situation in good shape, you will receive considerable notoriety and be a likely candidate for the presidency should the president be forced to resign. You will, however, need to be sure that you maintain the support of all the deans of the colleges, for their support is essential for your promotion. On the other hand, a major disruption at the university, in which you might lose support of the deans, would end any chances of your attaining your ambition. In fact, you might be fired along with the president!

Given the instructions from the president, there seems to be little you can do other than to assign reductions to the colleges. After reviewing the various programs within the colleges, however, you have decided that across-the-board cuts would be inappropriate and that some colleges could indeed stand to be cut more than others. You have, therefore, assigned differential reductions to each college, with Education receiving the greatest reduction (20 percent), Liberal Arts receiving the second-greatest reduction (10 percent), Science next (7 percent), and Business last (2 percent). You have chosen these figures based on your assessment of the quality of programs, the quantity of students (faculty/student ratios), the nature of the programs, and their suitability to the mission of your university.

The total reductions you have assigned to the deans exceeds the total the president has required you to complete. Your reasons for this strategy are twofold: (1) if any of the deans complain too loudly, you can fall back to the figure you actually need as a compromise, and (2) if you persuade all the deans to accept the assigned reduction, then you will have some money available for internal reallocations, which you would like to achieve anyway.

For the most part, you are willing to let the various deans assign reductions within their colleges as they see fit, so long as each seems to be doing a thorough job in the assignment. Later, if there is money available, you can make other needed reallocations to add needed new programs or strengthen others.

However, you are personally interested in a couple of particular areas. First, your favorite uncle chairs the oceanography program. Second, your own degree is in higher education administration, and you have enjoyed periodic classroom visits to that department. Third, the governor has expressed a strong interest in the integrity of the public administration program.

Dean Berryderry

College of Liberal Arts (target reduction — 10 percent). You approach the meeting with the vice president with some trepidation, for you realize that your college is likely to be high on the list of cuts. Obviously, you would prefer across-the-board cuts that would not place a special burden on your college. Several of your programs, however, are of minimal quality and simply have not been attracting students over the years. For example, your program in German has graduated an average of two majors per year over the past several years, while having a faculty of three. Several other programs, such as anthropology and geography, are showing similar results. These programs, however, are important to a broad-based liberal arts education. You feel that students should at least have the opportunity to enroll in such programs if they see fit.

On the other hand, there are some programs currently housed in your college you would just as soon see ended. For example, the graduate program in public administration is a professional program that you feel is inconsistent with the liberal arts perspective of the college. The total faculty salaries in this department would just about equal the total by which you need to reduce your budget. This is an obvious area to eliminate.

Next, it has occurred to you that your staff of professional advisors could be eliminated and all academic advising performed by members of your faculty. This could be accomplished with no faculty or program reductions.

You feel a natural alliance with the College of Science and would prefer to see reductions occur in either Education or Business rather than in Liberal Arts or Science. However, Dean Stevens of the College of Science has always been somewhat antagonistic toward you, perhaps because of your critical remarks about the oceanography program, which you think should be eliminated.

Finally, several personal considerations enter into your thinking. First, if the vice president were to become president, you would probably be the leading candidate for the vice presidency. You would find that very attractive. Second, though you don't want to appear to favor any department, your home department, the Department of Political

Science, is putting strong pressure on you to support expansion of the program. Across-the-board cuts *within* your college would make that impossible. Third, a member of your faculty was recently offended by sexual advances from the dean of the School of Business, Dean Dollar.

Dean Stevens

Dean of the College of Science (target reduction—7 percent). You have conducted a thorough analysis of the possibilities for reduction within your college. You feel that by eliminating one visiting professorship, four graduate teaching assistantship positions, and two staff positions, you'll be able to accommodate the reductions. You are quite aware, however, that others see your Department of Oceanography as a primary target for elimination. This is, however, one of your oldest and strongest programs, certainly one of the leading oceanography programs in the Midwest. You want to protect the program as it is; however, even if you are required to reduce that program, you wish to do so only by eliminating several faculty positions rather than the entire department. You also feel this program will be protected because the chair of that department is the vice president's uncle.

Several other personal considerations affect your thinking. First, you feel that the entire College of Education could be eliminated with no real loss to the university. Other programs within the state clearly produce enough graduates in that field. Eliminating the entire college would mean no reductions would be needed in any other college. Second, you think Dean Berryderry is an idiot. You were especially incensed by Berryderry's comments about oceanography. If Berryderry can't run his own college, why try to run yours? Third, one of your faculty members recently was offended by sexual advances from the dean of the School of Business, Dean Dollar.

Dean Dudley

Dean of the College of Education (target reduction—20 percent). You know you are in trouble! Over the past several years, enrollments have been dropping in Education to the point that you are considerably overstaffed. At the same time, other programs in the state have developed and now have better reputations. This is especially true for your Department of Higher Education Administration. The main campus of the university boasts one of the country's leading programs in this area. Your best hope is to argue for across-the-board cuts that would affect all colleges equally. Your suspicion is that the College of Business will receive the lowest reduction and the College of Liberal Arts and the College of Science will be somewhere above. One of them would probably benefit from across-the-board cuts as opposed to targeted reductions; the other would probably lose—but you don't know which one.

In addition, several personal considerations guide your thinking. First, nearly all the athletes who are part of the school's winning billiards program are students in your college. You doubt if they could pass their coursework elsewhere. Second, the chair of the Department of Higher Education Administration has been one of your strongest critics over the years, and eliminating that department would eliminate one of your biggest problems. Third, a member of your faculty was recently offended by sexual advances from the dean of the School of Business, Dean Dollar.

Dean Dollar

Dean of the School of Business (target reduction—2 percent). Though you realize that your college will have to take a token reduction, you are certain that your reduction is far less than that required from other schools. Consequently, you are highly supportive of the vice president's selective reduction and opposed to across-the-board cuts. Your college has grown by leaps and bounds in the past several years, and you are in desperate need of more faculty, not less. At the same time, salaries have increased dramatically in your field, and retention of capable faculty is a problem. You can probably accommodate the reductions assigned to you through minimal staff changes and will not have to fire faculty.

You see all this as a possibility for considerable reorganization of programs. One program that you would particularly be interested in bringing into the college is that in public administration. This program is viewed with great favor by the governor and, consequently, by those higher in the university's administration. Moreover, the program would seem to be consistent with the interest of your college in management. You wonder if perhaps somewhere in all of this redistribution of money you might be able to acquire a new program. If you can discredit Dean Berryderry's interest in public administration and champion that field, you should stand a good chance of receiving support from the higher administration. All in all, you see this process as opening the possibility of adding to your college rather than reducing it. This result, however, depends on selective reductions rather than across-the-board cuts and upon reallocations *beyond* the amount required for the president's stated budget reduction.

You also have several personal concerns. First, you think both the College of Education and the Department of Oceanography (in the College of Science) could be eliminated outright . . . and you could use the money. Second, you have heard that the chair of the Department of Oceanography is the vice president's cousin. Third, you have just met a very attractive person who is an advisor in the College of Liberal Arts. You think you are falling in love, again!

Do Not Read This Paragraph until after the Simulation

Following the simulation, the entire class should discuss each group's strategies and tactics. Sometimes it is helpful to ask first what others thought each dean was trying to do, then ask that group to describe its strategy. Pay particular attention to strategies of cooperation and competition, as well as to strategies that have little to do with actual budget reductions. (For example, shifting a program from one location to another doesn't save the university any money.) Note also the inevitable lack of information, as well as the roles of rumor and false impressions in the budget process. Both these features are more typical of budget decisions than you might imagine! Finally, just for fun, have Dean Berryderry read the last line of his or her description; then have Dean Stevens do the same; then Dean Dudley; then Dean Dollar.

For Additional Reading

Axelrod, Donald. *Budgeting for Modern Government.* New York: St. Martin's Press, 1988.

Briffault, Richard. *Balancing Acts.* Washington: Brookings Institution, 1996.

Clynch, Edward J., and Thomas P. Lauth, eds. *Governors, Legislatures, and Budgets: Diversity across the American States.* Westport, CT: Greenwood Press, 1991.

Frank, Howard A. *Forecasting in Local Government: Near Tools and Techniques.* New York: Quorum Books, 1993.

Garner, C. William. *Accounting and Budgeting in Public and Non-profit Organizations: A Manager's Guide.* San Francisco: Jossey-Bass, 1991.

Gosling, James J. *Budgeting Politics in American Governments.* White Plains, NY: Longman Publishing Group, 1992.

Jones, Vernon Dale. *Downsizing the Federal Government.* Armonk, NY: M. E. Sharpe, 1997.

Kettl, Donald F., and , John Dilulio, Jr. *Cutting Government.* Washington: Brookings Institution, 1995.

Light, Paul. *Thickening Government.* Washington: Brookings Institution, 1995.

Mikesell, John L. *Fiscal Administration.* 2d ed. Pacific Grove, CA: Brooks/Cole, 1986.

Miller, Gerald J. *Government Financial Management Theory.* New York: Marcel Dekker 1991.

Reed, B. J., and Swain, John. *Public Finance Administration.* Englewood Cliffs, NJ: Prentice Hall, 1990.

Reischauer, Robert D. *Setting National Priorities.* Washington: Brookings Institution, 1997.

Rubin, Irene S., ed. *New Directions in Budget Theory.* Albany: State University of New York Press, 1988.

Rubin, Irene S. *The Politics of Public Budgeting.* Chatham, NJ: Chatham House, 1990.

Shick, Allen. *The Federal Budget.* Washington: Brookings Institution, 1995.

Wildavsky, Aaron, and Naomi Caiden. *The New Politics of the Budgetary Process.* 3d. ed. New York: Longman, 1997.

Chapter 6

THE MANAGEMENT OF
HUMAN RESOURCES

Nothing is more critical for an administrator than to effectively manage the people who work in his or her organization. Yet the hiring and treatment of public employees often seem so bound up in rules, regulations, and "red tape" that effective management is extremely difficult. Many managers feel that civil service systems (and central personnel offices), originally designed to attract and retain competent personnel, exist merely to complicate the manager's life and make it more difficult to manage. Instead of simply hiring someone for a job, the manager must advise an applicant to take a competitive examination and join many other candidates on a register for the position (some of whom may be given special preferences in the hiring process) and then to wait until all the paperwork clears. After someone has been hired, the manager finds there are limits to the "rewards and punishments" that can be offered to encourage improved job performance; and, should the person fail to perform adequately, the paperwork and justifications required to terminate his or her employment seem endless. You may wonder how anything else gets done!

But there are good reasons for the way human resources or personnel management in government has developed. Even though it is true that some civil service systems have become overly rigid, even "fossilized," most of the requirements relating to government employment are deeply rooted in important political and ethical principles. So an understanding of how government personnel systems operate not only includes knowledge of personnel techniques, but also a sensitivity to the values that underlie human resources management in public organizations.

NETWORKING
For general information on personnel issues, see the International Personnel Management Association at http://www.ahrm.org/ipma/ipma.htm. For jobs and recruiting, see the following: http://www.aspanet.org/recruiter/recruit.htm (PA Times Recruiter), http://www.fedworld.gov/jobs/jobsearch.html (federal jobs search), http://www.usajobs.opm.gov/b3.htm (presidential management), http://www.JobsInGovernment.com/cgi-win/jobsrch.exe, and http://www.govtjobs.com/jobopp.html.

Nowhere is the contest between the competing values of efficiency and responsiveness played out more clearly than in the area of human resources or personnel. On the one hand, it is obvious that staffing government agencies with the most competent people available is essential to effective management. On the other hand, it is equally clear that those who staff the offices of government should be responsive to the citizenry. In any case, the human resources or personnel system for any public organization ultimately reflects the political priorities of the particular public involved. In some cases or in some periods, managerial concern for efficiency may receive preference; in others, the democratic concern for responsiveness may be uppermost.

MERIT SYSTEMS IN PUBLIC EMPLOYMENT

Because the Constitution made little mention of either administrative structures of government or how they would be staffed, early leaders at the federal, state, and local levels experimented with many different approaches to hiring, treatment, and firing. In the late 1800s, however, growing concern about the composition of the civil service led to a new focus on competence and professionalism and, in turn, to legislation establishing the merit principle in public employment. The **merit principle**, though widely varied in its application, generally means that selection and treatment of government employees should be based on merit or competence rather than on personal or political favoritism. Despite the apparent simplicity and appeal of this notion, the development of public personnel systems has been infused with controversy.

SPOILS VERSUS MERIT

Most of the early American presidents followed George Washington's lead in seeking persons of high competence and integrity—what he called "fitness of character"—to hold governmental positions. This approach resulted in a stable and fairly skilled government workforce, but not without several problems. Because there were few well-educated persons in society and because those with education tended to be from the wealthier classes, the newly formed civil service soon took on a somewhat elitist character. Moreover, partisan considerations began to enter into the process as well. Presidents and members of Congress began to recognize not only that government employees needed to be loyal to the new government (and presumably the party in power) but also that public offices (and salaries) could be rewards to the party faithful. Finally, there was the question of tenure—should civil servants hold office for life, thus providing experience and continuity, or should they change with each administration, providing loyalty (and jobs) to the incoming party?

All these concerns were dramatically illustrated in the administration of Andrew Jackson. Jackson was swept into office on a strong wave of democratic sentiment and was especially concerned with making government more accessible to those previously excluded, the "common people." Though Jackson was not the first to employ the **spoils system** (the notion that "to the victor belongs the spoils"—in this case, the ability to give government jobs to the party faithful), his administration was notable for its expansion of the system and for his elaborate justification of it. Jackson not only argued that the common people had as much right to government jobs as the wealthy, but that most government jobs could be done without special training.

Jackson is sometimes portrayed as something of a villain for his defense of the spoils system, though far greater abuses occurred later at all levels of government. At the same time, however, Jackson made several rather positive contributions to democratic government; for example, there is no question that he democratized the civil service of his era and set a tone for greater representativeness within government agencies for decades to come.

Even Jackson could not have foreseen the corruption and abuse that would soon become associated with the spoils system (see Box 6.1). Succeeding presidents went far beyond Jackson in applying the system, as did political bosses at the state and local levels. The quality of the civil service rapidly declined, and even those who found jobs in government became disenchanted with the financial contributions exacted from them each election year. The system also became a problem for each new president, as thousands of office-seekers came to press their claims for patronage positions, and presidents soon grew weary of the long lines of people seeking jobs.

These factors began to set the stage for reform, but even more important in eventually bringing about change was the increasing corruption in government. There were kickbacks from contractors, private sales of surplus public property, skimming of tax receipts, and many other abuses. Corruption was becoming a normal way of doing government business.

BOX 6.1

The Early Spoils System

By the late 1800s, the spoils system was firmly a part of political life in most jurisdictions. One aspect of the system was collecting funds from appointees to help sustain the party in power. Although such practices persisted in some jurisdictions well into the 1950s and even 1960s, they were hardly as blatant as the tribute requested in the letter from a state party committee in 1870.

Dear Sir:
(We) have great and imperative need of funds at once, to carry the campaign to successful issue. An assessment of one percent on the annual gross receipts of your office is therefore called for, and you will please inclose that amount, without delay, to the treasurer, E. S. Rowse, in the envelope inclosed. This assessment is made after conference with our friends at Washington, where it is confidently expected that those who receive the benefits of Federal appointments will support the machinery that sustains the party which gives them pecuniary benefit and honor. The exigencies are great, and delay or neglect will rightly be construed into unfriendliness to the Administration. We do not look for such a record from you, and you will at once see the propriety and wisdom of the earliest attention to the matter.

Isaac Sheppard
Chairman of Committee

SOURCE: Leonard D. White, *The Republican Era: A Study in Administrative History, 1869–1901* (New York: The Free Press, 1958), 332.

The various ills that grew from the spoils system eventually led to a strong and active reform movement, spearheaded by such groups as the National Civil Service Reform League. The reformers made both vigorous and eloquent appeals, but their eventual success was assured more by a historical accident, the assassination of President Garfield, than by eloquence. Though Garfield had hardly been a proponent of civil service reform and had indeed drawn criticism from the reform groups for his failure to support a reform bill, the fact that he was killed by a disappointed office-seeker made him a martyr for the reform cause.

A man named Charles Guiteau had hoped to be consul to Paris. After weeks of making his case and after repeatedly being turned away from Garfield's office, he followed Garfield into a train station and shot him twice in the back. As he did so, he shouted that now Chester Arthur, a noted spoilsman, would be president. The reformers capitalized on this comment, portraying the situation as the obvious result of the evil spoils system and, in a sudden change of heart (and reality), they described Garfield as a proponent of reform. After two more years of pressure, the Republican Congress finally acknowledged the rising sentiment for reform and passed the Pendleton Act, which was signed into law in January 1883.

The Pendleton Act is one of two landmark pieces of legislation in federal personnel administration (the other being the Civil Service Reform Act of 1978). The Pendleton Act was primarily an effort to eliminate political influence from administrative agencies and, secondarily, an effort to assure more competent government employees. It pursued these aims through the following major provisions:

1. A bipartisan commission, the U.S. Civil Service Commission, was created within the executive branch to establish and implement personnel rules and procedures for the federal government.
2. Open and competitive examinations to test job-related skills were developed wherever practical within the agencies covered by the law and were to become the primary basis upon which to make hiring decisions.
3. Employees were given protection against political pressures, such as assessments (mandatory contributions) or "required" participation in campaign activities.
4. **Lateral entry** into government positions (that is, entry at any level as opposed to entry only at the beginning level) was encouraged, thus maintaining an important element of Jacksonian openness.
5. Positions in Washington offices were to be apportioned among the various states, in an effort to provide geographical representation in the civil service.
6. The president was given the authority to extend coverage to other groups of government employees beyond the approximately 10 percent of federal employees covered by the act.

These provisions, especially the last, provided the basis for the gradual extension of the idea of a **merit system** throughout most of the federal government as well as state and local governments. A respected writer on public personnel provides the following definition of the civil service system that emerged: "Throughout its history, the civil service idea has rested on three basic principles: (1) that the selection of subordinate government officials should be based on merit—the ability to perform the work rather than any form of personal or political favoritism; (2) that since jobs are to be filled by weighing the merits of applicants, those hired should have tenure regardless of political changes at the top of organizations; and (3) that the price of job security should be a willing responsiveness to the legitimate political leaders of the day" (Helco, 1977, p. 20). The concept of "merit" is so central to the American approach to public personnel administration that "merit system" and "civil service system" have become almost synonymous.

The Pendleton Act, although it was important in establishing the notion of a merit system of public employment, merely provided a framework within which a more fullblown system might develop. Unfortunately, the development of the system was not well coordinated. Although the merit system was gradually extended to more and more government employees, the values of the system were not always the primary motivation for extension. For example, one unlikely set of agents for the extension of personnel reforms turned out to be out-going presidents, many of whom sought to "blanket in" those they had appointed to patronage positions by making their positions subject to the merit system. In this way, merit coverage was extended from its original 10 percent of all federal employees in 1883 to approximately 70 percent by the end of World War I and some 90 percent today.

Other changes in the system also occurred slowly. The Pendleton Act contained provisions for examinations, but other devices for improving the quality of the workforce, such as position classification, standard pay schedules, and objective performance appraisals, had not yet been developed. Over the next decades, however, these ideas too became a part of the federal system of civil service. The Classification Act of 1923, for example, established a system for classifying jobs according to qualifications needed to carry them out and tying them to various pay grades, thus providing uniformity throughout the system.

Changes were also required to respond to a newly professionalized workforce and a larger and more activist government. In the early days, the main jobs in government were essentially clerkships, but as government grew and entered new fields, there was a need for more professional and more highly specialized people. Similarly, especially through the Roosevelt years, a multitude of new agencies were created, each placing different demands on the personnel system. Prior to this time, the Civil Service Commission had assumed the role of the government's central personnel agency; now it was necessary to decentralize personnel responsibilities to the various agencies, with the commission setting regulations and monitoring implementation.

In any case, the merit system has now become firmly established at the federal level. Nine out of ten federal employees are covered by either the general merit system or by one of several special systems created by law to pursue merit principles within specific agencies—the Postal Service, the Federal Bureau of Investigation, the Foreign Service, and so on. The remaining positions are exempt because they are not amenable to competitive selection or to regular personnel procedures; they include seasonal workers, those in intelligence, and a limited number of policy-making/confidential positions. Any incoming president now has only about 2,400 positions to fill on a purely political basis—a number that many think is still too high.

Many questions have been raised in recent years about whether there are too many political appointees in the federal government or, in other words, whether the federal bureaucracy has become too highly politicized. This concern has been intensified as the growth in numbers of political appointees was accompanied by increasing centralization of the appointment process in the White House. At present, nearly all the several thousand political appointments that occur at the federal level—executives, as well as members of boards and commissions, ambassadorships, and judgeships—are cleared through the White House personnel office.

THE CIVIL SERVICE REFORM ACT AND ITS AFTERMATH

For nearly one hundred years, the Pendleton Act provided the primary statutory basis for federal civil service. That changed with the passage and implementation of the Civil Service Reform Act of 1978. During the 1960s and 1970s, it became increasingly clear that there were serious problems in the federal personnel management system. The problems were in large part a result of the fairly haphazard pattern through which the system had been established. Responsibilities for various aspects of personnel management were spread among the president, the Congress, the courts, the Civil Service Commission, and the various agencies; but there was often not agreement on the basic principles that should guide the development of the system.

Even within the Civil Service Commission itself, there was confusion about the direction of personnel policy. On the one hand, the commission existed to execute the president's personnel directives; on the other hand, it was also responsible for protecting employees from political abuse. At times, the two objectives came into conflict. As a result, the numbers of federal personnel rules and regulations were not only excessive, they often directly conflicted with one another.

President Carter made reform of the personnel system one of the central themes of his administration and targeted at least five problem areas.

1. *Technical overkill:* Critics charged that those in charge of the personnel function had, in their drive to achieve political neutrality, created overly detailed regulations for recruiting, testing, selecting, classifying, and releasing employees. In many cases, these technical rules became a maze that prevented rather than aided action, and sorting through the procedures to replace a key manager could take as long as two years. Firing one $8,000-per-year Commerce Department employee who consistently failed to show up for work without valid reasons took twenty-one months!

2. *Excessive protection of employees:* Similarly, many felt that the drive to achieve political neutrality created excessive protections for employees. Although these protections were initiated for the best of reasons—so that employees would not be unduly or arbitrarily punished or dismissed—they sometimes resulted in incredible outcomes, such as an award of almost $5,000 in back pay to a postal employee who had been fired for shooting a coworker in the stomach! On the other hand, protections were needed in other areas; for example, employees who pointed out cases of waste, fraud, and abuse in

public agencies—"whistle blowers"—were often subjected to harassment or even dismissal.

3. *Lack of management flexibility:* Managers, especially political appointees, claimed that civil service regulations were so inflexible that they could not manage effectively. In an effort to counter this tendency, one official in the Nixon administration prepared a document, known as the Malek Manual, suggesting 130 ways that managers could subvert the intent of the merit system and do what they wanted to do. One entry described how to get rid of someone who doesn't enjoy traveling: "[He] is given extensive travel orders criss-crossing the country to towns (hopefully with the worst accommodations possible) of a population of 20,000 or under. Until his wife threatens him with divorce, unless he quits, you have him out of town and out of the way. When he finally asks for relief you tearfully reiterate the importance of the project and state that he must continue to obey travel orders or resign."

4. *Inadequate incentives to eliminate inefficiencies:* It was also charged that a system that seemed to grant raises according to longevity rather than performance and that made raises and promotion appear almost automatic encouraged inefficiency. Over 99 percent of the nearly three million federal employees regularly received satisfactory performance ratings that entitled them to raises. Alan Campbell a leading advocate of reform, wrote: "The current system provides few incentives for managers to manage or for employees to perform."

5. *Discrimination:* Many—notably women and minorities—felt the federal personnel system was not adequately promoting their representation within the bureaucratic ranks. They wanted to make sure that any new system would be more attentive to their interests and better able to cope with the increasing number of complaints in this area.

The Civil Service Reform Act was proposed to "restore the merit principle to a system which has grown into a bureaucratic maze" (Carter, 1978). (See Box 6.2.) The act sought to deal with the often contradictory roles of the Civil Service Commission by creating a new office of Personnel Management responsible for policy leadership and a Merit Systems Protection Board to handle investigations and appeals. OPM is "the President's principal agent for managing the federal workforce"; it has responsibility for human resource management and enforcement of personnel regulations (Campbell, 1978, p. 100). The Merit System Protection Board, on the other hand, is the "watchdog" of the personnel system, hearing and resolving complaints, as well as protecting whistle blowers from reprisals. The previously conflicting responsibilities of the Civil Service Commission were split between the two new agencies.

Beyond establishing the two new agencies, perhaps the most striking feature of the Civil Service Reform Act was the creation of the Senior Executive Service (SES). Following ideas that had been discussed for nearly forty years and specifically proposed but not adopted in the Nixon years, the SES created a separate personnel system for the highest-ranking civil service officials, permitting greater flexibility in assignments and establishing a new system of incentives for top-level managers. Basically, eligible managers would apply for positions in the SES and, if accepted, would hold SES rank as individuals, rather than being limited to the rank of a particular position. This meant that, within certain limitations, SES managers could be moved from agency to agency depending on their talents and the needs of the agencies. A new system of performance evaluations and pay increases closely tied to performance was also developed, along with an elaborate system of bonuses for exceptional

BOX 6.2

Reinventing Human Resource Management

1. Create a flexible and responsive hiring system.

    Authorize agencies to establish their own recruitment and examining programs. Abolish centralized registers and standard application forms. Allow federal departments and agencies to determine that recruitment shortages exist and directly hire candidates without ranking. Reduce the types of competitive service appointments to three. Abolish the time-in-grade requirement.

2. Reform the general schedule classification and basic pay scheme.

    Remove all grade-level classification criteria from the law. Provide agencies with flexibility to establish broadbanding systems built upon the General Schedule framework.

3. Authorize agencies to develop programs for improvement of individual and organization performance.

    Authorize agencies to design their own performance management programs which define and measure success based on each agency's unique needs.

4. Authorize agencies to develop incentive award and bonus systems to improve individual and organization performance.

    Authorize agencies to develop their own incentive award and bonus systems. Encourage agencies to establish productivity gainsharing programs to support their reinvention and change efforts.

5. Strengthen systems to support management in dealing with poor performers.

    Develop a culture of performance which provides supervisors with the skills, knowledge, and support they need to deal with poor performers, and holds supervisors accountable for effectively managing their human resources. Reduce by half the time needed to terminate federal employees for cause.

SOURCE: Gore, Al. *From Red Tape to Results: Creating a Government That Works Better and Costs Less. Report of the National Performance Review* (New York: Times Books, 1993), 163.

executives. A 1991 "deal" involving pay plans and performance measures required SES members to be "recertified" every three years.

NETWORKING

The Office of Personnel Management is located at http://www.opm.gov/.

In addition to these major features, the Civil Service Reform Act made several other changes: giving agencies greater flexibility to administer their own personnel systems, establishing a new and more sophisticated performance appraisal system, creating a merit pay system for managers just below the SES range, providing protection for whistle blowers, assigning the federal Equal Employment Opportunity program (previously with the Civil Service Commission) to the Equal Employment Opportunity Commission, and creating a more independent Federal Labor Relations Authority.

After more than two decades, the Civil Service Reform Act is still receiving mixed reviews. The most favorable opinion is that there is little wrong with the act itself, but that implementation has been flawed by lack of funding and administration pressures to increase the number of political appointees. Others continue to suggest that the act was based on questionable assumptions about the nature of the federal workforce and was doomed from the beginning. In any case, the Civil Service Reform Act represented the first major change in personnel policy at the federal level since the Pendleton Act. Its confirmation of the principle of merit, its effort to sort out the multiple responsibilities of the personnel system, and its attempt to produce greater managerial flexibility have been significant.

NATIONAL PERFORMANCE REVIEW

More recently, Vice President Gore's National Performance Review (NPR), and the reinventing government movement generally, has had a dramatic impact on personnel systems within the federal government. The goal of NPR is to enhance government productivity by streamlining processes, increasing accountability, and decentralizing authority to encourage entrepreneurial behavior. Federal administrators have started searching for innovative ways of conducting the business of government while cutting costs. An immediate consequence of NPR has been a substantial reduction in the federal workforce. Within two years of NPR's release, more than 160,000 jobs had been cut and more than 2,000 federal field offices closed across the country.

A second consequence of NPR has been an overall shift in the culture of federal organizations. Decentralization and the focus on results has instituted a fundamental change in the way government agencies, and thus personnel systems, work. Public employees are now held accountable for customer service and productivity. And, they are rewarded based on their agency's efficiency and performance. (For some of the human resources recommendations from the National Performance Review, see Box 6.2.) The long-term impact of NPR, and the reinventing movement, remains to be seen. Some laud the approach as a key step in improving public service and restoring the public's trust, while others suggest that reinvention serves purely as a way of downsizing "big government." At the very least, the reinventing government movement has significantly changed the systems of management and human resources that underlie public organizations at all levels. (We will examine the National Performance Review in more detail later.)

STATE AND LOCAL PERSONNEL SYSTEMS

Many of the same problems that led to institution of the federal civil service system in the late 1800s also existed at the state and local levels—indeed, the problems were often even more severe. Although the federal government was certainly influenced by politicians interested in maintaining power through patronage, it was never so completely dominated by political bosses and machines as were the states and, especially, the cities.

Even after the federal government created its civil service system, states and localities were slow to follow. New York adopted the first state civil service law in 1883, followed by Massachusetts the next year. It was twenty years, however, before another state joined these two. By 1935, only twenty states had adopted merit systems. While, today, nearly all states have relatively sophisticated civil service merit systems, those systems don't cover everyone. Even today, only about 60 percent of state government employees are covered by merit systems.

The story is much the same at the local level: Albany, New York, was the first city to adopt a civil service system (1884), and a few other cities and counties followed prior to the turn of the century, but reform came slowly at the local level. Moreover, even where formal systems were adopted, patronage practices and political manipulation of the government workforce continued. Chicago and Cook County were among the first to adopt civil service systems; yet even today, mayoral candidates often run on a platform of reducing machine control in Chicago. In any case, today almost 90 percent of local jurisdictions with populations of over 50,000 have some type of merit system on the books.

Over the years, a primary motivator for adopting merit systems at state and local levels has been the number of federal laws requiring such systems in order for states and localities to receive federal funds. By 1980, every state and thousands of local governments had federal grants that required personnel systems that met a set of federal standards. The result has been that most state agencies receiving large amounts of federal funding are now covered by merit systems; those that receive limited or no federal funds are much less likely to have a merit system. In addition to these requirements, the courts have extended due process protections to many public employees and have supported affirmative action and other personnel-related actions that place greater burdens on state and local governments for detailed testing, classification, and reporting. Many states have thus found it advisable to establish or to extend merit concepts for their own protection.

Though these regulations have been somewhat relaxed in recent years, it seems unlikely that state and local governments will return to massive use of the spoils system. Indeed, there is some evidence that governments are pursuing many of the same reforms pursued at the federal level in the late 1970s, which some charge have led to greater politicization of the public workforce. For example, states and localities are experimenting with decentralization of personnel functions, greater responsiveness of managerial and political authority, and closer ties between performance appraisals and merit pay. Whether elected officials at state and local levels will be subject to the same temptation as were those at the federal level to employ the new devices in a more politicized approach to public personnel remains to be seen.

HIRING, FIRING, AND THINGS IN-BETWEEN

Most provisions of public personnel systems exist to protect public employees from excessive political interference; however, in some cases, they appear to make public personnel actions unduly complicated. Knowing the "rules of the game" will be a considerable help in your administrative work and will also be of help if you are looking for a job in a government agency.

CLASSIFICATION SYSTEMS

The key to most public personnel systems is the notion of **position classification,** the arrangement of jobs on the basis of duties and responsibilities and the skills required to perform them. A position classification system usually begins with a set of job descriptions, each based on a thorough analysis of the work and the required capabilities. A **job description** typically contains the following elements: job title, duties required, responsibilities associated with the position, and qualifications needed to carry out the job. A clerk-typist position, for example, might be described as including duties such as typing reports, maintaining correspondence records, answering telephone and walk-in inquiries, arranging for meetings and conferences on behalf of the supervisor, and other duties "as assigned." Qualifications might include such things as a high school degree or the equivalent, typing speed of forty words per minute, and two years' secretarial experience.

Typically, sets of jobs that are closely related are then grouped together in classes that indicate increasing levels of difficulty—Clerk-Typist I, Clerk-Typist II, Clerk-Typist III, and so forth. In larger jurisdictions, such as the federal government, various classes may also be grouped into grade schedules that group jobs of varying levels of difficulty. For example, the federal General Schedule, which covers clerical and professional positions, lists within one grade, GS-11, a variety of different occupations.

Organizations use personnel classification systems for several reasons: to maintain an objective inventory of positions, to provide equity across similar jobs, to connect tasks and the skills required to perform them, and to provide standards for judging the work of specific employees. Historically, such systems developed out of a concern for objectivity and equity consistent with the idea of protecting employees from political abuse. The Position Classification Act of 1923, for example, required grouping jobs into classes on the basis of duties and responsibilities and, in language sounding much more contemporary, committed the federal government to providing "equal compensation for equal work, irrespective of sex." With this early impetus, most public organizations have developed rather sophisticated classification systems that are usually more advanced than their private-sector counterparts.

While most people agree that the objective of current classification systems—equal pay for substantially equal work—is basically sound, many have argued that classification systems have become burdensome, inflexible, and unfair. Specifically, many argue that the complexity of the system creates excessive requirements that interfere with agency performance. Consequently, the National Academy of Public Administration has developed an alternative classification scheme that groups the existing 459 federal job categories into occupational "families" based on similarities in career progression, basic skills, recruitment training, and performance measurement. Families might include such areas as general support, office services, technical, engineering, health, or law enforcement.

Likewise, the National Performance Review (NPR), which we mentioned previously, identified existing classification systems as a primary target for reinvention. Key recommendations of NPR, for example, involved adopting "a broader system of classification, reducing the number of occupational families and using grade and pay banding" (Risher, Fay et al., 1997, p. 38). Proponents of NPR say that the traditional system relies on rigid job descriptions, which tend to constrict employee performance to a limited set of tasks. Instead, more flexible parameters should be used that allow for innovation and more businesslike performance on the part of public employees. Administrators should be given greater authority to establish classification systems that contribute to each agency's overall productivity and accountability.

THE RECRUITMENT PROCESS

Having objective statements of duties, responsibilities, and qualifications makes it possible to recruit personnel based not on who one knows, but on what one knows and what one can do. Recruitment efforts in the public sector must also be concerned with assuring fairness, openness, and representativeness. Typically, the recruitment process involves the following steps:

1. advertising or giving notice of a vacancy to be filled
2. testing or otherwise screening applicants
3. preparing a list of qualified candidates
4. selecting someone to fill the position

In most jurisdictions, a personnel officer within a particular agency or someone from a central personnel department is significantly involved in the first three steps.

Testing or screening processes have been subject to special scrutiny in recent years. Screening can occur through a review of written applications and recommendations, aptitude or ability testing, performance examinations, interviews, or assessment centers. Of the various aptitude or ability tests that public organizations use, some measure general knowledge, others measure personality characteristics, and still others measure specific job-related knowledge or abilities. Performance examinations, such as typing tests, measure specific job capabilities.

The method of testing should relate to the job to be filled. Though individual interviews are a common part of the hiring process, for example, they tend to be poor predictors of eventual job performance. Generally speaking, **structured interviews,** in which a previously developed set of questions is used with each applicant, and *panel interviews* involving more than one interviewer are preferable. Similarly, carefully constructed assessment centers using several independent raters may be used. (An *assessment center* involves putting several job applicants through a series of job-related simulations to observe their performance under nearly "real-life" conditions.)

For almost a decade, the primary examination for entry-level administrative and professional positions in the federal government was the Professional and Administrative Career Examination (PACE). In 1982, however, the Reagan administration bowed to repeated challenges from groups charging that the test unfairly discriminated against minority applicants and discontinued use of the test. (Over the years, only 5 percent of African Americans and 13 percent of Hispanics who took the PACE exam passed it.)

Through most of the 1980s, the federal Office of Personnel Management advised agencies to promote from within, to use noncompetitive appointments, or to use temporary appointments to fill vacancies—an approach that has obvious limitations in attracting and retaining "the best and the brightest" for government service.

In 1990, OPM implemented a hiring plan with two alternative recruitment possibilities. The first featured the use of a series of tests, which it called the Administrative Careers with America (ACWA) test; the second, known as the Outstanding Scholar Program (OSP), enabled agencies to select college graduates with a GPA of 3.5 or higher on a 4.0 scale. Both have been challenged. Critics of the ACWA argue that the tests pose a similar problem as other standardized assessments, limiting the number of minority candidates in the hiring pool. Likewise, they state that while OSP leveled the playing field somewhat, particularly when compared to the ACWA, the result was the same: more nonminority than minority candidates being considered by federal agencies.

In any case, after testing or screening, a small number of eligible applicants are certified and forwarded to the hiring agency, often with rankings based on the candidates' qualifications. Most merit systems require that at least the top three names be forwarded to the agency, so that the manager has some flexibility to consider personal or subjective characteristics in the final selection. This **rule of three** provision has proven controversial, however; many claim that it has been used as a device to discriminate against women and minorities. (Under this provision, for instance, a sexist employer could hire a male even if a woman candidate were objectively more capable.) An equally controversial provision of many merit systems requires that veterans (or sometimes even relatives of veterans) receive extra points in the ranking system. Obviously, such a provision works against the interests of nonveterans, most of whom are women; as you might imagine, however, it is strongly supported by veterans' groups.

The centralized process of recruitment traditionally underlying public personnel systems itself has come under fire in recent years, with many suggesting that it places decision-making authority in the hands of human resources staff as opposed to public managers. For example, NPR recommended that federal agencies be given the power "to establish their own recruitment and examining programs." The report concluded that managers in each policy area can be more effective in recognizing the type of skills and abilities needed to make the agency more productive, and that they are in the best position to determine when to increase hiring levels.

As a result, the tend toward decentralized recruitment has gained in popularity even in larger, more diverse agencies within the federal government. Decentralized processes may rely on similar selection criteria as a centralized system, but the primary difference is that agency heads, rather than personnel managers, select the viable candidates. Those with the greatest knowledge of the policy field, therefore, choose the individuals they believe will enhance the organization. Moreover, by not having to engage in the selection process, personnel staff are free to concentrate on broader concerns, such as diversity, affirmative action and others affecting the organization.

PAY SYSTEMS

Naturally, both the recruiting process and the individual's performance on the job are affected by compensation patterns, including both wages and benefits. Generally speaking, pay is determined by the nature of the work and the quality of performance in the job. But pay plans in the public sector are difficult to construct, for they must embody two often contradictory principles. On the one hand, to be fair and equitable, they must be highly structured; on the other hand, to be competitive, they must be responsive to changing political and economic conditions.

Most large personnel systems in government (including states and big cities) base their pay plans on their classification systems, which usually define a series of grades, each containing a set of jobs that are generally comparable in terms of difficulty, and a number of steps within each grade. These steps represent approximately equal increments of pay, with the highest generally about 20 percent to 30 percent above the lowest. In most cases, the grades are slightly overlapping, so that the first step in one grade is equal to one of the higher steps in the grade below. Individuals are assigned to a particular grade and step depending on how the position is described and on their individual qualifications for the position.

Employees in this type of system may receive pay increases in several ways. One way is to change grades; however, for an employee to change grades, either the particular position would have to be reclassified or all equivalent positions would have to be moved to a higher range. For an employee to receive increases within grade, either the entire pay plan can be adjusted upward, for example, through a legislative action to improve overall pay (e.g., through cost of living increases), or the individual can receive a raise. Raises can be based on several factors, ranging from seniority to merit pay, or pay for performance.

The idea of **merit pay** is simply that increases in salaries and wages should be tied to the actual quality of the work being done, so that those who perform better or more productively receive greater rewards. Although governments have used various merit pay systems, such systems have not always worked well. In many cases, the money available for merit raises for a few is spread so thinly that meritorious employees aren't differentiated from others. Part of the reason for this development is the difficulty of objectively measuring an individual's performance and the fact that many managers find it awkward to evaluate their employees' work.

As noted, the Civil Service Reform Act of 1978 sought to remedy this situation by requiring merit pay based on formal performance appraisal systems. Although agencies have been given considerable flexibility as to what systems they adopt, efforts have been made to base evaluations on critical elements of the individual's job or to develop results-oriented systems that tie evaluation to specific job outcomes. Any system of performance appraisal must be both accurate and fair:

Performance-appraisal systems must be based on the real requirements of the task. They must reflect realistic levels of performance, and be couched in terms that the workers understand, while at the same time providing workers with some insights on where and how performance improvements need to be made. (Siegel & Myrtle, 1985, p. 337)

One aspect of compensation policy that has received substantial attention over the years is the comparability of wages and salaries in the public and private sectors. Though nearly all efforts to make such comparisons have been plagued by the difficulty of comparing apples and oranges, early studies tended to show public-sector salaries considerably below those in the private sector, today ranging between 22 percent and 38 percent below, depending on grade level. (Incidentally, the greatest differences are at the top-level positions.)

Under these conditions, the federal Pay Comparability Act of 1990 required the federal government to close the gap between the public and private sectors, beginning by closing the gap 20 percent in 1993 and then 10 percent in following years. While both Presidents Reagan and Bush cited the country's economic problems as a reason to impose lower wages than those suggested by comparability studies, President Clinton, while proposing some increases, rejected the comparability targets, arguing that the law's formulas were based on flawed methodology.

CONDITIONS OF EMPLOYMENT AND RELATED MATTERS

There are several contemporary issues in personnel management that relate either to the conditions under which employees are hired or the conditions under which they must work. For example, increasing numbers of employers in both the public and private sectors are recognizing that substance abuse is responsible for greater absenteeism, higher accident rates, and generally lower productivity. Consequently, programs have been established to identify and to aid or dismiss employees who have problems with drugs or alcohol.

Testing for drugs, primarily through urinalysis, has become quite common. Despite the fact that such programs violate personal dignity and have a variety of technical problems, a substantial number of private companies now use drug testing. Whereas in 1983 only about 3 percent of private firms used drug testing, today over three-quarters do so. Employees in private firms have little protection from testing and, in the absence of collective bargaining agreements to the contrary, may be tested at management discretion. Because public employees (at least civilian employees) are more clearly protected against illegal search and seizure and are guaranteed equal protection and due process, programs to test public employees have frequently been challenged in the courts. For the most part, the courts have held that random mandatory testing is a violation of employee rights, but that testing may be required where there is reasonable suspicion of abuse or where testing is made a part of the hiring process. But questions continue to be debated; for example, what type of testing is appropriate for those in "sensitive positions," such as air traffic controllers or those in contact with nuclear or chemical weapons? (See Box 6.3.)

BOX 6.3

What Can Agencies Do about Sexual Harassment?

1. Agencies should find ways to capitalize on what is already known about the most effective actions that can be taken to prevent and eliminate sexual harassment; that is, they should publicize penalties and encourage assertive actions on the part of employees who are targets of unwanted sexual attention.
2. Managers and supervisors should be firm and consistent in penalizing proven harassers.
3. Agencies should diagnose the extent and seriousness of sexual harassment within their own organizations so that they know what kinds of solutions are appropriate and where resources should be concentrated.
4. Agencies should evaluate the effectiveness of the sexual harassment training they provide to ensure it addresses identified problems. Agencies should pay particular attention in the training efforts to the problem of sexual harassment by coworkers.

SOURCE: *Sexual Harassment in the Federal Workplace: Trends, Progress, Continuing Challenges.* (U.S. Merit Systems Protection Board, 1995).

NETWORKING

The following sites track contemporary issues in personnel management. Many others are available—just conduct your own search.
http://www.shrm.org/hrlinks/comp.htm *(sources on benefits)*
http://www.pcepd.gov/pubs/ek97/intro.htm *(Presidents Committee on Employment of People with Disabilities),*
http://ebn.ecommunications.com/ *(employee benefit news)*
http://www.feminist.com/fairpay.htm *(National Committee on Pay Equity)*
http://www.brta-lrta.org/links.htm *(AIDS links from CDC)*
http://www.lgu.com/em49.htm *(sexual harassment)*
http://www.nyper.com/aa_eeo.html *(newsletter on affirmative action)*
http://lawinfo.com/forum/sex-discrimination/edics-2.html *(overview of sex discrimination)*
http://www.faa.gov/acr/mwe/index.htm *(work environment diversity)*
http://www.backgroundbriefing.com/jobdiscr.html *(how to hire and fire)*
http://www.careermag.com *(Career magazine)*
http://www.unions.org/root-cgi/htmlscript?urn/index.hts+open *(unions listed by state and country)*
http://www.shrm.org/docs/HRmagazine.html *(HR Magazine)*
http://panoptic.csustan.edu/mgt/hrmlaw9.htm *(age discrimination)*

SEXUAL HARASSMENT

Another contemporary concern is establishing a work environment that is supportive of all persons and sensitive to their needs, regardless of gender. One aspect of this concern is **sexual harassment,** a topic that has received considerable national attention in the wake of several highly publicized cases, including the Clarence Thomas confirmation hearings in 1991, the inquiry into the behavior of Senator Bob Packwood in 1994, and the suit brought against President Clinton in 1994 for allegedly harassing a state employee while serving as governor of Arkansas. Sexual harassment may be defined as any unwanted and nonreciprocal verbal or physical sexual advances or derogatory remarks that the recipient finds offensive or that interfere with job performance. Sexual harassment especially includes (though is not limited to) situations in which one person in a position of power or influence uses his or her position to encourage or coerce a subordinate or coworker into undesired sexual activity, even to the point of withholding or taking away job advancements or promotions. The courts consider sexual harassment a type of inequality that employers must deal with, both in terms of eliminating offensive behaviors and creating a less hostile or intimidating work environment for both men and women.

NETWORKING

Two sites dealing with sexual harassment are http://www.cs.utk.edu/~bartley/index/ sexual harassment/ and http://panoptic.csustan.edu/mgt/hrmlaw5.htm.

Despite attention to sexual harassment in many public organizations, a survey by the Merit Systems Protection Board found that 44 percent of all women working for the federal government said they had been sexually harassed in the past two years. Incidents cited included actual or attempted rape, pressure for sexual favors, deliberate touching, suggestive looks, and sexual remarks. The board estimated that the practice cost the federal government $327 million over two years in lost productivity and turnover (Havemann, 1988b, p. 31).

Although there appear to be many instances of sexual harassment, many remain unreported. (The number of reported incidents has risen dramatically during the 1990s with the increase in public awareness.) One reason for this situation may be the complex and often ambiguous procedures many organizations have for dealing with complaints. Most tend to be lengthy, expensive, and psychologically draining. For this reason, public organizations are currently reviewing their policies on sexual harassment, establishing more clearly the seriousness of the offense, and developing strong enforcement and disciplinary measures, including dismissal. The goal is not only to eliminate specific instances of harassment, but also to create a work environment that is fully supportive of the potential of all employees, both men and women.

AIDS POLICY

Related issues having to do with creating a positive work environment arise as public organizations, like others, work to protect the rights of individuals with HIV/AIDS. The Office of Personnel Management provided one of the first directives for federal agencies, setting a policy that prohibits the discrimination against employees with AIDS and that allows managers to take disciplinary action against anyone who refuses to work with an employee who has AIDS. Among other things, the guidelines said that employees with AIDS "should be allowed to continue working as long as they are able to maintain acceptable performance and do not pose a safety or health threat to themselves or others in the workplace." Moreover, because there is no medical basis for someone to refuse to work with employees with AIDS, where managers feel that employees' refusal is "impeding or disrupting the organization's work, [the manager] should consider appropriate corrective or disciplinary action against the threatening or disruptive employees" (Haveman, 1988a, p. 34).

These considerations have become even more important with the passage of the 1990 Americans with Disabilities Act (ADA), which considers those infected with HIV/AIDS as disabled individuals. (The ADA will be discussed in more detail later in this chapter.) Consequently, many agencies are developing HIV/AIDS plans for the workplace. Despite this attention, though, a recent survey of local government officials suggested that much work remains to be done to create a positive work environment for this protected group. Most municipalities have yet to comply fully with HIV/AIDS-related provisions of the ADA. And the survey concluded that "the public workplace offers little protection" from discrimination for those with HIV/AIDS.

WORKPLACE VIOLENCE

In recent years, incidence and the threat of violence in the workplace has had a dramatic effect on work environments. While multiple murders and acts of terrorism, such as the 1995 Oklahoma City bombing, tend to capture the public's attention, other forms of violence pose an equally significant threat to workplace safety and quality. Of course, violent crime affects a variety of organizations in all sectors; however, the government remains a primary target. For example, the U.S. Justice Department reported that nearly one-third of the 1 million victims of workplace violence in 1994 were government employees. And, in a separate report, researchers found that in the U.S. Postal Service alone, twenty-nine employees were killed and sixteen wounded from August 1983 to May 1993.

The increase in violence over the past decade has prompted administrators to implement strategies for reducing the risk of workplace crime. Some preventive measures include improving the physical environment, adding security and related staff, and reducing hours of operation during high-risk periods. However, many public administrators have yet to realize the actual threat of violence that affects their organization. Some continue to view occupational violence as someone else's problem. Recent research on violent crime, though, suggests otherwise. The political nature of government, the deterioration in public perception of government workers, and the increase in stress loads among public employees combine to make public organizations likely targets for workplace violence.

REMOVING EMPLOYEES

For whatever reason, things occasionally don't work out on the job. An employee may not live up to expectations or may become unproductive. In cases such as these, your first step as a manager is to try to improve the individual's work (a strategy that is, of course, far easier than recruiting and training a replacement). You may encourage or counsel the employee, either personally or, better, through an employee assistance program. Or, in a surprising number of cases, you may be able to restructure the job so as to better motivate the employee. Concerns about an employee's work can often be addressed in positive and productive ways that are helpful to both the individual and the organization.

But if your efforts to help the employee fail, you may have to resort to disciplinary action, which might include formal reprimands, reduction of pay, suspension without pay, or outright dismissal. In all cases, it is important to be able to demonstrate that there is adequate cause for disciplinary action. Simply firing someone for personal reasons unrelated to the job opens both you and the organization to possible lawsuits; and, of course, firing someone for political reasons is contrary to the whole concept of merit employment in the public sector.

There is a strong presumption that public-sector employees are entitled to notice and an opportunity to be heard before disciplinary action or before dismissal. This does not mean that a person cannot be demoted, suspended, or terminated but rather that the employer cannot take such action in an arbitrary way.

At the federal level, the Civil Service Reform Act encourages development of performance appraisal systems that make it easier for managers to document employee incompetence and remove them from the organization. At the state and local levels, various court cases have indicated that employees being terminated have certain due process rights, such as advance notice and the opportunity for a hearing. In any case, if you decide to pursue disciplinary action, you should build a clear case to demonstrate the underlying reasons for your action.

THE CHANGING CHARACTER OF LABOR-MANAGEMENT RELATIONS

An interesting issue that cuts across the field of public personnel management is the rise and decline of public-sector unions. At the federal level, many rather narrow issues, having to do primarily with working conditions, are resolved through collective bargaining, though more controversial issues, such as compensation and hiring practices, are rarely considered. At state and local levels, there is a patchwork of labor relations practices, ranging from highly restrictive to extremely permissive labor legislation.

The early development of public-sector unions was tied to the reform of the patronage system. With the establishment of merit principles in public employment, employees had greater protection from political intrusions, but they also had fewer direct ways to get the attention of political leaders. To combat the possibility that they might simply be ignored, public employees began organizing in the late 1800s and early 1900s. At first, political leaders strenuously opposed these efforts; at least two presidents issued *gag orders* to prevent federal workers from pursuing wage demands except through departmental channels. In response, the newly organized employees, led by the postal workers, pressed Congress for recognition, which they finally received in the Lloyd-LaFollette Act of 1912. The only statutory basis for public-sector unionization for more than half a century, this act permitted federal employees to join unions (that did not advocate the right to strike) and to appeal directly to Congress.

With the early emergence of unions at the federal level, a few agencies, such as the Tennessee Valley Authority, developed rather advanced patterns of labor-management relations; elsewhere, however, public unions emerged relatively slowly, especially in comparison to their counterparts in the private sector. The slow development of public unions can be explained in part by the several difficult questions that public-sector unionization raised for those in public organizations.

First, there was the issue of sovereignty, the notion that the ultimate power to decide issues of public policy in a democracy lies with the people or their elected representatives and cannot properly be delegated, even partially, to some nongovernmental group such as a union. Illustrating this position, President Franklin Roosevelt wrote, "The process of collective bargaining, as usually understood, cannot be transplanted into the public service. . . . The very nature and purpose of Government makes it impossible for administrative officials to represent fully or bind the employer in mutual discussions. The employer is the whole people who speak by means of laws enacted by their representatives in Congress" (Klingner & Nalbandian, 1985, p. 292).

A second set of factors restricting the growth of public unions concerns the nature of governmental services, which are often considered either essential to the community (police, fire, national defense) or relatively unprofitable (systems of mass transportation). In the case of essential services, the ultimate union weapon—the strike—may be seen as holding the public interest hostage and can backfire; in the case of low-profit undertakings, the balancing factor of the market—the fact that a company may go out of business if pressed too far—does not appear to operate. In either case, the private-sector model of collective bargaining seems to apply only loosely.

NETWORKING

For information on labor-management issues, see http://www.igc.org/igc/labornet/ and http://www.dol.gov. On specific unions, see http://www.afge.org/splash/splash.htm and http://www.afscme.org/afscme/about/index.htm.

A third factor limiting the growth of public-sector unions through much of this century is the varied nature of government employment and the difficulties this presents for unionizing. Traditionally, unions have organized around occupational groups, such as truck drivers or garment workers. But government employs people in thousands of occupational groups; to have a union for each group would lead to endless and unsuccessful bargaining for both sides. The federal government is also characterized by geographic dispersion (only about 10 percent of the federal workforce is located in the Washington area), and the fact that there are so many white-collar workers in government, who have been historically reluctant to organize. Thus, the question of finding an appropriate focus for union activity has been especially difficult at the federal level.

Yet unions have been able to organize. Sparked at least partly by the success of unions in the private sector, where the right to bargain collectively was never seriously questioned after passage of the Wagner Act in 1935, public employees continued to press for recognition of their right to negotiate labor-management disputes. Soon even the sovereignty argument was eroded; Secretary of Labor Willard Wirtz commented, "This doctrine is wrong in theory; what's more, it doesn't work" (Levitan, 1983, p. 6). Bills providing recognition for unions in the public sector were introduced (although unsuccessfully) in every session of Congress from 1949 to 1961.

Just as another such bill seemed stalled in Congress, President Kennedy took the initiative in reforming public labor-management relations by issuing Executive Order 10988 in 1962. Kennedy's order affirmed the right of federal employees to form and join unions, set up conditions under which unions would be recognized for purposes of "meeting and conferring" (*discussing,* not necessarily *negotiating*) with management on certain issues, and established limits on the kinds of issues that could be discussed. Though the order placed a great deal of administrative authority in the hands of the various agencies, it did seek some uniformity in application through the Civil Service Commission.

The Kennedy order was expanded somewhat by several executive orders during the Nixon and Ford administrations. Principally, Executive Order 11491, issued in 1969, sought a more coherent labor policy at the federal level through establishment of the Federal Labor Relations Council and slightly expanded the scope of bargaining. The essential items of wages and benefits, however, remained outside the bargaining process.

The next landmark in federal employee unions was the Civil Service Reform Act of 1978. Though the CSRA did little to expand areas of bargaining or to alter administration of federal labor practices (other than replacing the Federal Labor Relations Council with a Federal Labor Relations Authority separate from the Office of Personnel Management), the act was important in that it based federal labor relations on a single, comprehensive statute rather than a series of executive orders.

Currently, some three out of every five federal workers are represented by unions, the largest of which is the American Federation of Government Employees (AFGE), a part of AFL-CIO. But because Congress has refused to permit a "union shop" among federal workers, though it exists in the private sector, the actual membership of federal unions is significantly less than it might otherwise be. (*A union shop* is an arrangement under which all members of an agency are required to join the union that represents them.) The AFGE, for instance, negotiates agreements that apply to three times its actual membership. Despite that fact, however, the percentage of federal workers who pay dues to unions compares quite favorably to that among workers in the private sector; public unions have done quite well in terms of membership (Levitan, 1983, pp. 14–20). Indeed, overall, public-sector union membership is higher than that in the private sector.

At state and local levels, there is incredible variety in the kinds of labor-management relations permitted by law. Though there has been occasional talk of uniform federal statutes to govern state and local practices, the case of *National League of Cities* v. *Usery* (1976) seemed to indicate that states have considerable sovereignty over public employees. More recently, however, the case of *Garcia v. San Antonio Metropolitan Transit Authority* (1985) again opened the possibility of further federal intervention. But until federal legislation is passed, states will continue to exercise control over labor relations in widely varying ways. At present, some states follow the "meet and confer" model of the Kennedy program, while others establish a "negotiations" process similar to the private-sector model. Some states differentiate between state and local employees, while others differentiate among various occupational groups as well. Some states require enforced arbitration of one kind or another, and eight states permit strikes by public employees.

In all, forty-three states have comprehensive labor relations laws, most of which are more favorable to unions than the existing federal legislation. Between 1960 and 1990, in fact, the two most rapidly growing unions in this country were the American Federation of State, County, and Municipal Employees and the American Federation of Teachers, both of which operate exclusively at the state and local levels.

STEPS IN THE BARGAINING PROCESS

The first and major steps in the bargaining process are recognizing the union's right to exist, determining the type of bargaining permitted, and determining the scope of bargaining. Scope of bargaining is a source of continuing debate in many jurisdictions. Legislation may prescribe areas where negotiation is permitted, areas where it is prohibited, and areas where it is required. But the applicable legislation may range from a prohibition on negotiating wages and salaries (as exists at the federal level) to situations in which wages and salaries are at the heart of the process (as in many states and localities). Even beyond these questions, many other issues are less clear. For example, does inclusion of "work methods and procedures" in a bargaining arrangement for public schools mean that teachers can negotiate class sizes?

The typical procedure requires that organizers who wish to represent employees petition the administrative authority to establish a **bargaining unit** that will represent the employees in conferring or negotiating various issues. (The decision to include or exclude certain groups in the bargaining unit is called **unit determination**.) Whereas the traditional standard for setting unit boundaries has been to establish a "community of interests," governments have loosely applied this concept, in some cases recognizing agency-based units (the Department of Social Services or the Department of Mental Health) and in others recognizing units based on occupational classes (nurses, custodians, or security officers). After deciding on the bargaining unit, some mechanism must be established to ensure coordination among the various groups and to prevent **whipsaw tactics** (arguing that pay or benefits negotiated by one group should apply to others as well).

A similar concern is where to draw the line between managers and workers; for example, are first-line supervisors part of the bargaining unit or part of management? The importance of this issue was illustrated in the case of *NLRB* v. *Yeshiva University* (1980), in which it was determined that faculty at Yeshiva University, a private university, are management personnel, participating in decisions such as curricula and scheduling, and therefore outside the coverage of federal labor laws. Similar questions are raised in almost any unit determination; inclusion or exclusion of supervisors in the bargaining process varies greatly from place to place.

After appropriate bargaining units have been established, the administrative authority may either voluntarily recognize a particular union, essentially by petition, as representing a group of employees, or it may conduct an election to determine which, if any, union will represent the employees in that area. Once a union has been recognized, it is usually granted exclusive representation of employees in the unit, including the ability to bargain on all issues required or permitted by law. (The reverse of this process, *decertification,* is rare, though it can occur.)

Bargaining may then begin, typically with both sides bargaining in *good faith*—attempting to resolve the issues at hand even while following the strategy they feel will be most advantageous to them. In most cases, the bargaining process results in an agreement; occasionally it does not. Where an *impasse* occurs, there are several possibilities for resolving the issue: mediation, fact finding, and arbitration.

1. *Mediation* involves the use of a neutral third party to attempt to work out a settlement. The work of the mediator is to assist the parties in communicating and clarifying their positions, but not to impose solutions. Though the mediator's recommendations are not binding, professional mediators are remarkably successful in helping parties reach agreements.

2. *Fact finding* employs the third party in a somewhat more investigatory and judicial role, to examine evidence on both sides of the issue, present the evidence, and, in most cases, make specific recommendations with respect to a settlement. Some jurisdictions require making the recommendations public, on the assumption that public pressure will then lead toward an agreement.

3. *Arbitration* is a form of impasse resolution involving fact finding followed by specific recommendations that are usually binding on the parties. One form of arbitration that has received attention recently is **final-offer arbitration,** a technique in which both parties must present their best offer with the understanding that the arbitrator will choose one or the other without modification. Presumably, since both parties know that unreasonable proposals will lead to the arbitrator's choosing the opposing proposal, it is in the interest of both parties to submit their most reasonable position.

TO STRIKE OR NOT TO STRIKE

If impasse resolution fails, the employee organization may consider a strike. Although most governmental jurisdictions prohibit strikes by public employees, they do occur. There are usually several hundred work stoppages in public agencies each year. These strikes raise difficult questions for public-sector, labor-management relations. Certainly public employees have the right to form associations, and one might argue that they should have the right to withhold services just as employees in the private sector do. On the other hand, the importance of public services, especially those such as fire or police protection, may justify different standards in the public sector.

Experts make the following arguments against public employee strikes:

1. Strikes violate sovereignty (conceding authority to any special interest group contravenes the public interest).
2. Public services are essential and cannot be interrupted. In effect, all government services are vital.
3. Traditional channels of influence on public policy exist for unions: lobbying and voting.
4. Whereas strikes in the private sector are usually of an economic nature, those in the public service are political. They are strategies that use the leverage of public inconvenience to cause a redirection of budgetary priorities (Siegel & Myrtle, 1985, pp. 377–378).

On the other hand, advocates of public employees' right to strike make these points:

1. Public employee strikes occur whether or not they are illegal and regardless of heavy penalties prescribed by law.
2. In strike situations, labor-management conflict becomes channeled and socially constructive—both labor and management gain greater understanding of each other and of the consequences of work stoppages.
3. The right to strike enhances a union's strength as a bargaining agent. Lack of the ultimate ability to withdraw services weakens labor's position at the bargaining table.
4. Many private workers doing the same work that public employees do (for example, in transit, health care, garbage collection, and communications) have the right to strike, and for many other public employees (clerks, for instance), the public consequences of striking would be little different from what they are when private-sector clerks strike.

Though strikes at the state and especially at the local level are more frequent, two landmark strikes at the federal level were especially dramatic. The postal workers' strike of 1970 occurred when members of the Manhattan-Bronx Branch of the National Association of Letter Carriers voted to strike against the U.S. Postal Service. The immediate issue was the low wage scale for carriers—a scale that left a substantial number of postal workers on welfare. Beyond this concern, the postal workers desired the right to negotiate wages and benefits, especially if the Nixon administration followed its plans to make the post office a government corporation. The strike began with about 25,000 postal workers in New York City, but soon spread up and down the East Coast and to several major cities around the country, ultimately involving some 200,000 union members. As the situation became more intolerable, President Nixon sent 27,500 National Guardsmen into New York to sort and deliver the mail. He also broke a long-standing precedent, however, and agreed to permit postal workers to bargain for wages. Following this agreement, the postal workers returned to work, most claiming victory in the strike. Eventually, the Postal Reorganization Act was passed, setting up the government corporation Nixon sought, and also providing for a bargaining pattern similar to that in the private sector.

A quite different result occurred when members of the Professional Air Traffic Controllers Organization went on strike in August 1981. PATCO had earlier established itself as one of the most powerful and most militant of the public unions, boasting 90 percent of the FAA's air traffic controllers as members (probably the highest percentage among federal-level unions at the time). Early in the year, the FAA was pressured into negotiating with the union concerning issues of wages and working conditions, even though it had no statutory power to do so and could only recommend wage increases to Congress. The union, arguing that the controllers were underpaid and subject to severe job stress, presented several demands, including a $10,000 across-the-board annual salary increase for the controllers and a four-day, thirty-two-hour workweek. Although the FAA did not meet these demands, Secretary of Transportation Drew Lewis agreed to support a $40 million package of improvements, including a $4,000 wage increase. However, 95 percent of the union membership rejected this proposal.

After a final round of negotiations was unsuccessful, the union decided to strike; union leader Robert Poli declared, "The only illegal strike is one that fails" (Steele, 1982, p. 38). As it turned out, this strike was to fail. What had begun as a confrontation between the union and the FAA now became a confrontation between the union and the White House. President Reagan acted decisively, fining the union and firing nearly 11,500 striking controllers for participating in an illegal strike. Although there was severe disruption in the air transportation system for several days, new controllers were hired, airline schedules were altered, and training programs were accelerated. The situation soon gave at least the appearance of a return to normalcy. Beaten in the strike and decertified by the Federal Labor Relations Authority (FLRA), less than a year later PATCO filed for bankruptcy.

UNIONS REDEFINED

The character and role of organized labor has undergone a fundamental change during the 1990s, as efforts to reinvent government and reform personnel processes have redefined the ties between labor and management. In some respects, the influence of unions has been diminished by the more businesslike approach taken by government agencies. Contracting out and privatization, too, have contributed to labor's troubles, due to more and more services being delivered by private or nongovernmental organizations. The net result has been a drop not only in the power of unions, but in some cases in the level of union membership. For instance, while AFGE still represents more than 640,000 employees, its roster of members nearly was cut in half during the last two decades. And, though a few public employee unions grew during this period, the overall trend has been a decline in union representation.

What remains the same, however, is the highly confrontational nature of the labor-management relationship, with many identifying collective bargaining as a key contributor to the problem. Though collective bargaining has been useful in private-sector contract negotiations, its application by public agencies often results in bitter contests between management and staff personnel. As a consequence, the National Commission on State and Local Government reported that an "adversarial climate . . . has predominated. It is a climate that can stifle innovation and government's ability to get the job

BOX 6.4

Labor-Management Cooperation

To strengthen relations between labor and management at Wisconsin's Department of Industry, Labor and Human Relations (DILHR), Secretary Carol Skornicka two years ago established a twelve-member Labor Management Advisory Council.

The council includes six management and six union representatives, including representatives from the department's six divisions. The group meets monthly with the following groundrules:

1. Decisions are by consensus.
2. Employees are surveyed on all major issues affecting them.
3. Communication with all employees is a priority.

The council is advisory, but operates under a strong presumption that the Secretary will act upon consensus recommendations on non-contractual issues.

The council's goal is to build labor-management policies that foster harmony, trust and cooperation. "We've got good relations at the top," says Tom Lonsdorf, a board member of the Wisconsin State Employees Union, Council 24, AFSCME. "Now we've got to move it down through the organization to get that team concept throughout" the department.

SOURCE: Copyright 1994 by the National Academy of Public Administration Foundation, 1120 G Street, N.W., Suite 850, Washington, D.C. 20005.

done." Public organizations often spend months, or sometimes years, trying to reach agreements or attempting to effectively manage existing contracts. Meanwhile, the relationship between managers and union employees becomes bogged down over what amounts to minuscule matters.

During the past few years, both labor and management have sought more peaceful, less adversarial alternatives to bargaining and dispute resolution (see Box 6.4 for an example). A major step toward this goal came in 1993, when President Clinton issued Executive Order 12871. The order encouraged the two sides to form partnerships and take a cooperative approach to labor issues. To carry out these objectives, the order created the National Partnership Council, which included representatives from public unions, management, and the Public Employee Department of the AFL-CIO.

Besides the president's formal challenge, change has been targeted not simply in the communication between management and labor, but also in the culture and leadership styles that characterize public organizations. Many public agencies have opted for a more participatory form of management, thus precluding the legalistic, not to mention lengthy, process of collective bargaining. Administrators work to dismantle bureaucratic hierarchies and distribute power throughout the organization. Public employees enjoy a more meaningful form of empowerment than could ever have been facilitated through traditional channels. The result is a more effective, productive organization.

Of course, such an alternative does not completely resolve the issue. The structural factors that pit the two sides against each other, for the most part, remain in place. Public unions still hold a level of power in government personnel administration, and the gains made on behalf of workers through lobbying and court decisions continue to influence the administrative process. However, the relationship is changing. Though the direction of this change remains to be seen, reform of the system and the search for alternative forms of communication between labor and management appears necessary.

CORRECTING PATTERNS OF DISCRIMINATION IN PUBLIC EMPLOYMENT

Whereas civil service systems have traditionally emphasized the concept of "merit" in public employment, other values have become increasingly important. Most prominent is a concern for correcting patterns of discrimination in hiring and treatment of workers in public agencies. The two terms that have been central to that debate are "equal employment opportunity" and "affirmative action." **Equal employment opportunity** refers to efforts to eliminate employment discrimination on the basis of race, ethnic background, sex, age, or physical handicap; it simply seeks to ensure that all persons have an equal chance to compete for and hold positions of employment based on their job qualifications. **Affirmative action,** on the other hand, involves the use of "positive, results-oriented practices to ensure that women, minorities, handicapped persons, and other protected classes of people will be equitably represented in the organization" (Hall & Albrecht, 1979, p. 26).

The concept of equal opportunity has a firm basis in constitutional and legal history, but the primary piece of federal legislation guiding current practices is the Civil Rights Act of 1964. (Many states had passed equal employment legislation in advance of the federal act.) Title VII of the Civil Rights Act banned employment discrimination in areas such as selection, promotion, and training based on race, national origin, sex, or religion and created the Equal Employment Opportunity Commission to investigate complaints of discrimination in the private sector. In 1972 the act was amended through the Equal Employment Opportunity Act to extend coverage to all public-sector employees (at the federal, state, and local levels) and to provide for stronger actions, including filing suits, against those who did not comply with the act.

The original Civil Rights Act did not require affirmative action to correct past patterns of discrimination; this requirement was included in an executive order issued by President Johnson. Executive Order 11246 sought to secure compliance with the Civil Rights Act by requiring that federal contractors not discriminate on the basis of race, creed, or national origin and that they develop affirmative action programs leading to equal employment practices. President Johnson's Executive Order 11375 later added women to the list of protected groups and specified requirements for affirmative action plans.

These requirements were first applied to federal contractors, but were soon adopted elsewhere in government and the private sector. The Civil Rights Act of 1964 had declared "that it shall be the policy of the United States to ensure equal employment opportunities for federal employees," but it was an executive order issued by President Nixon in 1969 that required agency heads to create "affirmative programs" in eliminating patterns of discrimination (Shafritz, Hyde, & Rosenbloom, 1981, pp. 185–186). Similarly, state and local governments were brought under the provisions of the Civil Rights Act in 1972 and were threatened with loss of federal funds in the event of noncompliance. Title IX of the Higher Education Act of 1972 was interpreted to require universities to provide equal athletic opportunities for both sexes in intercollegiate sports; the penalty was withdrawal of federal funds from universities found not in compliance.

There is reason to speculate, however, as to whether the trend toward further extension of equal employment opportunity has slowed. In 1986, for example, the Reagan administration seriously considered revising the Johnson executive order in a way that would effectively eliminate affirmative action requirements for federal contractors. The draft revision, proposed by the attorney general, would have eliminated numerical goals applied to recruitment and other employment practices and would have made it more difficult to prove discrimination. Presidential advisors argued that the existing rules had not significantly helped minorities, had discriminated against white males, and had proven excessively costly to businesses.

In a related area, Supreme Court efforts to limit the applicability of civil rights legislation have been the source of considerable controversy. In the case of *Grove City* v. *Bell* (1984), the Court narrowly interpreted the law as it regarded sex discrimination to mean that federal funds were to be restricted from the particular program receiving funds rather than from an educational institution as a whole. This meant that if an English department were found guilty of discrimination, its federal funds would be cut off, but funds to other parts of the institution would not be.

Obviously, the effect of the *Grove* case was to severely limit enforcement power of the federal legislation dealing with sex discrimination, and, by implication, similar legislation dealing with discrimination based on race, age, or handicap. Barely a week after the *Grove* ruling, for example, the Department of Education dropped charges against the University of Maryland's athletic programs because they did not receive federal aid—though the institution as a whole received substantial federal funding in scholarships, research money, and so on. Not surprisingly, legislation was soon introduced in Congress to put teeth back into the various civil rights laws. The Civil Rights Restoration Act, passed by an overwhelming bipartisan majority, applies not only to educational institutions, but to a wide range of other public and private organizations receiving federal funds.

Congress' effort to maintain a progressive stance on civil rights, however, faced a continued challenge from the more conservative judiciary. As will be discussed below, Supreme Court decisions during this period tilted the balance to employers and away from those petitioning against discrimination. While the election of a Democratic President in 1992 raised hopes for rolling back the rightward trend, those hopes quickly ended when Republicans took control of Congress in the 1994 midterm elections. Conservative lawmakers targeted the deconstruction of civil rights provisions, such as affirmative action, as a key tenet in their legislative agenda. Likewise, several states used the sea change in Washington as an opportunity to launch their own campaign against the legal framework of civil rights. And, in what many have called an important benchmark, California voters in 1996 approved Proposition 209, ending the state's practice of preference and limiting statewide protection from sex discrimination.

ADA

In 1990, the Americans with Disabilities Act was passed. The purpose of the ADA is to prohibit discrimination against 43 million Americans who live with some type of disability. Beginning in 1992, the ADA prohibited employers of twenty-five or more persons from discriminating against people with disabilities who can satisfactorily meet the expectations of the job they hold or seek, with or without reasonable accommodation. A disabled person must be qualified, meet educational and skill requirements, and be able to perform the essential functions of the position. However, the employer is required to make reasonable accommodations to the work environment so the disabled person can perform to the best of his or her ability (Bishop & Jones, 1993, p. 122).

With respect to public services, the ADA prohibits excluding a person from participating in programs or activities of a public entity or denying an individual benefits of its services. A public entity is defined to include not only the federal government but any part of state or local government. Other sections of the act deal with transportation, public accommodations, and telecommunications. Obviously, the ADA will substantially change both employment patterns and the design of public facilities in dramatic ways.

QUESTIONS OF COMPLIANCE

Early efforts to prove discrimination against an employer required proof of "evil intention"—evidence that the employer was knowingly discriminating. The difficulty of proving intent led to a new focus on "unequal treatment"—proof that an employer used different selection procedures for different groups or used the same procedure in different ways. Still, under this definition, minorities made little progress entering the workforce.

In 1971, however, the Supreme Court, in *Griggs* v. *Duke Power Company,* settled on a new definition, **adverse or disparate impact.** The *Griggs* decision held that it was no longer necessary to prove discriminatory motive or differential treatment; it was simply necessary to show that employment practices affect one group more harshly than another. The Court stated, "Practices, procedures, or tests neutral on their face, and even neutral in terms of intent cannot be maintained if they operate to 'freeze' the status quo of prior discriminatory practices" (Hays & Reeves, 1984, p. 354).

The notion of adverse impact has been articulated more fully in a set of *Uniform Guidelines* agreed upon by federal agencies. Under the Uniform Guidelines, employers are required to keep records indicating the relationship between those hired and minorities, including women, available in the community and the comparative success of various groups in selection for a position. If, for example, women constitute 50 percent of the labor market, yet only 20 percent of the workforce are women, there is evidence of adverse impact. (Actual figures show that about 41 percent of employees in local government are women, 41 percent of employees in state government are women, and 43 percent of employees in federal government are women. And, of course, women are disproportionately represented in lower-paying positions, such as secretarial or clerical jobs.)

The guidelines also follow another aspect of the *Griggs* case in requiring employers whose practices are found to have adverse impact to demonstrate the *job relatedness* of tests or procedures used in hiring or promotion decisions. That is, if a screening test cannot be shown to relate specifically to job performance, then it cannot be used as a criterion in making employment decisions. Elimination of the Professional and Administrative Career Examination (PACE), which we noted earlier, is a classic case of the job-relatedness issue. In a court challenge, it was ruled that the PACE exam, at that time the primary test given to applicants for federal managerial positions, was not related to the eventual jobs these persons would hold and had an adverse impact on African Americans and Hispanics. For this reason, the exam was shelved.

A conservative shift in the Supreme Court, however, led to an end in these protective standards. In *Wards Cove* v. *San Antonio* (1989), the court reversed the *Griggs* interpretation of Title VII and ruled that plaintiffs, not employers, must substantiate their position in discrimination cases. In particular, the court deemed unconstitutional the earlier ruling that allowed the establishment of a prima facie case based on the so-called "four-fifths rule" — that is, when minority hires constitute less than 80 percent of the nonminority hires. While the Wards Cove packing plant paid minority employees less and segregated their living and dining quarters, justices said that the workers would have to prove that such practices created a gap between the percentage of minorities actually employed and the percentage in the workforce.

Federal lawmakers tried repeatedly to counter the Wards Cove ruling and restore the more progressive provisions of *Griggs,* finally adopting the Civil Rights Act of 1991. In many respects, though, the act only confused the issue of Title VII protection. Progressive critics argued that too much had to be sacrificed in order gain the act's approval. While it contained several important provisions, such as extending the definition of discrimination to personnel decisions other than hiring and promotion, the act still placed in the court's hands the final decision on what can be considered discrimination in the workplace.

AFFIRMATIVE ACTION AND REVERSE DISCRIMINATION

To correct past patterns of discrimination against minorities and women, many employers are now required to implement *affirmative action programs*. Such plans typically include (1) a statement of policy indicating a commitment to correct discrimination with respect to employment practices; (2) an analysis of existing practices and their results; and (3) a statement of goals to improve those practices.

Unfortunately, a great deal of popular and legal confusion has developed around the notion of goals and quotas, often resulting in charges of *reverse discrimination* against white males. Although quotas require hiring specific numbers of people from specific groups (and are rarely used in actual practice), goals or timetables are intended to be flexible and are to be established internally by the employer. Both goals and quotas may involve numbers (and this causes some of the confusion), but the goals are merely intended to show a direction in which an employer wishes to move; generally, a good faith effort in that direction will be viewed as satisfactory in terms of providing opportunities for equal employment.

Even the Supreme Court has found it difficult to clarify exactly what is acceptable and what constitutes reverse discrimination. In *Bakke* v. *The Regents of the University of California* (1978), the Supreme Court ruled that it was illegal for a university to reserve a specific number of slots in its medical school for minority applicants who were less qualified than other students who were rejected. The Court agreed that race could be considered one factor in an admissions decision, but only one among several.

On a slightly different issue, the Court held in *United Steel Workers of America* v. *Weber* (1979) that a training program that admitted black workers before white workers with more seniority was acceptable. The key here seemed to be that the company initiated the program voluntarily to eliminate obvious patterns of discrimination and that it did not necessitate the discharge of white workers (Stewart, 1983). On the other hand, in *Firefighters Local Union #1784* v. *Stotts* (1984), the Court held that a lower court could not order an employer to lay off more senior employees in favor of less senior employees on the basis of race to preserve a specific percentage of minority employees. The emerging consensus, reflected in such recent cases as *United States* v. *Paradise* (1987) and *Johnson* v. *Transportation Agency* (1987), seems to be that affirmative action programs will be limited to specific needs and circumstances. Broad-scale programs are not likely to be accepted.

This outcome seems to have been confirmed by the Civil Rights Act of 1991, which provides that race, color, religion, sex, or national origin cannot legally be a motivating factor for an employment decision. While on its face, this provision would appear to encompass affirmative action programs related to the selection of candidates for hiring and promotion, there remains considerable ambiguity about the legislative history of the act and about how the courts will interpret its provisions (particularly with regard to what may be considered employment discrimination).

Given the increasingly conservative view in Washington and, as evident in California's Proposition 209, in many states, the future of affirmative action seems questionable. Some suggest that while preferences and so-called "set asides" leveled the playing field somewhat, they no longer offer what the nation needs to ensure a diverse workforce. Unfortunately, though, the discourse on the issue often degenerates into political rhetoric with both sides losing sight of an important principle—that is, not only must all have an equal opportunity to serve but also the distinct contribution made by each person must be appreciated. By pursuing an agenda to enhance diversity, organizations may gain important contributions from a broader range of viewpoints.

A few alternatives have been offered for promoting and sustaining such diversity, including several strategies that target the underlying culture of organizations. The process begins with creating a shared sense of purpose toward diversity, then empowering those at all levels to contribute action steps for achieving this goal. Periodic assessments can be used to determine how successful the organizational change has been and to identify any future barriers the group may need to overcome. The U.S. Forest Service, for example, has been working on the issue of diversity for a number of years. The Forest Service takes the position that since the character of the nation's workforce is changing, the character of the Forest Service must also change. "To be competitive in the business sense, the Forest Service must have a multicultural workforce that is representative of our multicultural society. Such a workforce will increase the productivity and quality of the organization" (Denhardt, 1993, p. 118).

THE GLASS CEILING

Unfortunately, extending diversity throughout the organization, especially at the highest levels of management, has proven difficult. While the representation of women and minorities in the federal workforce has generally improved along with their representation in the middle- and upper-management levels, certain groups remain underrepresented in the overall workforce, and white women and all minorities remain underrepresented in the key jobs that lead to middle- and upper-management positions. Similarly, at the state and local level, about 41 percent of government employees are women, but they still fill only 27 percent of the management positions.

The "glass ceiling" encountered by many women and minorities has been recognized in several recent studies. Data from OPM revealed that "women were promoted less than men who had comparable amounts of formal education and experience and who entered government at the same grade levels as the women; and women face obstacles to advancement at lower levels in the pipeline. For those women who have advanced, it usually meant staying late, relocating, or working longer hours" (Desky, 1992, p. 1). Recognizing these concerns, the Civil Rights Act of 1991 set up a "glass ceiling" commission to study the barriers to the advancement of women and minorities in the private sector. We can expect similar efforts in the public sector, at the federal, state, and local levels.

THE DEBATE OVER COMPARABLE WORTH

One more aspect of the affirmative action question focuses on what has come to be called **comparable worth**. The idea of comparable worth is that men and women in jobs that are not identical but require similar levels of skill and training should be paid equally. To understand this distinction, consider two questions:

1. Studies have shown that female electricians make less money on the average than male electricians doing the same work. In situations like this, should employers be required by law to increase women's pay to equal that of men?
2. Studies have shown that nurses, who have greater job skills and more extensive responsibilities than electricians, make less money on the average than electricians. Most nurses are women and most electricians are men. In situations like this, should employers be required by law to increase nurses' pay to match their job skills and responsibilities?

The first question raises the familiar issue of equal pay for equal work; the second rests on the concept of equal pay for comparable work.

The comparable worth issue has its roots in Title VII of the Civil Rights Act of 1964, which prohibited discrimination based on sex, and in the Equal Pay Act of 1963, which provided for equal pay "on jobs the performance of which requires equal skills, effort, and responsibility, and which are performed under similar working conditions." These two pieces of legislation (primarily the former) provide the basis upon which action can be taken to redress past patterns of discrimination.

Here's how it works. Persons in a female-dominated field seeking to prove discrimination would have to convince a court that their work requires equal skills, effort, and responsibility, and is performed under working conditions similar to those in a comparable male-dominated field. If these matters could be proven, the defendant company or agency would then have to convince the court that the reason for the difference was not sex discrimination but rather something that occurred under one of the Equal Pay Act's exceptions. These exceptions permit paying workers of different sexes different wages where there is (1) a seniority system, (2) a merit system, (3) a system that measures earnings by quantity and quality of production, or where the differential is based on a factor other than sex; for example, where there is a scarcity of people to fill a particular job.

Those who argue against the concept of comparable worth hold that even the best available job analyses cannot properly compare apples and oranges and that, even if they could, it would be improper (as well as excessively costly) to intervene in wage setting. It is much better, they contend, to let the market decide prevailing wages in various occupations and for women who desire higher pay to train for different jobs. On the other hand, those who favor the notion of comparable worth point out that the full-time earning power of women has consistently been about 60 percent of that of men over the past decade and that where pay differentials are clearly the result of patterns of sex discrimination, corrective action should be taken.

Again, regardless of the outcome of specific cases, it is clear that managers in public and private organizations need to be attentive to shaping employment policies so as to eliminate discrimination from the workplace. Whether in the area of affirmative action generally or in the area of comparable worth, a manager is well advised to understand the issues clearly and to take positive measures to create more equitable circumstances in the public workplace.

POLITICAL APPOINTEE–CAREER EXECUTIVE RELATIONS

The tension between political responsiveness and managerial effectiveness that characterizes public management is especially well illustrated in the relationship between political appointees and career executives. Each newly elected administration, whether at the federal, state, or local level, has a certain number of top-level managerial positions to fill with persons of its choosing. These appointees become the "bosses" of career civil servants who staff the various agencies of government. As you might imagine, there is occasionally some tension between the two groups. Incoming presidents are usually elected on a platform of change and view career employees as representing opposition to change (Colvard, 1992, p. 17). The political executive wants to move in new policy directions, but often has little experience in government operations; the career executive, on the other hand, has both knowledge and expertise, but, aware of potential problems, may appear reluctant to change.

The inevitable tension between political executives and careerists has become even more pronounced in recent years. Many argue that both the Carter and Reagan administrations came into office with a serious misunderstanding of the role of civil servants and, consequently, encountered difficulties in their relationships with the career service. Both presidents had, in a sense, run "against the bureaucracy," pledging to "clean up the mess" in Washington. Consequently, during the early days of their administrations, both presidents seemed mistrustful of career bureaucrats and felt that civil servants were inflexible and tied to the policies and programs of previous administrations. Both Presidents Bush and Clinton were more tempered in their criticism of the federal bureaucracy and indeed sought to establish more positive relations with career civil servants.

In any case, sorting out the relationship between politically appointed executives and career executives returns us to the old question of politics and administration. One interpretation suggests that the role of the career executive is solely to execute orders given by superior authorities—elected officials and their appointees. In the most extreme formulation of this view, the career executive should be isolated from any involvement in policy development and should concentrate on implementing policies handed down from above.

In contrast to this extreme position, career executives and many others find another interpretation of the politics-administration issue more appealing. This view holds that there are important reasons for career executives' involvement in policy development (see Box 6.5). Certainly, career executives have the background and expertise to con-

BOX 6.5

Education of Political Appointees

I recall an instance in which I was instructed by a new cabinet secretary to award a sole source contract of substantial dollar value to an individual who had been active in the presidential campaign which had just ended. The contract would have provided a service for which many other firms were qualified, and one clearly could not make a reasonable ease of unique capability which would justify a sole source procurement. I indicated to the secretary that while a sole source procurement in this instance violated federal procurement regulations, he possessed the authority to approve it. I further advised, however, that to award the proposed contract would be a serious error since it would be perceived as political favoritism which would only embarrass him and undermine his credibility,

[In another case], I had pointed out to an assistant secretary, who had been an executive with a major bank, the advisability of consulting with, or at least providing advance notice to, the chairman of the appropriate congressional committees on action to be taken. In rejecting my advice, I was told "at the bank when we decided to change minimum deposit requirements, we merely posted an announcement. We'll decide and then tell them what we've done." Needless to say, throughout the assistant secretary's tenure, he never had good relations with the Congress.

SOURCE: Excerpted from Alfred M. Zuck, "Education of Political Appointees," *The Bureaucrat* 13 (Fall 1984): 17. Reprinted by permission.

tribute substantially to developing practical and effective public policies. In addition, these executives are likely to be more effective in implementing policy if they have been involved in developing it, if they understand the need for policy changes, and if they feel some sense of "ownership" of the new policies.

Political appointees, on the other hand, generally come to government with relatively little knowledge about their subject matter (at least compared to career bureaucrats) and certainly with little understanding of how policies are developed in a governmental setting. While the average tenure of career civil servants is over thirteen years, political executives last an average of only eighteen to twenty-two months. If the stereotype of the bureaucrat is one of hostility to any change, the stereotype of the political appointee is someone brash, inexperienced, and intent on "quick and flashy change" (Lorentzen, 1985, p. 411).

THE RELATIONSHIP BETWEEN POLITICAL AND CAREER EXECUTIVES

Assuming that political appointees and career executives are going to work side by side, how might their relationship be improved and their work together be made more effective and more responsible? Paul Lorentzen, a former federal executive, summarizes the major problems in the relationship:

1. the new political appointee's lack of knowledge of and prior experience in the public sector
2. the need of career staffs to learn about the new leadership's policy goals and directions
3. the joint need of the political appointees and executives to understand each other's perceptions, attitudes, role perspectives, and values (Lorentzen, 1984, p. 8)

There have been several efforts to define a more effective relationship between political appointees and career executives. Al Zuck, a former career official in the Department of Labor and elsewhere emphasizes the responsibility of the career executive. Zuck writes, "Career executives have a distinct advantage and, therefore, a distinct educational responsibility, as it relates to the substantive knowledge of program content and history, as well as the knowledge of government processes to get things done. They possess invaluable institutional knowledge which can be of great assistance to political executives" (Zuck, 1984, p. 18). Based on this perspective, Zuck makes the following suggestions as to how the career executive can relate most effectively to the political appointee:

1. A successful relationship between career executives and political appointees must begin with the career person's recognition that policy changes can and will occur and that the career staff will be used as an instrument of change.
2. Career executives need to act professionally; the career executive should offer the best advice, information, and insight that his or her experience has provided.
3. The career executive must be careful not to be too "bureaucratic" — so bound by procedures and processes that nothing gets done.
4. Options or alternative courses of action should be provided to political officials so they have full and complete information about their various choices.
5. The career executive should expect to have one's advice ignored or rejected. "Not

only is it likely that one's advice is not always sound, but also each administration and political appointee has the right to fail" (Zuck, 1984, p. 18).

There appear to be at least three areas in which further improvements might be made in the relationship between political appointees and career executives. First, political appointees must receive the training and orientation they need to effectively manage public organizations and to work with career executives both in developing and implementing policies. Second, an exchange of views between political leaders and careerists, including team-building sessions between politically appointed executives and career executives, may help to develop greater understanding between the groups and forge more effective working relationships. Third, Congress should reassess the structure of executive management in government and make whatever structural changes are needed to establish a more balanced political-career interface. But the basic dilemma continues: the political appointee must make sure that the bureaucracy is responsive to the policy directives of the current president; the career executive must maintain high standards of professionalism so that the work of the organization is carried out in the best way possible.

SUMMARY AND ACTION IMPLICATIONS

Personnel systems in the public sector have evolved in response to a variety of competing demands. Much of the earliest personnel legislation at the federal level was directed toward assuring a neutral and competent bureaucracy protected from the potentially corrupting influences of politics. More recent efforts have sought greater responsiveness on the part of the bureaucracy to political leadership. Personnel systems in the public sector—like systems of budgeting and financial management—reflect important, though sometimes changing, values.

The development of merit systems of public employment reflects such concerns. At the root, policies governing recruitment and classification in the public sector reflect the fact that public organizations must, by definition, operate in the public interest. Similar concerns significantly affect the way contemporary issues such as conditions of employment (drug testing, etc.), labor-management relations, and comparable worth are played out in the public sector.

As a manager, you must obviously be concerned with recruitment, training, and retention of the best possible people to work in your organization. You may often feel that public personnel systems and the people who monitor them are simply roadblocks to effective management. Fortunately, in many jurisdictions, the relationship between manager and personnel officer is shifting in a more positive direction.

Obviously, personnel managers have been given the responsibility of protecting the merit system from abuse by maintaining detailed records of personnel transactions and enforcing personnel rules and procedures. Personnel officers have thus often been placed in the position of exercising control over the activities of program managers. But public personnel officers, like their private-sector counterparts, have always had another role as well—helping managers employ and utilize personnel effectively.

Although this service aspect of the personnel officer's role has often been treated as a secondary function, there is every reason to believe that the more progressive personnel systems will increasingly emphasize this aspect. Increasingly, personnel officers are shifting from the traditional emphasis on compliance to a new emphasis on consultation. In this role, those in personnel will be available to help with human resource management questions of all kinds; for example, a personnel specialist might be called in to help develop a productivity improvement program or to advise on legal questions. As this new orientation becomes established, line managers will tend to view the personnel officer more as an ally than as a protagonist.

Consequently, you are likely to be more effective as a public manager if you are able to develop a good understanding of the technical details of personnel transactions and an effective working relationship with the personnel professionals in your agency. The support of trained experts in the field of personnel management can help improve your organization's performance and, in turn, its service to the public.

Terms and Definitions

Adverse or disparate impact: Criterion for showing that employment practices affect one group more harshly than another.

Affirmative action: Use of positive, results-oriented practices to ensure that women, minorities, handicapped persons, and other protected classes of people will be equitably represented in an organization.

Bargaining unit: The organization that will represent employees in conferring and negotiating various issues.

Comparable worth: Notion that men and women in jobs that are not identical but require similar levels of skill and training should be paid equally.

Equal employment opportunity: Refers to efforts to eliminate employment discrimination on the basis of race, ethnic background, sex, age, or physical handicap; ensures that all persons have an equal chance to compete for employment and promotions based on job qualifications.

Final-offer arbitration: Technique in which both parties must present their best offer with the understanding that an arbitrator will choose one or the other without modification.

Job description: A thorough analysis of the work to be done and the capabilities for a job; typically contains these elements: job title, duties required, responsibilities, and job qualifications.

Lateral entry: Entry into government positions at any level.

Merit pay: Increases in salary and wages that are tied to actual quality of work performed.

Merit principle: Concept that selection and treatment of government employees should be based on merit or competence rather than personal or political favoritism.

Position classification: Analyzing and organizing jobs on the basis of duties, responsibilities, and knowledge and skills required to perform them.

Rule of three: Provision of most merit systems that requires at least the top three applicants' names to be forwarded to the hiring official to allow some flexibility in selection.

Sexual harassment: Any unwarranted and nonreciprocal verbal or physical sexual advances or derogatory remarks that the recipient finds offensive or that interfere with his or her job performance.

Spoils system: The ability to give government jobs to the party faithful; "to the victor belongs the spoils."

Structured interviews: Those in which a previously developed set of questions is used with each applicant.

Unit determination: Decision to include or exclude certain groups in a bargaining unit.

Whipsaw tactics: Argument that pay or benefits negotiated by one group should be applied to others.

Study Questions

1. "To the victor belongs the spoils" was a phrase used to define the spoils system for filling vacancies of government jobs. Discuss the historical use of this system and its contemporary manifestations.
2. What was the Pendleton Act, and how did it help to reform federal personnel procedures?
3. Explain the basic principles of the civil service system.
4. Discuss some of the basic problems President Carter faced regarding personnel/civil service reform.
5. The Civil Service Reform Act provided for various changes in personnel procedures. Explain the importance of this legislation and discuss the impact of major provisions on the civil service system.
6. What are some of the criticisms of the Civil Service Reform Act?
7. List the steps in recruiting for a government position.
8. Identify various methods of testing and screening applicants.

9. Discuss government methods to combat discrimination in employment activities.
10. What are some of the tools governments use to ensure compliance with equal employment opportunity regulations?
11. Discuss the pros and cons of comparable worth in pay systems.
12. With changing labor-management relations, public unionization has become an issue. Explain the factors public managers must recognize to unionize the public sector.
13. Discuss the major components of the bargaining process.
14. Identify arguments against strikes by public employees and give a few examples of strikes that have occurred.
15. Discuss the relationship between political appointees and career executives and how it might be improved.

Cases and Exercises

1. Consider the following case: You are Steve Style, a programming director in a large city's data-processing department. You manage five sections of computer programmers, each made up of a senior programmer and three to four trainees. The department generates computer systems for the other city departments, thus requiring you and your staff to spend a lot of time with the users of the systems. Your staff has a reputation throughout the city for being highly professional. For some time, your boss, Tom Traffic, has been talking about the need to expand the programming staff by adding a database administrator.

A few months ago, a new police chief was hired, brought in from another city. In the past, when a new department head came in, if he or she were married, the spouse also found a job somewhere in city government. You had heard that the police chief's wife has a degree in computer science. On Monday, Tom calls to tell you he has just hired Muffy Mann as the database administrator in your area. Tom is happy to get someone with Muffy's education and background, which includes working for several software companies. Tom also tells you that Muffy is the police chief's wife and that she will be making more money than any of your current senior programmers.

Excited about the addition of a database administrator, you go to tell the staff about the program expansion. Rather than the positive reaction you had expected, theirs is quite negative. David Denman, the most experienced programmer, is upset for two reasons. First, isn't she the police chief's wife? It sounds to him like a deal was made. And, second, why didn't any of the current staff have a chance to interview for the new position? Another staff member leaves the meeting grumbling about how much money Muffy will be making in comparison to the other senior programmers.

You go back to your office trying to figure out how to deal with this problem. You're looking forward to having a database administrator, and from what Tom tells you, Muffy is well qualified. You are concerned about the staff's reaction. You know you will face an uphill battle to convince the users that Muffy is qualified for the position.

- As a practical matter, how does an administration deal with the problem of a "qualified spouse"?
- How do you justify to your staff the fact that Muffy is making a higher salary than any of them and that they didn't have the chance to interview for the position?
- How does the personnel office handle this problem in light of the city's civil service system?

SOURCE: The preceding case was provided by Perri Lampe.

2. Through contacts with the U.S. Office of Personnel Management, the state's personnel office, and the city's personnel office, learn as much as you can about finding employment in a government agency in your area. Address such questions as

- What kinds of positions are typically available?
- What should you expect in terms of the salary range for entry at the bachelor's or master's level?
- What benefits and salary increments are associated with these positions?
- What is the hiring process (how do you apply; what types of tests or interviews are required; who makes the final decision)?

In addition, contact a variety of nonprofit organizations in your community or a representative of the American Society of Association Executives to discuss career possibilities in the nonprofit sector. Make your report available to students on campus through your academic department and through your school's placement center.

3. Obtain a copy of your school's policy (or policies) on sexual harassment regarding administrators, faculty, staff, and students. Based on conversations with knowledgeable faculty and other school officials, as well as your own reading and research, analyze the policy in terms of the following questions:

- Does the policy define sexual harassment in terms that are generally understandable?
- Does the policy specify particular types of actions that will be considered harassment?
- Are there clearly defined procedures through which charges of harassment can be brought and heard?
- Are there specific penalties, including dismissal from the school, for prohibited actions?
- Has the policy been employed in actual cases with success?
- Does the policy act as a deterrent to sexual harassment?
- Are there training programs or other educational materials available to help administrators, faculty, and students understand the issue of sexual harassment specifically and gender sensitivity more generally?
- What would you suggest to strengthen, to clarify, or to more easily enforce the policy?

SOURCE: The preceding exercise was adapted from material provided by Charles Sampson of the University of Missouri-Columbia.

4. Form small groups to complete the following exercise.

You have just accepted membership on the Energy Resources Commission Recruitment Task Force. This task force was recently created by the newly elected governor. The purpose of the task force is to develop recruitment strategies to staff the ERC, which has just been established to fulfill the following functions:

- Determine the future energy needs for the state.
- Develop strategies to meet these needs.
- Provide technical assistance to the public utilities and agencies involved in meeting these needs.

Special recruitment problems are anticipated because this is a completely new agency that will require a significant number of professional and technical personnel. The task force has been charged with the responsibility for developing specific action plans to recruit the required personnel over the next three years. The ERC will require approximately 250 employees by the end of this three-year period, in the following categories:

1. management and management staff (50 employees)
2. clerical support staff (65 employees)
3. professional/technical personnel (100 employees)
4. blue-collar/maintenance-type personnel (35 employees)

Factors that may or may not complicate the recruitment effort include the following:

1. The primary sources of employment in the state are in agriculture, mining, and transportation.
2. The population of the state totals 10 million, but almost 40 percent of the population resides in a single upstate metropolitan district.
3. The political environment has traditionally been characterized by conflict between upstate Democrats and downstate Republicans.
4. This political competition has produced extensive reliance on patronage as the means for staffing most public agencies.
5. Control of state government has just shifted to the Republicans after twelve years of Democratic control, but one of the new governor's major campaign promises was to professionalize the personnel system and expand civil service coverage to most state employees.
6. During the campaign, the governor also committed himself to hiring within the state whenever possible.
7. The state is currently involved in two employment discrimination lawsuits: one brought by the National Organization for Women, and the other by the NAACP.
8. Racial minorities compose 15 percent of the population, but most of these individuals reside in the upstate metropolitan area.
9. Of the total state workforce, 22 percent are women and 4 percent are classified minority.
10. The unemployment rate for the state is 12 percent, but most of the unemployed reside in the upstate area.

11. The unemployment rate by occupational class is as follows: 18 percent blue-collar, 7 percent white-collar, and 3 percent professional/technical.
12. The unemployment rate for minorities is 21 percent, and the rate for women is 16 percent.
13. Public-sector unionization is in its early stages of development in the state. Unions are competing for membership and becoming more and more militant. A key demand, which is currently before the legislature, is to establish an "agency shop" for public utility employees.
14. Citizens' groups and professional associations actively lobbied for the creation of the ERC.
15. The ERC is being partially funded by a federal grant-in-aid program that, in addition to requiring 50 percent matching funds from the state, also requires establishment of a merit system to ensure nondiscrimination in employment.

The task force is to design a specific recruitment strategy to meet all the staffing needs of the new Energy Resources Commission. Besides paying particular interest to the characteristics delineated above, you might also consider the following in your deliberations:

1. need and approach for determining the commission's specific staffing requirements
2. characteristics of the labor market geographically and by occupational field
3. level and availability of the state's labor resources
4. extent of search process for candidates geographically and occupationally; type of institutions/organizations/agencies to be covered in recruitment process
5. qualification standards (education, training, work experience, residency, physical characteristics, and so on) that should be required for each occupational category in the commission
6. implications of these standards for the recruitment effort
7. selection devices (tests, practical or aptitude type; credentials examination; interviews, and so on) and their effect on recruitment
8. whether recruitment should be for specific jobs, or for a career (and the implication of this decision for qualification standards, selection devices, and so on)
9. recruitment approaches for each occupational category; for example, job announcements, written brochures and materials, recruitment visits (and institutions that will be covered, if any), use of professional/collegial contacts (whose?), and so on
10. consideration of the factors to emphasize to prospective candidates (that is, what would be the attractive aspects of a job/career in this agency in this locale)

For Additional Reading

Beaumont, P. B. *Human Resource Management: Key Concepts and Skills.* Newbury Park, CA: Sage Publications, 1993.

Capozzoli, Thomas, and R. Steven McVey. *Managing Violence in the Workplace.* Delray Beach, FL: St. Lucie Press, 1996.

Cayer, N. Joseph. *Public Personnel Administration in the United States*. 2d ed. New York: St. Martin's Press, 1986.

Coleman, Charles J. *Managing Labor Relations in the Public Sector*. San Francisco: Jossey-Bass, 1990.

Farnham, David. *Managing People in the Public Service*. Basingstoke: Macmillan Business, 1996.

Goldstein, Irwin L. *Training in Organizations: Seeds Assessment, Development, and Evaluation*. 3d ed. Pacific Grove, CA: Brooks/Cole, 1993.

Guy, Mary E., ed. *Women and Men of the States*. Armonk, NY: M. E. Sharpe, 1992.

Huddleston, Mark, and William Boyer. *The Higher Civil Service in the United States*. Pittsburgh: University of Pittsburgh Press, 1996.

Ingraham, Patricia, and Ban, Carolyn, eds. *Legislating Bureaucratic Change: The Civil Service Reform Act of l978*. Albany: State University of New York Press, 1984.

Jackson, Susan E., ed. *Diversity in the Workplace: Human Resource Initiatives*. New York Guilford Press, 1992.

Klingner, Donald E., and John Nalbandian. *Public Personnel Management*. 4th ed. Englewood Cliffs, NJ: Prentice-Hall, 1997.

Lane, Larry M., and James F. Wolf. *The Human Resource Crisis in the Public Sector: Rebuilding the Capacity to Govern*. New York: Quorum Books, 1990.

Maranto, Robert, and David Shultz. *A Short History of the United States Civil Service*. Lanham, MD: University Press of America, 1991.

National Academy of Public Administration. *Modernizing Federal Classification: An Opportunity for Excellence*. Washington, DC: National Academy, 1991.

Nigro, Lloyd G., and Felix A. Nigro. *The New Public Personnel Administration*. 4th ed. Itasca, IL: F. E. Peacock Publishers, 1993.

Risher, Howard, Charles H. Fay et al. *New Strategies for Public Pay*. San Francisco: Jossey-Bass Publishers, 1997.

Robinson, Dana Gaines, and James C. Robinson. *Performance Consulting*. San Francisco: Berrett Koehler Publishers, 1995.

Selden, Sally Coleman. *The Promise of Representative Bureaucracy*. Armonk, NY: M. E. Sharpe, 1997.

Shafritz, Jay M., Albert C. Hyde, and David H. Rosenbloom. *Personnel Management in Government: Politics and Process*. 4th ed. New York: Marcel Dekker, 1991.

Sloane, Arthur A., and Fred Witney. *Labor Relations*. 8th ed. Englewood Cliffs, NJ: Prentice-Hall, 1994.

Sylvia, Ronald D. *Critical Issues in Public Personnel Policy*. Pacific Grove, CA: Brooks/Cole, 1989.

Thompson, Frank J. *Classics of Public Personnel Policy*. Pacific Grove, CA: Brooks/Cole, 1991.

Chapter 7

PLANNING, IMPLEMENTATION, AND EVALUATION

Developing policies and programs, putting them into operation, and measuring their success or failure constitute an important and recurring cycle for public managers. A new weapons inspection program in Iraq is initiated. To support that policy the U.S. Navy organizes a fleet of vessels to patrol those waters, while political and military leaders assess the operation and decide what to do next. Similarly, a new policy involves sending literature on AIDS to all households in the United States. A group in the surgeon general's office is convened to monitor the operation. Both the efficiency of getting the mailing out and its effectiveness as an educational device are discussed. Meanwhile, a local parks and recreation department develops a program for handicapped athletes. After staff and money are acquired to support the program and it begins operations, the department director asks whether the program is worth the time and energy it seems to be taking from other tasks. Repeatedly, plans are made, policies and programs are implemented, and the work of the organization is evaluated.

Recently these issues have taken on increased importance as public managers have been asked to do more with less, while at the same time providing more and better services. This has led many to call for "managing for results," that is, clearly stating goals and objectives in terms of public outcomes, designing and implementing programs, then measuring the performance of the government or other agency against established standards. The idea of "managing for results" or "performance management" suggests the importance of bringing together careful planning, implementation, and evaluation.

While planning, implementation, and evaluation all require knowledge of the political and ethical context of public administration and certain personal and interpersonal skills, various technical aids have been developed during the past decade to assist the manager in each of the three areas. These techniques range from strategic planning to specific quantitative methods for measuring government performance. Moreover, these techniques reflect a change in the way public organizations account for their actions. Citizens, lawmakers, and other advocacy groups increasingly hold government agencies accountable not only for their efficiency in expending public resources but also their effectiveness in achieving public outcomes. Techniques such as strategic planning, reengineering, and performance measurement link the actions of public organizations with specific, measurable results. Through the use of such techniques, public administrators may account both for their efforts and for the impact their efforts have in each given policy area.

NETWORKING

The NPR Web site at http://www.npr.gov/initiati/mfr/ provides resources about, and examples of, managing for results. For additional resources on productivity and performance management, see the National Center for Public Productivity (http://newark.rutgers.edu/~ncpp/ncpp.html) or the American Productivity and Quality Center (http://www.apqc.org/).

PLANNING

On a daily basis, all managers engage in planning. But organizations, and indeed entire governments, engage in more formal planning processes, often involving a wide range of participants and the development of considerable data and other information. Planning typically leads to the development of alternative courses of action that must each be examined to decide which way to go. Depending on the level of the problem, the process of examining and choosing from among alternatives may involve the manager in either "policy analysis" or "program design."

STRATEGIC PLANNING

Strategic planning is one approach that has been increasingly employed in the public sector. A number of writers have commented on the rapidity of the social and technological changes we are now experiencing and on the turbulence and complexity that such changes generate. In an effort to recognize and respond to such changes many private corporations began programs in the 1960s and 1970s to systematically plan for future development. The success of these programs is now confirmed by the fact that more than half of publicly traded companies use strategic planning in some form.

Strategic planning helps an organization match its objectives and capabilities to the anticipated demands of the environment to produce a plan of action that will ensure achievement of objectives. William Glucek (1980, p. 9) points out that a strategy is a plan that is unified (ties all the parts of the enterprise together), comprehensive (covers all aspects of the enterprise), and integrated (all parts are compatible with one another and fit together well). Similarly, Robert Shirley (1982, p. 262) writes that "strategy (1) defines the relationship of the total organization to its environment and (2) gives guidance to administrative and operational activities on an ongoing basis."

We can differentiate strategic planning from more familiar long-range planning activities in several ways. Long-range planning primarily concerns establishing goals or performance objectives over a period of time; it is less concerned with specific steps that must be undertaken to achieve those goals. Strategic planning, on the other hand, implies that a series of action steps will be developed as part of the planning process and that these steps will guide the organization's activities in the immediate future. Strategic planning takes the future into account, but in such a way as to improve present decisions.

A second way that strategic planning differs from long-range planning is its special attention to environmental complexity. The organization is not assumed to exist in a vacuum; rather, both the organization's objectives and the steps to achieve them are seen in the context of the resources and constraints presented by the organization's environment.

A final distinction between the two types of planning is that strategic planning, especially in the public sector, is a process that must involve many individuals at many levels. As most managers know quite well, effective changes in organizational practices are most readily accomplished by involving all those who will be affected by the change. This general rule is especially applicable to changes generated through a process of strategic planning.

Public organizations undertake strategic planning efforts for many reasons: (1) to give clarity and direction to the organization, (2) to choose from among competing goals and activities, (3) to cope with expected shifts in the environment, and (4) to bring together the thoughts and ideas of all participants in the work of the organization. Most importantly, planning activities provide an opportunity for the widespread involvement of leaders and citizens in defining the direction of the community or the agency as it moves into the future, thus building trust and commitment.

PLANNING FOR PLANNING

As a manager, you may wonder whether such activities are appropriate for your jurisdiction or agency. Whatever your work—at any level of government or in a nonprofit organization—you will find precedents for planning. Many federal, state, and local agencies have begun strategic planning programs over the past several years, as have voluntary associations, human service organizations, and job training programs. The key seems to be that any organization is a candidate for strategic planning if, by allocation of resources, it can significantly influence either formulation or implementation of public policy.

You may, of course, question whether strategic planning is worth the costs in terms of consultant fees, research and data analysis, and time away from other duties. The best gauges for assessing costs are (1) is it likely that careful planning will lead to reduced operating costs or increased productivity over the long run? and (2) what might the organization lose in the absence of a more comprehensive and integrated approach to the future?

The latter question has become increasingly important to those in local governments, who now realize that they must compete with other communities in attracting industry, providing amenities, and maintaining the population base. The issue, however, must be treated differently when an administrative agency such as a state government department is considering planning. Although strategic planning might make the agency more competitive in attracting resources from the executive or legislature, this clearly should not be the purpose of planning. Rather, the agency should use strategic planning to involve all important "stakeholders" in assessing the unit's work and the possibilities for improving its services (Ackoff, 1981). The process may indeed lead to requests for further funding, but it may also suggest ways to more effectively utilize existing resources or even ways to reduce the scope of activities.

You may also question, because of budgetary uncertainties, whether the time is right for planning activities. Some say that planning can't take place without solid information about funding levels. But the opposite argument is compelling—that planning is most essential in times of uncertainty, for these are exactly the times when you most need to be in control of your own destiny. Times of uncertainty do not mitigate the need for planning; they intensify it.

Managers in the public sector voice a related argument—that periodic changes in political leadership make planning more difficult than in private industry. Again, the opposite argument is compelling: in times of transition, planning can provide continuity. Even when the new leadership wishes to change the directions specified in an earlier planning effort, changes can be made with greater clarity and aimed more readily toward critical concerns if a plan is in place.

Finally, you may wonder whether strategic planning efforts are consistent with your organization's commitment to democratic or participatory processes. Here lies the most significant difference between strategic planning in the public and private sectors. Whereas planning in the private sector may involve many people throughout an organization, it remains centered and directed at the top, because that is where the private interests of the firm are most clearly articulated. In the public sector, however, every effort must be made to significantly involve all those who play an important role in the jurisdiction or the agency. For example, a local government planning effort should involve not only elected leadership and city staff, but also many others with a stake in the outcome—unions, neighborhood associations, chambers of commerce, civic organizations, and so forth. Similarly, a state government agency's planning effort should involve persons from all levels of the organization, members of constituent groups, elected officials, persons from other agencies and other levels of government, and representatives of the general citizenry.

Strategic planning in the public sector must be a highly participatory process, but this participation opens the possibility of building new understanding among various groups. Many communities that have engaged in strategic planning have found that the process brought together various groups in a way not previously possible. Strategic planning may therefore be undertaken to achieve both direction and commitment.

ORGANIZING FOR PLANNING

The planning process can proceed in a number of different ways, but the most common approach is to form a central planning group to work closely with an outside consultant to obtain information and make commitments to various new directions. In a local community, the group might include the city's political leadership; representatives of city administration (for example, the city manager); representatives of business, industry, and labor; members of neighborhood associations; and so on. For a federal or state agency, on the other hand, the major planning group might comprise the agency director, managers from the next organizational level below, and selected program directors. The planning group in a nonprofit organization might include the executive director, members of the board, staff members, and representatives of constituent groups.

STEPS IN PLANNING

Once it has been brought together, the planning group will want to give its attention to four primary concerns: (1) the organization's mission or objectives, (2) an assessment of the environment in terms of both opportunities and constraints, (3) an examination of the organization's existing strengths and weaknesses, and (4) the values, interests, and aspirations of those important to the organization's future (see Box 7.1). Consideration of these issues will lead to several strategic alternatives, perhaps stated as "scenarios for the future," and to the choice of a particular direction in which the organization should move. Finally, a set of action steps or implementation items will be developed to indicate what must be done immediately to put the organization in the proper position to face the future most effectively.

Mission or Objectives

Arriving at a concise, yet inclusive, statement of the mission of the organization is a difficult step in the planning process. Although most organizations have a general sense of their mission, questions often arise that cannot be readily answered in terms of stated objectives. Having a specific mission statement, however, provides an identity for the organization, as well as a guideline for future decisions and a standard against which to measure specific actions.

Because arriving at a mission statement may imply certain strategies, care should be taken to consider alternative approaches to the organization's goals. A statement of mission might indicate, for instance, whether a city wishes to seek a broad industrial base or focus on particular types of businesses, such as tourism or high-tech industries. Similarly, a university mission statement might indicate whether the institution seeks a broad range of programs in all areas or a limited number of exceedingly high-quality programs. The mission statement of a state agency might comment on the desired range of clientele, responsiveness to changes in the environment, or quality of service. If there is doubt or debate about items, they should be carried forward as elements of strategy for later consideration.

BOX 7.1

Steps in Strategic Planning

1. Statement of mission
2. Environmental analysis
3. Strengths and weaknesses
4. Values of organizational leaders
5. Development of alternative strategies

Environmental Analysis

After developing a mission statement, the planning group should move to an analysis of the environment within which the organization operates. This assessment should include legal and political considerations, social and cultural trends, economic circumstances, technological developments, and, where appropriate, the organization's competitive or "market" position. Each area should be examined in terms of the present environment and how it is likely to change in the future. This assessment leads the group toward identifying possibilities for reducing constraints and extending opportunities.

Strengths and Weaknesses

At this point, the planning group can turn its attention toward assessing the organization's existing capabilities—its strengths and weaknesses. The analysis should be as forthright and inclusive as possible, taking into account financial resources (including changing patterns of funding), human resources (including political and managerial strengths and weaknesses), the operation of both technical and organizational systems, and quality of work. This assessment of capabilities should relate as directly as possible to the stated mission of the organization. For example, an agency involved in facilities design and construction might want to consider the age and condition of facilities, the number and abilities of architects and engineers, the number and frequency of design projects, and the unit's standing among other similar organizations. Examining strengths and weaknesses should be accompanied by some attention to programs that might significantly improve capabilities in one or more areas.

Values of Organizational Leaders

A final step in preparing to develop strategic alternatives is to take into account the values, interests, and aspirations of those who will guide the organization into the future. People will respond to the same environmental and organizational analysis in different ways. In business, for example, some will be perfectly satisfied with the security of a stable market share, while others will be willing to take greater risks in the hope of greater payoffs. Leaders vary in terms of creativity, energy, and commitment. Yet to effectively implement a plan, it must reflect the concerns and interests of those who will play major roles in shaping the future of the organization.

DEVELOPMENT OF ALTERNATIVE STRATEGIES

At this point, the planning group can move to formulate alternative strategies. These strategies can take several forms; however, one useful way to proceed is to draw up alternative "scenarios of the future," indicating what the organization might look like five, ten, or twenty years into the future. The scenarios should indicate new directions the organization might take; pessimistic, realistic, and optimistic interpretations of its future; and factors likely to influence these future patterns. It is helpful to develop more than one scenario, then use them as competing viewpoints from which to debate the merits of various alternatives. From a thorough discussion of the scenarios, one or more strategies will emerge. The strategy should be chosen that most effectively moves the organization toward its mission, given environmental opportunities and constraints, organizational strengths and weaknesses, and the values, interests, and aspirations of the leadership. After developing the strategic orientation, the planning group should be pressed to identify specific action steps for implementing the strategy. A local job-training program, for example, went through an extensive planning exercise involving thorough analysis of environmental opportunities and constraints as well as organizational strengths and weaknesses. Based on the information developed, and especially on expectations of future funding patterns, the program's directors chose to de-emphasize subsidies for local businesses to employ those without work and to try for longer-term benefits through skills training and job preparation.

THE LOGIC OF POLICY ANALYSIS

One possible outcome of a formal planning process is that the need for new policies will be identified. (The need for new policies can be generated in other ways as well, many of which we discussed in Chapter 2.) A local group considering economic development issues might recognize the need for new tax incentives for industries interested in locating in the community. A state welfare department planning group might focus on the relationship between providing day care and job training. Or a nonprofit organization might decide there is a need for a new publications program. In each case, a problem is identified and the question arises as to whether a new approach to the problem—a new policy—might help.

Many issues may come up. Exactly what is the nature of the problem? What would we be trying to achieve with the new policy? What might be alternative approaches? What might we expect from each alternative? What criteria would we use to evaluate alternatives? Which alternative would best meet our criteria? Answering questions like these is the basis of analysis of public policies. We can therefore define **policy analysis** as the process of researching or analyzing public problems to give policy makers specific information about the range of available policy options and the advantages and disadvantages of various approaches. There are several ways you might become involved in policy analysis. All managers engage almost daily in a sort of informal analysis of public policies; they encounter new problems and consider alternative policies. But often a more formal review of policy options is called for. Sometimes staff members can do the analysis; many public organizations employ policy analysts to work on just such problems. In other cases, another governmental agency may be able to help; for example, the Office of Management and Budget, as well as its counterparts in many states, develops policy reports. Policy analysis might also be performed by legislative staff or legislative research groups. Finally, many analyses are performed by consultants, including university consultants, where the public manager acts as a client, issues the contract, monitors the work, and receives the final report. Even though, as a manager, you may perform the analysis yourself, you must be able to distinguish between high-quality analysis and work of limited usefulness.

Broadly speaking, most policy analyses attempt to follow a "rational" model of decision making, involving five major steps: formulating the problem, establishing criteria for evaluation, developing policy alternatives, considering the expected impact of the various alternatives, and ranking the alternatives according to the established criteria (see Box 7.2). As a simple illustration, think about how you might decide what would be the best route from home to work (Quade, 1989, pp. 33–34). If we assume at the outset that the "best" route is the shortest, then we could simply lay out the alternative routes on a map and select the shortest. (Using a map would in effect create a "model" that would help in our analysis.) As in almost all policy analyses, however, there may be more than one criterion involved. For example, the shortest route might involve more traffic and take longer to drive. The shortest travel time might then constitute a second criterion, but would require a more sophisticated model than a map, taking into account traffic congestion and perhaps other variables. Just thinking through the various complications that might arise in this "simple" example, you can get some sense of the difficulties you might encounter in moving through the five stages of a more comprehensive policy analysis.

Problem Definition

There are obviously many problems facing any public organization and, correspondingly, many opportunities to analyze policy alternatives. Someone, however, must decide about the problem to be analyzed and about how the analysis will proceed. This someone—the *sponsor* of the analysis—may be a legislator, an elected chief executive, or an agency manager. But, in any case, the one who will perform the analysis—the *analyst*—should seek as clear a statement of the problem as possible and as much information about the nature of the problem and the range of solutions. Why has the problem surfaced? Who is affected? How does this problem relate to similar problems? What policy options have already been tried? What is the range of policies that would be feasible, both economically and politically? What resources are available to support the analysis?

Obviously, how the question is initially formulated will guide the analyst toward certain possibilities and away from others, so it is important at the outset to be as clear as possible, without unnecessarily cutting off alternatives. The sponsor might ask, for example, "How can we provide adequate shelter for the homeless in our community this winter?" This statement of the issue permits exploring alternatives ranging from subsidizing existing shelters to building new shelters. If, however, certain options, such as building new shelters, are clearly out of the question by reason of time or money, then the analyst should be advised of these limitations.

BOX 7.2

Steps in Policy Analysis

1. Problem definition
2. Setting objectives and criteria
3. Developing alternatives
4. Analyzing various policies
5. Ranking and choice

Sometimes the problem is only vaguely understood at the outset, and part of the analyst's job is to develop a background statement or issue paper formulating the problem. In some cases, gathering information at the library will be helpful, especially in laying out the history of the problem, discovering approaches used in other jurisdictions, and in becoming aware of technical developments in the field. Additionally, the analyst may want to talk with other people, perhaps in other jurisdictions, to see what their experience has taught them. People in other governments, other levels of government, and other agencies at the same level can be helpful. The analyst can also gather information from those involved. In our example, the analyst would probably want to talk with those already involved in providing shelter. A statistical survey might even be possible. Finally, agency records and statistics might be helpful. Throughout these initial information-gathering efforts, the analyst wants to develop an idea of how different people and different groups perceive the problem and possible solutions.

Setting Objectives and Criteria

As we have seen, establishing objectives for a new policy or criteria for judging alternatives is often quite difficult. In some rare agencies, the existing values and preferences are clear enough to guide choices. The manager might be able to say, "It's worth much more to our agency to achieve result A than result B, C, or D. Therefore, whenever the choice presents itself, choose A." But in most policy areas, there are likely to be multiple and often conflicting objectives. To route a highway through an urban area, for example, one must consider factors such as the cost of the project, how many and who might use the highway, the number of houses and other properties that might be displaced, and the impact of noise and pollution on adjacent neighborhoods. How does one begin to rank all the factors?

There are other problems in selecting criteria. For example, criteria may differ among different levels of the organization. A constant problem for decision makers is to be sure that criteria used at one level are consistent with those at another level. A particular course of action might fit the criteria developed at one level, but so distort the use of resources at the next higher level as to make the choice inappropriate. Criteria must also be stated as completely as possible. An analyst might be told to seek a solution that maximizes output at minimum cost, then discover that no single alternative can meet both criteria. Which is more important?

Finally, choosing criteria depends on individual perspective. Most policy areas have many different **stakeholders**—many different people who are involved in the policy decision and affected by the result. These may include legislators, agency personnel, client groups, and other interest groups, and each group may feel quite differently about what is most important. In the design of a new highway, for example, a neighborhood association might place highest value on environmental concerns, while someone who lives in the suburbs might be most concerned with finding the shortest, quickest route to work. Many different criteria are likely to compete for prominence in any policy analysis. And, often, which criteria receive greatest prominence is a political decision of legislators or high-ranking administrators.

Developing Alternatives

Developing alternative policies is without question the most creative phase of policy analysis, for it is here that the analyst must move beyond easy solutions and develop innovative approaches to public problems. Different alternatives often derive from different assumptions about the problem. For example, should the welfare system be oriented toward providing support at home for impoverished mothers or should it enable mothers to work by providing day care? Should day care be addressed by building new centers or by providing tax credits or vouchers to subsidize attendance at existing centers? Obviously, answers to questions about alternative approaches to child support depend on interpretation of both the causes of poverty and the motivations of the mothers. To develop a complete range of alternatives, the analyst must assume the perspectives of many different stakeholders.

Another way to develop far-ranging alternatives is to consider the relationship between the particular problem and other similar issues. For example, adequate care for the homeless ties to issues of health care, financial support for housing, welfare policy, and perhaps such areas as mental health and Social Security. Again, alternatives that take the various interrelated concerns into account are likely to be generated if the analyst takes into account the views of many different stakeholders. Rather than saying, "How can my organization solve this problem?" the analyst should ask, "How can this problem be solved?"

Analyzing Various Policies

Having generated a number of realistic policy alternatives, the analyst must now assess the likely impact each alternative will have. Obviously, how one analyzes impacts will vary according to the particular type of policy. In some policy areas, including some of major importance, only limited information about possible impacts will be available. The analyst can only make intuitive judgments based on his or her experience and the experience of others. In other cases, however, one can gather specific data and analyze it by means of quantitative techniques. In the urban highway example, data could be gathered and analyzed to determine cost per mile, load-bearing capabilities, travel time for users, and a variety of other factors.

Occasionally, actual experiments with several policy options may be possible, sometimes with an experimental design similar to that used in the natural sciences. That is, the behavior of a particular target population may be compared to that of a control group when only one variable (the policy) is changed. Applied to large-scale social problems, such experiments may be quite costly, but they may also save considerable time and money in the long run. Sometimes it is appropriate to spend millions to save billions. (We should also note the ethical problems associated with providing a treatment expected to be beneficial to one group, but intentionally denying it to another "control" group. Is it ethical to deny some persons a treatment you think will be beneficial?)

A less formal means of policy experimentation occurs when one state or locality tries a particular policy approach and makes the results available to other communities. Sometimes this form of experimentation is simply the result of different groups trying different programs, but sometimes it is conscious. When state and local groups pressured the Carter administration to move the administration of the small cities portion of the Community Development Block Grant program to the states, two states—Wisconsin and Kentucky—were asked to run the program on an experimental basis. Their success in tailoring programs to local needs led to legislation allowing all other states to assume administration of the program (Jennings, Krane, Pattakos, & Reed, 1986).

Ranking and Choice

The final step in the analytic process is to compare the impacts associated with various alternatives and the criteria for evaluation established earlier. Alternatives can then be ranked in terms of their respective impacts. When both the criteria and the impact levels arc fairly straightforward, a simple comparison of possible effects may readily show which choice should be made; other cases may be more complex. The highway construction example, for instance, might yield three or four alternative proposals and as many as twenty criteria by which to evaluate the alternatives. One way to treat such cases is to simply lay out the expected results of each alternative in terms of the various criteria, leaving the task of comparing the data and ranking the alternatives to the decision maker. Sometimes more sophisticated quantitative techniques are available to the analyst.

COSTS AND BENEFITS

One of the most straightforward quantitative techniques is the *cost-effectiveness* approach, which "permits analysts to compare and advocate policies by quantifying their total costs and effects" (Dunn, 1981, p. 250). Costs are usually measured in monetary terms, but effects may be measured in units of any type.

Typically, the cost-effectiveness approach takes one of two forms. First, the level of effectiveness can be fixed, and one can search for the alternative that achieves this level at the least cost. If, for example, we want to increase the number of houses in a community tested for radon by 25 percent, would it be cheaper to hire inspectors or to spend money on advertising so that homeowners would do the inspection themselves? A second approach fixes the budget amount, then asks which alternative will provide the highest level of effectiveness for that amount. If we want to spend no more than $50,000 a year on radon inspections, which of our two approaches will result in a higher number of inspections?

The cost-effectiveness model is widely used because it is quite flexible and does not demand the same degree of precision as other approaches. Cost-effectiveness is especially useful when the relative merits of competing proposals, such as different child-care delivery mechanisms, are being debated. It is not as useful in comparing questions of absolute merits, however, such as whether to allocate resources to early childhood programs or to radon testing. Moreover, the cost-effectiveness approach may be somewhat limited where criteria and impacts are more complex.

A closely related approach is cost-benefit analysis. Essentially, the **cost-benefit** approach involves identifying and quantifying both negative impacts (costs) and positive impacts (benefits) of a proposal, then subtracting one from the other to arrive at a measure of net benefit. In contrast to cost-effectiveness analysis, the cost-benefit approach seeks to establish both the total monetary costs and total monetary benefits of a proposal (Dunn, 1981, p. 244). The logic of cost-benefit analysis is obvious, but applying it to policy proposals that involve large expenditures and produce difficult-to-measure results can be quite complicated.

There are several advantages to cost-benefit analysis (Sylvia, Meier, & Gunn, 1985, pp. 48–49). If programs can be evaluated in terms of costs and benefits, the approach can result in rather precise recommendations. But even if it is difficult to calculate costs or benefits, focusing on the two areas may help clarify the manager's thinking about a proposal. Legislation often requires that cost-benefit analysis precede particular policy changes, especially in environmental or regulatory policy.

Several factors make it difficult to assess the costs and benefits of a particular program. First, the analyst will be asked to come up with measures of both costs and benefits and reduce them to a common unit of measure (usually money). But in analyzing a proposed new highway, can we accurately portray the fatality rate for similar highway segments as a measure of safety? And, if so, how can we translate the rate of fatalities into dollars? Second, we should always remember that the final calculated cost-benefit ratio is not the only basis for choosing one alternative over another. Despite the ratio of costs and benefits in our highway example, a particular level of fatalities may simply be considered too high, either politically or ethically.

Typically, costs are thought of as inputs and benefits as outputs. Costs might include one-time items such as research and development, buildings and facilities, land acquisition, equipment purchases, and so on, and recurring budgetary items such as personnel, rent, maintenance, administrative overhead, insurance, and so forth. Because these expenditures take place over time, calculations usually take into account the *time value of money*—the fact that people generally are not as willing to pay for something in the future as in the present. Although the particular calculations are beyond the scope of this text, taking time into account enables us to answer questions such as whether Project A with low initial cost but high maintenance is better than Project B with high initial cost but low maintenance.

Benefits, based on outputs, include both positive and negative effects. (The negative effects of a program obviously might be calculated either as increases in cost or decreases in benefits. They are usually the latter.) Positive benefits might include reduction in disease or improved drinking water or increased highway safety; negative benefits might include increased noise and pollution from constructing a new airport. Again, some effort to translate positive or negative benefits into monetary terms would have to be made.

Obviously, measuring outputs and translating them into dollars are exceedingly difficult tasks. For example, eliminating a disease might increase productivity, which could be measured, but also reduce pain and suffering, which would be more difficult to measure. Omitting these factors because they are hard to measure biases the analysis, but assigning a dollar value to them might do the same. Consequently, the quantitative presentation of costs and benefits is often accompanied by an explanation of additional qualitative considerations.

OTHER QUANTITATIVE TECHNIQUES

In addition to cost-effectiveness and cost-benefit analyses, there are many other techniques to aid policy analysis. It is not necessary to examine the mathematical formulas, but it is helpful to understand the logic they depend on. Let us examine the following *payoff matrices* with that goal in mind. Assume a simple example: hiring an office worker who will need proficiency in computer operation and budgeting. After interviewing two applicants, A and B, you feel that A is stronger than B in both areas. Your thoughts might be modeled like this:

	Value Measures	
Possible actions	Computers	Budgeting
Choose A	+	+
Choose B	−	−

Your choice here is simple, because one candidate is clearly superior in both respects. But what if your decision appears to be structured like this:

	Value Measures	
Possible actions	Computers	Budgeting
Choose A	+	−
Choose B	−	+

Now there is no clear choice. Even if you thought computer skills were more important than budgeting skills, you couldn't choose, because candidate A might be a little better with computers, but candidate B may be much better in budgeting. To decide, you need either more sophisticated measures of ability or a way to weight the two factors, as we do in our next example:

	Computers	Budgeting	Combination
Choose A	.9	.3	.8
Choose B	.5	.8	.6
Weight	.7	.3	

Here we are assuming that we can measure ability in the two areas on a ten-point scale and that we have established that computer skills are more important than budgeting skills. By multiplying the scores by the weights, we obtain a combined value measure for the two candidates, thus enabling us to choose the better candidate. (This example is adapted from Latane, 1963.)

We could extend the logic of the payoff matrix even further. One way is to combine scores under differing working conditions. Indeed, following the logic of the payoff matrix, we could accommodate large numbers of weighted variables, as might be involved in a large-scale policy analysis; the logic remains much the same. Remember that one can adopt different decision rules and that the choice of criteria is subjective.

Another tool of policy analysis is **decision analysis,** a technique for use where decisions are likely to be made sequentially and with some degree of uncertainty. Decision analysis is applicable to a variety of complex problems, such as choosing airport sites or developing plans for commercial breeder reactors, but the underlying logic is fairly straightforward and often quite helpful. Consider the following case:

> The officer in charge of a United States Embassy recreation program has decided to replenish the employees' club funds by arranging a dinner. It rains nine days out of ten at the post, and he must decide whether to hold the dinner indoors or out. An enclosed pavilion is available but uncomfortable, and past experience has shown turnout to be low at indoor functions, resulting in a 60 percent chance of gaining $100 from a dinner held in the pavilion and a 40 percent chance of losing $20. On the other hand, an outdoor dinner could be expected to earn $500 unless it rains, in which case the dinner would lose about $10. (Stokey & Zechauser, 1978, p. 202)

Using decision analysis to structure the officer's dilemma involves first constructing a **decision tree** to show the various possible outcomes, given the risks associated with each (see Figure 7.1).

Obviously, the decision tree drawn here merely lays out the options, the probabilities of various occurrences, and the anticipated outcomes in much the same way as a payoff matrix. It is easy to imagine how much more complicated the situation could become, however, with the addition of other variables or other decision options. Even in this simple case, matters might be complicated by other variables, such as whether the weather will be hot or cold, whether there are other ways to increase attendance (advertising, and so on), and whether the commanding officer prefers indoors or outdoors. You can imagine the sequences and variables involved in a decision concerning location of a nuclear facility.

Indoors	.6 Attendance fair	+$100
	.4 Attendance very poor	−$20
Outdoors	.1 No rain; attendance excellent	+$500
	.9 Rain; attendance poor	−$10

FIGURE 7.1

Decision Tree

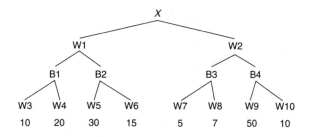

FIGURE 7.2

Chess Match Decision Tree

And, as if this weren't enough, consider what happens when you take into account competition from others. Let's imagine a chess match in which we have decided upon some evaluation criterion, such as king safety or center control, that we can measure (see Figure 7.2). That is, we have identified a way to place a value on each outcome that might result from a given set of moves. Let's say that White is ready to move and has two options, W1 and W2, leading to the following decision tree. (If we move W1, then Black can move either B1 or B2; if we move W2, then Black can move either B3 or B4; and so on. We will take the values across the bottom to be the outcomes.) We would obviously prefer to choose W2, then have Black choose B4, so that we could choose W9, the alternative with the highest value for us. But taking into account what Black is likely to do, we recognize that if we take W2, then Black will take B3, leading us to the two lowest payoffs. Recognizing this probability, we will instead take W1, expecting that Black will take B1, and we will have a satisfactory outcome.

Although our examples have been quite simple, their logic can support far more sophisticated applications of policy analysis. Moreover, the discipline these techniques imposes makes them useful for even relatively simple applications. The models force us to examine our assumptions, structure the problem clearly and logically, and consider the full range of available options. The models also allow us to more effectively communicate our analysis to others.

That brings us to one final point. No matter how sophisticated the analysis and how rational its conclusions, a policy analysis must be effectively communicated to the actual decision makers. Communication is often quite difficult, because decision makers are extremely busy and have a variety of conflicting demands on their time and interests. Sometimes even those who are invited to do a policy analysis find themselves and the analysis swept aside by political or other considerations and, indeed, that is the prerogative of major decision makers. A noted sociologist, Amitai Etzioni, spent several years as a senior advisor to the White House during the Carter administration. After trying unsuccessfully to interest the administration in a reindustrialization program, he wrote with some frustration: "Outsiders who seek to promote policy ideas uninvited, especially without the backing of an organized societal group, lobby, or pressure group, will usually find the process tortuous. Those who choose to travel this road should understand that as a rule they are in for a long haul" (Majchrzak, 1984, p. 92). A rational analysis is helpful in the decision process, but political considerations, in the positive sense, must also be taken into account before actions are taken.

IMPLEMENTATION

In the cycle of planning, implementation, and evaluation, implementation is the action phase. Once plans have been made and policies decided upon, you must put them into operation. Financial and human resources must be allocated and mobilized, organizational structures and systems must be devised, and internal policies and procedures must be developed. During implementation, you may be involved in issuing and enforcing directives, disbursing funds, awarding grants and contracts, analyzing programmatic and operational problems, taking corrective action, and negotiating with citizens, business, and those in other public and nonprofit organizations.

Recently, a body of literature dealing with the implementation process has emerged. Some of the literature merely uses new terms to talk about the general processes of administration in the public sector, whereas other parts of the literature focus on the relationship between policy development and program implementation, specifically alerting us to the difficulty of effective implementation and to how implementation of programs may distort or even subvert the intent of policy makers. Most pointedly, one commentator has written, "It is hard enough to design public policies and programs that look good on paper. It is harder still to formulate them in words and slogans that resonate pleasingly in the ears of political leaders and the constituencies to which they are responsive. And it is excruciatingly hard to implement them in a way that pleases anyone at all, including the supposed beneficiaries or clients" (Bardach, 1977, p. 3).

A classic study of the relationship between policy and implementation was suggestively titled *Implementation: How Great Expectations in Washington Are Dashed in Oakland; or Why It's Amazing That Federal Programs Work at All* (Pressman & Wildavsky, 1973). Implementation described a particular economic development program in the Oakland, California, area that was less than successful. Pressman and Wildavsky conclude that "what seemed to be a simple program turned out to be a very complex one, involving many participants, a host of different perspectives, and a long and tortuous path of decision points that had to be cleared" (p. 94). Implementation was characterized by multiple and conflicting interests, each trying to influence the program's direction to suit their many and divergent needs. The major recommendation of the study seemed to be that persons involved in designing public policies "pay as much attention to the creation of organizational machinery for executing a program as for launching one" (pp. 144–145).

This lesson has been clearly recognized in the literature of strategic planning. Plans remain sterile without implementation, so there has always been a close connection between planning and execution. As noted, planning is most beneficial where it can help make immediate decisions in light of future impact. Thus, a final step in any planning process is to arrive at a series of specific actions to take in the near future—the next six months, or the next year or two years—who does what, when and to what effect. These steps, which may detail new policy positions or new organizational processes, will form a new action agenda for the community or the agency.

ORGANIZATIONAL DESIGN

Some of the classic approaches to implementation, or what was formerly called simply "organization and management," focused on the structure and design of new organizations and their work processes or flows. The traditional organization chart expresses both the division of labor within an organization and the structure of command or control.

In the late 1930s, Luther Gulick advised managers developing new organizations that there were several ways they could divide work (Gulick, 1937, pp. 21–29). Among these were (1) purpose, (2) process, (3) persons or things, or (4) place. Dividing work according to purpose might result in distinctions such as that between providing education or controlling crime, while dividing it according to process might lead to a legal unit, a medical unit, or an engineering unit. One could also divide work according to the persons served or the things being dealt with; for example, the Veterans Administration deals with all problems that veterans face, whether legal, medical, and so on. Finally, one may organize according to geographic area, as would a state welfare department that has regional or county offices.

NETWORKING

Online resources and case studies relating to the planning and implementation of productivity initiatives can be found at http://www.alliance.napawash.org/alliance/index.html. Additional resources can be found at the NPR site (http://www.npr.gov/library/studies/list.html) and at the U.S. Conference of Mayors site (http://www.usmayors.org/uscm/best_practices/).

Gulick and his contemporaries also talked about the number of levels that would be appropriate to an organization. Obviously, many organizations are fairly "tall"—they have many levels; others are "flat"—they have relatively few levels. The number of levels is guided to a degree by the type of work and by the number of people who report to any one manager. The term *span of control* signifies the number of people that one individual supervises; though there are significant variations depending on type of work, it is generally considered difficult to supervise more than six to ten people.

In addition to developing organizational structures, early writers urged charting work processes as an aid to organizational design. **Process charting** or **flowcharting** can provide a graphic demonstration of the various steps in an operation, the people performing each step, and the relationships among these elements. Figure 7.3 shows a simple illustration of process charting, though charts can become far more sophisticated in actual applications. This process chart uses a variety of symbols to indicate

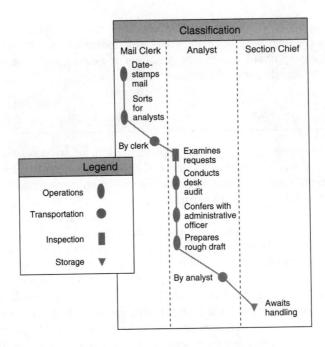

FIGURE 7.3

Process Charting

different activities. The vertical lines set the basic framework of the chart. The columns show the flow of work from one unit or person to another and vary depending on the complexity of the process and the degree of analysis desired. The column headings indicate the elements under study. In this example, the larger circles on the chart refer to a specific task (filling out a form, testing a sample, and so on); the smaller circles indicate transportation of the work from one unit or person to another. The triangles indicate storage, a period in which the item or operation is stationary. Finally, the square indicates an inspection of the work item, usually to check for quality or quantity. As illustrated here, one can make notations on the chart to indicate the nature of particular steps in the process.

Process charting is most useful where a considerable number of clerical or nonprofessional employees perform the same general classes of work and follow the same general sequence of operating steps. Although process charting is less useful in analyzing the work of professionals, there are possible applications here as well. For example, charting a professional operation may reveal bottlenecks, excessive periods of review, or excessive check points that inhibit the flow of work. As with other techniques, process charting can become quite complex, but its logic is both simple and compelling. Process charting simplifies analysis because it sharply points out backtracking, excessive detail, unnecessary repetition, poor distribution of functions, and other administrative defects. For this reason process charting has enjoyed a revival of interest by those implementing total quality management programs.

SYSTEMS ANALYSIS

There are many other sophisticated devices that have been developed for analyzing the design and operations of both public and private organizations. Many of the approaches are based in **systems theory,** an effort to identify, in logical fashion, the interactions of various internal and external elements that impinge on an organization's operations. The systems approach has been used in a variety of fields, including physics, biology, economics, sociology, and information science, but the basic concepts are much the same regardless of discipline. Generally speaking, a **system** is a set of regularized interactions configured or hounded in a way that differentiates and separates them from other actions that constitute the systems environment; thus, we can speak of a biological system, a physical system, an economic system, or a political system. Any such system receives *inputs* from its environment, then translates these through some sort of *conversion process* into *outputs* that are returned to the environment. These outputs in turn affect future inputs to the system through a *feedback loop.* Presumably, if the outputs of a system are valued by the environment, new inputs will be forthcoming and the organization will survive. (A basic systems model is illustrated in Figure 7.4.)

Following this model, consider the operation of a thermostat. The thermostat takes in information about the heat in a room, then measures the heat against some standard. If the level of heat is below the standard, the thermostat causes more heat to be put out into the room. The additional heat becomes part of the environment and creates new information (feedback), which becomes part of the next input into the system.

The systems concept works similarly in human organizations. A business might receive input from its environment that customers are demanding more red shoes. A

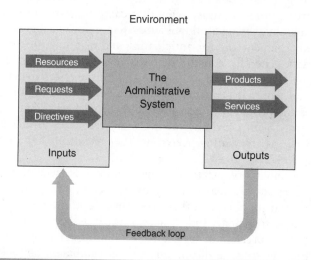

FIGURE 7.4

A Basic Systems Model

decision might be made to produce more red shoes, and those shoes would be part of the organization's output. The new red shoes become part of the environment and affect new inputs into the system, which might range from comments about the quality of the shoes or information that the demand has not yet been met. This new information guides the operation of the system in the future.

Like many of the other models we have discussed in this chapter, the systems approach has been used in highly sophisticated applications ranging from analysis of organizational design and processes to creation and modification of major weapons systems. Indeed, the first major applications of systems analysis occurred in the military during and soon after World War II. For some time thereafter, the Department of Defense was the major user of systems analysis, depending on a variety of contractors, most notably the Rand Corporation. This is why techniques such as PPBS (discussed in Chapter 5) found their earliest and warmest reception in the Department of Defense. Yet it is possible to apply systems logic to a variety of problems public organizations face, and, as with other techniques, the systematic discipline that the approach brings to problem solving is perhaps its greatest strength.

Systems analysis emphasizes the relationship between the organization and its environment, suggesting that public managers carefully consider factors in the environment that impinge on their operations. These factors include legal and political matters, support and opposition generated by interest groups and client organizations, human and financial resources, and applicable technology. Naturally, the environment also includes a large number of other organizations with which the agency interacts, such as the chief executive's office, the legislature, the budget office, related agencies at the same level of government, parallel agencies at other levels of government, and a variety of private and nonprofit groups and associations.

Many systems analysts tend to ignore what occurs within the system itself, preferring to think of it as a black box into which inputs go and from which outputs come. Others speak of several different subsystems that carry forward the organization's work. In a classic formulation, the **institutional subsystem** is responsible for adapting the organization to its environment and for anticipating and planning for the future. People involved in this activity generally constitute the organization's leadership cadre. The technical subsystem, on the other hand, is concerned with the effective performance of the organization's actual work. If the work of the organization is building rockets, the **technical subsystem** is the people who actually build the rockets. Finally, the **managerial subsystem** is concerned with providing the necessary resources for accomplishing the technical task, as well as mediating between the technical and institutional subsystems (Thompson, 1967, pp. 10–11).

Outputs of public organizations range from goods (such as highways or buildings) to services (such as student loans or employment counseling), but also include regulations, adjudication, and support for other programs. To know the effect of their efforts, managers need some sort of feedback mechanism. Feedback often occurs naturally: clients write letters of appreciation; legislators inquire about program operations; a program may even become an issue during an election campaign. Sometimes, however, you will want to secure more systematic and accurate feedback, for which you can use devices such as questionnaire surveys, field testing, or spot checks of service provision. Recall that systems analysis helps focus on how an organization interacts with its environment; developing effective feedback mechanisms helps the manager in that process.

PERT/CPM

Another technique for guiding implementation of public programs is the *Program Evaluation Review Technique (PERT)* or the *Critical Path Method (CPM)*. (The two techniques were developed separately and have minor differences, but we can treat them as one, using the title PERT.) **PERT** is a system for organizing and monitoring projects that have a specific beginning point and a specific ending point. NASA used the system extensively in developing the manned spacecraft program; it can accommodate quite substantial projects. We will focus on the basic logic underlying the system.

A *PERT* chart uses a series of circles, designating events, and arrows, designating time or costs, to indicate various activities for completing a project and the necessary sequence. One circle might show the beginning of a particular effort and be connected by an arrow to another circle, which might show the end of the first activity and the beginning of a second. Any activity that must be completed before the start of another activity should appear to the left of that activity. Thus, the key elements in a PERT chart might look like this:

Put on socks → Put on shoes

Activities that are independent of one another are shown in separate sequences; for example, if you could put on your shirt while you are putting on your shoes, that activity could be parallel to putting on your shoes.

A more complex PERT chart appears in Figure 7.5, showing a variety of activities that might be undertaken to hold a conference. As in all PERT charts, no activity can take place until all events logically prior to that event occur. For instance, to print and mail the brochures (I), it is necessary to develop a budget (H), contract for the space (D), and identify the conference speakers (K). Each event is necessarily preceded by others. Time estimates for each activity are entered above each line. (Some PERT charts give a normal, an optimistic, and a pessimistic time projection, but we give one figure—the expected time in days. PERT charts can also be constructed with cost estimates substituted for time estimates.)

Various paths lead from the decision to hold the conference (A) to the opening session (G). If you add the times required to complete all the steps along any particular path, you arrive at an expected time to complete that path—ABCDEFG requires twenty-two days; ABJKIFG requires forty-two days. The path that takes the most time is the *critical path* (in this case, path ABHKIFG) and is usually highlighted in some way. Any delay in the critical path will delay the entire project. Other paths may have built-in slack times, where small delays will not cause that path to exceed the time required for the critical path. The critical path in this example tells us that the conference organizers have forty-three days to complete their project. If for some reason the conference must be held sooner, they must find some way to decrease the time required to complete the critical path.

In summary, program implementation involves the full range of administrative skills and concepts, but implementation can occasionally be facilitated by using certain

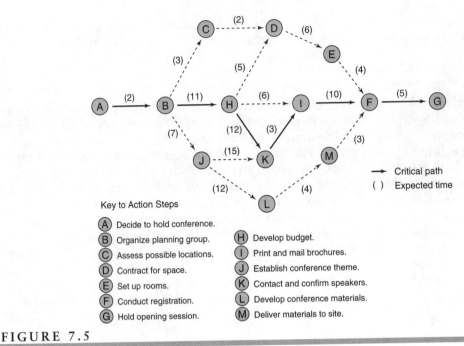

Key to Action Steps

- (A) Decide to hold conference.
- (B) Organize planning group.
- (C) Assess possible locations.
- (D) Contract for space.
- (E) Set up rooms.
- (F) Conduct registration.
- (G) Hold opening session.
- (H) Develop budget.
- (I) Print and mail brochures.
- (J) Establish conference theme.
- (K) Contact and confirm speakers.
- (L) Develop conference materials.
- (M) Deliver materials to site.

→ Critical path
( ) Expected time

FIGURE 7.5

Chart for Organizing a Conference

techniques. Our examples are simplified to illustrate the logic of the technique. All the techniques, however, can be applied to projects of much greater magnitude and complexity. Regardless of the complexity of the application, the result should be the same—a more disciplined and precise view of the implementation of one's program.

Reengineering

Recently, some public administrators have adopted a more comprehensive, even radical technique for enhancing organizational performance, called reengineering. The core tenet of reengineering centers on redesigning work processes and organizational structures to be in line with agency outcomes. Proponents of the technique view existing bureaucracies as relics from the industrial age and seek to restructure public organizations. Through this technique, they attempt to make public organizations more flexible and capable of responding to the dynamic conditions in contemporary society.

In some respects, reengineering builds upon systems theory, PERT/CPM and other techniques in that it involves the recognition of core processes and the systemic context of staff behavior. However, the outcome of reengineering goes well beyond simply making alterations within the existing bureaucratic structure. Its goal is to overhaul rigid government agencies into what one author calls seamless organizations: "In contrast to the fragmented bureaucracies of the past, seamless organizations provide a smooth, transparent, almost effortless experience for their customers. Staff in seamless organizations perform the full job, in direct contact with their end users" (Linden, 1994, p. xii).

Implementation of a reengineering process begins with an identification of the organization's desired outcomes. These include the short- and long-term impacts the agency wants to achieve. Then, the organization is redesigned around the core and support processes that will produce these outcomes. Given the hierarchical, inflexible nature of many public organizations, though, this is not as simple as it may seem.

Reengineering requires that public administrators change their current assumptions, those equating organization with traditional bureaucracy. Such a reorientation helps to transform work processes and agency structures to those driven by meaningful outcomes—a shift from segmentation to integration, from division of labor to seamless work (Linden, 1994).

Reengineering involves enhancing those activities that may be considered value-added—that is, activities that give customers more of what they are willing to pay for and cutting functions that merely stand in the way. Of course, some of the functions in this latter category remain crucial for the organization's success. Central administration activities such as budgeting, accounting, and quality inspections cannot simply be removed from the picture. On the other hand, these functions often hinder the completion of the more value-added activities. The key to successful reengineering is to separate the core processes from the other tasks, enabling the critical activities to be carried out more effectively.

While management plays a central role in any reengineering effort, the technique's success depends upon the capacity of key teams engaged in project design and implementation. The first team is responsible for identifying organizational processes in need of change. Next, the second group leads the change initiative. Individuals from throughout the organization, as well as members of the organization's stakeholder groups, are brought in to inform the process and to develop indicators that will help keep the initiative on track. Leaders emerge from each of these teams—individuals who guide the reengineering process by ensuring that it has adequate resources, administrative support, and overall organizational commitment (Hammer & Champy, 1993; Linden, 1994).

EVALUATION

The sequence of planning, implementation, and evaluation is completed by asking whether the goals and objectives of the program have been achieved in a way that was both efficient and effective. Such evaluations may, however, operate at a variety of different levels. Some may respond to the interest of the legislature in knowing whether the intended benefits of legislation were achieved; others may be designed to communicate to the public what is happening in areas of broad citizen interest; still others may be oriented toward improvements either in the design of the policy being implemented or in the way it was conducted. An understanding of the contemporary approaches to evaluation requires attention to both the performance measurement movement mentioned earlier and more traditional program evaluation approaches.

While program evaluation offers insight into each policy or program's direction, effectiveness, and sustainability, performance measurement generates information concerning the organization or network as a whole. When combined within the framework of evaluation research, these strategies not only assist in the decision-making process, they improve the overall accountability of public organizations. In turn, evaluation research enhances legislative oversight and administrative control.

Several legislative groups conduct or "sponsor" evaluation research at the federal level. These include the General Accounting Office (GAO), the Congressional Budget Office, the Congressional Research Service, and the Office of Technology Assessment, as well as various legislative committees, primarily those concerned with the budget and with oversight of specific programs. Executive agencies, such as the Office of Management and Budget and the Executive Office of the President, also conduct evaluation research. Much of this research, however, is sponsored by the various agencies themselves, as managers seek to determine how they can better manage or generate greater productivity from their organizations.

There is also great interest in performance measurement and program evaluation at the state and local levels, although resources to support such activities have often been limited. State governments have developed analytic capabilities within the executive branch, often through the budget office. In recent years, many states have restructured their budgets to be in line with predetermined performance standards. This has enabled state governments to link fiscal resources to the desired results targeted by each agency. Evaluation research is then used to help the state government determine how successful it has been in achieving its performance goals. Consequently, state legislatures and citizens can now see what services and impacts were gained with public resources.

Again, at the state and local levels and in most nongovernmental organizations, as at the federal level, a great deal of evaluation research is done as part of the agency or program manager's ongoing responsibility. Particularly in the era of "reinvention" and the National Performance Review, public administrators increasingly must show not only the efficiency of their actions but also the results of their actions within the broader stakeholder community. Examples of performance measurement and program evaluation range from complex, detailed, one-time studies to the ongoing, integrated monitoring of performance goals. Regardless of the level of sophistication, evaluation research offers important details in support of the organization's overall strategic planning and to assist the organization in determining the direction of individual programs.

PERFORMANCE MEASUREMENT

The most recent addition to the field of evaluation research, performance measurement, emerged during the late 1980s, as citizens, legislators, and advocacy groups started to demand more value from public organizations. Government was pressured not only to show its efficiency in expending public resources but also to prove that substantive results, or outcomes directly related to the effect a program has on the public, had been generated by its activities. As the call for "reinventing government" gained in strength in the early 1990s, the move toward performance measurement occurred at all levels of government. Federal agencies developed performance standards at the program level and in their management and administrative functions. State and local governments followed suit, both as a means of assessing their activities and of enhancing their reporting under federal programs (Wholey, Hatry, & Newcomer, 1994).

NETWORKING

The federal government provides updates and related information concerning evaluation strategies under its Goverment Performance and Results Act (GPRA) at the GPRA Report site (http://www.ombwatch.org/www/ombw/gpra/gpra1.html) and the Congressional Institute (http://www.conginst.org/). For information concerning evaluation activities by state and local governments, visit these sites: (1) http://policyworks.gov/org/main/mg/nprgate/gsaresults.htm and (2) http://www.auditor.leg.state.mn.us/ped.htm

In 1993, performance measurement became the law under the Government Performance and Results Act (GPRA). The act mandated that federal agencies undergo a strategic planning process to identify five-year performance outcomes. Organizational activities toward these outcomes, then, would be measurable through annual performance reviews. The performance review plans would be required starting in FY 1999. Within these plans, federal agencies must identify performance indicators—specific, quantifiable goals that the agency strives for in pursuit of its more substantive objectives. These indicators reflect each agency's outputs and outcomes.

A distinction should be made here between inputs, outputs, and outcomes: inputs are those resources—financial, human, and otherwise—available to the organization; outputs are the actual goods or services produced by an organization; and outcomes, as we have mentioned, are the long-term objectives that the organization wants to achieve. As an illustration, the Federal Aviation Administration issues regulations, which constitute one type of its outputs. But someone measuring the performance of this organization would be only moderately interested in the number of regulations it issues. More important would be the effect of the regulations on desired goals, such as improved air safety. Improved air safety would be an outcome. (Generally speaking, objectives are likely to be narrow and specific, directly tied to each organization's particular activities; outcomes, on the other hand, are related to the larger purposes to be served by the organization's work.)

The move toward performance measurement goes well beyond GPRA and its requirements for federal agencies. Public organizations at all levels have begun to tie evaluation research to their planning and implementation functions. Most state governments, for instance, now use performance measurement as a means of assessing their activities in terms of both outputs and outcomes. Accordingly, these states can associate budget decisions and program directives with specific performance standards set by each agency. And, as a result, the states enjoy a more effective system of accounting for their efficiency and effectiveness to citizens and other stakeholders.

Several years ago, for example, the state of Texas instituted a performance budgeting system as a means of enhancing agency accountability and productivity. Under the new system, state agencies must determine the resources necessary to accomplish performance goals, then negotiate the goals and resources with the state legislature. Once the outcomes and allocations have been established, lawmakers grant spending authority based on the performance goals. The move away from program categories and line items, thus, gives administrators in Texas greater flexibility in meeting their performance objectives. And, the budget system ensures that evaluation and measurement is based on productivity rather than on agency processes (Carter, 1994). However, as we see in Box 7.3, the task of identifying measures is not always easy.

In identifying performance standards, public organizations may pull from a variety of sources. This is usually done in what is called a process of benchmarking. Benchmarking features the targeting of specific goals based on previous performance levels, standards set by similar organizations, objectives created through a strategic planning process, or any combination of these and other relevant sources. Public administrators then assess agency performance, using comparisons with these predetermined indicators. Through benchmarking, administrators are able to connect their evaluation research directly with the agency's planning and implementation strategies.

Indeed, the most effective application of performance measurement integrates evaluation and measurement within the broader context of performance management. A recent report on one successful performance management exercise was developed by Jay Hakes, administrator of the Energy Information Administration of the U.S. Department of Energy, based on his work with the agency. Specifically, based on the EIA experience, Hakes suggests that organizations that attempt to pattern assessment strategies, without first sequencing these strategies in the overall process of organizational change, may lose sight of important organizational barriers both to performance measurement and to the change itself. These groups may fall into the trap of monitoring activities without linking them to the targeted goals and outcomes of the organization.

To prevent this, Hakes suggests several action steps that lay a foundation for successful performance measurement, which include:

- analyzing goals deriving from statutes and historic practices
- discussing desired outputs and outcomes with major customers in and out of government
- writing a strategic plan
- drawing an input/output map of the organization (Hakes, 1997, p. 10)

However, it is important to note that these steps represent merely the beginning of successful performance management. Commitments from top leadership, organizational members, stakeholders and those overseeing agency resources must be gained in order for the change strategy to be effective. The performance measures themselves must be linked with the organization's budget allocations and reward systems. In this regard, creating an effective measurement strategy means transforming the organization into a performance-based organization.

BOX 7.3

Altering the Outcomes

These days, discussions of welfare reform invariably turn to outcomes. Historically, welfare programs used measurements that assessed process efficiencies. In an entitlement system, the measurement of error rates and the number of cases per caseworker were appropriate, since the business was focused—as its primary driver—on determining eligibility.

In the new world of welfare reform, with time-limited benefits and workfare programs, the objectives are more complex than getting the applicant a check.

The new paradigm involves helping recipients develop enough self-sufficiency so that they do not need state-provided financial supports. It is no longer acceptable that welfare programs are just efficient; they must also be effective. The only way to confirm that they are effective is to measure their effectiveness against some agreed-upon criteria. Therefore, the discussion of outcome measures is critical to welfare reform.

William Kilmartin, comptroller for Massachusetts, who is a strong advocate of management accountability in the public sector, said:

> Clarifying the outcomes we desire is important. Let me give an example of a situation that makes outcome measurement so tricky in the field of human service. Take an example of a hypothetical mother and child that were getting assistance under the old Aid to Families with Dependent Children (AFDC) program; the child was removed from the home and put into the care and protection of the state in its foster care program. The child welfare worker that removed the child from the mother's care was supposed to inform the welfare caseworker that the child was out of the household, so that the benefit to the mother was reduced. The assumed measure of program success for welfare was to reduce the caseload level; we went one case down in AFDC and one up in child welfare. But a positive outcome measure for the child welfare program was to get the children in foster care back to their mothers. Working toward that outcome, the child welfare caseworker would not have informed the AFDC program of the foster care placement, because doing so would have reduced the mother's income level. The child welfare caseworker worried that the reduced resources available to the mother would reduce the likelihood that she could create the conditions necessary for the return of the child. The finance people went nuts when this type of situation occurred, but from the perspective of the child welfare worker it was a rational decision because of the assumed outcome of reunification. From the welfare agency's perspective it was a poor outcome—fraud! . . . I think that you would find that every public servant is in vociferous agreement with the concept of performance measurement. . . . The difficulty is converting policy objectives into metrics for accountability. A lot of people have tried to use the budget process as a tool for holding agencies accountable for outcomes, but I don't know if that works. In the private sector, goals and objectives can be converted to financial terms easily. In the public sector, it is a stretch beyond reason to think that all things can be measured in terms of budgetary outcomes.

SOURCE: Singer, Larry. "Altering the Outcomes: Assessing Welfare Program Effectiveness Requires More Than Just Caseload Count." *Government Technology* 10 (December 1997): 143.

The next steps in the process involve integrating the measures throughout the organization. This can be done, according to Hakes, by involving organizational members in the process and by gaining feedback to enhance the measures. Data sources, complete with baseline indicators, should be established and a benchmarking process initiated to ensure that the goals will be measurable and the activities geared toward predetermined performance standards.

Finally, clear decisions must be reached on how the performance measurement system will be used. Some may opt for a more punitive application of assessment, choosing to use the techniques to play a watchdog role. Hakes encourages public administrators to employ measurement strategies in a more constructive way: "If workers can use measures for self correction and continuous improvement without risk of punishment or with some prospect for reward, progress on providing value for dollar (maximum outputs and outcomes for minimal inputs) will surpass the expectations of most observers" (1997, p. 17).

As with any successful approach to organizational change, Hakes reveals that the most meaningful attempt at performance management will occur when leadership engages members from throughout the organization and, in turn, connects the assessment strategy to the organization's long-term outcomes. More important, Hakes suggests that public administrators must become less concerned with strictly the quantitative indicators and more concerned with creating a culture of success within their organizations.

An interesting approach to performance measurement in the private sector that balances concerns for financial performance, customer service, internal business processes, and learning and growth is Kaplan and Norton's "Balanced Scorecard." The Balanced Scorecard seeks to track various dimensions of an organization's performance in a way that can readily communicate common information to decision makers throughout the organization. Kaplan and Norton point out, however, that the Balanced Scorecard is not a just technique to control behavior or evaluate past performance. Rather it should be used to communicate, to inform, and to enable learning and growth. Through the use of this technique managers should be able to monitor and adjust the implementation of their strategies and make fundamental changes in the way the organization operates (Kaplan & Norton, 1966, pp. 18–24).

Not only those in the United States, but government agencies around the world have begun to develop strategies to help them evaluate their efforts and assume more client-centered approaches to meeting public outcomes. A recent study, for example, examined reform efforts in member states of the Organization for Economic Cooperation and Development (OECD) and selected nonmember nations.

Nations such as Canada, Spain, and Sweden were targeted for their efforts to develop and implement performance measurement techniques on a nationwide basis. Other countries, like the United States, Germany, Korea, Mexico, and the Netherlands, were cited for implementing performance monitoring in specific policy areas. The areas sampled included health care, police and public safety, and policy advice.

The findings from this research indicated that several requirements influence the success of performance monitoring by public organizations, including the need for "strategic leadership from central units," "the establishment of the proper organizational incentives which support and encourage results-based management," and "the use of program evaluation as a complement to ongoing performance measurement systems to address performance issues that performance measurement cannot well deal with so as to make the best use of these two measurement tools" (Mayne, 1997, p. 16).

The research indicated that the dynamic environments in which the organizations functioned had a significant impact on each agency's capacity for performance and its measurement. In fact, the study showed that the ability of an organization to adapt to changing conditions exceeded raw performance as the primary indicator of organizational success. Mayne (1997) wrote, "Maximizing flexibility may be more important than maximizing short-term utility" (p. 16). The study concluded that organizational survival depended on each group's ability to integrate performance measurement with the organization's overall capacity for problem solving and strategic management.

Of course, such a capacity depends on each agency's ability to monitor both the broader organizational performance as well as the effectiveness of individual programs. We have noted the significance of the first of these evaluation strategies in our discussion of performance measurement. However, additional attention should be given to program evaluation, which generates valuable insight into organizational processes and the programmatic impacts produced by policies and initiatives. If performance measurement connects the organization as a whole to specific results and outcomes, then program evaluation reveals how actions by an organization contribute to the objectives within each policy area.

PROGRAM EVALUATION

There are a variety of ways to classify the approaches to program evaluation. These are, for example, outcome evaluations and process evaluations. *Outcome evaluations,* which are closely tied to the type of assessment in performance measurement, focus on the results of program activity, the extent to which a program meets its objectives in terms of impact on the environment. If the work of an organization is to pave and repair city streets, then an evaluation might measure the number of miles of streets paved and repaired. That information would likely then be related to program inputs to show, in a cost-benefit ratio, the number of miles paved per thousand dollars spent. In general, an outcome evaluation seeks to determine whether X causes Y, where X is the activity of the program and Y is the desired outcome or goal. As you can imagine, outcome evaluations are particularly valuable to legislators and others concerned with performance of various programs.

In contrast to outcome evaluations, **process evaluations** focus on ways program implementation might be improved to better meet the program's objectives. The question here is what can be done to X, the program's management, to improve Y, the desired outcome. Where an evaluator interested in outcomes might spend a great deal of time developing systematic measures of program results, someone interested in process evaluation would analyze the organization and management of the agency's activities, including distribution of financial and human resources and design of service delivery mechanisms (Sylvia, Meier, & Gunn, 1985, p. 136). Process evaluations also determine if legally prescribed processes are being followed and assure that individual rights are not violated.

Relevant measures here would fall more on the input side, and might include such items as workload measures or data on resource allocation. In such studies it may be important to distinguish between efficiency and effectiveness. **Efficiency** is concerned with the relationship between inputs and outputs, usually expressed in a ratio per unit of input. For example, a measure of streets paved per thousand dollars spent would be a measure of efficiency. **Effectiveness,** on the other hand, is concerned with the extent to which a program is achieving or failing to achieve its stated objectives (Poister, McDavid, & Magoun, 1979, p. 3). Effectiveness measures are outcome-oriented; they focus on the real changes the program produces, such as a decrease in airline deaths.

Sometimes process evaluations occur after the fact, that is, upon completion of the program; but often they occur during program operation. Indeed, some process evaluations are almost continuous in their ongoing review of program operations (Poister, 1983). In either case, the information that emerges in the course of a process evaluation is likely to be of greatest interest to the program manager who hopes to improve his or her organization's performance.

Program evaluations may therefore be directed toward many different audiences and serve many different purposes. The specific kinds of information required vary from evaluation to evaluation. Eleanor Chelimsky, former head of the General Accounting Office's Program Evaluation and Methodology Division, lists the following types of information that may be developed retrospectively:

- information on program implementation (such as the degree to which the program is operational, how similar it is across sites, whether it conforms to the policies and expectations formulated, how much it costs, how stakeholders feel about it, whether there are major problems of service delivery or of error, fraud, and abuse, and so on)
- ongoing information on the current state of the problem or threat addressed by the program (Is the problem growing? Is it diminishing? Is it diminishing enough so that the program is no longer needed? Is it changing in terms of its significant characteristics?)
- information on program outcomes (What happened as a result of program implementation?)
- information on the degree to which the program made, or is making, a difference (That is, what change in the problem or threat occurred that can be directly attributed to the program?)
- information on the unexpected (as well as the expected) effects of the programs (For instance, was a program of drug education accompanied by an increase in the use of drugs?) (Chelimsky, 1985, pp. 8–9)

EVALUATION DESIGNS AND TECHNIQUES

Approaches to the evaluation of public programs range from historical analysis to sophisticated experimental designs. Indeed, over the years, there has been a recurring debate over the proper approach to evaluation. Some argue that such research should be primarily qualitative, concerned with tracking program development and indicating forces that helped shape the program. Advocates of this approach tend to be most interested in process questions, such as reasons for success or failure and unanticipated consequences of the program; they ask, "What happened?" Others argue that program evaluations should, wherever possible, employ the most rigorous scientific methods appropriate to the subject matter, including the design and execution of formal experiments. These analysts tend to be more interested in program outcomes"; they ask, "Does it work?" (Chelimsky, 1985, p. 14).

Whatever the approach, those involved in program evaluation must confront two challenges to the validity of their work. The first question, concerning *internal validity*, asks whether the approach measured what was intended. Was the design consistent with the goals of the program and the needs of the sponsor? Were the methods most appropriate for answering the questions that needed to be asked? Were the results as free from bias as possible? A second question, concerning *external validity*, asks to what extent the findings may be applicable to more general circumstances. What does the study say about similarly situated programs? Can the study be replicated and expected to produce similar results? These and other questions can be directed toward the various techniques employed in evaluation research.

Qualitative Techniques

Many program evaluations depend on qualitative information derived from reading about the program, from interviewing important actors (including agency personnel, clients, and others), and sometimes from actually participating in the work of the program. The initial step in a qualitative evaluation project is usually to read everything available about the program and the subject matter, including background material on the subject of the program (flu vaccines, child nutrition, rapid transit systems, and so on), agency documents, operating procedures, internal memoranda, newspaper and magazine articles, articles on similar programs elsewhere, and reports issued by various concerned groups. The researcher would also likely make a few phone calls to identify the significant actors in the program and determine where the most important activities are taking place.

Following an initial reconnaissance, the analyst settles on a limited number of sites (schools, hospitals, highway systems, and so on) as the focus of the investigation. Most qualitative evaluations are largely **exploratory**, designed to explore a variety of hunches or intuitions about the program's operation. For these cases, the analyst will probably try to select sites that vary widely along several crucial dimensions. Some evaluations, however, are *hypothesis-guided,* designed to demonstrate the plausibility of a particular hypothesis, so the analyst might choose a limited number of crucial sites that are especially illustrative of the issue under investigation (Murphy, 1980, pp. 38–47).

Once the research sites have been chosen, the analyst may choose to gather most of his or her information through *intensive interviews,* detailed information-gathering sessions involving major actors both inside and outside the agency responsible for the program. Interviewing skills include establishing the interviewer's credentials, setting the proper climate, arranging questions effectively, asking reasonable but challenging questions, and keeping a good record of all that is said. Perhaps most important, the interviewer must keep the discussion on the subject, in a way that is neither obvious nor embarrassing to either party. Immediately following the interview, the interviewer should review and expand upon the notes taken during the interview session. These notes will form an important basis for drawing conclusions about the program.

An alternative means of gathering qualitative information is the use of a **participant-observer,** someone involved in either the target population or the agency itself who makes observations and draws conclusions based on that firsthand data. For example, an evaluation of an antipoverty program in eastern Kentucky some years ago employed a participant-observer who lived in the community, talked daily with others in the community about the program, and reported back to the overall evaluation staff.

Either technique can be questioned with respect to both internal and external validity. Biased information and questions about internal validity can arise if the wrong people are chosen to interview or if those interviewed provide misleading information, intentionally or unintentionally. Participant-observers can affect the program's operation through their own presence, leading to outcomes far different from what would otherwise have happened. Questions concerning external validity (or generalizability) might be raised with either technique based on the choice of only a limited number of sites for investigation.

Quantitative Techniques

Policy evaluations often endeavor to approximate the scientific methods of the physical sciences, though such efforts are extremely difficult. In its classic formulation, an *experimental design* involves examination of two or more groups under carefully controlled conditions. One group, the *experimental group,* receives a treatment or intervention; in the case of program evaluation, members of the experimental group receive the benefits of the program being evaluated. Another group, the *control group,* consists of individuals who are as similar as possible to those in the experimental group and who act under the same general conditions, yet do not receive the intervention. Members of both groups are tested before and after the experimental intervention (pretest and posttest measures) and the results are compared. If the program has had either a positive or negative effect, the differences should show up in the data.

We can illustrate the difficulties in designing a rigorous experimental design with respect to social programs by imagining that we are interested in analyzing the effectiveness of a new approach to mathematics education in the fourth grade. One classroom might be designated an experimental group and be taught using the new approach; another classroom might be designated the control group and be taught using traditional methods. The mathematical abilities of all students would be measured both before and after the period in which the new program was being taught. If the new technique is indeed more effective in educating children in mathematics, the posttest scores of the children in the experimental group should be higher than those of the children in the control group.

Very generally, this is an application of an experimental design to a social program, and you can easily imagine how similar designs might be used to measure other programs, ranging from immunizations to welfare incentives to highway designs. But we can readily observe the difficulties in such designs, some of which relate to questions of internal validity. One might respond to the study by saying that the students in the experimental group were smarter to begin with, or that the absence rate was higher among those in the control group. Or you might suggest that one teacher was better than the other, and that made the difference. Or, even if the same teacher taught both groups, you might speculate that he or she taught the new material with more enthusiasm. Similar questions might be raised about external validity. For instance, if the results were obtained in a rural school, would they apply as well to an urban setting?

Some, if not all, of these questions could be anticipated by slightly altering the research design. For example, students could be randomly assigned to the two groups, thus eliminating any possibility of bias in group composition. But questions such as these show the difficulty of achieving true experimental conditions in measuring social programs. For this reason, most evaluations of social programs are called quasi-experimental.

Quasi-experimental designs retain the requirement for systematic data gathering that should be part of any quantitative approach, but free the researcher from some of the difficulties of developing experimental designs, such as the need for random assignment of subjects to various groups. Here again, different groups may be compared, but an essential task for the researcher is to separate the effects of a treatment from effects of other factors. Only the effects caused by the treatment are of interest.

Quasi-experimental approaches are not only more adaptable to social situations; they also better fit the situation in which program evaluators often find themselves—assigned to the evaluation long after the program has begun and having little way to influence patterns of intervention. In such a case, a historical approach may be of special value. For example, one quasi-experimental design, **time series analysis**, involves making a number of observations about the target population both before and after the program intervention. (These observations may even be made retrospectively, by gathering historical data.) In one case, basic information about neighborhood crime was developed for a period of years prior to the introduction of a new patrol pattern, then similar data followed after the new approach was introduced.

SUMMARY AND ACTION IMPLICATIONS

As a public manager, you will become quite familiar with the cycle of planning, implementation, and evaluation. In practice, the phases of the cycle will rarely appear as distinct as in our discussion, but you will still find that you must devote a portion of your time to each phase. In middle and upper management, the planning, implementation, and evaluation cycle will become especially complex, because you will find yourself engaged in all three phases almost simultaneously. That is, you will be planning for one project at the same time that you are implementing a second and evaluating a third, and so on. Obviously, maintaining a good sense of the timing of the various projects and knowing when and how to shift from one to the next will be extremely important.

As we have seen, techniques have been developed to help you work through the typical problems you will encounter in each phase of the cycle. Although many of the techniques can be elaborated in highly complex ways, the logic upon which they are based can be helpful in dealing even with fairly simple and immediate problems.

Throughout the planning, implementation, and evaluation cycle, you should remember that, whereas we have focused on technical aids to your administrative work, each of the three areas will be strongly affected by how you interact with the *people* in your organization (and elsewhere). Planning, implementation, and evaluation are human processes, and are thus subject to people's shifting values, attitudes, and behaviors. In planning, implementation, and evaluation, as with budgeting, financial management, and personnel, techniques are only successful when you use them with full regard for democratic values, clear leadership, and humane management.

Terms and Definitions

Benchmarking: Targeting of specific goals based on previous performance levels, standards set by similar organizations, objectives created through a strategic planning process, or any combination of these and other relevant sources.

Cost-benefit: Identifying and quantifying both negative impacts (costs) and positive impacts (benefits) of a proposal, then subtracting one from the other to arrive at a net benefit.

Decision analysis: Technique wherein decisions are likely to be made sequentially and under some degree of uncertainty.

Decision tree: Technique that identifies various possible outcomes, given the risk associated with each.

Effectiveness: Extent to which a program is achieving or failing to achieve its stated objectives.

Efficiency: Relationship between inputs and outputs.

Institutional subsystem: Responsible for adapting the organization to its environment and for anticipating and planning for the future.

Managerial subsystem: Concerned with providing necessary resources for accomplishing a technical task and mediating between the technical and institutional subsystems.

Outcome evaluations: evaluations that focus on the results of program activity, the extent to which a program meets its objectives in terms of impact on the environment.

Participant-observer: Someone in either the target population or the agency who makes observations and draws conclusions based on firsthand experience.

Performance indicators: specific, quantifiable goals that the agency strives for in pursuit of its more substantive objectives.

Performance measurement: Careful and detailed measurement of the achievement of program objectives and outcomes by a program or agency.

PERT: A way to monitor the time or costs of various activities required to complete a project, showing the sequence in which the activities must be completed.

Policy analysis: Process of researching or analyzing public problems to provide policy makers with specific information about the range of available policy options and advantages and disadvantages of different approaches.

Process charting or flowcharting: Graphically demonstrating the various steps in an operation, the people who perform each step, and relationships among those elements.

Process evaluations: Seeking ways to improve program implementation so as to better meet program objectives.

Reengineering: Radically redesigning work processes and organizational structures to be in line with agency outcomes.

Stakeholders: The many different persons who are involved in policy decisions and are affected by the results.

Strategic planning: Matching organizational objectives and capabilities to the anticipated demands of the environment to produce a plan of action that will ensure achievement of objectives.

System: Set of regularized interactions configured or "bounded" in a way that differentiates and separates them from other actions that constitute the system's environment.

Systems theory: Effort to identify the interactions of various internal and external elements that impinge on an organization's operations.

Technical subsystem: Concerned with effective performance of an organization's actual work.

Time series analysis: Making a number of observations about the target population both before and after program intervention.

Study Questions

1. Planning is one aspect of the policy process. Discuss the various types of planning and their objectives.
2. In organizing a planning process, what are the primary concerns of the planning group?
3. Discuss the necessary steps for comprehensive policy analysis.
4. Identify some of the quantitative techniques used for policy analysis.
5. The second phase of the policy process is implementation of plans. Discuss some of the techniques available to help in the beginning stages of the implementation process.
6. Compare and contrast the several different subsystems that carry forward an organization's work.
7. What does the phrase "managing for results" mean? How might such a program be implemented?
8. What are the different types of evaluation approaches? Discuss the distinctions among them.

Cases and Exercises

1. As a class or working in small groups, assume the role of a task force that the governor has asked to develop plans for a new university the legislature has created in a rapidly expanding area in the corner of your state. Your plan should be based on whatever assumptions you wish to make by explicitly stating them in writing; however, all your assumptions should be consistent with the following guidelines:

a. Assume that you have full legal authority to develop the university, including the power to develop a full range of undergraduate programs and a limited number of graduate programs in areas of special interest to the state. Assume a high degree of political support within the corner of the state where the university will be built, and general support throughout the state, but assume major opposition from the state's leading public university.

b. Assume that the area where the new university is to be located already houses a community college, which the university will take over, and a couple of small, private liberal arts colleges. Assume that the community college has two thousand freshmen and sophomores and operates in two large buildings on a large tract of otherwise undeveloped land, which will be sufficient to accommodate the new university.

c. Assume that the area in which the university will be built has traditionally had an agricultural and tourist-based economy, but is experiencing rapid growth in high-tech industry, primarily because companies are attracted to the area's natural beauty and comfortable climate.

d. Assume that you can anticipate a budget starting at $12 million for the first year of operations (this is inclusive of the community college budget), but rising at a rate of $7 million a year for the next nine years. Assume also that, in addition, there is adequate financing available for whatever new construction will be required during the first ten years of the university's existence.

e. Assume that you have full control over the curriculum of the university and authority to propose to the Coordinating Board on Higher Education any new program offerings. Assume, however, that the major university in the state will fight hard to protect its engineering and computer science programs from competition.

You should create a plan for development of the new university over the next ten years. You should take into account all aspects of development, including all academic programs, student services, administrative support (including the physical plant, personnel, and financial and accounting systems), capital construction, and intercollegiate athletics. You may wish to establish subcommittees or task forces to work on particular areas; however, all reports should be combined into one single planning document to be submitted to the governor's office.

2. Imagine that your city council is considering a proposed ordinance to require a 5-cent deposit on each beverage container sold in the city. Each beer can, soft drink bottle, or other container would carry a city sticker or imprint. Retailers would collect the deposit on each container sold and would be required to pay 5 cents for each empty container returned to the store. Proponents of the bill argue that it would help clean up the city and provide better recycling of containers. Opponents argue that the bill would be difficult for stores to adhere to and a nightmare for the city to enforce. Develop a research design—that is, a plan for conducting research—that would enable you to report to the city council on the potential costs and benefits of the proposed ordinance.

3. Complete the following exercise: The newly elected governor of a large Middle Atlantic state has asked you to assist in developing a plan to revise the method of patrolling the highways. The problem stems from a report by the federal Department of Transportation showing that an independent sampling of traffic in the state indicates

far too many motorists are exceeding the federally mandated speed limit. The report goes on to threaten a cutoff of all federal highway funds to the state if something is not done. Perhaps of greater urgency, however, is the finding that the number of accidents per 1,000 miles driven is rising dramatically.

The governor's office has provided you with a set of alternative strategies for patrolling the highways and the associated costs and probable reductions in both accidents and speeders. Also included in the materials is a study of the revenue generated by the issuance of citations. You are asked to write a report indicating the various payoffs associated with each strategy. The types of patrols are:

stationary radar trap patrol

cruising car patrol

airplane/chase car patrol

The costs per shift for each patrol type are:

stationary = $600 per patrol

cruising = $800 per patrol

airplane = $1,500 per patrol

The cost of servicing each accident that occurs during a patrol is $250. The likelihood of accidents, however, differs depending on the type of patrol: the stationary patrol results in a .50 probability of two accidents; the cruising patrol results in a .30 probability of two accidents; and the airplane patrol results in a .25 probability of two accidents. Finally, the number of citations issued varies by type of patrol: stationary patrols issue eight citations on average; cruising patrols issue five citations on average; and airplane patrols issue three citations on average.

A previous study indicated that accident rates of less than an average of one per patrol were typical of states where the Department of Transportation found acceptable levels of speeding.

In a concluding paragraph, the governor indicates that it costs the state $50 to process a citation (which averages a fine of $85), but the governor goes on to say that may not be relevant to the choice of patrol type since the whole idea is to prevent accidents by slowing traffic to the legal speed limit (and preventing a cutoff of federal money).

How would you go about developing the report to the governor?

SOURCE: The preceding case was adapted from material provided by Barry Hammond of Slippery Rock University.

4. Complete the following exercise: You have been hired by Expert Analysis consulting firm to work on a project for New York City. The city has hired the firm to analyze the advisability of contracting out garbage collection, expanding city garbage collection capacity, or going to a twenty-four-hour collection system.

The city currently operates a sanitation department of 2,538 people using 781 garbage trucks of two different sizes. The large trucks carry 35 tons per trip and make two trips per day. The small trucks carry 15 tons and make three trips per day. There are 537 small trucks and 244 large trucks. The cost of one day for a large truck is $720 in wages for three people (eight-hour shift) and $200 for maintenance. The cost of one day for a small truck is $480 for wages for two people (eight-hour shift) and $150 for maintenance. The collective bargaining contract calls for a "shift differential" of 15 percent above the standard $30 per hour for the truck crews, if the crews work other than 6:00 A.M. to 3:00 P.M. The contract has three years to go before it expires. A recent study indicates that the amount of garbage to be collected in the city will increase 14 percent in the next year and 18 percent in the following year. The study also shows that many of the larger firms in the city are contemplating using a private garbage service (We-Haul, Inc.), which has recently begun competing with the city. The study concludes that, although the amount of garbage to be collected will rise, the amount the city will be required to collect might fall slightly or remain steady.

A quick check of the maintenance records for the large trucks indicates that you can expect a 20 percent increase in maintenance costs if you operate the trucks twenty-four hours a day and a 30 percent increase for the small trucks. You call the Tidy-Truck manufacturer and get a quote of $82,000 for a new large truck and $59,000 for a new small truck if you order this year. They expect a 6 percent price increase next year.

Just as you put down the phone, your liaison with the city calls to tell you that the private contractor (We-Haul, Inc.) has offered to collect the additional garbage at a "special rate" for the city of $18 per ton for the first year and $20 per ton for the second year.

Making reasonable assumptions about information you may need, develop a recommendation as to whether the city should expand its service by buying more trucks and hiring more people, operate its service twenty-four hours a day, or contract with the private service to pick up the increase.

SOURCE: The preceding case was adapted from material provided by Barry Hammond of Slippery Rock University.

5. The governor of a large Midwestern state has recently introduced a performance management initiative to enhance the activities of state agencies and, more specifically, to reverse downward trends in educational achievement and increases in juvenile crime. The governor, responding to increasing public outcry, has encouraged her cabinet to develop ten outcomes in the area of human and social services, then identify performance indicators that can be used in monitoring the state's progress in achieving these outcomes. As a senior cabinet member, you have been called upon to play a leadership role in this process. What are the primary outcomes that the state would need to accomplish in order to reverse the downward trends? What performance indicators could be used to help keep the statewide initiative on track? How would you ensure that these performance measurement strategies are implemented throughout the state and that the necessary organizational change has occurred to ensure their effectiveness?

For Additional Reading

Bryson, John M., ed. *Strategic Planning for Public Service and Non-Profit Organizations.* New York: Pergamon Press, 1993.

Bryson, John, and Farnum Alston. *Creating and Implementing Your Strategic Plan.* San Francisco: Jossey-Bass, 1995.

Bryson, John M., and Robert C. Einsweiler, eds. *Strategic Planning Threats and Opportunities for Planners.* Chicago, IL: Planners Press, 1988.

Forester, John. *Planning in the Face of Power.* Berkeley, CA: University of California Press, 1989.

Goggin, Malcolm L., Ann O. Bowman, James P. Lester, and Laurence O'Toole, Jr. *Implementation Theory and Practice: Toward a Third Generation.* New York: HarperCollins, 1990.

Kaufman, Roger. *Strategic Planning Plus: An Organizational Guide.* 2d ed. Newbury Park, CA: Sage Publications, 1992.

Kearns, Kevin. *Managing for Accountability.* San Francisco: Jossey-Bass, 1996.

Keehley, Patricia, et al. *Benchmarking for Best Practices.* San Francisco: Jossey-Bass, 1996.

Koteen, Jack. *Strategic Management in Public and Nonprofit Organizations.* 2d ed. Westport, CT: Praeger Publishers, 1997.

Linden, Russell. *Seamless Government.* San Francisco: Jossey-Bass, 1994.

Meehan, Eugene. *Assessing Governmental Performance.* Westport, CT: Greenwood Press, 1993.

Meier, Kenneth J., and Jeffrey L. Brudney. *Applied Statistics for Public Administration.* 3d ed. Belmont, CA: Wadsworth, 1993.

Mercer, James L. *Strategic Planning for Public Managers.* New York: Quorum Books, 1991.

Nutt, Paul C., and Robert W. Backoff. *Strategic Management of Public and Third Sector Organizations: A Handbook for Leaders.* San Francisco: Jossey-Bass, 1992.

Quade, E. S. *Analysis for Public Decisions.* 2d ed. New York: North-Holland, 1989.

Rabin, Jack, W. Bartley Hidreth, and Gerald J. Miller, eds. *Handbook of Strategic Management.* New York: Marcel Dekker, 1989.

Starling, Grover. *Strategies for Policy Making.* Pacific Grove, CA: Brooks/Cole, 1988.

Sylvia, Ronald, et al. *Program Planning and Evaluation for the Public Manager.* 2d. ed. Prospect Heights, IL: Waveland Press, 1997.

Vines, David. *Information Strategy and Public Policy.* Cambridge, MA: B. Blackwell, 1991.

Wholey, Joseph, Harry P. Hatry, and Kathryn Newcomer, eds. *Handbook of Practical Program Evaluation.* San Francisco: Jossey-Bass, 1994,

Wye, Christopher G., and Harry P. Hatry, eds. *Timely Low-Cost Evaluation in the Public Sector.* San Francisco: Jossey-Bass, 1988.

Zey, Mary, ed. *Decision Making: Alternatives to Rational Choice Models.* Newbury Park, CA: Sage Publications, 1992.

Chapter 8

MANAGING IN A
POLITICAL CONTEXT

A public administrator needs a good understanding of the values and principles underlying work in the public sector, knowledge of how public policy is developed and executed, and familiarity with a number of administrative techniques peculiar to the public sector. But the real key to managerial success in public organizations is not what you know, but what you can do. How effectively and how responsibly can you deal with the seemingly endless series of problems and opportunities that confront you? A legislator calls to ask for an immediate report on a matter you know will require a week to examine properly; a subordinate confesses that he has grown dependent on drugs and needs your help; someone in a meeting becomes outraged over what you perceive as a minor matter and threatens to have you fired; your boss asks your assistance in designing a completely new program and asks if you would be interested in running it. These situations and many more like them constitute the real challenges of public administration.

Your response to each event, of course, is spontaneous; yet your actions will soon add up to a pattern that reflects your knowledge, values, and most of all, skills in dealing with other people. If, time after time, you can act effectively and responsibly in situations that arise unexpectedly and require immediate answers with little time to think through the "theoretical" possibilities, you will likely be considered a highly successful manager.

Fortunately, the skills required for managerial effectiveness can be developed over time. In this and the following chapters, we will examine how your knowledge and values can be brought to bear in real-world situations. We will focus on the specific personal and interpersonal skills a manager requires and on some ways you might further develop those skills. In this chapter, we will look at several broad approaches to understanding the structure and design of public organizations as well as people's behavior in those organizations.

IMAGES OF ORGANIZING IN THE PUBLIC SECTOR

All managers carry around in their heads ideas or images of how public organizations should operate and how individual managers should act. These images, built up through experience, reading and discussion, and reflection, include notions about the most effective structures for public agencies, the best way to manage employees, and the proper relationship between elected and appointed officials. Depending on your particular view of public organizations, you will tend to look for and emphasize certain things and ignore others. The images you carry in your head will lead you to emphasize certain aspects of organizational life and de-emphasize others.

Some of these images derive from our experiences in our families; others derive from school experiences; still others derive from our work in other organizations. Some are general lessons we learned about topics such as power and authority, communications and cooperation, and so forth. Others are more specific to the world of work or the world of public service. Some are fairly conscious; others lie far beneath the surface.

Whatever their form, these images direct our actions in specific ways. They cause us to see the world in a particular way and, correspondingly, to act in a particular way. So it is important to carefully consider how each of us thinks about public organizations. What images do we have, and how do they direct us to think about public organizations? Which images allow us to be most successful? Which images hold us back or get in our way?

As you begin to think more carefully about the images that shape your work in public organizations (or elsewhere), and especially as you begin to accumulate experiences in public organizations, you will begin to identify areas where your insight (and consequently your actions) might be improved. One way to sharpen your images of public organizations is to consider what scholars and practitioners in the field of management generally and public management in particular have said and written. Fortunately, there is a considerable and growing body of material to draw upon that offers many categories and approaches you might use in thinking about your involvement in public organizations.

For the most part, this literature has developed out of the experiences of practicing managers. Reflective practitioners and thoughtful academics have asked over and over how public managers can be helped to select those features of organizational life that will be most helpful to them. Many students and practitioners of public administration have contributed to our understanding of the management of public agencies. They have developed "word pictures" (often simply called theories) to suggest what will be most helpful when you approach similar problems.

Each theoretical approach directs attention toward certain topics or ideas and away from others. It is up to you to select the most relevant and most helpful approaches to your particular situation. In this chapter, we will review some of the most influential ways of thinking about management in the public sector. Some early approaches focused on fairly obvious points; more recent approaches seem more complex and sophisticated.

THE FUNCTIONS OF MANAGEMENT

Writing early in the twentieth century, French management theorist and practitioner Henri Fayol (1949) identified five general functions managers should perform: planning, organizing, commanding, coordinating, and controlling. Several years later, Luther Gulick arrived at a similar list. Gulick, at the time an advisor on federal government reorganization, described the functions of public management in terms of an acronym,

POSDCORB: Planning, Organizing, Staffing, Directing, Coordinating, and Budgeting (Gulick, 1937). To Fayol and Gulick, these activities were the essence of management and identified functions that had to be performed if organizations were to be managed effectively. They constituted advice to managers about what they should be doing.

Planning involves preparing yourself and your organization to move effectively into the future. All managers engage in planning at least to some extent, and for some managers, such as those on strategic planning staffs, planning is almost a full-time activity. Some managers make plans for the entire organization, others make plans for the units they directly supervise, and all managers plan for their own activities. Unfortunately, as we noted earlier, planning is one managerial function that is often easy to overlook. Managers get caught up in the hectic pace of conversations, meetings, and deadlines and often neglect planning. Yet the most effective managers are aware that time taken out for planning, whether for the organization or for oneself, pays rich dividends.

Planning is closely related to decision making, an aspect of managerial work that cuts across many of the other areas. The ability to make thoughtful decisions seems to distinguish the more successful managers. Because decision making is so fundamental to managerial work, it has been studied intensively for many years. In most organizations, decision making is a central activity.

Organizing refers to many different activities, including division of the organization into different departments, creating levels in the organization's hierarchy, and deciding who reports to whom. In a specific department or division, organizing also includes the task of defining specific positions and jobs. Note that organizing includes job design, but the assignment of individuals to specific jobs involves the staffing rather than the organizing function.

Staffing is the process of acquiring, training, and developing the personnel to conduct the organization's activities. Staffing is today more generally described as "personnel management" or sometimes "human resources management." As we saw in Chapter 6, specific tasks such as hiring, training, firing, and so forth are examples of the staffing or personnel function. Obviously, dealing with people involves important skills in communication and motivation, as well as the ability to make sound decisions about whom you hire to work with you.

Directing is often the most dynamic and most visible management function. It includes three critical management activities: leading, motivating, and changing things when necessary. Providing direction to an organization is a subtle and complex task that involves the full range of personal and interpersonal skills.

Coordinating the work of many different people in many different places is also a central managerial function. The complexity and diversity of most modern organizations means that a great deal of time must be spent making sure that all the "pieces" fall into place at the right time. Coordinating involves special skills in problem solving—how to make things work—but also involves skills in communicating and negotiating.

Budgeting involves managing the organization's resources, especially financial. Budgeting involves securing, planning for, and managing the organization's funds. As we saw in Chapter 5, budgeting is a technical field, but it also involves considerable human skills, especially those of developing funding for one's programs and allocating scarce resources among many different competing programs and people.

In addition to these standard management functions, there are also a number of miscellaneous tasks that are usually considered managerial work. One of the most important is dealing with people from outside the organization. Skills in presenting your organization and point of view to others are becoming increasingly important as the relationships among organizations at many different levels become more intense. Representing your organization before outside groups and organizations has come to be known in the literature on management as **boundary spanning.**

THE EARLY WRITERS: A CONCERN FOR STRUCTURE

The question of how managers might be guided in their work has occupied theorists and practitioners for many years. Early writers on public administration thought of management in highly mechanical terms and considered questions of organizational structure and design of paramount importance. Recall that the birth of public administration as a separate field of study occurred during a time of impressive gains in science and industry; new ideas and new products were changing society almost overnight, as were the industrial and organizational processes that made them possible. It was a time of rigid control by "captains of industry"; it was also a time of fostering the birth of the assembly line.

In such an era, the machine became the leading image for how to organize technical and human processes. Just as the machine was precise, mechanical, and efficient, so should the organizations that built machines show the same characteristics. The result was a highly mechanical approach to organization that valued the idea of developing proper structures and operating them with great efficiency.

This orientation was epitomized in the influential work of Frederick W. Taylor, who developed what he termed **scientific management,** an approach based on carefully defined "laws, rules, and principles" (1923, p. 7). Taylor focused first on the individual worker, designing detailed measurements of time and motion to discover how the worker might become more efficient. For example, one might measure the distance from where a particular piece of equipment was stored to where it was used, then try to reduce that distance and the time and motion required to use the equipment. (In one example, Taylor sought to develop a "science of shoveling" based on the premise that the size of each individual shovel load would affect the daily output of "first-class shovelers." After careful and detailed experiments, it was determined that the greatest tonnage per day would be achieved with an average shovel load of about twenty-one pounds!)

Obviously, Taylor's approach could be applied to a wide variety of work-process problems, from the design of assembly lines to the arrangement of items on one's desk. But beyond these efforts to turn workers into highly tuned machines, Taylor's work provided guidance for managers throughout the organization. The manager's role became that of making the organization more efficient through the application of detailed "scientific" information. The smooth-running organization was to be highly mechanical, with the human elements strictly controlled to contribute to overall efficiency. The manager's job was to ensure the efficient operation of the system.

NETWORKING

The Academy of Management Online (http://www.aom.pace.edu/), the Society for Industrial and Organizational Psychology (http://www.siop.org/), and the Institute for Operations Research and the Management Sciences (http://www.informs.org/) offer research and information sources concerning the general principles of organization theory and behavior. For an alternative, visit the Electronic Journal of Radical Organisation Theory at http://www.mngt.waikato.ac.nz/depts/sml/journal/ejrot.htm. This site is published by the University of Waikato School of Management Studies in New Zealand.

Just as Taylor and others emphasized the efficient operation of industrial systems, others soon applied this emphasis in public administration. Leonard White wrote, "The objective of public administration is the most efficient utilization of the resources at the disposal of officials and employees" (1926, p. 2). "In the science of administration, whether public or private, the basic 'good' is efficiency," Luther Gulick concurred (1937b, p. 192). Though several writers objected, pointing out that other values, such as responsiveness, need to come into play in public organizations and that mechanical efficiency is "coldly calculating and inhuman" (Dimock, 1936, p. 120), efficiency was clearly the primary interest of most early public administrationists.

From the field of business, the early writers in public administration transferred other lessons about the design and structure of organizations, specifically the importance of establishing single centers of power controlling basically top-down structures. At the top of the organization there was to be one single authority to whom all subordinate personnel ultimately reported. Though the organization would be characterized by many managers and perhaps many organizational units, the ultimate responsibility and authority lay at the top.

To reconcile this view with the democratic requirement that public organizations should be responsive to the popular will, the early writers suggested that the organization's head, the single source of power and authority, should simply be accountable to the legislative body in much the same way a corporate chief executive officer is accountable to a board of directors. (Recall this idea as "the doctrine of neutral competence.") In describing the role of an agency chief executive, the advice of the early writers was to vest all administrative authority in a single executive, who would be given appropriate powers to carry out the work and responsibility for seeing that it was done. According to W. F. Willoughby, this was the first step in making the executive branch a "single, integrated piece of administrative machinery" (1927, p. 37). (This advice was at odds with the standard political practice of that period, the election of many administrative officers and the use of many large executive boards. As we saw earlier, even today, most states elect officers such as secretary of state or treasurer rather than having such officers report to a single chief executive, in this case the governor.)

The early writers who put forth the administrative management viewpoint were practical people who drew on their experience in managing public agencies. Consequently, when they described their work, they tended to emphasize how organizational structures might be built. Luther Gulick, for example, wrote extensively about the formation of agencies. After the agency was created and an executive chosen, Gulick saw the next question as one of dividing the work necessary to the organization, then establishing proper means of coordination and control. In other words, the new organization would move through four phases in which the legislature or chief executive would (1) define the job, (2) select a director, who would (3) determine the nature and number of required unit and (4) establish a structure of authority through which he or she would coordinate and control activities of the units (1937a, p. 7).

The division of labor, which amounted to creation of an organizational structure, was a critical element. The logic was compelling: since people differ in knowledge and skills and since the amount of time any one person can contribute to solution of large-scale problems is limited, it is necessary to divide the work of the organization into manageable portions. As we saw earlier, division of labor could be accomplished in a limited number of ways. Recall that Gulick suggested organizing on the basis of (1) the major purpose served (education, welfare, etc.), (2) the process (engineering, medicine, etc.), (3) the persons or things being dealt with by the unit (veterans, convicts, etc.), or (4) the place or geographic location where the work is done (1937a, pp. 21–29).

Having established a division of labor, the next problem facing the new director or manager was to create a structure of authority to coordinate and control the various parts of the organization. Gulick's answer to this question, like others during this period, was again drawn from orthodox practice in business—the organization should feature unity of command exercised through a hierarchical structure of authority. By the turn of the century, hierarchical organizations, like those symbolized in the standard organization chart (see Figure 8.1), had become models for industry (as they had previously been in the military and the Catholic Church). Gulick and many other early scholars and practitioners in public administration suggested a similar approach in the public sector.

Guidance for creating such structures was given by two former General Motors executives, James Mooney and Alan Reiley, (1939). Mooney and Reiley described four main principles for structuring large organizations. The first, coordination through unity of com-

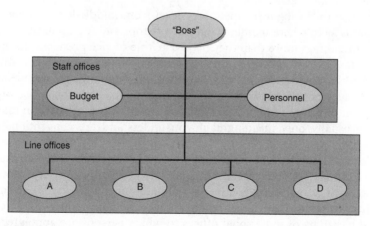

FIGURE 8.1

Typical Organization Chart Showing Line and Staff

mand, emphasized the importance of strong executive leadership exercised through a specific and formal chain of command. In this structure, each person would have only one boss, and each boss would have a limited span of control—that is, a limited number of people reporting to him or her. Mooney and Reiley argued that there should be no question about whose orders to obey. The second principle was the **scalar principle,** which described the vertical division of labor among various organizational levels. (In military terms, the difference between a general and a private reflects the scalar principle.) Third was the **functional principle,** describing a horizontal division of labor. (Again, in military terms, the difference between Infantry and Air Force would be a functional difference.) Finally, Mooney and Reiley discussed the relationship between line and staff, with line offices representing the direct flow of authority, and staff offices (such as personnel or finance) available to advise the chief executive, but not exercising direct authority over line offices.

The language of hierarchical structures became somewhat standard. And, just as distinctions were often drawn between line and staff, managers were (and are today) often classified as top, middle, or supervisory. Supervisory managers are at the bottom of the hierarchy, top managers at the peak, and middle managers in between. A supervisory manager directly manages the people involved in producing the organization's output. The supervisory level is the first level of management, so supervisors are sometimes called first-line managers. There are normally no managers below the supervisory level. An example of a supervisory manager is the person to whom your mail carrier reports at the post office.

Supervisors report to middle managers, usually defined as "managers who manage other managers!" If the organization is small, there may be only one level of middle managers; large organizations usually have more than one middle-management level. The highest level of management, the top level, usually has the fewest managers of the three levels. Top managers, often called "executives," are responsible for entire organizations, whereas middle- and supervisory-level managers focus on increasingly smaller sections of it at each level. Top managers are usually the most involved in relationships with other groups and agencies.

It is easy to distinguish supervisory-level from middle-level managers, but it is often ambiguous as to where middle management stops and top management begins. Titles often confuse things more than they help. The title of vice president, for example, indicates a top manager in some organizations; in others, the vice president is only a middle manager. Banks are particularly well known for having many vice presidents, most of whom are obviously not part of top management. Similarly, titles in public organizations, such as division director, branch chief, and department head, are used in many different ways and are usually only meaningful if you understand the conventions of the particular organization.

Independently of the American writers we have mentioned, German sociologist Max Weber examined the concept of bureaucracy early in this century, though Weber's work was not well known to the earlier public administrationists. Weber used the term *bureaucracy* to refer to any large organization, public or private, characterized by a clearly defined hierarchy of impersonal offices to which persons are appointed based on technical qualifications and through which they are subject to strict discipline and control (Weber, 1947, p. 328). Though we now often use *bureaucracy* pejoratively, Weber's more technical use carries no negative connotation. Indeed, Weber argued that bureaucracy is an attractive way to organize because it is so efficient: "Experience tends to universally show that the purely bureaucratic type of administration . . . is . . . capable of attaining the highest degree of efficiency and is in the sense formally the most rational known means of carrying out imperative control over human beings" (p. 337).

In any case, early writers on public administration generally sought to apply what they saw as the correct "principles" of administrative management to the conduct of public organizations. In doing so they implied that the problems facing government and their solutions were much the same as those in industry: centralization of authority and the development of hierarchical structures. But this assumption sidestepped several important issues essential to the operations of public agencies. Is the criterion of efficiency the only criterion by which the work of public organizations should be evaluated? Is it incompatible to create highly authoritarian structures to carry out the work of a democracy?

There were also questions about whether approaches to organization based on structural analyses alone were even the most efficient. In both the public and private sectors, for example, managers and researchers began to ask whether the rigid structures described in the principles of administrative management could effectively adapt to change. And, perhaps most important, where does the individual enter into the equation, other than as a potential machine? The structural lens through which many early scholars and practitioners viewed the world proved to be somewhat limiting; something else was needed.

RECOGNIZING HUMAN BEHAVIOR

In the mid-1920s, an impetus to further investigation of the informal or human factors in organizational life came from studies conducted by a group of Harvard researchers at the Hawthorne Works of the Western Electric Company. The studies, which began in a way largely consistent with the scientific management tradition, were designed to measure the relationship between working conditions (such as lighting, temperature, and humidity) and worker productivity (including monotony and fatigue). In the experiment, certain groups were isolated from their coworkers and placed in carefully controlled environments where conditions could be varied systematically. But, as the experiment developed, regardless of the changes in environmental conditions—lighter or darker, hotter or colder, more or less humid—the productivity of the experimental group tended to increase. Can you guess why?

The researchers' answer was that the experimental group was responding not to the conditions around them, but to the fact that they had been singled out for special attention. As a result, the researchers developed a new interest in the human aspects of organizational life. Those involved in the Hawthorne study began to see organizations as not only meeting the stated goals of producing goods or services but as being concerned also, even if implicitly, with the distribution of "satisfactions"—some monetary, others social and psychological—to the members of the organization. The informal organization, the human interactions that paralleled those prescribed by the organizational structure, was viewed as important or even more important than the formal organization. If this were the case, then it made sense that the manager's role involved attention to both the formal structure of the work process and the pattern of informal relationships among the workers. Either one could affect efficiency and effectiveness.

There was, of course, abundant advice on how to manage the formal structure, but only speculation about how to manage the informal or the human side of organizations. Consequently, a number of studies were undertaken that dealt with the critical human relationship between manager and worker. Many of the studies suggested that changes in one's approach to managing, or management style, could lead to important differences in productivity. By treating workers differently, you could affect the work they did.

An example of this orientation was Douglas MacGregor's discussion of Theory X and Theory Y. After reviewing other work on management, MacGregor suggested that a better theory of human behavior (not structure) might make it possible to more effectively control workers in organizations. Specifically, MacGregor contrasted a set of assumptions about human behavior that appeared to form the basis for traditional management techniques (Theory X) with a set of assumptions he felt would underlie a new and more enlightened approach (Theory Y). Traditionally, MacGregor argued, managers seemed to assume that human beings are lazy and dislike work, that they must therefore be coerced to produce, and that most in fact want such direction. MacGregor suggested in contrast that work is quite natural, that people do not need to be coerced, that they will devote energy to objectives to which they are committed, and that they will make commitments to objectives that, when completed, will lead to rewards. As a consequence, MacGregor suggested that most workers were not being utilized to their full potential. The lesson was straightforward: managers must take care to determine the needs and desires of their employees, then help orient the individual's objectives so that they are met by work toward the organization's objectives.

TWO CLASSIC WORKS

Two writers on organizational behavior, both stimulated by the new attention to human factors in organizational life, wrote "classics" on the subject during the forties and fifties. One author, Herbert Simon, came from the field of public administration; the other, Chris Argyris, began his work in the field of industrial psychology. Both have influenced all fields of management even to the present.

Simon began by suggesting that the reason we have large organizations in the first place is that individual human beings are limited or "bounded" in their rationality or capacity to solve the complex problems we face in the modern world. "The capacity of the human mind for formulating and solving complex problems is very small in comparison with the size of the problems whose solution is required for objectively rational behavior in the real world or even for a reasonable approximation to such objective rationality" (1957, p. 198). Organizations are seen as devices for molding our sometimes erratic behavior to rational patterns of obtaining our objectives.

In the abstract, it's really not difficult to design a rational system for reaching organizational objectives. The difficulty comes when human beings, with all their emotions and interests, are inserted into the system. Because they are human, they often appear "irrational" in terms of the system, even though what they are doing, from their point of view, may be perfectly rational. The chief problem for Simon, therefore, became how to understand and direct human behavior in such a way that it aids in pursuit of the organization's objectives in a rational (that is, efficient) way.

Simon described the organization as a decision-making system involving two primary sets of decisions on the part of the individual: the decision to be a part of an organization and the decision to contribute desired behaviors to the organization. Simon approaches each problem through a rational calculation of costs and benefits. For example, a person may be expected to remain a member of an organization as long as the benefits provided by the organization appear to exceed those that might be obtained elsewhere.

The same approach is used with respect to the individual's contributions to the organization, an issue closely tied to the question of authority. Simon argued that each individual establishes an **area of acceptance** within which the subordinate is willing to accept the decisions made for him by his superior" (Simon, 1957, pp. 74–75). But since it is in the interest of the organization to have the "zone" as wide as possible, the organization, through its managers, offers certain "inducements" designed to increase the individual's "contributions." Inducements obviously include money and status, but they also involve creating a state of mind in which individuals will tend to obey rather than disobey.

In establishing this state of mind, Simon argues that you cannot expect people to make perfectly rational decisions. Indeed, most human beings act with **bounded rationality;** they seek the best possible solution, though not necessarily the one that is most rational from a purely economic standpoint. The member can be made to fall in line with the organization's expectations by means of inducements that are just good enough to elicit the desired contributions. In this way, what Simon terms "administrative man" (in contrast to "economic man") becomes a part of a rationally behaving system.

Chris Argyris, rather than focusing on the design of rational systems, focused on the interaction of the individual and the organization, and suggested, much like MacGregor, that formal organizational structures and traditional management practices were inconsistent with a natural human striving for growth and development. Individuals in our society, Argyris concluded, develop from infancy through adulthood along several important dimensions: from passivity to activity, from dependence to independence, from a limited to a greater range of behaviors, from shallow to deeper interests, from a shorter to a longer time perspective, from a position of subordination to a position of equality or superordination, and from lack of awareness to greater awareness. Movement along each dimension contributes to what we know as the healthy adult personality.

Yet, argued Argyris, these goals are exactly those that traditional management practices prevent. For example, standard patterns of management give the individual little control over his or her work. Workers are expected to be passive, submissive, and limited in the range of their responses. They are basically expected to behave like children. Moreover, if individuals express frustration at such a situation, managers often see their behavior as hostile and dysfunctional. The typical managerial response is to crack down, to assert even more severe methods of control.

A healthier approach, suggests Argyris, would be to understand the basic tendencies of the human personality for growth and development, then to "fuse" these tendencies with the objectives of the organization. Achieving this congruence or fusion is the task of the manager. This requires that the manager develop "skill in self-awareness, in effective diagnosing, in helping individuals grow and become more creative, in coping with dependent-oriented . . . employees, and in surviving in a competitive world of management" (1962, p. 213).

In the work of both Simon and Argyris, there is a dramatic shift from concerns with structure to concerns with human behavior. Each offers a new way of looking at organizations and the people in them. The manager, according to this new view, needs to take structure into account (for that will affect human behavior), but the "bottom line" is how people behave. And, of course, the behavior of human beings is affected by much more than the structures in which they reside. In these works, the attention of the manager is redirected from structure to behavior. In this new view, the job of the manager is to mold human behavior toward the purposes of the organization.

THE ORGANIZATION AND ITS ENVIRONMENT

Both the early emphasis on structure and the later emphasis on human behavior proved helpful in focusing attention on important aspects of life in complex organizations. But neither viewpoint even considered the relationship between the organization and its environment. This missing element began to appear, however, as writers in the field of public administration returned to issues of structure, though they viewed it in a quite different way. The new concern for structure was stimulated by two emerging approaches to public organizations: systems theory and the **political economy approach.** The **systems approach** suggested that public (or other) organizations could be viewed in the same general way as biological or physical systems as whole "organisms," independent of their parts and pursuing specific purposes within a complex environment; the political economy approach focused on politics and economics as categories for analyzing organizational behavior.

SYSTEMS THEORY

We will discuss the basic ideas associated with systems theory in more detail later. For the time being, you should know that the systems model suggests that the organization receives from its environment the human and material resources it requires to function, as well as requests and directives about how it should operate; these resources, requests, and directives are processed through the organization and transformed by it; the resulting outputs (products, services, and so on) are transmitted back into the environment. In turn, these outputs are taken into account as new inputs are developed, and, over time, a balancing point is reached that makes possible the survival of the organization.

While we will discuss applications of systems theory of organizational design later, we should note here that the systems approach led those in public administration to think more carefully about the environment in which they worked and to begin to consider what influences were most important. A classic study of the relationship between an agency and its environment was Selznick's analysis of the Tennessee Valley Authority in the 1940s. Selznick argued that, in contrast to the closed, mechanical systems implied in many approaches to public organizations, those organizations are in fact open systems. That is, they exist within an institutional framework, which includes political parties, pressure groups, and special interests, and, though the groups' demands may appear "irrational" from the perspective of the organization, they simply cannot be ignored.

The Tennessee Valley Authority sought to involve already existing local agencies in planning power distribution systems and other programs. One reason was to enable the TVA to anticipate potential demands and be prepared to respond. A second reason was to try to get local groups committed to the TVA program by making them feel part of the organization. By bringing outside groups into the structure of the organization (by placing persons on advisory groups or negotiating service contracts with them), TVA sought support for its own programs. You will recall this idea as co-optation, a term Selznick defined as "the process of absorbing new elements into the leadership or policy-determining structure of the organization as a means of averting threats to its stability or existence" (Selznick, 1949, p. 13).

Another study examining the influence of environmental factors on the operations of public agencies was Herbert Kaufman's analysis of the U.S. Forest Service (Kaufman, 1960). The Forest Service faced the problem of how to secure compliance and consistency from forest rangers scattered across the country and subject to all kinds of pressures from their local communities. Rangers often served, of course, in isolated locations. While they sought to carry out the policies of the Forest Service, they also developed loyalties to their local communities. They often had to carry out regulations that would adversely affect their friends and neighbors in the local areas and, in such cases, might be tempted to deviate from central office directives. The agency's response was to devise a series of training programs, procedural devices, inspections, and sanctions as efforts to reduce the influence of the local environment and to ensure that central office orders were actually carried out in the field.

Looking at how environmental factors influence public organizations led other writers to characterize public agencies as interdependent systems operating in a complex environment. No longer could one agency's work be viewed in isolation from other public and private agencies; one would simply not be able to understand how an agency operated without understanding the myriad external influences on the agency. Imagine, for example, the difficulty of implementing a new set of standards for water quality in a city such as Cincinnati, located on a state boundary. Think of all the agencies, public and private, that would have to be notified and would wish to express their views. Think of the various political jurisdictions—states, cities, counties, and possibly many special districts. Think of the various bodies within each jurisdiction that might want input—the mayor, legislature, and administrative agencies.

The complexity of administrative activities (as in this example) have led some scholars to suggest that it is no longer even meaningful to focus on a specific agency's contribution to implementing a particular policy, but to think instead in terms of programs. We have already noted that many federal programs operate through a pattern of funding in which money, rules, and guidelines are established for programs that are actually delivered at the state and local levels through both public and private agencies. For example, in the delivery of social services, such as drug prevention efforts, state and local governments use federal money to fund private or nonprofit providers of the services. In many cases, the money goes to fund programs, not specific agencies, so that these programs operate through rather diffuse networks of loosely joined groups rather than through traditional hierarchical structures. In such ill-structured "structures," older notions of organizational control necessarily give way to new emphasis on bargaining and negotiation, in which the systems perspective has much to offer.

FROM POLITICAL ECONOMY TO ORGANIZATION DEVELOPMENT

Interest in interorganizational policy networks was further stimulated by the emergence of the political economy approach to understanding public organizations. Wamsley and Zald suggest that public organizations can best be understood in terms of the conjunction of political and economic factors influencing their operation. These factors affect the organization both internally and externally, leading to four categories through which we might view organizations. First, the external political environment involves the interplay of various interest groups and other organizations that affect the organization's political climate. Second, the external economic environment consists of market exchanges that influence the available supply of resources. Third, the internal political category focuses on the distribution of power and authority; and fourth, the internal economy concerns the allocation of resources and how they are used.

The Wamsley-Zald approach is related to a more sophisticated and complex approach most often associated with Vincent Ostrom. Ostrom's public choice approach begins with examining how individuals might make choices if they were free to act rationally and in their own self-interest. Under some circumstances, people might be expected to engage in collective action, especially where "public goods" are involved, or where situations are neither purely public nor purely private. (Public goods are distinguished from private goods—those that can be measured, marketed, and maintained—by the fact that they are highly indivisible; a public good such as the national defense is available to all once it is provided for one.)

Following this logic, Ostrom sees public organizations as "a means for allocating decision-making capabilities in order to provide public goods and services responsive to the preferences of individuals in different social contexts" (Ostrom & Ostrom, 1971, p. 207). Ostrom argues that the best structures for satisfying individual preferences are not centralized bureaucratic agencies, but rather more fragmented, multiorganizational arrangements.

Although earlier behavioral studies like Simon's and Argyris's were important in countering the field's dependence on a structural interpretation of organizational life, they were limited in certain ways. First, most of the behavioral literature failed to question the top-down pattern of organizational authority, so many thought it merely provided more sophisticated mechanisms for managerial control. Second, there seemed to be little interest in organization change processes at a time that rapid social change was becoming a dominant feature of the landscape. Third, as the open systems theorists pointed out, the perspective failed to comprehend the complexity of interorganizational bargaining and negotiation. Similarly, the political economy approach seemed to unnecessarily limit the creativity and communications possibilities of those in public organizations, and seemed, at least to some, to place values in a secondary position.

Among major critics of earlier approaches were a group of scholars in the early 1970s whose collective work came to be known (and, despite the passage of time, is still known) as "the New Public Administration." In contrast to older approaches that emphasized efficiency and control, the New Public Administration heralded openness and change, equity, and involvement. In a rapidly changing society populated by diverse groups, the New Public Administrationists felt that the key element in the survival of organizations—indeed, of the society—was the capacity to adapt to rapid social change. Organizations would have to find ways to deal with an increasingly "turbulent" environment.

Doing so would require stimulating the creativity of everyone involved in any public program, both within the agency and in the environment. Involving the organization's members and its clients in the decision-making process would, the New Public Administrationists felt, foster creativity. Moreover, such an approach seemed far more consistent with democratic norms and practices than operating through top-down structures of control. The key words in the New Public Administration were *equity* and *involvement*.

Many of those associated with the New Public Administration became students of organizational change processes and sought ways to help organizations implement needed changes. One of the most important approaches they employed was **organization development,** a process-oriented approach to planned change. Organization development suggests many techniques for change that we will examine later, but it also offers another approach through which to view the work of organizations.

Robert Golembiewski, a leader in the application of organization development strategies and techniques to the public sector, points out that organization development represents a particular philosophy of management that is considerably at odds with traditional top-down tendencies. It values:

1. mutual accessibility and open communications
2. a willingness to experiment with new behaviors and to choose those that seem most effective
3. a collaborative concept of authority that emphasizes cooperation and willingness to examine conflicts openly
4. creating mutual helping relationships involving a sense of community and acceptance of responsibility for others
5. authenticity in interpersonal relationships (Golembiewski, 1972, pp. 60–66)

ORGANIZATIONAL CULTURE, ORGANIZATIONAL LEARNING, AND STRATEGIC MANAGEMENT

During the past generation, many discussions of management and organizations, especially in the private sector, have emphasized the importance of understanding the "culture" of the organization. Most writers refer to organizational culture as the basic pattern of attitudes, beliefs and values that underlie the organization's operations. An organization's culture consists of the shared assumptions that members of the organization hold. Edgar H. Schein (1997, p. 8–10) notes that culture can be manifested in many ways, including the following:

1. *Observed behavioral regularities when people interact:* The language they use, the customs and traditions that evolve, and the rituals they employ in a wide variety of situations.
2. *Group norms:* The implicit standards and values that evolve in working groups, such as the particular norm of a "fair day's work for a fair day's pay" that evolved among workers in the Hawthorne studies.
3. *Espoused values:* The articulated, publically announced principles and values that the group claims to be trying to achieve.
4. *Formal philosophy:* The broad policies and ideological principles that guide a group's actions toward stockholders, employees, customers, and other stakeholders.
5. *Rules of the game:* Implicit rules for getting along in the organizations and "the ropes" that a newcomer must learn to be an accepted member—"the way we do things around here."
6. *Climate:* The feeling that is conveyed in a group by the physical layout and the way in which members of the organization interact with each other, with customers, or with other outsiders.
7. *Embedded skills:* The special competencies group members display in accomplishing certain tasks, the ability to make certain things that gets passed on from generation to generation without necessarily being articulated in writing.
8. *Habits of thinking, mental models, and/or linguistic paradigms:* The shared cognitive frames that guide the perceptions, thought, and language used by the members of a group and are taught to new members in the early socialization process.
9. *Shared meanings:* The emergent understandings that are created by group members as they interact with each other.
10. *"Root metaphors" or integrating symbols:* The ideas, feelings, and images groups develop to characterize themselves that may or may not be appreciated consciously but that become embodied in buildings, office layout, and other material artifacts of the group.

As these manifestations suggest, some of the most important aspects of an organization lie outside of the explicit characteristics shared in normal group interaction. The unique ways in which an organization communicates internally and externally, its system of reward and punishment, and the way group members perceive themselves and the outside world all stem from the deeper, mostly undiscussed system of values and beliefs that define the group as a whole (Schein, 1997).

These layers of culture represent key concerns in their own right, in that they yield insight in very different ways about the nature of the group. However, organizational culture becomes even more critical as it relates to planned organizational change. Organizations face dynamic conditions in their internal and external environments, a variety of social, economic, and political factors that impact group performance. The successful organization is one that remains flexible to meet these changing conditions. Yet given the multiple levels of organizational culture, change within the group cannot simply occur on the surface level. The organization's underlying system of beliefs and values must be transformed in order for change to be sustainable (Schein, 1997; Senge 1990).

In this context, the notion of organizational culture becomes closely related to another important management concept, what is called **organizational learning.** Learning organizations recognize that the primary contributors to error, or the disparity between what the group intends to happen and what actually occurs (Argyris, 1993) and thus the barriers to organizational change, are embedded deep within the organization's collective consciousness. They are not talked about, nor even immediately acknowledged by group members. Therefore, groups that succeed in becoming learning organizations, those which are able to correct error and overcome their barriers, can much more successfully bring about change both in surface behavior and in the underlying levels of culture in the organization.

For example, say an organization's performance has started to suffer because of a decline in employee satisfaction and a rise in infighting among staff members. An immediate response may be to alter the group's behavior in a way that reduces the infighting and, in some ways, improves the quality of work life. This type of surface-level change would be a form of single-loop learning. However, such behavioral change more than likely would not resolve the deeper problem that produced the infighting in the first place. To resolve this more tacit concern, double-loop learning, or a change in the underlying system of beliefs, would need to occur. Both the actions and the values of the group would need to be affected.

Peter Senge, writing in *The Fifth Discipline,* suggests five elements that contribute to building a learning organization. These are:

Personal Mastery: A discipline that connects individual learning, personal skills, and spiritual growth with organizational learning. It involves one's inherent capacity to continuously focus on what's most important, while ensuring that the view of reality remains clear and truthful (Senge, 1990, p. 141).

Mental Models: A discipline that links the way in which we view the world—our assumptions about "how things work"—with innovation and learning. Our mental models may pose substantial barriers to new ideas, those that conflict with our current understanding of reality, or they may become a source of new knowledge and creative learning (Senge, 1990, p. 174–178).

Shared Vision: A discipline in which an image or idea becomes transformed into a powerful force that is shared throughout the organization or group. The organization that has a shared vision is "connected, bound together by a common aspiration" (Senge, 1990, p. 206).

Team Learning: A discipline that reflects the capacity of a group of individuals to coalesce, to engage their respective energies into an integrated team. The team remains connected through its shared vision, thus ensuring that the individual learning that occurs becomes translated into a group—indeed, a shared—experience (Senge, 1990, p. 234–235).

Systems Thinking: A discipline that shows how human action—whether in business, government or other pursuits—represents a systemic, interrelated set of events. Thus, we may understand and effect change by recognizing the interconnectedness of our actions and their consequences in the broader system. Those who are able to achieve this type of systems thinking—what Senge calls the fifth discipline—have embodied the concept of individual and organizational learning (Senge, 1990, p. 7).

The convergence of the concepts of organizational culture and organizational learning provide an important foundation for understanding organizational change. Yet they also relate to an older concept, but one which remains crucial in contemporary society: **strategic management.** Several years ago, Peters and Waterman's *In Search of Excellence* (1982) introduced this concept in its analysis of implicit philosophies that guide most successful American companies. Much of the work remains just as valuable today as it did nearly two decades ago. In particular, Peters and Waterman state the importance of establishing a core set of values that comprise the mission of the organization and shape decisions throughout the structure. They suggest the importance of constant interchange between managers and workers, the organization and its clients. Though terms like "MBWA," or Management by Walking Around, may seem dated, the supporting principle of leadership remaining in close contact with members of the organization has perhaps even grown in significance.

NETWORKING

For a less formal introduction to organizational culture, begin with a Web site developed by graduate students at the University of Toronto at http://www.oise.utoronto.ca/ ~vsvede/culture.htm. Next, visit MIT's Society for Organizational Learning at http:// www.sol-ne.org/. This site discusses research about organizational culture and change.

Some of the specific features of successful companies cited by Peters and Waterman (1982, pp. 13–16) include:

1. *A bias for action:* a willingness to experiment and to take risks
2. *Close to the customer:* a near obsession with service and quality
3. *Autonomy and entrepreneurship:* allowing a freedom to develop new ideas and to compete with other parts of the company
4. *Productivity through people:* treating people as adults, and giving them trust and respect
5. *Hands on, value driven:* paying attention to their values and managers working hard to express those values
6. *Sticking to the knitting:* doing what you know best; don't diversify excessively
7. *Simple form, lean staff:* avoiding top-heavy and complex organizational structures
8. *Simultaneous loose-tight properties:* the coexistence of firm central direction and maximum individual autonomy

These criteria for excellence can be translated into a public-sector context without great difficulty. For example, the International City Management Association and the

Center for Excellence in Local Government adapted the Peters and Waterman criteria to define "excellence in local government":

1. *Action orientation:* Excellent local governments identify problems and deal with them quickly, fighting through structural, political, legal, and environmental constraints that make action more difficult than in the private sector.
2. *Closeness to citizens:* This criterion includes establishing and maintaining a variety of close links with citizens who are served by the local government, including those who are regulated against their will. Excellent local governments listen and are sensitive and responsive to public input.
3. *Autonomy and entrepreneurship:* Excellent local governments have developed climates conducive to conceiving ideas and doing new things to solve problems. They have track records for implementing creative solutions, even in the face of declining resources.
4. *Employee orientation:* This criterion demands more than lip service to employees and their needs. Excellent local governments insist on intensive, pervasive treatment of employees as human beings and adults.
5. *Values:* Excellent local governments have a defined set of values. Their overall focus is on being the best by providing superior quality service to the public. Their values are communicated clearly and demonstrated regularly to employees. Those values also provide the source of enthusiasm and pride among employees.
6. *Mission, goals, and competence:* Mission is the underlying premise of the organization. Excellent local governments have evaluated their missions based on changing resource levels and citizen demands, and have used mission statements as the foundation for establishing community and organizational goals. Within their defined mission, excellent local governments provide consistent, uniform service levels.
7. *Structure:* In excellent local governments, the potential negative effects of antiquated, bureaucratic structures have been minimized. These organizations have fewer management levels and fewer centralized support staffs. They provide firm central direction while giving maximum autonomy to employees.
8. *Political relationships:* Political relationships refer to more than how the elected governing body and management staff work together. In excellent local governments, managers and policy makers are tuned in to the political environment; have established positive, open, and respectful relationships with each other; and have established political stability (Barbour et al., 1984).

Most recently, Robert B. Denhardt (1993) has elaborated several approaches to public management based on interviews with highly successful public managers in Australia, Canada, Great Britain, and the United States. Denhardt's research has shown that these managers, highly regarded by their peers for improvements in quality and productivity in their organizations, have a distinctive style from the traditional rule-driven bureaucratic mode of operations, yet they have much in common. Among the approaches used by these "revolutionary" public managers are the following:

1. *A commitment to values:* The manager seeks organizational change less by attention to structure than by developing a pervasive commitment to the mission and values of

the organization, especially the values of professionalism and integrity, service and quality. Values are clearly articulated by the chief executive and shared throughout the organization.

2. *Serving the public:* The manager gives priority to service to both clients and citizens. That priority is supported by high standards of performance and accountability and by a constant emphasis on quality. Most important, the manager recognizes that technical efforts alone will fail unless equal or even greater attention is given to the human side, especially to building a sense of community within the organization and a sense of cooperation outside.

3. *Empowerment and shared leadership:* The manager encourages a high level of participation and involvement on the part of all members of the organization in efforts to improve the quality and productivity of the organization (see Box 8.1). Leadership from the top is complemented by empowering individuals throughout the organization to assume leadership within their own realms.

4. *Pragmatic incrementalism:* Change occurs through a free-flowing process in which the manager pursues a wide variety of often unexpected opportunities to move the organization in the desired direction. The manager views change as a natural and appropriate feature of organizational life and employs a creative and humane approach to change, taking into account the personal concerns and interests of members, clients, and others.

5. *A dedication to public service:* Individuals throughout the organization understand and appreciate the special character of public service, especially the role of public organizations in the process of democratic governments. The manager insists that members of the organizations maintain high levels of standards and encourages them to make their organization a model of integrity for similarly situated groups.

Denhardt argues that these approaches to public management are not merely techniques to be used in pursuit of the organization's interest, but are ideas consistent with the history and tradition of public service. For many public managers and many public employees the driving motive behind their best efforts is not the pursuit of self-interest, but rather the pursuit of the sense of meaning or significance in their work. As managers become more aware of this factor and take it into account in the way they manage, public organizations can become more flexible, more creative, and more responsive to both clients and citizens.

TOTAL QUALITY MANAGEMENT

Many of the themes in the organizational culture literature and the literature dealing with strategic management are coming together under the heading of Total Quality Management (TQM). While some consider TQM merely another set of techniques to be used in improving quality and in turn productivity, others consider TQM as embracing a variety of the most contemporary approaches to public management. They would say that TQM is a broad-scale approach to changing an organization's entire culture to focus it on establishing and maintaining high standards of quality, especially with respect

BOX 8.1

Empowering an Organization

Because I like to think I have learned a few things in 25 years (in the field of urban management), hopefully there are also some things I now do differently. At the front end of my career, for example, my concern was in making sure everybody in the organization knew I was in charge. Reorganization, replacement of key personnel, and formal control mechanisms were the hallmarks of my early days. They were meant to define me as a "take charge" person and to signal that change had occurred. . . .

In reflecting on my earlier approach, I have now come full circle. The kinds of changes I made back then were clearly visible and so probably satisfied those who wanted to see change. I have learned, however, that it is relatively simple to bring about physical, visible change but that to cause actual improvement in the way an organization functions is a far more difficult trick. . . . Obedience as the basis for organizational success has given way in my mind to the need for trust. A successful relationship is based upon mutual give and take rather than on "you give and I take. . . ."

What impresses me as more productive now is to figure out how you get those in the organization to feel confident about what they do, to move the organization where it needs to go. The values that permeate an organization have the power to override, at least in the long run, any other changes that may be made. What is new for me now in the second half of my career is an understanding that if dysfunctional and counterproductive values do not change, not much else of importance will either. And if management is not trying to improve the organizational culture's value system, no one else will.

A related lesson I have learned is that management cannot "order" values to change. This kind of change takes place relatively slowly, and it occurs only if management talks a lot about what is expected, sets the right example, creates the right kind of organizational climate, and uses the personnel and compensation system to support the right behavior.

So I am preaching. I am talking about organizational values important to success—customer responsiveness, treating people right, supporting city policies, being a good source of information, getting and giving "more bang for the buck," and providing anticipative rather than reactive management. . . .

The point of all this is to empower the people in the organization to exert themselves by their own volition, in the right direction. A manager can indicate the proper direction. A manager can encourage needed values and can create the climate in which employees will choose to make the organization's success their goal. Managers used to see success as a function of the assertion of their own power. Now they see the empowerment of others as a more likely avenue to success.

SOURCE: Excerpted from Roy R. Pederson, "Empowering an Organization," *Public Management* (August 1989): 23, International City Management Association, Washington, DC. Reprinted with permission.

to meeting "customer" expectations. The key of TQM is to serve the "customer," whether the customer is internal to the organization or someone outside. In this chapter we will consider the broad thematics of TQM; in the next we will note particular applications of TQM techniques.

The OMB circular describing TQM for federal executives calls it "a comprehensive management approach for meeting customer needs and expectations that involves all employees in improving continuously the organization's processes, products, and services." Specifically, TQM involves bringing together everyone in the organization in a manner that creates a new "culture of excellence" that emphasizes:

top management leadership and support

strategic planning and implementation geared to long-term success

focus on the customer

commitment to training and recognition

employee empowerment and teamwork

reliance on measurement and analysis of process and outputs

quality assurance (OMB Draft Circular A-132, 1990)

The emphasis in TQM is first on improving quality, not productivity. Indeed, the assumption is that if the quality of the organization's work is improved, its productivity will also improve. Improvements in quality are sought through a variety of tools or techniques, each tailored to the specific work of the organization. One organization might develop a series of quality control teams to oversee and control quality throughout its delivery of services; another organization might choose to develop a more detailed measurement system to pinpoint errors in its production processes. In all cases, however, the commitment to quality must be strongly expressed by top management and throughout the organization. It should also be long-term; TQM is not seen as a quick fix but as a never-ending process of improvement (see Box 8.2).

TQM Beginnings

The idea of quality management began in the late 1920s with Walter Shewart's development of a method for measuring variance in production systems, called statistical process control. During World War II, quality control methods were critical and the War Department incorporated Shewart's methods, hiring W. Edward Deming, who was actually a student of Shewart's, to teach the statistical process control method.

After World War II, American industry and government, blessed with a rapidly expanding economy, became very powerful yet eventually complacent. The Japanese faced a very different situation after the war. While they had never been blessed with abundant natural resources, they were quick to adopt progressive industrial management techniques. Deming traveled to Japan to help rebuild industry and taught the sta-

BOX 8.2

Norfolk Naval Shipyard: A TQM Success Story

How do you make sure that a shipyard older than the country itself will still be a leader in the ship repair industry in the twenty-first century? This is the problem that Captain Edward S. McGinley faced when he took command of the Norfolk Naval Shipyard in Norfolk, VA, in 1987.

To McGinley, TQM was the answer. In September 1987 he sequestered the shipyard's top managers in a local hotel for two days. They devised a list of objectives for the shipyard, ranging from reducing the cost of overhauls by at least 25 percent to improving compliance with environmental regulations.

To implement the goals, Norfolk uses a highly structured TQM program. At the top is the shipyard's Quality/Productivity Improvement Council, chaired by McGinley and composed of top managers and representatives of two of the shipyard's eight employee unions. The council creates overall quality initiatives and monitors their implementation.

Council recommendations for process improvements are turned over to a Quality Management Board of managers and union representatives for action. . . .

Quality Management Boards recommend that specific processes be examined and improved by Performance Action Teams. This is where TQM gets down to the nitty gritty. Each team is made up of people who actually work on the process designated for improvement. The team recommends specific improvements and implements them. "You could easily have a thousand teams," says Fred Porter, a TQM adviser at Norfolk.

The TQM process has been applied in the shipyard's sheet metal shop, where designs for equipment such as ventilation systems are turned into working sketches. Before TQM, as many as 23 percent of such sketches were going to the shop floor with errors even after workers were given eye exams and the lighting in the sketch area was improved.

So a Performance Action Team was appointed. Under its guidance, every completed sketch was inspected. Different types of errors were categorized and posted on charts in the sketch area. In addition, individual errors were noted and shown to employees. Managers did not see these personal evaluations.

Larry Kiser, who works in the sketch area, says it worked. "I knew where I was making errors, so the next time I did something I was aware of the problem." Fred Mullins, a supervisor, says that checking every sketch took time, but every 15–20 minutes spent in checking saved 15–20 hours on the shop floor. In the sketching of ventilation systems, the error rate dropped to 8 percent.

Efforts like this have made Norfolk one of the federal government's most prominent TQM success stories. In 1989 the shipyard won an award from the Office of Management and Budget for its TQM program. The award noted that all eight of the ships repaired at the shipyard from April 1988 to March 1989 were completed at or under estimated cost, and that seven were returned to the fleet early or on time.

SOURCE: Excerpted from Tom Shoop, "Norfolk Naval Shipyard: A TQM Success Story," *Government Executive* (March 1990): 21. Reprinted with permission.

tistical control method to the Japanese, as did another important figure in the development of TQM, Joseph Juran. Juran taught that quality should be defined as "fit for customer use." He also developed the concept of "cost of quality," a type of cost-benefit analysis. Under the guidance of Deming and Juran, the Japanese extended quality control methods to production and inspection. Eventually, the Japanese learned how to increase their competitiveness by improving the quality of the goods and services they produced.

Throughout this period, American industrial leaders felt no need to learn a new way of thinking. However, a remarkable renaissance occurred during the second half of the twentieth century. In the 1950s, Japanese products were considered very shoddy, while "Made in America" meant strength and competence. By the 1970s, the image had been reversed; Japanese products were now considered of higher quality and consequently fared better on world markets. Today, American industry (and American government), guided by such contemporary leaders in quality improvement as Philip Crosby, is taking a long, and at times skeptical, look at the quality management methods used by Japanese industry. The TQM movement represents a major initiative in this reassessment.

NETWORKING

The Council for Continuous Improvement (http://www.cci.org/) and the Public Sector Network of the American Society for Quality (http://deming.eng.clemson.edu/pub/psci/psn/) provide resources and other information concerning TQM and quality improvement activities in the governmental and nongovernmental sectors.

TQM stresses customer satisfaction, examines relationships between existing management processes, improves internal communications, and responds to the valid demands of all customers, internal and external (Milakovich, 1991). Among the questions advocates of TQM seek to address are the following:

1. How can an organization assess and improve its basic services and product quality in the eyes of its clients and customers?
2. How should it plan process redesign, organizational restructuring, participative management, and employee development to aid in this effort?
3. What coordination and evaluation mechanisms need to be put in place to facilitate quality management?
4. What measurement systems must the organization develop and how should the information generated be used in its pursuit of quality?

SOME CONCLUDING GUIDELINES FOR PUBLIC MANAGEMENT

What lessons can you draw from these various perspectives that might guide your actions as a public manager? One way to begin to answer that question is to summarize some of the thinking about management in terms of guidelines for practice.

The recent literature on strategic management seems to suggest the following guidelines:

1. Maintain clarity about organizational priorities, goals, and objectives. Although some ambiguity is often unavoidable in stating organization priorities, goals, and objectives, most organizations are far too confused on these issues. This confusion leaves people throughout the organization, including people who are required to make frequent decisions about organizational direction, without an appropriate basis for making such decisions. The direction of the organization should be stated as clearly as possible and widely communicated to all members.

2. Make decisions today in terms of the most likely future circumstances. Strategic management implies making all organizational decisions in terms of "futurity"—that is, how they will meet expected changes in the environment. It suggests taking every action in light of anticipated conditions, thus putting the organization in the best position to take advantage of future opportunities.

3. Be attentive to the context in which you operate, especially relationships with other actors in the governmental system. There is a natural but unfortunate tendency toward "tunnel vision" in most organizations. Actions are viewed in immediate terms, without duly considering who will be affected by the action. Acknowledging the importance of the environment is essential to strategic thinking.

4. Understand clearly the organization's capacities and limitations. New programs and policies can be effectively implemented only if they fall within the existing capacity of the organization or provide sufficient opportunity to build capacity. There are dangers in both underutilization of resources and becoming overextended.

5. Balance program goals with attention to organizational values and processes. It is important to state programmatic objectives clearly; however, the organization's culture and the prevailing norms, beliefs, and values of its members are equally important. Organizational processes, such as leadership, communications, motivation, group dynamics, and so forth, need constant attention, because they are essential to goal accomplishment.

6. Create diverse mechanisms, both temporary and permanent, for constantly renegotiating programs and processes. Both programmatic concerns and organizational processes are constantly changing in ways that affect persons throughout the organization. Thus, clarity with respect to priorities, goals, and objectives must not lead to rigidity. Mechanisms must permit and, in fact, encourage the entire membership of the organization to contribute regularly to refining programs and processes.

7. Build trust and commitment through open communications and genuine participation. Guidelines by which we might measure the degree of participation the organization encourages include members' access to information and to forums of decision making, their ability to open any issue without fear of retaliation, and their feeling that their ideas will at least be considered by major decision makers (Redford, 1969, p. 8).

Much of the work reviewed here applies equally to management in the public and private sectors. But it is interesting to note that some of the most recent general trends in management have been anticipated in public-sector management. Public organizations' dependence on pluralistic decision processes—that is, processes through which many different people and groups are likely to be involved in any particular decision—makes the process of managing change in the public sector quite complicated. It also means that a high degree of ambiguity and uncertainty is likely to surround most efforts to implement or alter programs, and that managers must be especially skillful in negotiating across organizational boundaries rather than expecting to control circumstances "from the top." In addition, public organizations must have a service orientation—specifically, an understanding of and an attempt to act in accord with the public interest. We noted that organizations seeking public purposes must operate openly, be cognizant of client interests, and understand the political context within which they operate.

Under these circumstances, it is not at all surprising that the values and perspectives that now seem so much a part of "modern management," such as those associated with strategic management or Total Quality Management, have always been central (if not dominant) in public administration theory. Thus, for example, Marshall Dimock's (1936, p. 120) comment that "successful administration is warm and vibrant. It is human" sounds very much like a quotation from Peters and Waterman. One might thus argue that, in contrast to Woodrow Wilson's admonition that public agencies should operate like businesses, it seems that public organizations and the values and interests they represent today should be and are becoming models for organizations of all types.

However, in this age of reinvention and managerialist government, there are reasons to be concerned that business values have overshadowed the ethic of citizenship that accompanies our theory of democracy. Public administration sometimes seems to be more concerned with promoting the entrepreneurial spirit than fostering meaningful engagement and sustaining citizen participation in civil society. There is a danger of devoting ourselves to satisfying the customer while neglecting to ensure equity, justice, and equality for citizens.

We will note later, in discussing recent critiques of the reinvention movement, that citizens are more than mere customers of government, that they are its owners, and that placing this relationship in economic terms reduces the role (and responsibility) of the citizen in the governance process. This critique carries important implications for our notions of public management. Specifically, in the current framework, public administrators can afford to view citizens in instrumental terms, and thus believe that by achieving an efficient, market-oriented system of service delivery that citizen trust and participation will be maintained. Citizen engagement, in this context, may be limited to a source of legitimation for public decisions that have already been made in more rational forms (for different perspectives, see Bryson & Crosby, 1992; Chrislip & Larson, 1994; Thomas, 1995).

Such a limited concept of engagement not only weakens our systems of public management and administration, in that it removes decision-making processes from the public realm, but also threatens to destroy the remaining level of citizen trust we as public servants enjoy. Citizens have expressed that their confidence is less contingent on managerial pursuits, such as efficiency and performance, and more so on the values of responsiveness and equity. Yet sometimes it is tempting to forget this important message and to continue to strive simply for greater productivity.

The question we encounter once again is, "How can we balance efficiency and responsiveness in the operation of public programs?" The field of public administration has generally leaned toward the efficiency side of the equation. Now, however, there is growing evidence that emphasizing responsiveness is not only consistent with democratic principles, but, in the long run, may also be the most effective way of operating. Whereas a structural view of organizations tends to emphasize internal efficiency, it is apparent that greater attention to external relationships and the ability to negotiate across organizational boundaries will become more and more necessary in our increasingly complex society, as will an organizational environment that fosters creativity.

Developing a "democratic" approach to management has often been attractive to public administration theorists because it seems only proper that government institutions in a democracy should operate democratically. What we are finding more and more is that such an approach is not only appealing but necessary for organizations of all types—not only those in the public sector—to survive.

SUMMARY AND ACTION IMPLICATIONS

As we have seen, your behavior is guided by the images you carry around in your head. Some of these images will have to do with the role of public agencies in a democratic society, others will have to do with the most effective and responsible way to run a complex public organization, and still others will have to do with the relationships you establish with other actors, both within and outside the governmental system. Over your career, you will develop and refine your images based on experience and on careful reflection and self-critique. You will also benefit from comparing your images (and approaches) to those that others recommend.

Through the years, students and practitioners of public administration have spent considerable time reflecting on the nature of their work and sorting out the many factors that make for successful public management. Each resulting "theory" represents an attempt to suggest where you should cast your attention. Because you can't attend to all things at once, a certain amount of selectivity goes into theory building. Each theory implies evaluating what is most important to be aware of and to do to manage successfully.

Early writers thought that issues of organizational structure were most important, so they spent considerable time detailing concerns for structure. Later theorists (some of them practitioners) felt that structural issues should be balanced, if not outweighed, by a concern for the behavior of individuals in the organization. Still others sought further refinements, moving from behavior to structure and back again. Contemporary approaches tend to emphasize the organization's culture or value structure, but these approaches will probably, in time, yield to still others.

For the time being, however, we should note the special sensitivity that those in public organizations have always shown for value questions. We have seen time and again how the values of public service—the pursuit of the public interest—affect the work of those in public organizations. The concern of contemporary writers in business and related fields for service and human values is something that those in public administration have always had to contend with, especially as they have been challenged to find a form of management compatible with the requirements of a democratic society.

Terms and Definitions

Area of acceptance: Area within which the subordinate is willing to accept the decisions made by the supervisor.

Boundary spanning: Representing an organization to outside groups and organizations.

Bounded rationality: Seeking the best possible solution, but not necessarily the most rational from a purely economic standpoint.

Functional principle: Horizontal division of labor.

Organization development: Process-oriented approach to planned change.

Organizational culture: Basic patterns of attitudes, beliefs, and values that underlie an organization's operation.

Organizational learning: the process of correcting error through recognizing the disparity between what the group intends to happen and what actually occurs and then drawing appropriate lessons for the future from this fact.

Political economy approach: Focusing on politics and economies as categories for analyzing organizational behavior.

Scalar principle: Vertical division of labor among various organizational levels.

Scientific management: Approach to management based on carefully defined laws, rules, and principles.

Strategic management: A systems-based approach to management that seeks clarity with respect to goals and objectives, strategies to achieve those goals and objectives, and processes of evaluation to measure accomplishments.

Systems approach: Suggestion that public (or other) organizations can be viewed in the same general way as biological or physical systems.

Study Questions

1. Discuss the approaches to public management espoused by early writers in the field.
2. Explain Douglas MacGregor's Theory X and Theory Y management concepts.
3. Compare the management approaches of Herbert Simon and Chris Argyris.
4. Two management approaches combine the human element with the structural aspect of the organization. Discuss the differences between the systems approach and the political economy approach.
5. What shared assumptions, as outlined by Edgar H. Schein, seem consistent in organizational cultures? What features do Peters and Waterman contribute to the list?
6. What basic philosophies underlie recent work in organizational culture and strategic management?

Cases and Exercises

1. Divide the class into four small groups (or multiples of four). Have each group analyze your class as an organization, taking into account questions of power and authority, communications, motivation, group dynamics, and so on. One group should employ only a structural perspective; the second group should employ only a behavioral perspective; and the third group should employ only a systems perspective. The fourth group should employ whatever perspective (or combination of perspectives) that its members consider most modern and most complete.

   Have each group (or a representative of each type of group, depending on the numbers) report their conclusions to the entire class. Think of each perspective as allowing you to see certain things and preventing you from seeing others. What do you see from the structural perspective? What about the behavioral perspective? The systems perspective? The combination perspective is likely to seem most complete, but consider the possibility that this modern viewpoint also overlooks a great deal, and that, though we think it is complete (as those using earlier perspectives considered them complete), there may be much left to understand about organizations, even small ones. What other questions might we encounter in the future?

2. As a class, study the interorganizational relationships of one small organization. The organization might be a unit at the university (either an academic or a staff unit); a unit in city, state, or federal government; or a local nonprofit organization. Pick an organization that is clearly identifiable and, if possible, that appears to have considerable autonomy. Based on interviews with its top administrators and top staff people, develop a chart showing the organization's relationships with others in its environment. (A model something like one of a molecular structure might be appropriate.) Indicate the importance of each relationship, the degree to which that relationship is considered positive or negative, and the degree to which it is considered essential. Try to develop some sense for how much time administrators and staff members spend on external relations versus internal organizational work.

3. The following statement was included as part of a statement of management philosophy for the Greensboro, NC, District of the Internal Revenue Service about a decade ago:

   Our first priority as managers will be to identify and focus on eliminating the barriers to our employees doing their work with the highest degree of quality. We will communicate in such ways as to provide information which will enhance understanding and involvement by our employees in the district decision-making process. We will encourage our employees to speak out and we will be receptive to their questions and/or criticisms of management directions. We will support, guide, and develop our employees to assist them in reaching maximum potential. We will promote positive feelings among our employees toward each other and their work. We will do everything possible to enhance the professional image of the IRS.

First, this statement deals with internal operations of the district; it is primarily concerned with the relationship between managers and employees. What elements would you wish to add to the statement? How has time and politics changed what you might want to include today?

Second, think about the relationship between a tax collection agency and its clients. What statements of philosophy dealing with the relationship between agency and clients would be appropriate to add?

Third, given the statement and your modifications, what specific steps would you recommend to the managers of the agency for putting their commitments (and yours) into practice?

For Additional Reading

Ban, Carolyn. *How Do Public Managers Manage?* San Francisco: Jossey-Bass, 1995.

Baum, Howell S. *The Organization of Hope.* Albany: State University of New York Press, 1997.

Bennis, Warren, Jagdesh Parikh, and Ronnie Lessem. *Beyond Leadership.* Cambridge, MA: Basil Blackwell, 1994.

Block, Peter. *Stewardship.* San Francisco: Berrett Koehler Publishers, 1993.

Bryson, John M., and Barbara C. Crosby. *Leadership for the Common Good: Tackling Public Problems in a Shared-Power World.* San Francisco: Jossey-Bass, 1992.

Caiden, Gerald. *Administrative Reform Comes of Age.* Berlin: W. de Gruyter, 1991.

Carnavale, David G. *Trustworthy Government.* San Francisco: Jossey-Bass, 1995.

Cohen, Steven, and Ronald Brand. *Total Quality Management in Government.* San Francisco: Jossey-Bass, 1993.

Davis, Charles R. *Organization Theories and Public Administration.* Westport, CT: Praeger, 1996.

Denhardt, Robert B. *The Pursuit of Significance.* Belmont, CA: Wadsworth, 1993.

Denhardt, Robert B. *Theories of Public Organization.* 2d ed. Belmont, CA: Wadsworth, 1993.

Diamond, Michael A. *The Unconscious Life of Organizations: Interpreting Organizational Identity.* Westport, CT: Quorum Books, 1993.

Dunn, Delmer. *Politics and Administration at the Top.* Pittsburgh: University of Pittsburgh Press, 1997.

Farmer, John David. *The Language of Public Administration.* Tuscaloosa, AL: University of Alabama Press, 1995.

Fox, Charles, and Hugh Miller. *Postmodern Public Administration.* Thousand Oaks, CA: Sage Publications, 1995.

Fredrickson, H. George. *New Public Administration.* Tuscaloosa: University of Alabama Press, 1980.

Golembiewski, Robert T. *Humanizing Organizations.* Mt. Airy, MD: Lomond Publications, 1985.

Harmon, Michael M., and Richard T. Meyer. *Organization Theory for Public Administration.* Boston: Little, Brown, 1986.

Kass, Henry D., and Bayard L. Catron, eds. *Images and Identities in Public Administration*. Newbury Park: CA: Sage Publications, 1990.

Kettl, Donald, et al. *Cutting Government*. Washington: Brookings Institution, 1995.

Koehler, Jerry W. *Continual Improvement in Government*. St. Lucie, FL: St. Lucie Press, 1996.

Koehler, Jerry W. *Quality Government*. St. Lucie, FL: St. Lucie Press, 1996.

Lee, Dalton M. *The Basis of Management in Public Organizations*. New York: R. Long, 1990.

Milakovich, Michael. *Improving Service Quality*. Delray Beach, FL: St. Lucie Press, 1995.

Morgan, Gareth. *Images of Organization*. 2d ed. Thousand Oaks, CA: Sage Publications, 1997.

Omar, Ray. *Management Analysis in Public Organizations: History, Concepts, and Techniques*. New York: Quorum Books, 1992.

Peters, B. Guy. *The Future of Governing*. Lawrence, KS: University Press of Kansas, 1996.

Peters, Guy, and Bert Rockman. *Agenda for Excellence 2*. Chatham, NJ: Chatham House, 1996.

Rainey, Hal G. *Understanding and Managing Public Organizations*. San Francisco: Jossey-Bass, 1997.

Schein, Edgar H. *Organizational Culture and Leadership*. San Francisco: Jossey-Bass 1987.

Senge, Peter M. *The Fifth Discipline*. New York: Currency Doubleday Dell Publishing, 1990.

Senge, Peter M., et al. *The Fifth Discipline Fieldbook*. New York: Currency Doubleday Dell Publishing, 1994.

Shafritz, Jay M. *Classics of Organization Theory*. Pacific Grove, CA: Brooks/Cole, 1992.

Stever, James A. *The End of Public Administration: Problems of the Profession in the Post-Progressive Era*. Dobbs Ferry, NY: Transnational Publishers, 1988.

Stivers, Camilla. *Gender Images in Public Administration: Legitimacy and the Administrative State*. Newbury Park, CA: Sage Publications, 1993.

Terry, Larry D. *Leadership of Public Bureaucracies*. Thousand Oaks: Sage Publications, 1995.

Wamsley, Gary, et al., *Refounding Democratic Public Administration*. Thousand Oaks, CA: Sage Publications, 1996.

APPENDIX A

Description of Total Quality Management (TQM)

Total Quality Management is a total, integrated organizational approach for meeting customer needs and expectations that involves all managers and employees and uses quantitative methods and employee involvement to improve continuously the organization's processes, products, and services. The description provided below presents TQM as it would exist in an advanced phase in an organization.

Top Management Leadership and Support

Top managers are directly and actively involved in the TQM process. They take the lead in establishing an environment and culture that encourage change, innovation, risk taking, pride in work, and continuous improvement on behalf of all customers. They exhibit a highly visible, personal leadership and communicate the organization's quality vision, goals, and values to all members. Managers provide the resources, time, and training necessary for the organization to improve quality and productivity. They show by example that open communication (vertically and horizontally) and information sharing are the organizational norm. They understand that quality improvement is a long-term process, not to be compromised by short-term considerations. Managers remove barriers to improvement; e.g., they delegate authority to the lowest feasible level, deregulate work, and discourage the "quick-fix" mentality that seeks short-term results at the expense of long-term goals. Managers establish trust, encourage cooperation among organizational units to achieve better service, and reward behavior that reflects the organizations TQM goals. They establish an organization structure that fosters effective implementation of the quality improvement process.

Strategic Planning

Strategic planning drives the organization's improvement efforts. Short- and long-term goals for quality improvement are established across the organization and are integrated into the strategic plan. Customer needs and expectations as well as issues relating to improved supplier relationships are considered and incorporated into the strategic plan. Resources are allocated to support the quality improvement objectives the organization wants to achieve.

Focus on the Customer

Management actively seeks ways to make all employees aware of customers and their need. Employees can identify both the internal and external customers of all their products and services. They understand that their primary task is to satisfy customer requirements and expectations. Communication with customers, as with suppliers, is open, continual, and two-way to ensure that clear definitions of needs and expectations are received and problems and concerns are understood. Customer perceptions of performance are continually measured, evaluated, and reported to responsible managers and employees. Feedback data are used to improve processes and services and provide input for strategic planning. Access by customers to information about the organization's products or services is easy and trouble-free. Complaints about aspects of the organization's services are solicited and corrected. Trends in customer satisfaction indicators are positive. The validity and objectivity of monitoring methods is ensured. Where expectations, desires, and perceptions of different customer groups are in conflict with each other, the organization strives to achieve a balance among them that best fulfills the organization's mission.

Commitment to Training and Recognition

Managers and employees receive ongoing training to enable them to keep abreast of changing job requirements and prepare for greater responsibilities. A key element of training for all managers and employees is quality awareness and the use of tools, technologies, and techniques to support continuous improvement.

Employees are motivated to achieve total quality through trust, respect, and recognition. Managers believe that employees want to do a good job; they personally, regularly, and fairly recognize individuals and teams for measurable contributions to quality improvement. Rewards and recognition are broad-based and innovative, encompass all levels of the organization, are centered on team quality and productivity improvement, and include peer recognition as a part of the reward structure. Celebration of small successes is common. Performance plans for managers include measurable quality improvement objectives. Evaluations focus on the degree to which the objectives are met.

Employee Empowerment and Teamwork

Management provides an environment that supports employee involvement, contribution, and teamwork. Where unions exist, union leaders are involved in high-level policy and decision-making groups, such as Quality Councils or Policy Boards. Teamwork is the vehicle for cooperation and communication among managers, supervisors, unions, and employees in addressing quality improvement issues. The demands of quality, cost, schedule, and mission that cross organizational units are met through cross-functional team cooperation. Employees have clear avenues for participation and involvement; e.g., as members of self-regulating work teams responsible for an entire process or group of customers, contributors to developing and implementing improvement plans, suggestors of ideas for improvement, participators in establishing work unit performance measures and goals, evaluators of processes, and decision makers in many aspects of their work and work environment. Hierarchies are reduced in favor of cooperative teams and networks. Employees have a strong feeling of empowerment and team ownership of work processes because sufficient power, rewards, information, and knowledge are moved to the lowest levels of the organization to enable everyone to accomplish their work with excellence. As a result, everyone feels "ownership" of quality improvement and exhibits personal pride in the quality of their work.

Measurement and Analysis of Processes and Outputs

All information required to support total quality of processes and products/services is complete, timely, accurate, useful, and clearly communicated to those who need it. The scope of the data includes: customers and suppliers (both internal and external), internal operations, products/services, employees, comparisons or benchmarks of other organizations, and safety/environmental considerations (if appropriate). This information is the basis for developing quality measures that cover all aspects of work processes and all products and services provided a customer. Customer satisfaction measures are used extensively. These measures are used by employees to identify problems, determine root causes, identify solutions, and verify that proposed remedies produce the expected results.

Quality Assurance

Products, services, and processes are designed and verified to meet customer needs and expectations. Processes that produce the organization's products and services are controlled, optimized, and maintained. There is sufficient standardization within the organization to ensure compatibility. Comprehensive assessments of the quality assurance system as well as of products/services are performed at appropriate intervals. An approach exists for translating assessment findings into quality documentation supporting quality assurance. Quality assurance systems are updated to keep pace with changes in technology, practice, and quality improvement. Product and service performance standards are set for internal support functions such as finance and accounting, personnel, and administrative support. There is an established method to verify that the organization's quality requirements are being met by suppliers and other providers of goods and services. The organization compares (benchmarks) its products, services, and internal operations with the "best" in the private or public sectors (e.g., other federal agencies, state and local governments, and the governments of other countries).

SOURCE: Excerpted from office of Management and Budget, Draft Circular A-132, 1990.

Chapter 9

REINVENTING GOVERNMENT: IMPROVING QUALITY AND PRODUCTIVITY IN PUBLIC ORGANIZATIONS

Over the past few years, you probably have heard the expression "reinventing government," or perhaps even read Osborne & Gaebler's (1992) important work that popularized the concept in American public administration. The book voices a belief that public organizations or, more accurately, the systems underlying public organizations, lack the capacity to meet the challenges and opportunities of the twenty-first century. Thus, the concept of reinvention in many ways can be considered a new approach to a rather old issue: the drive to improve government performance and accountability.

However, reinvention should not be equated simply with a call for increased government productivity. Proponents of the more recent reform agenda recognize that public agencies, particularly in America, constitute some of the most productive institutions in the world, even more so than private institutions. (For example, over the past generation, government productivity has increased at double the national average.) Instead, reinvention and related reformist themes, such as "the new public management" and "the new public administration," suggest that government should not account merely for its own activities but should be assessed on its capacity to achieve substantial public outcomes.

Reinvention is, however, closely related to issues of quality and productivity in government. The two stem from similar sources. Concern about government productivity centers around issues of efficiency and accountability. These issues have, of course, been debated throughout the country's history; modern expression is typically dated back to the passage of Proposition 13, a tax limitation initiative passed by California voters in the late 1970s. Following the California example, other states and localities also began efforts to limit what voters perceived as the excessive cost of government services.

At the federal level, the desire to avoid new taxes meant reduction or elimination of numerous domestic programs, especially during the Reagan years. Many of these programs provided aid to state and local governments. When the reductions were combined with the desire to limit state and local taxation, many governments were severely constrained in trying to provide sufficient revenues to support important, even basic, services. But despite these limitations, these governments were often asked to do more, to provide increased services, with the same or even with reduced funding.

We examined some of the implications of this situation in Chapter 5 with respect to budgeting and financial management, as many governments were forced to search for alternate funding methods, including privatization, coproduction, user fees, and so forth. But the same governments also sought new ways to improve both the quality and quantity of work without extra cost. Many governments and agencies at all levels began new or at least intensified efforts to innovate new solutions, to break from the traditional assumptions and find more effective means of meeting their objectives.

Success stories emerging from this innovation had a weakening effect on the traditional assumptions in public administration, as even those in the mainstream started to question core principles that had defined the field since the Progressive Era. Around the world, public management and administration began to take a new shape. Public organizations started to lose their traditional bureaucratic structure, becoming instead more lateral systems of shared power and teamwork. Systems of management, too, were transformed into more equitable, less controlling forms of leadership. And, government agencies began to form meaningful partnerships with other institutions and citizens in response to public problems.

Advances in information technology (IT) played an integral role in transforming public administration worldwide. The impact was twofold. First, increased capacity for communication and information sharing redefined the distribution of authority within government institutions. Every member of the organization had access to the latest news and information, thus shared in one of the more important sources of power. Second, IT enabled public organizations to engage more effectively with their counterparts in other sectors and around the world, as well as citizens. Such a change restructured the ways in which governments and agencies responded to opportunities and challenges.

So, whether we call it an effect of reinvention, the new public management, or efforts to improve quality and productivity, the public administration we have at the beginning of the twenty-first century is quite different from that of merely a generation ago. The ways in which we organize ourselves, engage with others, and respond to public concerns have undergone dramatic change. Yet, as we explore the various aspects of reinvention and the new public management, keep asking: Have we improved service to the public? Is the work we are doing today consistent with our expectations for a system of democratic governance. Are we truly acting in the interest of our citizens?

REINVENTING GOVERNMENT

The reform movement that emerged from Osborne & Gaebler's (1992) landmark work, *Reinventing Government,* represented a response in public administration to what the authors call the bankruptcy of bureaucracy—that is, the ineffectiveness of government organizations. The authors believed that public agencies had failed to keep pace with changing social and economic conditions in the postindustrial society. They suggested that government still attempted to respond to public issues with a "one-size-fits-all" approach. As a result, the systems in which public administrators function had become the problem, not the solution, and consequently citizens had begun to lose faith in the capacity of government to serve their needs.

At the heart of reinvention lies the belief that only more entrepreneurial forms of government can effectively deal with problems and capitalize on opportunities in contemporary society. Yet, in contrast to most interpretations, Osborne & Gaebler (1992) avoided the more traditional view that government should be run like a business: "Government and business are fundamentally different institutions. Business leaders are driven by the profit motive; government leaders are driven by the desire to get reelected . . . Differences such as these create fundamentally different incentives in the public sector" (p. 20). While encouraging public administrators to derive insights from successful experiences in all sectors, Osborne & Gaebler maintain that the challenges confronting the public sector remained vastly different from those in the private sector.

Entrepreneurial government, then, refers to more streamlined, flexible, and responsive systems of public policy and administration. Osborne and Gaebler cite example after example of public organizations that had chosen innovative strategies for doing more with less strategies for increasing the value of public services without raising costs for public consumers. From privatization efforts in Phoenix, Arizona, which enhanced competition among service providers, thus raising significantly performance standards, to public school initiatives in East Harlem, New York, that empowered residents with greater choice for students' learning opportunities. The authors suggest that these common themes—competition and empowerment—combined with more attention to public outcomes and action based on customer priorities rather than bureaucratic imperatives, represent the future of successful government.

To carry out the reform agenda, Osborne and Gaebler (1992) provide ten principles underlying reinvention and public entrepreneurship:

1. Catalytic Government: Steering Rather Than Rowing
   Public entrepreneurs move beyond existing policy options, serving instead as catalysts within their communities to generate alternate courses of action. They choose to steer, recognizing a wide range of possibilities and striking a balance between resources and needs, rather than row or concentrating on a single objective. Those who steer define their future, as opposed to those who row that simply rely on traditional assumptions (Osborne and Gaebler, 1992, p. 35).
2. Community-Owned Government: Empowering Rather Than Serving
   Public entrepreneurs have learned that past efforts to serve clients produced dependence, as opposed to economic and social independence. Rather than maintain this approach, these entrepreneurs shift ownership of public initiatives into the community. They empower citizens, neighborhood groups, and community organizations to be the sources of their own solutions (Osborne and Gaebler, 1992, p. 52).
3. Competitive Government: Injecting Competition into Service Delivery
   Public entrepreneurs have recognized that attempting to provide every service not only places a drain on public resources but also causes public organizations to overextend their capabilities, thus reducing service quality and effectiveness. Public entrepreneurs counter this trend by fostering competition among public, private, and nongovernmental service providers. The results are greater efficiency, enhanced responsiveness, and an environment that rewards innovation (Osborne and Gaebler, 1992, pp. 80–83).

4. Mission-Driven Government: Transforming Rule-Driven Organizations

Public entrepreneurs have seen how excessive rule making in bureaucratic organizations stifles innovation and limits government performance. Such rule making is further supported by rigid systems of budgeting and human resources. In contrast, public entrepreneurs focus first on the mission of the group—what the organization strives for internally and externally. Then, the budget, human resources, and other systems are designed to reflect the overall mission (Osborne and Gaebler, 1992, p. 110).

5. Results-Oriented Government: Funding Outcomes, Not Inputs

Public entrepreneurs believe that government should be dedicated to achieving substantive public goals, or outcomes, as opposed to concentrating strictly on controlling the public resources expended in doing the job. Current evaluation and reward systems focus mainly on fiscal efficiency and control, rarely asking what impacts were gained from each public initiative. Public entrepreneurs transform these systems to be more results oriented that is, accountability based on government performance (Osborne and Gaebler, 1992, pp. 140–141).

6. Customer-Driven Government: Meeting the Needs of the Customer, Not the Bureaucracy

Public entrepreneurs have learned from their private-sector counterparts that unless one focuses on the customer, the citizen will never be happy. Since legislative bodies provide most public resources to government agencies, these agencies operate completely blind of their customer base. They function according to their own priorities, and those demanded of them by the funding source, instead of what they customers actually need. Public entrepreneurs stand this system on its head, serving the customer first (Osborne and Gaebler, 1992, p. 166–167).

7. Enterprising Government: Earning Rather Than Spending

Public entrepreneurs face the same fiscal constraints as their traditional counterparts, but the difference is in the way they respond. Rather than raise taxes or slash public programs, public entrepreneurs find innovative ways to do more with less. By instituting the concept of profit motive into the public realm—for example, relying on charges and fees for public services and investments to fund future initiatives—public entrepreneurs are able to add value and ensure results, even in tight financial times (Osborne and Gaebler, 1992, pp. 203–206).

8. Anticipatory Government: Prevention Rather Than Cure

Public entrepreneurs have grown tired of funneling resources into programs to resolve public problems. Instead, they believe the primary concern should be prevention, stopping the problem before it ever occurs. Government in the past prided itself on service delivery—on being able to put forth initiatives aimed at curing public ills. However, as the problems in postindustrial society became more complex, government lost its capacity to respond. By returning to prevention, public organizations will be more efficient and effective for the future (Osborne and Gaebler, 1992, p. 219–221).

9. Decentralized Government: From Hierarchy to Participation and Teamwork

Public entrepreneurs appreciate the role centralized organizations served in the industrial age. These institutions represented the first steps toward professionalization in the field of public administration. Yet, the age of the hierarchical institution has passed. Advances in information technology, improved communications systems, and increases in workforce quality have brought in a new age of more flexible, team-based organizations. Decision making has been extended throughout the organization, placed in the hands of those who can innovate and determine the high-performance course (Osborne and Gaebler, 1992, pp. 250–252).

10. Market-Oriented Government: Leveraging Change through the Market
    Public entrepreneurs respond to changing conditions not with traditional approaches, such as attempting to control the entire situation, but rather with innovative strategies aimed at shaping the environment to allow market forces to act. Each jurisdiction—whether a nation, a state, or a local community—represents a market, a collection of people, interests, and social and economic forces. Public entrepreneurs realize that these markets remain beyond the control of any single political body. So, their strategy centers on structuring the environment so that the market can operate most effectively, thus ensuring quality of life and economic opportunity (Osborne and Gaebler, 1992, pp. 280–282).

Osborne and Gaebler intend these ten principles to serve as a new conceptual framework for public administration—an analytical checklist to transform the actions of government. "What we are describing is nothing less than a shift in the basic model of governance used in America. This shift is under way all around us, but because we are not looking for it—because we assume that all governments have to be big, centralized, and bureaucratic—we seldom see it. We are blind to the new realities, because they do not fit our preconceptions" (Osborne and Gaebler, 1992, p. 321). By applying the ten reinvention principles in the context of any given policy area, a new universe of opportunity, an altogether different system of governance, would emerge.

Despite the immediate and pervasive impact of "reinventing government" on American government, though, the work itself should not be considered the beginning point of "reinvention." Efforts to reform public management to create government systems geared toward accountability and high performance had emerged years before the book's publication. Influenced by the fiscal crisis beginning in the late 1970s, as well as innovations by public-sector managers, scholars and practitioners began to develop new ways of thinking about public administration. As early as the mid 1980s, public managers began to restructure their bureaucratic agencies, redefine their organizational missions, streamline agency processes, and decentralize decision making (see Kamensky, 1996).

Many scholars refer to this more comprehensive reform agenda as the "new public management," a worldwide effort to transform the theory and practice of public administration. Some principles in the new public management may sound familiar, given our discussion of reinvention. For example, reformers seek to create organizations that are mission-driven, decentralized, and incentive-based. They strive for more flexible public organizations and more responsive interorganizational networks. Key principles in the new public management include accountability, responsiveness, and the commitment to achieving public outcomes (see Boston, 1996; Peters, 1994).

NETWORKING

Global perspectives on the New Public Management are available from the Canadian Centre for Management Development (http://www.ccmd-ccg.gc.ca/index.html), the OECD Public Management Service (http://www.oedc.org/puma/), and the Australian Public Service Innovations (http://www.innovations.gov.au). Specific information about the New Zealand government can be found at http://www.govt.nz/ or through the government's Management Development Centre at http://www.mdcentre.govt.nz/.

Perhaps the best example of the new public management in an international context can be seen in New Zealand's administrative reforms. Initiated in 1985, under the fourth Labour government, the revolution "down under" paved the way for our contemporary notion of reinventing government. New Zealand's central government cited as its primary goal the creation of more responsive and effective public organizations. To achieve this end, the government redeveloped its personnel system for top executives to be more performance-oriented, instituted a new process of measuring the productivity and effectiveness of government agencies, and reengineered departmental systems to reflect the government's commitment to accountability (Boston, 1991, 1996).

The effectiveness of New Zealand's reform agenda, as well as parallel activities in Canada, Great Britain and the United States, prompted public administrators around the world to adopt many of the principles from the new public management. Reports from the UN Commission on Global Governance and other international bodies reinforced this international movement, advocating decentralized decision making, civil society, empowerment and a reliance on third-sector organizations for achieving public outcomes (Commission on Global Governance, 1995).

However, critics of the new public management, and later of reinventing government, suggested that while certain aspects of the agenda contributed to meaningful improvements in public service, the application of these principles had produced a variety of negative externalities not envisioned by early reformers. In practice, the adoption of business practices and the reliance on market forces by public organizations degenerated into a sense of managerialism—a belief that government could and should be run like a business based on strictly economic principles. As public managers began to apply their reform agendas, many focused on the pursuit of administrative efficiency more than maintaining the democratic principles of effective governance.

Another point of concern in the reform movements centered on the customer-centered, as opposed to citizen-centered, public administration. Critics argued that "citizens are not the customers of government; they are its owners who elect leaders to represent their interests. A customer-centered model puts citizens in a reactive role limited to liking or disliking services and hoping that administrators will change delivery if enough customers object" (Schachter, 1995, p. 530, citing the argument by Frederickson, 1994). In contrast, citizen-centered public administration restores the public to an ownership position—a proactive relationship in which citizens engage with the institutions of governance to achieve public outcomes.

Despite this criticism, however, the new public management and reinvention movements have had a pervasive impact on public administration in this country and around the world. As we will discuss later in the chapter, the principles underlying these reform efforts have contributed to major initiatives to enhance government performance and accountability, particularly in the United States. Public organizations at all levels have embarked on strategies to streamline work processes and enhance the public service.

TECHNOLOGICAL INNOVATIONS AND REINVENTION

IT AND THE PUBLIC SERVICE

Advances in information technology (IT) have played a key role in the move toward a more entrepreneurial public service. Beginning with the PC revolution in the early 1980s, when personal computers started to appear in every office (not to mention every home), IT has been a central part in the drive to increase government performance. Yet in the age of reinvention, IT was transformed from being a tool for enhancing productivity to a metaphor for the very way in which we organize in government. We began to view ourselves as actors in wired organizations, members of virtual teams, and citizens in a growing web of cyber-democracy.

In the 1990s, the dramatic growth in the Internet, which began as an electronic network of researchers and scholars, into a global infobahn supported our change in perspective. We could, in real time, have a virtual chat with colleagues around the world on matters of public policy (or anything else for that matter), exchange insights on common challenges, or swap information relating to new innovations. Governments and agencies soon turned to online resources for many of their core functions, including economic development, human and social service delivery, and engagement with citizens. So, we can say that in less than a generation, the Internet and improvements in IT generally have helped to reshape our notions of governance and public space.

WIRED ORGANIZATIONS

From a public management perspective, the most immediate impact of IT has been to redefine our concept of organization. Intranets, electronic mail, and other networking resources have allowed or in some cases forced agencies to more effectively integrate work processes and create a team-based approach to meeting objectives. In fact, some even consider the two innovations linked in our contemporary understanding of organizing. Mankin, Cohen, and Bikson (1996), for example, suggested that "information technology can make teams more effective, and teams can help fulfill the promise of information technology. Together, teams and new information technology can catalyze dramatic improvements in organizational performance" (p. ix). Organizations that succeed in integrating teamwork with IT, and use IT to support team-based initiatives, will be more successful in managing organizational change.

Accordingly, IT became a key theme in Vice President Al Gore's National Performance Review (NPR). The NPR plan, as well as the Information Technology Management Reform Act of 1996, focused on the use of IT in the reengineering process of federal agencies. Specific NPR recommendations included the creation of an information infrastructure that would allow for a more effective use of government resources, as well as facilitate the modernization of processing and customer service centers; the development of an efficient electronic mail service, improving federal agencies with messaging and communications capabilities; and the implementation of an incentive system to reward innovation, a system that would enable agencies to reinvest dollars saved into information technology (Gore, 1993).

The NPR recommendations have translated into important innovations relating to the use of IT in the reinvention process (see Box 9.1). At a recent conference organized by the International Quality and Productivity Center, administrators from a variety of federal agencies shared their experiences and insights on one of the crucial advancements: the use of government intranets or internal Web sites for public organizations. Noted one participant, "An intranet is much more than a glorified email or groupware solution . . . (it) can be customized and tailored to a specific work environment, enabling employees to not just communicate internally, but collaborate, interact, and become part of a team connected through their desktop computers" (Kerwood, 1997, p. 1).

Of course, the application of IT in the reengineering process has not been limited to the federal government. New York City's Bureau of Law and Adjustment recently upgraded its technological capacity as a means of improving its organizational performance. Before the change, the Bureau struggled to process more than 32,000 claims per year using pre–twentieth century rules and regulations. The technological situation before the shift was not much better. "In 1990, we had one PC for 160 people," said Bureau Chief Michael Aaronson (cited in Newcombe, 1997, p. 20). In response, the bureau contracted with Universal Systems Inc. to manage the integration of IT and the organization's work processes. They primary goal was to reduce the bureau's paper trail by switching from hard-copy claims to an electronic processing system.

The contractor-consultant team ultimately developed the Omnibus Automated Image Storage and Information System (OAISIS) a relational database that uses software created by the Oracle Corporation. The new imaging-based system has enabled the bureau to cut in half its number of claims awaiting settlement, which allowed the organization to reach settlements on more cases without having to go to court. The savings from this alone topped $2.5 million. The automation also made redundant a number of city staff positions, which were later downsized at a savings of about $300,000. Finally, due to the system's efficiency, city staff has been able to spend more time investigating fraudulent claims, activity which has produced an additional $250,000 in savings (Newcombe, 1997).

IT APPLICATIONS

As this example indicates, IT can be particularly useful in merely processing the enormous amounts of data generated, and handled, by public agencies. Some governments and agencies, however, have created information systems that do more than merely "push paper." **Expert systems,** or other forms of artificial intelligence, mimic the decision-making processes that human experts use in a particular field. These programs have the ability to accept information and infer conclusions based on decision heuristics (or "rules of thumb"). The state of California, for example, has developed an expert system for determining eligibility for social services. The system takes the individual's data and compares that information with the applicable rules and regulations and makes recommendations with respect to eligibility (*Government Productivity News,* February 1992, p. 4).

Advancements in technology have also been experienced in the field of geographic information systems, or GIS. Technology of this nature, which is based on satellite imagery, allows planners and public administrators to more accurately map and analyze an

---

BOX 9.1

Service to the Citizen, by the Citizen

New technologies are alleviating the headaches of doing business with the government by enabling citizens to do much of the work themselves.

It's lunchtime—peak business hours at the Department of Motor Vehicles. A line of frustrated customers waits to step up to the service counter. Clerks register automobiles, administer driver examinations and try to reduce the waiting lines. But the same thought crosses the mind of almost everyone in the room: "Isn't there a better way?"

Until recently, the answer was no. Whether a citizen needed to register an automobile or obtain a Social Security card, it meant a harrowing day of hustling between agencies and waiting for a number to be called. For government employees, a day at work meant subduing dissatisfied customers and spending time on repetitious paperwork.

But in today's wired age, citizens are beginning to help themselves. Self-service kiosks, informational or interactive Websites and toll-free telephone lines are helping public agencies revolutionize the way they serve the public. And, for the most part, people love it. Experts say electronic government is unique because both parties can reap benefits. Consumers profit from increased government accessibility and faster response time, while governments can cut costs and improve reliability. Janet Caldow, director of IBM Corp.'s Institute for Electronic Government, said government is undergoing a dramatic technological transformation. "Electronic government has the potential to change the relationship between elected leaders and constituents," she said. "These vital technologies will change and empower both governors and the governed."

Government one day may resemble a neighborhood convenience store: one location that offers everything the citizen needs from public agencies, any time he or she needs it. The U.S. Postal Service's Web Interactive Network of Government Services (WINGS) is a step in that direction. WINGS is one of the first intergovernmental efforts to reduce the complexity and confusion people experience when dealing with the government.

The website, www.wings.gov, offers local, state, and federal government services and information by way of the Internet.

"The WINGS infrastructure provides the complete functionality to enable electronic commerce between the public and their government," said WINGS Program Manager Susan Smoter. "Basically, the Postal Service relieves other agencies of the burden of secured delivery, freeing them up to concentrate on the services that fall into their individual missions."

continued

continued from the previous page

Caldow said saving time and trouble is one of the prime benefits of systems like WINGS. "There is not a citizen in the world who wants to take a vacation day and stand in line to get a driver's license," she said. "That's why one of the trends we're seeing is the next generation of Websites for government, where it's not just information on government, but actually service that can be performed from a computer or kiosk." Experts predict that government-provided interactive kiosks, IVR (interactive voice recognition) systems and Web services soon will be commonplace. "Everyone is pursuing it quite aggressively," Caldow said. "Kiosks are going to be as common as bank ATMs in the not-too-distant future."

"The stuff you only find on the Internet now, it's going to be pervasive enough that anyone will feel it is common," Mechling agreed. Progress in voice systems means that in about a decade, "a lot of machines we'll be talking to, instead of using keyboards for," he predicted.

The days of waiting in line at government offices may be numbered. And that's good news for customer and agency staff alike.

SOURCE: Maxwell, Alison. "Service to the Citizen, By the Citizen." *Government Technology* 29 (special insert with *Government Executive,* Oct. 1997): 6–16.

---

entire jurisdiction. GIS technology links physical and other geographic features that can be depicted on a map (schools, roads, and sewer lines) with other records (including political, environmental, or statistical records), placing them into a large database. The system then allows these different databases to be layered and merged. While such systems are continuously being improved, they have created a large number of advantages for state and local governments (Brudney & Brown, 1992, p. 84–85).

In many cases, though, IT applications are no longer considered extraordinary in performing public services. As *Government Technology* (September 1997) recently reported, the use of IT last year became the law in Oakland, California, as Mayor Elihu M. Harris and city council members approved a measure that requires the jurisdiction's public housing units to be wired to the information superhighway. The program, which will place computer technology into each residential unit, is part of a citywide effort to give low-income residents greater access to public services and employment opportunities. City officials have formed a partnership with IBM to complete the venture, which will give each unit a network station connected to the city's local area network. It is this type of "connectivity," or linking citizens to the institutions of governance through IT and related technologies, that has reshaped our systems of public administration worldwide.

CYBER-DEMOCRACY

The concept of cyber-democracy stems from the growth during the early 1990s in electronic community networks. Alexander and Grubbs (1998) define community networks as "as a low cost, easy-to-use computer network that provides citizens with access to electronic mail, public bulletin boards, and electronic information relevant to their locality" (unnumbered, online journal). These networks are usually used to enhance local community organizations, facilitate neighborhood capacity-building programs, and foster citizen participation in public decision making. In recent years, these networks have gained in complexity and strength, with some even branching into providing Internet access, GIS technology, and computer-based civic and educational courses.

At the heart of these community networks lies a public-private-nongovernmental sector partnership, with administrative roles shared by the various actors. In some cases, universities also play an crucial role. In Delaware, for example, the University of Delaware's Center for Community Development and Family Policy houses the civic network, Diamond.net, a joint effort by the university, the Delaware Association of Nonprofit Agencies, the Division of Public Libraries, and other public and nongovernmental organizations. The network's mission "is to enhance collaboration and electronic communication among the state of Delaware's citizens, nonprofits, community-based organizations, and state and local government agencies" (Alexander and Grubbs, 1998, unnumbered, online journal). Membership and usage of the network is free and can be accessed by groups around the state through a toll-free dial-in number.

Community networks serve as models for what Grossman (1995) calls a key pad democracy—an electronic republic in which public participation occurs in virtual settings. He outlines several indicators of this emerging system of governance:

Greater communication with public officials and administrators is possible through electronic mail, faxing, and audio-video conferencing.

Information necessary for rational decision making can be disseminated to the public via the Web and advanced multimedia presentations.

Elections and public referenda may be conducted more accurately through electronic voting mechanisms (in Alexander & Grubbs, 1998, unnumbered, online journal).

While we may have to wait a few years until we can vote online, our capacity for interacting with public officials and building a virtual civil society has never been greater.

THE INTERNET

Although we have already mentioned the Internet in our discussions of IT, we must consider cyberspace in its own right, particularly with respect to the use of Internet-based technology by governments at all levels. The NPR, for example, has used the Internet to target a number of its efforts in what it calls Access America. NPR's U.S. General Store program—a virtual one-stop-shop for government services—expands the federal government into cyberspace. One of the General Store physical sites, in Atlanta, Georgia, uses the Internet to link a variety of federal, state, and local agencies into a single, virtual location for the purpose of community-based human and social service delivery. The

Portland, Oregon, site features a similar federal-state partnership, except out west the Internet site targets information on natural resources and recreational activities.

State governments, too, have uploaded a variety of services onto the Internet. Delaware and South Carolina have emerged as leaders in this area, particularly in advancing their economic development initiatives. These Internet sites feature regional information relating to incentive programs and other initiatives for business recruitment. On the South Carolina site, Web surfers can view the state's overall economic development plan, as well as link to a variety of other pages that give more detailed information about doing business down south. The Delaware site features similar information, aimed at keeping the state one of the leaders in state-level economic growth (Richardson, 1996).

THE HUMAN SIDE OF TECHNOLOGICAL INNOVATION

Whether in designing new vehicles for collecting garbage, developing new techniques for space exploration, or creating broad-based management information systems, the technical questions are always accompanied by a related set of "human" concerns, most having to do with how human beings work together to solve technical problems. For example, what is the proper relationship between government and industry in supporting research and development activities? How can technological innovations be transferred from one jurisdiction or organization to another? What are the human consequences for a particular organization in adopting particular approaches? How can people in the organization be helped in adapting to the new technology?

One group that has been deeply involved in responding to questions such as these is Public Technology, Inc. PTI began in 1969 when a group of local government managers joined together to establish a way to apply technologies developed by NASA to problems encountered by local governments (Mercer & Philips, 1981). (Throughout most of its history, NASA has had a special mandate to support civilian applications of space technology.) For example, local officials were concerned about inadequate or bulky air supply for fire fighters. As a result of conversations with NASA people who designed life support systems, the local officials gained access to high-pressure, lightweight air tanks, devices that see through smoke, and other similar tools (Toregas, 1988, p. 3).

In addition to specific technical contributions, Public Technology, Inc. focused on the human element of technology transfer. PTI felt that what came to be called orgware, that combination of human and interpersonal skills needed to cope with the frustration and fear associated with new technologies, was more important than the technical hardware or software (Toregas, 1988, p. 3). Emotional issues can often get in the way of applying improved technology; for example, firefighters viewed a new, automated, radio-controlled nozzle for fire trucks as such a threat to their jobs and their normal way of fighting fires that it was abandoned almost immediately.

Experiences such as this led Public Technology to adopt a formula for technology management: for every $5 spent on hardware, $15 must be spent on software, and $80 must be spent on "orgware" training, organization development, and so on.

Organizational members' concerns about introduction of new technologies can be dealt with effectively, but implementing a change to new technologies is time-consuming and costly. In any application of new technology, you must keep the human element very much in mind. For this reason, many agencies establish joint technology design committees to analyze how employees will respond to the changes brought about by new technology (*Government Productivity News,* September 1992, p. 4).

Other dimensions of the human side of advanced technology, especially advanced information technology, are also important. The first has to do with the impact of information technology on day-to-day work patterns. As we will see in later chapters, managers' work is not only information-based, but highly interpersonal as well. There is no question that computer networking, for example, will increase the information available to managers and decrease the time spent waiting for it. Moreover, extensive networking should improve managers' capacity to more effectively integrate the work of various groups within the organization. On the other hand, managers with access to computer networks may spend much less time in face-to-face conversations or in visits to various locations where the work is done, and these interpersonal tasks are essential.

Second, we should expect greater dependence on advanced information technology to raise several very personal concerns for those who work in or deal with public organizations. The depersonalized nature of computerized control and evaluation systems may prove highly stressful for either employees or clients. In the private sector, for instance, there have already been experiments with automated systems of accountability measuring the number of keystrokes a typist generates or the number of calls a salesperson makes. Similar applications in the public sector could well lead to the same negative reactions that have often occurred in the private sector applications.

Third, the use of advanced information technology raises questions about how organizations of the future are likely to be structured. Networking can simultaneously allow for greater centralized control or for greater decentralization. Some argue that "knowledge is power," and that making more information available to top officials on a timely basis will permit them to accumulate even greater power (perhaps to the detriment of others). Some argue instead that new technology will spread information throughout the organization and, consequently, power will be decentralized. The latest studies take a different position—that information technology in and of itself does not necessarily lead an organization toward either more or less central control. Rather, the organization's initial structure, history and culture, and the behavior of its managers are the determinants. Information systems, it seems, can be designed to either centralize or decentralize.

HUMAN RESOURCES AND PRODUCTIVITY IMPROVEMENT

Whereas advanced technology can improve productivity, far greater improvements are possible through more effective use of human resources. Many approaches for improving the commitment, motivation, and creativity of employees (including managers) have been developed over the years. Most today are considered merely good management practice, but many specific techniques are more often used in formal productivity improvement programs than as ongoing managerial processes. We will review four techniques: management by objectives (MBO), quality of work-life programs (especially job enrichment), quality circles (or similar group approaches), and incentive programs.

MANAGEMENT BY OBJECTIVES

One of the oldest productivity improvement techniques to be used systematically in business and government is **management by objectives** (MBO). Management by objectives became especially popular in the late 1960s and through the 1970s. President Nixon extended MBO concepts throughout many federal agencies, a pattern that was soon followed in a large number of state and local organizations. Although MBO has fallen into some disfavor in government agencies, many of its key elements, such as objective setting and performance appraisal, remain in place in many agencies.

Essentially, management by objectives is a highly participatory approach to establishing clear and measurable objectives throughout an organization. First, MBO assumes that the organization as a whole will benefit by clarifying its broad-range goals and by targeting the work of all organizational units and all individuals in pursuit of those goals. Second, MBO assumes that all elements of the organization, from top to bottom, will benefit from establishing realistic objectives each year and measuring progress toward the objectives as the year goes by. Third, MBO assumes that the process of establishing goals and objectives should involve a broad spectrum of organizational members, both to solicit the fullest range of ideas and to build patterns of effective communications and commitment.

Management by objectives is based on an image of the organization as a hierarchy of linked goals and objectives. The organization's broad goals are developed at the top of the hierarchy and become the basis for negotiating more specific objectives at the next level down. These objectives in turn become the basis for negotiating objectives at the next level and so on down through the organization, even to the level of setting objectives for each individual employee. In a fully developed MBO system, the broad agency goals theoretically provide a framework within which everyone in the organization, including both managers and other employees, has before him or her a set of performance objectives to guide his or her work during the course of the year (June 1976, pp. 15–16).

Note that the objective-setting process is not one in which objectives decided "from above" are merely handed down to each successive level. Rather, MBO involves a highly decentralized objective-setting process, in which each supervisor works with each subordinate manager or employee to arrive at a reasonable set of objectives. Ideally, this process of negotiation involves face-to-face conversations in which objectives at various levels are worked out; however, in many applications of MBO, the objective-setting process occurs through an exchange of memos and written forms.

For objectives to most effectively guide the work of those throughout the organization, you must pay special attention to the type of objectives being developed (Morley, 1986, p. 186). The most useful objectives are those that are:

Clear and specific: The objectives should state exactly what is to be done (e.g., to reduce response time to three minutes), rather than vague and subjective (e.g., to respond in the shortest possible time).

Realistic: The objectives should be challenging to the unit or the individual, but not beyond reach. It also should be clear that the resources and support necessary to meet the objectives will be available.

Measurable (or otherwise verifiable): There must be some way for both the supervisor and subordinate to know when the objective has been met.

Prioritized: Both the superior and subordinate should agree on which objective is most important, which is next most important, and so on.

The resulting objectives may be stated in several ways: in terms of amount of work (cases processed per week), effectiveness of work (applicants placed each month), quality of work (a minimum error rate), completion dates and target costs, or some combination of these (Morley, 1986, p. 186). You should follow the objective-setting process with a more detailed examination of what must be done to meet the objective. Usually an action plan is developed, indicating how, when, and by whom the actual work will be done to meet the objectives. (At this point, of course, it is important to agree on the resources and support necessary to attain the objective.) Finally, managers must assign specific responsibility to those in their units for completing the necessary task.

As mentioned, MBO has been tried in many different government and nonprofit organizations here and abroad. Recently, MBO has been widely criticized, largely because of the extremely detailed paperwork that many organizations required as part of their MBO system, but many places still use important features of MBO. For example, setting goals and objectives and developing accompanying action plans are central to more contemporary strategic management efforts. Similarly, one of the most important features of MBO systems, which has been retained in many organizations long after the demise of a full-blown MBO system, is the frequent review and revision of objectives, accompanied by detailed **performance appraisal;** that is, a specific evaluation with respect to an individual's progress in completing specified tasks. By setting a standard against which to measure performance (which is often especially difficult at the professional or managerial level), MBO-based performance appraisal systems provide a base against which results can be measured. Finally, the emphasis in MBO on frequent communications up and down the organizational ladder has clearly been maintained in other approaches to productivity improvement, as well as in management practice more generally.

QUALITY OF WORK-LIFE/JOB ENRICHMENT

For a period, management by objectives took on the aura of a "movement," complete with classic texts, disciples and other advocates, and strong commitment to "the cause." Much the same is true of the recent concern for Quality of Work-Life (QWL). The quality of work life (see Box 9.2) "movement" traces its ancestry back to

BOX 9.2

Judging the Quality of Work-Life

Adequate and fair compensation: Compensation for one's work should meet general standards for the work involved and should bear an appropriate relationship to the pay provided for other work.

Safe and healthy working conditions: The conditions of work should include reasonable hours and should not be detrimental to the health of the worker.

Immediate opportunity to use and develop human capacities: The job should allow for substantial autonomy and self-control, it should permit use of a wide range of capacities, and it should be meaningful to the worker.

Opportunity for continued growth and security: The job should allow for and indeed encourage personal growth and development on the part of the employee, as well as opportunities for meaningful advancement in a career.

Social integration in the work organization: The personal side of one's organizational involvement, one's interaction with others on the job, should be a source of satisfaction.

Constitutionalism in the work organization: The rights of the individual, including rights to privacy, free speech, equal treatment, and due process, should be protected.

Work and the total life space: One's work life should be adequately balanced with the other spheres of one's life, especially one's family life.

The social relevance of work life: If the organization is not seen as being socially responsible (for example, in its employment policies or approaches to energy conservation or waste disposal), workers will think less of their work and their careers.

SOURCE: Richard E. Walton, "Criteria for Quality of Working Life," Reprinted with the permission of *The Free Press*, a Division of Macmillan, Inc., from Louis E. Davis and Albert B. Cherns, eds., *The Quality of Working Life, Volume 1: Problems, Prospects and the State of the Art.* Copyright © 1975 by Louis E. Davis and Albert B. Cherns.

the development of child labor laws, passage of workers' compensation legislation, and more general concerns for human relations arising in the 1930s. Its more recent impetus, however, has come primarily from a group of European scholars and practitioners associated with the Tavistock Institute for Human Relations in London.

The Tavistock group was initially concerned with how organizations might become more adaptive to a society engaged in a shift from a production base to a service base, one expected to exhibit a high degree of social change and "turbulence." According to the Tavistock researchers, most organizations reflect their technological bases; that is, their organizational structure models their technology. Unfortunately, such a structure limits adaptability. The Tavistock group urged attention to the interaction of social and technical systems.

For at least some QWL advocates, creating a work environment of high quality was even more important than improving productivity. The most important question to ask, they argued, is whether a particular organization is doing all it can to contribute to a more humane and progressive work environment. Others, however, felt that one didn't have to trade productivity for quality. Rather, by improving the quality of work-life, the productivity would rise as well. Indeed, studies seemed to show that improving the quality of work-life led to decreased absenteeism and turnover, greater job satisfaction, and greater commitment to the organization and its goals—all features that should improve an organization's productivity as a whole.

Obviously, any movement directed toward concerns as broad as these may lack some focus, and that has been a problem with efforts to improve the quality of work-life; the term has become so embracing as to be unclear. Some scholars, however, have focused on three paramount concerns—the autonomy, the responsibility, and the authority granted to individual workers. "The general objective is to arrange organizations, management procedures, and jobs for the maximum utilization of individual talents and skills, in order to create more challenging and satisfying work and to improve organizational effectiveness" (Jenkins, 1983, p. 2). Another writer puts the objective of QWL efforts in this question: "How can jobs be designed so that effective performance is linked with meaningful, interesting, and challenging work?" (Suttle, 1977, p. 1).

This question leads to a specific productivity improvement effort—job enrichment— which is concerned with designing or redesigning particular jobs so that workers experience greater meaning and satisfaction from the work and, consequently, can be more productive. Job enrichment efforts usually assume that people will perform better (1) where they perform a diverse array of tasks; (2) where they have a high degree of autonomy in their work; and (3) where they get clear feedback on the quality of their work.

Diversity, autonomy, and feedback in a particular job can be enhanced through a variety of mechanisms. For example, you might combine tasks so that instead of a series of individuals each involved in only one part of an assembly process, each individual would be responsible for the entire product. Jobs might also be enriched through vertical loading—that is, giving individual workers responsibilities and controls previously reserved for management, such as responsibility for deciding on work methods or for training new workers (Hackman, 1983, p. 249). Presumably, workers in enriched jobs not only find the quality of work-life improved, but also become more productive.

QUALITY CIRCLES AND RELATED IDEAS

The "quality-circles" concept has been widely used over the past two decades, and hundreds of reports of documented savings and solutions to work-process problems—some involving public-sector organizations—have appeared in the popular and business press. More important, while the term *quality circles* seems to be fading from use, some of the principles underlying quality circles have reemerged under the concept of "self-managed teams" and through the application of the techniques of Total Quality management.

A **quality circle** is a small group of people who do similar or connected work and meet regularly (usually an hour a week) to identify, analyze, and solve work-process problems. Quality circles involve six to twelve employees, who are led by their first-line supervisor (often called a team leader) and assisted by a trained facilitator, usually from outside the work unit. The circle chooses its own problems to work on and approaches them through a structured, problem-solving process. Resulting recommendations are usually presented to the team leader's immediate supervisor, who in turn may carry the recommendations further up the hierarchy.

Since quality circles offer frontline employees the opportunity to get involved in decisions affecting their work, circles have proven popular among employees (as well as employers) in many organizations. In some places, employees have never been asked how they think work processes might be improved, yet they are the experts in providing patient care, processing tax returns, or developing procedures to remove hazardous wastes. The benefits for these employees are thus twofold: first, they are given time to solve problems that cause frustrations and that keep them from completing their jobs; and second, by taking greater responsibility for work-process problems, they gain a greater awareness of solutions and may have greater interest in the success of those solutions.

The team leaders, facilitators, and circle members receive training in quality-circle operations and in group dynamics and problem solving. An open atmosphere concerning circle activities helps managers to feel comfortable with the circle concept, a natural step toward acceptance and institutionalization of the entire program.

A key ingredient in the success of a quality-circle program is the support of top management. This factor needs careful attention at the beginning stages of a quality circle program. Without active support from the top, quality-circle members may feel their recommendations will not be taken seriously, and managers elsewhere in the organization may see no incentive to start quality circles in their work areas. Although quality circles are a bottom-up approach to problem solving, the implementation process is very much top-down; information about the concept must be presented to those at all levels of the organization.

Although managerial support is necessary for long-term success, the real core of any circle program is the participants themselves; without a large proportion of highly motivated and properly trained circle leaders and members, the circle program cannot succeed. Members of the organization must be introduced to the notion of quality circles, and team leaders, facilitators, and group members must be trained. Then the real work of the quality circles begins. Normally, circles meet regularly, perhaps once a week, for a specified time, usually an hour. The first task is choosing a problem to solve. Generally, circles choose a problem by brainstorming—generating long lists of topics without evaluation or comment. The group reviews the list and selects one problem to focus on. (This same process is used when the cycle is completed and a new topic is chosen.)

The circle members then analyze the problem and develop solutions. Analysis typically involves some data collection or information gathering, followed by efforts to identify both the causes of the problem and potential solutions. Each solution is examined with respect to its effectiveness in dealing with the problem and feasibility of implementation. Some solutions may be considered ineffective, others too costly, and others inconsistent with agency policies. When a solution has been settled on, the circle members prepare and make a formal presentation of the problem and their recommended solution to management. In most cases, management finds the solution acceptable and works with the circle members to implement it.

Although quality circles are usually employed to solve specific work-process problems, and are more frequently used in units where such problems are found, the basic quality-circle principles of widespread participation and group problem solving are applicable elsewhere. For example, **task forces** (groups brought together to work on specific organizational problems) may consist of members from different parts of the organization. They may address work-process problems or issues of organizational policies or broader public policies; however, the approach to problem solving may be much like that modeled by quality circles.

As an example, the North Island Naval Air Depot in California created a team of ten middle managers drawn from various departments and gave it the power and money to rescue a money-losing operation making replacement parts for the F/A-18 Hornet fighter planes. That team revamped the manufacturing process by listening to workers and giving them the tools to do their job. Over a period of a year and a half, the team's improvement saved the U.S. Navy at least $1.7 million. As a result, the time it takes to manufacture and deliver F/A-18 parts has dropped from 172 days to 100 days, a 42 percent decline. Combining the idea of group activity through task forces with the notion of listening to frontline workers, the group was able to even win work away from private contractors (*USA Today,* April 2, 1993, p. B-1).

INCENTIVE PROGRAMS

Many if not most personnel systems in public agencies emphasize merit considerations in deciding which employees receive larger and smaller raises. This is an effort to build into the system a reward or incentive for high-level performance. In addition to pay increases, there are several other types of incentive plans that reward extraordinary performance. The rewards are usually money, but may sometimes be nonmonetary incentives such as merchandise or time off. The incentives seek to reward increased output (measured quantitatively), improved performance (measured qualitatively), or improved behavior (such as reduced absenteeism or fewer accidents) (Morley, 1986, p. 118).

A variety of incentive plans are currently used in public agencies (Greiner et al. 1981, pp. 28–29). Among the most common are performance bonuses, piecework bonuses, gainsharing plans, suggestion awards, behavioral awards, and employee recognition.

Performance bonuses are one-time monetary awards based on superior performance on the job generally or in a particular task. Often used to reward professional or managerial employees, bonuses may be presented annually or upon completion of a specific task. There are, however, several difficulties with bonus systems in the public sector. Many people, including many legislators, seem to feel that performance evaluation is so difficult to manage that there is no fair basis for deciding which employees receive bonuses and which do not. Consequently, bonus systems may become mechanisms for rewarding friends and favorites in the organization. Although these concerns can be addressed in several ways, they have led, in many jurisdictions, to legislation prohibiting bonus systems.

Piecework bonuses are performance incentives that tie the worker's productivity in a given task to monetary rewards. These systems may either tie the monetary reward directly to the number of units produced or use some formula to determine which workers are exceeding a standard level of performance. For example, keypunch operators in many jurisdictions are paid according to number of entries. Similarly, painters and electricians in some areas are paid according to what degree they meet or exceed a standard of performance set in advance. The effectiveness of piecework bonuses depends on arriving at specific measures of performance that will be clear to all concerned.

Gainsharing plans provide a monetary award for a group of employees based on savings the group generates. Based simply on the idea of rewarding those who produce more, this kind of plan is easy for both employees and citizens to understand. Washington, for example, has operated such a program for nearly a decade; through the state's Teamwork Incentive Program, employees in groups that develop significant savings can receive up to 25 percent of the documented savings. State employees have received as much as $6,273 per employee (*Government Productivity News*, April 1989, p. 1).

Gainsharing can also be combined with a quality-circles program. If, for example, a quality circle designed a new computer program that saved a state government $6,000 a year, it might split as much as $600 among the circle members. Again, this system depends on careful documentation of the savings generated by the work of the group.

Suggestion award programs provide incentives for employees who make specific suggestions that result in savings for the organization. Such systems are widely used in American industry; firms such as General Motors have major suggestion "contests" that result in thousands of dollars, even hundreds of thousands, in awards to individuals and, of course, even greater savings for the companies. Suggestion programs have only recently become widespread in public agencies and are still less well established than in the private sector.

Such programs typically involve extensive advertising encouraging employees to participate. Suggestions are carefully scrutinized for originality and applicability to the organization. If a proposal seems workable, the savings to be generated are documented and an award, usually a percentage of the savings, is granted. Most systems limit the maximum award, but the limits can be quite high; in British Columbia, for example, the maximum award is $25,000. Suggestion systems can help increase productivity; in Phoenix, for example, a recent suggestion to reduce pavement thickness by one inch, which could be done while maintaining quality, saved the city $1.2 million in one year.

Behavioral awards reward specific behaviors that management wishes to encourage. If absenteeism is a problem, a system might be designed to reward good attendance; if workplace accidents are a problem, a system might be designed to reward excellent safety records. Again, it is important to establish clear standards for performance and relate them to specific benefits.

Employee recognition programs, although they do not provide monetary incentives, are often an effective way to acknowledge special contributions of certain employees or groups. An employee-of-the-month program, for example, allows top management (the governor, a department head, or a city manager) to recognize individuals who have done work "above and beyond the call of duty." Similarly, special recognition of groups of employees involved in quality circles or interdepartmental task forces is a good way to highlight work of exceptional quality. At little or no real cost, such programs provide a surprisingly good incentive for employees and emphasize the high-quality work that most employees of public organizations do. As one productivity leader pointed out, "You always hear about the bad things that happen in government. An employee-of-the-month program gives us an opportunity to talk about the good things that happen!"

All in all, incentive programs are effective mechanisms for encouraging employees to make more significant or more appropriate contributions to the organization. You must be careful, however, to identify specific behaviors that will lead to improved productivity, devise specific measures so you know when the objective has been met, and provide an appropriate and meaningful incentive. As the success of employee recognition programs testifies, incentive programs do not work merely because employees need more money. Employees also respond because they take pride in their work and in their contributions to the organization's success.

RECENT EXPERIENCES IN PRODUCTIVITY IMPROVEMENT

Public organizations at all levels have experimented with formal efforts to improve quality and productivity, including those carried forward under the "reinvention" banner. Generally speaking, public productivity is concerned with how organizations can achieve their objectives as efficiently and effectively as possible—how they can improve their performance. We will focus here on efforts that seek to "(1) increase service levels while holding costs constant, or (2) decrease costs for current service levels, or, ideally, (3) increase performance and service levels while simultaneously reducing costs" (Jarrett, 1982). Some emphasize technological innovation, while others emphasize human resources management; some operate through centralized productivity improvement staffs, while others are more decentralized. But most have successfully demonstrated the value of sustained attention to productivity concerns.

Success Stories at the Federal Level

A major campaign was undertaken in the 1980s and early 1990s to introduce TQM to all parts of the executive branch. The General Accounting Office completed a comprehensive survey of TQM in 2,800 federal agency installations in 1992 (*Government Productivity News,* January 1993). Over half stated they had quality initiatives under way, and the number is continuously increasing. Approximately 69 percent of all federal domestic, noncombat installations have introduced quality management. According to data reported by federal officials, TQM was being implemented in roughly two-thirds of all organizations. Most were in the preliminary phase. Of the remaining one-third, roughly half indicated that TQM would be started in the future. By mid-1992, 13 percent of federal employees and 20 percent of managers were involved in some type of TQM activity. Similarly, most federal leaders have had the opportunity to become familiar with TQM. By 1992, 91 percent of top federal managers had received TQM awareness training and 63 percent had participated in a retreat to learn more about it, according to the GAO survey.

Six types of problems were seen as inhibiting TQM's development in the federal government (and in others). These include:

1. resistance to participatory management
2. funding constraints

3. insufficient employee information about TQM and TQM tools

4. federal personnel regulations

5. lack of attention from senior management

6. employee resistance to change

More recently, in one of the more dramatic recent efforts to improve the management of the federal government, President Clinton announced in September 1993 a new set of initiatives to cut red tape, reduce the size of government, put customers first, empower employees, and consolidate various agencies. These recommendations were based on a six-month study chaired by Vice President Al Gore and known as the National Performance Review. In the Gore report, "Creating a Government That Works Better and Costs Less," a variety of proposals aimed at "reinventing government"—the phrase taken from the title of a popular book on creating more entrepreneurial government—were presented. Announcing "The government is broken and we intend to fix it," Clinton gave his support to ideas in the report, including recommendations to cut some 250,000 federal jobs and to save $108 billion over a five-year period. Among the many recommendations were the following:

institute two-year budgets and appropriations

allow agencies to carry over unspent funds at the end of the year

phase out the *Federal Personnel Manual* and decentralize the recruitment process

cut in half the time required to fire employees

require agencies to provide the best in business customer service

make agencies compete with one another and the private sector

issue governmentwide cost accounting

empower employees by decentralizing decision making

upgrade computer technology

establish new labor-management partnerships

extend quality management training

give the president authority to cut items from spending bills

eliminate or consolidate particular agencies where duplication exists

allow credit card payments to the IRS (*Washington Post*, 1993, p. A17)

NETWORKING

The NPR site (http://www.npr.gov/initiati/mfr/) gives some of the best information about reinvention and other NPR activities. Additional sites about NPR, reinvention, and reengineering include (1) ttp://policyworks.gov/org/main/mt/homepage/mtc/smartgov/re-re/re-re.htm and (2) http://www.reengineering.com/.

In 1997, the National Performance Review estimated that through its activities, federal agencies have saved more than $137 billion, established approximately 4,000 customer service standards, cut more than 16,000 pages of bureaucratic red tape and regulations, and reduced the federal workforce by 309,000 positions. While NPR initiatives have been documented in more than 570 organizations and programs, it may be helpful here to highlight a few case studies from the federal government.

The Social Security Administration (SSA), for example, focused its reinvention efforts on improving its customer service. Its first step involved conducting telephone and in-person interviews with more than ten thousand clients, asking them what would make SSA more customer-friendly. Next, it prepared action plans that laid out the changes necessary to achieve its customer service mission. Agency staff and clients reviewed the plans and made recommendations to SSA administrators. Finally, SSA embarked on a continuous-improvement program to implement the initial plans and to make improvements where needed.

Changes in the SSA customer-response process included upgrading payment delivery, increasing the number of bilingual support staff, and streamlining claims systems. The most immediate improvement, however, can be seen (or heard) in the SSA's toll-free service. SSA made a number of investments to enhance telephone access, including switching service centers previously dedicated to data processing to customer service and hiring more customer service representatives. Consequently, the improved toll-free service was recently ranked higher than even those provided by L. L. Bean and Disney.

The Department of Energy (DOE), though smaller than the SSA, faced a more complex reinvention mission. A primary concern of the agency involved redefining the organizational purpose in the post–Cold War era. So where did DOE go to better understand its future? To those individuals who knew the agency best: the employees. Agency administrators gained insights from hundreds of DOE staff, from which they compiled the organization's first strategic plan. The plan outlined the agency's core principles, mission, and priorities. It detailed the various activities needed to achieve this mission, as well as the performance indicators that would enable the agency to assess its activities and impacts.

With its purpose more clearly defined, DOE set out to enhance its performance internally and externally. First, it restructured its contract management to increase oversight and enhance competition among contractors. The agency even switched to a performance-based system of contracting. Second, DOE reengineered its internal management systems. The agency brought together thirty-seven of its most experienced staff members in what became the Strategic Alignment Initiative. The result was a more effective, responsive system of administration for stakeholders both within and outside of the organization (Gore, 1996).

Success Stories at the State Level

State governments, too, have adopted key reinvention principles into their governance practice. The state of Arkansas, for instance, was one of the case studies featured in the Osborne and Gaebler's (1992) work. Its Home Instruction Program for Preschool Youngsters (HIPPY), which was derived from an Israeli model initiative, reflects the need for government to concentrate on preventing rather than curing public problems. The program is built on the premise that parents can be the most effective teachers of their children.

In HIPPY, participating families receive training on ways to educate their youngsters at home. Program volunteers, often former HIPPY parents themselves, work with parents to develop weekly lesson plans. Families qualify based on income and educational level, or if their children have special needs. The impact of HIPPY, though, does not end with the children becoming strong learners. Indeed, in a single project nearly half of the parental participants themselves enrolled in educational programs. Recent reports from program administrators indicate that HIPPY reaches about 2,400 parents and 5,000 children (Alliance for Redesigning Government, 1995).

The State of Iowa's reinvention strategy focused on enhancing government performance and accountability. State officials recognized that existing systems failed to inform citizens on the value of public service. "Citizens don't see a connection between appropriations and their priorities, they don't know what they are getting for their tax money" (Weidner & Reavely, 1996, p. 1). This failure to connect had contributed to a sense of disengagement between the public and their government institutions. Citizen cynicism had degenerated into a lack of public participation.

State administrators responded to this crisis in confidence by transforming their assessment systems to be more results-oriented. First, the state compiled information from agency, as well as stakeholder, strategic plans as a means of identifying critical policy areas. Second, this and related information was compiled into measurable performance goals and benchmarks to allow for comparative analysis. Third, the state connected this planning information to the state's results-based budgeting initiative, a crucial link between performance objectives and fiscal resources. Fourth, the performance indicators, benchmarks and results-oriented budget data were integrated into policy decision-making processes.

These primary steps (which have been overly generalized here) not only succeeded in connecting public resources to meaningful public outcomes and allowed for continuous performance monitoring by agency and administrative staff, but also reflected agency missions and goals due to the link with the strategic planning processes. Thus, the Iowa case study reflects the important relationship between reinvention and responsible performance measurement (Weidner & Reavely, 1996).

Success Stories at the Local Level

The impact of reinvention also can be seen at the local level, as city and county governments find innovative ways of meeting public outcomes. For example, in Louisville, Kentucky, city workers rewrote the area's telephone directory as a means of facilitating more effective connections with citizens. Before the change, local residents who needed to reach public agencies were forced to struggle through a maze of bureaucratic listings. Garbage collection, for instance, remained hidden behind the hard-to-locate title, Department of Solid Waste Management. Thanks to the user-friendly listings, citizens can now contact agency personnel more effectively.

The phone book story exemplifies the efforts of CityWork, an initiative started in the early 1990s by Louisville's mayor Jerry Abramson. CityWork places decision-making authority into the hands of city employees on the front line, those who know best how to resolve snags in government systems. "Who better to talk about how to fill potholes than the people who fill the potholes," Abramson said (cited in Weil, 1996, p. 3). The program brings together people from throughout the municipal government, asking them to develop more effective ways of doing the public's business. If the group's recommendations are accepted by the Mayor's office, then they must be implemented within ninety days.

CityWork's success has even carried over into the rigid world of administrative law. Louisville's legal staff joined the group's brainstorming sessions to find ways to reduce its departmental expenditures. These sessions, and the follow-up inquiry, revealed that the city's practice of outsourcing some of its case work was actually more costly than if the city managed the cases in-house. By assigning the caseload to city attorneys, Louisville is saving nearly $100,000 per year (Weil, 1996).

The city of Wethersfield, Connecticut, targeted their reinvention strategy at another of Osborne and Gaebler's ten principles, namely that of community empowerment. When it embarked on its organizational change initiative in 1995, the city had just survived a period of profound economic crisis. Besides stagnant tax assessments, a graying population, and little promise of commercial redevelopment, Wethersfield was faced with growing demands for public services. To resolve the fiscal problems, city officials downsized several of its top administrative positions. Yet even this wasn't enough.

Wethersfield then initiated a strategic-planning process combined with efforts to improve service quality, performance, and customer satisfaction. More important, the city began to search for alternative strategies for meeting public outcomes. It joined with citizens to create collaborative approaches to service delivery, shifting ownership of the programs outside of the government bureaucracy. Public dialogue led to stronger power-sharing relationships between the city administration and citizens. And, city services began to be focused to meet more specific citizen-identified needs. The reinvention initiative is succeeding because citizens and government learned how to learn, together (Rusaw, 1997).

IMPLEMENTATION ISSUES IN QUALITY AND PRODUCTIVITY

Whatever approach to improving quality and productivity you undertake, the design of your intervention will be important to its success.

Productivity in public organizations, as in others, can often be improved through technological innovations. Many areas of federal, state, and local governmental activity rest on a strong technical base. In areas such as the design and construction of waste-to-energy plants, development of pollution control devices (including hazardous-waste treatment centers) or building of public housing, new technologies may help governments to be not only more effective in meeting their objectives, but also to be more cost efficient.

NETWORKING

Several organizations offer resources, case studies, and links to other sites on the issue of productivity, including NPR (http://www.npr.gov/initiati/mfr/), the Alliance for Redesigning Government (http://www.alliance.napawash.org/alliance/index.html), the National Center for Public Productivity (http://newark.rutgers.edu/~ncpp/ncpp.html), and the American Productivity and Quality Center (http://www.apqc.org/). The Benchmarking Exchange (http://www.benchnet.com/) also features information on benchmarking and performance measurement.

Think for a moment about the changes that are likely to occur in the country's transportation system over the next twenty years. In the not-too-distant future, high-speed intercity rail systems or vehicles that move on cushions of air may well displace planes, cars, and trains as the primary means of transportation between major urban areas. Designing the systems, regulating them, coordinating among various systems, providing communications and control—all these and many more functions will fall at least in part to government, and all will benefit from advanced technology.

Other efforts—such as many associated with the reinventing government movement—are more concerned with changing the culture and practices of the organizations, but these can vary in scope. Some programs simply require you to undertake new efforts to motivate your employees. Others are more programmatic; for example, you might emphasize greater responsibility on the part of lower-level personnel through a job enrichment strategy or you might develop a recognition program within the unit.

You might also work with a broader program, such as undertaking a reinvention effort throughout a local government or establishing a governmentwide employee suggestion award system.

STEPS TO PRODUCTIVITY IMPROVEMENT

Whatever the level or organization of the quality and productivity effort, there are certain basic issues to consider (Holzer, Rosen, & Zalk, 1986, pp. 9–15).

1. Identify ripe areas.
   Identify areas that are "ripe" for productivity improvement. Any program, however great its ambitions, must start small. It makes sense to start where you are most likely to achieve immediate gains, because you will identify savings most quickly here, and because a few early successes will encourage productivity improvement efforts elsewhere. To identify areas, managers should be particularly attentive to:

   functions continually faced with large backlogs of work or slipping deadlines

   operations where visible problems have already been hinted at (citizen complaints, high employee turnover)

   operations that appear to be using an unusually large percentage of resources operations where large numbers of employees perform essentially repetitive tasks (payoffs will be especially evident here because of the effect of multiplying any increase by the number of employees)

availability of new techniques or technology already proven workable elsewhere (e.g., computer installation to improve police response time)

receptivity of managers and supervisors to new ideas coupled with an ability to follow through (Holzer et al., 1986, p. 10)

2. Locate models in other jurisdictions.

Whatever your organization, it is likely that there are others like it and that others have experienced similar problems. Having some idea of how others approached the issues you are now confronting is especially helpful. Fortunately, such information is readily available, either through publications such as the Governmental Productivity News or through professional organizations such as the American Society for Public Administration or the International City Management Association. From these sources, you may discover new approaches to productivity improvement or you may find that approaches you are considering have either been successful or have failed elsewhere.

3. Define roles.

Define the roles of those who will be involved in planning and implementing the program. Some programs are oriented to a particular department, while others cut across several departments within a jurisdiction; in either case, some staffing for the productivity effort will be necessary. Staffing at the department level will provide a specific focus to the productivity program and will allow you to build technical expertise (e.g., in fire or police work). A centralized productivity staff will enable you to give broad impetus to the program and to build general expertise in productivity techniques. Presumably, this general knowledge can then be applied in various departments.

4. Set realistic goals and objectives.

As noted, productivity programs in public organizations have been stimulated by public demand for "doing more with less." You may thus be tempted to set high expectations for a new productivity improvement effort; resist the temptation. Setting realistic goals and objectives and actually meeting them is more helpful in the long run than setting too-high expectations and falling short.

5. Choose among alternative programs.

Different approaches range from changes in management style to technological innovations to specific productivity efforts, such as quality circles or incentive programs. In implementing a productivity program, it is advisable to fit the solution to the problem rather than the other way around. Though this advice seems obvious, you may find yourself tempted to pursue an immediate opportunity rather than engage in more careful planning. For example, a vendor might herald a new telecommunications system as the solution to all your problems. Even though you may not view communications issues as your highest priorities in terms of productivity improvement, you may be tempted to adopt the new technology "just because it's there." A more reasonable approach, of course, is to establish a prioritized list of problems, then seek to develop solutions that match your most important concerns.

6. Anticipate problems.

Many problems can arise in implementing a productivity improvement program, especially one of high visibility. Many of the problems are based on misconceptions about what productivity improvement is all about and can be anticipated and dealt with early in the program. Employees might feel that a quality circles program will lead to elimination of jobs, or they may feel that safety standards will be lowered; in fact, neither outcome is likely. But these are serious concerns that should be thoroughly discussed as the program is begun. To the extent possible, all participants and all persons likely to be affected by the program should have a chance to learn about and comment on the proposed program. Dealing with questions up front minimizes confusion and disruption later.

7. Implement the program.

After carefully analyzing the need for a productivity improvement program and deciding upon a course of action that will address the identified needs, you will face the difficult task of implementation. Implementation may, in fact, be the most difficult phase. Expectations may be too high; needed legislation may be difficult to pass; organization "turf" issues may interfere; there may not be enough money to invest in the program.

You can avoid some of the difficulties by starting the program on a modest basis, then expanding to other areas. Limiting objectives at the outset can help keep expectations from rising too high and will make it easier to demonstrate the viability of the effort. Beginning the program in an area where you might reasonably expect quick and identifiable gains will enable you to claim early success and in turn make the program more likely to be adopted elsewhere. Similarly, keeping a low profile for the program in its early days will make it less threatening to labor and management. Whatever publicity is accorded to the program (and many political leaders will want high-profile efforts), you should monitor the program carefully in its early days to avoid misconceptions.

The most serious limitations, however, are the difficulties in institutionalizing the program. Implementation is not merely a short-term concern; you should be concerned from the beginning about how durable the program is likely to be. Several factors work against institutionalization of productivity improvement programs. Programs may be dependent on a particular individual, such as a governor or mayor or a particular department head, and may be discontinued when that person leaves office. Many programs lack an organizational home and thus find it difficult to sustain support over a period of years (Bailey, 1987, pp. 19–20).

8. Evaluate the program.

Most productivity improvement programs require an initial investment of money and time; you have to spend money to save money, and many people may be skeptical of the program's value. Skeptics are likely to be unconvinced by general statements of program advocates; they will want to see specific, objective data. Types of information you should collect from the beginning are documented cost savings, increased output that has been achieved at a similar or reduced cost, or increased citizen satisfaction with the agency's services. This information can be made public through periodic reports to legislators or other decision makers or through press conferences or news releases.

An aspect of evaluation that needs special attention is the development of an appropriate measurement system to ensure that the proper information is being acquired at an appropriate time. You must be sure that information is gathered on a timely basis and that it is accurate. The information must also be fully relevant to measuring the improvement effort. It is difficult to develop a measurement system, but it may be critical to sustaining your program over time.

We have already discussed ways to measure objectives. (Indeed, much of our discussion of more general issues involving program evaluation is applicable here.) For example, a social service agency might measure the number of clients served, a police department might measure response time, or a public works department might measure numbers of miles of streets and highways paved. Matters are complicated, of course, by the fact that most organizations seek several objectives simultaneously. The social services agency is not concerned only with screening clients, but may also make referrals to other agencies or distribute money to certain clients. Each of these multiple objectives, and each of the activities that contribute to the objectives, may require its own separate measure.

Even more important, those who measure the effects of productivity improvement programs need to be attentive to what properly reflects the quality of work performed. Obtaining an increase in cost savings at the expense of courtesy or promptness is questionable at best; responding to requests for information or help "when it is convenient" to the agency may be less costly, but will probably not be acceptable in terms of quality. You may wish to consider either a separate measure of quality or implementation of a quality control system. You might also be able to develop composite measures that combine considerations for output and quality. For example, the streets department might measure repairs made within a certain number of working days, or the revenue department might measure the number of tax returns processed without error.

Three conditions appear to be required for productivity improvements to occur: "(a) the performance of individuals or groups must be assessed in a valid, objective manner, emphasizing the public purposes of the services provided by those employees, (b) such assessment should be closely linked to some type of reward or penalty, whether monetary or nonmonetary, and (c) there should be both early meaningful involvement by employee organizations as well as adequate advance participation and training for those affected, including supervisory as well as nonsupervisory employees" (Greiner et al., 1981, p. 411). Developing programs with these considerations in mind will help ensure not only early successes in productivity improvement, but will also help sustain the program through the years.

SUMMARY AND ACTION IMPLICATIONS

Technical innovations are often dramatic in their impact, sometimes saving thousands, even millions, of dollars. But technological innovations do not occur independently of the skills and attitudes of those who work in an organization. Innovations seem to flourish in a climate where human creativity is encouraged and usually require human changes — what one group calls "orgware" — to be successfully implemented.

Improved productivity appears to depend at least in part on a shift from the traditional authoritarian approach to management to a more open and participatory approach. This shift has been especially apparent in implementing productivity improvement programs at all levels of government. In many cases, we find a shifting orientation toward management that places greater emphasis on the involvement of all employees. (The resulting orientation was perhaps best expressed by the head of a state productivity council, who described his philosophy this way: "Those who do the work know the work best and know best how to improve the work.") The result is an approach to management that seems not only more human in scale and perspective, but that many authorities are coming to believe is far more productive as well.

A recent study by the Canadian government of "well-performing" governmental organizations in that country outlines some of the basics of this new approach. That study identified five factors leading to organizational success, which we may take as recommended patterns of action for managers to seek in trying to improve productivity:

Emphasis on people. People are challenged, encouraged and developed. They are given power to act and to use their judgment. There is a belief that high performance is a product of people who care rather than systems that constrain. People do not preoccupy themselves with the risk of failure, but are confident they can tackle virtually any challenge.

Participative leadership. Leadership is not authoritarian or coercive, but participative whenever possible. The leaders envision an ideal organization, define purpose and goals, then articulate these and foster commitment. Staff communicate easily. They feel comfortable consulting peers as well as those above and below them. Although formal levels exist for administrative purposes, there are no boundaries that inhibit collaboration in achieving goals.

Innovative work styles. Staff reflect on their performance. They learn from the effects of their actions. They seek to solve problems creatively. They maintain strong monitoring, feedback and control systems as useful tools. They are self-reliant, rather than dependent on control from an outside authority.

Strong client orientation. These organizations focus strongly on their clients, deriving satisfaction from serving the client rather than the bureaucracy. There is an alignment of values and purpose between the well-performing agency and their political and central agency masters.

A mindset that seeks optimum performance. People hold values that drive them to always seek improvement in their organization's performance. When conditions change, they adjust their methods, not their values. Because of this orientation toward performance and adaptability, the organization performs well even in a changing environment. This mindset may be the most important feature of all (*Government Productivity News,* December 1989, p. 4).

SOURCE: Extract originally from the Report of the Auditor General of Canada to the House of Commons for Fiscal Year ending 31 March 1988, Chapter 4: "Attributes of Well-Performing Organizations." Reproduced with permission of the Minister of Supply and Services, Canada, 1990.

As a manager, one of the primary technical concerns you will face is improving your organization's productivity. Whereas you may be able to accomplish great gains through technological innovations, the most significant long-term gains will come from a proper emphasis on the human factors in organizational effectiveness. To be judged successful, you will always have to balance your concern for the technical side of your agency's work and your attention to the human side of the organization, a topic to which we will turn in the next several chapters.

Terms and Definitions

Behavioral award: Used to reward specific behaviors that management wishes to encourage.

Employee recognition program: Effective way to acknowledge special contributions of certain employees or groups to the organization.

Expert systems: Computer programs that mimic the decision-making processes of human experts within a particular field.

Gainsharing plan: Monetary award for a group of employees based on savings generated by the group.

Management by objectives: Participatory approach to establishing clear and measurable objectives throughout the entire organization.

Performance appraisal: Specific evaluation with respect to an individual's progress in completing specified tasks.

Performance bonus: One-time monetary award based on superior performance on the job or in a particular task.

Piecework bonus: Incentive that ties the worker's productivity in a given task to the monetary rewards he or she receives.

Quality circle: Small group of people who do similar or connected work and meet regularly to identify, analyze, and solve work-process problems.

Suggestion award program: Incentive for employees who make specific suggestions that result in savings for the organization.

Task forces: Groups brought together to work on specific organizational problems.

Study Questions

1. Discuss the relationship between the growing use of computer-based systems and the human element involved in technology transfer.

2. What is management by objectives, and how can this approach benefit an organization?

3. Identify the eight categories for judging the quality of work-life.

4. Discuss the variety of incentive plans currently used in public agencies. Explain the usefulness of each approach.

5. Productivity improvement has become a major concern of public managers. What basic issues should one consider when undertaking a quality of productivity program?

6. Explain the basic ideas associated with President Clinton's National Performance Review.

Cases and Exercises

1. Review the criteria in Box 9.2 for evaluating the quality of work-life. Working in groups of five to seven, choose two or three jobs that members of the group have previously held and analyze the quality of work-life in those jobs. In each case, members of the group should interview the person who held the job, asking questions about each category in the chart. When everyone has a complete understanding of the nature of the job, the group as a whole should draw conclusions with respect to the quality of work-life for someone holding that job.

   Following this activity, choose two or three jobs to which members of the group might reasonably aspire in ten to fifteen years. Have one individual imagine in detail what the job would be like from day to day, then follow the same procedure to interview the "job holder" and draw conclusions about the quality of work-life. In what ways do you expect that future jobs will be of higher "quality" than those in the past? Why should there be any differences?

   Finally, choose one job from the "jobs already held" and one from those "to which you aspire." Then consider these jobs from the standpoint of the person to whom the individual job holder would report. How could the manager improve or "enrich" the particular job? Specifically, could adjustments in authority or responsibility improve the quality of work life for the job holder? How would those changes affect the individual's productivity? Report your conclusions to the class.

2. Divide the class into groups ranging from seven to ten members each. Have each group select a reasonably small public agency—federal, state, local, or nonprofit. Based on interviews with several top managers and a sampling of employees throughout the organization, analyze the organization's existing system of incentives. Design a new incentive program you think would result in improved quality and productivity. (If you have difficulty locating or gaining access to a particular organization, simply develop a research design through which you might test an incentive system. Assume an organization of two hundred people engaged in manual processing of tax receipts for a state government. What kinds of questions would you ask of which individuals in the organization?)

3. Academic departments, like other organizations, can benefit from information and advice from employees and clients (faculty, staff, students, alumni, potential employers,

and so on). Consider the department of your major. How would you design a comprehensive program of employee and client involvement that would help the department improve the quality of its offerings? (After designing a program, you might interview the department chair to find out what mechanisms are already in place.)

For Additional Reading

Anderson, David F., and Sharon S. Dawes. *Government Information Management: A Primer and Casebook*. Englewood Cliffs, NJ: Prentice Hall, 1991.

Barzelay, Michael. *Breaking through Bureaucracy*. Berkeley: University of California Press, 1992.

Cohen, Steven, and Ronald Brand. *Total Quality Management in Government: A Practical Guide for the Real World*. San Francisco: Jossey-Bass, 1993.

Dilulio, John, Jr., Gerald Garvey, and Donald Kettl. *Improving Government Performance*. Washington, DC: The Brookings Institution, 1993.

Gore, Albert. *Common Sense Government*. New York: Random House, 1995.

Gore, Albert. *Businesslike Government*. Washington: Government Printing Office, 1997.

Gore, Albert. *Serving the American Public*. Washington: Government Printing Office, 1997.

Holzer, Marc, ed. *Public Productivity Handbook*. New York: Marcel Dekker, 1992.

Holzer, Marc, and Arie Halachmi. *Strategic Issues in Public Sector Productivity*. San Francisco: Jossey-Bass, 1986.

Light, Paul C. *The Tides of Reform*. New Haven, CT: Yale University Press, 1997.

Matzer, John, Jr., ed. *Productivity Improvement Techniques*. Washington, DC: International City Management Association, 1986.

Morley, Elaine. *A Practitioner's Guide to Public Sector Productivity Improvement*. New York: Van Nostrand Reinhold, 1986.

National Performance Review. *From Red Tape to Results: Creating a Government That Works Better and Costs Less*. Washington, DC: U.S. Government Printing Office, 1993.

Osborne, David, and Ted Gaebler. *Reinventing Government*. Reading, MA: Addison-Wesley, 1992.

Osborne, David, and Peter Plastrik. *Banishing Bureaucracy*. Reading, MA: Addison-Wesley, 1997.

Reynolds, George W. *Information Systems for Managers*. 2d ed. St. Paul, MN: West Publishing, 1992.

Rosen, Ellen Doree. *Improving Public Sector Productivity*. Thousand Oaks, CA: Sage Publications, 1993.

Sacco, John F., and John W. Ostrowski. *Microcomputers and Government Management*. Pacific Grove, CA: Brooks/Cole. 1991.

Schachter, Hindy L. *Reinventing Government or Reinventing Ourselves*. Albany: State University of New York Press, 1997.

Swiss, James. *Public Management Systems: Monitoring and Managing Government Performance*. Englewood Cliffs, NJ: Prentice-Hall, 1990.

Wholey, Joseph S., Mark A. Abramson, and Christopher Bellavita. *Performance and Credibility: Developing Excellence in Public and Nonprofit Organizations.* Lexington, MA: DC Heath, 1986.

Wholey, Joseph S., and Kathryn E. Newcomer. *Improving Government Performance: Evaluation Strategies for Strengthening Public Agencies and Programs.* San Francisco: Jossey-Bass, 1989.

Chapter 10

PERSONAL SKILLS IN PUBLIC MANAGEMENT

All the ideas and approaches we have examined are helpful in understanding what is going on in public management. But those perspectives are sterile without the personal and interpersonal skills to put theory into practice. A manager must be able to size up a situation and take appropriate action, often within a matter of seconds. A division director to whom you report calls to tell you that the president is getting ready to announce a new breakthrough in a disease treatment your unit has been working on unsuccessfully for years. Or you hear on the radio that asbestos has been found in a building your organization recently pronounced "clean." Or your boss, the head of the state mental health department, calls to tell you he has just resigned in protest over the legislature's failure to support a new appropriation and you are in charge. In all these cases, you will necessarily and appropriately analyze and understand the situation in terms of your own approach or theory. But you will also have to act. You may have to talk with certain people; you may have to motivate others to act; you may have to judiciously exercise the power of your office.

All these examples test your skills as a manager. If you can communicate well, and if you can make decisions and motivate others to follow your lead, you will quite likely be judged effective. If you lack these skills, you will be judged ineffective. Managerial success is based largely on managers' ability to exercise various "interpersonal" skills.

Interestingly, however, effectively exercising interpersonal skills depends on several essential "personal" skills that are a part of one's social and psychological makeup. Some of these personal skills reflect your approach to the world, others have to do with your capacity for creativity or effective decision making, still others have to do with how you deal with ambiguity or lack of clarity. For example, the manager suddenly promoted to the directorship of the mental health department will certainly have important (and immediate) decisions to make, perhaps involving creative solutions to organizational problems left by the departing director. The new manager will also have to be able to operate, perhaps for months, in a highly ambiguous situation.

In this chapter and Chapter 11, we will examine the "personal" and "interpersonal" skills that underlie managerial effectiveness. Personal skills include management of stress and time, creativity and problem solving, individual decision making, and issues of power and leadership.

THE MANAGER'S DAY

What, specifically, do public managers do? Most important, how would you spend your time as a public manager? Obviously, the answer depends on your job and level in the organization. Nevertheless, several recent studies give us some idea of a typical manager's day. We will discuss five aspects of managerial work (Colin Hales, 1986): (1) the elements of managerial work, (2) distribution of managers' time between work elements, (3) interactions with other people, (4) the informal elements of managerial work, and (5) the themes of managerial work.

ELEMENTS OF MANAGERIAL WORK

Hales's review of what managers actually do at work closely parallels the classic descriptions of what managers "should" do, with some contemporary variations. Hales identifies nine elements as common, nearly universal, activities of managers:

1. *Playing the role of figurehead and leader of an organizational unit:* The manager symbolizes the organization to the outside world.
2. *Acting as liaison:* Liaison or boundary spanning is performed with individuals outside of the organization as well as with other organizational units and with managers of units higher and lower in the hierarchy.
3. *Monitoring:* Managers monitor affairs both internal and external to the unit, including the tasks of filtering and disseminating information.
4. *Allocating resources:* Managers make decisions with respect to appropriate distribution and use of human, financial, and physical resources.
5. *Handling disturbances:* Managers are frequently called upon to deal with disruptions in the flow of work in the organization.
6. *Negotiating:* Reaching agreement with a variety of parties, both inside and outside the organization, is an important part of the manager's work.
7. *Innovating:* Where there is the need to change, the manager often acts as a creative center or catalyst for change.
8. *Planning:* Managers must always be attentive to the future, especially as probable future conditions affect the work of the organization today.
9. *Directing subordinates:* The manager must spend considerable time developing a direction for the organization and securing the support and activities of the many individuals required to move the organization in that direction.

Like the classic descriptions noted earlier, these elements of managerial work identify a variety of activities. Nearly all the classic functions are included in the list (depending on how one classifies the elements), but several aspects deserve emphasis. First, note the wide diversity of activities in managerial work. Second, note the number of activities that involve other people. And, third, note the emphasis on change and innovation. Indeed, one might even say that the ability to handle change is a hallmark of modern management.

DISTRIBUTION OF TIME AMONG WORK ELEMENTS

Studies of how managers spend their time often use terms such as *tactical, frenetic, reactive, troubleshooting,* and *constant interruptions.* They describe the frequency of short, face-to-face meetings that move constantly from topic to topic. These findings, however, do not necessarily mean that the image of the manager as one who plans, thinks, and formulates strategy is a myth. To the contrary, effective managers have general agendas that enable them to quickly gather large amounts of information and make the correct decisions to further those agendas. Furthermore, managers work within networks that must be both developed and activated. These tasks require many interactions with people in the networks, and the interactions must of necessity be sporadic and informal (Kotter, 1982, p. 166).

What appears to be an absence of planning may sometimes be illusory; for some managers, planning is something that happens constantly. The seemingly disjointed nature of managerial interactions with others does not so much indicate disorganization, but rather the wide range of problems that must be handled. General agendas allow managers to deal with many situations opportunistically within the context of a larger framework or agenda that provides guidance for specific decisions.

MANAGERIAL INTERACTION AND COMMUNICATION

Descriptions of managerial time usage have identified the importance of interactions with other people, which typically involve some sort of communication. Hales found that between two-thirds and four-fifths of a manager's day is spent giving or receiving information, and that most of this giving and receiving takes place in face-to-face interactions. Communication is clearly a dominant activity in a manager's day.

Interestingly, and again despite appearances to the contrary, patterns of communication are not random. A majority of managerial communication is with managers of the same rank (lateral communication). Among the remaining communication, how much is vertical (i.e., up and down the hierarchy) varies widely with the manager's position, but regardless of position, the predominant pattern of communication is lateral.

Since much of their day is spent responding to requests for information, managers are often described as reactive. They spend more time responding to information requests than to initiating requests. To the casual observer, these interactions would appear extremely diverse, and often informal rather than official, but there is more to informal communication than meets the eye.

INFORMAL ASPECTS OF MANAGERIAL WORK

Unfortunately, it is difficult to provide universal descriptions of the informal aspects of management. There is, for example, considerable debate over whether the informal aspects of the manager's role are "good" or "bad"—that is, whether they contribute to or detract from the organization's goals. As in many such debates, it is probable that the informal work sometimes enhances and at other times detracts from the organization's goal achievement. For example, informal activities are often political in nature and involve negotiation; as such, these activities are extremely relevant. In any case, what is formal and what is informal is often a specific manager's perception as to what is actually part of his or her job; that which is really considered a part of the job is defined as formal, and that which is not is defined as informal.

THEMES OF MANAGERIAL WORK

We can draw a number of general conclusions about managerial work, one of which is that managerial work is extremely diverse and variable in terms of the different activities managers perform in a typical day. A manager may work on literally dozens of distinct topics during the course of the day and bring to bear a wide range of skills in dealing with those topics. A second conclusion is that managerial jobs are loosely enough defined to allow significant variation and choice by the specific manager in regard to both job content and style of performance. Two jobs that appear identical on an organizational chart are not necessarily composed of exactly the same tasks, nor will they necessarily be carried out in the same way. A central part of the work of managers is "the management of their work" (Hales, 1986, p. 101).

Another conclusion is that managerial work is pressured and conflictual. There are many demands on the manager, and these demands are often contradictory. Consequently, there may be competing claims on the same resources of time, energy, personnel, and equipment. Moreover, competing claims often occur simultaneously or within a short period, creating even more pressure and conflict. Fourth and finally, Hales (1986) reports that managerial work tends to be action-oriented, with emphasis on action rather than on reflective contemplation. So many problems arise so quickly that managers often develop a preference for concrete action to address problems and opportunities.

We can conclude that the manager's job is one of life's more challenging in the world of work. It is diverse, and that diversity implies the need for diverse skills. The need for many skills is compounded by the pace of managerial work and its unending stream of conflicting demands for action. (See Box 10.1 for a review of the diversity and complexity of a local government manager's job.) Fortunately, managers often have considerable latitude in building their positions and in developing their working styles.

STRESS MANAGEMENT

We have noted the importance of the skills, especially interpersonal skills, that are required to manage successfully. But effective use of interpersonal skills is predicated on a number of personal qualities and characteristics that form the basis for action.

Although not all managerial positions in public organizations are stress-filled, "pressure-cooker" jobs, there are certainly moments of tension, just as in management jobs elsewhere. The pressure of deadlines, questions about who is responsible for a particular problem, an angry flare-up at a staff meeting—these and other stressful situations arise in the course of the manager's job.

BOX 10.1

A Typical (?) Manager's Day

A typical local public manager's daily agenda might look something like this:

8:00 A.M.	Arrives at work to polish off leftover paperwork/dictation from yesterday.
9:15 A.M.	Meets with mayor to review next week's council agenda prior to its publication.
10:00 A.M.	Local business group offers ideas on newly proposed industrial park on east side.
10:45 A.M.	City engineer and city treasurer join group to brief them on construction/financial details of site development.
11:30 A.M.	Police chief and personnel officer review a pending grievance against the department by a member of the city employees' union.
12:15 P.M.	Leaves ten minutes late for luncheon speech at League of Women Voters' monthly meeting to urge their help with the water bond campaign.
1:30 P.M.	Back again for more discussion with the police chief on the same topic discussed in the morning.
2:15 P.M.	Rides with public works director to inspect north side residents' complaints of "smells" from nearby city dump; mentally drafts responses to their council members and neighborhood group on return to office.
3:15 P.M.	Returns stacked-up phone calls at office.
3:45 P.M.	Talks with local newspaper reporter about the importance to the city of next month's special water bond vote.
4:10 P.M.	Free time that was scheduled to review several pending budget items is interrupted by visit from two council members.
5:20 P.M.	Goes home for dinner.
7:10 P.M.	Leaves to attend meeting of south side citizen association, a predominantly poor black group that the manager wants to involve more closely in community public housing planning.
11:00 P.M.	Home to bed at last!

NOTE: Several managers from all levels of government, upon reviewing this schedule, commented that this particular day appeared rather light!

SOURCE: Excerpted from Wayne F. Anderson, Chester A. Newland, and Richard J. Stillman, II, *The Effective Local Government Manager* (Washington, DC: International City Management Association, 1983), 35. Reprinted with permission.

A variety of organizational factors can contribute to stress (see Box 10.2). In public organizations, stress is especially likely in situations of role conflict or role ambiguity. **Role conflict** occurs when there are two different and incompatible sets of demands on the individual; for example, if one is asked to complete two different projects simultaneously. **Role ambiguity** occurs when one does not clearly understand the rights and responsibilities of one's job. These two conditions seem to be especially prominent in public organizations.

Stress of any type, or continued stress over time, can be quite damaging to both the individual (mental or physical ill health can result) and the organization (managers operating under excessive stress are typically less competent in interpersonal relations and less productive generally). To prevent these problems and to have a happier, more satisfying work experience, public managers are finding it increasingly helpful to understand the nature of job-related stress and develop programs for reducing its negative consequences.

Hans Selye, the "father" of stress research, defines stress as the "nonspecific response of the body to any demand made upon it" (Selye, 1974, p. 27). Selye points out that stress can be good or bad, depending on the situation and the individual; stress can produce positive responses, such as joy and excitement, as well as harmful effects such as depression or ill health. Our concern is with excessive or continued stress leading to psychological or physiological impairment. Note, however, that people respond differently to sources of stress (or stressors)—a situation that one person may react to calmly may be a crisis for another.

Selye suggests that individuals respond to stress through a set of defense reactions that occur as a general syndrome. The first response phase is *alarm,* marked by increases in anxiety, fear, or depression (depending on the nature of the stressor). Muscles tense and heart rate and blood pressure increase. There is usually also a marked increase in psychological defensiveness. If the stressor is only momentary, the body soon returns to normal. But if the stressor continues, the individual may move to the next stage, *resistance,* wherein one engages in a variety of defense mechanisms to counter the stressor. These may range from (psychologically) attacking the stressor itself, attacking oneself or others, denying the stressor, or withdrawing either actually or symbolically from the situation (Whetten and Cameron, 1984, pp. 92–93). These mechanisms may reduce the level of stress, but where the stressor overwhelms the individual's defenses, a pathological state which Selye terms *exhaustion* may result. Exhaustion can lead to physical or mental difficulties, such as depression, alcoholism, or heart problems, or interpersonal problems, such as trouble with one's superiors or subordinates or one's family.

Fortunately, there are signals to help you recognize patterns of behavior that lead to excessive stress and specific techniques to reduce stress levels.

STRESS SIGNALS AND RESPONSES

Type A/Type B Behaviors

During the past twenty-five years, there has been growing interest in the relationship between various patterns of human behavior and the health problems that may result. A

BOX 10.2

Organizational Factors That Promote Burnout

- Continuously high stress levels
- A norm of constantly giving to others
- Discouragement of hierarchical staff interaction
- Constant demands for perfection
- Expectations of extra effort with minimal rewards
- No reinforcement for suggestions on improving morale
- Repetitive work activities
- Minimal additional resources available for extra-effort tasks
- Lack of encouragement for professional development
- Discouragement of mutual participation
- Evangelistic leadership styles
- Policy changes unrelated to problem priority
- Policy changes too frequent to be evaluated
- Rigid role-typing for workers
- A belief that playfulness is unprofessional
- Pervasive "isms" (ageism, sexism, nepotism, etc.)
- Emphasis on past success
- Constant shifting of ground rules for policy
- Minimal emphasis on positive feedback
- Minimal emphasis on comfort of environment
- High instance of work overload
- High number of dead-end jobs
- Poor communication and feedback

SOURCE: Excerpted from Linda Hopper, "Unstressing Work," *Public Management* (November 1988). Published by the International City Management Association (ICMA), Washington, D.C. Reprinted with permission.

substantial part of medical and psychological research on this issue has focused on cardiovascular disease, the leading cause of death in this country. Coronary heart disease (CHD), a form of cardiovascular disease characterized by an inadequate supply of oxygen to the heart, has been shown to be related to certain patterns of behavior often exhibited by managers in public and private organizations. Researchers have labeled these behaviors "Type A."

In the 1950s, cardiologists Meyer Friedman and Rav Rosenman became aware that many of their patients' illnesses could not be explained by the traditional factors related to CHD: heredity, high blood pressure, and high levels of cholesterol. Other factors seemed to be playing a major role in contributing to CHD. They began to describe this set of factors as the Type A behavior pattern, which included (1) an intense, sustained desire to achieve; (2) a profound eagerness to compete; (3) a persistent drive for recognition; (4) seemingly continuous involvement in many activities that were subject to deadlines; (5) a habitual propensity to accelerate the rate of execution of all mental and physical functions; and (6) an extraordinary mental and physical alertness (Price, 1982, p. 7).

In contrast, people who exhibit more relaxed, easygoing patterns are referred to as having "Type B" behavior. Studies indicate that Type A individuals are two to three times more likely to suffer CHD than Type B individuals.

Lifestyle Changes

Type A personalities, "workaholics," or others especially vulnerable to stress-related problems should obviously be attentive to ways of altering their behavior patterns to reduce the possibility of impairment (either illness or reduced effectiveness). Research shows that even those who are less vulnerable can improve the quality of their lives and the effectiveness of their work through sustained programs designed to reduce stress. Some involve merely recognizing and eliminating undesirable characteristics, such as Type A behaviors; others involve more specific efforts to alter one's lifestyle. For example, greater self-awareness—understanding oneself and how one reacts to different situations—allows one to anticipate and moderate reactions. One study showed that "receptive managers," those concerned with detail, are most affected by time pressures or information overload, whereas "preceptive managers," those who concern themselves with the "big picture" or the whole, are most stressed by role conflict or role ambiguity. Similarly, "systematic managers," who prefer logical solutions, are most affected by problems requiring creativity, whereas "intuitive managers" are most stressed by problems requiring logic and objectivity (Whetten and Cameron, 1984, p. 102). Obviously, if you can anticipate what problems will cause you the most difficulty, you can marshal your psychic resources to deal with them, enlist the help of someone better attuned to the particular type of problem, or simply avoid the issue.

Understanding the context of your work and how your work life relates to the rest of your life is also helpful in reducing the negative effects of stress. Having a sense of the meaning of your work, as opposed to just doing a job, provides a helpful way to assess what is really important and what is merely irritating. Similarly, exploring the relationship between your work life and family life will provide a clearer "grounding" for work activities. Life-work planning activities, offered either in groups or in one-on-one relationships with career counselors, give you an opportunity to step back from your work and develop an improved picture of where your career and your life may generally lead. Finally, developing a **support system,** a network of people with whom you can talk about problems you face, can be a great help.

Relaxation Techniques

Specific relaxation techniques can help moderate either immediate or long-term stress. Deep-breathing exercises, visualizing and rehearsing upcoming situations, or diverting your attention to more pleasant times are primarily techniques to deal with fairly immediate stressors. More long-term stress reduction can be accomplished through techniques such as meditation.

Psychologist Herbert Benson suggests that, just as the fight-flight syndrome is associated with overactivity of the nervous system, another response—the relaxation response—brings about a quieting of the nervous system. The relaxation response can be brought about through traditional techniques of religious meditation or more secular means, but the essentials are much the same. Four essential elements elicit the relaxation response:

1. a quiet environment
2. a mental device such as a word or phrase that should be repeated in a specific way over and over
3. adoption of a passive attitude (perhaps the most important of the elements)
4. a comfortable position

Practicing these four elements for ten to twenty minutes once or twice daily should markedly enhance one's well-being (Benson, 1975, p. 19). Regular use of any relaxation technique will help reduce tension and improve one's ability to handle stressful circumstances.

Exercise

The benefits of exercise to physical health are well known; researchers have found that individuals who exercise regularly are less tense and more self-confident as well. Cardiovascular conditioning, which strengthens the heart and lungs, is especially important in reducing stress and increasing one's sense of well-being (Cooper, 1978, p. 77).

STRESS AND THE ORGANIZATION

Many public organizations, like their counterparts in the private sector, recognize the tremendous drain on resources that stress can cause. Stress not only causes managers and employees to perform poorly because of distraction, poor concentration, and exhaustion, but can lead to more severe mental and physical problems and addictions. Consider the following facts:

Studies have shown that it costs companies $100,000 per year more to employ a smoker than a nonsmoker due to increased sickness and absence.

Over 1 million workers call in sick each day, resulting in over 330 million lost workdays.

Losing an executive at 41 years of age to death or disability can cost between $600,000 and $1 million. (Hopper, 1988, p. 4).

In addition to the direct costs of illnesses, through diminished productivity or having to replace workers, organizations suffer in other ways. For example, temporary workers or replacement personnel are not likely to be as effective as full-time permanent employees, thus limiting service delivery.

Many organizations have developed employee assistance programs to help employees through difficult times. The programs may deal directly with mental or physical problems through drug and alcohol counseling, smoking cessation sessions, hypertension control, and so on, or they may use a preventive approach, seeking to promote a healthier workforce through exercise and fitness programs, health screening, or nutrition and weight control. Many smaller organizations are not able to afford employee assistance efforts on their own, but there are abundant resources in most communities to provide needed help. The point is that if you or one of your employees could benefit from such a program, you shouldn't hesitate to become involved; both you and your organization will benefit.

TIME MANAGEMENT

Obviously, your ability to use time effectively will be one determinant of your success as a manager. It will be difficult to manage others' affairs if you cannot manage your own, especially because your activities will directly affect the people you will manage (see Box 10.3). It is not surprising that strategies and techniques for more effective time management have evolved and that time management training programs are popular today. (The techniques taught in such programs are as helpful to students facing the many demands of college life as they are to managers in public or private organizations.)

Time management begins with establishing goals. Goals are the heart of time management; everything else is just a tactic or a technique. Most approaches to time management tell you to set your own goals (though in some organizations, supervisors are involved in setting goals). Although your own goals may or may not equate with the goals of the organization, they will probably overlap at least to some extent.

Remember also that you do not necessarily set a goal for a lifetime; goals change, they are modified or abandoned, and this is normal, even desirable. One should consciously set goals, but reevaluate them periodically. New goals can replace old goals or goals that have been accomplished. Most people have more than one goal, which creates a potential problem if they are not managed properly. Not all goals are equally important; we constantly have to choose which goals to give priority. Many choices favor one goal at the expense of others, so if one's goals are not ranked, at least roughly, it will be difficult to use them to make choices.

Once you have established goals and your priorities among them, you can genuinely begin to manage your time better, which means you will be managing your work better. You can even answer the constant question, "What am I going to do today?" Part of your day is primarily under your control, but part of it is not. Effective time management can help you manage both parts.

You can manage the part of your day that is primarily under your control by using a "to do" list, one of the older time management technologies. Even as a student, you may currently be using some version of it. One of the best examples of an earlier manifestation of a "to do" list involves Charles Schwab, the president of Bethlehem Steel

BOX 10.3

Learning the Balancing Act in Public Life

If Sheryl Sculley ever thought being Kalamazoo city manager meant sitting behind a desk all day, she since has learned otherwise.

Take the time she inspected the inside of the Blakeslee Water Tank, which holds 3 million gallons of water in two compartments underground.

"Dressed in a suit, I stuffed my skirt in the oversized hip boots, size 11, and walked, as best as I could, to the entrance," she told an audience of Kalamazoo Network members at a recent meeting.

"Sticking out of a hole were two wooden ladders tied together in the middle extending to the bottom of the 30-foot tank. I stepped into the chlorine solution to sanitize my boots and reluctantly proceeded with no safety belt, in size 11 boots, down a slippery wooden ladder.

"I was as nervous as ever, but I couldn't retreat in front of all those employees."

When she returned from the bottom of the tank, Sculley recalled, "the employee holding the ladder must have noticed the look of relief on my face. He leaned over and quietly said, 'That's OK. It took me two days to develop the courage to climb down that ladder.'

"Needless to say, I had a few words for our utilities director as we drove back to city hall that morning—the first having to do with safety for our employees, the second about setting me up for such an experience with no advance warning."

Sculley came with her husband to Kalamazoo after they married and in the fall of 1974 was hired as a research writer in the city's planning department. She was named assistant city manager in 1977, deputy city manager in 1979, and acting city manager in 1984.

The mother of 6-month-old Collin and 2-year-old Courtney supports parental leave as an individual but does not champion it as a city spokeswoman.

"The highest increase in the rate of labor force participation has been in women with children under 3 years of age," she told the Network audience. "The number of mothers returning to work while their infants were less than 1 year old increased 95 percent between 1970 and 1984. At this rate, by the year 2000, four out of every five American infants will have a mother in the labor force."

Sculley's work as city manager consumes an average of 60 hours per week, so her time with her children is planned. "Our time together includes more than mere presence," she said. "We bike, ride, read, walk in the woods, paint, take swimming classes at the YMCA, and Courtney even comes to city hall with me on Saturday mornings, and that's one of the highlights of her week."

SOURCE: Excerpted from "Sculley Learns the Balancing Act in Public Life," *Public Management* 70 (November 1988): 19. Reprinted with permission of International City Management Association, Washington, DC.

early in the twentieth century (LeBoeuf, 1979, pp. 52–54). Schwab evaluated his work performance as president of the company and decided he was not doing as good a job as he should be. He hired Ivy Lee as a consultant to advise him on how to do a better job, and the two struck a rather unique agreement on how they would proceed. Lee was to observe Schwab at work and recommend ways Schwab could improve. Schwab would do whatever Lee told him, and he would pay Lee whatever he thought the recommendations were worth after trying them.

Lee's major recommendation was for Schwab to begin each workday by writing a list of everything he could think of that he might do that day. Schwab was then to examine the list and identify the most important thing he might do and begin work on that item immediately. If he completed the task during the day, he was to pick the second most important task to work on, and so forth. The next day, Schwab was to write out a completely new list, pick out the most important task on it, go to work on it, and proceed as he had on the preceding day. Schwab tried this recommendation for a few weeks, and he must have thought it was valuable, because he sent Lee a check for $20,000 (and that $20,000 was in 1910 dollars!). Lee's advice was basically what we know today as the "to do" list.

The "to do" list is simply a list of the things you intend to do during the day, usually ranked in some order of importance. Since Schwab and Lee's time, a number of systems have been developed to rank activities. One popular system is the ABC system (Lakein, 1973). Each activity is placed into one of three categories on the basis of how important it is (this is where your overall goals come into play). "A" activities are essential to complete; "B" activities, less so; and "C" activities are those that can wait. Another popular system is a five-category scale in which 1 = important and urgent, 2 = important but not urgent, 3 = urgent but not important, 4 = busywork, and 5 = wasted time.

Whatever system you use, the important thing is to prioritize your activities to identify which are most important. You should then plan to devote more time and energy to the important activities. Prioritized goals can serve as criteria for placing a particular activity in one category or another. Without prioritized goals, you will have to create a new criteria system for each "to do" list you write.

We have described the "to do" list as a daily time management system. It is actually very flexible, and some people create weekly or monthly "to do" lists in addition to or in place of a daily list. Charles Schwab wrote his list at the beginning of each day, but many people write theirs at the end of one day for the next, and some people write a tentative one at the end of the day and revise it when they get to work the next morning. Regardless of when you write the list, it is crucial that it be written down and the activities prioritized in some way. In this way, you are really managing your work as you manage your time.

We said earlier that a prioritized set of goals will help you manage the parts of your time that are not primarily under your control, just as they will help you deal with the parts of the day that are under your control. This is because the goals will help you determine how to respond to the uncontrolled parts of the day. They will help you decide how to react in terms of energy and concern about events beyond your control, and in this way manage some important internal resources.

CREATIVITY AND PROBLEM SOLVING

One of the most important personal skills for managers is the capacity for creative problem solving. There are many approaches to problem solving; indeed, if a random sample of people is given an identical problem or situation, individuals in the sample will approach the problem differently and often arrive at very different decisions about what to do. A psychological model developed by Carl Jung provides a compelling explanation for this phenomenon and for why the differences will be systematic. Jung's model of psychological types is a way to classify people according to differences in their psychological makeup. The model describes various psychic functions based on how we take in and process information.

Jung identified two fundamental ways in which people acquire information or perceive things and labeled the two modes *intuition* and *sensation*. Perception by sensing is information acquired directly by means of the senses (seeing, hearing, touching, and so on); sensing is a conscious form of information acquisition. Information acquisition through intuition is mainly an unconscious process, in which ideas are added indirectly to perceptions made through the senses and associations are made between elements perceived by the senses. A genuine hunch or insight (not a guess) is an example of an intuitive perception. Emphasis on one mode of perception or the other may lead the individual to different ways of approaching the world; some approaches may help in some situations, and other approaches may help in other situations. The sensing individual tends to see the details of a situation, whereas the intuitive person tends to see the whole, but not the parts. Similarly, the sensing person will be clear about what is actually occurring at the moment, while the intuitive person will look more creatively at the possibilities that lie ahead.

NETWORKING

An exploration into the works of Jungian psychology can begin at JungWeb (http://www.onlinepsych.com/jungweb/jungweb.html). This site provides information on the Swiss psychologist's work and has links to other resources, including research institutes. Next, a glossary of terms (http://www.cgjung.com/glossary.html) may help clarify some of the concepts in the research. Finally, the search may take you to The Round Table Review (http://www.cgjung.com/cgjung/rtreview.html), a journal dedicated to Jungian psychology.

After information is acquired, it must be processed; decisions must be made about what to do. Jung's model identifies two major modes of information processing and evaluation. Making choices based on *thinking* is the rational and logical way of dealing with information; one attempts to develop logical, objective conclusions. *Feeling*, on the other hand, emphasizes making a value judgment, deciding according to what is right or wrong, or based on a preference about what is better or worse. The evaluation is not necessarily illogical, but its basis is always a human value and thus ultimately subjective. There are advantages in each approach. An individual who relies on thinking will be careful and objective, though he or she may appear cold and uncaring. The person who relies on feeling will appear friendly and engaging, but may not be as exact or objective as some might want.

Jung argued that all people employ all four psychic functions from time to time, but over the years, each person comes to rely on some functions more than others. Some people tend to emphasize sensing, others emphasize intuition; some people emphasize thinking, others emphasize feeling. (Although we are discussing categories, when the dimensions are actually measured, people seem to differ more in degree than categorically.) Based on the combination of preferences, we can arrive at four different psychological "types," illustrated in Figure 10.1. Certain personal characteristics or predispositions have been found to be associated with each of the four types of information acquisition/evaluation.

The upper left-hand cell in our illustration is the *sensing/thinking* combination, which combines the realistic view of the sensing function with the logical and objective capacities of the thinking function. The sensing/thinking person is likely to be good at handling data and solving problems logically. People like this tend to gravitate toward occupations such as accounting, computer programming, and engineering.

In many ways, the lower right-hand corner is the opposite of the sensing/thinking combination, as it combines intuition and feeling. The *intuition/feeling* combination draws on the creativity of the intuitive function and the strong emotional sense of the feeling function. The intuitive/feeling person is likely to be concerned with the future and with creativity, but, at the same time, be sensitive to and caring about the needs of individuals. Characteristic occupations here are art, advertising, public relations, and personnel management.

The lower left-hand cell combines intuition and thinking. The *intuitive/thinking* combination brings together the creativity of the intuitive function with the logical, problem-solving ability of the thinking function. The intuitive/thinking person is likely to be cre-

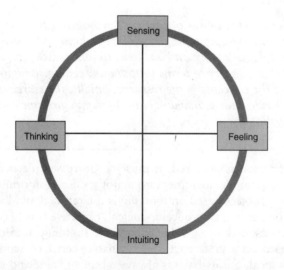

FIGURE 10.1

Jungian Psychological Types

ative with respect to problem solving but is also likely to work out the details of a particular solution logically and objectively. Many scientists and architects share these preferences, and, indeed, many middle and upper managers are found here. Top managers must be careful and objective, but are also relied upon to plan the work of the organization, a task that requires the future orientation that comes with intuition.

The upper right-hand cell combines sensing with feeling. The *sensing/feeling* combination brings together the preference of the sensing function for immediate data and the feeling preference for values and emotions. A sensing/feeling person sees the world in terms of immediate sense data, but is also concerned about the human implications of action based on that data. Teaching, counseling, and sales are associated with this combination, as are, again, significant numbers of managers.

The point is not that one or the other of these combinations is "better" than the other, but that they are different. Consequently, we would expect an individual's approach to solving problems to differ according to how the individual acquires and processes information. Presenting "identical" situations to a random sample would not seem at all "identical" to the people in the sample. Because the subjects would tend to use different modes of acquisition and evaluation, they would "see" very different things and reach very different conclusions. At least one result of the differences would be different decisions. How one sees things makes all the difference in the world when it comes to solving problems.

The implications of these differences for management are profound. We have already emphasized the diversity of situations in which managers find themselves. We can now say that different situations may require the use of different psychic functions. As an illustration, imagine two individuals who are about to buy a house looking in the window of that house. One, emphasizing the sensing function, might say, "This house is a wreck—the carpet is torn up; the ceiling is falling down; the walls are dirty." On the other hand, an intuitive person looking in the same window at the same time might say, "We could do great things with this room; if we fixed the carpet and the ceiling and if we painted the walls, this could be a real showcase." The two people see things quite differently.

Translating these differences in viewpoint into daily activity, you would surely acknowledge that the activity of balancing one's checkbook is not one where you want a great deal of creativity; instead you want to be careful about the immediate data and work with those data in the most logical and objective way possible. On the other hand, there are situations where you will need especially creative solutions to problems. In those situations, the intuitive capacity is very helpful. (Remember that we all have all the functions at our disposal, but we may have to work a little harder at those we don't ordinarily rely upon.)

Similarly, different management activities draw on different psychic functions. For example, monitoring work and performance is likely to be facilitated by carefully observing performance data. On the other hand, the planning function is likely to be aided by the creative potential of the initiative function. Depending on the situation, you may be required to emphasize one psychic function or another. If your normal preference is to emphasize the sensing function, you may wish to call more consciously on your intuitive capacities where long-term planning is required. You may sometimes want to bring together different people who typically rely on different functions to help solve various problems. You may, for example, want to bring in people you recognize as having strong sensing and thinking capacities to help solve accounting problems. Or, you may wish to bring in individuals noted for strong intuitive and feeling capabilities to help solve human resource planning issues.

MODELS OF INDIVIDUAL DECISION MAKING

One could argue that decision making is the most universal managerial activity because it is involved in all the other functions of management. It is impossible to plan, control, staff, direct, organize, or perform any of the miscellaneous management functions without making decisions. All management involves either explicit or implicit decisions. We will examine decision making at the individual level and explore several models of how decisions should be made and how decisions are actually made.

A great deal of research has been conducted concerning rational processes for decision making, some of which we discussed in terms of rational policy analysis. In its purest form, the rational model of decision making suggests the following steps:

1. Find an occasion for decision making ("decide to decide") and then formulate the problem in the best way possible.
2. Develop as many alternative solutions as possible.
3. Choose the alternative that maximizes the possibility that we will attain our goals or standards.

In essence, analyze the problem, generate alternative solutions, and choose from among the solutions. For our purposes, the most important lesson of the rational decision model lies at the beginning—becoming aware that a problem exists and correctly defining the problem. If you are not aware of a problem, you will not go through the rest of the process to solve it. Your chances of solving the problem are obviously low. (The probabilities are not zero, however, since problems are sometimes solved by accident.) Even if you are aware that a problem exists, your chances of solving it do not increase much if you do not identify it correctly.

Definition of the situation is one's perception of reality. Human beings need to make sense of things. We do not tolerate chaos well, and thus are continually defining and redefining situations we find ourselves in. Aside from our need to make sense of things, defining the situation is important because it is the basis upon which we act and make decisions to act. All mentally healthy individuals behave in a way consistent with their definitions of situations.

When it comes to problem solving, incorrect diagnosis of the problem (that is, an incorrect definition of the situation) can be disastrous; the correct definition is half the battle. An example from the Cold War days of the early 1960s illustrates this point. During this period, the United States and its allies had installed long-range radar systems to monitor the Soviet Union and to give warning of any Soviet attack by either missile or bomber. Soon after the radar systems were installed, the commander of an installation in

England was made aware of a set of images on the station's screens that looked as if the Soviet Union were launching a massive missile assault against the United States. It was the commander's job to evaluate the information, report it to Washington, and include a recommendation and evaluation of the accuracy of the information.

Obviously, since missiles travel pretty fast, the commander did not have a great deal of time to contemplate the situation. But, being a calm and collected individual, the commander thought things over a few moments before he made his report. He remembered that Nikita Khrushchev, then premier of the Soviet Union, was in New York City addressing the United Nations that day and thought it would be an unlikely time for the Soviets to attack. He also took into consideration the fact that the radar system was new, and that new systems sometimes have "bugs" in them. Putting all this together, he made his report, including in it his relatively low confidence in the information on his screens. He stated that he believed there was a malfunction somewhere in the system and recommended that the radar images not be interpreted as an attack on the United States. Obviously he was correct; there was no major attack by the Soviet Union. But what was actually happening?

It turned out that the radars were so powerful that some of the radiation they broadcast traveled far out into space. The system operated smoothly for about a week, but then the moon orbited into position to be hit by some of the radiation, which was reflected back to the radar antennas, in turn creating images on the screens that looked much like a flight of missiles heading toward the United States. The computers in the radar system had not been programmed to disregard the radiation coming back from the moon.

The commander was presented with a problem: the decision of interpreting the images and making his report. He had two interpretations. One was that the Soviet Union had started World War III, the other, that he had a malfunctioning system. One definition of the situation might have actually started World War III; the other avoided that catastrophe. You can easily see why correct definition of the problem is so critical in a problem-solving situation.

The rational decision model is often presented as the way people actually go about making decisions (or at least the way they should), and this is probably true to a certain extent. It is also clear that, in many cases, solutions to problems are arrived at in a far different way. The basis of the rational problem-solving process is the economic assumption that people attempt to maximize their outcomes when they make choices (i.e., decisions). Theoretically, people select a criterion, such as income or profit, then evaluate all decision alternatives in terms of that criterion, and select the alternative that will produce the best results.

Herbert Simon has studied decision-making behavior, especially in organizations, and concludes that the classic "economic man" assumption is seldom an accurate description of human problem-solving or decision-making behavior in real life. Simon (1957, p. xxvi) argued that maximizing outcomes is simply not possible in most situations and identified several reasons that it is usually impossible. All the reasons Simon offers add up to constraints on human beings' abilities to acquire and process information. There are time limits for making most decisions, and there are only so many resources available to gather information. Moreover, because we care more about some problems than others, our motivation to solve problems varies. We are willing to spend more mental and physical energy on some problems than on others.

Even if we had access to unlimited information about any problem, there are cognitive limits to how much information we can process at any given time. Furthermore, particularly in managerial situations, we seldom have the luxury of being able to deal with just one problem at a time. Other problems compete for our attention, time, and energy, which further taxes our cognitive limits.

Putting all these constraints together, Simon argues that human beings attempt to be rational, but they can be rational only within certain limits or bounds. What Simon calls "bounded rationality" (see Chapter 9) suggests that choices will be evaluated, but only within the bounds of these constraints. This results in a satisficing criterion for evaluating alternatives, rather than in a maximizing one.

A **satisficing decision** is one that is just "good enough" in terms of some criterion. Bounded rationality leads to satisficing decisions, and the process, in its pure form, operates as follows: When an individual faces a choice situation in which a decision must be made, rather than attempting to gather all possible information, generate all possible alternatives, and choose the alternative likely to produce the best results, the decision maker decides what level of outcome (in terms of some criterion) will be satisfactory or "good enough." The individual then examines choice alternatives one at a time and selects the first one that equals or exceeds the minimal ("good enough") criterion level. The process stops at this point, and the choice becomes the decision. No attempt will be made to examine other, potentially better, options.

That human beings vary in attempts to maximize suggests something of a continuum between satisficing and maximizing. But Simon's work suggests that most decisions, most of the time, fall much closer to the satisficing end of the continuum than the maximizing end, even where we are making important (and potentially costly) decisions. Marketing research shows, for example, that people tend to seek out most of the information they acquire about new cars after they purchase a new car rather than before.

Thus, the rational decision-making process can be considered a prescriptive model that tells us what we should do to make better decisions, but it does not give us an accurate picture of how human beings actually make decisions. Because we tend to satisfice rather than maximize, a modified and more limited version of this process, the satisficing model, provides the more accurate description. Hence, we can call it a descriptive model, which attempts to describe how things actually happen without regard to how they should happen. Given the nature of managerial work, satisficing may be the only way a manager can deal with the constant stream of problems and choice situations that arise daily.

Interestingly, one alternative model of decision making in the public sector claims to be both prescriptive and descriptive. Charles Lindblom's incremental model of decision making assumes that most governmental decisions (and others) usually begin by analyzing the existing situation and then move marginally or incrementally away from that position. In making a case for new programs, for example, managers often talk about how a new idea "builds on" existing strengths. This descriptive aspect of the model has a familiar ring. But, in a curious twist, Lindblom also suggests that the incremental model may even make sense normatively: because incremental proposals focus on well-known experiences, they reduce the number of alternatives to be considered and thus reduce the complexity of the problem at hand (Lindblom, 1968, p. 27).

POWER AND LEADERSHIP

The capacity to understand power, especially the capacity to recognize and use the resources one has available to influence others, is essential in modern organizations of all types. But power is a far narrower term than leadership. We will consider power as one aspect of the larger question of how one might develop greater skills in public leadership.

Many commentators have argued that improved leadership is essential for us to successfully meet the challenges of the coming century. Public opinion data reveal widespread loss of faith in the leadership of business, government, labor, and other private and public institutions. But many argue that the problem relates not merely to formal positions of power; rather the failure of leadership is pervasive throughout society. John Gardner, the former cabinet secretary and founder of Common Cause, stated, "In this country leadership is dispersed among all the segments of society and down through all levels, and the system simply won't work as it should unless large numbers of people throughout society are prepared to take leaderlike action to make things work at their level" (Gardner, 1987).

NETWORKING

For different perspectives on leadership, visit the James MacGregor Burns Academy of Leadership (http://academy.umd.edu/Academy/), the Center for Public Leadership (http://www-bushschool.tamu.edu/leader.html), the National Initiative for Leadership and Institutional Effectiveness (http://www2.ncsu.edu/ncsu/cep/acce/nilie/), or the Centre for Advanced Studies in Leadership (http://www.hhs.se/CASL/).

In this view, leadership is a pervasive phenomenon occurring in families, work groups, businesses, and at all levels of government, society, and culture. Leadership, then, should be seen not merely as a position someone holds, but rather as something that happens in a group or organization, something that comes and goes, something that ebbs and flows as the group or organization does its work. Anyone can be a leader, no matter how briefly.

As we have seen, modern society can be described as (1) highly turbulent, subject to sudden and dramatic shifts; (2) highly interdependent, requiring cooperation across many sectors; and (3) greatly in need of creative and integrative solutions to problems. Under such circumstances, ambiguity is increasingly a hallmark of decision making, and the involvement (rather than the control) of many individuals in group decisions will be necessary. "Leadership . . . will become an increasingly intricate process of multilateral brokerage, including constituencies both within and without the organization. More and more decisions will be public decisions; that is, the people they affect will insist on being heard" (Bennis, 1983, p. 16). Leadership for the future cannot be equated merely with the exercise of control by those in formal positions of power.

What do we know about leadership, especially shared or public leadership? What do we know about leadership in the increasingly common situations where no one is really "in charge"—student organizations, churches, political groups, and so on? Often, much of their work is done through committees or other even less formal groups. And those committees seem to waste a lot of time and energy, partly because of lack of leadership. Even though one person may be designated the "leader," rarely does he or she exercise much control. Usually, things drift for a while—maybe a long while—until someone finally puts forth a suggestion that people pick up on and begin to get excited about. At that point, we can say that someone has exercised leadership.

Somewhat more formally, then, we can define leadership as "the character of the relationship between the individual and a group or organization that stimulates or releases some latent energy within the group so that those involved more clearly understand their own needs, desires, interests, and potentialities and begin to work toward their fulfillment" (Denhardt and Prelgovisk, 1992, pp. 33–44). Where leadership is present, something occurs in the dynamics of the group or organization that leads to change. What is central to leadership is the capacity of the leader—whether or not called a leader—to "energize" the group.

Leadership involves helping the group become aware of a new direction in which to move. The leader merely taps and reshapes the "consciousness" of the group. Acts of leadership express a new direction, but one that is determined by the emerging interests of all members of a group. We can say that one exercises public leadership who (1) helps the group or organization understand its needs and potential; (2) integrates and articulates the group's vision; and (3) acts as a "trigger" or stimulus for group action.

The essence of leadership, therefore, is its "energizing" effect. But often the people we formally refer to as leaders don't really lead; at best, they "manage" things successfully by keeping the group running more or less smoothly.

Although power may be an important resource to the leader, one need not exercise power to bring about change (see Box 10.4). Efforts to control a group are often ultimately destructive of leadership. On the other hand, when the direction of the group or organization is selected through a developmental process that gives priority to group members' needs and desires, leadership is much more likely to be enduring. Leadership for the future will require much more than a formal position.

What skills will you need to be successful as a leader? They begin with those we ordinarily associate with effective management—the ability to use power and influence effectively, the ability to communicate with and motivate others, and the ability to work in and among diverse groups of people. (We will discuss most of these skills in the next chapter.) But leadership builds on these skills in some interesting ways.

To energize the group for example, the leader must know how to "sense" its underlying desires, sometimes even before those desires are clear even to the group members. The leader must also be able to act in ambiguous situations and to take risks; leadership involves change, and change is often difficult for both group and leader. Developing the personal strength to face change is important.

Leadership has often been viewed in terms of the exercise of power by one person or group over another—getting people to do what one wants them to do by manipulating power and influence. Leadership in the future will be more and more independent of

BOX 10.4

Bases of Social Power

Power is really much more complex than we often think. For example, the power we exercise is based on a number of different factors that operate in social situations. A classic research article describes the following "bases of social power."

1. *Reward power:* the ability to meet the needs of another, or control the other by rewarding the desired behavior. Pay, promotions, or bonuses may be ways that organizations exert reward power over employees.
2. *Punishment power:* coercive power, or the ability to deliver a painful or punishing outcome to others, and hence control them by their desire to escape the punishment. Firing, ridiculing, or disciplining an individual are common techniques of punishment.
3. *Expert power:* power based on the ability to understand, use, and deliver information that others need. Engineers or scientists may exert great influence in an organization based on their knowledge of scientific techniques for manufacturing a product, etc.
4. *Legitimate power:* control or influence exerted by virtue of one's holding a particular position in the organizational structure. The "power" is vested in the rights and responsibilities of the position, not the person. Thus, a company president or chairman of the board has power by virtue of the rights and responsibility given to whoever holds the office. Compliance with legitimate power occurs because other individuals in the organization respect the organizational structure and the rights and responsibility that accompany particular positions.
5. *Referent power:* liking, charisma, or the desire to comply with someone's wishes because you are attracted to him or her are examples of referent power. Control based on referent power depends upon the power-holder's ability to have others like and be attracted to him or her, and to follow his or her leadership because of this attraction.

SOURCE: Adapted from John R. P. French, Jr., and Bertram Raven, "The Bases of Social Power," in Dorwin Cartwright and Alvin F. Zander, eds., *Group Dynamics,* 2d ed., New York: HarperCollins Publishers, 1962). Copyright © by Dorwin Cartwright and Alvin F. Zander. Reprinted by permission of HarperCollins Publishers.

power, and the most critical leadership skills will be the personal (rather than interpersonal) skills associated with correctly empathizing with and "reading" a group, acting with a sense of direction in the presence of ambiguity, and having the courage to take risks when change is warranted.

Helgesen (1996) calls this new approach grass-roots leadership. She argues that today's organizations differ dramatically from those created in past generations. Power becomes shared throughout the group and, in turn, leaders "are to be found not only among those at the top, the 'lead horses,' but also among those who constitute what in the industrial era we called the rank and file" (Helgesen, 1996, p. 21). Accordingly, each individual plays a key role in shaping the organization; each helps the group deal with issues of organizational change.

Leadership, in this context, relates more to sharing power among the group rather than using power for the purpose of control. Such a change in power and leadership stems from the fact that most individuals within an organization, though not serving in traditional positions of power, represent the principal link between the group and its environment. Those referred to as the "rank and file" are those who ensure that the organization achieves its primary objectives.

So, in order for the new knowledge-based organizations of today to be successful, greater autonomy and decision-making capacity should be distributed to the front line, with those closest to the situation serving as the leaders of change.

SUMMARY AND ACTION IMPLICATIONS

Public management is a complex and diverse career. One moment you may be developing a budget for your agency; the next moment you may be leading a meeting on sick leave policy; and the next, you may be counseling an employee who is feeling burned out. The diversity of the work and its occasional intensity mean that you not only need to understand the ethical and political context of your work, but also to develop the personal and interpersonal skills to bring about action.

Skills based in the individual personality management of stress and time, creativity in solving problems, capacity for decision making, and skills in public leadership are played out in social settings, but each skill is deeply rooted in your own identity and character. Because they are so personal, these skills underlie nearly everything you do.

Thus, understanding yourself is an essential prerequisite to acting effectively and responsibly in public organizations. Moreover, to the extent that you are able to learn about yourself, your strengths and weaknesses, your desires and frustrations, you will be much more effective in your work with others. If you are able to reflect on your experiences and share them with others, and to learn from others' experiences as well, you will be a much more effective learner and a much more effective manager.

Nowhere is this admonition more appropriate than in the area of leadership. To lead others, you must first know yourself. Leadership involves more than power or control. Whereas power may be a resource, leadership capabilities are more likely to arise from the ability to understand the emerging desires of a group, to articulate the vision or direction the group wishes to follow, and to stimulate the group to action. Leadership unquestionably requires social or interpersonal skills, but it is based in empathetic understanding, the ability to express the aspirations of the group, and the confidence to undertake the risks associated with change. Nowhere is this more true than in the realm of public leadership.

Terms and Definitions

Role ambiguity: Occurs when the rights and responsibilities of the job are not clearly understood.

Role conflict: Occurs when one faces two different and incompatible sets of demands.

Satisficing decision: One that is just "good enough" in terms of some criterion.

Support system: Network of people with whom one can talk about problems.

Study Questions

1. Discuss the activities involved in a typical managerial day.
2. Discuss the concept of "stress management." What are some specific techniques for reducing stress levels?
3. The ability to effectively use the time available is one determinant of a successful manager. How do time management practices help improve success?
4. Explain how individuals vary in terms of creativity and problem-solving skills.
5. What features are present in rational decision making?

Cases and Exercises

1. Chapter 1 listed management skills developed by the U.S. Office of Personnel Management. Part of that list is reproduced here. Go through the list and assess your level of development in each of the skills. You might want to verify your evaluations by talking with others who know you well and have seen you operate in groups and organizations. After you have a sense of your own level of skill development, try to identify the activities (classes, workshops, readings, and so on) that would help you improve your skills in areas that need some work.

The "How" of Management Effectiveness Characteristics

Broad perspectives: Broad, long-term view; balancing short- and long-term considerations.

Strategic view: Collecting, assessing, analyzing information; diagnosis; anticipation; judgment.

Environmental sensitivity: "Tuned into" agency and its environment; awareness of importance of nontechnical factors.

Leadership: Individual; group; willingness to lead, manage, and accept responsibility.

Flexibility: Openness to new information; behavioral flexibility; tolerance for stress, ambiguity, change; innovativeness.

Action orientation: Independence, proactivity; calculated risk taking; problem solving; decisiveness.

Results focus: Concern with goal achievement; follow-through, tenacity.

Communication: Speaking; writing; listening.

Interpersonal sensitivity: Self-knowledge and awareness of impact on others; sensitivity to needs, strengths, and weaknesses of others; negotiation; conflict resolution; persuasion.

Technical competence: Specialized expertise (e.g., engineering, physical science, law, accounting, social science).

2. This instrument will help you determine, very roughly, your psychological preferences. After completing and scoring the questionnaire, note your preferred functions. In a small group, discuss the extent to which your personality tends to mirror the characteristics of your type.

Personal Style Inventory

Just as every person has differently shaped feet and toes from every other person, so we all have differently "shaped" personalities. Just as no person's foot shape is "right" or "wrong," so no person's personality shape is right or wrong. The purpose of this inventory is to give you a picture of the shape of your preferences, but that shape, while different from others' personality shapes, has nothing to do with mental health or mental problems.

The following items are arranged in pairs (a and b); each member of the pair represents a preference you may or may not hold. Rate your preference for each item by giving it a score of 0 to 5 (0 meaning you really feel negative about it or strongly about the other member of the pair, 5 meaning you strongly prefer it or do not prefer the other member of the pair). Scores for a and b must add up to 5 (0 and 5, 1 and 4, 2 and 3, etc.). Do not use fractions such as $2\frac{1}{2}$.
I prefer:

1a. being called imaginative or intuitive.
1b. being called factual and accurate.
2a. making decisions about people in organizations based on available data and systematic analysis of situations.
2b. making decisions about people in organizations based on empathy, feelings, and understanding of their needs and values.

3a. using methods I know well that are effective to get the job done.
3b. trying to think of new methods of doing tasks when confronted with them.
4a. drawing conclusions based on unemotional logic and careful step-by-step analysis.
4b. drawing conclusions based on what I feel and believe about life and people.
5a. thinking about possibilities.
5b. dealing with actualities.
6a. being thought of as a thinking person.
6b. being thought of as a feeling person.
7a. the abstract or theoretical.
7b. the concrete or real.
8a. helping others explore their feelings.
8b. helping others make logical decisions.
9a. possible views of the whole.
9b. the factual details available.
10a. using common sense and conviction to make decisions.
10b. using data, analysis, and reason to make decisions.
11a. ideas.
11b. facts.
12a. convictions.
12b. verifiable conclusions.
13a. carrying out carefully laid, detailed plans with precision.
13b. designing plans and structures without necessarily carrying them out.
14a. logical people.
14b. feeling people.
15a. imagining the nonexistent.
15b. examining details of the actual.
16a. experiencing emotional situations, discussions, movies.
16b. using my ability to analyze situations.

Personal Style Inventory Scoring

Instructions: Transfer your scores for each item of each pair to the appropriate blanks. Be careful to check the *a* and *b* letters to be sure you are recording scores in the right blank spaces. Then total the scores for each dimension. These scores are rough approximations of your psychological preferences as outlined in our discussion of the Jungian psychological types.

3. The following "classic" exercise in group problem solving will illustrate several important aspects of the decision-making process.

Your spaceship has just crash-landed on the moon. You were scheduled to rendezvous with the mothership 200 miles away on the lighted surface of the moon, but

Perception Dimension		Evaluation Dimension	
Intuiting *Item*	*Sensing* *Item*	*Thinking* *Item*	*Feeling* *Item*
1a. _____	1b. _____	2a. _____	2b. _____
3a. _____	3b. _____	4a. _____	4b. _____
5a. _____	5b. _____	6a. _____	6b. _____
7a. _____	7b. _____	8a. _____	8b. _____
9a. _____	9b. _____	10a. _____	10b. _____
11a. _____	11b. _____	12a. _____	12b. _____
13a. _____	13b. _____	14a. _____	14b. _____
15a. _____	15b. _____	16a. _____	16b. _____
Total	Total	Total	Total
Intuiting _____	Sensing _____	Thinking _____	Feeling _____

SOURCE: Adapted from R. Craig Hogan and David W. Champagne, "Personal Style Inventory," Organization, Design, and Development, Inc., King of Prussia, PA 19406. Reprinted by permission.

the rough landing has ruined your ship and destroyed all the equipment on board, except for the fifteen items listed below.

You and four to seven other people should take this test individually, without knowing one another's answers, then take the test as a group. Share your individual solutions and reach a consensus—one ranking for each item that best satisfies all group members.

Your crew's survival depends on reaching the mothership, so you must choose the most critical items available for the 200-mile trip. Your task is to rank the fifteen items in terms of their importance for survival. Place a 1 by the most important item, a 2 by the second most important, and so on through fifteen, the least important.

box of matches

food concentrate

50 feet of nylon rope

parachute silk

solar-powered portable heating unit

two .45-caliber pistols

one case of dehydrated evaporated milk

two 100-pound tanks of oxygen

stellar map (of the moon's constellation)

self-inflating life raft

magnetic compass

5 gallons of water

signal flares

first-aid kit containing injection needles

solar-powered FM receiver-transmitter

NASA experts have determined the best solution to this task. Their answers appear in Appendix A.

SOURCE: Jay Hall, "Decisions, Decisions, Decisions," *Psychology Today* 5 (November 1971): 51–88. Reprinted with permission from *Psychology Today Magazine*. Copyright © 1971 by Sussex Publishers, Inc.

4. Stress profile: Place your answer to each of the following questions in the space provided before each number. Answer with: (a) almost always true; (b) often true; (c) seldom true; (d) almost never true.

1. I hate to wait in lines.
2. I often find myself "racing" against the clock to save time.
3. I become upset if I think something is taking too long.
4. When under pressure I tend to lose my temper.
5. My friends tell me that I tend to get irritated easily.
6. I seldom like to do anything unless I can make it competitive.
7. When something needs to be done, I'm the first to begin even though the details may still need to be worked out.
8. When I make a mistake, it is usually because I've rushed into something without giving it enough thought and planning.
9. Whenever possible I will try to do two things at once, like eating while working or planning while driving or bathing.
10. I find myself feeling guilty when I am not actively working on something.

Scoring: a = 4, b = 3, c = 2, d = 1. Score: _____
    This exercise tests "Type A" behavior, characterized by impatience with delays, urgency, competitiveness and stress-related illness. A total score of 26 or above indicates that you tend toward this type.

SOURCE: Daniel A. Girdano and George S. Everly, Jr., *Controlling Stress and Tension: A Holistic Approach* (Englewood Cliffs, NJ: Prentice-Hall, 1979), 108–109. Copyright © by Prentice-Hall. Adapted by permission.

5. Although power should not be equated with leadership, it can certainly be an important resource to public managers. To illustrate some of these types of power, think

back over the past week or two as you attended class and worked in various groups and organizations, and answer the following questions:

a. Who were the two or three people during this period who exercised the greatest power over you?
b. Who were the people during this period over whom you exercised the most power?

Now return to the "Bases of Social Power" in Box 10.4. What was the basis for the power that others exercised over you? What was the basis for the power that you exercised over others? How might you most effectively build up your power base in groups and organizations to which you belong?

For Additional Reading

Bingham, Richard D., et al. *Managing Local Government: Public Administration in Practice.* Newbury Park, CA: Sage Publications, 1991.

Bozeman, Barry, and Jeffrey D. Straussman. *Public Management Strategies: Guidelines for Managerial Effectiveness.* San Francisco: Jossey-Bass, 1990.

Cohen, Stephen R. *Principle-Centered Leadership.* New York: Simon and Schuster, 1991.

Conger, Jay A. *Learning to Lead: The Art of Transforming Managers into Leaders.* San Francisco: Jossey-Bass, 1992.

Covey, Stephen R. *The Seven Habits of Highly Effective People: Restoring the Character Ethic.* New York: Simon and Schuster, 1990.

Garnett, James L. *Communicating for Results in Government: A Strategic Approach for Public Managers.* San Francisco: Jossey-Bass, 1992.

Whetten, David A., and Kim S. Cameron. *Developing Management Skills.* 2d ed. New York: HarperCollins, 1991.

APPENDIX A

"Lost on the Moon" Exercise: Answers from NASA Experts

1. Two 100-pound tanks of oxygen: most pressing survival need
2. Five gallons of water: replacement for tremendous liquid loss on lighted side
3. Stellar map of the moon's constellation: primary means of navigation
4. Food concentrate: efficient means of supplying energy requirements
5. Solar-powered FM receiver-transmitter: for communication with mothership; but FM requires line-of-sight transmission and short ranges
6. Fifty feet of nylon rope: useful in scaling cliffs, tying injured together

7. First-aid kit containing injection needles: needles for vitamins; medicines, etc.; will fit special aperture in NASA spacesuits
8. Parachute silk: protection from sun's rays
9. Self-inflating life raft: CO bottle in military raft may be used for propulsion
10. Signal flares: distress signal when mothership is sighted
11. Two .45-caliber pistols: possible means of self-propulsion
12. One case of dehydrated evaporated milk: bulkier duplication of food concentrate
13. Solar-powered portable heating unit: not needed unless on dark side
14. Magnetic compass: magnetic field on moon is not polarized; worthless for navigation
15. Box of matches: no oxygen on moon to sustain flame; virtually worthless

Chapter 11

INTERPERSONAL SKILLS
AND GROUP DYNAMICS

The ability to work effectively with other people is absolutely central for the public manager. To persuade people on issues, to encourage and motivate your employees, to represent your organization well before external groups—these and many other interpersonal skills contribute to your success as a public manager. Whereas it was once thought that managers were "born, not made," we now know that the skills managers need can be learned and improved. By carefully considering and constantly practicing good management skills, you can become more effective.

COMMUNICATIONS

As we saw in Chapter 10, most of a manager's typical day is spent in some form of communication activity; some days are devoted almost exclusively to communications. The ability to communicate well is necessary for any adult to function successfully in American society. Indeed, research has shown that, on the average, adult Americans spend 70 percent of the waking day in some form of communication activity (Rankin, 1929). He classified how people spent their communication time, and found that 9 percent of the time was spent writing, 16 percent reading, 30 percent speaking, and 45 percent listening.

We will discuss the communication modes of listening, speaking, and writing. (We will not address reading, except to note that the special skill known as "speed reading" is probably one a manager would find useful.)

LISTENING

We do more listening than we do any other form of communication. Recent research focusing exclusively on managers reveals that managers spend a greater than average portion of their time listening—about 63 percent of the day. Recall that the studies of managerial activities we discussed in the last chapter indicate that a majority of a manager's communication interactions are initiated by others. Because most are in the form of face-to-face interactions, this finding implies a lot of listening.

But doing a lot of listening does not mean that managers listen well. Listening is not the same as hearing, and, although hearing cannot be altered without medical or technical intervention, one can substantially improve the quality of one's listening with proper

BOX 11.1

Principles of Effective Listening

1. Have a reason or purpose.
2. Suspend judgment initially.
3. Resist distractions.
4. Wait before responding.
5. Rephrase what you listen to in your own words.
6. Seek the important themes.
7. Use the thinking-speaking differential to reflect and find meaning.

motivation and training. Let us first review some basics of effective listening (see Box 11.1).

Have a Reason or Purpose

This is the most important principle of those we will discuss. Having a purpose or a reason to listen provides the motivation to listen, and, generally speaking, anything you are motivated to do, you will do better than if you are not motivated. Listening is no exception. One must be motivated to listen well; it does not just happen. Without motivation, you will not use the other six principles, or you will not use them as well as you could.

But, you ask, what if I don't have a reason to listen? Then find one. Actively search for a reason to listen to what is being said. Ask yourself, "How can this information help me do my job better?" Or, "How can I use this information in some way, on the job or elsewhere?" Finding a reason to listen will provide the motivation to use all the other principles and techniques.

Suspend Judgment Initially

The key word in this phrase is "initially." You will obviously need to evaluate the material you listen to, but you should wait until you hear the entire message before you begin the evaluation. This can be difficult. In an election year, for example, if we know a particular candidate's party, we are likely to evaluate what the candidate is going to say before he or she even begins speaking. It is not coincidental that television and radio advertising for many candidates does not prominently identify the candidate's party. The advertisers want to increase the chances of having the message heard rather than losing half the audience immediately by identifying the speaker as a Democrat or Republican. To make a judgment before listening carefully to what someone is saying is the opposite of the "suspension" principle.

Resist Distractions

Many things can distract us when we are trying to listen. The "distraction' principle tells us to fight back, to actively resist whatever may be distracting us. Among the many things that distract us, various sounds are usually the most powerful. The sound may be a nonverbal noise, such as the siren from a passing fire engine or ambulance, or the voices of several people speaking at once, or something about the way the speaker talks. Regardless of what type of sound is creating the distraction, the remedy is to resist, to try harder.

In this case, "trying harder" means that you should increase your concentration. If you are in a face-to-face situation with a speaker, make sure you maintain constant eye contact. You can also lean a little bit in the direction of the speaker. By increasing your level of concentration, you can resist distractions you would have thought impossible to overcome. And that is the problem with distractions—they become an excuse for not even trying to listen, because "It's impossible to hear what she's saying."

A common classroom demonstration in listening skills illustrates the "distraction" principle (as well as others). Two volunteers read a short paragraph to the class. The volunteers are positioned in front of the class, about fifteen feet away from each other. Each has a sheet of paper containing a short (thirty- to forty-second) paragraph. Each student in the class is assigned to listen to one or the other of the two volunteers, but not to both. The students are instructed not to take notes while the paragraphs are being read, but, at the end of the reading, to write down something about each of the major points their speaker has read.

The trick is that each volunteer has a different paragraph and they read the paragraphs simultaneously! After the first round of the exercise, checking usually reveals that only a small number and sometimes none of the students in the class are able to write down something about every major point their speaker read. The instructor then reviews the eye-contact and leaning points, picks two new volunteers, gives them two new paragraphs, and repeats the exercise. The second time around it is not unusual to find that 20 percent to 25 percent of the class has written down something about each major point.

This exercise demonstrates that there is variability in the quality of listening, both between and within individuals. It also demonstrates that it is possible to resist even a major distraction. The effectiveness of the demonstration lies in the fact that it shows that our ability to resist distractions is much higher than we realize, and that we can overcome a great deal to improve the quality of our listening.

Some distractions are less obvious, perceived only semiconsciously. One such distraction for many Americans is English spoken with a foreign accent or with a different regional accent. Professor Allen Bluedorn recalls learning this lesson while he was in the U.S. Army, taking part in a listening course. The course made the same point about distractions that we have made, and he wondered if he had been allowing the fact that people spoke with different accents to become excuses not to listen. (He was stationed at Fort Bliss in El Paso, Texas, and had ample opportunities to hear English spoken with a Spanish accent.)

The approach he used to test the principle was to simply concentrate harder the next time he encountered someone who spoke with a Spanish accent. To his surprise, by concentrating harder, he was able to understand completely what the person said. He concluded that he had indeed been succumbing to the distraction of the accent, and it had become an excuse not to listen well. This lesson is important in today's increasingly multicultural organizations, where English is often spoken with a wide variety of accents. But the larger and more important lesson is that even substantial distractions can be overcome.

Wait before Responding

The "response" principle suggests that one relax and wait for natural opportunities to speak, instead of jumping into the conversation immediately. When we are burning to contribute to a discussion or conversation, we become too excited about getting into the conversation; we concentrate on whatever it is we want to say and stop concentrating on and listening to what the speaker is saying. The "response" principle suggests that one wait for a natural opportunity to contribute; try to flow with the conversation as an event rather than disrupting it by speaking at the wrong time.

Rephrase What You Listen to in Your Own Words

The "rephrasing" principle suggests an incredibly simple, yet powerful, way to check one's understanding. The idea is merely to take something you hear (an idea, instructions, and so on) and put it into your own words. You then repeat it to the person who gave you the information and ask if that is what was meant. As easy as it seems, this is an excellent way to check understanding and avoid mistakes. When you give instructions, you can ask the person who is receiving them to do the same thing. You can say, for example, "I'm not sure I explained that very well. Please tell me what you got out of that."

Seek the Important Themes

The "thematic" principle indicates that the main ideas are more important than facts—so important that they are the general keys to understanding and retaining what is said. Understanding the main ideas provides a framework for organizing the facts, which makes the facts themselves easier to remember.

The man usually credited with starting the listening movement over thirty years ago, Ralph Nichols, demonstrated this point in his research. He discovered that A and B students reported different listening habits than C and D students. In surveys of hundreds of students, he discovered that the A and B students gave a much different response to the question, "What do you listen for first when you attend a lecture?" than did the C and D students. The A and B students predominantly gave a response like, "I listen for the main ideas first," whereas C and D students said, "I listen for the facts." (This finding probably does not entirely explain the differences in these students' GPAs, but it is undoubtedly part of it.)

Use the Thinking-Speaking Differential to Reflect and Find Meaning

The "meaning" principle reflects the fact that people think faster than they speak. Although it varies by region, people in the United States speak at a rate of about 150 words per minute, but in terms of language, they think at a rate of about 500 words per minute. Thus, we normally think more than three times faster than we speak. This differential creates an opportunity to listen more effectively, but the opportunity can also be a temptation to do things that interfere with our listening. The extra time can also be used for things that distract from the listening process—concentration lapses, daydreaming, thinking about something other than what the speaker is saying, and so forth. All these things interfere with good listening, so the extra time is a two-edged sword—both opportunity and temptation.

Listening is both the most widely used and the most widely misused communication skill. It is also the skill least often taught in the American education system, from kindergarten through graduate school (Steil, Barker, & Watson, 1983).

SPEAKING

Most of the speaking managers do is informal, one-on-one or small group communications in their offices, on the phone, and in meetings. To show how we can improve our speaking, we will focus on giving instructions because a significant amount of manager-initiated communication consists of giving instructions to others. The managerial activity of delegation, in fact, would be virtually impossible without instruction giving. The key to giving instructions successfully is the ability to put yourself in the position of the person who will receive the instructions. Ideally, you want to give exactly the right amount of information—neither too much nor too little; however, if one must depart from the ideal, it is usually better to give too much rather than too little.

Two questions help you put yourself in the position of the individual who will receive the instructions:

1. What does the person need to know to carry out the instructions?
2. What does the person want to know to carry out the instructions?

The ability to decide what information is really needed is, incidentally, a justification for promotion from within—making managers out of the people who have done the jobs they will be managing. People who have done the job should be able to determine more accurately what their subordinates need to know when they receive instructions. Unfortunately, not everyone who is promoted to the management level takes full advantage of this knowledge.

To demonstrate how difficult it is to identify what information to transmit, let's consider another classroom exercise to illustrate how you can put yourself in the position of the person who will be receiving the instructions. Students form pairs, and one member of each pair is given a diagram. The students are seated back-to-back, and the one with the diagram gives the other one instructions for drawing the diagram on a piece of paper. Only the instruction giver is allowed to speak, and he or she is not allowed to look at the copy as it is drawn. After the copy is completed, the diagram is evaluated according to a set of scoring rules. Roles are then exchanged in the pairs, a new diagram is distributed, and instructions are again given to produce copies of the diagram, all rules remaining the same.

It is common for the scores in the second round to be higher than those in the first, even if the second diagram is more complex. Why? The answer seems to be that the instruction giver in the second round has been in the position of the instruction receiver during the first round and, thus, has a better idea of what information is really needed. Furthermore, the instruction givers during the second round know the scoring rules and can focus on what elements of the diagrams will be scored when the copies are evaluated. Most important, however, the instruction giver who understands what information someone needs is better able to provide that information.

WRITING

Writing is a less common form of managerial communication than speaking and listening, but it is important nevertheless. Most managerial writing is brief, often one or two pages. The memo is the most common type of written communication for many managers. Sussman and Deep (1984) offer six rules for effective managerial writing that they call the "Six Cs":

Clarity: To be clear, one must put oneself in the reader's position—much as the instruction giver must put himself or herself in the receiver's position. Write in the active voice (i.e., Dave painted the house) rather than the passive (i.e., The house was painted by Dave); avoid jargon; and try to use the simple format of introduction, body, and conclusion.

Courtesy: Courtesy involves knowing your readers, adapting to their moods, and writing at their level, providing neither too much nor too little information. Again, there are clear parallels with instruction giving.

Conciseness: This is the rule of brevity; be short and to the point. Sometimes you may want to repeat something for emphasis, but the general rule is the shorter the better. Think of it this way: which are you more likely to read, a fifty-word memo or a ten-page report? You are likely to read the fifty-word memo on the spot; the ten-page report goes into the pile you will "get to when I can."

Confidence: Always write with confidence. Confidence is really a matter of judgment on the writer's part, based on one's knowledge of one's readers. Judgment is especially important in avoiding two extremes: overbearing (too confident) and wishy-washy (not confident enough).

Correctness: You must be correct in grammar and composition, the technical rules of writing which include spelling and punctuation. Inaccurate spelling is especially conspicuous.

Conversational tone: To achieve a conversational tone, try to write in about the same way you talk, and try to imagine one specific person to whom you are writing. Thinking of a specific individual rather than an abstract category makes it much easier to write. It is much easier to write to John Jones than to "all economics professors." Occasionally, conversational writing calls for violating some formal rules of grammar, but this breach often makes things smoother, and thus more understandable and easier to follow.

Communications will affect nearly every aspect of your work as a public manager. Your ability to persuade others of your position, your clarity in sharing ideas, and your ability to deal effectively with difficult people will shape your image as an administrator (see Box 11.2). Fortunately, you can improve your ability to listen, to speak, and to write. So, practicing your communication skills whenever possible will pay dividends whatever your career.

BOX 11.2

Secret Weapons for Organizational Communication

Here are several methods for dealing with difficult situations in the work setting. (1) Remember that people do things for their own reasons, not yours. Someone's anger may mean he or she actually sees the situation from a completely different perspective, so try to understand that view. (2) When under attack, use a calm, even tone of voice and low-key body language. The content of what you say can be the same, just modify your delivery; in face-to-face communication, words carry 7 percent of your message, tone of voice 38 percent, and body language 55 percent. (3) Use conversational fantasy to anticipate a really sticky situation by saying exactly what you want to say. Then tone it down to what you know you should say. (4) Remember to rehearse so that you are prepared to cope with the situation when it arises. Practice receiving and returning "verbal hardballs." (5) If necessary, use emotional jujitsu. The principle of jujitsu is to flow with your opponent's strength, to turn his own force against him by redirecting it rather than resisting it. Rather than defending yourself, agree. Your critic will be instantly disarmed, and then you can begin to deal with the causes of the emotion rather than the emotion itself.

SOURCE: Excerpted from "Personal Productivity: Organizational Communication," *Government Productivity News* 3 (September 1989): 4.

DELEGATION AND MOTIVATION

Management can be defined as "the process of getting things done through others." To get things done through others, it is necessary to communicate with others and, often, to motivate them as well. Much of the time, those "others" are the people you supervise. After all, if you can do all the work yourself, you should just go ahead and do it. As a manager, however, you are not there to do the actual work but to do the managerial work, as illustrated in this case study:

After a long and distinguished career as a research scientist, Fraser Parks became manager of a well-known research and development laboratory. Soon after his appointment, a major new project was assigned to the lab. The task was clear in Fraser's mind; as a good scientist he knew how to do the work and how to ensure a high-quality, technically flawless piece of equipment. With a couple of years alone in the lab, he knew he could do the whole project by himself and do it well. The problem was that the equipment was needed in less than three months. Fraser knew that most of the work would have to be delegated to newly hired and reassigned staff, but he knew these people would never be able to do the high-quality job that he alone would have done. After two and a half months of trying to get the job done right, Fraser collapsed in his office one night and was immediately hospitalized.

Delegation is the process of assigning tasks to others. Like so many other managerial tasks, it may be done poorly or it may be done well. As Fraser Parks discovered, poor delegation can be nearly fatal. To delegate well, you need to try to delegate an equal amount of authority and responsibility for a job. Authority is the legitimate power to do the job, and responsibility is the accountability the individual has to you for getting the job done. The idea that an individual should have equal amounts of both is the **parity principle.** Managers often complain that they will be held responsible for something, but have not been given enough authority to get the job done. Less frequent, but equally troublesome, is an individual who has authority but is not held responsible for its use.

Generally speaking, you should delegate jobs with complete and clear instructions, and you should delegate tasks to the appropriate level. Holding everything else equal, the appropriate level is the lowest level in the hierarchy where the task can be accomplished competently. You should also provide support for the delegated tasks. This support can take many forms, including delegation of authority in a public statement (such as saying at a meeting, "Betty is in charge of inspections in the northern district now").

It is often helpful to involve subordinates in the process of delegation, encouraging them to make suggestions about the kind of work they can or should be doing. Delegation should be a two-way process. On the other hand, do not fall victim to the upward delegation phenomenon. Upward delegation occurs when subordinates bring problems to their managers that the subordinates should be solving themselves. This is the opposite of effective delegation. You should refuse to accept these problems. An effective technique is to insist that any subordinate who wants advice about a problem (the way the upward delegation attempt is often presented) should first think of at least one potential solution before coming to you to discuss the problem. To allow for creativity and motivation in the delegation process, it is best to hold subordinates accountable for results and leave the "how" up to them. This principle assumes, of course, that the "how" will be within the constraints of legal and ethical behavior as well as the constraints of public or organizational policies. Finally, tasks should be delegated consistently when the work load is light as well as heavy and when the jobs are fun as well as nasty.

Besides getting things done through others, delegation helps to develop employees, thereby making them more valuable to you and to the organization. Some managers are threatened by the idea that they may be developing possible replacements (i.e., competitors). But there is another way to look at this situation. Unless you are at the very top of the organization, you probably want to be promoted. But you cannot be promoted if you cannot be replaced. Developing your subordinates through delegation is a way of providing, to your advantage, your own potential replacements!

MOTIVATION

Whether members of an organization perform well depends partly on ability and partly on motivation. A person must have or be able to call upon the right mix of skills and abilities to do a job and must be motivated to do the job well. When you can help develop your employees' skills through instruction, training programs, and so forth, you are likely to have a significantly greater impact on their motivation.

Pay and Job Satisfaction

When one thinks of motivation in a managerial context, pay is a subject that naturally comes to mind. Frederick Taylor based the entire incentive system of his scientific management program on economic factors. Contemporary thinking about motivation is more sophisticated than Taylor's, however, as pay is seen to interact with other motivators in complex ways.

Even as early as the 1950s, Frederick Herzberg developed a model of motivation known as the **two-factor theory.** Herzberg (1959) argued that two sets of variables were relevant to the question of motivation. One set, "hygiene factors," related to job dissatisfaction; the other set, "motivators," related to job satisfaction.

Hygiene factors included variables such as pay and working conditions; motivators were factors such as chances for achievement, recognition, and advancement. Herzberg argued that improvements in hygiene factors such as pay would not increase job satisfaction; instead, any improvements would simply reduce dissatisfaction. If an individual's pay got worse or did not increase fast enough, dissatisfaction would increase. Conversely, motivators such as achievement or advancement would not affect dissatisfaction, but would increase or decrease job satisfaction. The lesson for managers was that motivating employees is a far more complex task than simply changing salary levels.

Other approaches to motivation were based on psychologist Abraham Maslow's theory of human development, the assumption that everyone has a need to grow and develop and to establish a sense of meaning in their lives. Maslow (1954) suggested a *hierarchy of needs* that all human beings must fulfill. At the first level, we must meet our physiological needs for food, clothing, and shelter. Next we have a need for safety and security. Beyond these basic needs, we have social needs, which we meet by being a part of a group. Next, we have a need for ego satisfaction and self-esteem. Finally, at the highest level, we have a need for development or self-actualization. This final level, which can only be reached after the other four levels have been achieved, describes that state of psychological development through which we reach our greatest human potential.

Controversy about the effect of job satisfaction goes back at least as far as the Hawthorne studies conducted during the mid-1920s and early 1930s. Recall that these studies began as a research project to investigate the effects of physical working conditions such as lighting on workers' productivity. Given some unexpected findings early in the studies, the investigators changed the focus of the research to investigate the impacts of social and supervisory variables on performance.

Some authors interpreted the results of the later studies as indicating that higher levels of job satisfaction led to higher levels of worker performance, a conclusion that some argue was never present in the original research reports and is thus a misinterpretation (Organ, 1986). But misinterpretation or not, the Hawthorne studies are usually credited for the "discovery" that a "happy worker is a productive worker." Other studies of the job satisfaction–performance relationship produced mixed results. Some theorists argued that the job-satisfaction-leads-to-better-performance thesis was wrong in terms of the causal ordering—that it was actually the other way around, with higher levels of performance causing higher levels of job satisfaction.

Although there is still not complete agreement on this issue, support is accumulating for a third interpretation of the job satisfaction–performance relationship—that there will only be a relationship between job satisfaction and performance if the rewards one receives are based on one's performance. If rewards are based on performance, there should be a positive correlation between job satisfaction and performance (the higher the performance, the higher the job satisfaction) because higher performance will lead to higher rewards, which will produce higher job satisfaction. If this is true, one part of the manager's job will be to make sure that performance is directly linked to rewards—pay as well as others. One method to achieve this linkage is reinforcement theory.

Reinforcement Theory

Reinforcement theory and related approaches have been given various labels, including behaviorism, operant conditioning, stimulus-response psychology, and Skinnerian psychology. The labels all refer to more or less the same thing, an approach to explaining behavior based on Thorndike's law of effect: "Of several responses made to the same situation, those which are accompanied or closely followed by satisfaction (reinforcement) . . . will be more likely to occur; those which are accompanied or closely followed by discomfort (punishment) . . . will be less likely to occur" (Daft & Steers, 1986, p. 51).

The law of effect has been studied for over a century, as it relates to learning in both animals and human beings. Results of this research have produced a number of generalizations about the specifics of reinforcement. There are four basic scenarios or results that may follow a specific behavior. If a reward follows the behavior, the individual is more likely to repeat the behavior; this is called positive reinforcement. Reinforcement will also occur when behavior is followed by the removal of something unpleasant, called negative reinforcement.

On the other hand, if an unpleasant event or punishment follows the behavior, the individual is less likely to repeat it. Note that negative reinforcement is not the same as punishment, even though the terms have become synonymous in ordinary usage. From the standpoint of the recipient, punishment would be considered a bad outcome, whereas negative reinforcement would be considered a good outcome. The final possibility is that nothing will happen following a behavior, or at least no reinforcement will occur in connection with it. When this is the case, the individual is less likely to repeat the behavior and will eventually stop repeating it altogether. This cessation of behavior is called extinction.

Regardless of which of the four possibilities one is considering, a common theme, and one of the key principles of the reinforcement approach, is that whatever response is given to the behavior, the response should follow the behavior as soon as possible. If there is too long a delay following the behavior, the response (reward, removal of an unpleasant situation, and so on) may be misinterpreted and associated with other behaviors that have occurred in the interval.

Other important considerations of the reinforcement approach are the patterns, frequency, and basis for providing the response. In terms of frequency, responses can be given every time the behavior occurs (continuous reinforcement schedule) or for only a certain proportion of occurrences (partial reinforcement schedule). The basis for making the responses can be either the number of times an event occurs (ratio schedules) or the passage of time (interval schedules). The pattern of responses can be either consistent (fixed schedules) or random (variable schedules). Research indicates that fixed schedules lead to faster learning, but to quicker unlearning or forgetting when the schedule is abandoned. Conversely, variable schedules lead to slower learning, but once the behavior is learned, the unlearning or forgetting is much slower when the schedule is abandoned.

This description of reinforcement approaches probably conjures up images of laboratory animals running through a maze to earn food pellets or to avoid electric shocks, and these are indeed how reinforcement has been studied in the laboratory. An obvious and natural parallel applying reinforcement theory in a managerial context is to link pay in some way to an individual's performance. This can be done, but pay (wages or salaries) tends to be set only once a year, and, since organizational policies often dictate pay levels, many managers have only a partial impact on establishing their subordinates' pay levels. This limits the extent to which the manager can use pay as a motivational tool.

Goal Setting

Goal setting is another method of motivating that can be used by itself or in conjunction with reinforcement techniques. In fact, you can use it to motivate yourself as well as other people. A goal is a desired state of affairs one attempts to realize, and, as research has shown, merely setting goals seems to increase the probability of attaining them. But some ways of setting goals are better than others in terms of motivational impact. Research indicates at least eight necessary characteristics for a goal to have maximum motivational impact.

1. It is best to write down a goal rather than to just keep it in mind. In a technical sense, one does not "do" a goal—one achieves a goal; therefore, the proper way to write a goal statement is with the word to followed by an action verb for example, "To finish this chapter by 5 o'clock today." Something about writing down a goal creates greater commitment on the part of the writer. It is harder to ignore, and seeing it on your desk or in your notebook constantly makes the goal harder to forget. Writing down a goal can also facilitate planning, as you consciously identify the actions you must take to achieve the goal.

2. Because specific goals are much better motivators than general goals, a properly stated goal should be as specific as possible.

   A field experiment on goal setting at the Weyerhauser Lumber Company several years ago tested the relative impacts of general and specific goals. The objects of the experiment were truck drivers who hauled logs from one location to another in Oklahoma for processing.

   The federal government established safety standards for how much weight the truckers could carry, and this amount was taken to be the maximum capacity of the trucks, 100 percent. The researchers and managers at Weyerhauser noted that the truckers normally only hauled about 62 percent of capacity. The first part of the experiment consisted of management informing the truckers that they wanted more weight to be carried on each load and that the truckers were to do their best to achieve this goal.

   The truckers' performance was tracked for the next three months and there was little or no improvement (1 or 2 percent at most). The truckers were then informed that a goal had been set for them; the goal was to haul 94 percent of capacity on each load—a much more specific goal than "Do your best." After three months, the truckers were averaging over 90 percent of capacity per load, very close to the 94 percent goal the managers had set for them.

No pay increases were given for the increase in weight hauled, although the truckers were told they would not be asked to make any more runs than they normally did as a result of hauling more weight. This remarkable change in behavior saved Weyerhauser over $250,000 annually, and subsequent checks on the truckers have found this level of performance to have been maintained for many years. A specific goal indeed makes a difference.

NETWORKING

Information on organization development and management is available online through the OD Pages (http://z.simplenet.com/od/index.html) and the Organizational Issues Clearinghouse (http://ursus.jun.alaska.edu/). For specific information on conflict resolution, visit the Conflict Resolution Center (http://www.ConflictRes.Org/) or the National Association for Community Mediation (http://www.igc.org/nafcm/).

---

3. The means for verifying whether a goal has been achieved should be specified. In the study at Weyerhauser, the truckers weighed in at the delivery location for the logs, which provided a precise way to measure the amount of weight they were hauling and, in turn, how close they were to the goal. (Incidentally, the weigh-in procedure was not added by the experiment; the truckers had been following it for many years as part of their job.)

4. A date or time by which the goal is to be accomplished should be specified. The presence or absence of a deadline is a critical attribute of any goal-setting exercise. Deadlines stimulate action, and the closer the deadline, the more motivation to act. The absence of a deadline makes the urgency of the goal indefinite and hence less motivating.

   For example, there are a disproportionately large number of plays during the last few minutes of a football game because the team that is behind faces a deadline for scoring more points or losing the game. Similar increases in activity occur toward the end of the trading period each day on the New York Stock Exchange. Think of your own behavior as a test date approaches and you begin to increase your preparation activities. These examples illustrate the motivational force of a deadline, a crucial ingredient in any goal statement.

5. A goal should be perceived as attainable. Impossible goals often are demotivating because there is no reason to try if they cannot, by definition, be attained. (Problems may occur, however, if the goal is too attainable.)

6. Although a goal should be attainable, it should also be challenging. There is little or no satisfaction in achieving a goal that presents too little challenge. The best goal in terms of motivation is one that is perceived as attainable yet challenging—as one that can be achieved, but only with significant effort.

   Psychologist David McClelland demonstrated this phenomenon many years ago. Children were asked to throw bean bags into a box from various distances, including a position located right next to the box. After they had thrown from various distances, they were asked from which position they preferred to throw. Very few picked the location next to the box; most picked a position farther away, a decision consistent with the properties of attainability and challenge. In effect, the children were setting their own goals, and the goals they set were challenging but attainable.

7. When setting a goal for someone else, the goal must be understandable to the people for whom you are setting them. If they cannot understand the goals, how can you expect them to achieve them? As in so many areas, clarity is highly important.

8. It was originally thought that if the people did not take part in setting goals, they would reject them. Subsequent research, such as the Weyerhauser study in which the truck drivers did not take part in establishing the goals, has shown that people are quite willing to accept goals that others set for them. This does not mean, however, that involving people in establishing goals is a waste of time. Among other things, if the people who will actually be trying to accomplish the goals take part in formulating them, there is a greater chance that they will more completely and accurately understand the goals. And although people may be willing to accept goals established by others, there may be greater motivation if they participate.

Managers often worry about involving subordinates in decision making, including decisions about goals and goal levels. A study comparing goals that managers set for their subordinates to goals for the same activities set by the subordinates themselves revealed that the subordinates set the more difficult goals (Hitt, Middlemist, & Mathis, 1983, p. 289). Although this may not happen all the time, it is an intriguing finding that supports the notion of including subordinates in the goal-setting process.

CONFLICT, BARGAINING, AND NEGOTIATION

Differences and conflicts inevitably arise in public organizations. Finding a way to equitably resolve differences is a key interpersonal skill for public managers. Some problems are relatively minor; others are quite substantial. Two employees raise a concern about which one is to manage a particularly valued program. A labor union demands increased wages and changes in working conditions for city workers. The secretary of state discusses arms control with his counterpart from Russia. Where differences exist, some means of resolving them is necessary.

Roger Fischer and William Ury of the Harvard Negotiation Project have suggested that negotiation is a natural process that occurs where two parties share certain interests but are opposed with respect to others. Negotiations often move quickly to positions that are held by one party or another. For example, a union representative requests a 10 percent raise, while the city negotiator takes the position that only a 2 percent raise is possible. Moving quickly to a position and allowing it to become hard and fast tends not only to produce undesirable results, but to damage the continuing relationship between the parties. Positional bargaining seems to move participants to one of two postures: a soft posture that tends to emphasize the ongoing relationship and seeks agreement among participants, or a hard posture that assumes an adversarial relationship and in which each party seeks victory over the other.

BOX 11.3

Guidelines for Successful Negotiations

1. Separate the people from the problem.
2. Focus on interests, not positions.
3. Generate a variety of possibilities before deciding what to do.
4. Insist that the result will be based on some objective standard.

SOURCE: Roger Fischer and William Ury, *Getting to Yes* (Boston: Houghton Mifflin, 1981), 98.

Fischer and Ury suggest an alternative method called "principled negotiation." Principled negotiation is based around four elements of negotiation: people, interests, options, and the criteria for solution. Four guidelines emerge from these elements (see Box 11.3).

According to Fischer and Ury, following these guidelines leads to negotiated settlements that are more equitable and more likely to lead to continued effective working relationships than are more traditional modes of bargaining. Remember that negotiations occur in all kinds of situations, from deciding which movie to see to resolving matters of war and peace; however, the same general guidelines may be employed in all negotiations to generate more effective and responsible solutions.

GROUP DYNAMICS

Individuals acting alone make a majority of organizational decisions, but sometimes two or more people combine efforts to solve a problem or make a decision. Research has shown that sometimes a group should make a decision and that certain advantages come from group decision making, but there are also disadvantages. Similarly, studies of group dynamics have established fairly predictable patterns of interactions.

ADVANTAGES OF GROUP DECISION MAKING

An old cliché has it that two heads are better than one—probably because two heads hold more information than one. Put any two people together, and each one will know something the other does not. Create a group of five or six, and there is even more information available. We have already seen that generating alternatives is one of the fundamental steps in the rational decision-making process, even under satisficing conditions. Because there is more information in a group, there is greater potential for generating more alternative solutions to a problem than could be generated by a single decision maker. But these advantages will surface only if the group is managed properly.

Groups may also benefit from synergy, the notion that the whole is greater than the sum of the parts. Synergy can occur in a group, but it is a precious commodity that is not easy to create. Consider the following case:

Three people get together to solve a problem. Bob proposes a solution, then Allen proposes a different solution. Betty has been listening to the proposals, which stimulates an idea to solve the problem in a completely new way. The idea represents something new that was not present before in the group. If it were possible to quantify the information in the group at the beginning of the discussion, the total information would equal the sum of the information held by the individual members. With Betty's new idea, an idea stimulated by the group discussion, the sum is now greater than the sum of the individual parts.

How much and how often synergy occurs in a group is often a function of the nature of the group's communications. In small groups (ten or fewer), a number of characteristic communication patterns or networks tend to develop, some of which promote synergy more than others. A fundamental way communication networks differ from one another is in terms of how centralized the networks tend to be. The more centralized a communication network, the more one or a few people are at or near its "center." In such a group, the people near the center of the network are involved in receiving and transmitting all or most of the messages that are communicated within the network. The less centralized or more decentralized a network is, the more everyone can communicate with everyone else without having to transmit the message through intermediaries.

As shown in Figure 11.1, the Wheel is the most centralized of the networks, the All-Channel is the least centralized, and the Circle and the Chain fall between the two extremes. Research has shown that decisions are made more quickly in centralized networks when a simple problem is being handled, and that groups with centralized networks also tend to produce more accurate solutions to simple problems than do decentralized groups.

Decentralized networks, however, are both faster and more accurate in reaching decisions about complex problems, and they will also produce more accurate solutions. Complex problems, by their nature, involve more information, and the decentralized networks make it easier to tap and process the information held by each member. Complex problems also tend to benefit more from synergy in developing solutions, and the ability of everyone to be involved in the discussion and to listen to the discussions of

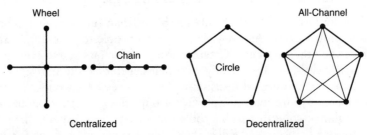

FIGURE 11.1

Communication Networks

others promotes synergy. Thus, decentralized communication networks tend to promote synergy more than do centralized networks.

There is also evidence that centralized, one-way communication also tends to promote information loss. A well-known study followed messages sent from the boards of directors in one hundred companies to see what happened to them as they worked their way down the hierarchy in each company. The messages passed from the board of directors, to vice presidents, to division managers, to plant managers, to supervisors, and finally to the operating managers. By the time the messages reached the operating managers, only 20 percent of the original content was left!

We want to do more than just make a good decision. The final step in the decision-making process is always implementation. Especially if the people who make the decision are the ones who will be implementing it, commitment to the decision should help with implementation. Research also reveals that satisfaction with the group and its processes increases as the networks become more decentralized. Satisfaction is not exactly the same thing as commitment, but the two are closely related. In most cases, then, as participation in making the decision increases, so should commitment to the final decision.

An interesting property of group decision making, the risky shift, can be either an advantage or a disadvantage. The **risky shift** refers to how daring the decisions would be if made as a group compared to the average risk of the same decision if each member made it alone. It was originally thought that groups would always make riskier decisions than would individual members. As more research was conducted, however, it was discovered that sometimes the shift will be in the opposite direction—that groups sometimes make decisions that are less risky than those made by members working alone.

Sometimes a daring decision produces better results, but sometimes it makes things worse. Since the same can be said about more conservative decisions, the dilemma is that it is often impossible to predict whether a more conservative or more daring decision will yield better results. The most we can say is that a group decision will normally be either more daring or more conservative than the average riskiness of a decision made by each member acting individually.

DISADVANTAGES OF GROUP DECISION MAKING

In addition to the several advantages that are possible with group decision making, there are potential problems too. One of the obvious constraints on human beings that results in our "bounded rationality" is the constraint of time. Time not only limits the efforts of individual decision makers to acquire and process information, but it also limits the possibilities for groups to make decisions. Normally, it takes a group much longer to make a decision than it takes an individual to make a decision about the same problem. Time thus becomes an important constraint on a manager's ability to use group decision making.

Another constraint may be cost. Even if group decision making and individual decision making were equally fast, the group is still more expensive. Compare a single decision maker, whose pay amounts to $100 per hour, taking one hour to reach a decision to a committee of five managers, each of whose salaries amount to $100 per hour. The cost to the organization for the single decision maker is $100, whereas the cost of the committee is $500.

Another property of groups, which is the opposite of synergy, is groupthink. If synergy is the notion that the whole is greater than the sum of the parts, groupthink makes the whole (the group) less than the sum of the parts. Groupthink was first defined and analyzed by Irving Janis as "a mode of thinking that people engage in when they are deeply involved in a cohesive in-group, when the members' strivings for unanimity override their motivation to realistically appraise alternative courses of action" (Janis, 1983). Because the group is so cohesive, greater emphasis is given to conformity than to making good decisions.

Janis identified characteristics of groups victimized by groupthink and cautioned managers to interpret the presence of these characteristics in a group carefully. For example, groups experiencing groupthink have an illusion of morality, a belief that the group's position, whatever it may be, is inherently ethical and moral in comparison to positions held by other individuals and groups. Such groups also engage in negative stereotyping of other people and groups, often viewing outsiders as the "enemy" and as being too different to negotiate with. Groupthink tends to produce an illusion of invulnerability, which makes decisions seem less risky than they really are. Rationalization is commonly employed as a way to discredit information critical of the group or its decisions, and there is frequent self-censorship of dissenting views, which minimizes the amount of critical or contrary information to which the group is exposed. A strong conformity pressure permeates the group and puts further pressure on group members to agree with the dominant position. Finally, an illusion of unanimity results in the belief that everyone in the group believes in the group's decision and judgment. Obviously, groups that are victimized by groupthink are limited in their constructive abilities.

INTERPERSONAL DYNAMICS IN GROUPS

Interpersonal relationships affect the work of groups or teams. To illustrate the problems that can arise, imagine that two people who despise each other are assigned to the same committee. Obviously, these two individuals will not work as well together as two people who are neutral toward each other or who like or respect each other. Even if the conflict is not manifested, personal animosity may contribute to building a **hidden agenda**, where privately held goals and priorities motivate actions more directly than the overt and publicly stated reasons. Obviously, the operation of hidden agendas disrupts the group and diminishes its effectiveness.

But the interpersonal dynamics of groups in action are much more subtle and complex than these examples suggest (Gardner, 1974, pp. 8–11). For example, groups often follow a fairly predictable pattern of development. Typically, at the outset of the group's work, its members are highly dependent on the leader of the group. They ask for direction and become quite frustrated if specific direction is not given. If the leader allows the group to become overly dependent, however, its effectiveness will suffer in the long term. The leader can resist dependency by referring questions back to the group's members for input.

Often, however, a period of counterdependence will follow, in which members may show hostility toward the leader. Still wanting some direction, the group's members are now also experiencing a need for independence, just as an adolescent may simultaneously love and hate his or her parents. Counterdependency seems especially likely to occur in authoritarian work environments, where members' actions are too closely regulated.

On the other hand, in a group where members feel they can openly express themselves and their ideas without fear of retaliation, feelings of interdependence may develop. At this stage, group members recognize the purposes they hold in common and come to have greater trust and respect for one another. The group will probably be most effective when it reaches this stage.

As the group moves through these stages of development, certain patterns of behavior are likely to occur. Early in the group's development, some members may seek flight, through actual withdrawal from the work of the group or through silence, irrelevant comments, or self-serving remarks. Most flight behavior is an implicit attempt to say that nothing significant will happen unless the leader gives in to the group's desire for explicit direction. In the counterdependent stage, members may engage in fight behavior or in pairing. Fighting the group's leader in some symbolic fashion is, of course, a fairly straightforward act of rebellion; pairing or breaking off into small groups or alliances is somewhat more subtle, yet expresses the same emotion. Finally, as the group reaches the stage of interdependence, the actual work of the group can be accomplished in reasonable and satisfying ways.

At this stage, a variety of leadership functions must occur for the group to maintain its effectiveness (see Box 11.4). These functions can all be performed by a single person, typically the group's formal leader, but they can also be performed by a variety of different people active at different times in the group's development. In either case, if you wish to help the group meet its objectives, you should be attentive both to the stages of group development and to the extent to which the various leadership functions are being fulfilled.

CHANGING THE COMPOSITION OF THE GROUP

An open group is one that experiences a great deal of turnover among its membership, whereas a closed group has a stable membership (Ziller, 1965). Because of their stability, closed groups tend to become very cohesive, but this feature often makes it difficult for a newcomer to become integrated with the group. Whereas lack of acceptance of a newcomer is a group property, it may be perceived as the result of unsatisfactory interpersonal relationships between the newcomer and individual group members.

American organizations are becoming more multicultural in composition at both the managerial and nonmanagerial levels. As more and more women and members of minority groups come to be included in what were previously relatively homogeneous groups, other types of problems, often interpersonal, will tend to occur, and the people involved will often not consciously know the reasons for them. Rosabeth Kanter (1977) explains what happens when a previously homogeneous group is joined by a newcomer who differs in some socially salient way from the group members as the "theory of relative numbers." The insights it provides can be useful to managers working in multicultural environments.

BOX 11.4

Leadership Roles in Group Dynamics

1. *The coordinator role:* Communicate to all members about meetings, schedules, tasks, procedures, and similar matters; act as an information clearinghouse for all group members and as a contact person with other groups or outsiders.

2. *The facilitator role:* Set up procedures and a structure for group work; assist members in identifying problems, defining issues, summarizing progress, and working together. (This role involves minimal direct influence on the group task. It concentrates on establishing an interpersonal network that helps members work together to solve problems.)

3. *The trainer role:* Teach group members ways of approaching problems; provide the group with methods of learning from their own experiences; arrange for outside consultants to train the group.

4. *The observer role:* Be alert to how the group is functioning and particularly to which functions are not being met; describe to members what is happening in terms of the group process; show the group areas in which change might facilitate their work.

5. *The gap filler role:* Fulfill those functions that are not being handled by anyone else, particularly the functions of summarizing, clarifying, synthesizing, or facilitating compromise.

6. *The monitor role:* Once the group has determined a procedure to follow or a solution to a problem, see to it that the group is reminded of responsibilities, functions, and assignments necessary for implementation of the decision; provide copies of budgets, schedules, assignment sheets, and agendas to members so they can complete their work on schedule.

SOURCE: Excerpted from Ernest Stech and Sharon Ratliffe, *Working in Groups* (Lincolnwood, IL: National Textbook Company, 1976), 220–221. Reprinted by permission.

The theory of relative numbers is proposed as a universal explanation for the phenomena that occur when a homogeneous group is joined by someone who differs from the existing group members. Groups defined by occupation, age, religion, political preference, marital status, and many other characteristics all fit the theory and its explanation. The theory then presumably applies to many situations other than groups defined by race or gender, although these are the characteristics with which we are concerned. The theory begins by asking what happens when an all-white group is joined by a black member, or when an all-male group is joined by a female member.

When a group is homogeneous in terms of a characteristic such as race or sex, members may differ in terms of individual personalities, but they will not stand out, by definition, because of race or gender differences. Kanter illustrates such a group with the letter "X" and calls all of the group members Xs (members of a single race).

XXXXXXXXXX   (1)

Kanter represents a member of a different race with the letter "O"; when an individual of this race joins the group, the group is diagrammed as follows:

XXXXXOXXXX   (2)

This new group, new in terms of composition, will experience different dynamics now that O is present. Diagram (2) illustrates what happens in this situation. Which letter sticks out in row (2)? It is the O, who experiences extra visibility as a result of the racial difference. The extra visibility itself, to say nothing of prejudicial attitudes that may prevail in the group, will create problems for O. Because always standing out is inherently stressful, O faces more personal stress. Moreover, O will also have problems with informal aspects of the organization because Xs tend to become involved with other Xs rather than Os. This makes it harder for Os to become part of the informal networks that exist in organizations. It also means that Os tend to be unsponsored or unmentored, since Xs tend to mentor other Xs.

One of the more intriguing things that happens to O is a form of stereotyping. As we have mentioned, human beings do not tolerate chaos well and create order by defining and redefining situations to explain what is happening. This is especially true in trying to understand human behavior, as we all tend to develop explanations for why other people behave as they do. Explanations for O's behavior will tend to take the form "O is behaving that way because that is the way all Os behave." Explanations for O's behavior will often be based on O's status as an O. These attributions are often detrimental to O's standing because, among other things, they tend to depersonalize O.

In terms of solutions or remedies, adding more Os to the group may be helpful. Kanter suggests that the extra visibility and its attendant effects tend to diminish as the proportion of Os in the group increases to about 15 percent, but she believes they do not become inconsequential until the group is composed of about 40 percent Os. The key is the proportion of Xs and Os in the group, not absolute numbers; for example, two Os in a group with ten members will experience the same visibility as four Os in a twenty-member group.

It is not always possible to solve or significantly reduce many of these problems by increasing the proportion of Os. African Americans, for example, compose about 15 percent of the American population, which means that, on the average, only enough blacks could be added to a predominantly white group to begin to reduce the visibility-created problems. Thus, having managers become aware of the visibility phenomenon and acting appropriately in their own behaviors toward Os will become particularly important as more diverse types of people become part of organizations.

MANAGING GROUPS IN ACTION

After examining the pros and cons of group decision making, the manager's strategy should be obvious. If a group is to make a decision, it should be managed so as to enhance the advantages of the group technique and minimize the disadvantages. How,

BOX 11.5

How to Be an Effective Group Leader

Effective group leadership requires:

1. A solid knowledge of and dedication to the history, goals, values, achievements, and current directions of the organization.
2. An ability to keep issues in focus and matters in perspective; to demonstrate emotional stability in times of stress and conflict.
3. To value the opinions of each member, to judge each on its merits alone and not be persuaded or intimidated by displays of emotion or aggressiveness.
4. A willingness to give credit to others and to accept the blame for failures without being overly dramatic or obvious.
5. A good sense of humor, the ability to keep meetings lively and interesting, will contribute as much as anything to good attendance, morale, and overall achievement.
6. To find enjoyment in the meeting and be able to infect others with enthusiasm.
7. To be responsive to the individual members but to be firm when necessary in order that the members know where they stand.

SOURCE: Excerpted from Bill D. Schul, *How to Be an Effective Group Leader* (Chicago: Nelson-Hall, 1975). Reprinted by permission.

---

exactly, does one manage the group to accomplish this? Because most group decision making takes place in meetings, one answer would seem to be in good meeting management (see Box 11.5).

The meeting has nearly the worst reputation of any managerial tool, and much of this reputation is probably justified. Most of the blame should not be on the meeting as a technique, however, but on the way meetings are usually managed (or mismanaged). The first point in improving the effectiveness of meetings is that they are activities that require active management: a successful meeting does not just happen, it requires a lot of work.

Not surprisingly, the fundamentals of managing a meeting are similar to the fundamentals of management generally. For example, a meeting must be planned. When will we have it? Where? What do we intend to accomplish? These questions should be answered well before the meeting begins.

A meeting must also be staffed. Who do we want to attend? Who will we invite? These questions often depend upon the reasons for meeting, which further emphasizes the importance of planning, but there are other factors in selecting participants. Are there people who might have hidden agendas, or who might not work well together? How well did the people you are considering work together last time? How productive were they?

An effective meeting manager must organize the meeting, which also involves a substantial amount of planning. What roles will you create at the meeting? Will you have anyone serve as parliamentarian? In what order will topics and problems be discussed?

Will you divide the group into subcommittees to work on special projects? If so, should they work on them before, during, or after the meeting?

Directing the meeting—providing the actual leadership of the ongoing meeting—is itself complex. Some necessary skills are obvious, such as starting the meeting on time; others are subtle, such as the ability to inhibit a too-vociferous participant. If you have planned well, you will have a good general idea of what the meeting is intended to accomplish and will try to move the meeting in that direction.

As meetings often produce decisions, the manager must also see that the decisions are implemented. This is often achieved through a form of delegation at the meeting, when assignments for future action are made. Indeed, it is often a good idea to review assignments as part of the meeting's conclusion. Finally, conducting a critique of the meeting after it is over, perhaps introspectively, may prove helpful in moving the manager closer to the goal of better meeting management.

SPECIALIZED TECHNIQUES FOR GROUP DECISION MAKING

Brainstorming is a technique that was developed to enhance the alternative-generation portion of the decision-making process. The goal is to generate as many ideas about some problem as possible, while suspending judgment about each idea. The task before the group is to develop ideas about a problem, or even solutions to the problem, and the more generated, the better.

Once the assignment is announced, group members begin to generate ideas. The ideas are described orally, and someone records each idea on a blackboard or flipchart for everyone to see. No evaluations of ideas are permitted during brainstorming, and the session continues until everyone is out of ideas or the leader feels the session has lasted long enough. The purpose is to bring out the information held by different group members and to encourage synergy by stimulating new ideas.

While brainstorming helps enrich the alternative-generation portion of the decision-making process, the nominal group technique generates both alternatives and solutions. A major purpose of the design is to avoid groupthink. A **nominal group** is a face-to-face meeting that allows only very limited interaction among participants. A problem is presented, but unlike brainstorming, the group is expected to make a decision about how to solve the problem. After the problem has been presented, each member, working alone, writes down as many solutions to the problem as he or she can formulate. When everyone is finished writing, the leader calls for the solutions. Each person in the room presents one solution until all the possible solutions have been heard.

The solutions are recorded publicly as they are presented, again usually on a blackboard or a flipchart. Other members may ask questions for clarification if they do not understand a solution, but only clarifying questions are allowed. Members may not debate the merits of particular solutions. After every solution has been presented and all questions answered, the group makes a decision by means of a written poll, taken as a secret ballot. Each member rank-orders the different solutions from best to worst. The rankings are submitted to the meeting leader without any identifying material on the ballot. The leader or someone assisting the leader tabulates the ballots, and the solution that receives the highest average preference becomes the group's decision.

In many ways, quality circles are the most comprehensive specialized technique for group decision making in that they are explicitly concerned with every step in the decision-making process, from recognition that a problem exists through implementation of solutions. Quality circles also incorporate other specialized techniques such as brainstorming.

Now that we have examined the advantages and disadvantages of group decision making, how do we know when to use group decision making rather than an individual decision maker?

PARTICIPATION IN GROUP DECISION MAKING

The Vroom-Yetton model of participation in decision making focuses on the manager's decision concerning the extent to which subordinates should participate in making a specific decision (Vroom & Yetton, 1973; Vroom & Jago, 1988). The most impressive study supporting the model was an investigation of two hundred actual managerial decisions. Managers made these decisions as part of their jobs without the aid of the model; the model was then applied, after the fact, to determine the effectiveness of various patterns of involvement in decision making.

Vroom and his associates identified the two hundred decisions and gathered data about how much subordinate participation was involved in making each decision. The researchers were also able to gather information about the consequences of each decision specifically, whether each decision produced successful results. When decisions were made using a level of subordinate participation consistent with levels that would have been recommended by the Vroom-Yetton model (remember, none of the managers knew anything about the model at the time they made the decisions), 68 percent of the results or outcomes were judged to have been successful. When the amount of participation by subordinates was not at a level consistent with the model's recommendations, only 22 percent of the outcomes were judged to have been successful.

This is a remarkable difference. In both relative and absolute terms, the managers who involved subordinates to a degree consistent with the model's recommendations had extremely good results. In relative terms, the outcomes were more than three times better than the decisions whose level of subordinate participation was inconsistent with the model. In absolute terms, 68 percent success is excellent, because factors other than how a decision is made determine whether it produces good results. We would not expect any decision-making method to produce successful outcomes 100 percent of the time, so the results in the study were quite impressive.

The Vroom-Yetton model involves the choice of various levels of involvement in decision making; the choice is not merely between a single individual and an entire group. These are two alternatives that frame a continuum with several other levels of participation in-between. As Vroom and Yetton conceptualized them, there are five levels of participation along this continuum (see Box 11.6). The Vroom-Yetton model indicates which level of participation is appropriate in a particular situation. (Note that for some situations, two or more participation levels are equally likely to produce decisions that will generate successful results.)

To use the model, you must understand (1) how to identify the different situations, and (2) how to match different situations with the appropriate levels of participation.

BOX 11.6

Types of Management Decision Methods

Symbol	Definition
AI	You solve the problem or make the decision yourself using the information available to you at the present time.
AII	You obtain any necessary information from subordinates, then decide on a solution to the problem yourself. You may or may not tell subordinates the purpose of your questions or give information about the problem or decision on which you are working. The input provided by them is clearly in response to your request for specific information. They do not play a role in the definition of the problem or in generating or evaluating alternative solutions.
CI	You share the problem with the relevant subordinates individually, getting their ideas and suggestions without bringing them together as a group. Then you make the decision. This decision may or may not reflect your subordinates' influence.
CII	You share the problem with your subordinates in a group meeting. In this meeting you obtain their ideas and suggestions. Then you make the decision, which may or may not reflect your subordinates' influence.
GII	You share the problem with your subordinates as a group. Together you generate and evaluate alternatives and attempt to reach agreement (consensus) on a solution. Your role is much like that of chairperson, coordinating the discussion, keeping it focused on the problem, and making sure that the critical issues are discussed. You can provide the group with information or ideas that you have, but you do not try to "press" them to adopt "your" solutions and you are willing to accept and implement any solution that has the support of the entire group.

SOURCE: Reprinted from Victor H. Vroom and Phillip W. Yetton, *Leadership and Decision-Making* (Pittsburgh: University of Pittsburgh Press, 1973). Reprinted by permission. © 1973 by University of Pittsburgh Press.

Both issues are resolved by the use of two tools in combination: (1) the set of alternative courses of action listed in Box 11.6 and (2) the decision tree shown in Figure 11.2.

The decision tree initially appears complex but is simple to use. One begins under point A by answering question A (all questions must be answered either "yes" or "no"; "maybe" or "sometimes" is not allowed). Depending on the answer, you proceed to either question D (for a "no" response to A) or to question B (for a "yes" response to A). One continues answering the questions as indicated by the decision tree until you reach an end point.

Each end point is numbered, with a set of participation levels listed after each end point. These are feasible sets; all the participation levels listed in a feasible set are equally likely to result in a successful outcome. This does not mean, however, that there is no

A. Does the problem possess a quality requirement?
B. Do you have sufficient information to make a high-quality decision?
C. Is the problem structured?
D. Is acceptance of the decision by subordinates important to effective implementation?
E. If you were to make the decision by yourself, is it reasonably certain that it would be accepted by your subordinates?
F. Do subordinates share the organizational goals to be attained in solving this problem?
G. Is there likely to be conflict among subordinates over preferred solutions?

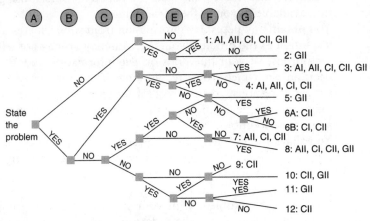

FIGURE 11.2

Decision Tree Governing Group Problems

SOURCE: Reprinted from Victor H. Vroom and Phillip W. Yetton, *Leadership and Decision-Making* (Pittsburgh: University of Pittsburgh Press, 1973). Reprinted by permission. © 1973 by University of Pittsburgh Press.

reason to pick one style over another within the feasible set. The decision styles are arranged in the order of the amount of time it will take to reach a decision using the styles. The style listed first is the fastest, followed by the second fastest, and so on. In most situations, one should choose the fastest style in the feasible set.

Again, the answers to the questions along the path reaching the particular end point define the situation, and the participation levels indicated in the feasible sets provide guidance concerning the appropriate level of involvement. Although the model, even as presented here in simplified form, may initially seem cumbersome and complex, managers who practice it for several days seem to be able to utilize it without notes thereafter.

ORGANIZATION CHANGE AND DEVELOPMENT

The capacity to bring about needed changes effectively and responsibly may be the key determinant of success or failure as a public manager. Change is ubiquitous in public organizations; some changes are small and little noticed, others are major and widely publicized. New programs and procedures must be developed, new organizational arrangements are required, and new attitudes and behaviors must be encouraged. Especially as the pace and complexity of modern life impinges on those in public organizations, a high degree of flexibility, creativity, and adaptability on the part of the organization and its members is increasingly required.

But change does not come easily in modern organizations, so it is important to understand the nature of the change process and the reasons that people sometimes accept and support changes and sometimes resist. Some people are simply more open to change than others. The intuitive person, for example, is attracted by the future and is eager to embrace new ideas and concepts; the sensing person, on the other hand, lives more in the here and now and may need more convincing that a proposed change is a good idea. But regardless of personal differences, there are things managers can do to increase the likelihood that organization members will agree to a particular change (see Box 11.7). If people trust the per-

---

BOX 11.7

Major Objectives of Typical Organizational Development Programs

To create an open, problem-solving climate throughout the organization so that members can confront problems rather than fight about or flee from them.

To build trust among individuals and groups through out the organization, whether through vertical linkages between superiors and subordinates, horizontal linkages among peers, or diagonal linkages among individuals of different ranks in different units.

To supplement the authority of role or status with the authority of knowledge and competence.

To locate decision-making and problem-solving responsibilities as close as possible to the information sources.

To make competition, where it exists, contribute to meeting work goals (organization units compete to produce a good or service more efficiently and effectively) as opposed to win/lose competition.

To maximize collaboration between individuals and units whose work is interdependent.

To develop a reward system that recognizes both achievement of the organization's mission (profits or service) and human development (growth of people).

To increase the sense of ownership of organization objectives throughout the work force.

To help managers manage according to relevant objectives rather than according to "past practices" or to objectives that do not make sense for one's area of responsibility.

To increase self-control and self-direction for people within the organization.

To create conditions where conflict is brought out and managed.

To increase awareness of group "process" and its consequences for performance that is, to help people become aware of what is happening between and to group members while the group is working on the task (e.g., communication, influence, feelings, leadership styles and struggles, relationships between groups, how conflict is managed, etc.).

son who is proposing the change, either based on his or her skill and expertise or his or her record in past change efforts, then they will be more likely to accept the change. Similarly, if people fully understand the implications of the change, and if they have been involved in developing the new idea, they will be more likely to accept the change. Finally, if the manager is sensitive to the implications of the change for individuals in the organization and for their relationships with one another, people will be more likely to accept the change.

Unfortunately, these basic guidelines for implementing change are regularly violated, often leading to confusion and turmoil. Take the following case as an example:

> Jane Sanford knew the work of the health services agency better than anyone else; she also knew the importance of employee involvement in organizational changes. As she listened to proposals from her staff for ways to implement a new immunization program, however, she knew that the plan she had formulated earlier in her office was far superior. Just as consensus seemed to be building around one particular suggestion, Jane jumped in and announced her plan, asking for quick implementation. To Jane's surprise, the members of her staff were furious.

Obviously, as Jane Sanford discovered, if a change is ordered abruptly and dictatorially with little advance notice or preparation, the chances of its ready adoption are severely reduced. Moreover, if some perceive a proposed change as threatening, its chances of success are lessened. These outcomes are especially likely when the organization is already marked by poor working relationships; the proposed change may become a target for other real or imagined frustrations and will not be considered on its merits at all.

DIAGNOSING THE NEED FOR CHANGE

Ideas for change often occur in response to a feeling that something is wrong with the existing situation. As a manager, you will often scan the organization for "blips" or trouble spots that need attention; from these reviews, you may recognize symptoms of underlying problems. Sometimes you may wish to undertake a more thorough and detailed analysis that could possibly lead to a major change activity. These are standard topics to consider:

NETWORKING

Resources on organizational learning and change are available from MIT's Society for Organizational Learning (http://www.sol-ne.org/) or the Stanford Learning Organization (http://www-leland.stanford.edu/group/SLOW/). Additional information can be found at the Academy of Management Online (http://www.aom.pace.edu/).

---

1. *Context:* What is the purpose and history of the organization? What have been major strengths and weaknesses over the years? What are the political and economic constraints on operations?
2. *Outputs:* At the organizational level, what are the levels of citizen satisfaction, effi-

ciency, and productivity? At the group and individual levels, what is the satisfaction level of the employees and their commitment to the organization?

3. *Organizational culture:* What are the dominant beliefs, attitudes, and values in the organization? Are there different values in different parts of the organization? Are some sets of values in conflict with others?

4. *Task requirements:* What are the principal tasks that members of the organization must perform? Do employees clearly understand organization goals? How highly developed (or overdeveloped) are organizational rules and procedures?

5. *Formal organization:* How is the work organized? What is the organization structure? How many levels of management are there? How is work planned and coordinated? What are the formal modes of communication through the organization?

6. *People:* How many employees does the organization have and where do they work? What is the mix of skills and abilities among employees? How many managers are there, and how do they relate to other employees?

7. *Physical setting and technology:* What is the condition of the organization's buildings and equipment? How does the physical environment affect the work being done? What is the level of technology, and how effectively is it employed? (Lippitt, Langseth, & Mossop, 1985, pp. 6–13.

STRATEGIES FOR ORGANIZATIONAL CHANGE

Having diagnosed the need for changes, the manager may wish to undertake a fairly broad-scale effort to revitalize the organization. As we saw earlier, one set of approaches to change efforts is generally termed organization development Those involved in organization development, or "OD," tend to focus on the human side of the organization, though their work may lead to recommendations about physical or programmatic matters as well. OD practitioners see the primary problem in most organizations as restrictive patterns of behavior, often based on misunderstanding and mistrust, that limit the capacity of the organization and its members to deal effectively with a complex and changing environment. The problem then becomes one of "unfreezing" past patterns of behavior, replacing them with more open and trusting relationships, and "freezing" these in place. Because these behavior patterns are largely based on the implicit images or "theories" of organization that guide our eventual behaviors, it is important not only that behaviors change, but that real learning—that is, adjustment of one's "theories"—occur.

Most students of organizational development find that efforts to change established patterns of behavior are easier with the help of an outside educator or **interventionist,** an external consultant brought in to work with members to reveal dysfunctional behaviors and to try to develop more effective working relationships. It is important to have changes develop internally rather than be imposed from outside. Chris Argyris suggests that the interventionist's role involves three efforts: "(1) to help generate valid and useful information; (2) to create conditions in which clients can make informed and free choices; and (3) to help clients develop an internal commitment to their choice" (Argyris, 1970, pp. 12–13).

A variety of techniques are available to the interventionist, including the following:

Team building: Much of an organization's work is done in groups; a program of team development may help improve group effectiveness. Usually, one begins with a careful review of how team members communicate and work together. Following a diagnosis of interpersonal group problems, the facilitator leads the group in designing an action plan to overcome those difficulties. Many of these "interventions" can be accomplished without an outside facilitator.

Intergroup problem solving: Occasionally conflict or competition arises among groups; for example, two divisions of a small organization may fight over resources and prestige, overlapping responsibilities, or confusion about allocation of responsibilities. An interventionist might bring the groups (or representatives) together to identify problem areas and begin to devise ways to deal with the problems. As you might expect, confrontations are often difficult—sometimes even tumultuous—but a trained group facilitator can help keep the group focused on resolving the real issues that divide them.

Goal setting and planning: In goal-setting efforts, superior-subordinate pairs or groups throughout the organization are asked to systematically assess their capabilities and set specific targets for future performance. After a specific period, the individuals or groups meet again to evaluate their work and establish goals for the next period. (As we have seen, one broad approach to organizationwide efforts to engage in formal planning and goal setting is described as management by objectives, or MBO.)

Sensitivity training: As we saw in Chapter 9, the values heralded by students of organization development emphasize openness and trust among people at all levels of the organization. One way to significantly improve openness and trust is to help individuals and groups identify and explore their deep-seated feelings about their work and, perhaps, about one another. A trained facilitator is almost essential here, for serious personal and interpersonal issues often emerge and must be handled with great care.

SUMMARY AND ACTION IMPLICATIONS

All the knowledge, values, and skills you possess are expressed in the moment of action. Whether you are a manager or a policy analyst, or hold some other position in a public organization, your ability to act effectively and responsibly "in the real world" will determine your success. Your actions will usually occur in social settings and require working with others. Especially in a managerial position, you will engage in almost constant interaction with other people. So, no matter how much you know or how proper your values, your effectiveness will be limited if you cannot work well with others.

Today we recognize that interpersonal skills, like other skills, can be developed and improved over time. Just as artists or athletes can improve proficiency, so can you improve your skills in areas of communications, delegation, negotiation, and group dynamics. The key to improving your skills in public management, as in other areas, is practice and repetition, accompanied by self-reflection and self-critique.

If you want to be a better communicator, for example, you should seek opportunities to practice communicating with others. Find opportunities to make presentations; practice listening with special concentration and sensitivity; try to develop your writing skills. As you practice, be conscious of your own and others' reactions. Reflect upon your successes and failures and try to learn from both. Over time, you'll improve your skills and find yourself far more effective.

Throughout this book, we have described public management as involving cognitive, conceptual, technical, and human skills. In the moment of action, however, the areas cannot be separated. Indeed, your capacity to bring together knowledge, technique, and interactive skills at the moment of action will determine success or failure in most situations. Public management can be studied in the abstract, but it must be lived in the real world—a world of stress, complexity, and uncertainty. In few other fields do so many aspects of the human personality have to come together. But it is this very difficulty that makes public service so challenging and rewarding.

Terms and Definitions

Brainstorming: Technique for enhancing the alternative-generation portion of the decision-making process.

Delegation: Assigning tasks to others.

Hidden agenda: Privately held goals and priorities.

Interventionist: External consultant brought in to reveal dysfunctional patterns of behavior and to try to develop more effective working relationships.

Nominal group: Face-to-face meeting that allows only limited interaction among participants.

Parity principle: Idea that an individual should have equal amounts of authority and responsibility.

Risky shift: Difference in the daringness of decisions group members make as a group compared to the average risk of the same decision if each member made it alone.

Two-factor theory: Model of motivation involving two variables: job satisfaction and job dissatisfaction.

Study Questions

1. What are the seven basics of effective listening?
2. Why is speaking an important interpersonal skill?
3. Discuss the "Six Cs" for effective written communication.
4. Management can be defined as "the process of getting things done through others." Discuss how delegation and motivation enable the work of management to occur.
5. Explain reinforcement theory and its four basic scenarios or results.

6. Goal setting is another motivation technique. Discuss what characteristics a goal should have for maximum motivational impact.

7. What are the elements of "principled negotiation"?

8. Discuss advantages and disadvantages associated with group decision making.

9. Explain the fundamentals of managing group dynamics.

10. Identify and discuss various techniques for group decision making.

11. Change is an important aspect of administrative work. Discuss the necessary steps for organizational change and development.

12. Define the techniques available to interventionists involved in organizational change and development.

Cases and Exercises

1. Divide your class into groups of three. Taking turns, have one person choose a topic from the list that follows and begin a conversation with the group. Try to follow the rules of effective communication.

   a. You are short of cash and want to take a winter vacation to an island off the coast of Mexico. You need to borrow at least $300 for the trip. You are pretty sure you can pay it back in three months.

   b. The two classmates you are talking with have been working with you on a class project. Actually, the problem is that they haven't been working! You have to do something to get them busy, or your grade will suffer. You need at least a "B" in the course to graduate.

   c. You have been working in behalf of the homeless in your community for the past two years. A march on Washington has been scheduled for next week, and a bus has been chartered to take people from your community to Washington, at a cost of $83 each. The problem is that unless you can find two more people to make the trip, the bus won't go. You want to convince your two friends to go with you.

2. Imagine that you are an administrative assistant to the director of the Department of Social Services in your state government. The director is interested in starting a new quality-circles program and wants to send a letter to all the managers and employees in the department describing the new program and enlisting their support. You have been asked to draft the letter. Using the information about quality circles in Chapter 8, draft an appropriate letter.

   After everyone in the class has drafted a letter, each draft should be shared with and analyzed by at least one other student. Your analysis should take into account the specifics of the situation (what should be said, how much should be said, how it should be said) as well as the more general Six Cs of effective communications listed in this chapter.

3. Divide the class into task groups of five persons each, with three observers assigned to each group. The task groups should complete the following task:

   List what you consider the five most important guidelines for effectively managing a large organization.

After the task group completes its work, the observers should lead a discussion of the group dynamics they observed in the work of the task group.

For observers only: During the discussion, you should silently watch the discussion and take notes about the operation of the group. Try to identify patterns of group development such as those presented in the chapter. Pay special attention to shifting patterns of leadership and communications. If this same group were to perform a similar task, what would you suggest to improve its effectiveness?

4. Divide the class into groups of three. Have one person in each group play the role of Chris, the supervisor, and another play the role of Lynn, the employee. (Each person should read only his or her own role description and not that of the other person.) The third person in each group should observe the discussion between Chris and Lynn, then comment on the motivation strategies employed. The scene begins as Lynn walks into Chris's office and says, "Someone said you wanted to see me."

Chris: You are twenty-eight years old and recently received your MPA from a fairly prestigious school in the East. You have worked for the federal government for four years, moving rapidly from a presidential management internship to your current position supervising a small unit that produces health and safety brochures for industry. Lynn has worked with the agency for twenty-three years as a design specialist. Throughout this period, from what you understand, Lynn has done an excellent job. In the few months you have been with the agency, however, you have noticed a decided drop in both the amount and quality of Lynn's work. With a heavy workload anticipated over the next several months, you decide that you have to do something to improve Lynn's performance. You have asked that he come in to visit.

Lynn: You have worked for twenty-three years as a design specialist for a small federal government unit that produces health and safety brochures for industry. Throughout your career, you have taken great pride in your work and have done an excellent job. Over the last few months, however, you have been increasingly troubled by painful back spasms, the source of which you have not been able to identify. The problem with your back has triggered a lot of concerns about your health, your age, your work. Although you haven't shared these concerns with anyone, you find that you spend long periods daydreaming about them. Even drinking a few martinis each evening hasn't calmed your fears. You still enjoy your design work, but somehow the projects you have had recently just don't seem all that exciting. What's worse, your supervisor, a kid probably half your age, has been hinting that your work may not be up to par.

5. Consider the following case. You have recently been appointed head of a new agency established to monitor pollution emissions from coal-based power plants throughout the Midwest. The data you collect will have a direct impact on an anticipated presidential decision concerning "acid rain" in the Northeast and Canada. You must try to develop the most comprehensive and precise measures possible, then monitor as many plants as you reasonably can during the relatively short period prior to the presidential decision.

Your staff, most of whom have been in the pollution control field much longer than you and are highly committed to the goals of your agency, have been arguing that a new piece of equipment, an Emission Systems Monitoring Instrument (ESMI), is the only device that is capable of precise measurements of the particular pollutants with which you are concerned. The problem is that the ESMI is both extremely costly and would require nearly half the time you have available just to be delivered. You are skeptical about whether the ESMI is worth the cost, but even more concerned that its limited availability will mean that you will fail to meet your deadline. You also think though you are not sure that the rough estimates generated by the existing equipment will be sufficient for the purposes of your report to the president. Do you go ahead with the existing equipment, or do you buy the ESMI?

Using the Vroom-Yetton model for decisions about delegation, work through the various aspects of this problem to determine the appropriate level and pattern of delegation.

For Additional Reading

Bass, Bernard M., and Bruce J. Avolio, eds. *Improving Organizational Effectiveness through Transformational Leadership*. Thousand Oaks, CA: Sage Publications, 1993.

Bechard, Richard. *Changing the Essence: The Art of Creating and Leading Fundamental Change in Organizations*. San Francisco: Jossey-Bass, 1992.

Denhardt, Robert B. *The Pursuit of Significance: Strategies for Managerial Success in Public Organizations*. Belmont, CA: Wadsworth, 1993.

Fischer, Roger, and William Ury. *Getting to Yes*. 2d ed. New York: Penguin Books, 1991.

Gortner, Harold F., Julianne Mahler, and Jeanne Bell Nicholson. *Organization Theory: A Public Perspective*. Pacific Grove, CA: Brooks/Cole, 1987.

National Academy of Public Administration. *Leading People in Change: Empowerment, Commitment, Accountability*. Washington, DC: National Academy, 1993.

Stewart, Debra W., and G. David Garson. *Organizational Behavior and Public Management*. New York: Marcel Dekker, 1983.

Vroom, Victor H., and Arthur G. Jago. *The New Leadership*. Englewood Cliffs, NJ: Prentice Hall, 1988.

Chapter 12

THE FUTURE OF THE PUBLIC SERVICE

For those considering work in the public service, whether for a relatively short period or for an entire career, several considerations may shape your thinking. As we have noted, the rewards of public service are not likely to be primarily financial. Salaries in most public organizations lag somewhat behind comparable salaries in business or industry. At the same time, however, those in public organizations are likely to be given a broader range of responsibilities earlier in their careers than their counterparts in business or industry. Moreover, the challenges and complexities of public service provide a special excitement that comes from being a part of unfolding major events—local, state, national, or even international.

If you want to be a part of what's happening in a changing society, then the public service is the place for you. Think about the incredible variety of work in the public sector. Public managers are key actors in foreign affairs, the human services, environmental policy, educational reform, the space program, and an endless variety of other important areas. Indeed, it is fair to say that every major local, state, national, or international issue now being discussed will provide challenges and opportunities for public managers in the future. If you are interested in meaningful work—work that makes a difference in people's lives—then you should find involvement in the public service quite appealing.

THE CHANGING IMAGE OF THE PUBLIC SERVICE

Throughout most of our country's history, public service has been recognized as an important undertaking that contributes to the betterment of society, supported by citizens and politicians alike. Unfortunately, for the past twenty-five years or so, support has wavered. From the late 1960s through the middle 1980s, the public service seemed to be under fairly constant attack. Through the candidacies of both Jimmy Carter and Ronald Reagan, national politicians of both parties organized their campaigns at least in part around attacks on Washington and the bureaucracy. Public administrators were criticized as both unresponsive and overly responsive—unresponsive to the common citizen and overly responsive to special interests. Public organizations were accused of being highly ineffective and inefficient, failing to achieve their objectives and wasting enormous sums of public funds.

Fortunately, the environment of the public service has changed considerably over the past several years, leading us to be somewhat more optimistic about its future image. Both the Bush and Clinton presidencies have been far more supportive of the federal public service, with Clinton involving many career public servants in designing his major management change program, the National Performance Review. In addition, part of the more positive perspective on government was brought about as the result of policy and program shifts in response to questions about government activism; part reflects a growing acceptance of the initiatives that gave rise to dissent; and part is the reemergence of a positive view of government. In addition, the emergence of state and local governments as both significant and professional in their dealings with the public has had a positive effect.

In policy areas, over the past decade, Americans have seen tax reductions and tax reform at the federal level, as well as tax limitations at the state and local levels. These actions have helped to mitigate the view that the government tax machine is running wild. In addition, after years of soaring budget deficits, the Clinton administration seems to have brought that issue at least somewhat under control. Similarly, throughout the last four presidential administrations, there has been a move to deregulate certain activities. Some areas (such as transportation) were significantly deregulated, while others were put under special scrutiny by the Office of Management and Budget. In general, an impression developed that excessive government intervention was being brought under control.

Finally, the political climate has been changing, even to the point that we might suggest the reemergence of a positive view of government. Such a view has been most evident at the state and local levels. In several important areas—notably education, economic development, and environmental concerns—the states were taking positive actions. And, at the same time, public confidence in state and local governments was growing.

Moreover, with growing national concern about such problems as AIDS, hazardous waste, ocean dumping, the greenhouse effect, drugs, foreign competition, the homeless, and child care for working families, we might even speculate that a new era of national action is on the horizon. Indeed, the success of the Clinton administration in reducing the size of government and the size of the federal deficit, while at the same time encouraging substantial economic growth may permit the beginning of a more activist era, as well as one in which the men and women who constitute the public service will be treated with greater dignity and respect.

These efforts in support of the public service return our country to a long-standing tradition. At other periods—and even today in other countries—the public service has been considered a proud and honorable profession. John F. Kennedy's inaugural statement continues to have relevance today. Recall that Kennedy said, "Ask not what your country can do for you, ask what you can do for your country." In another speech, Kennedy amplified the point: "Let the public service be a proud and lively career. And let every man and woman who works in any area of our national government, in any branch at any level, be able to say with pride and honor in future years: I served the United States Government in that hour of our nation's need." Those who work in the field of public administration at all levels of government carry forward that long and proud tradition.

EFFORTS TO SUPPORT THE PUBLIC SERVICE

Despite recent attacks on the public service, more and more people are coming to recognize its tradition of excellence. Recognition of the importance of public service has been fostered by several groups and organizations, among them the American Society for

Public Administration. Always an advocate of public service, a decade ago, ASPA developed a "National Campaign for the Public Service," to promote the dignity and worth of the public service. Activities of ASPA's National Campaign for the Public Service have included joining with other groups, such as the Public Employees Roundtable, in publicizing the benefits and contributions of public servants, developing award programs and other forms of recognition for outstanding public officials, and developing curriculum projects at elementary and secondary school levels to introduce young people to the public service and the benefits of public-service careers.

One particularly prestigious body that actively supported the public service was the National Commission on the Public Service, chaired by former Federal Reserve Board Chairman Paul A. Volcker. The commission was formed in 1987 following a symposium in Washington, D.C., "A National Public Service for the Year 2000." Those at the symposium concluded that a private, nonprofit organization should be assembled to prepare action recommendations to the president and Congress on what many saw as a "quiet crisis in government." The group felt that "too many of the best of the nation's senior executives are ready to leave government, and not enough of its most talented young people are willing to join." Moreover, conferees felt that "this erosion in the attractiveness of the public service at all levels—most specifically in the federal civil service—undermines the ability of government to respond effectively to the needs and aspirations of the American people, and ultimately damages the democratic process itself" (National Commission, 1989). Following a period of study and deliberation, the commission made the following general recommendations (see also Box 12.1):

First, the president and Congress must provide the essential environment for effective leadership and public support.

Second, educational institutions and the agencies of government must work to enlarge the base of talent available for, and committed to, public service.

Third, the American people should demand first-class performance and the highest ethical standards, and, by the same token, must be willing to provide what is necessary to attract and retain needed talent.

Specifically, the commission called upon the president and the Congress to:

Take action now by word and deed to rebuild public trust in government.

Clear away obstacles to the ability of the president to attract talented appointees from all parts of the society.

Make more room at senior levels of departments and agencies for career executives.

Provide a framework within which those federal departments and agencies can exercise greater flexibility in managing programs and personnel.

Encourage a stronger partnership between presidential appointees and career executives.

Develop more student awareness of, and educational training for, the challenges of government and public service.

BOX 12.1

Main Conclusions of the Volcker Commission

The central message of this report of the Commission on the Public Service is both simple and profound, both urgent and timeless. In essence, we call for a renewed sense of commitment by all Americans to the highest traditions of the public service—to a public service responsive to the political will of the people and also protective of our constitutional values; to a public service able to cope with complexity and conflict and also able to maintain the highest ethical standards; to a public service attractive to the young and talented from all parts of our society and also capable of earning the respect of all our citizens.

A great nation must demand no less. The multiple challenges thrust upon the Government of the United States as we approach the twenty-first century can only reinforce the point. Yet, there is evidence on all sides of an erosion of performance and morale across government in America. Too many of our most talented public servants—those with the skills and dedication that are the hallmarks of an effective career service—are ready to leave. Too few of our brightest young people—those with the imagination and energy that are essential for the future—are willing to join.

Meanwhile, the need for a strong public service is growing, not lessening. Americans have always expected their national government to guarantee their basic freedoms and provide for the common defense. We continue to expect our government to keep the peace with other nations, resolve differences among our people, pay the bills for needed services, and honor the people's trust by providing the highest levels of integrity and performance.

At the same time, Americans now live in a stronger, more populous nation, a nation with unprecedented opportunity But they also live in a world of enormous complexity and awesome risks. Our economy is infinitely more open to international competition, our currency floats in a worldwide market, and we live with complex technologies beyond the understanding of any single human mind. Our diplomacy is much more complicated, and the wise use of our unparalleled military power more difficult. And for all our scientific achievements, we are assaulted daily by new social, environmental, and health issues almost incomprehensible in scope and impact issues like drugs, AIDS, and global warming.

Faced with these challenges, the simple idea that Americans must draw upon talented and dedicated individuals to serve us in government is uncontestable. America must have a public service that can both value the lessons of experience and appreciate the requirements for change; a public service that both responds to political leadership and respects the law; a public service with the professional skills and the ethical sensitivity America deserves.

SOURCE: Excerpted from The National Commission on the Public Service, *Leadership for America: Rebuilding the Public Service* (Washington, DC, 1989), 1–2.

Develop new channels for spreading the word about government jobs and the rewards of public service.

Enhance the efforts to recruit top college graduates and those with specific professional skills for government jobs.

Simplify the hiring process.

Increase the representation of minorities in public service.

Build a pay system that is both fair and competitive.

Rebuild the government's chief personnel agency to give it the strength and mandate it needs.

Set higher goals for government performance and productivity.

Provide more effective training and executive development.

Improve government working conditions.

While the Volcker Commission focused on the federal government, a more recent National Commission on the State and Local Public Service examined other levels of government and came to similar conclusions. The commission, chaired by former Mississippi Governor William F. Winter, pointed out that the 15 million people who work at the state and local level do much of the real work of domestic governance. Members of the commission agreed that some important institutional changes were necessary in order for these people to meet the challenges of the future. Their proposals call for movement away from the old rule-bound bureaucratic governments of the past to a new, more responsive system. Among the recommendations of the commission were the following:

Strengthen executive authority to act by reducing the number of independently elected cabinet-level officials.

Temper the fragmentation of government by consolidating or eliminating as many overlapping or underperforming units as possible though a "base-closure" approach.

Use the executive budget approach and give state and local executives more opportunity to have their program considered as a whole in the legislative process.

Flatten the bureaucracy by reducing the number of management layers between the top and bottom of agencies and thinning the ranks of the managers who remain.

Deregulate government by (1) reforming the civil service, including reducing use of veterans' preference and seniority; (2) streamlining the procurement process; and (3) making the budgeting process more flexible.

Create a learning government by (1) restoring employee training and education budgets; (2) creating a new skills package for all employees; (3) basing pay increases on skills, not time in position; (4) insisting on a new kind of problem-solving manager, not merely a paper passer; and (5) encouraging a new style of labor-management communication.

Open the books on government by providing detailed information on campaign financing and lobbying.

Limit the political fund-raising season to six months before an election, and limit the use of carryover campaign funds.

Encourage citizen problem solving by experimenting with citizen liaison offices and setting up a national service corps.

Begin to deal with the financing crisis in health care, with the federal government leading, following, or getting out of the way (National Commission, 1993).

With the efforts of groups such as ASPA, the Volcker Commission, and the Winter Commission, and with renewed support of political leaders at the national, state, and local levels, we can expect the reemergence of a greater sense of respect and appreciation for the work of those engaged in public service at all levels. The work of the public service, the work of building a better world, requires the best possible talent and deserves both commitment and support. As the Volcker Commission puts it, "A great nation must demand no less" (National Commission, 1989, p. 1).

TRENDS IN THE PUBLIC SERVICE

The challenges that will face those in the public service over the coming years are substantial, for they not only require resolving important public-policy problems, but resolving them in a way that restores and then maintains public confidence. The efforts to restore meaning and integrity to the public service are much needed in our society, but they should be accompanied by a clear understanding of several important trends in our field that are reshaping the values and commitments of public service itself. What are the major trends that those entering the public service in the next decades are likely to experience?

ECONOMIC CHANGES AND REDEFINING GOVERNMENT

First, remember that a significant redefinition of the public service is now taking place. Note specifically that changing economic conditions are affecting both the mission and structure of the public enterprise. Our economy is shifting in several ways from a production base to a service base, from a national base to a global base, and from a growing public commitment to a limited commitment. In each case, there are direct implications for those in the public service:

Challenges face public managers in areas where traditional industries, such as steel or timber, have suddenly declined, as "high tech" and "high touch" have become banners for economic growth.

Challenges face those at the state and local levels who must play new and important roles in economic development, including international economic development, which may require them to know as much about business decisions in Japan as in their own state capital.

Challenges face those operating public programs, especially in the human services, who have found government spending severely restricted at a time when the need for the services seems ever increasing.

Our economy is presenting important challenges to government, but in responding to these challenges, government is not alone. The challenges have led to new ways of thinking about public/private relationships in the provision of public services. As a result, public-service work is no longer the work only of government, but an effort in which governmental agencies, nonprofit and third-sector organizations, and corporate and business interests participate. Consider these examples:

In many states, the number of persons employed by private security forces exceeds the number employed by local police departments.

In some cities, the chamber of commerce is so involved in public programs that it receives more funding from government than it receives from private business.

In major urban areas, less than half of human services are delivered by government; the majority are delivered by nonprofit and private agencies.

Some of these trends, such as privatization and contracting for specific goods and services, are becoming familiar; others are quite distinctive, as they involve third parties' discretion in the use of public authority and in spending of public funds. This development suggests a significant reshaping of the public service and raises serious questions about equity and accountability in the management of public programs.

Trends associated with "reinventing government" and the National Performance Review reflect more recent responses to our changing social and economic condition. We have noted that the reform agenda stems from the belief that government has failed to keep pace with the dynamic environment in the postindustrial world. Consequently, the reinvention movement already has had a dramatic impact on the character and processes of government organizations at all levels. And, given the attention this reform movement has received, such trends promise to continue into the future.

An important consideration with respect to reinvention and "the new public management" relates to the application of entrepreneurial practices and business values in the public service. While transforming the government-citizen relationship to economic terms—that is, viewing the citizen as a customer—may generate cost savings and lead to more streamlined public organizations, the question remains as to what the long-term impact will be for issues of citizenship and public participation. For although creating a government that "does more with less" may produce a stronger bottom line, it could have harmful effects for issues of citizen engagement with the institutions of governance.

GLOBALIZATION

Second, changing economic conditions have combined with technological developments to make the international dimensions of public administration more important than ever. Understanding the activities of political and administrative officials in other countries is important not only for those who will spend part of their careers outside the United States, but also for those who will work at home. Increasingly, city managers, for example, find that to be effective in local economic development activities, they must be experts in international business. But global interdependencies will affect us in other ways as well; for example, the deforestation in Brazil, Africa, and the Philippines will directly affect the quality of our own environment. And, of course, we cannot overlook our obligation to help reduce poverty and hunger throughout the world.

Several diverse—indeed, competing—views have emerged relating to this globalization trend. They range from a critical perspective, in which the trend is seen as an attempt by developed nations to introduce Western values into other regions, to what supporters believe to be a chance to extend employment opportunities and wealth creation into impoverished nations. This latter view suggests that, over time, all of us in the global village will benefit from the forces of globalization and the internationalization of economic markets.

NETWORKING

For information concerning international perspectives on governance and public administration, visit the OECD (http://www.oecd.org) or the United Nations (http://www.un.org/ecosocdev/). Local issues on a global scale, including decentralization and sustainable development, can be researched online at the ICMA (http://www.icma.org/resources/index.htm) or at the International City Government Resource Centre (http://www.geocities.com/).

The impact of globalization on public administration should not be underestimated. However, relating to the internationalization process is a pattern which carries perhaps even greater implications: decentralization. Central governments increasingly are handing over new powers and responsibilities to local and regional authorities. Whether triggered by declining revenues at the national level, or the nation-state's diminished power-base, the result has been growing demand for services and decision-making by subnational administrations. And, in many cases, these administrations lack the capacity and resources to deal effectively with their newfound authority.

To better understand these trends, and what they mean for public administration, the development of more globalized, comparative forms of analysis will be critical. Such analysis serves both as a source of understanding international issues, as well as enhancing the way we deal with issues in our own communities. So, as we continue to live in our "global village," we will be challenged to deal with opportunities and threats that defy national boundaries. Our systems of governance, consequently, will need to reflect our concern for the public interest—both at home and abroad.

TECHNOLOGY AND THE WORK ENVIRONMENT

A third area of concern is the changing environment in which public servants work. New people and new values are entering the public workplace. Greater diversity in public agencies has had important and positive impacts on the values of those agencies. Public organizations have taken on entirely new shapes, a feat that would have been impossible with the established, more traditional views of organizing that characterized public bureaucracies in the past. In turn, this diversity has contributed to important changes in the way we understand leadership, as diverse cultural and organizational views become translated into more equitable, power-sharing systems of authority (see Box 12.2). One hopes that present trends toward equity and involvement will continue.

Similarly, we have experienced a transformation in the public workplace brought on by new forms of technology. The influence of information technology, in particular, on how we conduct the public's business has been remarkable, and there is no reason to expect that the technological revolution is over. Pressure to integrate work

BOX 12.2

Global Perspectives on the Future of Public Administration

The UN General Assembly recently opened a dialogue on the importance of public administration in building civil society and ensuring sustainable development worldwide. The following statements by discussion participants, which appeared in the UN press release, "Good Government Cited as Positive Stimulus to Progress, as Assembly Continues Public Administration Debate" (April 17, 1996), give a snapshot of the global dimensions of public administration:

S. R. Insanally (Guyana) said that in recent years there had been a marked tendency to diminish the importance of public administration. That accompanied the belief that more things could be left to the "magic hand of the market." In some countries, he added, "it even became fashionable to see government as a problem, to denounce 'big' government." Economic progress was due, however, both to good public administration and to individual initiative, which good governments have actively facilitated and fostered, he said.

Soliman Awaad (Egypt) said public administration was one of the main means through which governments could respond to the wishes of their people. State administrative organs were faced with the burden of seeking to promote social and economic development, preserve the environment, control overpopulation, and provide employment for increasing numbers of young people.

continued

continued from previous page

Joseph Chiteyeye (Malawi) said that his country had implemented a number of development programs that were aimed at raising the standard of living of its people. He said one of the government's roles in that respect was to mobilize resources, both locally and in the donor community, which could be provided directly to local communities for the construction of such things as schools, water schemes and health centers.

Gerhard Walter Henze (Germany) said public administration had to be based on the rule of law and democracy. Transparency and accountability for all public institutions were essential to combat all forms of mismanagement and corruption.

Mehmet Atalay (Turkey) said that public administration and development were inseparable. Since 1980, Turkey had applied an outward-oriented and private sector–based development strategy, parallel to the major trends in global conditions. The succeeding Turkish governments recognized the need for privatization, development of new markets, decentralization, and accountability, among other measures. All of those had now become pivotal issues in the field of public administration in the world today.

Ascar Aitmatov (Kyrgyzstan) said that evidently, as demonstrated by the General Assembly's dedicating a resumed session to the theme of public administration, "we have come to the stage where the need for a fundamental review of that role is urgent" and more apparent than ever. Training was one of the most urgent needs; the government's administration and management system had not kept pace with the changes in modern society. The earlier predominance of central planning meant that many public servants had technical skills, but almost no training on policy analysis, evaluation, or modern implementation methods. "New management methods and techniques are almost unknown," he said.

Ramtane Lamamra (Algeria) said that, since independence, Algeria had sought to establish solid institutions which could lay the groundwork for an economic and social progress. In that process, a web of industries had been set up and the needs of a deprived population had been addressed. Free enterprise and private initiative had been encouraged. The challenges facing public administration today called for a refocusing towards promoting the well-being of all society. Attention was being devoted to preserving macroeconomic stability, achieving national consensus in an open society, and restructuring the state's presence in the economic arena.

Alyaksandr M. Sychou (Belarus) said his country had set itself a series of tasks to effect the move from a planned to a market economy. The effectiveness of public administration had been a key factor in the success of that transition effort in Belarus. Reform of the public administration currently involved focusing on leading-edge technology, while stimulating long-term capital investment and direct foreign investment.

Diallo Amadou Ousmane (Mauritania) said that after independence, his country found itself confronted with the urgent need to build a nation state. This required the rapid organization of civil society and the building of the appropriate state structures; it then had to take over the key sectors of the economy. The state thus found itself as chief employer and chief driving force in the economy at all levels, and in development, he continued. The government set up a broad program of structural adjustment, in the context of the economic policies of the time. To achieve the decentralization and institutional development, the government focused on modernizing its administration and strove for the establishment of a pluralistic democracy.

Vianney Shumbusho (Rwanda) said the recent war and catastrophic genocide of 1994 had resulted in destruction of approximately one-seventh of the population, most of whom were in the productive labor force. It had also involved destruction of infrastructure and equipment, the collapse of institutions, a severe setback in agricultural and industrial activities, an exodus of between 1 million and 2 million people, a demanding inflow of former refugees for voluntary repatriation, and a traumatized surviving population.

Imre Verebelyi (Hungary) said that Hungary was a European country in transition from the previous totalitarian, centralized, one-party system. It was currently undergoing "an administrative revolution, rather than a simple reform." This administrative revolution focused on the changes of basic functions, role, and structure of public administration. The institutional side of change was underlined and emphasized, while the operational side had been "rather pushed into the background."

Joseph Cassar (Malta) stressed the important role played by public administrations in promoting economic growth and sustainable development. There had been unprecedented political, economic, and technological changes in recent years, which also impacted on public administrations. The United Nations played a pivotal role as a clearinghouse and service-oriented catalyst for governments to improve their public management capacities.

SOURCE: United Nations. "Good Government Cited as Positive Stimulus to Progress, as Assembly Continues Public Administration Debate." Press release issued by the United Nations General Assembly, Press Release #GA/9062, 17 April 1996.

processes and create more flexible, networked organizations will continue to fuel the drive for more effective forms of communicating and sharing information. We will, more and more, work in virtual groups, with much of our interaction being transferred into cyberspace.

Of course, the most prevalent argument for technology remains grounded in the more instrumental purpose that is, the use of technology to enhance government performance. The changing character of government organizations reflect this purpose, as virtually all systems and work processes feature some form of automation. However, we should not lose sight of the fact that technology may also help us achieve more value-oriented goals of public service. Technology in the form of civic networks and other resources may help us shift the orientation of our public organizations to be more external in nature. We may, through our emerging technology, be able to enjoy more meaningful forms of engagement with citizens.

Still, as this trend develops, it raises important concerns for the human consequences of advanced technology. How technology affects the relationship between government workers and their clients, how to cope with the seemingly inevitable impersonality of the information age, and how to resolve the difficult ethical questions relating to privacy and abuse—these and many other issues will continue to confound us over the coming decades as the technological society pursues its present course.

THE ROLE OF CITIZENS IN THE GOVERNANCE PROCESS

The fourth issue involves the participation of citizens in the governance process and the notion of civil society. More and more, public decisions are being made through meaningful interaction with citizens. This means that citizens are playing an important role not as recipients of government services but as contributors to the policies and programs that affect their lives. In many ways, this emerging form of citizen participation represents a return to important principles that underlie our system of democracy. It appears that we are becoming more concerned with equity and justice, as opposed to merely efficiency and performance. Yet the change from the more traditional representative democracy to a direct form poses unique challenges for elected and administrative officials.

As it stands, many public administrators view citizen participation as a source of tension. That is, they associate civic engagement with public hearings, legal and administrative arbitration, and other formal mechanisms that tend to be time consuming and highly confrontational. Public involvement, accordingly, comes to represent a hindrance to efficient management. In turn, public involvement is limited to being a source of legitimation, through hearings and similar forums, of decisions that have already been made through more rational approaches. However, such limited forms of civic engagement not only result in policies which are detached from the actual needs of affected populations, but over time create barriers between the local institutions of governance and citizens.

In recent years, a few public officials have started to open decision-making and governance processes to more substantive forms of engagement. In Orange County, Florida, for example, local officials have incorporated principles of direct democracy into the processes of government through a program called "Citizens First!" "Citizens First!" starts with the fundamental ideal that people acting as citizens must demonstrate their concern for the larger community, their commitment to matters that go beyond short-term interests, and their willingness to assume personal responsibility for what happens in their neighborhoods and the community. After all, these are among the defining elements of effective and responsible citizenship. But the theme also cuts in another way, suggesting that those in government must be willing to listen and act in a responsive manner. Only by pursuing this "two-way street" between citizens and government will the most healthy relationship between government and citizens be brought about. For those in public administration, the challenge will be, particularly in this era of reinvention, to sustain these meaningful forms of engagement and civil society.

THE ETHICAL CHALLENGES FACING THE PUBLIC SERVICE

Establishing a proper ethical basis for public action is itself one of the most important challenges facing the public service. If your generation has one significant contribution to make to the development of the public service, it may be to identify and elaborate the moral and ethical dimensions of public administration and to assert moral leadership.

As we have seen, early writers in the field portrayed public administration primarily as a managerial concern with the technical processes of implementing public policy. Over the years, public administrators have developed considerable skill in managing public programs—probably more than they are usually given credit for.

Others soon came to recognize that public administration is also a political concern—that administrators at all levels are deeply involved in shaping public policy. Despite recent rhetoric in Washington, there is every reason to expect that those in public organizations will increasingly be called upon to do more than simply respond to legislative mandate; they will be asked to identify and to articulate important public interests.

Beyond a view of public administration as a managerial or a political concern, public administration today is increasingly an ethical concern. Indeed, all the "spontaneous" little actions you will take as an administrator will carry important value implications. At the root of every act of every public servant, whether in developing or executing public policy, lies a moral or ethical question.

What does it mean, then, to recognize public service as not only a managerial and political concern but also as a moral and ethical concern? For one thing, it means that public administrators must demonstrate in their own actions the highest standards of behavior. Beyond that, to see the public service as a moral and ethical concern requires recognition that every action an administrator takes involves an effort to discover or to clarify the public interest.

The future public servant will likely be both active in policy development and responsive to the public interest. Our constitutional structure not only permits but encourages an active executive and administrative role. Even more important is the implicit philosophical directive of the Constitution that public service is a special calling in a democracy and that those who participate in the public service, regardless of background or occupation, are guardians of a public trust.

This point is most critical at a time when our definition of public service is shifting. As we have noted, the public service is no longer merely that group of political and administrative officials employed by government agencies. Public service today involves a wide range of private and nonprofit organizations in the delivery of public goods and services. This development raises managerial concerns, political concerns, and most of all, moral and ethical concerns. Under these conditions, public administrators must assume leadership in establishing a high moral tone for the public service generally. In contrast to the often-heard advice that public administrators should follow the model of business, we might propose just the opposite—that public organizations and the values and commitments they represent should become models for all organizations, at least those involved in the management of public programs.

For the public service to regain its proper role in our society, we will have to establish and maintain throughout government and the public service a true commitment to the values of democracy. Trust in the public service and the public willingness to participate in the work of government will occur only if the public is convinced that those in office, whether political or administrative, seek the public interest (not merely their own), and that they do so with skill and responsibility. Only when our commitment to democratic practices and ideals is clear to all will we once again be able to establish public service as the highest calling in our society.

Commitment to democratic ideals involves concerns such as responsiveness and involvement, but also commitment to equity and justice. Think for a moment of the reasons that bring people to the public service. No doubt high on the list would be "concern for the well-being of others." At one point in our history, we seemed to feel that the primary measure of success of the public service was the elimination of human suffering. Public officials are still at the forefront of dealing with the complex and difficult issues of homelessness, poverty, and drug addiction. Perhaps more than any other group, public administrators are uniquely situated to see and understand these concerns. They certainly should be able to pinpoint the failures of past policies, to suggest alternatives, and to work actively toward implementation with elected leaders. Indeed, they have a moral responsibility to do so.

A FINAL NOTE

The challenges to the public service are substantial and pose managerial, political, and ethical questions for all who participate in public programs. They will require careful analysis and effective action on the part of academics and practitioners in the field of public administration and beyond. Most of all, they are challenges that will require responsibility both in the sense of acting responsibly and in the sense of accepting responsibility for our ideas and actions. The frontiers of public service will present quite difficult personal and professional choices. But responsible public servants will find their solution very rewarding. Albert Schweitzer once said, "I don't know where you will go or what you will do, but the ones among you that will be most happy will be those who serve." We would only add that especially happy will be those who serve the public, well and faithfully.

Study Questions

1. Discuss some of the changes in the image of public service over the last thirty years.
2. What are some recommendations of the National Commission on the Public Service for attracting and retaining the "best and the brightest" in the public service?
3. Discuss future trends in the field of public administration.

Cases and Exercises

1. By most objective measures, public agencies are, on the average, highly productive—at least in comparison to their private-sector counterparts. (Obviously, there are wide variations in both sectors, but the general conclusion seems valid.) The general public, however, seems to have exactly the opposite impression—that government agencies are hopelessly inefficient and unproductive. Part of the problem seems to be that people are more critical of government in the abstract than where it directly touches their lives. In fact, one study found most people highly critical of the coldness and inefficiency of government in general, but highly complimentary of specific government employees with whom they had dealt most recently.

   In any case, there seems to be some disparity between image and reality—a disparity that is often quite damaging to the morale of the public workforce. Write an essay explaining why you think governments are considered less productive and less efficient than they really are. Consider the issue from several viewpoints. How would the issue appear from the perspective of a legislator? A public manager? A citizen? On the basis of your analysis, what should be done to improve the image of the public service?

2. In this chapter, we have considered a number of trends that are likely to affect the public service over the next decade or more. What do these trends mean in terms of the skills that individual public managers will require? Review once more the set of public management skills in Chapter 1, then, in small groups, discuss the following questions: What specific skills will public managers likely utilize more frequently in the future than in the past? What, if any, will be de-emphasized? To what extent will the demands of the future public service change the mix of conceptual, technical, and human skills needed for effective public management? Finally, how will the values that underlie the work of public managers shift as we move through the coming years?

For Additional Reading

Chandler, Ralph Clark. *A Centennial History of the American Administrative State.* New York: The Free Press, 1987.

Chrislip, David D., and Carl E. Larson. *Collaborative Leadership.* San Francisco: Jossey-Bass, 1994.

Denhardt, Robert B., and Edward T. Jennings, Jr. *The Revitalization of the Public Service.* Columbia: University of Missouri, 1987.

Goodsell, Charles T. *The Case for Bureaucracy.* 3d ed. Chatham, NJ: Chatham House, 1994.

Ingraham, Patricia W., and Donald F. Kettl. *Agenda for Excellence: Public Service in America.* Chatham, NJ: Chatham House, 1992.

Ingraham, Patricia W., and Barbara Romzek. *Governance and the Public Service: Rethinking the Research Agenda for Public Sector Change.* San Francisco: Jossey-Bass, 1994.

Lappe, Frances Moore, and Paul M. Du Bois, *The Quickening of America.* San Francisco: Jossey-Bass, 1994.

Lerner, Allan W., and John Wanat. *Public Administration: A Realistic Reinterpretation of Contemporary Public Management.* Englewood Cliffs, NJ: Prentice-Hall, 1991.

Mills, Claudia. *Values and Public Policy.* Fort Worth: Harcourt Brace, 1992.

National Commission on the Public Service. *Leadership for America.* Washington, DC: National Commission, 1989.

Nye, Philip D. Zelikow, and David C. King, eds. *Why People Don't Trust Government.* Cambridge, MA: Harvard University Press, 1997.

Thomas, John C. *Public Participation in Public Decisions.* San Francisco: Jossey-Bass, 1995.

Thompson, Frank J., ed. *Revitalizing State and Local Public Service: Strengthening Performance, Accountability, and Citizen Confidence.* National Commission on the State and Local Public Service, 1993.

Wamsley, Gary, et al. *Refounding Public Administration.* Newbury Park, CA: Sage Publications, 1990.

REFERENCES

Chapter One

Appleby, Paul. *Policy and Administration.* University, AL: University of Alabama Press, 1949.

Blumenthal, W. Michael. "Candid Reflections of a Businessman in Washington." In *Public Management,* by James L. Perry and Kenneth L. Kraemer. Palo Alto, CA: Mayfield Publishing, 1983.

Dimock, Marshall E. "Criteria and Objectives of Public Administration." In *The Frontiers of Public Administration,* edited by John M. Gaus, Leonard D. White, and Marshall E. Dimock, pp. 116–134. Chicago: University of Chicago Press, 1936.

Flanders, Loretta R., and Dennis Utterback. "The Management Excellence Inventory." *Public Administration Review* 45 (May/June 1985): 403–410.

Gulick, Luther. "Science, Values, and Public Administration." In *Papers on the Science of Administration,* edited by Luther Gulick and L. Urwick, pp. 189–195. New York: Institute of Public Administration, 1937.

Katz, Robert L. "Skills of an Effective Administrator." *Harvard Business Review* 52 (September/October 1974): 90–102.

Redford, Emmette S. *Democracy in the Administrative State.* New York: Oxford University Press, 1969.

Rosenbloom, David. *Public Administration.* New York: McGraw-Hill, 1993.

Rumsfeld, Donald. "A Politician-Turned-Executive Surveys Both Worlds." In *Public Management,* by James L. Perry and Kenneth L. Kraemer. Palo Alto, CA: Mayfield Publishing, 1983.

Simon, Herbert A., Donald W. Smithburg, and Victor A. Thompson. *Public Administration.* New York: Knopf, 1950.

White, Leonard D. *The Study of Public Administration.* New York: Macmillan, 1948.

Willoughby, W. F. *Principles of Public Administration.* Baltimore, MD: Johns Hopkins Press, 1927

Wilson, Woodrow. "The Study of Public Administration." *Political Science Quarterly* 2 (June 1887): 197–222.

Chapter Two

Abney, Glenn, and Thomas P. Lauth. "Councilmanic Intervention in Municipal Administration." *Administration and Society* 13, no. 4 (February 1982): 435–456.

Anderson, James E., David W. Brady, and Charles Bullock. *Public Policy and Politics in America.* Pacific Grove, CA: Brooks/Cole, 1984.

Archibald, Samuel J. "The Freedom of Information Act Revisited." *Public Administration Review* 39, no. 4 (July/August 1979): 311–317.

Behn, Robert D. "The Fortune 500 and the 50 States." Durham, NC: Institute of Policy Sciences and Public Affairs, Duke University (February 1990).

Bowman, Ann, and Richard C. Kearney. *The Resurgence of the States.* Englewood Cliffs, NJ: Prentice-Hall, 1986.

Caldwell, Lynton. *Administrative Theories of Hamilton and Jefferson.* Chicago: University of Chicago Press, 1944.

Cooper, Phillip J. "Due Process, the Burger Court, and Public Administration." *Southern Review of Public Administration* 6, no. I (Spring 1982): 65–98.

Cooper, Phillip J. *Public Law and Public Administration.* Palo Alto, CA: Mayfield Publishing, 1983.

Cooper, Phillip J. "Conflict or Constructive Tension: The Changing Relationship of Judges and Administrators." *Public Administration Review* 45, special issue (November 1985): 643–652.

Cooper, Phillip J. "By Order of the President." *Administration and Society* 18, no. 2 (August 1986): 233–262.

Crenson, Matthew A. *The Federal Machine.* Baltimore, MD: Johns Hopkins University Press, 1975.

Davidson, Roger H., and Walter J. Oleszek. *Congress and Its Members.* Washington, DC: Congressional Quarterly Press, 1990.

Dodge, William R. "The Emergence of Intercommunity Partnerships in the 1980s." *Public Management* (July 1988): 2–7.

Elling, Richard C. "State Legislative Casework and State Administrative Performance." *Administration and Society* 12, no. 3 (November 1980): 327–356.

Federal Administrative Procedures Source Book. 2d ed. Washington, DC: Administrative Conference of the United States. 1992.

Fisher, Louis. *Congressional Conflicts between Congress and the President.* 3d ed. Lawrence, KS: University Press of Kansas, 1991.

Gilmour, Robert S. "Agency Administration by Judiciary." *Southern Review of Public Administration* 6, no. I (Spring 1982): 26–42.

Henry, Nicholas. *Governing at the Grassroots.* Englewood Cliffs, NJ: Prentice-Hall, 1980.

Hill, Larry B. "The Citizen Participation-Representation Roles of American Ombudsmen." *Administration and Society* 13, no. 4 (February 1982).

Johannes, John R. *To Serve the People.* Lincoln: University of Nebraska Press, 1984.

Johnson, Stephen F. "The Legislative Veto in the States." *State Government* 56, no. 3 (1983): 99–102.

Karl, Barry D. *Executive Reorganization and Reform in the New Deal.* Cambridge, MA: Harvard University Press, 1963.

Kingdon, John W. *Agendas, Alternatives, and Public Policies.* Boston: Little, Brown, 1984.

Lowi, Theodore. "Four Systems of Policy, Politics, and Choice." *Public Administration Review* 32 (July/August 1972): 298–310.

McLaughlin, Curtis. *The Management of Nonprofit Organizations.* New York: Wiley, 1986.

Meier, Kenneth J. *Politics and the Bureaucracy.* 2d ed. Pacific Grove, CA: Brooks/Cole, 1987.

Municipal Year Book. Washington, DC: International City Management Association, 1992.

Nelson, Michael. "A Short, Ironic History of American National Bureaucracy." *Journal of Politics* 44, no. 3 (August 1982): 747–778.

PA Times (April 29, 1988): 1.

Reich, Robert B. "Public Administration and Public Deliberation: An Interpretive Essay." *Yale Law Review* 94 (1985): 1617–1641.

Ripley, Randall B., and Grace A. Franklin. *Congress, the Bureaucracy, and Public Policy.* 4th ed. Pacific Grove, CA: Brooks/Cole, 1987.

Rourke, John T. "The GAO: An Evolving Role." *Public Administration Review* 38 (July/August 1978): 453–457.

Walsh, Annmarie Hauck. *The Public's Business.* Cambridge, MA: MIT Press, 1978.

White, Leonard D. *The Federalists.* New York: Macmillan, 1948.

Wolf, Thomas. *The Nonprofit Organization.* Englewood Cliffs, NJ: Prentice Hall, 1984.

Young, Dennis R. *If Not for Profit, for What?* Lexington, MA: Lexington Books, 1983.

Chapter Three

Aldrich, Howard, and David A. Whetten. "Organization-sets, Action-sets, and Networks: Making the Most of Simplicity." In *Handbook of Organizational Design,* vol. 1, by Paul C. Nystrom and William H. Starbuck. Oxford: Oxford University Press, 1981.

Barlas, Stephen. "States, Locals Battle for ISTEA." *American City & County* 112 (March 1997): 12.

Beam, David R. "New Federalism, Old Realities." In *The Reagan Presidency and the Governing of America,* by Lester M. Salamon and Michael S. Lund. Washington, DC: The Urban Institute, 1984.

Beckman, Norman. "Developments in Federal-State Relations." In *The Book of the States, 1988–1989 Edition.* Lexington, KY: The Council of State Governments, 1988.

Berman, David. "State/Local Relations." In *Municipal Yearbook.* Washington, DC: International City Management Association, 1992.

Blackstone, Edwin, and Simon Hakim. "Private Ayes: A Tale of Four Cities." *American City & County* 112 (February 1997): 4–8.

Bowman, Ann O'M., and Michael A. Pagano. "The State of Federalism, 1989–1990." *Publius* 20 (Summer 1990): 1–25.

Bowman, Ann O'M., and Michael A. Pagano. "The State of American Federalism, 1991–1992." *Publius* 22 (Summer 1992): 1–20.

Brennen, David A. "Treasury Regulations and Judicial Deference in the Post-Chevron Era." *Georgia State University Law Review* 13 (February 1997): 387–430.

Carrington, Tim, and Edward T. Pound. "War Games." *The Wall Street Journal* (June 27, 1988): 1, 4.

Council of State Governments. *Private Practices: A Review of Privatization in State Government.* Lexington, KY: Council of State Governments, 1997.

Cooper, Phillip J., Linda P. Brady, Olivia Hidalgo-Lardeman, Albert Hyde, Katherine C. Naff, Steven J. Ott, and Harvey White. *Public Administration for the Twenty-First Century.* Fort Worth, TX: Harcourt Brace College Publishers, 1998.

Cooper, Phillip J. "Understanding What the Law Says about Administrative Responsibility." In *Handbook of Public Administration*, 2d ed., edited by James L. Perry. San Francisco: Jossey-Bass, 1996.

Eggers, William D. "There's No Place Like Home." *Policy Review* 83 (May/June 1997): 43–47.

Forester, John. "The Effects of the Elimination of General Revenue Sharing on U.S. Cities." Unpublished manuscript, 1988.

Gold, Steven D. "The Federal Role in Fiscal Stress." *Publius* 22 (Summer 1992): 33–47.

Gore, Al. *From Red Tape to Results: Creating a Government That Works Better and Costs Less. Report of the National Performance Review.* New York: Times Books, 1993.

Harter, Philip J. "The APA at Fifty: A Celebration, Not a Puzzlement." *Administrative Law Review* 48 (Summer 1996): 309–311.

Hatry, Harry P. *A Review of Private Approaches for Delivery of Public Services.* Washington, DC: The Urban Institute, 1983.

Howard, S. Kenneth. "A Message from Garcia." *Public Administration Review* 45, special issue (November 1985): 738–741.

Hult, Karen M., and Charles Walcott. *Governing Public Organizations.* Pacific Grove, CA: Brooks/Cole, 1990.

Kadlecek, James M. "Cooperation among Local Governments." *National Civic Review* 86 (Summer 1997): 175–179.

Katzen, Sally. "Administrative Perspectives on the 1995 Regulatory Reform Legislation." *Administrative Law Review* 48 (Summer 1996): 331–333.

Kettl, Donald F. *The Regulation of American Federalism.* Baton Rouge: Louisiana State University Press, 1983.

Kettl, Donald F. *Government by Proxy.* Washington, DC: CQ Press, 1988.

Kincaid, John. "From Cooperative to Coercive Federalism." *Annals of the AAPSS* 509 (May 1990): 139–159.

Kincaid, John. "Reinventing Federalism." *PA Times* 16, no. 2 (February 1, 1993).

Kincaid, John. "Dual to Coercive Federalism in American Intergovernmental Relations." In *Globalization and Decentralization: Institutional Contexts, Policy Issues, and Intergovernmental Relations in Japan and the United States*, edited by Jong S. Jun and Deil S. Wright. Washington, DC: Georgetown University, 1996.

Koch, Edward I. "The Mandate Millstone." *The Public Interest* 61 (Fall 1980): 42–58.

Kolderie, Ted. "Two Different Concepts of Privatization." *Public Administration Review* 46 (July/August 1986): 285–291.

Kostro, Charles. "The Road to Cheaper Services." *American City & County* 109 (August 1994): 16.

Kurtz, Howard. "In an Era of Reduced Federal Aid, Newark Stays Afloat." *The Washington Post National Weekly Edition* 5, no. 35 (June 20–26, 1988): 31–32.

MacManus, Susan. "Enough Is Enough," *State and Local Government Review* (Fall 1992): 103–111.

Meese, Edwin, III. "Taking Federalism Seriously." *Intergovernmental Perspective* 13 (Winter 1987): 8–10.

Murray, Sylvester. "Privatization: Myth and Potential." *Urban Resources* 2 (Summer 1985): 3–5.

Nathan, Richard P., Fred C. Doolittle, and associates. *Reagan and the States.* Princeton, NJ: Princeton University Press, 1987.

Nice, David C. *Federalism: The Politics of Intergovernmental Relations.* New York: St. Martin's Press, 1987.

Osborne, David, and Ted Gaebler. *Reinventing Government: How the Entrepreneurial Spirit is Transforming the Public Sector.* Reading, MA: Addison–Wesley, 1992.

Reagan, Michael D., and John G. Sanzone. *The New Federalism.* 2d ed. Oxford: Oxford University Press, 1981.

Reagan, Ronald. "Inaugural Address." Washington, DC, January 20, 1981.

Schwartz, Bernard. "Administrative Law Cases during 1994." *Administrative Law Review* 47 (Summer 1995): 355–371.

Schwartz, Bernard. "Administrative Law Cases during 1995." *Administrative Law Review* 48 (Summer 1996): 399–418.

Schwartz, Bernard. "Administrative Law Cases during 1996." *Administrative Law Review* 49 (Summer 1997): 519–548.

Stone, Charles F., and Isabel V. Sawhill. *Economic Policy in the Reagan Years.* Washington, DC: The Urban Institute, 1984.

Walker, David B. *Toward a Functioning Federalism.* Cambridge, MA: Winthrop, 1981.

Walker, David B. "The Advent of an Ambiguous Federalism and the Emergence of New Federalism III." *Public Administration Review* 56 (May/June 1996): 271–280.

Wallin, Bruce A. "The Need for Privatization Process: Lessons from Development and Implementation." *Public Administration Review* (January/February 1997): 11–20.

Wright, Deil S. "A Century of the Intergovernmental Administrative State." In *A Centennial History of the American Administrative State,* by Ralph Clark Chandler, pp. 219–260. New York: The Free Press, 1987.

Wright, Deil S. *Understanding Intergovernmental Relations.* 3d ed. Pacific Grove, CA: Brooks/Cole, 1988.

Zimmerman, Joseph F. "Changing State/Local Relationships." In *The Book of the States, 1988–1989 Edition.* Lexington, KY: The Council of State Governments, 1988.

Chapter Four

American Society for Public Administration. *Ethical Dilemmas.* Washington, DC: ASPA, n.d.

Arendt, Hannah. *Eichmann in Jerusalem.* New York: Viking Press, 1963.

Bailey, Stephen K. "Ethics and the Public Service." In *Public Administration and Democracy,* edited by Roscoe C. Martin. Syracuse, NY: Syracuse University Press, 1965.

Blum, Lawrence A. "Gilligan and Kohlberg: Implications for Moral Theory." *Ethics* (April 1988): 472–491.

Bowman, James S. "Ethical Issues for the Public Manager." In *Handbook of Organization Management,* edited by William B. Eddy, pp. 69–102. New York: Marcel Dekker, 1983.

Bowman, James S. "Whistle Blowing: Literature and Resource Materials." *Public Administration Review* 70 (May/June 1983): 271–276.

Congressional Quarterly Weekly. Washington, DC: Congressional Quarterly Press (March 6, 1993): 511.

Cooper, Terry L. *An Ethic of Citizenship for Public Administration.* Englewood Cliffs, NJ: Prentice Hall, 1991.

Cooper, Terry L., and N. Dale Wright, eds. *Exemplary Public Administrators.* San Francisco: Jossey-Bass, 1992.

Council of State Governments. *Book of the States, 1992–1993.* Lexington, KY: Council of State Governments, 1992.

DeGeorge, Richard T. *Business Ethics.* New York: Macmillan, 1982.

Denhardt, Kathryn G. *The Ethics of Public Service.* New York: Greenwood Press, 1988.

Denhardt, Kathryn G. "Managing Ethics." Unpublished manuscript, 1989.

Devroy, Ann. "Late for Appointments," *Washington Post* (March 12, 1993): 197.

Finer, Herman. "Administrative Responsibility in Democratic Government" In *Bureaucratic Power in National Politics,* edited by Frances Rourke, pp. 165–175. Boston: Little, Brown, 1972.

Fleishman, Joel L., and Bruce L. Payne. *Ethical Dilemmas and the Education of Policy Makers.* Hastings-On-Hudson, NY. The Hastings Center, 1980.

Friedrich, Carl J. "Public Policy and the Nature of Democratic Responsibility." In *Bureaucratic Power in National Politics,* edited by Frances J. Rourke, pp. 176–186. Boston: Little, Brown, 1972.

Hilberg, Raul. *The Destruction of the European Jews.* Chicago: Quadrangle Books, 1961.

Ignatius, David. "U.S. Civil Servants Are Cowed into Silence." *Manchester Guardian Weekly* (February 22, 1987): 15–16.

Kohlberg, Lawrence. "From Is to Ought." In *Cognitive Development and Epistemology,* edited by T. Mishel, pp. 151–235. New York: Academic Press, 1971.

Lewis, Carol. *The Ethical Challenge in Public Service.* San Francisco: Jossey-Bass, 1991.

Masters, Marick F., and Leonard Bierman. "The Hatch Act and the Political Activities of Federal Employee Unions." *Public Administration Review* (July/August 1985): 518–526.

McKeon, Richard. *Basic Works of Aristotle.* New York: Random House, 1941.

Meier, Kenneth J. *Regulation: Politics, Bureaucracy and Economics.* New York: St. Martin's Press, 1985.

Milgram, Stanley. *Obedience to Authority.* New York: Harper & Row, 1974.

Pastin, Mark. "The Thinking Manager's Toolbox." In *Ethical Insight, Ethical Action,* Washington, DC: International City Managers Association, 1988: 91–104.

President's Commission on Federal Ethics Law Reform. *To Serve With Honor: Report and Recommendations to the President.* Washington, DC: U.S. Department of Justice, 1989.

Rawls, John. *A Theory of Justice.* Cambridge, MA: Belnap Press of Harvard University Press, 1971.

Reich, Robert B. "Public Administration and Public Deliberation: An Interpretive Essay." *Yale Law Review* 94 (1985): 1617–1641.

Rubin, Hank. "Dimensions of Institutional Ethics." In *The Nonprofit Organization,* edited by David Gies, J. Steven Ott, and Jay Shafritz. Pacific Grove, CA: Brooks/Cole, 1990.

Time (May 25, 1987).

Tong, Rosemarie. *Ethics in Policy Analysis.* Englewood Cliffs, NJ: Prentice Hall, 1986.

Truelson, Judith A. "Protecting David from Goliath: On Blowing the Whistle on Systematic Corruption." *Dialogue* (Spring 1986): 1–23.

Washington Post (September 5, 1992).

Chapter Five

Axelrod, Donald. *Budgeting for Modern Government.* New York: St. Martin's Press, 1988.

Bahl, Roy. *Financing State and Local Government in the 1980s.* New York: Oxford University Press, 1984.

Berne, Robert, and Richard Schramm. *The Financial Analysis of Government.* Englewood Cliffs, NJ: Prentice Hall, 1986.

Berry, Mike, and Judy Ikerd. *Outcome Budgeting: Catawba, North Carolina.* Washington, DC: American Society for Public Administration, 1997.

Botner, Stanley B. "The Quiet Revolution in State Financial Management." *State and Local Government Review* 15 (Fall 1983): 134–139.

Botner, Stanley B. "Impact of Data Processing Techniques in Budgeting and Financial Management in Federal Nondefense Departments and Agencies." Unpublished manuscript, 1988a.

Botner, Stanley B. "A Presidential Item-Veto: Assessment of the Issues." *Economic and Policy Information* (University of Missouri) 31, no. 8, 1988b: 1–3.

Brown, Richard E., Thomas P. Gallagher, and Meredith C. Williams. *Auditing Performance in Government.* New York: Wiley, 1982.

Caiden, Naomi. "The Boundaries of Public Budgeting." *Public Administration Review* 45 (July/August, 1985): 495–502.

Congressional Quarterly Weekly. Washington, DC: Congressional Quarterly Press (March 20, 1993).

Council of State Governments. *Book of States, 1992–1993.* Lexington, KY: Council of State Governments, 1993.

Joyce, Philip G., and Robert D. Reischauer. "The Federal Line-Item Veto: What Is It and What Will It Do?" *Public Administration Review* 57 (March/April 1997): 95–104.

King, John L., James N. Danziger, Debora E. Kunkle, and Kenneth L. Kraemer. "In Search of the Knowledge Executive: Managers, Microcomputers, and Information Technology." *State and Local Government Review* 24, no. 2, Spring 1992: 48–57.

Kraemer, Kenneth L., William H. Dutton, and Alana Northrop. *The Management of Information Systems.* New York: Columbia University Press, 1981.

Lee, Robert D. "A Quarter Century of State Budgeting Practices." *Public Administration Review* 57 (March/April, 1997): 133–140.

Leloup, Lance T. *Budgetary Politics.* Brunswick, OH: King's Court Communications, 1977.

Levine, Charles H. "Organizational Decline and Cutback Management." In *Managing Fiscal Stress,* edited by Charles H. Levine, pp. 13–32. Chatham, NJ: Chatham House Publishers, 1980.

Levine, Charles H., Irene S. Rubin, and George G. Wolohojian. *The Politics of Retrenchment.* Beverly Hills, CA: Sage, 1981.

Lyden, Fremont J., and Marc Lindenberg. *Public Budgeting in Theory and Practice.* New York: Longman, 1983.

Lynch, Thomas D. *Public Budgeting in America.* 2d ed. Englewood Cliffs, NJ: Prentice Hall, 1985.

McGowan, Robert P., and Gary A. Lombardo. "Decision Support Systems in State Government." *Public Administration Review* 46, special issue (November 1986): 579–583.

Mikesell, John L., and Kurt C. Zorn. "State Lotteries as Fiscal Savior or Fiscal Fraud." *Public Administration Review* 46 (July/August 1986): 311–320.

Palmer, John L., and Isabel V. Sawhill. "Overview." In *The Reagan Record,* edited by John L. Palmer and Isabel V. Sawhill. Cambridge, MA: Ballinger, 1984.

Pechman, Joseph A. *Federal Tax Policy.* 4th ed. Washington, DC: The Brookings Institution, 1983.

Pfiffner, James P. *The President, the Budget, and Congress.* Boulder, CO: Westview Press, 1979.

Pyhrr, Peter A. "The Zero-Base Approach to Government Budgeting." *Public Administration Review* 37 (January/February 1977): 1–8.

Rubin, Barry M. "Information Systems for Public Management." *Public Administration Review* 46, special issue (November 1986): 540–552.

Schick, Allen. "The Road to PPB: The Stages of Budget Reform." In *Perspectives on Budgeting,* 2d ed., edited by Allen Schick. Washington, DC: American Society for Public Administration, 1987.

Thomassen, Henry. "Capitol Budgeting for a State." *Public Budgeting and Finance* 10 (Winter 1990): 72–86.

Thurmaier, Kurt. "Information Resources Management Expenditures in the States." *Public Budgeting and Finance* 10 (Winter 1990): 28–46.

Towns, Steve. "Number Crunching: A New Spreadsheet Literally Puts San Francisco Commissioners on the Same Page." *Government Technology* 10 (November, 1997).

Wildavsky, Aaron. *The New Politics of the Budgetary Process.* Glenview, IL: Scott, Foresman, 1988.

Wolin, Sheldon. "Democracy and Counterrevolution: Powerlessness Is Not an Unintended but a Calculated Consequence of the System." *The Nation* 262 (April 22, 1996): 22–24.

Chapter Six

Bishop, Peter C., and Augustus Jones, Jr. "Implementing the Americans with Disabilities Act of 1990." *Public Administration Review* 53, (March/April 1993): 121–128.

Campbell, Alan K. "Civil Service Reform: A New Commitment." *Public Administration Review* 38 (March/April 1978).

Carter, Jimmy. "State of the Union Address." January 19, 1978.

Chi, Keon S. "Comparable Worth." *State Government* 2 (1984): 34–45.

Coil, James H., and Charles M. Rice. "Managing Workforce Diversity in the 90's." *Employee Relations Law Journal* 4 (Spring 1993): 547–563.

Colvard, James E. "Invigorating the Civil Service." *Government Executive* (December 1992): 17.

Cooper, Phillip J., Linda P. Brady, Olivia Hidalgo-Lardeman, Albert Hyde, Katherine C. Naff, Steven Ott, and Harvey White. *Public Administration for the Twenty-First Century.* Fort Worth, TX: Harcourt Brace College Publishers, 1998.

Denhardt, Robert B. *The Pursuit of Significance.* Belmont, CA: Wadsworth, 1993.

Desky, Joanne. "Glass Ceiling Slows Down Women in Government." *PA Times* (December 1992): 1.

Gore, Al. *From Red Tape to Results: Creating a Government That Works Better and Costs Less. Report of the National Performance Review.* New York: Times Books, 1993.

Hall, Francine, and Maryann H. Albrecht. *The Management of Affirmative Action.* Santa Monica, CA: Goodyear, 1979.

Havemann, Judith. "The Government Takes a Stand on AIDS in its Office." *Washington Post National Weekly Edition* (March 28–April 3, 1988a): 34.

Havemann, Judith. "Sexual Harassment." *Washington Post National Weekly Edition* (July 11–17, 1988b): 30–31.

Hays, Steven W., and Zane T. Reeves. *Personnel Management in the Public Sector.* Boston: Allyn and Bacon, 1984.

Heclo, Hugh. *A Government of Strangers.* Washington, DC: Brookings Institution, 1977.

Ingraham, Patricia W., and David Rosenbloom. "The State of Merit in the Federal Government." In *Agenda for Excellence,* edited by Patricia W. Ingraham and Donald F. Kettl, Chatham, NJ: Chatham House, 1992.

Kamensky, John M. "Role of the 'Reinventing Government' Movement in Federal Management Reform." *Public Administration Review* 56 (May/June 1996): 247–255.

Kearney, Richard C. "Managing Relations with Organized Employees." In *Handbook of Public Administration,* 2d ed., edited by James L. Perry. San Francisco: Jossey-Bass, 1996.

Kearney, Richard. "Federal Labor Relations 2000: Introduction to the Symposium." *International Journal of Public Administration* 16, no. 6 (1993): 781–791.

Klingner, Donald E., and John Nalbandian. *Public Personnel Management.* 2d ed. Englewood Cliffs, NJ: Prentice Hall, 1985.

Lee, Robert D., Jr., and Paul S. Greenlaw. "The Legal Evolution of Sexual Harassment." *Public Administration Review* 55 (July/August 1995): 357–364.

Levitan, Sar. *Working for the Sovereign.* Baltimore, MD: Johns Hopkins Press, 1983.

Lorentzen, Paul. "A Time for Action." *The Bureaucrat* 13 (Fall 1984): 5–11.

Lorentzen, Paul. "Stress in Political-Career Executive Relations." *Public Administration Review* 45 (May/June 1985): 411–414.

Marcus, Ruth. "Push Comes to Shove on Grove City." *Washington Post National Weekly Edition* (March 14–20, 1988): 31.

Moore, Mary V., and Yohannan T. Abraham. "Comparable Worth: Is It a Moot Issue?" *Public Personnel Management* 21, no. 4 (Winter 1992): 470.

Nigro, Lloyd G., and William L. Waugh Jr., "Violence in the American Workplace: Challenges to the Public Employer." *Public Administration Review* 56 (July/August 1996): 326–333.

PA Times (April 1, 1984).

PA Times (May 1, 1984).

PA Times (September 15, 1985).

PA Times (October 1, 1985).

Rabin, Jack, Thomas Vocino, W. Bartley Hildreth, and Gerald J. Miller, eds. *Handbook on Public Personnel Administration and Labor Relations.* New York: Marcel Dekker, 1983.

Risher, Howard, Charles H. Fay, and associates. *New Strategies for Public Pay: Rethinking Government Compensation Programs.* San Francisco: Jossey-Bass, 1997.

Roberts, Alasdair. "Performance-Based Organizations: Assessing the Gore Plan." *Public Administration Review* 57 (November/December 1997): 465–478.

Schroeder, Patricia. "Is the Bridge Washed Out?" *The Bureaucrat* 13 (Fall 1984): 22–24.

Shafritz, Jay M., Albert C. Hyde, and David H. Rosenbloom. *Personnel Management in Government.* 2d ed. New York: Marcel Dekker, 1981.

Siegel, Gilbert B., and Robert C. Myrtle. *Public Personnel Administration: Concepts and Realities.* Boston: Houghton Mifflin, 1985.

Slack, James D. "Workplace Preparedness and the Americans with Disabilities Act: Lessons from Municipal Governments' Management of HIV/AIDS." *Public Administration Review* 56 (March/April 1996): 159–167.

Steele, Randy. "Strike Zone." *Flying* (March 1982): 34–41.

Stewart, Debra W. "Assuring Equal Employment Opportunity in the Organization." In *Handbook of Public Personnel and Labor Relations,* edited by Jack Rabin, Thomas Vocino, W. Bartley Hildreth, and Gerald J. Miller. New York: Marcel Dekker, 1983.

Washington Post (July 15, 1992): 197.

Zuck, Alfred M. "Education of Political Appointees." *The Bureaucrat* 13 (Fall 1984): 15–18.

Chapter Seven

Ackoff, Russell L. *Creating the Corporate Future.* New York: Wiley, 1981.

Bardach, Eugene. *The Implementation Game.* Cambridge, MA: M.l.T. Press, 1977.

Carter, Karen. "Performance Budgets: Here by Popular Demand." *State Legislatures* 20 (December 1994): 22–25.

Chelimsky, Eleanor. *Program Evaluation: Patterns and Directions.* Washington, DC: American Society for Public Administration, 1985.

Dunn, William N. *Public Policy Analysis.* Englewood Cliffs, NJ: Prentice Hall, 1981.

Glueck, William F. *Strategic Management and Business Policy.* New York: McGraw-Hill, 1980.

Gore, Al. *From Red Tape to Results: Creating a Government That Works Better and Costs Less. Report of the National Performance Review.* New York: Times Books, 1993.

Gulick, Luther. "Notes on the Theory of Organization." In *Papers on the Science of Administration,* edited by L. Gulick and L. Urwick, pp. 1–46. New York: Institute of Public Administration, 1937.

Hakes, Jay E. "Performance Measurement and Organization Change." *PA Times* 20 (July 1997): 10, 17.

Hammer, Michael, and James Champy. *Reengineering the Corporation: A Manifesto for Business Revolution.* New York: Harper, 1993.

Jennings, Edward T. Jr., Dale Krane, Alex N. Pattakos, and B. J. Reed, eds. *From Nation to States.* Albany: State University of New York Press, 1986.

Kershaw, David N. "A Negative-Income-Tax Experiment." In *The Practice of Policy Evaluation,* edited by David Nachmias. New York: St. Martin's Press, 1980.

Latane, Henry A. "The Rationality Model in Organizational Decision Making." In *The Social Science of Organizations,* edited by Harold J. Leavitt. Englewood Cliffs, NJ: Prentice Hall, 1963.

Linden, Russell M. *Seamless Government: A Practical Guide to Reengineering in the Public Sector.* San Francisco: Jossey-Bass, 1994.

Majchrzak, Ann. *Methods for Policy Research.* Beverly Hills: Sage Publications, 1984.

Mayne, John. "Public Sector Reforms: International Perspectives on Performance Monitoring." *PA Times* (July 20, 1997): 1, 16.

Mayne, John, and Eduardo Zapico-Goni. *Monitoring Performance in the Public Sector: Future Directions from International Experience.* New Brunswick: Transaction Publishers, 1997.

Murphy, Jerome T. *Getting the Facts.* Santa Monica, CA: Goodyear, 1980.

Osborne, David, and Ted Gaebler. *Reinventing Government.* Reading, MA: Addison-Wesley, 1992.

Poister, Theodore H. *Performance Monitoring.* Lexington, MA: Lexington Books, 1983.

Poister, Theodore H., James McDavid, and Anne Hoagland Magoun. *Applied Program Evaluation in Local Government.* Lexington, MA: Lexington Books, 1979.

Pressman, Jeffrey, and Aaron Wildavsky. *Implementation.* Berkeley: University of California Press, 1973.

Quade, E. S. *Analysis for Public Decisions.* 2d ed. New York: North-Holland, 1989.

Shirley, Robert C. "Limiting the Scope of Strategy." *Academy of Management Review* 7 (April 1982): 262–268.

Stokey, Edith, and Richard Zechauser. *A Primer for Policy Analysis.* New York: Norton, 1978.

Sylvia, Ronald D., Kenneth J. Meier, and Elizabeth M. Gunn. *Program Planning and Evaluation for the Public Manager.* Pacific Grove, CA: Brooks/Cole, 1985.

Thompson, James D. *Organizations in Action.* New York: McGraw-Hill, 1967.

Wholey, J. S., H. P. Hatry, and K. E. Newcomer, eds. *Handbook for Practical Program Evaluation.* San Francisco: Jossey-Bass, 1994.

Chapter Eight

Alexander, Jason Hansen, and Joseph W. Grubbs. "Wired Government: Information Technology, External Public Organizations, and Cyberdemocracy." *Journal of Public Administration and Management* 3 (January 1998): unnumbered, on-line journal.

Alliance for Redesigning Government. *Anticipatory Pre-school Education in Arkansas Prevents Future Problems.* Washington, DC: National Academy of Public Administration, 1995.

Bailey, Mary Timney. "A Model System for Institutionalizing Productivity Improvement Efforts." *Public Productivity Review* 44 (Winter 1987): 19–28.

Barbour, George P., Jr. "Improving Productivity for Better Service Delivery." *Management Information Service Report* 8, no. 6. Washington, DC: International City Management Association, 1976.

Boston, Jonathan, ed. *Reshaping the State: New Zealand's Bureaucratic Revolution.* Auckland, New Zealand: Oxford University Press, 1991.

Boston, Jonathan, ed. *Public Management: The New Zealand Model.* Auckland, New Zealand: Oxford University Press, 1996.

Brudney, Jeffrey L., and Mary M. Brown. "Geographic Information Systems Meet Public Managers Expectations?" *State and Local Government Review* (Spring 1992): 84–90.

Burstein, Carolyn. Presentation to the Governor's Advisory Council on Productivity, State of Missouri, November, 1988.

Business Insurance (August 3, 1992).

Commission on Global Governance. *Our Global Neighborhood.* Report issued to the United Nations. Oxford, United Kingdom: Oxford University Press, 1995.

Coursey, David H., and R.F. Shangraw, Jr. "Expert Systems Technology for Management Applications." *Public Productivity Review* 12, no. 4 (Spring 1989): 237–262.

Dilworth, Robert L. "Artificial Intelligence: The Time Is Now." *Public Productivity Review* 12, no. 2 (Winter 1988): 123–130.

Dineen, Carole. "Productivity Improvement: It's Our Turn." *The Bureaucrat* 14 (Winter 1985–1986): 10–14.

Frederickson, H. George. "The Seven Principles of Total Quality Politics." *PA Times* (January 17, 1994): 9.

Gore, Al. *From Red Tape to Results: Creating a Government That Works Better and Costs Less. Report of the National Performance Review.* New York: Times Books, 1993.

Gore, Al. *The Best Kept Secrets in Government.* Washington, DC: U.S. Government Printing Office, 1996.

Government Productivity News (April 1989): 1, 3.

Government Productivity News (July/August 1989): 1, 4.

Government Productivity News (December 1989).

Government Productivity News (February 1992): 4.

Government Productivity News (April 1992): 4.

Government Productivity News (September 1992): 4.

Greiner, John M., Harry P. Hatry, Margo P. Koss, Annie P. Miller, and Jane P. Woodward. *Productivity and Motivation.* Washington, DC: The Urban Institute Press, 1981.

Grossman, Lawrence K. *The Electronic Republic: Reshaping Democracy in the Information Age.* New York: Penguin, 1995.

Hackman, J. Richard. "Designing Work for Individuals and for Groups." In J. Richard Hackman, Edward J. Lawler, and Lyman W. Porter, *Perspectives on Behavior in Organizations.* 2d ed. New York: McGraw-Hill, 1983, pp. 242–257.

Holzer, Marc, Ellen Doree Rosen, and Constance Zalk. "Steps in Productivity Improvement." In *Productivity Improvement Techniques,* edited by John Matzer, Jr. Washington, DC: International City Management Association, 1986.

Jarrett, James E. "Strategies and Innovations in Productivity Improvement." Unpublished manuscript.

Jarrett, James E. "Productivity." In *The Book of the States 1981–1982.* Lexington, KY: Council of State Governments, 1982.

Jerkins, David. "Quality of Work Life." In *The Quality of Work Life and the 1980s,* edited by Harvey Kolodny and Hans van Beinum, pp. 1–32. New York: Praeger, 1983.

Jun, Jong S. *Management by Objectives in Government.* Beverly Hills, CA: Sage Publications, 1976.

Kamensky, John M. "Role of the 'Reinventing Government' Movement in Federal Management Reform." *Public Administration Review* 56 (May/June 1996): 247–255.

Kaplan, Robert S., and David P. Norton. "Strategic Learning and the Balanced Scorecard." *Strategy & Leadership* 24 (September/October 1996): 18–24.

Kerwood, David. "Government Intranets." (Article submitted to the Federal Communicators Network, National Performance Review, December 15, 1997). Washington, DC: National Performance Review, 1997.

Mankin, Don, Susan G. Cohen, and Tora K. Bikson. *Teams and Technology: Fulfilling the Promise of the New Organization.* Boston: Harvard Business School Press, 1996.

Mercer, James L., and Ronald J. Philips. *Public Technology.* New York: American Management Association, 1981.

Morley, Elaine. *A Practitioner's Guide to Public Sector Productivity Improvement.* New York: Van Nostrand Reinhold, 1986.

"Oakland Wires Public Housing." *Government Technology* 10 (September 1997): 12.

Osborne, David, and Ted Gaebler. *Reinventing Government.* Reading, MA: Addison-Wesley, 1992.

Peters, B. Guy. "New Visions of Government and the Public Service." In *New Paradigms for Government: Issues for the Changing Public Service,* edited by Patricia W. Ingraham and Barbara S. Romzek. San Francisco: Jossey-Bass, 1994.

Richardson, Kari. "Using the 'Net' to Lure Business." *PA Times* (September 19, 1996): 1, 24.

Rubin, Barry M. "Information Systems for Public Management." *Public Administration Review* 46 (November/December 1986): 540–552.

Rusaw, Carol. "Reinventing Local Government: A Case Study of Organizational Change through Community Learning." *Public Administration Quarterly* 20 (Winter 1997): 419–432.

Schachter, Hindy Lauer. "Reinventing Government or Reinventing Ourselves: Two Models for Improving Government Service." *Public Administration Review* 55 (November/December 1995): 530–537.

Suttle, J. Lloyd. "Improving Life at Work." In *Improving Life at Work,* by J. Richard Hackman and J. Lloyd Suttle, pp. 1–29. Santa Monica, CA: Goodyear, 1977.

Toregas, Costis. "Technology and Our Urban Communities: Who Shall Lead?" *Public Management* 17 (May 1988): 2–5.

USA Today (April 2, 1993): B-l.

Walton, Richard E. "Criteria for Quality of Working Life." In *The Quality of Working Life,* edited by Louis E. Davis and Albert B. Cherns. New York: The Free Press, 1975.

Weidner, Mary, and Mary Noss Reavely. *The Council on Human Investment: Performance Governance in Iowa* (Task Force on Government Accomplishment & Accountability, Case Study S1). Washington, DC: American Society for Public Administration, 1996.

Weil, Nancy. "City Workers Figure Out How to Cut Red Tape." *PA Times* (September 19, 1996): 3.

Chapter Nine

Argyris, Chris. *Interpersonal Competence and Organizational Effectiveness.* Pacific Grove, CA: Brooks/Cole, 1962.

Argyris, Chris. *Knowledge for Action: A Guide to Overcoming Barriers to Organizational Change.* San Francisco: Jossey-Bass, 1993.

Argyris, Chris, and Donald A. Schon. *Theory in Practice.* San Francisco: Jossey-Bass, 1974.

Barbour, George, P., Jr., Thomas W. Fletcher, and George A. Sipel. *Handbook: Excellence in Local Government Management.* Washington, DC: International City Management Association, 1984.

Bryson, John M., and Barbara C. Crosby. *Leadership for the Common Good: Tackling Public Problems in a Shared-Power World.* San Francisco: Jossey-Bass, 1992.

Chrislip, David D., and Carl E. Larson. *Collaborative Leadership.* San Francisco: Jossey-Bass, 1994.

Cohen, Steven. *Total Quality Management in Government: A Practical Guide for the Real World.* San Francisco: Jossey-Bass, 1993.

Denhardt, Robert B. *The Pursuit of Significance: Strategies for Managerial Success in Public Organizations.* Belmont, CA: Wadsworth, 1993.

Dimock, Marshall E. "The Criteria and Objectives of Public Administration." In *The Frontiers of Public Administration,* edited by John M. Gaus, Leonard D. White, and Marshall E. Dimock. Chicago: University of Chicago Press, 1936.

Fayol, Henri. *General and Industrial Management.* Translated by C. Storrs. London: Isaac Pitman and Sons, 1949.

Golembiewski, Robert T. *Renewing Organizations.* Itasca, IL: Peacock, 1972.

Government Productivity News (June 1989): 3.

Government Productivity News (January 1993)

Grubbs, Joseph W., and Jason Hansen Alexander. "Citizen Trust: Examining Trends in Public Confidence in Government and the Implications for Civic Engagement." Paper presented at the American Society for Public Administration national conference, Philadelphia, July 1997.

Gulick, Luther. "Notes on the Theory of Organization." In *Papers on the Science of Administration,* edited by Luther Gulick and L. Urwick, pp. 1–46. New York: Institute of Public Administration, 1937a.

Gulick, Luther. "Science, Values, and Public Administration." In *Papers on the Science of Administration,* edited by Luther Gulick and L. Urwick, pp. 189–195. New York: Institute of Public Administration, 1937b.

Kahn, Robert, and Daniel Katz. "Leadership Practices in Relation to Productivity and Morale." In *Group Dynamics,* edited by Dorwin Cartwright and Alvin Zander. Evanston, IL: Row, Peterson, 1953.

Kaufman, Herbert. *The Forest Ranger.* Baltimore, MD: Johns Hopkins University Press, 1960.

Milakovich, Michael. "Total Quality Management in the Public Sector." *National Productivity Review* (Spring 1991): 195–213.

Mooney, James, and Alan C. Reiley. *The Principles of Organization.* New York: Harper & Row, 1939.

Office of Management and Budget. OMB Draft Circular A-132 (1990).

Ostrom, Vincent, and Elinor Ostrom. "Public Choice: A Different Approach to the Study of Public Administration." *Public Administration Review* 31 (March/April 1971): 203–216.

Peters, J. Thomas, and Robert H. Waterman. *In Search of Excellence.* New York: Harper & Row, 1982.

Rainey, Hal G., and Brinton H. Milward. "Public Organization: Policy Networks and Environments." In *Organization Theory and Public Policy,* edited by Richard H. Hall and Robert E. Quinn, pp. 133–146. Beverly Hills, CA: Sage Publications, 1983.

Redford, Emmette. *Democracy in the Administrative State.* New York: Oxford University Press, 1969.

Schein, Edgar H. *Organizational Culture and Leadership.* San Francisco: Jossey-Bass, 1987.

Schein, Edgar H. *Organizational Culture and Leadership,* 2d ed. San Francisco: Jossey-Bass, 1997.

Selznick, Philip. *TVA and the Grass Roots.* Berkeley: University of California Press, 1949.

Senge, Peter M. *The Fifth Discipline: The Art and Practice of the Learning Organization.* New York: Currency Doubleday, 1990.

Simon, Herbert A. *Models of Man.* New York: Wiley, 1957.

Taylor, Frederick W. *Scientific Management.* New York: Harper & Row, 1923.

Thomas, John Clayton. *Public Participation in Public Decisions.* San Francisco: Jossey-Bass, 1995.

Washington Post (September 8, 1993): A17.

Weber, Max. *The Theory of Social and Economic Organization.* New York: Oxford University Press, 1947.

White, Leonard. *Introduction to the Study of Public Administration.* New York: Macmillan, 1926.

Willoughby, W. F. *Principles of Public Organization.* Baltimore, MD: Johns Hopkins Press, 1927.

Chapter Ten

Bennis, Warren. "The Artform of Leadership." In *The Executive Mind,* edited by Suresh Srivastya. San Francisco: Jossey-Bass, 1983.

Benson, Herbert. *The Relaxation Response.* New York: Morrow, 1975.

Cooper, Kenneth H. *The Aerobics Way.* Toronto: Bantam Books, 1978.

Denhardt, Robert B., and Kevin Prelgovisk. "Public Leadership: A Developmental Perspective." In *Executive Leadership in the Public Service,* edited by Robert B. Denhardt and William H. Stewart. Tuscaloosa: The University of Alabama Press, 1992.

Gardner, John. Remarks to the National Conference of the National Association of Schools of Public Affairs and Administration, Seattle, October 23, 1987.

Hales, Colin P. "What Do Managers Do? A Critical Review of the Evidence." *Journal of Management* 23 (1986): 88–115.

Helgesen, Sally. "Leading from the Grassroots." In *The Leader of the Future: New Visions, Strategies, and Practices for the Next Era,* edited by Frances Hesselbein, Marshall Goldsmith, and Richard Beckhard. San Francisco: Jossey-Bass, 1996.

Hopper, Linda. "Unstressing Work." *Public Management* 17 (November 1988): 1–4.

Kotter, John P. *The General Manager.* New York: The Free Press, 1982.

Lakein, Alan. *How to Get Control of Your Time and Your Life.* New York: Signet Books, 1973.

Leboeuf, Michael. *Working Smart.* New York: McGraw-Hill, 1979.

Lindblom, Charles E. *The Policy-Making Process.* Englewood Cliffs, NJ: Prentice Hall, 1968.

Price, Virginia Ann. *Type A Behavior Pattern.* New York: Academic Press, 1982.

Selye, Hans. *Stress without Distress.* Philadelphia: Lippincott, 1974.

Simon, Herbert A. *Models of Man.* New York: Wiley, 1957.

Whetten, David A., and Kim S. Cameron. *Developing Management Skills.* Glenview, IL: Scott, Foresman, 1984.

Chapter Eleven

Argyris, Chris. *Intervention Theory and Method.* Reading, MA: Addison-Wesley, 1970.

Blanchard, Kenneth, and Spencer Johnson. *The One-Minute Manager.* New York: Berkley Books, 1982.

Daft, Richard L., and Richard M. Steers. *Organizations: A Micro/Macro Approach.* Glenview IL: Scott, Foresman, 1986.

Gardner, Neely. *Group Leadership.* Washington, DC: National Training and Development Service, 1974.

Herzberg, Frederick. *The Motivation to Work.* New York: Wiley, 1959.

Hitt, Michael A., Dennis R. Middlemist, and Robert L. Mathis. *Management Concepts and Effective Practice.* St. Paul, MN: West, 1983.

Janis, Irving. *Groupthink.* 2d ed. Boston: Houghton Mifflin, 1983.

Kanter, Rosabeth Moss. *Men and Women of the Corporation.* New York: Basic Books, 1977.

Lippitt, Gordon L., Peter Langseth, and Jack Mossop. *Implementing Organizational Change.* San Francisco: Jossey-Bass, 1985.

Maslow, Abraham. *Motivation and Personality.* New York: Harper & Brothers, 1954.

Organ, Dennis H. "A Review of Management and the Worker." *Academy of Management Review,* 11, no. 2 (April 1986): 459–464.

Rankin, Paul. "Listening Ability." Proceedings of the Ohio State Educational Conference, Ninth Annual Session, 1929.

Steil, Lyman K., Larry L. Barker, and Kittie W. Watson. *Effective Listening.* Reading, MA: Addison-Wesley, 1983.

Sussman, Lyle, and Samuel Deep. *Comex.* Cincinnati, OH: Southwestern, 1984.

Vroom, Victor H., and Arthur G. Jago. *The New Leadership.* Englewood Cliffs, NJ: Prentice-Hall, 1988.

Vroom, Victor H., and Philip W. Yetton. *Leadership and Decision Making.* Pittsburgh, PA: University of Pittsburgh Press, 1973.

Ziller, R. C. "Toward a Theory of Open and Closed Groups." *Psychological Bulletin* 64 (1965): 164–182.

Chapter Twelve

Goodsell, Charles T. *The Case for Bureaucracy.* 2d ed. Chatham, NJ: Chatham House, 1985.

National Commission on the Public Service. *Leadership for America.* Washington, DC: National Commission on Public Service, 1989.

National Commission on the State and Local Public Service. *Hard Truths/Tough Choices.* Albany, NY: The Nelson A. Rockefeller Institute of Government, 1993.

APPENDIX

Journals

Academy of Management Review
Ohio Northern University
P.O. Box 209
300 South Union Street
Ada, OH 45810

Administration and Society
Virginia Polytechnic Institute and State University
Center for Public Administration and Public
   Affairs
Blacksburg, VA 24061

Administrative Science Quarterly
Cornell University
Johnson Graduate School of Management
425 Caldwell Hall
Ithaca, NY 14853-2602

American Review of Public Administration
University of Missouri-Kansas City
Cookingham Institute of Public Affairs
Bloch School of Business and Public
   Administration
Kansas City, MO 64110

Australian Journal of Public Administration
University of Queensland
Royal Institute of Public Administration
Department of Government
St. Lucia, Queensland 4067
Australia

California Management Review
University of California, Berkeley
Haas School of Business
350 Barrows Hall
Berkeley, CA 94720

Canadian Public Administration
Journal of the Institute of Public Administration
   of Canada
Revue de l'Institut d'administration publique de
   Canada
150 est, av. Eglington Ave. East, Suite 305
Toronto Ontario Canada M4P IE8

The Executive
Ohio Northern University
Academy of Management Executive
Academy Office
P.O. Box 39
300 South Union
Ada, OH 45810-0039

G.A.O. Journal
U.S. General Accounting Office
Office of Public Affairs
Room 6901
Washington, DC 20548

Governance
Blackwell Publishers
238 Main St.
Cambridge, MA 02142

Governing
Congressional Quarterly Inc.
2300 N. St., NW, Suite 760
Washington, DC 20037

Government Executive
National Journal Inc.
1730 M St., NW, 11th Floor.
Washington, DC 20036

Government Productivity News
P.O. Box 17433
Austin, TX 78755-0435

Harvard Business Review
P.O. Box 52622
Boulder, CO 80321–2622

International Journal of Public Administration
Pennsylvania State University
Institute of State and Regional Affairs
Harrisburg, PA 17057

Journal of Management
Indiana University
Graduate School of Business
Bloomington, IN 47405

Journal of Policy Analysis and Management
University of California
Association for Public Policy Analysis and
    Management
Graduate School of Public Policy
Berkeley, CA 94720

*Journal of Public Administration Research
    and Theory*
Rutgers University
J-PART
Department 4010
Transaction Periodicals Consortium
New Brunswick, NJ 08903

Journal of State Government
The Council of State Governments
P.O. Box 11910
Lexington, KY 40578

Journal of Urban Analysis and Management
State University of New York
Harriman College for Urban and Policy Studies
Stony Brook, NY 11790

National Civic Review
National Civic League Press
1445 Market St. Suite 300
Denver, CO 80202-1728

*New Directions in Public Administration
    Research*
Florida Atlantic University
School of Public Administration
220 E. Second Ave.
Fort Lauderdale, FL 33301

Organizational Dynamics
American Management Association
P.O. Box 408
Saranac Lake, NY 12983

Organization Studies
University of Cambridge
The Judge Institute of Management Studies
Fitwilliam House, 32 Trumpington Street
Cambridge, CB2 IQY

Policy Studies
Policy Studies Institute
100 Park Village East
London, NWI 3SR
England

Policy Studies Review
Arizona State University
Policy Studies Organization
School of Justice Studies
Tempe, AZ 85287

Public Administration
Royal Institute of Public Administration
P.O. Box 87
Oxford, OX2 ODT
England

Public Administration and Development
RIPA International Ltd.
22 Bedford Square
London WC1B3H
England

Public Administration Review
ASPA
1120 G St., NW Suite 700
Washington, DC 20005-2885

Public Budgeting and Financial Management
Pennsylvania State University
Institute of State and Regional Affairs
Middleton, PA 17057

Public Finance Quarterly
University of New Orleans
College of Business Administration
New Orleans, LA 70148

Public Management
ICMA
777 N. Capitol St., NE
Washington, DC 20002-4201

The Public Manager
The Bureaucrat Inc.
12007 Titian Way
Potomac, MD 20854

Public Personnel Management
IPMA
1617 Duke St.
Alexandria, VA 22314

Public Productivity and Management Review
Jossey-Bass Publishers
350 Sansome St.
San Francisco, CA 94104

Public Productivity Review
National Center for Public Productivity
John Jay College
City University of New York
445 W. 59th St.
New York, NY 10019

State and Local Government Review
University of Georgia
Carl Vinson Institute of Government
Athens, GA 30602-4582

Organizations

Academy for State and Local Government
444 N. Capitol St. NW, Suite 349
Washington, DC 20001

American Consortium for International Public
    Administration
1120 G St. NW, Suite 225
Washington, DC 20005

American Planning Association
1776 Massachusetts Ave. NW, Suite 800
Washington, DC 20036

American Public Health Association
1015 15 St. NW, 3rd Floor
Washington, DC 20005

American Public Power Association
2301 M St. NW, 3rd Floor
Washington, DC 20037

American Public Welfare Association
810 First St. NW, Suite 500
Washington, DC 20002

American Public Works Association
1313 E. 60th St.
Chicago, IL 60637

American Society for Public Administration
1120 G St. NW, Suite 500
Washington, DC 20005

Council of State Governments
P.O. Box 11910
Lexington, KY 40578

Education Commission of the States
1860 N. Michigan Ave., Suite 800
Chicago, IL 60601

Government Finance Officers Association
180 N. Michigan Ave., Suite 800
Chicago, IL 60601

International City Management Association
777 N. Capitol St.
Washington, DC 20002

International Institute of Municipal Clerks
160 N. Altadena Drive
Pasadena, CA 91107

International Personnel Management
  Association
1617 Duke St.
Alexandria, VA 22314

National Academy of Public Administration
1120 G St. NW, Suite 540
Washington, DC 20005

National Association of Counties
441 First St. NW, 8th Floor
Washington, DC 20001

National Association of Schools of Public
  Affairs and Administration
1120 G St. NW, 5th Floor
Washington, DC 20005

National Association of State Budget Officers
400 N. Capitol St. NW, Suite 295
Washington, DC 20001

National Civic League
1445 Market St.
Denver, CO 80203

National Forum for Black Public Administrators
777 N. Capitol St.
Washington, DC 20002

National Institute of Governmental Purchasing
115 Hillwood Ave., Suite 201
Falls Church, VA 22046

National League of Cities
1301 Pennsylvania Ave NW, 6th Floor
Washington, DC 20004

Public Administration Service
1497 Chain Bridge Road
McLean, VA 22101

Public Technology Inc.
1301 Pennsylvania Ave. NW, Suite 704
Washington, DC 20004

GLOSSARY

Accounting: The process of identifying, measuring, and communicating economic information to permit informed judgment and decision making.

Adverse or disparate impact: Criterion for showing that employment practices affect one group more harshly than another.

Affirmative action: Use of positive, results-oriented practices to ensure that women, minorities, handicapped persons, and other protected classes of people will be equitably represented in an organization.

Agenda setting: Phase in public policy process when certain problems come to be viewed as needing attention.

Allotments: Amounts that agencies are authorized to spend within a given period.

Apportionment: Process by which funds are allocated to agencies for specific portions of the year.

Appropriation: Legislative action to set aside funds and create budget authority for their expenditures.

Area of acceptance: Area within which the subordinate is willing to accept the decisions made by the supervisor.

Authorizing legislation: Legislative action that permits establishment or continuation of a particular program or agency.

Autocracy: Government by one.

Bargaining unit: The organization that will represent employees in conferring and negotiating various issues.

Behavioral awards: Used to reward specific behaviors that management wishes to encourage.

Block grants: Grants in which the money can be used for nearly any purpose within a specific functional field.

Bond: Promise to repay a certain amount (principal) at a certain time (maturity date) at a particular rate of interest.

Boundary spanning: Representing an organization to outside groups and organizations.

Bounded rationality: Seeking the best possible solution, but not necessarily the most rational from a purely economic standpoint.

Brainstorming: Technique for enhancing the alternative-generation portion of the decision-making process.

Budget padding: Proposing a higher budget than is actually needed.

Business cycle: Periods of economic growth featuring inflation and high employment followed by periods of recession or depression and unemployment.

Capital expenditures: Spending for items that will be used over a period of several years.

Capital grants: Grants for use in construction or renovation.

Categorical or project grants: Grants requiring that the money may be spent for only a limited purpose; typically available on a competitive basis.

Charter: Local government's equivalent of a constitution.

Cohesion: Degree to which members of a group are uniformly committed to the group and its goals.

Comparable worth: Notion that men and women in jobs that are not identical but require similar levels of skill and training should be paid equally.

Constituent policy: Policy designed to benefit the public generally or to serve the government.

Continuing resolution: Resolution permitting the government to continue operating until an appropriations measure is passed.

Cooperative federalism: Greater sharing of responsibilities between federal and state governments.

Co-optation: Situations in which citizens are given the feeling of involvement while exercising little real power.

Coproduction: Using volunteer activity to supplement or supplant the work of government officials.

Cost-benefit: Identifying and quantifying both negative impacts (costs) and positive impacts (benefits) of a proposal, then subtracting one from the other to arrive at a net benefit.

Councils of government: Oversight bodies representing various localities to help coordinate local affairs.

Cross-cutting requirements: Rules that apply to most grant programs.

Debt capacity: Value of a city's resources combined with the ability of the government to draw on them to provide payment.

Decision analysis: Technique wherein decisions are likely to be made sequentially and under some degree of uncertainty.

Decision tree: Technique that identifies various possible outcomes, given the risk associated with each.

Deferral: Decision by the president to withhold expenditure of funds for a brief period.

Delegation: Assigning tasks to others.

Democracy: A political system in which decision-making power is widely shared among members of the society.

Deontology: Belief that broad principles of rightness and wrongness can be established and are not dependent on particular circumstances.

Dillon's Rule: Municipalities have only those powers granted in their charters; cities are creatures of the state.

Direct orders: Requirements or restrictions that are enforced by one government over another.

Discretionary spending: That portion of the budget still open to changes by the president and Congress.

Distributive policy: Policy involving use of general tax funds to provide assistance and benefits to individuals or groups.

Dual federalism: Pattern in which federal and state governments are struggling for power and influence with little intergovernmental cooperation.

Effectiveness: Extent to which a program is achieving or failing to achieve its stated objectives.

Efficiency: Relationship between inputs and outputs.

Employee recognition program: Effective way to acknowledge special contributions of certain employees or groups to the organization.

Entitlement grants: Grants that provide assistance to persons who meet certain criteria.

Entitlement programs: Programs that provide a specified set of benefits to those who meet certain eligibility requirements.

Equal employment opportunity: Refers to efforts to eliminate employment discrimination on the basis of race, ethnic background, sex, age, or physical handicap; ensures that all persons have an equal chance to compete for employment and promotions based on job qualifications.

Equality: The idea that all persons have an equal claim to life, liberty, and the pursuit of happiness.

Ethical or moral relativism: Belief that moral judgment can be made only by taking into account the context in which action occurs.

Ethics: Process by which we clarify right and wrong and act on what we take to be right.

Ethics audit: Evaluation of the value premises that guide an organization's action.

Excise tax: Tax applied to the sale of specific commodities.

Executive order: A presidential mandate directed to and governing, with the effect of law, the actions of government officials and agencies.

Expert systems: Computer programs that mimic the decision-making processes of human experts within a particular field.

Exploratory evaluation: Investigating a variety of hunches or intuitions about program operations.

Fiduciary funds: Funds used when government must hold assets for individuals or when government holds resources to be transmitted to another organization.

Final-offer arbitration: Technique in which both parties must present their best offer with the understanding that an arbitrator will choose one or the other without modification.

Fiscal policy: Public policy concerned with the impact of government taxation and spending on the economy.

Fiscal year (FY): Government's basic accounting period.

Formula grants: Grants that employ a specific division rule to indicate how much money any given jurisdiction will receive.

Franchise: Exclusive award to one firm (or a limited number) to operate a certain business within a jurisdiction.

Functional principle: Horizontal division of labor.

Gainsharing plan: Monetary award for a group of employees based on savings generated by the group.

General fund: Fund that handles "unrestricted" funds of government.

Grants: Transfers of money (and/or property) from one government to another.

Grantsmanship: Skills needed to compete successfully in the grant process.

Gross National Product (GNP): Measure of total spending in the economy; includes total personal consumption, private investment, and government purchases.

Hidden agenda: Privately held goals and priorities.

Home rule: Provision allowing cities greater autonomy over local activities.

Impoundment: Withholding of funds authorized and appropriated by law.

Independent agencies: Agencies intentionally created outside the normal cabinet organization.

Individualism: The idea that the dignity and integrity of the individual is of supreme importance.

Institutional subsystem: Responsible for adapting the organization to its environment and for anticipating and planning for the future.

Intergovernmental relations: A term encompassing all the complex and interdependent relations among those at various levels of government.

Interorganizational networks: Pattern of relationships within and among various groups and organizations working in a single policy area.

Interventionist: External consultant brought in to reveal dysfunctional patterns of behavior and to try to develop more effective working relationships.

Iron triangle: Term given to a coalition of interest groups, agency personnel, and members of Congress created to exert influence on a particular policy issue.

Item veto: Allows a governor to veto specific items in an appropriations bill.

Job description: A thorough analysis of the work to be done and the capabilities for a job; typically contains these elements: job title, duties required, responsibilities, and job qualifications.

Lateral entry: Entry into government positions at any level.

Legislative veto: Statutory provision that gives Congress the authority to approve or disapprove certain executive actions.

Liberty: The idea that individual citizens of a democracy should have a high degree of self-determination.

Line-item budget: Budget format for listing categories of expenditures along with amounts allocated to each.

Management by objectives: Participatory approach to establishing clear and measurable objectives throughout the entire organization.

Managerial subsystem: Concerned with providing necessary resources for accomplishing a technical task and mediating between the technical and institutional subsystems.

Mandate: Order requiring a government to do something.

Merit pay: Increases in salary and wages that are tied to actual quality of work performed.

Merit principle: Concept that selection and treatment of government employees should be based on merit or competence rather than personal or political favoritism.

Morality: Practices and activities considered right or wrong and the values those practices reflect.

Negotiated investment strategy: Bringing together representatives of all affected groups to set priorities for funding.

Neutral competence: The belief that a neutral public bureaucracy following the mandates of a legislative body will meet the requirements of democracy.

Nominal group: Face-to-face meeting that allows only limited interaction among participants.

Nonprofit organizations: Organizations prohibited by law from distributing surplus revenues to individuals.

Objective responsibility: Assurance of responsiveness through external controls.

Oligarchy: Government by the few.

Ombudsman: Permanent office that receives complaints and acts on behalf of citizens to secure information, request services, or pursue grievances.

Operating grants: Grants for use in development and operation of specific programs.

Organization development: Process-oriented approach to planned change.

Organizational culture: Basic patterns of attitudes, beliefs, and values that underlie an organization's operation.

Parity principle: Idea that an individual should have equal amounts of authority and responsibility.

Participant-observer: Someone in either the target population or the agency who makes observations and draws conclusions based on firsthand experience.

Performance appraisal: Specific evaluation with respect to an individual's progress in completing specified tasks.

Performance auditing: Analysis and evaluation of the effective performance of agencies in carrying out their objectives.

Performance bonus: One-time monetary award based on superior performance on the job or in a particular task.

Performance budget: Budget format organized around programs or activities; includes various performance measurements that indicate the relationship between work actually done and its cost.

PERT: A way to monitor the time or costs of various activities required to complete a project, showing the sequence in which the activities must be completed.

Picket-fence federalism: Pattern of intergovernmental relations in which the horizontal bars represent levels of government and the vertical slats represent various substantive fields.

Piecework bonus: Incentive that ties the worker's productivity in a given task to the monetary rewards he or she receives.

Planning-programming-budgeting system (PPBS): Effort to connect planning, systems analysis, and budgeting in a single exercise.

Policy: Statement of goals and intentions with respect to a particular problem or set of problems.

Policy analysis: Process of researching or analyzing public problems to provide policy makers with specific information about the range of available policy options and advantages and disadvantages of different approaches.

Policy analysts: Persons who provide important information about public programs through research into the operations and impacts of the programs.

Policy entrepreneur: A person willing to invest personal time, energy, and money in pursuit of particular policy changes.

Political economy approach: Focusing on politics and economies as categories for analyzing organizational behavior.

Position classification: Analyzing and organizing jobs on the basis of duties, responsibilities, and knowledge and skills required to perform them.

Preaudit: Review in advance of an actual expenditure.

Preemption: Federal government efforts to preempt an area traditionally associated with state government.

Privatization: Use of nongovernmental agencies to provide goods and services previously provided by government.

Process charting/flowcharting: Graphically demonstrating the various steps in an operation, the people who perform each step, and relationships among those elements.

Program managers: Persons ranging from the executive level to the supervisory level who are in charge of particular governmental programs.

Progressive tax: One that taxes those with higher incomes at a higher rate.

Proportional tax: One that taxes everyone at the same rate.

Proprietary funds: Used to account for government activities that more closely resemble private business.

Public administration: The management of public programs.

Public corporation: An essentially commercial agency in which work requires greater latitude and acquires at least a portion of its funding in the marketplace (e.g., Tennessee Valley Authority).

Public policy: Authoritative statements made by legitimate governmental actors about public problems.

Quality circle: Small group of people who do similar or connected work and meet regularly to identify, analyze, and solve work-process problems.

Reconciliation bill: Legislative action that attempts to reconcile individual actions in taxes, authorizations, or appropriations with the totals.

Redistributive policy: Policy designed to take taxes from certain groups and give them to another group.

Regressive tax: One that taxes those with lower incomes at a proportionally higher rate than those with higher incomes.

Regulatory commission: Group formed to regulate a particular area of the economy; usually headed by a group of individuals appointed by the president and confirmed by the Senate.

Regulatory policy: Policy designed to limit actions of persons or groups to protect all or parts of the general public.

Rescission: Presidential decision to permanently withhold funds.

Revenue sharing: Grant pattern in which the money can be used any way the recipient government chooses.

Risk management: Ways that public organizations anticipate and cope with risks.

Risky shift: Difference in the daringness of decisions group members make as a group compared to the average risk of the same decision if each member made it alone.

Role ambiguity: Occurs when the rights and responsibilities of the job are not clearly understood.

Role conflict: Occurs when one faces two different and incompatible sets of demands.

Rule making: Administrative establishment of general guidelines for application to a class of people or a class of actions at some future time.

Rule of three: Provision of most merit systems that requires at least the top three applicants' names to be forwarded to the hiring official to allow some flexibility in selection.

Satisficing decision: One that is just "good enough" in terms of some criterion.

Scalar principle: Vertical division of labor among various organizational levels.

Scientific management: Approach to management based on carefully defined laws, rules, and principles.

Sexual harassment: Any unwarranted and nonreciprocal verbal or physical sexual advances or derogatory remarks that the recipient finds offensive or that interfere with his or her job performance.

Special districts: Local governments created for a specific purpose within a specific area.

Spoils system: The ability to give government jobs to the party faithful; "to the victor belong the spoils."

Staff managers: Persons who support the work of program managers through budgeting and financial management, personnel and labor relations, and purchasing and procurement.

Stakeholders: The many different persons who are involved in a policy decision and are affected by the results.

Strategic planning: Matching organizational objectives and capabilities to the anticipated demands of the environment to produce a plan of action that will ensure achievement of objectives.

Structured interviews: Those in which a previously developed set of questions is used with each applicant.

Subjective responsibility: Assurance of responsiveness based on an individual's character.

Suggestion award programs: Incentives for employees who make specific suggestions that result in savings for the organization.

Sunset law: Provision that sets a specific termination date for a program.

Sunshine law: Provision that requires agencies to conduct business in public view.

Supplemental appropriation: Bill passed during the fiscal year, adding new money to an agency's budget for the same fiscal year.

Supply-side economies: Argument that decreased taxes and government spending will stimulate capital investment and economic growth.

Support system: Network of people with whom one can talk about problems.

System: Set of regularized interactions configured or "bounded" in a way that differentiates and separates them from other actions that constitute the system's environment.

Systems approach: Suggestion that public (or other) organizations can be viewed in the same general way as biological or physical systems.

Systems theory: Effort to identify the interactions of various internal and external elements that impinge on an organization's operations.

Task forces: Groups brought together to work on specific organizational problems.

Technical subsystem: Concerned with effective performance of an organization's actual work.

Time series analysis: Making a number of observations about the target population both before and after program intervention.

Two-factor theory: Model of motivation involving two variables: job satisfaction and job dissatisfaction.

Unit determination: Decision to include or exclude certain groups in a bargaining unit.

Urban renewal: Government program designed to provide cities with money for public housing and urban redevelopment.

Utilitarianism: Philosophy of the greatest good for the greatest number of people.

Whipsaw tactics: Argument that pay or benefits negotiated by one group should be applied to others.

Zero-base budgeting: Budget format that presents information about the efficiency and effectiveness of existing programs and highlights possibilities for eliminating or reducing programs.

INDEX